THE GREEK CONNECTION

THE GREEK CONNECTION

The Life of
Elias Demetracopoulos
and the Untold Story
of Watergate

JAMES H. BARRON

 MELVILLE HOUSE

Brooklyn
London

The Greek Connection

Copyright © James H. Barron 2019
All rights reserved
First Melville House Printing: May 2020

Melville House Publishing
46 John Street
Brooklyn, NY 11201
and
Melville House UK
Suite 2000
16/18 Woodford Road
London E7 0HA

mhpbooks.com
@melvillehouse

ISBN: 978-1-61219-828-6
ISBN: 978-1-61219-829-3 (eBook)

Library of Congress Control Number: 2020931413

Design by Richard Oriolo

Printed in the United States of America
10 9 8 7 6 5 4 3 2 1

A catalog record for this book is available from the Library of Congress.

To Margie, with infinite love,
and to journalists worldwide who take great
risks to gather news and tell uncomfortable truths.

History is malleable . . . Memory is imperfect, but its inherent instability allows our past, which we usually see as fixed, to remain as it actually is: malleable, changing not just as new information emerges, but as our interests, emotions and inclinations change.

KEN BURNS

CONTENTS

INTRODUCTION   xi

  1. Growing Up   3

  2. Resisting the Germans   19

  3. Locked Up   34

  4. December Uprising   47

  5. A Tubercular Education   55

  6. The Young Journalist   66

  7. Celia   79

  8. Persona Non Grata   91

  9. Elias and Ethnarch Makarios   100

 10. "I Don't Sit at My Desk"   111

 11. Blowback   120

 12. A Dark Side of Camelot   129

 13. Moving Left   143

 14. The Koumparos and the Star Reporter   158

 15. From Reporter to Activist   175

 16. Escape   191

 17. Exiled in America   199

 18. Junta-gate and the O'Brien Gambit   214

 19. Fighting the Dictatorship   237

 20. "Senator, are you telling me it's a trap?"   253

 21. Pushing Congress   270

 22. Campaign 1972   289

 23. Fallout from a Mutiny   302

24. Watergate, Window Dressing, and a Counter-Coup   314

25. Crisis on Cyprus   327

26. After the Junta   342

27. "The Plot to Snatch Demetracopoulos"   353

28. Fighting for Vindication   369

29. Later Years   387

AUTHOR'S NOTE   403
ACKNOWLEDGMENTS   405
ENDNOTES   407
BIBLIOGRAPHY   448
INDEX   474

Introduction

FOREIGN MEDDLING IN AMERICAN ELECTIONS didn't start in 2016.[1] In 1968, the Greek military junta, which had overthrown its country's democratic government the year before, tried to buy influence by secretly funneling $549,000—almost $4 million in today's dollars—to the Nixon campaign, money that likely began as "black budget" US aid to the Greek equivalent of the CIA.

The winning margin in that election, the second-closest presidential contest in the 20th century, was less than 1 percent. The bagman for the illegal funds was tycoon and Republican Party fundraiser Tom Pappas, who later became known on the Watergate tapes as "the Greek bearing gifts." Timely disclosure of this transfer could have meant a Hubert Humphrey victory, no President Nixon, no Watergate, and a different course of history.

At a 2009 fundraiser for the New England Center for Investigative Reporting, of which I am a founding board member, I told our guest speaker Sy Hersh I was considering writing something on this unexplored transaction, a stillborn October Surprise. He recommended I contact Greek journalist Elias Demetracopoulos in Washington, the person who tried unsuccessfully to expose the money-laundering plot. When I did, I quickly realized that this episode was but part of Elias's much larger and even more compelling life story.

As a boy he was brutalized for fighting his homeland's Nazi occupiers and imprisoned. He survived being shot in the Greek Civil War and nearly died of tuberculosis incubated during his incarceration. Inspired to become an investigative journalist by the 1948 assassination in Greece of CBS correspondent George Polk, Elias became a fiercely independent and scoop-hungry reporter, exposing truths others wanted hidden.

In 1967 he escaped Greece's military dictatorship and fled to Washington, where for seven years he led the fight to restore democracy in his homeland. He became a target of Greek plots to kidnap and execute him, as well as of CIA, FBI, and State Department attacks on his reputation and effectiveness. Unbroken, he resolutely stood up for himself, his country, and his sense of honor.

Elias Demetracopoulos was a difficult subject. He gave me full power under the Freedom of Information and Privacy Acts to access all his government files, and he provided reams of articles and documents concerning better-known aspects of his career, but opened up only slowly about his multifaceted personal life. He steadfastly resisted divulging the names of sources to whom he had pledged confidentiality, even long after the sources had died. Nevertheless, for more than five years I visited him frequently and talked with him by phone, often daily, as I tried to peel back the layers of his story, getting him to confirm or disconfirm information I'd discovered elsewhere, and reveal more of himself. Eventually he gave me access to his personal files, shared once-hidden stories, and permitted friends who held his confidences to speak openly with me.

Journalist, information broker, lobbyist, Wall Street financial consultant, trusted advisor, tipster, troublemaker, "dangerous gadfly," suspected foreign agent, desired extra man for Georgetown dinner parties, impassioned democracy fighter and free press advocate, a man with friends and sources spanning the political spectrum, Elias always cultivated an air of mystery and carefully compartmentalized the different parts of his life. When he died in 2016, obituaries in both the *New York Times* and the *Washington Post* described him as "enigmatic"; he was said to have negotiated "a unique and controversial swath through Washington's political and social thickets."[2]

Elias P. Demetracopoulos was never as famous as celebrity mononyms like Bono, Oprah, Liberace, and Madonna, but for decades he was known around the nation's capital and in major European cities as simply "Elias." And being famous in Washington is different from being famous in music or Hollywood.

When Susan Margolis sought to explain fame in her 1977 book of that name, she chose Elias as her exemplar of fame in Washington.[3] Fame, for Margolis, involved having power, having access to power, or appearing to have such access. Elias had it all. The essence of his success, she wrote, was his ability to be both an outsider and an insider, projecting an attractively reassuring savoir faire; to be a trusted keeper and sharer of secrets who had mastered the game of knowing what and how much to disclose or tantalizingly hold back until the next time.

We can see the impact of Demetracopoulos's reputation in the difference between two 1976 receptions held in honor of the publisher of *To Vima*, the then-influential Greek newspaper, following the restoration of Greek democracy. The Greek ambassador invited celebrity journalists and government officials to his embassy, but the gathering was small and unnoticed. The only "A-list invitees" who attended were Margaret Truman and her husband Clifton Daniels of the *New York Times*. [4]

The next evening, Elias borrowed the mansion of his friends Walter and Lydia Marlowe and threw a party for the same publisher that became the talk of the town. The guests included forty-two senators, with names like Fulbright, Kennedy, and Javits, thirty-four congressmen, cabinet officials, leading Washington socialites, financiers, reporters, columnists, editors, broadcast journalists, bureaucrats, and twenty-two ambassadors, including the Greek ambassador.

It was a remarkable achievement for someone who for many years was deemed persona non grata by both Greek and American officials.

There are lessons for us in Elias's unyielding battles against powerful and abusive governments and for human rights and democratic values; his dogged pursuit of news and would-be news leakers; his belief in the potential of congressional investigations and hearings to expose wrongdoing; and his effectiveness in working across partisan political aisles.

There are eerie echoes today of Elias's world of the 1950s, '60s and '70s: when foreign money tainted and undermined free and fair elections, when fragile democratic norms buckled under popular susceptibility to authoritarian impulses, when human rights were deemed expendable, when independent journalists and political critics were harassed, subjected to disinformation campaigns, and disparaged as purveyors of fake news.

It's my hope that the saga that follows will illuminate the real story behind this extraordinary Greek patriot and relentless champion of democracy and a free press.

THE GREEK CONNECTION

I.

Growing Up

HE WAS A JOURNALIST BEFORE he was a journalist. A gatherer and disseminator of information, he never considered doing anything else.

Elias Demetracopoulos grew up in a modest but comfortable four-room stone house at 51 Dafnomili Street, near the base of the north side of the greatest vantage point in Athens, Mount Lycabettos. From his yard, he could look up at its coniferous slopes and looming limestone prominence. His close-knit neighborhood was less than a mile from downtown Athens. The central street was an uneven dirt road flanked by Mediterranean pines, its quiet interrupted only by sounds of roosters and of street vendors passing through with pushcarts and donkey wagons noisily hawking their wares and services.

Little distinguished his stolidly middle-class home from the others in a neighborhood of shopkeepers and small merchants—except for the books. The house was filled with anthologies, mythologies, histories, and biographies in Greek and, most unusually, in English.

Elias's father, Panagiotis, was born in tiny Leondarion, about six miles from Megalopoli, a mountainous village in the province of Arcadia, in the east central Peloponnese. To poets, playwrights, and painters, Arcadia is a utopian idyll of unspoiled wilderness and natural beauty. At the end of the 19th century, Panagiotis's hardscrabble agrarian parents found it inhospitable land from which to eke out a living and an inauspicious place to raise a family. They moved to Athens in his early childhood.

Panagiotis Demetracopoulos shaped his own life. In his late teens, he sought his fortune in America. In Chicago, the destination of choice for Arcadian Peloponnesians, he worked at odd jobs, from construction to food carts, until the Great War came. Unlike fellow Greek emigrants, disparaged in ethnic lore as *koulourakia* (crumbly cookies) or *kotes* (hens), for remaining abroad in times of trouble, Panagiotis returned home to fight. He volunteered to defend the fatherland, and he was almost killed in the process.

Afterward, still seeking better economic prospects, he returned to Chicago, where he worked until the mid-1920s. He settled in the growing "Greektown" enclave along Halstead Street. It was a difficult time to be a Greek in America; Greek immigrants were discriminated against for being "strange," "undesirable," and "dangerous."[1] Panagiotis started his own fruit stand and did modestly well at first. Instead of sending his meager earnings home, he invested in the rapidly rising stock market of the Roaring Twenties. But, like many of the unsuspecting public, he was unaware of then-legal stock price manipulation schemes, and his losses soon outpaced his gains.

Growing nativism and exclusionary US immigration quotas on those coming from southern and eastern Europe, prompted Panagiotis to consider naturalization. But the pull of home was strong, and he did not want to be one of the many single Greek males to start an American family with a "picture bride."[2]

When Panagiotis returned to Athens, his English was good enough to provide him steady work as an interpreter for businessmen and tourists. But he wanted something more. A lover of history, antiquity, and the Greek classics, he was proud of his heritage and taught himself the elements of archaeology. He enrolled in the necessary courses, then passed the qualifying examination to be a state-certified, official guide to archeological sites throughout Greece. Panagiotis spent much of his life as a *xenagos*—a guide for foreigners at the Acropolis and Athens museums. For decades, "Mr. Demetracopoulos" was the big hotel concierges' guide of choice for visiting celebrities and other VIPs.[3]

Home for good, Panagiotis met Panagiota Bokolas, who had grown up in a moderately wealthy family with extensive farming and business interests in the northern Peloponnese town of Aigion, not far from the bustling port of Patras. Panagiota's good-natured demeanor masked her fiercely protective and take-charge personality. After a brief courtship, they married in Athens on February

25, 1928. Panagiotis was 40, a decade older than his bride. Less than ten months later, on December 1, they had their first and only child, Elias Panagiotis Demetracopoulos.

Elias was named for Elijah, the zealous prophet-saint who sternly reproves the lawlessness of Ahab and Jezebel, challenges the injustice of the King, slays false prophets and priests for leading the people astray, and ultimately rides to heaven in a flaming chariot. Given his father's Greek mythology predilections, Elias may also have been named for Helios, the all-seeing sun god who each day traversed the sky in his golden chariot. Either way, his name would prove prophetic.

■

MODERN GREEK HISTORY is a tale of tangled and conflicting dualities, including Byzantine and Western, authoritarian dictatorships and fragile democracies, alternating monarchies and republics. Its roots intertwine Hellenistic paganism and Christian orthodoxy and are expressed in both its liberal cosmopolitanism and provincial conservatism.[4]

From the fall of Constantinople in 1453 to its creation as a sovereign state in 1830, Greece was a peripheral province of the Ottoman Empire, a dusty backwater, outside the pale of basic economic development. The educational and cultural benefits of the Renaissance and Enlightenment had largely passed it by. Even the glories of ancient Greece were alien to the impoverished inhabitants. It was foreigners educated in the classics who rekindled interest and helped the new nation rediscover both its Hellenic and Byzantine pasts.

The oppressive Turkish occupation, rife with intrigue, corruption, favoritism, greed, opaque bureaucratic legerdemain and arbitrary enforcement of draconian laws, weighed heavily on Greek life. It took an assortment of Greek expatriates, wealthy westernized aristocrats and merchants, later joined by *kleftes*—guerrilla brigand leaders operating in rural mountainous regions—to ignite the Greek liberation movement. The insurgents knew that even though the Ottoman Empire was crumbling from within, their success ultimately depended on support from major European powers. In what would become a pattern over much of the next two centuries, they sought foreign patronage.

The governments of Britain, France, and Russia were slow to act. However, European and later American writers, poets, intellectuals, academics, and travelers, fueled by a romantic idealization of ancient Greece, ignited public opinion that engaged politicians and diplomats.[5] They celebrated ancient Greece as the progenitor of Western civilization. Periclean Athens was mythologized as the apotheosis of democracy in its purest form, the pinnacle of Western humanism and artistic achievement.

When Greeks launched their sporadic war of independence from the Ottoman Empire on March 25, 1821, the revolutionaries were riven by factional dissent. Politicians clashed with military leaders, and civil strife became civil war. The sultan, using support from Egypt, besieged and then captured Athens and the Acropolis.

In disarray, the Greeks cleverly enticed the self-interested involvement of the English, French, and Russians. The three powers proposed an armistice, warning the warring sides that if both did not accept the treaty offered, they would intervene. The Greeks accepted. The Turks did not. In the ensuing Battle of Navarino, the Allied squadrons destroyed the Ottoman fleet, effectively ending the war.

But the path to independence was perilous. The country split into regional blocs and moved closer to anarchy. In 1832, the Great Powers decided that Greece was too unstable to govern itself and would be better off as a monarchy. They shopped the royal houses of Europe and created a Kingdom of Greece with Bavarian Prince Otto Friedrich Ludwig imposed as its first ruler. Seventeen-year-old Otto, a Roman Catholic who never converted to Greek Orthodoxy, came with a regent, a retinue of Bavarian advisors, and more than 3,000 Bavarian troops. He later married a teenaged German Lutheran duchess, whose troublesome interference in affairs of state was a harbinger of 20th-century royal practices.

A minority of modernizers struggled against a majority of traditionalists to build a European-style government. After an 1843 military coup, the King was compelled to allow a constitution, modeled after that of France, but it was effectively a royal dictatorship. A form of democracy was established, but democratic rule was often twisted by violence, fraud, and clientelism. Childless, Otto was overthrown, and the royal line of succession was changed to become part of the historic German ducal House of Glucksburg, which includes the royal houses of Denmark, Norway, and Windsor.

DURING PANAGIOTIS'S ABSENCE from Greece, his homeland witnessed the collapse of the "Megali Idea": a type of manifest destiny that sought to incorporate large parts of the Byzantine Empire, including millions of Greece-identifying co-religionists or Greek speakers living in Ottoman lands.[6] By 1913, Greece had nearly doubled its territory and population.

The leading advocate for expansion was a charismatic young Cretan politician, Eleftherios Venizelos, who sought to transform his country at home and abroad. Dubbed "the Greek Bismarck," he became during the first decades of the 20th century the leading republican reformer, statesman, prime minister, and a national hero. However, in so doing, he clashed with King Konstantinos, whose ambitions were more modest. Their political battles led to a National Schism that would haunt the country for decades.[7]

Educated in Germany and married to Kaiser Wilhelm II 's sister, Konstantinos continued the crown's linkage to Germany. Believing Germany would easily win the Great War, the Germanophile royal palace decided to remain neutral and share in the victory of the Central Powers.

In stark contrast, Prime Minister Venizelos greatly admired Britain and France. Convinced that the British navy would eventually be victorious, Venizelos enthusiastically advocated that Greece ally itself with the Triple Entente Powers, a decision for which the country would be well rewarded.

The King's provocative and unconstitutional interference in foreign policy-making led to Venizelos's elected government's resigning, getting reelected, and resigning again in October 1915. In the ensuing National Schism, Konstantinos ruled from Athens, while Venizelos established a rival provisional government in Thessaloniki (known colloquially as Salonika).

The Allies recognized the Venizelos government. On the morning of December 1, 1916, twelve years to the day before Elias was born, after the Anglo-French fleet had surrounded the Greek capital and the King failed to negotiate a diplomatic solution, French warships bombarded the palace and other targets, killing and wounding civilians and Greek soldiers. Konstantinos abdicated and Venizelos formed a new national government, but he was defeated in the next plebiscite and went into exile. Konstantinos returned.

In dividing the spoils of World War I, the Allies, in the Treaty of Sèvres, gave Greece administrative control of the heavily Greek-populated Asia Minor coastal region of Smyrna (now Izmir), which had a Greek population more than half that of Athens, and Western and Eastern Thrace, not far from Constantinople. Turkey, however, refused to honor the treaty.

Ignoring diplomatic efforts of the Great Powers to find a peaceful solution to the impasse, Konstantinos and the new Greek government launched an ill-prepared invasion of Turkey, stretching out indefensible supply lines and failing in its assault on Ankara. Turkey struck back, intent on expunging 3,000 years of Greek history from its soil.

In August 1922, in what Greeks refer to as the "Great Catastrophe," at least several hundred thousand Greeks, some of whom traced their ancestry to the time of Homer, were killed, the result of gruesome tortures, rapes, and massacres that culminated in a monumental blaze at least partially set by Turkish forces: the Great Fire of Smyrna. It is estimated that more than a quarter-million Greeks died in the overall conflict.[8]

Violent ethnic cleansing, which had occurred to varying degrees in both countries for more than a decade, gave way to the diplomatically controlled ethnic cleansing stipulated in the Treaty of Lausanne: the forced exchange of religious minorities. Some 500,000 Moslem Turks were expelled from Greece, and more than 1,300,000 Christian Greeks from Asia Minor[9] were turned into refugees, most crowding into Greater Athens, Macedonia, and Western Thrace. They shared the same religion, but many were poor, culturally distinct, and did not speak Greek. Difficulties in assimilating them economically and socially would affect the political landscape for generations.

■

THE LATE-1920S GREECE in which Panagiotis and Panagiota were married was quite different from the one they'd grown up in. A vibrant shipping and trade center, Athens had seen its population nearly double. According to the 1928 national census, only a third of the nearly half-million Athenians had been born there, a third had moved from other parts of Greece, and a third were refugees from Asia Minor.

An expanding network of beige electronic streetcars had replaced the horse-drawn trams of Panagiotis's youth. Apartment blocks supplanted low-rise homes with gardens. Touches of modern architecture, from Bauhaus to Art Deco, dotted the 19th-century neoclassical skyline. The air was perfumed with fragrances of currants, cotton, olive oil, and tobacco, export crops that would soon crash in world markets.

But Greece's extended political upheaval had taken a toll. Mourning for the dead and the dashed irredentist dream gave way to a military takeover of the government and the scapegoating of competing partisans.[10] Officers of an anti-monarchist Military League purged officers loyal to the King, much the way Konstantinos had removed those loyal to Venizelos. Tribunals led to executions, and abdications led to a republic that could not stand. Multiple short-lived governments and several attempted military coups followed, capped by a successful military coup d'état whose leader was overthrown a year later. A republican constitution was passed in 1927, but the Populists, then the primary opponents of the republicans, refused to support it. Even the electoral system itself was a matter for dispute. High-minded rhetorical fights about whether Greece should be a republic or a monarchy continued, but the real stakes were patronage jobs and personal power.

Venizelos returned to power in 1928 committed to fostering a bourgeois democracy and improving international relations. He embarked on ambitious programs to reform education, build the nation's transportation infrastructure, and transform its traditional agriculture system. But in 1929, Elias Demetracopoulos's first year of life, the Wall Street crash and global Great Depression hit Greece hard. Emigrants' remittances, exports, and agricultural prices fell precipitously. New foreign loans were unavailable, and Greece suspended interest and payments on past obligations. Venizelos's ambitious modernization strategy unraveled.[11]

Venizelos lost control of Parliament. Unsuccessful coups and failed assassination attempts followed. In March 1935, Venizelos fled the country, opening the floodgates of retribution, purges, and executions of Venizelos loyalists. A rigged plebiscite paved the way for the restoration of the monarchy with Konstantinos's son, King George II, at its head.

In the January 1936 election, royalist parties won 143 seats and republicans 141. The Communists, with only a few thousand members, received about 50,000 votes, or 6 percent of the total. With only fifteen seats in Parliament, they held the balance of power. Despite public protestations to the contrary, both royalists and republicans shamelessly tried to cut secret deals with the Communists.[12]

General Alexander Papagos, the minister of war in 1936, told King George II that any government that included Communists was unacceptable to the military. The king reacted first by replacing Papagos with staunch royalist General Ioannis Metaxas. Then, after unsuccessful efforts to form a ruling coalition, he appointed Metaxas to run the government. The Parliament ratified the decision and adjourned. It did not meet again for a decade. The Metaxas dictatorship had begun.

The years since the National Schism had exposed profound differences between cosmopolitan and parochial, urban and rural, republican and monarchist impulses in Greek society. Venizelists and new immigrants were generally supportive of reforms, expanding educational opportunities, democratizing the language, and paving the way for capitalist modernization. In contrast, royalists and those whose families had lived in Old Greece for generations were largely defenders of traditional, often rural, staunchly conservative and deeply held religious values. They feared the pace and direction of social, economic, and cultural changes. The stage was set for battles to come.

■

FROM EARLY CHILDHOOD, Elias looked much older than his age. Taller and heavier than his friends, he had a deeper voice and started shaving earlier. His childhood friends recall him being gregarious but serious. George Enislides, a contemporary who grew up a few houses away from Elias, described him as being "always the gentleman," polite, respectful, and solicitous of others' feelings, a good listener, who detested bullies and saw no humor in mimicking boys or teasing girls.[13]

At the age of six, he eagerly walked the few blocks to his grammar school. It wasn't an especially rigorous education, and Elias remembered affectionately his first years in a classroom. Most of his chums enjoyed such childhood amusements as playing hide-and-seek, shooting marbles, and practicing soccer on back streets, where play was more often interrupted by street vendors with donkey carts than by a passing automobile. Elias joined in neighborhood pickup games but dropped out when soccer became an organized neighborhood-against-neighborhood activity.

An only child, Elias preferred the company of his elders, eavesdropping or sitting with them as they gathered by radio newscasts and discussed current events. He was, as he recalled, "too serious to have fun." But, he added with a twinkling eye and smile, he started early on his lifelong interest in women, young and old, actively listening to their perspectives on most everything.

He faced his first challenge at eight, when his parents thought it important for him to be trained at the Peiramatikon Gymnasium, the experimental school of the University of Athens. The city's most prestigious secondary school, it offered eight years of rigorous education and was limited to 30 boys per grade. Two cousins on his mother's side already attended upper classes there and were standout students. Admission to Peiramatikon was on the basis of a highly competitive entrance examination, which Elias passed on his first attempt.

In October 1937, two months before his ninth birthday, he entered the modern, spacious building on the corner of Lykavittou and Skoufa streets. The school was socially mixed, with a few children of the rich driven by their parents or chauffeurs in private cars, then still a rarity in Greece. Most, like Elias, came on foot from nearby.

Elias began as an unremarkable pupil. His more sophisticated peers considered him "naïve," somewhat insecure, and less articulate. He lacked the give-and-take common to those who grow up with siblings. His friends teasingly called him *boudalas*, a pejorative term for an awkward person, which in this case probably had more to do with his nerdy formality than with any physical clumsiness.

Elias's academic epiphany occurred when his professor of Greek, as part of an oral examination in front of the entire class, asked to see his copybook. Elias replied that he had forgotten it at home. "Go and bring it," demanded the teacher, knowing how close to the school Elias lived. Elias responded by confessing that he had never written the assigned lesson. Then, recalled a classmate more than 70 years later, "the professor scolded and ridiculed him in an abominable way."[14]

The public humiliation deeply hurt his pride. Afterward, Elias turned to his academic subjects with a vengeance. By the end of the term he was at or near the top of his class, and he stayed there. "It was a big achievement that made him self-confident and energetic, performing whatever he was doing with exactitude and diligence," said classmate Antonis Drossopoulos. Elias's favorite subjects were history, geography, and mathematics.

Elias had fond memories of the school's rigorous curriculum and the stern teachers who challenged and inspired him, but he was quick to acknowledge his father's leading role in his education: Panagiotis filled him with stories of the greatness of Greece from ancient days to the 1821 fight for independence. Adventures described by Homer and Xenophon weren't remote tales but living history. He learned from Herodotus the art of storytelling, and from Thucydides the importance of observation and careful reporting.

His father stressed the unwavering importance of truth, integrity, and the "majesty" of character. Repeatedly, he extolled *philotimo* as the highest of all virtues.[15] The roots of this very Greek word are: *philos* (friend) and *timi* (honor), but its meaning goes far beyond those simple words to an all-embracing way of life that encompasses the concepts of pride in one's heritage, country, community, family, and self. "You have a duty to do good" and "do the right thing eagerly," his father explained, "even at great personal sacrifice."

Some of the best times of his childhood were his private tours around the Acropolis, escorted by his father, who described Neolithic encampments more than 7,000 years earlier, mythological legends, twists of history, recent archaeological discoveries, and architectural details of the Parthenon itself. Although sometimes it seemed to Elias his father was practicing parts of his archaeological spiel, the message was so personalized that he thought it had been designed just for him. His father told him about the heroes of the Golden Age of Athens, the difficulty of transporting the thousands of large blocks of marble from a new quarry on Mount Penteli, and how sculptors ingeniously shaped the Parthenon's Doric columns to create the illusion of perfect symmetry. Panagiotis also described how different occupiers had turned sacred Acropolis buildings into a church, a mosque, a harem, and barracks. He pointed out the spots where the Turks had desecrated the Parthenon by using its interior for storage of ordnance and for target practice.[16]

Both father and son had a special affection and reverence for the sublime Erechtheion, built on the site where Athena and Poseidon were said to have fought over who should be the city's patron. Sometimes the two mortals would stand silently near the temple of the gods, gazing at the Porch of the Caryatids, where exquisite statues of women in diaphanous robes serve as columns, their forms basking in the lambent sunshine.

Elias never tired of trips to the Acropolis, scurrying up the broad stone steps as fast as his legs could carry him, always careful not to trip on the slippery marble surfaces. It was a magical time, with the expanding city stretched out below. No crowds, no tourists. Just the two of them, alone, the wind blowing, and a profound feeling that ghosts of their Hellenic heritage were everywhere. His father lectured him, tested him with questions, and dropped aphorisms, often quoting Plato on overcoming ignorance through education and Aristotle on the importance of friendship. Panagiotis also taught his son English from early childhood, at a time when speaking any second language was rare, and when, for the educated elites, the second language of choice was French. These lessons would prove fateful.

Large in stature and lean in build, with powerful hands and big ears, Panagiotis was imposing in personality and forcefully conservative in his beliefs and politics. He neither smoked nor drank, dismissing these habits as intemperate vices and personal failings. He had difficulty expressing affection, and Elias could not recall moments of tenderness or sentimentality with him. This reticence carried over into a reserved demeanor in his public life, which some of Elias's childhood friends remembered as being cold and unfriendly.

Politically, Panagiotis was more a cafeteria conservative than a true believer. He was not a regular churchgoer and did not particularly like Ioannis Metaxas or the trappings of his dictatorship. He was, however, sympathetic to the King and the royalist cause, and in recent years he had been quick to criticize Venizelos, his followers, and the failings of successive republican governments.

At first, Elias echoed his father's views, but at an early age he began asking questions, cultivating a slight contrarian streak. By age twelve he thought of himself as a liberal republican. To his father's surprise and sometimes displeasure, he became a youthful Venizelist, espousing the late statesman's cosmopolitan and reformist views.

Elias's first lessons in democracy had come from his father's inspirational descriptions of Hellenism and the golden age of Pericles, a romantic vision of freedom and portrait of ancient Greece as the "cradle of democracy." In school, however, he became increasingly impressed with stories about the American and French revolutions. He started to think through the meanings of democracy, from the 5th century B.C.E. to the 1930s, in all their nuanced complexity. The son began to pick at inconsistencies and uncomfortable truths in his father's unqualifiedly glorious legends. Elias liked part of the story of Socrates, the "gadfly" biting the steed of state for its own good,[17] but he was troubled that in doing so the philosopher brought about his own death by hemlock. He also was disturbed that the much-celebrated Periclean Athens denied rights to women and relied on the labor of slaves. He saw disconnects between aspects of modern Western democracies and the classical Greek version. Though Elias shared his father's nationalist pride, he was more open to questioning uncomfortable realties about his homeland.

Elias revered his father and respected his toughness, but chafed at his strictness. He had tremendous difficulty winning paternal praise or approval. It was his warm-hearted mother, indulging her only child, who acted as a gentle buffer against his father's sometimes overbearing pressures. Petite, but powerful in spirit, she ran the household and, although the youngest of her siblings, was the linchpin of her family's Athenian network. Although her inheritance was a critical safeguard for the family in hard times, she lived modestly and never used her relative wealth to diminish her husband's role as paterfamilias.

Elias's mother was deeply pious and went for vespers almost daily to the nearby church of Saint Nicholas, but she never forced her religiosity on her son. As a boy, he had often joined her at services, but as he got older he, like his father, preferred to stay away. In this, as in other activities, Panagiota encouraged Elias to find and express himself.

The life lessons his mother tried to instill in him complemented those of his father: Stand up for yourself but be tolerant of others. Keep your eyes open. Listen carefully. Be careful not to make snap judgments. She too impressed on him the importance of *philotimo*, doing the right thing, modestly, even when no one was watching.

Elias was fiercely protective of his mother, whose hearing difficulties became progressively worse. The sonorous voice and carefully modulated diction he developed early on to ensure that Panagiota would not be left out of conversations evolved into a speaking style that some later would describe as affected.

■

PANAGIOTIS NEVER DISCUSSED the discrimination he must have experienced while living in America. With close friends and family, he expansively praised the United States as a land of opportunity where liberty and democracy flourished together. America to him was "the apotheosis of nations," the likely and best world leader, then and in the future. On this issue, Elias did not challenge his father's views.

Elias's first encounter with an American was with its highest-ranking representative in Greece: Lincoln MacVeagh, the former publisher of the Dial Press, appointed ambassador by President Franklin D. Roosevelt in 1933 and famous for giving his inaugural public address in classical Greek. In the 1930s there was no US ambassadorial residence, so MacVeagh and his family had moved into the American School of Classical Studies on Souidias Street, an imposing stone edifice across from the home of one of Elias's uncles, whom Elias often visited. Occasionally the silver-haired MacVeagh would engage young Elias and his cousins warmly in street conversations about life in Greece and books they might consider reading.

Elias's father had met MacVeagh on a few of the diplomat's frequent archeological outings on the Acropolis—the finds from which MacVeagh contributed to the Greek National Museum—and Panagiotis respected the legate's keen interest in Greek antiquities. At the same time, MacVeagh's trenchant, often acerbic telegrams and dispatches provided Washington with a steady stream of information describing the "labyrinthine complexities" of the various royalist and Venizelist intrigues, coups, and counter coups in the immediate pre-war period, and the King's blessing of Metaxas's right-wing dictatorship.

For a long time, the United States had not had close relations with Greece, a country largely irrelevant to its interests.[18] The United States waited until 1837 to appoint its first consul in Greece and did not establish full diplomatic relations until 1868. For more than a hundred years, the United States had left nation-building in the Balkans to the Europeans, with Greece predominantly a region of British influence. MacVeagh, however, in monitoring signs of a second World War, first promoted, then managed the American transition from passive observer to active participant in that Southern European arena.

■

GENERAL METAXAS HAD a soft square face, Charlie Chaplin moustache, round wire-rimmed spectacles, thinning hair combed back over a high widow's peak, and an avuncular appearance. He believed his people needed a paternalistic popular autocracy, more discipline and efficiency. When he took over in 1936, he declared his Fourth of August Regime to be the Third Hellenic Civilization, blending the best of mythic ancient Athens, the First Hellenic Civilization, and Byzantium, the Christian apogee. And he paid unsubtle homage to Hitler and Mussolini, demanding to be called *Kyvernitis* ("Governor") and requiring people give him the Fascist salute. Having trained with the German army, he had a proclivity for Teutonic values and culture.

Metaxas declared a state of emergency, annulled parts of the constitution, decreed martial law, imposed press censorship, and curtailed freedom of speech. He created a secret police apparatus to restore public order, crushing the incipient Communist Party. As dictator, he larded the civil service with his friends and purged liberals and centrists.

During his four and a half years, Metaxas did much that could be characterized as tyrannical, reactionary, sanctimonious, and absurd.[19] But notwithstanding his Teutonic predilections, he maintained British ties and did not embrace the Axis. He significantly reorganized the armed forces to prepare for any incursion from Bulgaria across a newly fortified border called the "Metaxas line."

Metaxas overreacted to the Communist threat. In suppressing countless supporters at home and expelling thousands to intolerable island prisons, he fostered a wellspring of sympathy to their cause internationally. With the benefit of hindsight, Elias agreed with historians who described the Metaxas regime as fascism lite, a variety closer to Salazar's Portugal than Hitler's Reich. For one thing, he lacked "one of the most important hallmarks of fascism, an ideologically radicalized mass base,"[20] even if he did create a state-organized youth movement. Nevertheless, Elias felt that his parents, who despite their royalist leanings were not enthusiastic with life under Metaxas, should have been stronger in their criticism. Elias and his family did not know any Communists and did not feel any particular affinity for their ideological cause, but as early as age nine Elias made clear his distaste for the dictator. His role model for these views, and many others, was the family's eloquent 40-year-old doctor and close friend, Kostas Giannatos, a debonair scion of a notable Athenian family.

The Demetracopoulos household followed the news closely, from the Third Reich's annexation of Austria to its takeover of Czechoslovakia in 1938 and the invasion of Poland in 1939. Their polished wooden shortwave radio, with its bright dial, impressive buttons, and cloth-covered speaker, held a place of honor in the living room. It was usually tuned to a BBC broadcast or local news. From time to time, friends who didn't have such radios came by to listen and discuss the day's events and ponder the future. Through this medium, more than the newsreels preceding movies at the cinema, Hitler, and his strident staccato oratory, became an increasingly palpable presence in the Demetracopoulos household.

Newspapers were their most important source of information. The family's daily paper was *Kathimerini*, the preferred choice of conservative Greeks. Every day Panagiotis sat quietly in his big armchair in the living room, methodically reading the broadsheet. Elias also picked up copies of the center-left *Ta Nea* on daily trips to the local kiosk. Whether he did this out of an early interest in multiple news sources, or simply to tweak his father, is not clear. Elias got his first paying job at the age of nine, distributing a variety of newspapers in the neighborhood. He was a familiar sight, out before breakfast, freshly scrubbed, wearing a clean shirt, short pants, and polished shoes, pulling a wagon piled high with papers along his route. It was the first money he earned in the news business.

■

AT THE OUTBREAK of war in 1939, ten-year-old Elias eagerly advocated for the British-French side. His mother was generally apolitical. His father did not like the Germans but respected their prowess. Sensitive to the royal family's historic ties to Germany, and aware of the economic benefits of maintaining good trade relations with the National Socialist government, he was not eager to see Greece enter the fray. The country was bitterly divided between the royalists and Venizelists. Panagiotis felt that the best choice for Greece, as during the Great War, was to remain effectively neutral.

One issue on which the whole family could agree was their contempt for Italy, the country that posed the most immediate threat to Greece. After the fall of France and other German conquests, Benito Mussolini became increasingly restive, resentful that Germany had, without telling him, moved into Romanian oil fields that he regarded as part of Italy's sphere of influence. He wanted to show his Axis partner that Italy too could achieve significant victories. Il Duce's vision of a new Roman Empire included the takeover of Greece, and he set about finding ways to provoke a Greco-Italian war, whipping up propaganda at home, authorizing flyovers of Greek territory, and encouraging sporadic attacks on Greek vessels.

The August 15, 1940, torpedoing of the light cruiser *Elli,* moored at the island of Tinos for the annual Feast of the Dormition holy pilgrimage, was particularly odious. Sailors were killed. Onlookers panicked. Greek government officials pretended they didn't know the perpetrators, but many citizens disbelieved them. That date, the name day for both of Elias's parents, marked the moment when Elias's father ceased to support Greek neutrality.

■

ITALY APPROVED WAR plans to attack Greece on October 26. Two days later, at about three in the morning, Italy's ambassador in Athens, Emanuele Grazzi, left the Italian Embassy for Metaxas's house in the suburb of Kiffisia. There, he woke up the Greek leader and handed him an ultimatum from Mussolini in which Il Duce demanded safe passage for his troops to occupy unspecified "strategic points" inside Greek territory. A heated exchange in French ensued. Italy was in effect asking to be invited to invade Greece. Metaxas rejected the ultimatum, shouting: "Alors, c'est la guerre" ("and so it's war"). In this surprisingly brave act of defiance, he voiced the will of the Greek people to resist, a spirit popularly expressed in the single word *ochi* ("no").

Air-raid sirens sounded in Athens at the first light of dawn. Within hours of the diplomatic confrontation, Italy began attacking Greece from Italian-occupied Albania. A country of 40 million with the second-strongest military on the continent invaded a nation of fewer than eight million. The outcome seemed obvious. In London, His Majesty's government, which had signed a declaration in April 1939 proclaiming that, if Greece's independence were threatened, it would be honor-bound to provide "all the support in their power," decided there wasn't much that could be done. Mussolini had been assured by his staff that Greece could be defeated in a matter of weeks.

Metaxas rallied the nation. It helped that Italy's planning and mobilization were incompetent, and that the Italians lacked the manpower, supplies, and expertise to do battle in the mountainous terrain of northern Greece. Although it was already late autumn the invaders, expecting a short conflict, did not even bring winter coats. Fortuitously, unseasonably bad weather rendered Italy's superior air force ineffective. In the Pindos Mountains in Epirus and West Macedonia, the invading Italians were soundly defeated and pushed back into Albania. By mid-November, it became clear that the Italian version of a blitzkrieg had failed miserably. The two sides positioned themselves for a long winter slog.

The Demetracopouloses and their neighbors cheered the early upbeat, fragmented reports they received from the BBC and Radio Athens. They laughed at the anti-Mussolini songs and jokes that ridiculed their Italian enemy. At first, they tracked battles on a regional map tacked to a living-room wall, using colored pins to mark Greek military progress. But, as time wore on and they heard more stories of returning soldiers maimed and deeply frostbitten, their mood darkened. For much of Elias's young life, the word *polemos* (war) had been something once-removed. He had read about its ravages in Tolstoy and other works of literature and in his history books. There was even a touch of unreality to the reports of conflicts in remote parts of Europe and nearby Albania. But increasingly, Elias's parents expressed deep concerns about impending danger. *Polemos* was coming much closer to Dafnomili Street.

2.

Resisting the Germans

SPRINGTIME IN GREECE IS PRECIOUS. Clear blue skies and sparking cobalt water. Roses, oleander, bougainvillea, and a splash of scarlet poppies. The fecund soil, aromatic citrus trees, and other scents enhance "rosy-fingered" dawns and the soul-lifting warmth of morning sunshine. But in 1941 the sensual attractions of the country's natural beauty were suffused with the sounds, sights, and stench of war.

In January, Greece, grossly underestimating German troop strength in Romania, refused British offers of an expeditionary force as not worth the risk of alienating Hitler.[1] Unbeknownst to Greece, Hitler had already signed a directive to invade. By early February, following the sudden death of General Metaxas and a growing unease that neither Turkey nor Yugoslavia could withstand a German invasion, Greece concluded it had to take some action. King George, then effectively in charge, asked for British anti-aircraft and anti-tank support, but was still reluctant to accept troops or RAF squadrons. At the same time, his new government overruled defeatist generals, officers, and politicians who proposed seeking a peace agreement with the Axis rather than fighting.[2]

In early March, the Italian offensive again failed to break through the Greek lines. Harsh spring weather and the wretched conditions of roads and bridges provided an added defense. But Greece lacked the guns and ammunition to mount a serious counteroffensive. Finally, the king turned to Britain.

Churchill's first priority had been the protection of his home front, which had been battered by air raids. His second priority was the campaign in North Africa. But with the situation calming in England, and recent military successes in Egypt and Libya, he considered transferring an Allied expeditionary force, mainly New Zealanders and Australians, from Egypt to Greece. The British War Cabinet's decision to provide troops was not an easy one. Churchill himself equivocated in the face of pressure from Antipodean leaders fearful of their troops being slaughtered in an ill-planned campaign. Quarter-century-old memories of the vast casualties at Gallipoli still haunted the Allies. But there were strategic reasons to get involved, from control of the Eastern Mediterranean to the possible opening of a Balkan front. Furthermore, Churchill was an unabashed champion of British imperial grandeur and by extension Greece's King George II, who was related to the British royal family.

In Berlin, war planning focused on Operation Barbarossa, the massive invasion of Russia. News from Greece about the travails of the faltering Italians was an unwelcome distraction, but it also convinced the Germans that mounting the Russian campaign with an exposed southern flank was too risky. They had no choice but to delay Operation Barbarossa and come to the aid of their embarrassed Axis partner. Rather than occupying Greece, the German high command expected to win decisively and then share the follow-on administrative responsibilities with the Italians and Bulgarians.

The Demetracopoulos family, like their neighbors, waited anxiously in anticipation of a German onslaught. *Kathimerini* publisher George Vlachos, in a March 8 front-page open letter, proudly declared Greek independence and appealed to Hitler not to invade. The letter concluded: ". . . this land which may be small but is also great. This land that taught the world to live will now teach it how to die." Elias and his parents were moved by the message, but such nationalist paeans were no match for armored steel. On Sunday April 6, panzer and infantry units of the German Twelfth Army attacked Greece and Yugoslavia from Bulgaria, overcoming resistance, and circumventing the vaunted Metaxas Line.

With lightning speed, they moved south. Defenses quickly fell apart. Three days later Thessaloniki, the country's second largest city, fell to the invaders. Other areas followed, isolating the Greek Army. British forces withdrew from strategic Thermopylae, not wanting to become trapped in the narrow pass as Leonidas and the 300 Spartans had 2,000 years before.

More than 15,000 Greek and 3,700 Allied soldiers were killed. Many others were taken prisoner. More than 50,000 British, Australian, New Zealand, and Free Polish divisions and brigades, in hasty retreat, evacuated the country under Luftwaffe fire. Allied soldiers left to fend for themselves turned to locals for help escaping.[3]

The roar of gunfire over Athens shattered the morning quiet of Easter Sunday, April 20, as German Stukas dive-bombed the city.[4] Messerschmitts, flying terrifyingly low over rooftops, strafed nearby towns and ports, their machine guns drumming densely populated areas. People ran for cover where they could. Some went to nearby shelters. Most simply cowered in their homes. Athens looked abandoned. Meanwhile, the government vacillated.[5] More than a few Greek generals and high officials viewed armed opposition as suicidal, but King George, in a response long appreciated by Churchill afterward, urged the Greek army to fight as long as possible.[6] It was a noble gesture, but too little too late. The demoralized Greek prime minister, Alexandros Koryzis, committed suicide.

On April 20, Greek Army Corps Commander Lt. General Georgios Tsolakoglou offered the Army's unilateral surrender to the Germans. Tsolakoglou acted quickly to avoid the greater dishonor of surrendering to the Italians. An enraged Mussolini insisted that the surrender ceremony be repeated three days later with Italians included.[7]

On Sunday, April 27, 1941, the conquering Germans entered Athens with an imposing display of tanks, trucks, motorcycles, and armed troops on horseback. Believing classical Greece to be the progenitor of the Third Reich, and Greek soldiers "the valorous descendants of Alexander's hoplites,"[8] Hitler praised the non-Aryan Greek fighters for their bravery and ordered honorable armistice terms.[9] Keeping the structure of the Metaxas regime, the Germans established a puppet government in Athens, with General Tsolakoglou as the quisling prime minister.

During the first agonizing hours of occupation, 12-year-old Elias had hundreds of questions. Though he never imagined his own death, he fantasized dark and fearful images of his parents being tortured and killed, his neighborhood and country destroyed. He felt the urge to resist but had little idea of exactly what that meant.

Some families made plans to send their children to stay with relatives in rural villages or the islands, or even out of the country, where they might be safer. There were no such discussions in the Demetracopoulos household. Elias always thought his father to be a "tough fellow" and "not a pushover," but didn't see him rush to take arms or join a group. Neither did he see his other relatives act. His mother fretted about the situation and worried that her strong-willed son would behave precipitously. Knowing he would not spend all his days at home, his parents cautioned him to think carefully before acting.

Surprisingly, Elias's mother was one of the first to take decisive action. Two days before the Easter surrender, at about seven o'clock on Good Friday morning, she went to meet several friends to prepare garlands to decorate the makeshift wooden "tomb" outside her beloved St. Nicholas church. Coming down the church steps were some black-clad women, jabbering nervously. They told her to go inside. There they pointed out two gangly, hungry, scared Australian soldiers who had been hiding in the sanctuary. The soldiers knew only a few phrases of Greek, and the ladies collectively knew little English. Germans were out to capture or kill enemy Allied soldiers left behind. The apolitical Panagiota Demetracopoulos took charge. She directed a friend to "find Elias quickly" and, tell him, without explaining the reason, that his mother wanted him in church *tora* (right now). School cancelled; Elias had been at home reading. He came immediately to serve as interpreter, interviewer, and information broker.

The Aussies wanted to join their comrades on Crete but didn't know how to do it. They did not want to wander the streets of Athens in their uniforms. Elias first found someone who had civilian clothes that would fit. Then, with the help of Dr. Giannatos, he contacted people helping to smuggle Allied soldiers out of the country. He was proud, scared, excited, and still only twelve years old.

■

THE GREEK FLAG was still flying at the eastern end of the Acropolis when the occupiers rolled into Athens and ordered that it be replaced by the German swastika. To fiercely proud Greeks, there could not have been a greater affront than hoisting and unfurling at the Parthenon an enormous red-and-black Nazi flag. To a man like Panagiotis Demetracopoulos, who had spent much of his life studying and teaching others about Greece's greatest achievements, this gesture, symbolizing rape and domination, evoked humiliation and outrage.

Panagiotis and his archaeologist colleagues reacted differently to the occupation. The director of the Acropolis resigned in disgust and was soon in the mountains looking to organize a resistance. Others, scared silent, remained at their posts. Many German officers expressed their reverence for ancient Hellas. A highly idealized understanding of classical Greek culture, literature, and artistic creations was an essential part of German education.[10] They made it a point on their arrival to visit major ancient historical locations and pose for photos as war tourists. Some requested personally guided tours of the Parthenon and other sites at the Acropolis. When asked to provide such a service, Panagiotis Demetracopoulos refused, went home, and did not return to the Acropolis until after the war.

Late on Friday night, May 30, two eighteen-year-old Athens University freshmen climbed up the eastern side of the Acropolis and tore down the fluttering swastika flag. Under the cover of darkness, they fled with it to safety, burying it in an Acropolis well. Word of the act was disseminated through drippingly sarcastic editorials in the censored press "condemning" the "despicable seizure" of the German flag, which everyone knew was a "symbol of the New Reich, created by the mind of the genius Adolf Hitler, . . . the flag of a great nation, . . . symbol of the restoration of an era of peace, as a symbol of justice, the rule of law and civilization."[11] The two leftist students were never caught. Elias understood the irony in the editorial message and marveled at the power of the press to make its point, even under oppressive circumstances. Word of the flag caper spread rapidly and inspired some Greeks to discuss making other dramatic gestures of "heroic madness,"[12] but young Elias, however self-confident and prideful, did not see the point of taking on the Nazis singlehandedly.

Residents were put on notice that harsh punishments would be imposed for unlawful assemblies and organizational memberships, strikes and demonstrations, possession of firearms and short-wave radios, listening to foreign broadcasts, distributing anti-German propaganda and sabotage. Some locals spontaneously cheered and tossed precious cigarettes to British prisoners being convoyed across Athens, and others painted graffiti on walls or punctured tires of occupier vehicles, but overt acts of resistance were few and scattered. The conquerors did not sense much antagonism. An unusually eerie calm prevailed.

The occupiers jettisoned their initial restraint, confiscating homes and automobiles. German reverence for Greek antiquities gave way to pilferage, looting, and destruction.[13] Soon people realized that the token amounts Germans made for purchases were in worthless currency. Greek patients were discharged from hospitals to make space for Germans. Despite the harsh heat of summer, shutters were ordered closed. The curfew forced people indoors from 6 p.m. to 7 a.m. Stories of random acts of cruelty, such as breaking a little girl's forearm as punishment for taking bread, became common.

The spirit of national unity that had prevailed during the Italian invasion soon fractured. The dominant mood in Athens was one of disillusionment, bitterness, resignation, and private recrimination. Few took immediate action, although some politicians followed King George into exile, first to Crete, then to Cairo or London. They sought to create a government-in-waiting, prepared to build international support for the Greek cause and then, after the war, return to power. Meanwhile, the king and his initial government-in-exile cautioned those left behind against "involvement in politics,"[14] a directive interpreted as not advocating resistance. In a prescient analysis, Ambassador MacVeagh warned Washington that the Greek people would long remember the King's role in the Metaxas dictatorship, and his flight from the country. MacVeagh sensed that the King's return after the war, even with the support of the British, would not be a simple matter.[15]

Some Athenians left the city for isolated mountain encampments and from there, in the following months, joined with small bands of guerrillas. Other Greeks chose to collaborate to various degrees with the occupiers for personal gain. Most people simply stayed home, unsure of what else to do. It took months before the *antartes* (resistance fighters) came together under the banner of a National Liberation Front and its military arm ELAS, and to a lesser extent the anti-Communist EDES.[16] There were also smaller groups, in Athens and elsewhere, tied to the secretive British MI6 and MI9.[17] The resistance of these units largely took the form of intelligence-gathering, facilitating propaganda, organizing escape networks for Allied operatives and prisoners of war, and engaging in small acts of sabotage. For much of the war, this was Elias's world.

Shortly after the April invasion, Peiramatikon was taken over by the Germans and used for administrative offices, and the school was forced to scatter its students to various places, with Elias's classes moved across the street to the St. Denis Church. The school let out early for summer vacation. When lessons resumed in October, all grades were crowded into the church annex, a little house located just behind the sanctuary. Only four rooms were available, so the school operated in shifts, with classes limited to about two hours each and the curriculum dramatically reduced. Because of the lack of wintertime fuel, schools would operate only in the autumn and spring months until liberation.

Elias had time to find a resistance group. He sought out Dr. Giannatos, who told Elias about OAG, a relatively small group operating early in Athens.[18] Its acronym stood for *Organosis Anastaseos Genous*, roughly translated as Organization for the Resurrection of the Race, with the last word having cultural Hellenistic rather than genetic implications.[19] Giannatos explained to Elias that he, his brother, and his sister-in-law were part of the group. With a touch of clandestine excitement, he introduced his young friend to some OAG members and later, in his book-lined Kolonaki study, encouraged Elias to join. Not insignificantly, he also tried to allay the concerns of Elias's anxious parents.

In the ideological taxonomy of Greek politics, OAG was "a group of the Right,"[20] deeply conservative and staunchly anti-Communist, composed largely of professionals such as doctors, lawyers, journalists, Greek military officers, and English expatriates. Though some were republican, most were unabashed royalists and sympathetic to the king's plight while he was in exile. Dr. Giannatos advised Elias to keep his anti-royalist reservations to himself. The organization was headed by Ioannis "John" Bobotinos, a chemistry teacher and decorated army officer from Kalamata who had recently fought the Nazis in Crete,[21] and previously served in the Asia Minor Wars. For Bobotinos, a fierce nationalist, defending the homeland was tantamount to a religious obligation. He was never interested in being part of the National Liberation Front (EAM) and its army (ELAS) because of the paramount roles played in those organizations by the KKE, the Greek Communist Party. And he viewed EDES, which at the beginning of the war espoused republicanism, as also too far to the left.

The world of OAG became Elias's new classroom. The boy fast became an active, albeit entry-level, member. His new mission was helping his comrades, whose identities were often unknown to him, with intelligence-gathering and sabotage. His English was not especially good at this point, but it was better than that of most in the group. Bobotinos welcomed the young recruit and came to praise him for his energy, honesty, and reliability.

At the beginning, he was simply a gatherer of general information, picking it up from different vantage points by unobtrusive observation. Then he became an active intelligence source, who could elicit the answers to assigned questions quickly and pass on the responses. Bobotinos later claimed that OAG was the first of the resistance groups to focus on sabotaging military targets and had done such jobs well before EAM and ELAS. Disabling the military airport at Tatoi, north of Athens, was an early objective. Six members conducted surveillance and then blew up the airfield's underground gas storage facility along with 15 airplanes. Others cut telephone lines in the Irakleio area to block communications between Tatoi and Nazi headquarters in downtown Athens. Another OAG cell committed daytime sabotage at the Maltsinioti munitions factory and repeatedly raided Chasani Airport at night. Escapes were harrowing. The Germans retaliated brutally, sometimes torturing and murdering someone who merely looked like an OAG member. Elias often collaborated with a member named Angelos Barkas and his brother, carrying incendiary devices, lighting fuses, and acting as their lookout.

Elias still met with his old friends and joined in family routines, but his life had changed dramatically.[22] He would go to local movie houses or open-air theaters and watch German propaganda newsreels and films that were not banned. But traveling to beaches on hot days and taking other day trips outside Athens were pleasures of the past. His customary practice was to stay close to his house, reading and listening to outlawed broadcasts, waiting for someone to send a courier to tell him he was needed at a particular place, usually without delay. Not infrequently he was out all night, since he did not want to risk returning home during the curfew.

Disregarding the immediate danger to his life, the boy repeatedly talked his way into opportunities to gather secret information. Elias learned quickly how to ferret out actionable intelligence and developed a nose to distinguish fact from fiction, reliable sources from blowhards. With just a few carefully crafted questions, a thoughtful cultivation of active listening skills, and knowledge gleaned from picking up salient nonverbal cues, he was usually able to discern whether a would-be informant was telling the truth, did not have any useful answers, or was leading him astray. He learned how to acquire the "who, what, when, and where" of newsgathering under the pressure of tight deadlines and pass the news on to his handlers. And, like the good reporter he would one day become, he cultivated a widening network of reliable contacts. Many of Elias's school friends were involved to varying degrees in different resistance activities, but they regarded Elias as the most close-lipped. He never revealed anything about his exploits.[23]

One of his proudest activities was making the nearly 300-mile trip from Athens to Salonika (Thessaloniki) with OAG confederates in early August 1943 to help with the escape logistics, burials, and language needs of some English-speaking fliers. The airmen had been shot down in the daring and disastrous treetop-level Allied bombing raid on the oil refineries in Ploesti, Romania, a mission in which 177 planes left from Benghazi, Libya, and only eighty-eight returned.

Elias's parents thought of themselves as patriotic, but they were not among the rare Greek families who made their homes safehouses or otherwise provided shelter for Allied soldiers in hiding. Their greatest risk, until Elias started storing guns and ammunition at home, was listening to prohibited BBC and other Allied broadcasts on their outlawed shortwave.

They gathered each evening around the radio and strained to hear the BBC Greek broadcast signal through German jamming devices. The transmission began with the four opening notes of Beethoven's Fifth Symphony—mimicking the "dot, dot, dot, dash" sound of the Morse code letter *V*, the symbol adopted for "victory." Before the news came the prologue: "Greeks. Our thoughts are near you. You are the heroes who said the big 'No' to a strong enemy. You are the ones who offered the first victory to the Allies. We admire you and we are grateful. The time is approaching when your country again will be free and glorious. Our struggle continues until the final victory . . ."[24]

The broadcasts carried Allied propaganda, coded operational messages from British intelligence, and brief communications from loved ones in London and Alexandria. As one Athenian remembered the experience, the broadcasts filled "us with hope [. . .] The radio broke our isolation, animated our spirit of national pride, and reinforced our souls' resistance."[25] With strict press censorship, accurate news was hard to come by. Great dangers lurked for people caught reading or simply having banned papers at home. People met in parks and other public places to exchange a blend of facts and rumors. Panagiotis and Panagiota were frequently more pessimistic than hopeful. For the most part, they just kept their heads down and tried to survive. Elias's father withdrew into his world of books. Elias's mother had her beloved church. Both were proud of their only child and understood why he wouldn't share the details of his activities with them. They worried about his safety, but never tried to stop or discourage him. His mother gave him a medallion to wear that depicted St. Barbara, the protector of those who work with artillery and explosives.[26]

■

IN ATHENS, THE increasingly strict rationing became painful. But then things got worse. Winter 1941–42 was brutal. For most Greeks who lived through the era, the very word *katochi* (occupation) still evokes dreadful memories of the privations of war and the pains of oppressive foreign occupation. Elias Demetracopoulos, who only reluctantly shared stories of the years of subjugation, was no exception.

There had been food in the countryside, but much of that, along with raw materials and cash reserves, was forcibly requisitioned for the Reich. Resources that made it to Athens, from olive oil to pack animals, were confiscated or purchased with nearly worthless currency by the occupiers. The Germans also imposed "forced loans" and levied an onerous taxation scheme that forced the locals to pay for their own occupation.[27] To make matters worse, peasants played their own games with the food supply, and the quisling government lacked the competence and integrity to handle the overall logistics. On top of all that came a disastrous British blockade that diverted wheat and other necessities.

The breakdown of food transportation and distribution hit Athens the hardest. Rationing and long queues for scant foodstuffs set the stage for an active black market. Buses stopped running. Everyone walked. Refugees huddling in the slums and shantytowns on the outskirts of the city bore the brunt of the famine. It was unusually cold, with snow in the streets of Athens. Houses went without heat. Food rations disappeared altogether. Stray dogs and cats were hunted for food; then rodents, which were skinned and sold as "rabbit." Bread was made from lupine, and coffee shops brewed ground chickpeas. Per-capita nourishment dropped to between 400 and 800 calories a day.[28]

The acute food shortage led to malnutrition and starvation. Cadaverous children, with festering sores, bulging eyes, threadbare clothes, swollen feet and stomachs, scavenged scraps from rotting garbage. People collapsed and died from hunger and disease. Municipal trucks would drive by to pick decaying corpses off the streets or from underground air-raid shelters. Some families intentionally left their relatives' bodies stripped of identification in cemeteries or parks, so they could keep their ration cards—but there were no longer any rations.

Signs of deprivation were everywhere. Men without jobs turned to peddling used clothing and household items or simply begging. Women went without food to provide for their children, turning to soup kitchens serving watery gruel. Others gathered and boiled wild grass and weeds to feed their families. An estimated 300,000 people died of hunger and related causes in the Great Famine of the first winter, between 40,000 and 100,000 in Athens alone.[29]

Occasional support from Panagiota's family, along with her inheritance—which included gold sovereigns, jewels, and gold jewelry squirreled away under floorboards and other hiding places at home—was enough to permit the Demetracopoulos family to weather the worst, even when inflation ran rampant and barter became the means of exchange.[30] But, unsure of how long the war would last, they knew they needed other income. Panagiotis worked odd jobs, but steadier employment was critical, and ultimately he turned to Panagiota's wealthy brother, Costas Bokolas. Among Bokolas's business interests was a highly successful eponymous patisserie and coffee shop in Kolonaki. Costas doted on his youngest sister and had ample resources to help out his many family members, but, according to Elias, he made Panagiota's husband grovel for the hard-to-get job, then intemperately bossed his more intellectual employee around the store in front of customers. The shop flourished during all the privations, and Panagiotis's long hours working the counter selling sweets and waiting on tables were indispensable to the family's survival. But the image of his taciturn, lean, and proud father bending over a broom, hectored by his short, pudgy uncle, lingered long with Elias.

The boy, sensitive to his parents' embarrassment and wanting to contribute to the meager family budget, had already dropped out of Peiramatikon. A childhood friend remembered an awkward encounter when some of his former classmates saw Elias trudging down a street, carrying a large sack, hawking cigarettes and candies. Elias tried to make light of the situation, offering free caramels to his friends. They, knowing how important each *lepto* (a hundredth of a drachma) was to him, declined, but also bought nothing.[31]

Besides running with OAG and peddling cigarettes and caramels, Elias arose early to help distribute various censored publications to a public hungry for news. OAG found hidden print shops that were willing to publish its resistance leaflets and illegal newspapers. It was risky business. Producers, editors, and distributors of free underground newspapers such as *Eleftheria* were hunted down. Thirty-year-old Efangelos Votsadopoulos, who performed all of those roles for OAG's illicit publications, was executed. Others were sent to a facility in the northern suburb of Chalandri, which was used for forced labor and as a transit depot to death camps. The children who distributed the one-page news flyers house-to-house were mercilessly targeted. Elias was one of them. He had some close calls, but for a long time he eluded capture.

In autumn 1941, OAG's resistance activities grew in audacity and impact with the arrival of the dashing Polish-born Allied-forces commando Jerzy Iwanow-Szajnowicz, who would become another important figure in Elias's life.[32] To some he was known as Georgios Ivanof, simply Ivanov, or by his cover name, Kiriakos Parissis. To British intelligence he was cryptonym "033B." Son of a Polish mother and a Tsarist Russian colonel father, he was born in Warsaw on December 14, 1911. His mother divorced the colonel, married a Greek (Giannis Lamprianidis), and moved to Thessaloniki. In that cosmopolitan community, the dashing Ivanof, with wavy dark hair and blue-gray eyes, blossomed. He became a multilingual scholar and an outstanding athlete: an Olympic-level swimmer, he went to Warsaw on holidays to star on the Polish championship water polo team.

When the war broke out, Ivanof, using his contact with the Polish consul in Thessaloniki, went to Palestine to become an officer in the Independent Carpathian Rifle Brigade and fight the Germans in the Middle East and North Africa. He then joined the British Special Operations Executive Unit No. 004 in Cairo. Trained in Alexandria, he was transferred to Greece by submarine, going ashore near Marathon under cover of darkness on October 13, 1941.

Ivanof's OAG connection was established by Mariana Giannatos, the sister-in-law of Elias's mentor Dr. Giannatos, who worked at the Polish Embassy in Athens. She was married to the doctor's brother Dimitrios, a butcher who was also an early OAG member. For tactical reasons the conspirators decided that Ivanof would be better trusted within OAG if he were presented as Mariana's brother. Equipped only with a pistol, a switchblade, and a small radio transmitter, Ivanof contacted Bobotinos, then set himself up within the OAG intelligence network. His goal was to help the English by interrupting German logistical chains as materially as possible, whether they operated by air, land, or sea. Young Elias was instantly impressed when he met Ivanof and was eager to work for him in whatever way he could be useful.

A polyglot whose languages included Polish, Russian, French, Greek, German, Italian, and English, Ivanof had a remarkable ability to infiltrate installations and sabotage equipment. He readily found "work" at different facilities and used the positions to gather information on Italian and German supply transports heading from the port of Piraeus and other locations to Rommel's Afrika Korps. On some of his undercover jobs, he gained access to German submarines, on which he planted magnetic mines, once destroying a base of German frogmen. Ivanof and OAG made it their business to know the location of Axis naval vessels, especially submarines, and would radio the details to British bombers. Elias's longtime interest in military matters dated from this period. He wanted to learn everything about the planes and ships, the men who made the decisions about when and how to deploy them, and when and how to destroy them.

To reduce the risks of betrayal, Ivanof usually worked alone. Believing that Mussolini was coming to Athens, he posed as a German officer to infiltrate the crowded Grande Bretagne Hotel, then serving as German headquarters. He stealthily set explosives in the basement, but, when Il Duce failed to come, he snuck back in, disarmed the bomb, and removed it, at the same time stealing secret German documents. On the rare occasions when Ivanof felt it necessary to work with others, he chose from former naval and police officers and boys who liked fireworks. "The Greeks are brave people," he supposedly said, "but they don't like the bangs of explosives." His carefully selected team targeted rebuilt fuel tanks, anti-aircraft gun positions, and the routes of German convoys. Elias understood that the death penalty awaited anyone convicted of assaulting or sabotaging the occupying armed forces or their property. He volunteered but was not selected.

Elias engaged in other sabotage. One of his targets was the local radio station, located in the back of the massive Zappeion Hall near the Palace Gardens.

"Anything you destroy counts in the effort," Ivanof would often say. Everyone had a role to play. Elias wasn't one of the more agile saboteurs. But he was quick-witted and had a fierce work ethic, and his fluency in English was unequaled by most others in the group. He used it to help communicate local developments to British operatives and MI6 contacts in Cairo.[33] He became a low-profile but important combatant and was increasingly respected as such.

OAG was a small organization that grew to about 200, but within it were smaller units that operated in strict secrecy from one another. No more than two from each group were given assignments in advance of their missions. Precautionary measures were critical. When a safehouse was exposed or its activities compromised, the group would disband and then regroup. A favorite song was "My Peaceful Night," which included the line "the less you know, the better you sleep." Counterespionage was a constant problem, with Axis forces aggressively injecting informants into resistance organizations and setting up "false flag" philhellene groups as traps. There were many betrayals during missions, Bobotinos later wrote, "because of bribes from the enemy, but also because of personal conflicts, egotism and lack of selflessness."[34]

The sustained attack on the Maltsinioti engine maintenance factory was one of the best sabotage operations of World War II. OAG members had infiltrated the plant before Ivanof arrived, putting a mixture of metallic and rubber powder into the crankcases of the engines, which caused the engine oil to decompose. After dozens of planes crashed unexpectedly, interrogations led to discovery of the plot. Five OAG members were executed. Two of them were the Barkas brothers, who had trained Elias in sabotage.[35]

Underground activities had become increasingly dangerous in early 1942. Growing urban resistance forced the German occupiers to bring to Athens two units of *Feldpolizei* that specialized in breaking up spy networks. Captured "patriotic amateurs" were routinely tortured by the Abwehr and the Gestapo, who used forced confessions to further erode local networks. It was at this time that Elias Demetracopoulos developed his lifelong habit of compartmentalizing relationships. Because of ongoing security concerns, Elias knew relatively few of the others involved, and then only briefly. He respected the roles they played, but never formed lasting friendships with any of them.

Though Elias knew nothing of Ivanof's plans in advance, he shared the reflected glory of the underground leader's daring deeds. He especially admired the story of how on the Ides of March 1942 Ivanof swam alone to the submarine U-133, based in the nearby Saronic Gulf, and sank it with a magnetic depth charge. Ivanof followed this with other aquatic heroics, and his activities assumed mythic proportions. Twice he was arrested, convicted, and sentenced to death. The first time, on December 18, 1941, he was betrayed by a childhood acquaintance from his schooldays in Salonika. Conviction was swift, and Ivanof was sent to Averof Prison to await execution. While being transferred by car to Gestapo headquarters for further interrogation, Ivanof surprised his guards and escaped. Wanted posters, with large pictures of Ivanof's face, were plastered around Athens.

For months Ivanof eluded his pursuers, moving house-to-house. He arranged an escape to Egypt via the island of Evia, but the ubiquitous bounty posters kept him trapped in Athens. On September 8, 1942, he was betrayed again, this time by a policeman who had pretended to be cooperating with the OAG but was likely a garden-variety double agent and collaborator. The arrest led to a court martial and triple death sentence.

This time Ivanof was held full-time within the confines of Averof, with extra attention from guards who were not pleased about his earlier escape. On the way to his execution on January 4, 1943, Ivanof tried again to break free, but was shot in the leg and fell. He got up, tried to run, but was shot in the back. He was then fastened to a wooden post and executed by the SS. Three other OAG members arrested with him, including Dimitrios Giannatos, Dr. Giannatos's brother, were also executed. Greek and Polish histories claim that Ivanof's last words were "Long live Greece. Long live Poland."[36]

News of the 32-year-old Ivanof's death hit Elias hard. The teenager had grown accustomed to seeing in the streets bodies of those who had starved, been shot, or been hanged from lampposts. He had known others in their group who had been killed, even hacked to pieces. But Ivanof had seemed larger than life and indestructible. For Elias, his death reinforced the sense of palpable risk shared by everyone in the OAG.

3.

Locked Up

WHILE OAG PLAYED A SMALL and largely unheralded role in maintaining the resistance spirit in Athens, the largest and most famous resistance group was the National Liberation Front (EAM), a coalition open to all who wanted to liberate Greece from the occupation. EAM was heavily populated by groups opposed to General Metaxas and the King; its original rank-and-file members were largely non-Communist, attracted principally to the immediate cause, but also supportive of a vision of a better future in which they would be free to choose their form of government.

The EAM leadership shaping this ecumenical message was drawn from the Greek Communist Party, the KKE. This group had been the one most forcefully oppressed by the Metaxas dictatorship, and its members were zealously committed to a life-or-death struggle for control of the country. They created and dominated the People's Liberation Army (ELAS), the military arm of EAM. Liberation to them was not a goal, but a means to an end: a Communist-controlled peoples' democracy that would largely follow an agenda shaped in Moscow. Whether these long-term ends could best be achieved through "peaceful penetration and subversion from within" or armed struggle was a matter of tactics, and the KKE vacillated between the two approaches.[1]

Many non-KKE resistance activists fighting under the EAM banner did not particularly care about the Communist agenda. For them the battle against occupation surmounted old political divisions.[2] Some who mistrusted Communist intentions organized an alternative resistance group, the National Republican Greek League (EDES). This group started out with a socialist, anti-monarchist philosophy, and reached out to London, not to Moscow, to guide and fund their activities. As the war progressed, the roster of warring factions became increasingly complex. Superimposed on the traditional divide between monarchists and republicans were conflicts between Communists and anti-Communists and other splits spawned by opportunistic alliances and shifting priorities.

The Germans played one group against the other, convincing both ELAS and EDES that the other was secretly working with them. The collaborationist government also formed armed *Tagmata Asfaleias* (Security Battalions) composed of Greeks whose hatred of the Nazis was less than their fear of the Communists, and sometimes drew into their orbit EDES supporters. The legitimization of the Battalions' role would have far-reaching implications in the Greek Civil War and beyond.

ELAS increasingly viewed itself as the legitimate alternative to the government-in-exile and was positioning itself to take power after liberation. When, during the summer of 1943, the Allies tried to trick the Germans into believing that Greece and not Sicily was the intended target of an upcoming invasion, KKE leaders fell hard for the deception. Believing an Allied landing was imminent, ELAS attacked its non-Communist Greek enemies to clear the field. Then, in August, it prematurely rushed to British headquarters in Cairo to assert its postwar demands. The movement then got slapped down hard (and repeatedly)—primarily by the British—and this set the stage for violent clashes in autumn 1943 that have been characterized by some historians as the first round of the Greek Civil War.[3]

To the extent that he was aware of the larger forces at play, Elias, now fourteen but looking twenty, was probably most sympathetic to the manifesto of EDES in its early anti-monarchist, social-justice phase. Those were clearly the views of some of his neighbors and most of his Peiramatikon classmates. Although he respected Churchill greatly, Elias, like Dr. Giannatos and a minority of OAG members, was opposed to the return of the King, especially if the monarchy were imposed before the holding of a free and fair plebiscite.

At the time, however, he didn't pay much attention to the convoluted schisms, backstabbing, secret agendas, and looming battles among the *antartes* and other larger Greek resistance organizations. Elias's focus was on the quotidian tasks of information-gathering, interpreting, and doing whatever else he was asked to do to support the work of Giannis Bobotinos and his OAG confederates. Circumstances soon conspired to remove him from the scene entirely.

■

REPORTS OF MUSSOLINI'S swift downfall in a July 1943 palace coup in Rome shocked the Italian troops in Greece, and the Italian capitulation on September 8 had a profound impact on resistance activities in Athens. When the surrender became known, demoralized Italian troops, eager to go home, were ready to sell guns, hand grenades, and other equipment to resistance contacts. OAG and like-minded groups were eager to obtain urgently needed weapons, ammunition, and radio sets, but did not have the resources to purchase them in the volume they wanted.

It was a chaotic time. At first, the high spirits and good cheer following the Italian surrender made Athens feel like an "endless market festival."[4] But within days that mood changed. Stories of Wehrmacht atrocities committed against the defeated Italians, notably in the Cephallonian massacre fictionalized in *Corelli's Mandolin*, were shared. And word spread quickly when the Germans, who had already largely destroyed the 500-year-old Sephardic community in Thessaloniki, targeted the Jews of Athens. With the Italians out, the Third Reich was fully in charge and eager to impose *eine gewisse Brutalität* ("a certain brutality").[5] Greek hostages were executed in reprisal for the slightest offenses, and those trafficking in guns and other weapons were often shot on sight.

Despite the risks, the British in Cairo urged resistance groups to get weapons, and lots of them. OAG members determined that their immediate priority must be to disarm the defeated Italians. According to one account, Elias had "proved a real master in drawing up plans for the escape of patriots held in custody."[6] In recent months he had been part of a cell that was able to free at least eight Greeks and three British soldiers from the Vouliagmeni Street military prison. After that operation, he walked slowly down the long hill with the *sang froid* of strong self-assurance.

Elias was becoming more vocal in the organization. He audaciously suggested to his OAG elders that one way to comply with the British request was for him to secure a forged identification card displaying a photograph of himself in a German uniform, and then proceed to the Italian military and political headquarters on Amalias Avenue, ground zero for Italian weapons. Not all Italians had bolted. Some were still loyal to their Axis allies, and others were waiting to leave under better conditions. OAG had been told that there were still Italians working inside.

Disguises had been commonplace among OAG members. Ivanof often dressed in Italian and German uniforms, and Bobotinos also passed in Axis garb, learning appropriate gestures and shouting, "Heil Hitler." At first, Elias's confederates were reluctant to put the boy at risk by letting him pose as a German. However, seeing a high potential payoff and no viable alternative, they approved the plan and created his fake ID. The next step was to find a suit and tailor it to fit Elias.

In the early afternoon of September 13, 1943, wearing civilian clothes and a somber tie with a meticulously tied Windsor knot, Elias was stopped by an Italian guard at the grand entrance. Saying nothing, he flashed his forged German identification card, and the guard opened the headquarters building to him immediately. Inside, three Italian officers were on duty. Elias strode forward with an air of authority. The soldiers casually greeted him and inquired, "What do you want?"[7]

Again, without replying, the bold young Greek displayed his German identity card. The three men jumped to attention. The "German officer" then calmly searched and disarmed them, emptied the contents of their desk drawers into a satchel he carried, took all the bullets, two hand grenades, and five small dynamite sticks, and departed as quickly as he had come. To his great surprise, none of the other Italians nearby tried to stop or question him.

Over the next several weeks, OAG learned that Italian officers stationed at Zappeion in the National Gardens would surrender their guns if their personal safety were guaranteed. So, on October 12, Elias, again with false identification, met with an Italian staff officer named Guido Gozanni to arrange a gun transfer on the 15th. During their negotiations, three SS officials barged in with three German officers and an interpreter and demanded: "Who are you, and what do you want?"

At first Elias tried to fake his way through in German, but his ruse was obvious. They attacked him and he fought back, punching the interpreter in the face. German guards with machine guns rushed in. Elias was taken to the radio station in the Zappeion for interrogation.

About an hour later, two black cars stopped at the Zappeion back door. Four more Germans arrived, two in grey-green SS uniforms and two in civilian clothes, escorting their Greek interpreter, Menelaos Giantiskos, a notorious sadist known commonly as "the beast." Elias tried hard not to show his fear at falling into the hands of Giantiskos.

As soon as they entered the building, the duty officer read the text of the usual inquiry with clenched fists. Turning abruptly to Gozanni, he asked: "How had your gun been found on this man?"

"He disarmed me, under the pretense he was a German," Gozanni replied, trembling.

"How?"

"He threatened me with a gun."

Elias's heart beat faster. This was a critical moment. Persons caught armed were subject to the death penalty. However, although all the others had testified against him, the second Italian officer, who had been with him during the gun negotiations, stated that Elias knew absolutely nothing; furthermore, he doubted whether "this Greek" even knew how to use a gun, intimating that Gozanni had stupidly handed over his gun voluntarily, even knowing that Elias was not a German.

Elias could hardly believe what he was hearing. The Italian officer might pay dearly for this response. Elias never learned the man's name but remained grateful for his heroism, which was made even greater because, as became apparent later, he had also destroyed the map Elias had been carrying. If discovered by the Germans, the map would have disclosed the whereabouts of Greek resistance fighters and British soldiers, surely leading to their arrests and probably to their deaths.

Gozanni's statement complicated matters. To please his masters, the Greek interpreter Giantiskos shook Elias hard by the shoulders and in a "dramatically wrathful tone" threatened, "If you don't reveal where you conceal the British and the guns, your blood will run in the streets."

Elias stifled his fear and, swallowing hard, viewed him with utter contempt. "You can kill me, but you won't get anything from me," he said with teenage bravado. "One day you will pay for your crimes, traitor," and spat in his face.

Then his tortures began. They went after soft tissue and organs, muscle, and bone. Elias was certain he was going to die. When Giantiskos finished beating him, they handcuffed him, brought him downstairs, and threw him into a car. An officer holding a gun sat on one side of Elias. On his other side was a Greek collaborator, also with an unholstered gun, who snarled at Elias: "Don't move or I'll shoot you."

Elias later described the episode:

I was not sure whether the Italian officer had given the map to the
Germans and my head was splitting. There was no way to warn the
others. I could endure their tortures, I could even commit suicide,
if necessary. But the map was my nightmare still, and, unable to do
anything else, I placed my faith in God. Finally, I saw the car turn [onto]
Korai Street, and the black building of the German Kommandatura.[8]

Inside the occupied government building, his captors shoved Elias into
Room 41, marked "Feld Polizei." A short SS officer glanced at the inquiry report, abruptly arose, and shouted: "*Spriech*!" When Elias refused to answer,
the interpreter flogged him until he fainted. When he regained consciousness,
Elias found himself still in handcuffs. He understood they wanted to search
his home.[9]

The Germans drove to Dafnomili Street and barged in brandishing machine guns.

Panagiota took one look at her son's bloodied and beaten face, let out an
anguished scream, and collapsed in a heap on the floor. "Fortunately, the day
previous to my arrest, I had carried away two dynamite cases, and other con-
traband material," Elias later recalled. The Germans ransacked the house looking for guns and, at the end of their fruitless search, demanded that his
trembling mother disclose where he had concealed the weapons. Ashen and
worried more for her son than for herself, she merely shrugged her shoulders
and nodded silently in negation. The home invaders redoubled their search
and this time found five pistols Elias had squirreled away. These were capital
offenses.

The Germans shoved Elias back into the car and drove him the short distance to what before the war had been the fortified Ethniki Insurance Mansion
at 4 Korai Street. The complex, part of which had been imported from Germany before the war, was requisitioned by the occupiers in 1941.[10] There they
yanked him out of the vehicle and forced him, still handcuffed, to the top floor,
which was used by the Gestapo and SS for interrogations. After reading the
report to another officer, the duty officer ordered Elias taken to a nearby room.

From the ceiling hung a contraption involving a pulley from which dangled
a thick rope. There were also four blood-stained whips. When Elias did not reply

to SS questions, his hands were tied behind his back. Then, in a variation of *strap-pado*, he was suspended by a pole, tied to the rope, and slowly lifted off the ground.

Afterward, half-dead, he was moved to a small sub-basement cell in one of the two floors of underground rooms that had been specially built as an air raid shelter. There were heavy iron doors and structures to protect insurance-company personnel against gas attacks.

During the war, these rooms became underground detention wards used for holding prisoners before it was officially determined whether they'd be sent to one of the Athens jails at Averof Prison, to Gestapo headquarters on Merlin Street, or to Chaidari, where they'd frequently be tortured, put to forced labor, and then loaded onto trains going to German concentration camps. Some prisoners scheduled for imminent transfer only stayed at Korai for a few hours or days. Others, like Elias, who were ordered to trial, were kept longer. Conditions were sometimes overcrowded and, with just a single bathroom on each floor, nauseatingly fetid. Graffiti scrawled on the walls pleaded for water and food.

Once a day, the prisoners were taken up from their basement dungeon and permitted to walk slowly in a circle on the plaza at the entrance, under the gaze of heavily armed German guards. Friends, family, and curiosity-seekers would gather nearby, some throwing assorted edibles to them.

Elias's mother prepared a food package and asked a Peiramatikon classmate to take it to her son. He gave it to the *Feldkommandatur*, who never passed it on to Elias. Afterward, while observing the somber ritual of slow trudging inmates, the friend was surprised to see a teenaged walker raise his right fist and break the silence, proclaiming: "My name is Elias Demetracopoulos. I am Greek, and I am proud to be Greek." And then he repeated, "My name is Elias Demetracopoulos and I'm a proud Greek." Such flamboyant temerity did not go unnoticed. Again, he was punished.[11]

A journalist recounting Elias's experience at Korai Street wrote in *Stavros* magazine: "It is impossible to describe how the Greek patriot suffered. For two weeks, morning, noon, and evening, he underwent the most inhuman torture of the Inquisition. Yet, he did not utter a sound, did not even open his mouth. He groaned and bit his tongue, to cut it if necessary. But, until the last day when he was bound and taken to the Parnassos auditorium for a trial and sentenced to death on two counts, Demetracopoulos bore all tortures bravely."[12]

After sentencing, Elias was taken, along with six other convicts, to the infamous Averof Prison, the dreaded gray stone bastion on Leoforos Alexandras Avenue, which loomed as a dark blot against the azure sky. For decades, incarceration at Averof was the penultimate punishment imposed on political prisoners of the left and right who'd been condemned to death. During World War II it reeked from overcrowding and fear, with resistance fighters randomly pulled from their cells and executed in the courtyard.

The boy tried to keep up an unflappable demeanor as his new German handlers roughly pushed him into a seven-by-eight-foot cell, but that effort soon evaporated. Incarcerated and alone, he felt his body tingling with a strong sense of foreboding. He remembered that the "superhuman" Ivanof had tried twice to escape these walls and armed guards, but that even he had been caught and shot to death. In November 1943, fourteen-year-old Elias was feeling quite human and terribly vulnerable. Moved to a larger, crowded cell, Elias met airmen and soldiers from Australia and New Zealand and was able to practice his English. He tried to help smuggle out a letter from a Captain J. K. Lewis to his family in Sydney but was caught and punished.

"The days passed," Demetracopoulos later wrote, "without any hope of salvation. Exhausting gymnastics, whipping, and other tortures were a part of the daily schedule."[13] He heard stories of inmates given severe beatings for simply pleading to be fed. Some prisoners were battered in their cells every two hours, their floors flooded with water between the beatings to keep them from resting. Others, condemned to execution, spent their last night out of the main building in a special underground cell called the *Arapis,* a covered pitch-black hole.

One afternoon, two boyhood acquaintances named Zampetakis and Levantakis, were brought from the Parnassos Court Martial. They smiled wanly and told Elias of their death sentences. The following day, when the Germans came to escort them to the place of execution, the two teenagers, both a little older than Elias and originally from Crete, turned to the other prisoners and said: "Don't worry, boys, Greece cannot die because we will go [sacrifice ourselves]!"[14]

Elias Demetracopoulos awaited his turn. He remembered how he had once thought the job of underground wireless operator was the worst in the OAG, because the Germans used tracking equipment to pinpoint the location of transmitters and shot the operators on the spot. It was a task he'd been relieved he'd never been assigned. The operators claimed with gallows humor that they were the lucky ones, since their immediate execution prevented torture. Now, Elias had the worst of both worlds. He'd experienced the torture and was now preparing for his execution. Every day he heard the sounds of firing squads coming from the courtyard, as he waited to die.

■

SHORTLY BEFORE CHRISTMAS 1943, Archbishop Damaskinos, Spiritual Leader of Athens and All Greece, paid a holiday visit to the prison. The inmates were let out of their cells and ordered to line up for his blessing. Resplendent in black vestments and a sparkling pectoral cross, the fifty-two-year-old Damaskinos, with his flowing white beard, soulful eyes, and wise countenance, was an imposing presence, well beyond the fact that he symbolized church power. At six feet four inches tall, with his pastoral staff and wearing a *kalimafkion*—his tall cylindrical hat—the archbishop towered over the guards. Damaskinos fought hard to protect his flock during the famine and hardships of war.[15] He repeatedly challenged both the occupiers and the quisling government. He also famously intervened to save thousands of Athenian Jews facing deportation, directing his prelates to provide baptismal certificates to those fleeing and arranging hiding places for others. Threatened with a firing-squad execution, Damaskinos—alluding to the fate of Patriarch Gregory V of Constantinople in 1821 who had been lynched by an Ottoman mob at the start of the Greek war of independence—told an SS commander that Greek religious leaders are hanged, not shot. "I request that you please respect our traditions," he said.[16]

Elias, the youngest of all the prisoners, was startled to see the important visitor. To him, Archbishop Damaskinos was more than just a venerated church leader. He was a dear friend of his Uncle Costas, and Elias had met him. When it came time for the boy to kneel down, kiss the prelate's hand, and receive a benediction, he said in a barely audible whisper, "Please tell my uncle I'm okay." Then he paused, adding for emphasis, "today."

Damaskinos didn't respond as he worked his way down the line. After he left, the prisoners were again locked away. The next morning, the day before Christmas, German guards roused Elias early, shackled his wrists and frog-marched him outside in the early dawn.

Armed guards walked him at a brisk pace down the street across from the empty soccer field and past the unoccupied US ambassador's residence. At that hour, as they turned down Panormou and Zaharof streets, the loudest sounds were the clacking of hobnail boots hitting pavement. Elias had no idea where they were taking him. After just a kilometer, they stopped at a sprawling and imposing topaz-toned building, about a mile from his house.

To his great surprise, instead of being led to the firing squad, Elias had been transferred to the Eginition Home for the Insane. The Germans brought paperwork that declared him a "psychopathic" case. This was not a matter of sudden German respect for the mentally ill. Somebody on the outside had made the appropriate connections. For the time being, his young life had been spared.

Since Elias's arrest, his father had been stoic, but Panagiota was distraught. Working different approaches simultaneously, she beseeched friends and family to call in all favors and explore any avenue to get Elias out of Averof Prison. She repeatedly pressured her brother Costas Bokolas to use all his customer and business contacts. She even demanded that her brother-in-law Christos Apostolou, a retired naval commander, ask for help from a collaborator judge advocate in the German courts who as a young sailor had worked part-time for Costas.

Willing to pay anything for his release, Panagiota offered bribes to anyone she thought could free her son, but apparently no money ever changed hands.

Most effectively, Panagiota turned to her St. Nicholas priest, P. Vamvakas, who energetically worked his network up the ecclesiastical chain and together with Costas directly approached Archbishop Damaskinos. Elias later speculated that Damaskinos had probably played the decisive role in sparing his life as part of a Christmas goodwill package. He could hardly conceive that he was still alive.

At Eginition, Elias, now just past his fifteenth birthday, was first placed in a two-bed room with another inmate, who asked him all manner of questions. He quickly concluded, probably correctly, that his roommate had been put there to ascertain if he were really mentally ill or just avoiding his death sentence. Twice a day he was let out to exercise by walking the narrow corridors in a serpentine line with other inmates, under the watchful eyes of Greek staff, including assumed collaborators, and armed German guards. Elias didn't know how he was supposed to act, but felt he had to play along with the diagnosis. When he protested loudly that he wasn't insane (which he thought an insane person would do), other inmates mocked and mimicked him, pointing at him, some cackling hysterically. This apparently confirmed to the guards the correctness of his incarceration. They moved him to a ward with seriously mentally ill patients.

To Elias's great surprise, one of the first people he saw during the asylum walks was Dr. Kostas Giannatos, whose whereabouts and fate had been unknown to him since shortly after Ivanof's death. For the two years following his arrest, Giannatos had faked insanity to escape execution. To help make his case, the previously impeccably mannered doctor smeared himself with his own feces and even ate it. The two exchanged furtive glances and whispered brief comments from time to time while passing, but never had a real conversation.

One can only begin to imagine the emotional and physical impact of the Eginition experience, especially on a teenager. Though there were no accounts of eugenic programs, "crude, odd, and unproven" psychiatric treatments were used, including special diets, laxative treatments, bloodletting, hot and cold showers, mechanical restraints, opiates, malaria experimentation, hypnotherapy, insulin-induced fits, and lobotomies.[17] Elias was spared the worst of these, but only because the medical and nursing staffs were so shorthanded.

Whatever hardships Greece suffered during this time, asylum life was worse. Parts of the building were used as barracks and arsenals, making conditions more crowded. Food was tightly rationed and often inedible. Inmate-prisoners were sexually abused by hospital personnel. Windows, tables, and chairs removed for firewood during the winter famine were not replaced. The death rate of mentally ill patients in Greek hospitals during the war was 50 percent.[18]

The sickening smells and frightening sights of broken humanity, most with serious psychopathological problems; the constant moans, shouts, and keening, the lack of light and fresh air, the coughing, sneezing, and spitting in overcrowded conditions that enabled diseases to pass readily from one inmate to another, shaped a life in extremis. Whenever Elias tried to shut out his new world, vivid memories of his tortures in Averof Prison came flooding back. He had been helpless in the face of powerful forces. He promised himself that if he ever got out alive, he would never live in fear nor let anyone bully or brutalize him again.

The seasons changed from winter to spring to summer and then autumn. During nearly a year in Eginition, Elias was cut off from the climax of the war. Before his arrest he had been vaguely aware that Communist and non-Communist resistance fighters seemed to be more at each other's throats than united in the struggle against the occupiers. He knew almost nothing about what had happened since his incarceration.

In October 1944, the German occupiers, fearful of the advancing Red Army, withdrew from Athens and mainland Greece. They took down the swastika flag from the Acropolis and, with no shots fired, convoyed north out of the city, blowing up bridges and highways and despoiling the countryside on their way.

Shortly after dawn on Thursday, October 12, Elias and some of the other inmates realized that no one was guarding them. Sympathetic medical staff opened the doors of the rooms of those they thought to be political prisoners and not actually insane. Elias was free to go home. Without looking back, he simply walked out through the main door.

All alone, Elias blinked at the daylight and beheld his new surroundings near central Athens. The aptly named Eleftherias ("Freedom") Park was just ahead. Starting with a brisk walk, interspersed with brief trots, he took in snatches of the familiar streets and buildings of Kolonaki with fresh appreciation. As he approached the southwest corner of the great black rock of Mount Lycabettos that, according to legend, Athena had dropped while carrying it to her temple on the Acropolis, Elias took a shortcut, away from the concrete sidewalks and through the forest of Mediterranean pines near its base. He inhaled the intoxicatingly sweet, clean smell of the resinous sap, his footsteps muffled by the silken needles. As he rejoiced in his newly regained liberty, an unsettling phantasmagoria of scenes from the past year flashed in his mind. He picked up his pace.

Less than half an hour after leaving Eginition he was on Dafnomili Street. The heavy wooden door at his house was unlocked. When he walked in, his parents were alone. His mother screamed with joy and embraced him, smothering his face with kisses. His father, wearing a warm but reserved smile, said matter-of-factly: "Good to have you back home." Neighbors treated him as a local hero.

Already thinner in mid-1943 than he had been at the start of the war, Elias had lost more than twenty pounds during his incarceration. He was wan and malnourished. Somewhat under six feet tall, his weight was down to the low 130s. His thick black hair had started to thin. Sunshine hurt his dark brown eyes. But he had an appetite. To help him recover, his mother prepared his favorite spaghetti dishes, followed by freshly made chocolate ice cream she had obtained despite the widespread scarcity.

■

TWO DAYS LATER, British forces arrived by sea to a festive welcome, followed by the Greek government-in-exile, which had delayed its debarkation because, superstitiously, it did not want to return on a Tuesday, the day that Constantinople had fallen to the Ottoman Turks in 1453. On Wednesday, October 18, liberation was celebrated. Hundreds of thousands thronged into central Athens to celebrate the end of the war against the Axis. Elias Demetracopoulos, scrawny, deflated but exhilarated, stood with his family, friends, neighbors, and strangers, wearing a broad smile.

There were church bells and fireworks, tears and embraces, parades of soldiers and resistance fighters, street dancing and grand oratory from returning former minister and political leader George Papandreou. Elias didn't sing, cheer, or wave flags, but he was immensely proud of what had been achieved and glad for his small role in the national victory.

The joys of the end of the occupation were short-lived.[19] The devastation facing the survivors was profound. Some 550,000 Greeks had been killed, about 8 percent of the country's population—a much higher rate of casualties than in France or Britain. Greek losses compared more closely to those suffered in Russia and Poland.

Greece's economy and infrastructure were in ruins, its currency worthless. Nearly half a million homes had been destroyed, along with more than half of the country's national road system, 73 percent of its commercial fleet, 66 percent of its trucks, and 60 percent of its large farm animals. Half its urban population was unemployed. Inflation was spiraling out of control, exacerbating a crisis in which old animosities and fresh political confrontations would soon intensify.

4.

December Uprising

LIBERATION FROM THE GERMANS DID not bring a political resolution or reconstruction to Greece, as it did to much of formerly occupied Europe. Instead, the end of the occupation ushered in increasingly brutal phases of civil conflict. Even before the German surrender, Greece became a battlefield of the coming Cold War.

The British believed that a peaceful solution to post-occupation conflict in Greece was unlikely. To minimize the negative consequences of a violent struggle, they tried to ensure they had a free hand by keeping the Russians out of any coming fray. Stalin, desiring a similarly free hand in Romania and elsewhere, readily agreed. Over several months of meetings, the two erstwhile allies arrived at an understanding of postwar spheres of influence in the Balkans, and their agreement was finalized in Moscow on October 11, 1944 with the so-called "Percentages Agreement."[1] According to Churchill's memoirs, this handwritten agreement gave Russia 90 percent predominance in Romania, the UK 90 percent of the say in Greece, and gave them a 50–50 split regarding Yugoslavia. Post–Cold War declassification of East European archives reveal that, months before this understanding, Soviet leaders had already decided to avoid contact with representatives of the Greek left.[2] The Greeks themselves were unaware of how the gods were playing with their fates. How Stalin honored this agreement in the coming years had a decisive impact on the battles ahead.

■

ANTICIPATING GERMANY'S WITHDRAWAL, and dreading the prospect of the Communist-leaning National Liberation Front (EAM) stepping into a power vacuum before the exiled Greek government could be established, the British arranged a meeting of the different Allied wartime factions in Greece, including EAM, in a villa near Caserta, Italy on September 26, 1944, to bridge partisan differences and design the country's political future. They agreed to formalize a Greek "government of national unity," with membership from all camps, to run the country until elections were held. George Papandreou was put in charge, with heavy British influence.

Papandreou was probably the best choice for such a herculean task. Born February 13, 1888, the son of an impoverished Orthodox archpriest in Kaletzi, Achaia, in western Greece, he studied law at the University of Athens, then political science in Berlin, where he refined a lifelong philosophical commitment to social democracy. A protégé of Venizelos, he was exiled under the Metaxas dictatorship and escaped imprisonment during the occupation. A resolute anti-Communist and devoted republican, Papandreou tempered his anti-royalist sentiments to negotiate a compromise solution to the crisis.

Of all the issues facing the coalition National Unity government, the most daunting were disbanding the various resistance groups and forming a new national army. How to disarm and reconcile the *antartes* on the left, particularly from ELAS, the Greek People's Liberation Army that controlled most of the country outside of Athens, and, on the right, the pro-royalist Mountain Brigades and often Nazi-collaborationist Security Battalions?

Those on the right passionately believed that the leaders of EAM/ELAS sought a Communist takeover of Greece. It might be done clandestinely, in stages, under the deceitful cover of democratic rhetoric and legalistic procedures. It might be achieved directly, either on the battlefield, or through a coup d'état. The outcome, they feared, would be the same unless they took drastic action.

Those on the left, meanwhile, believed that the so-called National Unity forces wanted to disarm the heroic ELAS resistance fighters to better serve British economic and geopolitical interests and restore the Greek "Monarcho-Fascists" who had been discredited through their inaction, sympathy, or outright collaboration with the Axis occupiers. EAM and their sympathizers feared that the new government would never share real power with the left, but would instead turn the clock back to the prewar political arrangements. This was not the better world for which they had fought and died. There were elements of truth in both caricatures, but they remained oversimplifications.

■

LIKE MANY OF their war-weary neighbors, the Demetracopoulos household didn't want to be drawn into the growing conflict. They just wanted to be left alone. In the weeks since Elias came home, things had been settling down into a more normal routine. Panagiotis had gone back to work at the Acropolis. Panagiota gave daily prayers of thanks at St. Nicholas for her reunited family. Her top priority was feeding her son to help him gain back the weight and health lost during his incarceration.

Elias's first order of unfinished business was to go to the Hellenic Red Cross and reconstruct from memory a letter guards had taken from him that was to have been sent to the family of Australian 7th Corps Captain J. K. ("Jack") Lewis, whom he had befriended in Averof Prison two years before. As Elias explained to Red Cross officials, he'd discovered that Lewis had been sent to Germany in March 1944. He didn't know if Lewis had survived the war but considered it his duty to pass on to Lewis's brother in Sydney the information and what may have been his last words. It took him several tries and almost a year to get the letter sent. He never received a reply.[3]

After that, he reconnected with friends and made plans to return to school.

■

PAPANDREOU'S GOAL WAS to achieve national unity without conceding anything to the Communists. His government, under pressure from the British, declared the resistance over as of October 31, 1944. The transferring of the Third Mountain Brigade to Athens on November 9, followed by British Commander General Ronald Scobie's demand that EAM fighters disarm unilaterally, were the provocations that led to December's violence.[4]

Left-wing groups, in response, pressured the government and its British protectors with street demonstrations, marches, and the smearing of buildings with political graffiti. EAM refused to dissolve its military arm unless the government also demobilized the Third Mountain Brigade, the Sacred Squadron, and the extreme right-wing organization "X." "Recriminations and charges of collaboration or treason replaced the sudden exhilaration of freedom. "Accusations became the national discourse," wrote the Canadian historian André Gerolymatos. "Indeed, fear stalked every corner of Athens, grinding down the little trust that remained and diminishing any hope for the future."[5]

On December 1, 1944, Elias celebrated his sixteenth birthday. It was also a pivotal day in Greek history.

■

LATE ON THE first night of December, the EAM ministers concluded that the organization's differences with Papandreou's British-guided regime were irreconcilable, and resigned from the governing coalition, criticizing British interference in Greek affairs. The government of national unity came apart.

The next day, a cold and rainy Saturday, EAM stalwarts roamed the city with cardboard megaphones calling for a massive protest. To ensure a large turnout, EAM agitators warned that those who failed to participate could face reprisals.

On Sunday morning, December 3, the streets were still wet, but it was bright and sunny.[6] Well over 100,000 demonstrators of various classes and political shades poured into Syntagma (Constitution) Square in the heart of Athens. Along with Greek flags, marchers held aloft the colors of the United States, the Soviet Union, and even Great Britain.

Accounts differ as to who fired the first shot, with pro-government writers blaming police panic. Others noted that police and members of the extreme-rightist "X" organization, both positioned strategically high up in surrounding buildings, opened fire. Some witnesses remember a man dropping to one knee and shouting: "Shoot the bastards!"[7] Nikos Farmakis, then a 15-year-old gun-wielding member of "X," said the signal to open fire was given by then–Athens police chief Angelos Evert, who waved a handkerchief out of a police headquarters window. Fourteen years later, Evert admitted that he had directed the forceful breakup of the demonstration, according to orders he said came from Churchill by way of Scobie and Papandreou.[8] In the end, more than two dozen people were killed, including a six-year-old boy,[9] and 148 were injured. George Papandreou offered his resignation to General Scobie, but Churchill would not let his chosen Greek leader off the hook, and instead of a government of national unity, Papandreou found himself presiding over several weeks of urban warfare. Those weeks of intra-Greek carnage became known collectively as *Dekemvriana* (the "December events"), a series of bloody confrontations, fixed battles, and outright massacres involving diehard political enemies—the Liberation Army, the Greek government, and the British forces. The goal of the British: to wrest control of Athens from the ELAS fighters.

A general strike and mass rally were called for the next day, Monday, December 4. Participants were peaceful until dispersing demonstrators were violently attacked by a variety of right-wing bands, including notably those of "*X*," led by Colonel Georgios Grivas, who would later play a pernicious role in the Cyprus conflict. More than one hundred people were killed. In retaliation, ELAS overran police stations, inflicting casualties and taking weapons. Scobie proclaimed martial law. Churchill took charge, ordering: "Do not hesitate to act as if you were in a conquered city where a local rebellion is in progress . . . This is no time . . . to imagine that Greek politicians of various shades can affect the situation."[10]

For about two weeks, EAM/ELAS refrained from attacking British troops directly, and even proposed an armistice. The response from Churchill was un-equivocal: "The clear objective is the defeat of EAM. The ending of the fighting is subsidiary to this."[11]

IN THE WEEKS after the mass demonstrations, it became risky just to step out-side, let alone travel between neighborhoods. The Demetracopouloses lived on the outskirts of the only section of Athens effectively protected by the British. However, Dafnomili Street and the rest of Athens, its environs, and most of the country was essentially controlled by ELAS.

Blocks from Elias's house, street fighting raged, with snipers on rooftops tar-geting those below and people running for cover. British tanks rolled through city streets. Bursting shells seemed to be everywhere, and RAF planes, trying to take back territory, dropped ordnance and caused serious civilian casualties.

About a week into the battles, the war hit home. Mid-morning, Panagiota's oldest sister, Angeliki Handrinos, who lived in the next house, banged on the Demetracopouloses' heavy wooden front door. Distraught, she explained that her husband Vassilis and son Spyros had been picked up late the day before by what she believed was one of the local Communist groups and taken to some unknown location.

Uncle Vassilis was a small merchant. Cousin Spyros, five years older than Elias, had been an honor student at Peiramatikon. Although both were conser-vative, neither had been actively political, not even from the sidelines. Around the neighborhood, stories had been circulating about Communists recruiting foot soldiers off the streets or randomly picking people from whom to extract useful information. More serious were reports that ELAS and OPLA (Organiza-tion for the Protection of the People's Struggle) had been exacting revenge on those they believed had betrayed their cause, had made disparaging remarks, or, as members of the Athenian upper class, could be useful hostages. Many of those unsympathetic to the left were deemed "traitors," and hundreds were said to have been executed with sadistic passion. Some victims were shot in the head and dumped ignominiously in fields, street corners, or alleys. Others were dismembered alive, then killed.[12] Lucky ones were kidnapped and, in stages, moved out of the country, to Albania and Bulgaria.

Angeliki, the anxious wife and mother, did not want to believe that any of this could be happening to her family. She didn't know where to turn, but thought that Elias, now known in the neighborhood as a "war hero," might be able to do something. Without knowing what he was getting into, and somewhat cocky because of his local-celebrity status, the teenager assured his aunt that he would go search for his relatives.

He didn't trust using the telephone, but, even if he had, electric power was shut off. From the Hotel Grand Bretagne's beehive of political gossip and intelligence, Elias learned more about the street snatchings. But it was largely speculation, and, if he made a mistake, he might not only fail in his mission but be taken captive himself.

Under the curfew, civilians were allowed to cross sectors only from noon to 2 p.m. to fetch water and food. Valuable time ticked away as Elias dug for more reliable information. Finally, he was told his uncle and cousin had been taken by Communists to a particular building in Nea Ionia, a suburb in the north of Athens, northeast of Patissia. Approaching one o'clock, a safe time to cross neighborhoods, Elias left the relatively secure British-controlled area for the nearby "no man's land" and beyond. The December sun was bright, but the air was chilly. With a heady mix of swagger, fear, and excitement, Elias worked his way on foot through the expanding battlefield of his hometown.

Unarmed, he walked for about two hours on a secondary road. But when he got to the identified place, no one was there. He made further inquiries, was pointed in one direction, then another. For more than an hour, he trudged farther north, in the direction of Lykovrysi, over rolling hills, past farmlands and groves of pines and fruit-bearing trees, but found few dwellings. Elias didn't want to return home empty-handed. More than a day had passed since the abduction. He didn't know if his uncle and cousin were dead or alive.

Following another tip, Elias approached a three-story stone house in a residential area somewhere between Irakleio, and Nea Ionia. It was now about 4 p.m., shortly before dusk would cast an eerie pall on his mission. Suddenly, armed sentries appeared from nearby shadows, stopped him, and took him inside the house to the commander in charge. After Elias presented his identification and told his story, one guard claimed to have known about his arrest, torture, and incarceration. The men did not treat him roughly. In a first-floor room in the darkening house, Elias saw his uncle and cousin sitting on wooden chairs, unshackled, with surprised looks on their faces.

The leader was middle-aged, heavyset, full-bearded, and had a mane of thick black hair—the caricature of a guerrilla from central casting. He was flanked by two scruffy associates, all seated at a table illuminated by a flickering hurricane lamp. The fighters exchanged mild pleasantries with the teenager, who was trying hard to mask his anxiety. After a short conversation during which both parties uttered anti-British diatribes cursing "perfidious Albion," Elias seemed to convince the commander that holding his relatives served no purpose because they knew nothing of value and any allegations against them were baseless. Without much ado, the commander released the two men. As Elias and his relatives walked out, the captors, it appeared, had already turned to other business.

The three crossed the street toward Athens. But after they had walked less than thirty yards, someone shouted at them from the doorway to stop or they'd shoot. This time Elias's instinct, the opposite from that when taken from Averof Prison, was to flee as fast as possible. Remembering the tales of Ivanof's escapes, he yelled encouragement to his relatives and led them as they zigzagged away from the encampment, bullets whizzing near their heads. Then Elias stumbled. He'd been shot in the left leg, about six inches above the ankle. Fortunately, the bullet went all the way through, missing his tibia and fibula, wounding but not disabling him. They kept running.

After losing their pursuers, they caught their breath. Elias tore his shirt to make a bandage. Years later he reflected that being shot had been a blessing in disguise, forcing the threesome to decide that their return to the Anglo-royalist stronghold should not be a straight trip. If they had not been attacked they might have been less wary, taken a more direct route back, and been captured or killed. As night fell and it grew colder, the trio cautiously worked their long way back through the hilly outskirts of the city, their presence sporadically illuminated by the piercing brightness of flares dropped from Royal Air Force planes to expose ELAS troop movements.

When they got closer, they decided it was safer to spend the night at Uncle Costas's house than to return to Dafnomili Street. The house was about a mile away, near the US ambassador's residence at the American School of Classical Studies, which had been spared from the fighting. The accidental hero returned home the next day to tears of relief, words of gratitude, and medical treatment. He would later speculate that the interrogators' change of heart may have come from their sudden realization that Elias's OAG had royalist sympathies.

■

IT DID NOT sit well in Western capitals, especially in Washington and in the House of Commons, that British forces were battling members of a Greek resistance movement that had so recently been lauded for its bold stand against the Axis.

Even FDR, who had earlier made it clear to Churchill that the British would have carte blanche in Greece, was taken aback. The US secretary of state told American representatives in Athens to remain strictly neutral. American newspapers excoriated the return of naked British imperialism.[13] Even in England, the prime minister was attacked from the left and the right.

Churchill, seemingly obsessed with the Greek crisis, made a surprise Christmas visit to Athens, where he learned first-hand the importance of the King waiting to return until a plebiscite was held. Archbishop Damaskinos, who Churchill now realized was not the reprehensible "pestilent priest" he and some of the British command had disparagingly dismissed, was appointed regent.[14]

Eventually, the British prevailed. The new year brought a cease-fire. General Nikolaos Plastiras, an aging war hero and political moderate, became prime minister. In the preceding month there had been more Greek casualties than in the entire 1940–'41 war with Italy.[15] On February 12, 1945, the different sides, meeting in the seaside town of Varkiza, reached an agreement to end the "second round" of the civil war.[16] The peace would not last.

5.

A Tubercular Education

DURING THE HARROWING WEEKS FROM early December 1944 to early January 1945, Panagiotis and Panagiota Demetracopoulos felt their lives were even more precarious than during the German occupation. And Elias's recent experience rescuing his relatives seemed to prove he had as much to fear from Communists as he ever had from the Germans. The bloody fighting in the bullet-riddled streets of Athens brought to the city the full terror of civil war. The political assassinations and taking of civilian hostages by ELAS soured the non-Communist resistance on EAM and its leadership. Elias and his neighbors were terrified that the Communists might destroy their world.

When EAM/ELAS forces withdrew from the capital and the Varkiza ceasefire was signed, Athenians could begin to breathe more comfortably. Nevertheless, stories about the forced marches of hostages into ELAS-held territory in the north and the numerous casualties along the way cost the KKE the support of all but a small minority of their wartime allies. The December kidnapping of their relatives was still disturbingly fresh.

Elias's father and mother were center-right conservatives, sympathetic to the monarchy and staunchly anti-Communist. They admired Churchill for his role in saving Greece from the Axis powers and regarded Britain as their bulwark against a Communist takeover. They also opposed the involvement of former

German collaborators in positions of authority in the army and other parts of the Greek government.

Elias differed from them in his republican sympathies but leaned to the conservative side until well into the 1950s. He later reflected that, under other circumstances, he and his parents might have responded positively to certain leftist social-reform positions. Elias, in particular, had always supported voting rights for women. But the near-escape of Elias and his relatives during the *Dekemvriana* largely tainted their view of all left-wing programs. Certainly, they acknowledged, EAM had included moderate members. But they didn't believe that EAM/ELAS could ever separate itself from its Communist leadership or that the Communists were honest in their promises. Their actions during the Athens uprising proved it: if the KKE ever attained power, they surmised, the Party would soon subvert any free and democratic government to ends determined in Moscow.

The heavily negotiated February 1945 Varkiza Agreement called for the demobilization of ELAS, creation of a national army, amnesty for political crimes committed during *Dekemvriana*, and purging Axis collaborationists from the civil and security services. It declared that within the year there would be a plebiscite allowing Greeks to choose whether they wanted a republic or a monarchy. Parliamentary elections would follow.[1]

These terms offered a reasonable compromise, but none of the parties fully abided by their provisions. ELAS surrendered many weapons but hid a substantial amount of their best weaponry in the mountains. The so-called national army, which had been purged of almost all liberal and republican officers, was anything but popular. And the amnesty provision protected only EAM/ELAS leadership, leaving many rank-and-file ELAS soldiers subject to harassment, arrest, and imprisonment.

As public opinion swung decidedly against the left in the wake of the December uprising, Nazi collaborators used their vitriolic anti-Communism to escape being purged from positions of authority and became the vanguard of a new terror campaign. Demobilized ELAS soldiers used this terrorism to mount their own attacks in "self-defense," but the government and its British allies controlled the cities and major centers of power. Disproportionate revenge attacks against the left for real or imagined transgressions troubled Elias and his family, but personal security trumped their concern for civil liberties.

The post-Varkiza interlude was short-lived. The agreed voting procedure was to choose the form of government, then to elect members of a constituent assembly. But the British insisted that a government be formed first, followed by a vote on whether to allow the return of King George II from London. With right-wing gangs exacting "White Terror" upon left-wingers of all shades, and a policy of prosecution that rounded up even marginal former ELAS members, prospects for a fair vote were bleak. After the British refused demands from Communists, centrists, and liberals to postpone the March 1946 election until a less-tumultuous time, those parties urged their followers to boycott the country's first election since 1936. Since the boycott ensured the absence of about half the electorate, the results gave artificial legitimacy to an unrestrained, hard-right coalition government.[2]

Elias and his parents welcomed the clear conservative electoral victory, but were dismayed by the left's policy of organized abstentions. The absence of even a modest parliamentary opposition undermined Greek democracy and encouraged the opposition's "extra-parliamentary" temptations. Several months later, a plebiscite restored the royal family. Throughout 1946, cooperation among the major wartime allies deteriorated, but Stalin maintained his hands-off attitude toward the Greek Communists. The KKE leadership, however, had a loyal supporter in Josip Broz Tito, who had consolidated his own rule in nearby Yugoslavia. Gradually they turned from strikes and demonstrations to organized violence, with guerrilla bands effectively targeting villages. In late 1946, the KKE reorganized ELAS as the Democratic Army of Greece, and the Greek Civil War entered its third and most atrocious final round. The rural northern and southern countrysides became killing fields, with peasants savagely victimized by both sides.

Once the fighting moved out of Athens, the Demetracopouloses and their neighbors were spared the terrorism and violence that beset their compatriots in Macedonia, Thrace, Thessaly, and the Peloponnese. But daily life remained difficult.[3] The Germans had destroyed more than one-third of Greece's national wealth and devastated its railways, roads, port facilities, power grids, and communications networks, and much of its merchant marine force. The decimation of livestock, poultry, and draft animals imperiled urban food supplies. Illness was rampant, and runaway inflation had wiped out many families' life savings. While other parts of war-torn Europe engaged in reconstruction, Athens struggled. United Nations Relief and Rehabitation Administration (UNRRA) packages of food and basic necessities kept people alive, but barely.[4]

As conservative anti-Communists, Elias and his family avoided the discrimination affecting Greeks branded with so-called forbidden views, who found difficulty obtaining from the police certificates of national loyalty required to get driver's licenses, passports, public jobs, contracts, and benefits. Panagiotis Demetracopoulos worked as an Acropolis guide, leading relief-agency VIPs and visiting military officers around the major sites, but business was far from brisk. Elias's mother's family lived in a peaceful region on the nearby Gulf of Corinth, and they replenished her dwindling supply of British sovereigns and provided vital foodstuffs, from olive oil to fresh vegetables. Panagiota strategically bartered away her family heirlooms piece by piece, often at bargain prices. This support buffered the Demetracopoulos family from the shocks of runaway inflation and the economic privations that beset most of their neighbors.

After recovering from his December 1944 bullet wound, Elias turned his attention to school. He had not wanted to return to Peiramatikon, from which his classmates had already graduated while he was locked up. So, he went to a general public high school, the 5th Boys High School in nearby Exarcheia, and made up the missing credits for graduation. He passed his examinations in 1946 and received a certificate for "Excellent Behavior."

Elias next enrolled in the well-regarded Athens School of Economics and Commercial Sciences, the precursor of the Athens University of Economics and Business. He immersed himself in his studies and excelled early on. Soon, however, a nagging, intermittent cough turned into a persistent and enervating hack. An overwhelming fatigue forced him to drop out of school. Months later he re-enrolled but dropped out again.

Already quite thin, the eighteen-year-old lost his appetite and with it still more weight. Then he came down with fever, chills, and night sweats. His mother gently palpated his neck to check lymph glands she hoped would not be swollen. He started coughing up blood and phlegm. Finally, blood samples and an X-ray confirmed a serious case of tuberculosis. The time he had spent in crowded, unheated Averof Prison and the Eginition Asylum had finally taken its toll.

He was ordered immediately to Sotiria, once the best sanatorium for TB care. Located near Neo Psychiko, with a pine orchard bathed in fresh air drifting down from nearby Mount Hymettus, Sotiria had been stripped by the occupying Germans and, because of the latest wave of civil conflict, lacked equipment and competent staff. The clinic represented hope more often than salvation. A TB survivor whose sister died there remembered that at that time there were no medicines or food save for what could be purchased at inflated black-market prices. "With little to eat, patients had to be provided [for] by parents or relatives, most trekking many kilometers on foot to do so, sharing what little they had and expending their own caloric intake in the process."[5]

For months, Elias's mother walked to the bus stop and waited for unreliable buses that dropped her near the hospital. On good days, the trip took more than an hour. On days when the bus didn't come, she'd hike nearly three-miles, carrying her son's homemade care package. Each afternoon she'd make the journey in reverse.

Panagiota would have continued this routine willingly, but she had her doubts about the quality of care her son was getting. Nurses were little more than well-intentioned servant girls, and she was afraid that, convalescing in an ill-equipped, ill-staffed medical warehouse, Elias would not get the treatment he needed. He might even get worse and die. The air on Dafnomili Street was un-polluted, with the pine trees on Mount Lycabettos wafting a fresh aroma. Panagiota reasoned that Elias could recuperate better at home, in his own bed, with her overseeing his care and feeding. She negotiated his release with the doctors and administrators. It did not hurt her case that the chief of the Sotiria clinic, Nikolaos Karditsis, had helped OAG obtain medicines and explosives during the war.

For more than a year, his parents organized Elias's health care. But drugs were in short supply and, in mid-1947, when it seemed he was better, he tapered off and then stopped taking his medications. He suffered a relapse, became chronically weak and exhausted, and prolonged his recovery. After he was deemed no longer contagious, family, friends, and some of his current and former teachers home-schooled him. Individually and together they brought text-books and works of non-fiction—particularly on economics, politics, and history—and discussed the different subjects with him. He also read and debated great works of literature, taking a particular interest in the works of Leo Tolstoy and George Bernard Shaw. In coming years, Elias would have many opportunities to reflect on a line from the preface to *Heartbreak House*: "Truth telling is not compatible with the defence of the realm." Elias had time to read omnivorously, not simply to prepare for examinations, but for the pure joy of learning. He regarded this time of recuperation and home schooling as the most intellectually stimulating period of his life. Economics, especially political economics, was his favorite topic.

His most steadfast link to the outside world during his convalescence came from newspapers, particularly *Kathimerini*, the highly respected conservative daily and, to many, the most influential publication in Greece. He devoured it daily, front to back. He thought often not just about the selection and ordering of the stories themselves but about how they must have been gathered and assembled. Elias was especially taken with the articles by two brothers working at *Kathimerini* as financial news correspondents, Efangelos and George Androulidakis. They had already distinguished themselves by secretly publishing and distributing the praised World War II resistance publication *Fighting Greece* and had become leading reporters and commentators on issues of political economics. Elias imagined himself covering stories, writing them, seeing them in print, and having an impact on shaping reader opinion. The outlines of a possible career were beginning to take shape.

■

IN LATE 1946, Britain decided it was unable to carry the burden of Greek reconstruction.[6] Widespread unmet Greek needs, enduring corruption, mounting inefficiencies, and the emerging insurrection in particular proved overwhelming. Economic problems at home and worsening finances elsewhere only made matters more urgent. London told Washington on February 21, 1947, that Britain's program of military and economic aid to Greece (and Turkey) would stop on March 31 and requested immediate help.

On Wednesday evening March 12, 1947—early in his recovery from tuberculosis—Elias and his family listened to a live broadcast of President Harry S. Truman speaking in Washington to a joint session of the US Congress to announce what would become known as the "Truman Doctrine," now seen as a landmark in the accelerating Cold War between Soviet-style Communism and the West.

Truman gave an "all-out speech," a flamboyant, evangelical invocation designed to electrify an indifferent American public and win over a parsimonious Republican Congress.[7] He began by telling this audience that he had received from Greece "an urgent appeal for financial and economic assistance" that was "imperative if Greece is to survive as a free nation." The President warned that "the very existence of the Greek state is today threatened by the terrorist activities of several thousand armed men, led by Communists . . . The Greek government is unable to cope with the situation. . . . Greece must have assistance if it is to become a self-supporting and self-respecting democracy . . . There's no other country to which democratic Greece can turn."[8]

Truman conceded that the Greek government had made mistakes, that the United States did not condone everything it had done or would do. But the country was operating in an atmosphere of chaos and "desperately need[ed] our support now."

The Demetracopouloses listened intently, wondering about the implications of the speech. The family had welcomed British aid and influence and was unprepared for the news that the UK could no longer afford to be engaged. United States involvement introduced a new unknown, but Elias's father appreciated his earlier experiences in America and encouraged his extended family and neighbors to embrace US support. They hoped that a substantial American presence would crush the Communist insurgency and open the way to a Greece that would flourish economically, socially, and politically. For his part, Elias welcomed the change in Western patron from the royalty-loving British to a country with republican roots.

It was not until late summer of 1947 that the first shipments of American aid arrived. Meanwhile, eruptions of violence increased, and the central government lost control of more of the countryside, making major parts of the plans to rebuild the economic infrastructure "inoperative."[9]

Initially, Greece's Democratic Army leaders were firm believers in guerrilla warfare. This strategy of gradually wearing down the Greek government had served them well. But the influx of massive American aid made a marked difference. In May 1948, rebel leader Markos Vafeiadis, then in Belgrade, concluded that there was no way the insurgents could win and proposed a cease-fire. But Nikos Zachariadis, the secretary general of the Greek Communist Party and the power behind the insurgent struggle, refused to give in. Instead, he ordered Kapetan (Commander) Markos to abandon guerrilla strategy and operate in conventional small brigades of three or four battalions. This was a grave error.[10] Setting up for fixed battles behind barbed wire and concrete barriers made the Democratic Army better targets, tipping the advantage to the larger, better-trained and -equipped government forces.

■

In the spring of 1948, a high-profile example of the critical role played by journalists in shaping the course of events made a lasting impression on Elias. On Sunday, May 16, a grisly news report described a fisherman's discovery of CBS correspondent George Polk's bound, bloated, and barnacled body floating in Salonica Bay. He had been shot in the head at close range. The thirty-four-year-old

American broadcaster had disappeared while seeking an exclusive interview with Markos Vafeiadis. There were few leads or clues, and fingers pointed in all directions.

Elias was mesmerized by the Polk assassination and its aftermath. He followed accounts of Polk's personal story and his controversial journalism and was struck by reports of Polk's fearlessness in covering both the left and right wings in Greece.[11] Unsparing in his criticism of the atrocities committed by the Communists, Polk had also uncovered the corruption and venality of members of the Greek government who skimmed American aid, and he had criticized Greek politicians who were "unwilling to serve anybody except themselves."[12] Elias admired Polk's independence and doggedness of purpose.

Various theories proliferated in American and Greek press coverage. Initial suggestions of a right-wing—perhaps even a government—plot were matched and soon overtaken by right-wing theories that the Communists were behind the murder. It was counterintuitive to believe that the guerrilla leader Markos would have ordered Polk assassinated rather than taking advantage of Polk's platform to broadcast the Communist commander's views, especially given the growing rift between him and KKE head Nikos Zachariadis. But the alternative theory of a right-wing government plot could have fatally undermined the American public's willingness to support a war that was just beginning to show signs of making progress.

The competing theories about George Polk's murder came to an end a few months later with the arrest and "confession" of a Communist-ordered "conspiracy" whose principal actor was Grigoris Staktopoulos, one of the last people who had seen Polk alive. Staktopoulos was a Greek journalist who had once briefly joined the Communist Party and had more recently contributed to the center-left Salonika newspaper *Makedonia*. The confession confirmed Communist involvement in the plot, a story line clearly in the interest of both the Greek and American governments. Elias carefully followed press accounts of the government's activity, the subsequent arrests, trial, and convictions, and the related news coverage. He even mulled what his own behavior might have been had he found himself in Polk's shoes. He also sensed a disturbing official rush to judgment. Several years later he would understand just how unfair that judgment had been.

■

FAR FROM ATHENS, the American-backed war ground on. Using a strategy later repeated in Korea and Vietnam, government forces relocated inhabitants of whole villages to deny raiding partisans supplies, recruits, and information. In the south this was effective, but costly. Thousands of displaced persons became refugees, needing food, shelter, and clothing. Their number rose to an estimated 700,000. Also brutally efficient was the introduction of American-supplied Napalm B, a powerful and long-lasting incendiary substance used to defoliate landscapes and attack guerrillas' hideouts. Meanwhile, Greek Communist fighters, who had earned ignominy for their savage treatment of civilians and prisoners, lost much of any remaining support in 1948 by ruthlessly kidnapping thousands of children from peasant villages and taking them into the mountains or out of the country to be trained as soldiers. Some of these "recruits" were as young as four.

In the fight between Tito and Stalin over Yugoslavia's growing independence, the KKE and the Democratic Army of Greece struggled not to choose sides. Eventually they chose the more powerful Stalin and Soviet orthodoxy. In July 1948, Tito retaliated by closing Yugoslavian borders to Greek guerrillas. Stalin ignored Secretary Zachariadis's loyalty by declaring that "the uprising in Greece must be stopped, and as quickly as possible."[13] Undeterred by Stalin's lack of support, the KKE's "Radio Free Greece," operating from Romania, took a slap at Tito and endorsed an independent Macedonia, a stance favored by Moscow.[14] The move demoralized the majority of soldiers in the Democratic Army, who thought of themselves as Greek patriots and had no interest in the dismemberment of their homeland.

Resistance to the government's 1949 spring offensive was minimal. From south to central Greece, the insurgency was destroyed, and thousands were captured and killed. In August, General Alexander Papagos, a hero of the Greco-Italian War who had taken charge of the National Army, inflicted major damage in a northern counteroffensive code-named "Operation Torch."[15] At about the same time, Royal Hellenic Air Force Spitfires and US navy surplus Curtis Helldivers equipped with napalm bombs destroyed many well-camouflaged targets.[16] With Albanian supply lines and escape routes effectively closed, the remaining Democratic Army of Greece was routed. On October 16, 1949, KKE radio declared a cease-fire. The civil war was finally over. More had been killed than during the entire German occupation. Economically, the country was in worse shape than it had been in 1944. The scars would last for generations.

■

WHILE ASSIDUOUSLY FOLLOWING the progress of the hot war in his homeland and the beginning stages of the Cold War on the world stage, Elias studied the history of Greek news publishing, from its earliest handwritten broadsides, to its role in the revolution, to the growth of opposition papers and restrictive press laws imposed by authoritarian governments.

He didn't want to be a doctor, lawyer, businessman, or engineer. He wanted to be a journalist. He thought of the Androulidakis brothers and George Polk, their courage, integrity, independence, and willingness to criticize both sides if the facts justified it. Elias wanted to be an *investigative* reporter—one who would be the first to uncover important stories. He also reckoned that, if he did it well, he could even be more famous than the people he covered. He wanted to make news by getting news. And he wanted to start at the top, at *Kathimerini*.

When he was finally well enough to return to college, he told his parents he didn't want to interrupt his education by enrolling again in school. Given the growing American presence in Greece, he thought his ability to read, write, and speak English, especially colloquial and idiomatic American English, could help him land a reporter's job. But he also knew that his English-language skills needed improvement. So, in early 1949, he applied for a job at the Athens branch of the British insurance firm White Star, where he learned the King's English. After work he attended a language school near Syntagma Square with instructors from the United States.

Processing commercial and maritime property claims was deadly boring, and in his second year he quit to pursue his dream. Journalism was a closed profession, but, through a combination of well-placed family friends like Dr. Giannatos, Elias lined up a call with the *Kathimerini* editor, Aimilios Chourmouzios. After several increasingly long telephone conversations with different people, Elias was invited to the paper to meet with its business editor, Epameinondas Efetas. Elias was bright, ambitious, and had boundless enthusiasm for the job, but all of that would not have secured a position at the paper. Once again, his ability to read, write, and speak English, even if imperfect, made him a valuable resource.

When he first walked into the open newsroom on Sokratous Street with the high ceiling, big windows, desks lined up in rows, telephones ringing and typewriters click-clacking, he experienced a mixture of awe and comfort. He was oblivious to the acrid smell of stale cigarettes. Efetas talked to Elias about Greek politics and international business issues, Dr. Giannatos, and his own extended family's circle of friends. Elias then met the editor, Chourmouzios. He was shorter than Elias, but his firm handshake, handsome face, strong jaw, and piercing eyes gave him a commanding aura. The interviewee was introduced to George Vlachos, the paper's legendary owner, and his attractive daughter, Eleni. He looked for the Androulidakis brothers, whose writing he much admired, but they weren't around.

The interview process lasted nearly two hours. Elias talked about himself, OAG, a range of current events, and personalities in the Greek government. Chourmouzios steered the conversation to the American Embassy, international economics, and the paper's reputation and traditions. At the end, Elias shook hands, left, and walked home. He was told politely and noncommittally that the paper would get back to him with its answer.

For three long days, he waited near the telephone as the paper weighed its hiring decision. Then Chourmouzios called personally to tell him that he was not only being offered a job, but that he would be a diplomatic correspondent, reporting primarily on the American community in Greece. It was one of the happiest days of his life.

6.

The Young Journalist

I N SUMMER 1950, NOW A young man of 21, Elias felt he was on top of the world, writing for arguably the most prestigious and influential paper in Greece, with immediate access to powerful figures in both Greek and American circles in Athens.

Having replaced Great Britain as the country's primary benefactor, the United States's military, diplomatic, economic, and political influence in Greece was paramount. "Millions of dollars in aid and thousands of personnel were flooding the country. The American community in Greece was the biggest story," Elias recalled, "and the paper wanted to cover it well. I determined that to be effective as a journalist would require me to be especially aggressive and indefatigable."

There were potential stories everywhere. The American presence in Greece had grown from the hundreds to the thousands, but the juggernaut was far from monolithic. The large embassy competed frequently with semiautonomous parts of the American mission, particularly an acronym jungle of economic-aid organizations spawned by the Marshall Plan, the various military contingents, and the CIA in its different guises. Each of these entities established a distinctive relationship with a variety of Greek organizations and individuals.

Beyond bringing the *Amerikanokratia* that dominated Greek political and economic decision-making, American culture permeated everyday Athenian life.[1] Movies were a cheap form of entertainment. In theaters, for a couple of hours, people with threadbare clothing and rumbling bellies could vicariously experience the lives of beautiful women, dashing men, and the American dream. Few women could resist the allure of synthetic hosiery with seams down the back. Young men coveted aviator sunglasses, the kind worn by the flamboyant General Douglas MacArthur. By the early 1950s, Brits were replaced by Yanks, who were invested with a similar exalted status.

IT WAS AN unusually hot August afternoon when Elias Demetracopoulos took his first taxi trip from the *Kathimerini* building on Sokratous Street to the American Embassy on historic Vasilissis Sofias Avenue, not far from the Royal Palace and Constitution Square. The warren of offices, disparaged by those who worked there as dilapidated, was a grand old building and a cool oasis to the outsider entering it. The embassy staff and foreign correspondents who frequented the building were welcoming. But, afraid of being taken in, Elias remained skeptical of the bonhomie.

According to Elias, the press corps would customarily gather at the embassy for 10 a.m. briefings. Staff would usually bring news releases. The reporters would take the official press handouts and rework them into articles, often including something from notes they jotted down at the press conference. Reporters, whether present at the briefings or not, were often encouraged to rewrite the handouts and check back with public affairs officers before filing the articles. Filing early in the day made it easier to have long lunches at local tavernas and take in the pleasures of the Greek capital.

Reporters who were somewhat more enterprising would conduct follow-up interviews to amplify the embassy release or develop stori⟨ ⟩their own. But even then, some reporters would run their pieces by the ⟨ ⟩officers for an informal "fact-checking" review. John Rigas, lon⟨ ⟩ a variety of publications and a Demetracopoulos con⟨ ⟩ Elias's characterization fits the description of ma⟨ ⟩ cially those who were just in for a visit, it painted ⟨ ⟩ the regular press corps.[2] Nevertheless, Rigas ⟨ ⟩ welcome independent reporting.

Elias chafed at the cozy way embass⟨ ⟩ never been to journalism school, but, fr⟨ ⟩ thought it important to be skeptical.[3]

review his stories prior to publication. He later remembered embassy staff and many of his new press colleagues being taken aback at his brash attitude. But Chourmouzios, his editor, backed him up and told him he was proud of his stance. "And that opinion," said Elias, "is what mattered most."

Elias refined the same skills he first developed in the OAG underground, trying to build trusting relationships and ferret out information. He was the youngest reporter at the paper and possibly the youngest in the press covering the embassy, which brought out his competitive nature. He eagerly sought angles to stories other reporters didn't have and impatiently grappled with the reality that scoops would not come to him on a platter. "I began to develop my own sources," he recalled, "obtain exclusive stories and interviews and expose official wrongdoing."

He learned the various press hangouts where reporters ate, drank, and exchanged gossip.[4] "France," at the beginning of Stadiou Street in downtown Athens, was a large cafe with small marble tables and wrought-iron chairs. For next to nothing, low-wage reporters could patiently nurse their *kremes*—bowls of warm milk, corn flour, and sugar—and while away hours in the close, smoke-filled atmosphere. For fancier fare, reporters and some publishers went to Pappos Gallery, a small restaurant located near three printing-press shops. Apotsos served arguably the best delicatessen, good for the stomach while one drank ouzo. And nearby, the Ideal was the bar of choice for a quick drink after work. Other popular tavernas were tucked away in nearby cellars and side streets.

Elias visited these places from time to time, but he wasn't a regular anywhere. He chose to work independently and saw more value in socializing with possible sources at diplomatic receptions and dinners. The information was fresher, the food better (and free), and these events seemed to take place almost every day. As he got to know members of the American community, he also became a regular visitor in their homes and offices. When he hosted important sources, he preferred to splurge at the Grand Bretagne Hotel.

During Elias's early months at the paper, he developed what would become his signature practice: conducting long-form interviews, often providing written questions to the subjects in advance. He was trying to turn a liability into an ~~a~~dvantage. Although his English had improved significantly, he was self-con~~~~ ~~a~~bout his ability to take notes during a rapid-fire exchange in a non-native ~~espe~~cially when the topics were complex.

~~The s~~ubject would respond to his inquiries in writing. More often ~~he opted~~ for taping, using the subject's equipment or, if that wasn't possible, lugging or wheeling a large reel-to-reel tape recorder into the interviewee's office. The tapes would then be transcribed by the interviewee's secretary or a one-woman secretarial service near the Court of Justice, on whom Elias came to rely. Afterward, he'd return to have the interviewee approve, in writing, the accuracy of the transcript. Only then would he prepare a story using all or part of the interview.

Elias's method lent itself well to *Kathimerini*, which was generally regarded as Greece's national newspaper of record. The Androulidakis brothers befriended him, but his main mentor and protector at the paper was Chourmouzios, who pushed back at those who would tease Elias for his youth or his non-smoking, non-drinking habits. The editor came from the cosmopolitan Cypriot port of Limassol, where his family had a long tradition of literary publishing excellence. In his youth he'd praised socialism, but his awareness of the atrocities committed in the Soviet Union moved him to the political right.

Chourmouzios critiqued Elias's stories, shared his own approaches to working sources and newsgathering, and gave young Demetracopoulos the latitude to develop his style. He also introduced him to his circle of friends, including the renowned author Nikos Kazantzakis, who had been a *Kathimerini* correspondent. The editor risked stoking the jealousy of some reporters at the largely no-byline paper by letting Elias, early in his career, attach his name to some of his articles. And he encouraged Elias to pitch other news outlets for stories that didn't make sense for *Kathimerini* and would not compete with it.[5]

Elias felt that a respected but undoctrinaire conservative paper was a good fit for him. On the political spectrum his views were decidedly center-right, but he believed himself an independent thinker. He sympathized with General Nikolaos Plastiras, the progressive victor of the 1950 general el ~tion, but disagreed with his domestic plan for reconciliation and amnest   ~unists who had been exiled and imprisoned. Acknowledging the   ~s and those being held who were not security threats, Elias   reviews, but thought the menace of international Com amnesty too risky. He also came quickly to doubt th larly the Queen, accepted the limits of a constit found in countries like Great Britain and Sweder ical activities had been curtailed. Elias supp Alexander Papagos, hero of the Albanian ar the political arena.

At first, Elias viewed the ever-changing coalitions that struggled to govern the country as the price of a robust democracy and was opposed to changes in the election law that would narrow choices. But he soon acknowledged the importance of a stable government to the country's economic recovery. US Ambassador to Greece Henry F. Grady, Papagos, and Chourmouzios all favored a variation on majority rule for parliamentary elections, which led to fewer and larger parties, instead of the modified proportional representation system then in place. Elias did too, but thought Greeks themselves should drive the reform changes, without outside pressure.

When Elias started working for *Kathimerini*, the big domestic story was American plans to reduce the amount and scope of US aid, then over a billion and a half dollars for rehabilitation alone. The commitment of the Economic Cooperation Administration (ECA), created by the US Congress in 1948 to administer the Marshall Plan, extended only through 1952, and was in the process of being replaced by the Mutual Security Administration (MSA), a multilateral alliance that would focus on security rather than economic development. During his two years as ambassador, Grady advocated for carefully weaning Greece off its heavy American economic dependence, worrying that Greeks of all stripes were falsely assuming that reconstruction aid would continue indefinitely. The increased Soviet threat, the rise of Communist China, and the Korean War dramatically accelerated the change in American policy.

When Grady was reassigned to Iran, Elias wondered what changes might take place at the American Embassy. Little did he know that the incoming ambassador, John Emil Peurifoy, would become one of his life's great antagonists, responsible for triggering three decades of personal and professional travails.

■

DURING HIS FIRST months on the job, Elias did a lot of "meet-and-greet" and tried to cultivate relationships with a wide range of new contacts. He learned the faces and personalities behind the letterhead names in the alphabet soup of agencies on his beat. At first, he didn't report any significant exclusive stories. In general, he found it easier to talk with admirals and generals than with diplomats. The military brass was blunter and "gave good quotes," whereas the embassy crowd ...ed to be more circumspect. Initially, he was insensitive to potential prob-...s creating by favoring different agencies for coverage and pitting ...e another. He later used the technique as part of his newsgath-

That autumn he was informed that he wouldn't have to interrupt his new work to serve in the army. The Greek government advised him that his participation in OAG and imprisonment had satisfied his military-service obligation. He was promoted to second lieutenant. Along with the good news, he was chagrined to find that the letter crediting him for his stay in Eginition included a diagnosis of "schizophrenia." He immediately called Dr. George Pampoukis, the longtime director of the hospital's Department of Psychiatry, demanding that the letter be revised to reflect the diagnosis as feigned. The doctor simply replied, "That's what it says in the records." Elias exploded: "Just because it's written on a paper doesn't mean it's true. This was the cover used by Archbishop Damaskinos and others to save me from execution. I don't want a false diagnosis to follow me all of my life and hurt my reputation and employment opportunities. Check with your superiors." A couple of days later he received a second letter that complied with his request.

Shortly thereafter, he learned that his wartime service would be rewarded.[6] On the balmy afternoon of October 4, 1950, His Beatitude the Patriarch of Alexandria, Msr. Christoforos, conferred upon "the Greek newsman Mr. Elias Demetracopoulos, sentenced by the Germans . . . for acts of sabotage, the decoration of the Gold Cross of Saint Mark, the highest distinction of the Alexandria Patriarchate." Attending the ceremony at the Cecil Hotel in Kifissia was the Greek minister of national defense and future prime minister, Konstantinos Karamanlis. The Greek aviation, marine, and agriculture ministers also came. Among the Americans were a general from the American Military Mission; the military, air, and naval attachés of the US Embassy and the director of the US Information Service.[7] Newspaper accounts noted "this attendance was significant" because of "the daring and patriotic activities of Mr. Demetracopoulos." Elias was especially happy that his mother attended, along with OAG leader Bobotinos, and OAG's deputy chief, Dr. Giannatos. Elias's latest girlfriend, Celia Was, sat next to his mother at the ceremony.

Almost four years later, on August 19, 1954, Elias received tive Medal of the National Resistance 1941–45 from the Greek of the Army for "outstanding services." The citation said: "M· was the most trustworthy link between the 'National Org· urrection of the Nation' and Ivanoff [sic] . . . and was ser sabotages he had performed, including at the Zappei having kept weapons and a secret radio transmitter at bodily injuries and lasting scars from being tortured. And on October 15, 1954, the Greek Ministry of National Defense awarded Elias the Golden Cross of the Royal Order of George I "for his national activity during the enemy occupation."

In coming years, the validity of each of these awards and the heroism they acknowledged would be denied by enemies attempting to destroy his reputation.[8]

Meanwhile, Demetracopoulos was doing everything he could to burnish that reputation. Seizing on the recent outbreak of the Korean War as a news hook, he sought outlets beyond *Kathimerini* to showcase his reporting. He successfully pitched stories to *Pathfinder News Magazine*, a right-wing publication that also published articles by FBI director J. Edgar Hoover; to the weekly magazine *Thisavros*, and to the short-lived English language journal *Greece*. He became Mediterranean correspondent for the North American Newspaper Alliance, also known as NANA, a worldwide syndicate that employed an eclectic group of writers including Ernest Hemingway, Ian Fleming, and Lucianne Goldberg over its nearly 60-year existence. To expand his network, he volunteered as press director for the Greek-American Cultural Institute and informally helped promote programs of the American-Hellenic Chamber of Commerce. Most significantly, in late 1951 he became a political contributor to *Makedonia/Thessaloniki*, a popular liberal morning-evening newspaper in northern Greece and one of the oldest publications in the country.

■

JOHN EMIL PEURIFOY arrived in Athens on September 15, 1950, to take over the position of ambassador from Henry Grady.[9] Matinee-idol attractive, jaunty, and "good ol' boy" informal, the five-foot-nine Peurifoy had launched his political career in 1935 by utilizing a patronage appointment as elevator operator in the House of Representatives. Three years later, he climbed the State Department ladder, where his rapport with individual members of Congress helped advance the Foggy Bottom agenda with legislators generally hostile to State Department personnel. "Smilin' Jack" came from wealthy South Carolina bluebloods and had set his sights on being president or a US senator. In eight years, he advanced from clerk to under-secretary of state.

A zealous anti-Communist in charge of security at the State Department, Peurifoy helped stoke the national paranoia about "the enemy within," exposing ᵥosexual "perverts" and other serious "shady" security risks.[10] In March ᵥbetted Senator Joseph McCarthy's Congressional witch hunt by tell-ᵥAppropriations Committee that, because of his loyalty-checking vigilance, at least ninety-one "undesirable" individuals in the State Department had either resigned or been dismissed from their jobs during the previous three years. In September he took over the Greek ambassadorship with a mandate larger than simple diplomacy.

Initially, after the Greek Civil War, the United States and NATO held the view that Greece had limited international strategic value. The Korean War, which turned the Cold War quite hot, changed that strategic thinking. Washington came to believe that Soviet expansion from the Balkans posed an imminent threat. Peurifoy was tasked to be point man in the transformation of Greece into a front-line bulwark against the worldwide Communist menace. To that end, he advocated for Greeks to change their electoral system to effect a center-right government and threatened aid cuts if they refused. The idealistic democratic rhetoric of Truman's speech would have to take a back seat.[11]

Lacking any background in Greek affairs, Peurifoy repeatedly clashed with both American economic-aid administrators and the US military mission. Colleagues agreed that, in Greece, Peurifoy had "no political sense at all."[12] He was much more comfortable working in lockstep with, if not under the tutelage of, CIA Chief of Station Thomas Karamessines, an old hand in Greece for nearly a decade before the new ambassador's arrival.

Born in 1917, Thomas Hercules Karamessines had worked as a prosecutor for New York District Attorney Thomas E. Dewey and during World Was II was assigned to OSS and SSU in Greece. Karamessines joined the CIA at its creation in 1947 and became its second station chief in Athens. From his fifth-floor office in the pink stone Tamion Building's downtown headquarters, he focused on enemies both within and outside Greece's borders.

Greece had had its own state security services since the 1920s, most recently the Central Intelligence and Investigation Service, created in 1949. Claiming that Greece needed a more sophisticated operation, Karamessines helped the Greek Government create an independent structure tasked with safeguarding "national security, the security of military forces, and public security." The Central Intelligence Service (KYP) was effectively the CIA, FBI, NSC, Defense and State departments' intelligence services, all rolled into one.[13]

Karamessines was more reserved than Al Ulmer, his CIA station chie⸍ decessor, who had boasted: "We were in charge. We ran things. We we⸀ kings" and exulted: "we did what we wanted … God we had fun!"[1⸍ league later wrote about Karamessines that "[t]here was no flam¹ and he shunned publicity."[15] When Elias first approached Karamessines at a dip-lomatic reception, he saw a dour, dark-haired man with a prominent nose and dark-framed glasses. He came away from the encounter "not greatly impressed." He recalled Karamessines as "a smart cookie," but "not a man whose opinion I would ask for, because I knew he would never give me a straight reply." Karamessines probably regarded Demetracopoulos with similar disdain. For him, the press was an asset to be manipulated or a nuisance to be avoided.

The new ambassador, Peurifoy, viewed Elias's journalistic independence as a direct affront to his mission. Particularly offensive was Demetracopoulos's eagerness to report stories that raised questions of malfeasance in the imple-mentation of US aid programs. While Elias was grateful for the American in-volvement, and believed the reconstruction support had saved his country from some form of East European Communism, he wasn't going to let his apprecia-tion deter him from reporting stories of wrongdoing. He was eager to publish scoops like American investigators finding "huge supplies of food aid rotting in warehouses at a time when 75 percent of Greek children were suffering from malnutrition."[16] And he readily shared the critical assessments of others, such as American columnist Joe Alsop, who wrote that "Most Greek politicians had no higher ambition than to taste the profitable delights of a free economy at American expense."[17]

Peurifoy had much bigger issues to deal with than thwarting Elias Demetra-copoulos, including transforming American economic aid marked for recon-struction into a program of security-related support, and restructuring the Greek parliamentary system in a way that would help Papagos and his conserva-tive Greek Rally party win elections. Nevertheless, Elias's reporting became a persistent nuisance, and both the ambassador and the CIA Station Chief com-plained repeatedly. In phone calls and in person they protested to editor Chour-mouzios, and publisher Vlachos that Elias was being "too aggressive and that his articles were embarrassing the United States." The paper's management, they maintained, had a professional responsibility to rein in Elias. A lesser publica-tion would have complied. However, as Demetracopoulos recalled: "Mr. Vla-chos and Mr. Chourmouzios backed me fully and refused to limit my reporting."

American officials and press colleagues began referring snidely to twenty-two-year-old Demetracopoulos as "the Scooper." However, when Elias heard the nickname, he crowed with delight; he was proud to wear it as his personal brand.

In mid-1951, the paper, pleased with Elias's stories about American activities in Greece, approved his first visit to the United States. His assignment: to conduct a series of interviews with high-level US officials. For months he wrote letters arranging appointments and providing supportive letters of introduction. He was aided in his efforts by American military officials such as Major General Reuben Jenkins, chief of the Joint US Military Aid Group, who referred to Elias as "a friend" who "has always presented our efforts to the reading public in a most favorable light."[18] Brigadier General Leigh Wade, the USAF air attaché in Athens, wrote to the Pentagon asking that assistance be extended to one whose "war record is most outstanding."[19]

Before leaving for the United States, Elias visited former prime minister George Papandreou at his modest whitewashed villa in Kastri. He wanted the statesman's views of the people he planned to meet. After luncheon, they continued their discussion in the garden, during which Papandreou expressed his deep desire that his son Andreas return home and get involved in Greek politics. He explained that Andreas had left for the United States during the Metaxas dictatorship in 1939 and had built a successful university career there as an economics professor. The former prime minister had not seen his son in all the years since, save for one brief reunion in Washington, the year before, which had not gone well.

When it was time to leave, the older man bent down by the doorway and picked a sweet-smelling fresh sprig from a dark-green basil plant. He gently pressed it into Elias's palm. "When you see my son, Andreas," Papandreou said, tears rolling silently down his cheeks, "please give this to him and tell him this is coming from his father." Elias, knowing the significance of *basilikos* in Greek religious celebrations, was greatly touched by the gesture.

■

ELIAS MADE HIS first transatlantic crossing in July 1951 on the aging steamship *Nea Hellas*.[20] The fifteen-day voyage from Piraeus to New York included stops in Malta, Naples, Genoa, Lisbon, and Halifax. *Nea Hellas* wasn't one of the new glamorous four-stack luxury liners, but for generations of Europeans, particularly Greeks, it was a "ship of dreams." War refugees used it to escape Hitler; economic emigrants to find better lives. During the war it was a troop ship, convoying thousands of American and British soldiers and airmen who, crowded on board, affectionately nicknamed it "Nelly Wallace."

The trip was quite comfortable, with good food and entertainment. Looking out at glorious sunsets and sailing on calm midsummer seas, young ⌐

tracopoulos imagined himself an explorer setting out to discover the "New World." He thought of his father and imagined the lesser conditions of that passage and the sensations Panagiotis might have experienced getting off another boat more than three decades earlier. Arriving in New York was a spectacular experience, the city's skyline providing a backdrop to the Statue of Liberty in unfiltered sunlight. Elias was struck by the size of Manhattan's skyscrapers, the bustling crowds, the ceaseless cacophony of the streets. After spending several days in New York, largely playing tourist, he took a train to his meetings in D.C.

Elias's most memorable first impression of the nation's capital was the sweltering, oppressively humid and breezeless Washington summer, which drove people indoors or out of town. It was much more uncomfortable than Athens in August. Compared to New York, Washington felt remarkably quiet, if not abandoned.

He tried to contact Andreas Papandreou to give him the gift of basil and deliver his father's message. But Andreas was in Nevada, establishing residency so he could get a quick divorce from his wife, Christina, and marry Margaret Chant.[21] Discarding the sprig, Elias wondered what might cause a son not to visit his father in their homeland for more than a decade.

The young reporter set himself up at the old National Hotel on I Street and went about his business. He had more than twenty-four letters of introduction to high-ranking officials, and those who hadn't left town were willing to schedule meetings on short notice. Among his interviews were the secretaries of the Air Force, Navy, and Commerce and senior officials in the Departments of State and Defense. They in turn recommended others to meet and invited him to diplomatic events and parties.

He also met President Harry S. Truman and Vice President Alben W. Barkley. As his photograph was being taken shaking hands with the President at a Mayflower Hotel reception, he thought back to the scene in 1947 in the living room of his Athens home, as his family listened to the fateful radio announcement of the Truman Doctrine.

·

AFTER ONE OF his scheduled meetings at the Pentagon, Elias's interviewee was apparently so impressed by the young reporter's sophisticated assessment of strategic issues that he requested Elias meet another official to exchange views about the situation in Greece and the Balkans. Eager to expand his network of sources, the young journalist accepted. According to a contemporaneous "SECRET" document prepared by the Covert Action Staff of the CIA's clandestine Directorate of Operations:

> Dimitrakopoulos [sic] provided intelligence information on Greek military, political and refugee matters to US Army intelligence officers in the Pentagon. His information was considered to be of value and the general impression of the Army interviewers was that Dimitrakopoulos was a man of excellent education background, well able to interrelate the political and military situation, that he showed remarkable aptitude in his appreciation of the general Balkan strategic picture and that he appeared to be a potentially valuable source for the Army Attaché in Athens ... Upon conclusion of their interrogation of Dimitrakopoulos the Army representative turned him over to their Requirements Branch for further exploitation by the Western Branch and ONI. The Defense Department then introduced Dimitrakopoulos to a CIA official in Washington in order to evaluate the recommendations Dimitrakopoulos had put forth.[22]

Later, at a diplomatic reception, John Zimmerman, an American intelligence official, approached Demetracopoulos and asked to meet with him privately. Within days, Zimmerman invited him to lunch at the New Baghdad Restaurant and afterward asked if he'd be interested in working for the CIA. Zimmerman told Elias that his career and income would benefit. He offered him a part-time job with the CIA starting at an outrageously high $17,000-per-year salary (about $164,000 today). This would have been an exponential boost to his earnings as a journalist. Of course, the offer may have been nothing more than tantalizing bait.

Elias would be asked, Zimmerman explained, to do things for which being a journalist was a good cover: intelligence-sharing from his activities at home and abroad; supplying names of sources; relaying gossip and rumors that could prove useful. If he agreed to work for the CIA, he would be contacted by a member of the American community in Greece, a US businessman who was also a covert CIA agent.

Demetracopoulos had already experienced pressure from Peurifoy and Karamessines to get on the team. He was aware that other journalists, economics advisors, public relations agents, and businessmen worked for the CIA. Indeed, guessing who was or wasn't working for the CIA had almost become a parlor game in Athens.

It was one thing to exchange perspectives and tidbits with intelligence sources, part of the "give a little, get a little" newsgathering ritual. But he rejected working as a paid agent for any government. Elias politely turned Zimmerman down.

Zimmerman quietly tried again several days later, at another social gathering in Takoma Park, just north of Washington. At first the twenty-two-year-old journalist began to explain the principles of his profession, including the importance of a free press, but he stopped himself. Realizing it was neither the time nor place, he simply said, "No, thank you" and moved to another cluster of guests. Though his decision made his career and reputation vulnerable to retaliatory attacks from the CIA, this would not be the agency's last overture.

7.

Celia

AT TWENTY-ONE, ELIAS DEMETRACOPOULOS WAS already a self-styled ladies' man who dated omnivorously. He was taller than most Greeks, with brown spaniel eyes and a well-trimmed full head of black hair carefully parted and slicked down. He favored tailored two-piece dark-blue pinstripe suits, repp ties, starched white shirts, pocket squares, and wing-tipped brogues. His cleft chin and pearly white teeth stood out on his full, handsome face. Ever fearful of becoming overweight, he skipped meals to permit himself to indulge regularly in his favorite vice, chocolate. He walked erect and quickly, believing it helped him deal with intermittent back pain, a legacy of his tortures.

Elias met Celia Was in his first days covering the embassy in late summer 1950. He was charmed by her looks, impressed by her savvy, and enchanted by her cosmopolitan sophistication and international experiences. She had just returned from State Department trips to Cairo, Beirut, and New York.

Svelte and tall, with warm brown eyes, an engaging smile, well-coiffed auburn hair, and stylish outfits, Celia had rejected the frequent attentions of her male colleagues since her arrival a few months earlier. But she found young Elias fresh and charming. Celia immediately liked what she saw as his odd combination of "diplomatic snobbery [and] cynical optimism," extroversion, and an intelligent, quiet reserve that she called "Jesuitical."[1] They started dating shortly after he started covering the embassy. Over time, he would learn the details of her dramatic past.

Celia was ten years older than Elias. She had been raised in New Britain, Connecticut, by her Polish-Austrian émigré parents, who were so economically stressed that Celia and her sister swapped dresses so it wouldn't seem they could afford just a single outfit. Unlike most of her contemporaries seeking to get married and raise a family, Celia wanted to be independent, get a job, and experience the world. After graduating from high school second in her class, she started out with local secretarial jobs, then moved to administrative positions with *Time* and *Life* in Washington and Paris. With enthusiastic recommendations from her employers and "the ability to adapt herself to unusual conditions or environment," Celia easily passed all security clearances and joined the US Foreign Service.[2]

While Elias had been scurrying around the streets of Athens as a teenage resistance fighter, Celia was working as a clerk-stenographer at the Office of War Information in Washington, and as a translator-secretary at its offices in London and Paris. When Elias was back at school, she was at the State Department. And when Elias was home battling tuberculosis, Celia, in part because of her multilingual skills (Polish, Russian, French, and English), had been transferred to Moscow as a foreign-service officer, part of the public-diplomacy section of the American Embassy.

Celia did editorial work on the State Department's popular glossy magazine, *Amerika*, designed to present to Russian-speaking people beautiful photographs and positive stories of life in the United States. Ambassador Walter Bedell Smith praised her work. In fall 1947, after she clashed with her department superiors over their mistreatment of Russian nationals working at the embassy, the ambassador moved her to the consular section. Celia, unostentatiously ambitious, thought she was on the way up. Soon, however, collateral damage from the activities of another embassy staffer jeopardized her career.

Celia had invited Annabelle Bucar, a Croatian-American, from Pennsylvania to share her small two-room apartment. The pair were not especially close, but they commiserated about the local food, travel difficulties, and problems at work. Annabelle was outspoken in her criticism of what she thought was an embassy rife with anti-Soviet paranoids, doltish staff members who refused to learn the local language, and too many spies posing as diplomats. Celia regarded her roommate's comments as overly harsh critiques, but not as evidence of disloyalty to America.

During this early period of the Cold War, Russians and Americans gleefully trumpeted tales of individuals defecting to their side for apparently ideological reasons. The embassy had specifically urged Celia to cultivate Yugoslavs and Poles in connection to her work with the cultural program and was aware that Celia had dated officers assigned to the Polish Embassy. Annabelle, meanwhile, fell hard for Konstantin Lapschin, a baritone at the Moscow Operetta Theater well-known for having courted many unattached young foreign women in Moscow, while also secretly working for the police responsible for internal political control.

On the night of January 25, 1948, Annabelle confided to Celia that she was not only deeply in love with Lapschin but was pregnant and had secretly married him. She said she was planning to resign and defect. Alarmed, Celia urged her to see the ambassador immediately and disclose everything. She recommended that Annabelle ask to be transferred back to the States. But the next day Annabelle did nothing, and an emotionally upset Celia left her post in the afternoon to go ice-skating alone. Distracted, she fell and broke her arm and wrist. The damage was so serious that she was told she would have to go to Stuttgart for treatment and might be away for a couple of weeks. Before leaving, Celia extracted a promise, unfulfilled, that her roommate would have a frank discussion with Ambassador Smith.

After Annabelle resigned, people at the embassy, notably Smith, treated the episode largely as the blind infatuation of a pretty thirty-three-year-old woman with an alluring singer, not a calculated political defection.[3] But the tone changed after Annabelle started delivering anti-American speeches, the KGB used her name as "author" of a book-length diatribe, and the European press publicized an unflattering portrait of US diplomats in Moscow.[4]

Annabelle Bucar's defection being the second in a year, Bedell Smith ordered a full investigation. Others at the embassy, acutely embarrassed by the fallout, lacked Smith's patience and objectivity and decided to make Celia the scapegoat. She lost her high-level security clearance and was assigned to stateside duties with the Office of International Education pending completion of investigations by multiple federal agencies including the State Department, CIA, and House Committee on Un-American Activities. Simultaneously, the FBI investigated her "character, reputation and loyalty." J. Edgar Hoover became involved. Interrogations went on for much of the year.

In a SECRET June document, the State Department's Personnel Security

Branch reported "she spoke willingly and freely on all matters on which she was questioned and gave the impression of candor and veracity," adding that she revealed "several interesting items" [redacted] that were not known to Ambassador Smith at the time of Bucar's disclosure and resignation, all of which could cast the matter, including Celia's reactions, in a different light.[5] Referring to her as "an important witness" instead of a target, the security investigators confidentially admitted "that the Department's handling of Miss Was has been, in certain respects, unfortunate," and expressed "the very real possibility that she may seek outside counsel pending final resolution of her implications, if any, in the [Bucar] matter."[6]

The misfired loyalty investigation raised internal red flags. "If Miss Was should seek outside assistance on one or more of these matters," wrote Chief of State Department Security Donald L. Nicholson to Under-Secretary of State John Peurifoy, before his Athens posting, "I believe considerable embarrassment could result to the Department." He asked Peurifoy, who would later confront both Elias and Celia in a different setting, to "spare an hour to hear her story" and persuade her of "the Department's sincere desire and intention to resolve her problems fairly."[7] There is no record of Peurifoy's having done so.

On October 4, 1948, the investigation bizarrely concluded that Celia was "an attractive person" who could again be "a valuable employee of the foreign service," but because of her temperamental "Slavic 'soul,' which is bound to be trying to her superiors [. . .] she should never again be assigned to a post inside the Slavic orbit of the Soviet Union."[8] Celia was shaken by her Moscow experience and its aftermath but put up an unflappable professional front. When she was offered a position with USIS in Athens in 1950, she took it.[9] Elias was not put off by Celia's story. Rather, he admired that she was not a pushover.

Their relationship became serious quickly. While she was away for three months in the States, her twenty-two-year-old suitor wrote: "I behave like women never existed. I finally discovered I don't feel passion for you but love— real love. I want you as my wife and think that you will be happy doing that." When Elias visited her in New Britain, Connecticut, during his summer 1951 trip, she accepted his marriage proposal.

They discussed getting married in two different religious ceremonies, no later than Christmastime 1951, because, as he explained to her, according to Greek superstition, it is unlucky to marry in a leap year. They talked about their future together, uniting her quiet composure and his "emotional" Greek spirit.

As she told him years later, the trait that endeared him to her most was not his forceful public persona, but his less-visible "tenderhearted generosity," captured best in his solicitude toward children with TB and his insisting that poor fishermen join them for dinner at seaside restaurants. Neither of the two thought through the wisdom and implications of their decision. He was just starting out, eager to engage with the world at warp speed. She was tired, wounded, and in many ways wanted to move back home to Connecticut. She frequently took extended stateside assignments for the State Department, and their courtship proceeded, largely by long distance.

THE FRUITS OF Elias's United States trip, published in *Kathimerini* as a series of page-one stories, elicited a cascade of responses. His interview with US Navy Secretary Dan Kimball was his first bylined piece.[10] He gushed to Celia, who had stayed behind in the USA, that he had received "a great reception" at the paper and from the King, Field Marshal Papagos, and Prime Minister Venizelos. "Think that I have got in my office about 500 letters!!!! from readers of *Kathimerini*—congratulating, complaining, and requesting favors from President Truman through me as if I was a personal friend of him!!!"[11]

With Greeks viewing those appearing to be close to the omnipotent Americans as having special powers, Elias "assiduously cultivated" the image of a man with access to the highest levels.[12] He embellished details of his Washington trip, exaggerating the public encounters with President Truman and Vice President Barkley into full-fledged private meetings. And he didn't correct those who would fabulize his exploits, turning simple hyperbole into outrageous whoppers.

Peurifoy and Karamessines were not pleased with Elias's high-level access and newfound celebrity. Soon after the articles appeared, Major General Petros Nikolopoulos, head of the Central Intelligence and Investigation Service, the Greek intelligence precursor to the KYP, called Elias and said he had been told by both Peurifoy and Karamessines that the Washington interviews were "fabricated."

"That's a lie," Elias responded indignantly. Outraged, he arranged to meet Nikolopoulos the next morning in the General's office. One after another, he showed Nikolopoulos the signed transcripts of his interviews and matched them to the articles. In each, Elias proved to Nikolopoulos the accuracy of the published versions.

The director of Greek intelligence apologized for having been set up. Alas, he was dependent on CIA support and US funding and could not, he said, publicly denounce Elias's critics. Without any third-party pushback on the journalist's behalf, Peurifoy and Karamessines stepped up their attacks. Contradicting the award ceremony the year before, they put the word out that Elias's war record was fabricated. Other American officials in Greece echoed the idea that Elias was an impostor. The American Embassy expanded its disinformation campaign by falsely charging that "the presentation of this award was disputed by other Greek members of the OAG," and a later CIA report elaborated that the presentation had been "disrupted." No evidence to support these bogus charges was ever provided.

Elias was outraged by the attacks on his personal character and war record. Embassy officials also hindered his daily newsgathering. Appointments for embassy and other agency interviews were scheduled, rescheduled, then cancelled. Other interviews couldn't even be scheduled.

Impetuously, the twenty-two-year-old decided to fight back. Taking a page from stories he had heard about Peurifoy's "Big Lie" McCarthyite smear tactics when in Washington, he rumored that four US officials in Athens were known to be accepting bribes and engaging in other financial irregularities. Then, in response to the ambassador's continued personal attacks, he poured gas on the flames, prodding Peurifoy's preoccupation with "pinkos and queers." Some of the corrupt officials, Elias alleged, were also Communist-connected homosexuals.[13] And "they appear to have someone in Washington powerful enough to keep them on the job," he added darkly "in the case of [one], unusually and suspiciously beyond the normal length of a foreign service duty tour."

For nearly five months, cables were sent from Athens to Washington and back to Athens referencing an intrusive investigation into the private lives of the four individuals named by Elias. American security thought it important to make the investigation, even if the charges were false, because, as one wrote confidentially: "Mr. Demetracopoulos appears to have an imposing background and the opportunity to acquire inside information."[14] Eventually all were cleared of wrongdoing. The only common trait they had was that each had been involved in blocking Elias from getting information or interviews he wanted.

At first, Elias felt no remorse for spreading false rumors as payback. He had accepted that these men's blocking of his news sources was part of a game that he too would have to play, only better. It was just business. The brutality and humiliations of Averof and Eginition were still fresh in his mind, and the mendacious personal attacks stoked by Peurifoy and Karamessines wounded his sense of honor. Young Demetracopoulos remembered his promise never to allow himself to be bullied. He was afraid of being thought of as someone who would not fight back.

Later, with hindsight, Elias would concede that his incendiary tactics had been counterproductive. US officials responded by concocting even more far-fetched Demetracopoulos tales. Some charged that he was neither a *Kathimerini* employee nor the author of his American trip articles, but merely a freelance "opportunist" whose name was known only "in an adverse way."[15] Another investigation declared: "No one has ever heard of the man."[16]

To Elias's claims of having discussed issues with General Papagos, Peurifoy lied, saying that the brash young journalist had never even met him. As for Elias's war record, his enemies tried to have it both ways. His resistance work and incarceration were said to be lies and his awards for heroism counterfeit. At the same time, other intelligence reports concluded that he was "mentally deranged . . . mentally impaired by the hardships of the occupation and the fact he had been imprisoned [for a long time and sentenced to death] by the Germans."[17] At the end of the year, the American Embassy concluded that Elias was "a definite mental case," "a definite security risk" and it was pleased to report to Washington that he "is completely 'out of circulation.'"[18]

Elias most certainly was not out of circulation. His American military contacts were still excellent, and he had good access to high-ranking Greek officials. A memorandum to the State Department, CIA, and FBI from the Department of Defense contradicted Peurifoy's assessment. It pointedly warned that Demetracopoulos "is a personal friend of Field Marshal Alexander L. Papagos [the head of the Greek government] . . . and has been handled carefully and courteously, albeit guardedly, by the [US] Army Attaché, Greece."[19]

Nevertheless, being cut off from State Department, embassy, and economic-development personnel had hurt Elias's work, and by early 1952, his editor had had enough. In a letter addressed to "Mr. Ambassador," Chourmouzios said that he "had examined carefully" Peurifoy's remarks about Demetracopoulos's writings made in "certain conversations we had in different occasions and I am obliged to answer you that I found them unfair."[20] In a two-page single-spaced letter, he drew Peurifoy's attention to facts that refuted all of the ambassador's erroneous allegations, starting with a summary of Demetracopoulos's "outstanding" war record on behalf of the Allied cause, his patriotism, arrest, torture, and death sentence, and added that "among the reasons for [the Nazis] condemning Mr. Demetracopoulos to death were that he contributed to the escape of seven American pilots, whose planes were shot down."

Turning to the October 4, 1950 official ceremony decorating Elias for his valor, Chourmouzios listed, name by name, US Embassy officials and staff, members of the US military mission, and Greek government officials who had been in attendance. He followed with a detailed list of names and titles of Washington officials whom Demetracopoulos had interviewed on his recent trip and added the dates and time of his meetings with President Harry S. Truman and Vice President Alben W. Barkley. Chourmouzios concluded: "For all these reasons and taking into consideration the professional abilities of Mr. Demetracopoulos as a very competent newspaperman, I am glad that I can state that Mr. E. P. Demetracopoulos has my complete respect, confidence and admiration."[21]

Unmoved, the ambassador declared Demetracopoulos persona non grata at the US Embassy, and urged American officials in Greece to deny him exclusive interviews.[22] Elias pushed back by joining in on an exclusive interview that visiting columnist Joe Alsop had arranged for himself with Peurifoy.[23] The ambassador was not pleased but did not throw Elias out.

Meanwhile, the Peurifoy diktat against Demetracopoulos caused a special problem for his USIS fiancée. Elias and Celia had accepted that getting married would make it difficult for Celia to keep working at the embassy. She first planned to resign effective the end of December 1951, but her worries about having to live on one salary caused them to postpone their wedding date and find a less-expensive place to live. They would get married the following summer in the United States, with her family, when he joined her there with plans to conduct more interviews. Submitting her resignation to the secretary of state, on June 20, 1952, she concluded: "I wish to express my gratitude for the many courtesies and kindnesses which it has been my privilege to receive while in the Foreign Service . . . I now leave with regret."[24]

The couple had no idea just how closely they both had been surveilled by US intelligence since they started dating in the autumn of 1950—in Greece by the CIA, and in the USA by the FBI. Elias's 1951 arrival in New York and entire stay at the St. Moritz Hotel had been monitored. From the time he met Celia in Manhattan and switched to the Henry Hudson Hotel, they were continually spied on. Their marriage by a clerk at City Hall on July 5, 1952, with Celia's sister and brother-in-law as witnesses, was dutifully logged, and the marriage certificate scrutinized. The document noted no previous marriages for either, and that a

Dr. Emanuel Kotsos was the physician certifying that neither the subject nor his prospective wife had any communicable diseases.[25] The FBI then reported that Celia and "the Subject took residence in Room 1015 of that hotel and as of 7 July 1952. [...] were still there."[26] On the day after their wedding, July 6, "There were no phone calls."[27] On July 7 at 5:27 p.m. the couple checked out, with a forwarding address at the Hotel National in Washington, D.C. In all, the FBI collected more than twenty-six pages of still heavily redacted surveillance reports.

Ambassador Peurifoy had learned from his Washington days how simple allegations could destroy lives. He escalated his anti-Demetracopoulos campaign, calling on the FBI to surveil Elias as a suspected Soviet or double agent. In an Orwellian touch, Peurifoy also twisted the Zimmerman meetings, in which the CIA had offered Elias a job, into a claim that Elias had been passing himself off as a paid American secret agent.[28] Elias, who compartmentalized his relationships and intentionally cultivated a mysterious persona, contributed to this misapprehension. Interacting with Americans was essential to his news beat, and he intentionally fostered the image of being close to those in power. Cryptically, he told those who suspected he might be an agent that there were some things he couldn't talk about. Of course, had he actually been an agent, he wouldn't have drawn attention to the fact.

■

IN ADDITION TO getting married, Elias had other priorities on his agenda in the summer of 1952. The first was to report for his current papers on the American presidential campaign. In early July, the Republicans nominated General Dwight D. Eisenhower, with Senator Richard Nixon for vice president. Later that month, the Democrats picked Illinois governor Adlai Stevenson and Tennessee senator Estes Kefauver. Other than Eisenhower's, these names meant little to Elias. What he did know was that, regardless of who won, a new administration could mean big changes in US-Greek relations. He set up appointments, conducted more interviews, and gathered new material. Wherever he went, whomever he saw, his activities were almost always closely monitored by the FBI.

Elias's other priority was to expand his news outlets. At the recommendation of former Greek prime minister Panagiotis Kanellopoulos, he contacted James A. Linen III, the publisher of *Time* magazine, who set up a meeting for him in New York with John W. Boyle, the assistant chief of correspondents at Time-Life, Inc. A few days later, on August 2, 1952, Elias was appointed a correspondent for Time-Life in Greece.

On the surface, his relationship with the American news empire looked good. He was given detailed instructions regarding payments and filing procedures and urged to pitch stories to both *Time* and *Life*.[29] When Elias returned to Athens, he prepared another series of stories and interviews, which were published prominently in September in *Kathimerini* and *Makedonia*, for the latter of which Elias had become political editor. The *Kathimerini* articles centered on his original beat: American policy toward Greece and the American community there. His writings as political editor for *Makedonia* were not so circumscribed.

In early October, Elias was astounded to receive a "PERSONAL & CONFIDENTIAL" letter from John Boyle in New York, dated October 1, terminating the relationship with Time-Life. The letter stated that Boyle had "received reports . . . which if accurate to any degree, indicate you face great difficulty in attempting to operate as our stringer." Boyle wrote that he had been told by "disinterested non-official sources, whom I know to be well-informed and reliable," that "although you are a contributor to Kathemerini [*sic*] you are not a member of the staff." Mr. Boyle also stated his concern that Demetracopoulos lacked direct access to key US and Greek officials "who make news." Effective immediately, Boyle "simply" terminated his arrangement as a correspondent for Time-Life.

In his reply of October 25, Elias explained to Boyle that the information he had received was incorrect, and enclosed documentation attesting to his status as a regular member and political correspondent of the *Kathimerini* staff, along with ten letters of recommendation from such figures as former prime ministers George Papandreou and Panagiotis Kanellopoulos and members of the United States mission in Greece. They extolled his virtues and confirmed his access to news at the highest levels of government.[30]

Boyle's letter was puzzling. Demetracopoulos had yet to submit any stories to Time-Life, and no news executive there had yet had an opportunity to evaluate his work. Less than a month later, Boyle replied, reaffirming his decision. He wrote: "I am sorry if I was misinformed about your status with *Kathimerini*. I appreciate the letters of endorsement which you have collected and forwarded. But they do not alter my judgment."[31]

The backstory did not become clear until, on a visit to New York in 1954, Elias met John Boyle at a party given by James Linen, the man who had made the original *Time* connection, for Kanellopoulos, then visiting as the Greek defense minister. Boyle told Elias, in the strictest of confidence, that Henry Luce had personally ordered that he be summarily fired at the behest of CIA director Allen Dulles, after Dulles received continuing complaints from Peurifoy and Karamessines. For decades, US officials would use this "firing" from *Time* as evidence of Demetracopoulos's "incompetence" and "untrustworthiness."

■

RETURNING TO GREECE in the fall of 1952, the newly married couple set up housekeeping in a four-room apartment on Vasillisis Sofias Avenue, near the Yugoslavian Embassy. Whatever intrusions each had felt individually from unremitting surveillance, as a couple the pressures increased exponentially. Celia's resigning did not stop the embassy and CIA from watching them, reporting on their personal and social activities, and checking up on them with their friends and neighbors. The spying was not subtle, but conducted outside their apartment, when they were shopping, visiting friends, attending to medical appointments, and simply going about the city. Celia was badgered by former embassy colleagues as to when Elias was going to apply for US citizenship as her spouse. When she said he wasn't, they speculated wildly about what mischievous agenda he had for not doing so. Simple acts of introducing people at social events or Celia's speaking Russian with a Soviet official at a Turkish Embassy reception invited intelligence reports suggesting they were making contacts with the Soviet Union.[32]

Elias's parents were warm and welcoming to Celia. The couple took some enjoyable trips together to Rome and Paris, but the incessant monitoring, whispering, innuendoes, and rumors of espionage were especially hard on Celia, who sometimes felt she was back in the pressure-cooker of Moscow. Celia suggested they move to America. Briefly, Elias seriously considered starting a new life there, perhaps as a US correspondent for a Greek newspaper or, as Celia would have preferred, changing careers entirely. As was his wont, he kept his emotions bottled up and experienced the first symptoms of what would develop several years later into a serious case of ulcers.

The couple believed that having a baby together would provide a joyful respite and could be a foundation for a strong marriage. Celia became pregnant in early 1953 and for a few months the pregnancy was the center of their attention and that of his parents. But the severe emotional strain of the outside pressures activated stress hormones, causing her to suffer a heartbreaking miscarriage.

The two of them looked at the arc of life from dramatically different perspectives. Elias wanted to explore new worlds, meet new people, and throw himself into his work. He was developing a tougher skin. Celia, no longer working, wanted to get away from the prying eyes, go home to Connecticut and her family, and return to her Roman Catholic roots, which she greatly missed.

They separated in October 1953, having lived together as husband and wife for only fifteen months. Celia wrote to Elias that she preferred to live among simple people at home to the "stupid pretentiousness of diplomatic life."[33] Elias might be able to function, even flourish, in a complex and intrusive world of secrets, deceptions, and white lies, she said, but she could no longer do so. Early the next spring, they halfheartedly discussed a reconciliation when Elias came to Washington with Defense Minister Kanellopoulos. The *Washington Post*'s "For and About Women" page featured a photo of Celia taken at a diplomatic reception with the caption: "Mrs. Demetracopoulos will visit relatives in Connecticut while her husband tours the United States installations with the [Greek] Defense Minister's party. They return to Athens this month."[34] However, Elias returned without her.

The parting was amicable. Elias stayed in Greece. Celia took charge of getting a Florida divorce, in the 1950s a preferred East Coast venue for uncomplicated marriage dissolutions.[35] Desertion was the stated grounds, with a Palm Beach newspaper gossiping incorrectly that Elias had left his wife because the pace of life in America was "too fast" for him.[36] The marriage may have ended, but their close relationship continued. Fully engaged on several fronts, Elias reasoned that he was better off single.

8.

Persona Non Grata

AMBASSADOR PEURIFOY HAD LITTLE SUCCESS dealing with the Greek Palace. From the moment of his arrival, the King and Queen made it clear that his efforts to influence Greek politics would go more smoothly if they were invited to Washington for a state visit. Giving in to such a request would have undermined Peurifoy's plans to restrict their Majesties' self-indulgent spending, and it did not happen during his tenure. Queen Frederika called State Department officials "fairies"[1] and much preferred dealing with the CIA, with whom she was developing warm relations—especially Allen Dulles, who counted her among his high-profile sexual conquests.[2]

Elias detected the friction and reported in early 1953 that the ambassador would be leaving his post.[3] The embassy issued strong denials, but, because the charge was made by Elias, decided to make its own inquiries, and discovered that his intelligence was correct: Frederika had indeed pressured the CIA, and Peurifoy's tenure would be cut short, if not as early as Elias had reported. In July 1953, Peurifoy left Greece for Guatemala, where he would play a role in the overthrow of the democratically elected Jacobo Arbenz, and later go on to Thailand, where he would die in an automobile accident. Queen Frederika and King Paul left for their desired visit to the US several months after Peurifoy's departure. CIA Station Chief Karamessines also left Athens for Rome and other important positions, though unfortunately Elias's connection with him would endure.

In Athens, Peurifoy and Karamessines had achieved their short-term missions. They had pressured the Greek parliament into restructuring the country's electoral system from proportional representation to weighted majority rule, paving the way for a clear conservative victory in the 1951 election, and insuring a decade of conservative governments.[4] They had seen to it that Greece was equipped with a domestic military and political structure tailored to serve America's security interests—as well as an intelligence agency, the KYP, created and funded by the CIA, that had a focus on internal espionage. Greece had become a loyal, if gelded, part of NATO, and an important Cold War listening post for the Balkans and the Middle East. They also had sown the seeds of later public discontent and fostered the dependent mindset of a clientist state. This was their lasting legacy.

■

MANY GREEKS BREATHED a sigh of relief at the departure of Peurifoy and Karamessines. Demetracopoulos's widely imposed persona non grata label at the American Embassy appeared to have been effectively removed. Embassy staff, however, continued to be split in their assessments of him, with some reports calling his newsgathering activities "shenanigans."[5]

He was becoming a player on a larger stage. In addition to visits to the United States, he travelled around the world twice, participated in international conferences, fact-finding missions, and NATO briefings, always pushing to get exclusive interviews. The newspapers he wrote for preferred, where possible, that others pick up his travel expenses, and the costs of his trips were often underwritten by the host governments or sponsoring organizations. The US flew him to Beirut, Amman, and several European cities to cover events and write stories about the US military.[6] He remained defiantly independent from his sponsors, believing that if he couldn't take their junkets and still write as he saw fit, well then, he didn't belong in the business.

Sometimes Demetracopoulos would be decorated by foreign governments for his past reporting or simply to curry favorable coverage. King Leopold made him an "Officer of the Order of the Crown of Belgium." Lebanon made him an officer of the Order of Cedar. And the United Arab Republic first made him an officer of the Order of the Republic and on a later trip elevated him to Commander. Even after their divorce, he would often send Celia picture postcards from his travels, noting his achievements and expressing affection.

Definitely not camera-shy, Elias would often get his picture taken with his news subjects and frequently appeared in published photos with assorted high-ranking Greek, British, and American officials. Such exposure enhanced his celebrity and refueled gossip about his connections. In confidential dispatches from Athens, Paris, Rome, Tokyo, and Washington, US intelligence agencies aggressively monitored Elias's travels, filing and sharing often uncorroborated and incorrect information. Although he made repeated trips to Europe and the Middle East, often with Greek elected politicians, he steadfastly refused all opportunities to visit the Soviet Union, either alone or in a group. This behavior puzzled the American Embassy and invited dark speculation.[7]

When his contacts with US diplomats were hindered, Elias nurtured his military connections, both Greek and American. In 1953, he met and formed an enduring friendship with General William W. "Buffalo Bill" Quinn, who came to Greece for a two-year tour as part of the Joint Military Aid Group. Quinn became a trusted source. In turn, Elias occasionally floated trial balloons on behalf of the American general. After his separation from Celia, he frequently relaxed in the Quinns' home enjoying Bette Quinn's southern cooking.

The following year he befriended Admiral Arleigh Burke when the World War II hero took over command of the Sixth Fleet in the Mediterranean, the major operational component of US Naval Forces in Europe. At a time when NATO and US military planners were privately disparaging the usefulness and future of the Greek Navy, Elias conducted a series of interviews for *Kathimerini* in which he succeeded in getting perhaps the three most important NATO commanders—Admiral and First Sea Lord Mountbatten, Chairman of the US Joint Chiefs of Staff Admiral Arthur Radford, and Chief of US Naval Operations Admiral William Carney—to go on record about the importance of Greek naval forces in a world of constant Soviet threats. Further, he wrote an essay about the strategic importance of the Greek navy, especially in the event of an atomic war, and the need for reinforcing the fleet with new vessels. Greek navy officials were so pleased with the articles that they reproduced the series as a bilingual book titled *The Royal Hellenic Navy in the Defense of Greece* and distributed copies in a successful lobbying campaign for greater NATO and US support.[8] This coverage earned Elias better access to an expanding circle of military sources.

■

WHEN DEMETRACOPOULOS SOUGHT to return to the United States in 1954, the State Department found no legitimate reason to deny him a visa but warned agencies that during his visit he might circumvent public-information officers in search of exclusive interviews. He was difficult to pigeonhole. His US intelligence dossier claimed he was aligned with both the liberal views of former prime minister George Papandreou and the conservative ones of Defense Minister Kanellopoulos. He was identified not only as a member of Kanellopoulos's delegation, covering the visit, but as the keeper of the minister's Washington schedule.

Relying on dogged persistence and his little black book of names and inside telephone numbers, Elias landed several high-profile interviews. After Army Chief of Staff General Matthew Ridgway responded to his written interview questions, Demetracopoulos extended their interview by accompanying the general and Kanellopoulos to the airport for the defense minister's departure and returned with Ridgway to the Pentagon. Army intelligence reported: "subject . . . is an aggressive newsman who specializes in contacts with top officials and takes advantage of opportunities to meet and chat with them."[9] However, he was not successful in getting an interview with Richard Nixon. Elias arranged a photo opportunity with a short exchange of pleasantries, but the Vice President declined to respond to his list of questions about Western preparedness in dealing with the Soviet Union after the Korean cease-fire.[10]

The CIA was particularly concerned that Demetracopoulos might try to interview CIA director Allen Dulles or make suggestions regarding American policy for Greece. It noted that the newsman was still "definitely persona non grata" with USIS, claiming he had created the impression in newspaper and political circles that "he is practically a covert employee of CIA." It recommended "caution and skepticism in anything concerning him." But, it added: "The fact is, however, that he is a good news man, has excellent contacts, particularly in military circles, and is associated with perhaps the best newspaper in Greece."[11]

■

CYPRUS HAS BEEN described poetically as the "beautiful sun-kissed birthplace of Aphrodite" and strategically as the "crossroads of conquerors for millennia." According to American diplomats, "No report from Cyprus is ever cheerful."[12] Its unresolved political status was a reoccurring theme of the 1950s for its residents, Greece, Britain, and Turkey. Over 80 percent Greek, less than 20 percent Turk, but only forty miles from the southwestern coast of Turkey, the island had for centuries been part of the Ottoman Empire, and its *enosis* or union with Greece part of the irredentist "Megali Idea."

Turkey, concerned about a looming Russian threat, gave Cyprus to Great Britain in 1878 to hold in trust. Later, Britain, upset with Turkish behavior during the Great War, offered Cyprus to Greece if Greece would join the fight against the Kaiser, but the Germanophile King Konstantinos passed up the opportunity. In the wake of the war, Turkey ceded its rights to Britain, and Cyprus became a crown colony. Greeks wanted to revisit the earlier offer, but overtures to unite it with the fatherland were repeatedly rebuffed by the British.

For more than three decades, one man was inextricably involved in the fate of the island. Born Michail Christodoulou Mouskos in the rural western village of Panagia in 1913 and educated in Athens and Boston, he returned in 1948, becoming Makarios III, Bishop of Cyprus. Two years later he was made archbishop and Ethnarch—the national leader of the Cypriot people. This office combined spiritual and temporal authority: Makarios was expected to be both religious ruler and the national political leader. In 1950, the charismatic Makarios organized a plebiscite on union with Greece and won the overwhelming support of Greek Cypriots. But the British, concerned about the strategic importance of the island to their Middle East oil interests, military bases, and listening posts, and not wanting to upset their Moslem subjects elsewhere, were unmoved by pleas for self-determination.

Remembering how important international backing was to Greek independence, Makarios traveled the world seeking support for the principle that Cypriots had the right to determine their own form of government. He pushed the Greek government to advocate self-determination at the United Nations. Britain, with the support of the United States, blocked the effort. Makarios, concluding that peaceful approaches alone were insufficient, quietly authorized the creation of the National Organization of Cypriot Fighters, known as EOKA, to agitate for liberation. This armed underground movement was led by a right-wing *enosis*-oriented fanatic, Colonel Georgios Grivas, who had formed the paramilitary group "*X*" during World War II and fomented White Terror during the Civil War.

EOKA detonated the first bombs on April 1, 1955. Greek Cypriots hoped such acts of sabotage would lead to a two-party negotiated resolution. Great Britain, however, used the island's pre-existing communal divisions as a means of adding Turkey to the mix. Engaged Turkish anger, it reasoned, would protect British interests. So, in violation of the 1923 Lausanne Peace Treaty, under which Turkey had waived its rights to territories including Cyprus, Britain allowed Turkey to raise once more its claims to the island. Egged on by the British, Turks rioted against Greek interests in Ankara and Istanbul, desecrating tombs, burning Greeks alive, and destroying churches. Local police stood by.

After a cease-fire, the United Kingdom, Turkey, and Greece met in London in September 1955. The conference ended in deadlock.[13] The Greeks didn't want any solution that failed to provide *enosis*. The Turks opposed any solution that did. In reaction, Makarios sought support from the emerging bloc of anti-colonial, non-aligned countries. He attended the world's first Afro-Asian Conference in Bandung, Indonesia, enlisting as allies Nehru, Nasser, Sukarno, and other Third World leaders, raising warning flags that Greece might turn away from its commitment to the Western alliance. On his return, he encouraged passive resistance and supported strikes.

The United States found itself in a difficult political and moral position. It was on record supporting, at least rhetorically, decolonization, self-determination, human rights, democracy, and majority rule. But concerning Cyprus, it repeatedly deferred to its ally, Great Britain. Geopolitical strategic considerations held sway, including fears of inter-communal violence that could encourage Soviet intervention and conflict between two NATO members.

Once the cease-fire broke down, the British blamed Makarios. On March 9, 1956, while at the Nicosia airport en route to Athens for discussions, he was seized by police and, without trial, deported to a British facility in the Seychelles.

•

READYING HIMSELF FOR a trip to the United States and Europe in 1955, Elias gathered more letters of introduction. Despite the CIA's reporting he was persona non grata with USIS, the Athens USIS Public Affairs officer, Theodore Olson, encouraged his counterpart in Rome to help arrange a 1955 interview for him with Ambassador Clare Boothe Luce, remarking that Elias "has done us many favors and I should like to do him one in return."[14] Brigadier General William W. Quinn wrote to General Maxwell D. Taylor, Army Chief of Staff to facilitate Pentagon meetings:

> Mr. Demetracopoulos has an excellent reputation and a very wide circle of acquaintances . . . In addition, he enjoys the full confidence and trust of the Royal Palace, the Greek Government, and the Greek National Defense Staff.
>
> Above all, however, he has been a very close and valuable friend of the United States and has materially assisted many times our Mission with his wise and timely counsel.[15]

STILL ONLY IN his mid-twenties, Demetracopoulos had established himself as a serious player.

Lurking in the background, however, was a fresh warning from the CIA's deputy director of plans, in charge of clandestine services, to security officials at State, the Army, the Navy, Immigration, and the FBI. The deputy director maintained that: "available information indicates [Demetracopoulos] is a megalomaniac who may have suffered impairment of his mental faculties as a result of his imprisonment by the Germans during World War II for sabotage activities."[16] And the State Department's Office of Coordination, recycling claims cooked up during Peurifoy's tour of duty in 1951, sent to its visa unit the false news that Elias "does not work for the newspaper 'Kathimerini' nor is he considered a journalist. Subject is considered an individual of unstable character."[17]

When Konstantinos Karamanlis became prime minister of Greece in 1955, he faced a full array of conflicting international and domestic pressures. He wanted economic integration with the Western European community and Cold War military protection but felt obliged to embrace an electorally popular *enosis* nationalism that pitted him against the interests of Britain, Turkey, the United States, and other NATO members who voted against Greece on Cyprus debates at the United Nations. Ideologically committed to the West, and fearing a Slav Communist—especially Bulgarian—attack from the north, he was sensitive to growing anti-Americanism and neutralist spirit at home. Indeed, Greek public opinion polling in 1956 and 1957 demonstrated strong support for pulling out of NATO, with 49.67 percent preferring that Greece adopt a policy outside the two major blocs.[18] Karamanlis decided to pursue an "autonomous foreign policy."[19]

In October 1956, after Elias returned from a successful trip to the US, his life at *Kathimerini* became harder. Aimilios Chourmouzios, his beloved editor, was seriously injured in a near-fatal automobile accident. Facing a long recovery, Chourmouzios took an extended medical leave from the newspaper. Without Chourmouzios, Elias felt the spirit of the paper was gone and his role threatened. Before his death in 1951, publisher George Vlachos had given control of the paper to his daughter Eleni. Although Elias thought he had a good relationship with her, he worried that she wanted to "take the paper in less-serious directions" in the interest of generating new revenues from a broader audience.

All newspapers in Greece had political orientations and tended to back one party or another. They also benefitted financially when their party was in power.

Kathimerini was clearly identified as a conservative paper, but under Chourmouzios it had earned a reputation as sober, fair-minded, and not unduly partisan. In
recent years Chourmouzios had written forceful editorials decrying "intellectual McCarthyism" and the behavior of the "Americans over here." Elias agreed
with these sentiments, but disagreed with his mentor when, after Greece's perceived "betrayal" by Britain and the US in the UN vote on Cyprus, Chourmouzios shouted "Shame!" in a page-one column, declaring that Greece should
consider leaving NATO and "fight alone."[20] At the time, Elias believed emotional
Greek nationalism should not undermine the importance of American and
NATO military protection.

The first sign that Elias's career at *Kathimerini* might be endangered came
when Eleni Vlachou installed Konstantinos Zafeiropoulos, then a political correspondent like Elias, as Chourmouzios's temporary replacement. Elias claimed
he wasn't jealous, that he did not want the position, but regarded Zafeiropoulos
as an unworthy placeholder and a political sycophant, elevated at the recommendation of recently elected Prime Minister Konstantinos Karamanlis.

Once Chourmouzios returned, some of the old spark also came back and
Elias found himself again assigned to some prominent "scoops," particularly
about Cyprus. Nevertheless, Elias sensed that the paper was increasingly being
run by the Vlachou-Zafeiropoulos alliance, which was itself responding to the
agenda of Karamanlis and his ERE Party. Elias challenged the paper's direction,
claiming that in overreacting to the Cyprus crisis *Kathimerini* was wronghead-
edly moving toward a risky neutralist stance.[21]

■

ELIAS'S RELATIONSHIP WITH his other major news outlet and its publisher grew
in importance during the 1950s. Founded in 1911, *Makedonia* was the oldest
paper in northern Greece, and publisher Ioannis Vellidis came from one of the
wealthiest and most powerful families in Thessaloniki. An avowed Venizelist,
Vellidis had been twice exiled as well as imprisoned during the Metaxas dictatorship. During the German occupation, he was forced to cease publishing
and moved to Athens; he didn't return until 1945. Politically, he and his paper
supported center-left parties and politicians, George Papandreou in particular. Vellidis was so impressed with young Demetracopoulos's assertive personality and breadth of contacts in the rapidly expanding and pivotal American
community that he added a bonus to his reporter's modest paycheck: a com-

mitment, unusual for a Greek publisher, to pay Elias's newsgathering expenses promptly. He not only kept to this commitment, but over time it grew into a generous expense account.

From his *Makedonia* connections Elias learned details of the case of journalist Gregoris Staktopoulos, who, after a forced confession and show trial, had been sentenced to death for his role in the 1948 assassination of CBS reporter George Polk.[22] When Gregoris Staktopoulos was finally released from jail in 1960, after twelve years, and was looking for a job, Elias urged that *Makedonia* hire him. Staktopoulos's story was a painful reminder of how easily an innocent reporter could have his life destroyed in a society in which the civil rights of journalists were not protected. It was eye-opening to learn how little truth, logic, and fairness mattered to both the Greek and American governments in their quest for so-called justice. But, for Elias, the most sobering lesson was discovering how celebrated leaders of his chosen profession, exemplars of the so-called free press, allowed themselves to be used in a cover-up of the murder of one colleague and the scapegoating and framing of another.[23]

9.

Elias and Ethnarch Makarios

I N THE MID-1950S, ELIAS MAY have remained a *bête noire* to several CIA and State Department officials, but he was held in high regard by both American and Greek military officers. The head of the Plans and Intelligence Division of the Greek National Defense General Staff, Theodosis Papathanassiadis, wrote that Elias had the "complete respect and confidence" of the defense minister and defense staff and, as a military correspondent, had been granted "secret" security clearance.[1] That access helped him interview American and European military and political leaders on changing foreign policies in a nuclear age.

At this time, Elias learned about the work of a Harvard professor and private advisor to Nelson Rockefeller named Henry Kissinger, who reportedly opposed Eisenhower's policy of massive retaliation as the deterrent to Soviet aggression in favor of a combination of conventional arms and tactical nuclear weapons. Anticipating a 1956 Kissinger visit to Athens, CIA station chief John Richardson suggested to Elias that the journalist take the future diplomat to lunch to exchange views.[2] Separately, General Konstantinos Dovas, made the same request, adding presciently, "He's not important now, but he will be. Get to know him."

Arrangements were made for Elias to take Kissinger to the Grande Bretagne hotel, but things didn't turn out as planned. Unexpectedly, Kissinger brought with him his first wife, Ann, and their two young children, Elizabeth and David. "It was not a setting conducive to a serious discussion," recalled Elias.

Although Demetracopoulos's *Kathimerini* beat had increasingly become more military, he was still one of its top diplomatic correspondents. His articles were carefully monitored by both the State Department and the CIA and occasionally even earned plaudits. In June 1956, the American chargé d'affaires in Athens wrote to the American ambassador in London that Demetracopoulos "is extremely well versed on the internal and external aspects of Greek life and has ready access to many of the leading personalities here. Although sharing, I am sure, the general Greek sentiments about the Cyprus question, he has always shown with me a very well-balanced attitude toward that difficult question."[3] That November, Demetracopoulos broke the story of the Greek government's decision to extend its territorial waters to twelve miles if the reported Turkish intention to extend its territorial limit to twelve miles were carried out. Warning that such a decision would turn the Aegean into a "closed sea" with serious international consequences, he added the observation that only a decisive American intervention in Ankara could avert this problem. In its review, the American Embassy widely circulated his article, describing Elias as *Kathimerini*'s "diplomatic correspondent," without any qualifications or snide remarks.[4]

■

IF THE BRITISH thought putting Makarios under house arrest in the Seychelles would provide an opening for a more moderate Cypriot alternative, they were wrong. Even Eisenhower asked that the archbishop be freed. Moreover, Britain's October 1956 invasion of Egypt during the Suez Canal nationalization crisis encouraged an anti-British backlash at the United Nations. After about a year, London released Makarios in exchange for "an ambiguous statement deploring violence" and the prelate's agreement not to return to Cyprus.[5]

Although many in Greece were prepared to give Makarios a hero's welcome, political leaders there debated privately how they should respond. After delicate discussions with Great Britain and the United States, both the King and Prime Minister Karamanlis—fearful of hurting relations with Turkey—decided not to send a welcoming party for his release or to greet him in public ceremonies in Athens. Instead, politically influential shipping magnate Aristotle Onassis redirected one of his freighters to pick up the Ethnarch and bring him to Nairobi. Hearing this news, *Kathimerini* sent Demetracopoulos to meet and interview the Cypriot leader. This plum assignment pleased Elias enormously and made some of his colleagues quite jealous.[6] Elias left on an arduous journey, taking planes from Athens to Paris to Casablanca to Nairobi to Madagascar and then catching a boat to meet the *Olympic Thunder* carrying the archbishop and his entourage from the Seychelles.[7]

Kathimerini announced Elias's historic role on the front page of the paper's April 5, 1957 special edition that later carried the first exclusive interview, wired from Madagascar, along with a photo of the two men sitting side by side aboard the ship. For days, Chourmouzios ran front-page stories with interviews and descriptions of the public outpouring in Kenya, a country struggling for its own independence from Britain and quite responsive to Makarios's statements about freedom and justice.[8]

Elias had never met Makarios before and found him to be a difficult interview. The prelate sometimes sounded more like an evasive Delphic oracle than a newsmaker, with such replies as "You should never mix people with politics." The archbishop acknowledged the role of the United Nations in his release and said that the Cypriots desired *enosis*. He talked about his interest in going to London to meet with the British Labour Party and opinion-makers, and that he didn't want to negotiate until he was permitted to return to Cyprus.[9]

Makarios asked Elias for his insights about how American attitudes might influence British behavior. It was clear to Elias that Makarios had been out of touch with international news and opinion during his incarceration. The Ethnarch tended to downplay, if not dismiss, the "Turkish factor." And when bishops accompanying the archbishop made some incendiary remarks, Elias ignored them, restraining his newsman's impulse to wire that story for publication.[10] As a CIA report noted, Elias believed that Makarios could bring down the Greek government "almost overnight," so it was vital that he be careful in his reporting.[11]

Amidst the international press scrum in Nairobi, Makarios invited Elias to accompany him on a visit to the zoo. They went together, obliging British photographers who asked them to pose for a picture. A day later, Elias received a call from an outraged Greek ambassador in London berating him for allowing the two men to be placed in a photo under a sign warning: "Danger, Wild Animals." Only years later did the Greek newsman think the image funny.

Demetracopoulos continued to file stories, but for the rest of the trip he largely stood back from Makarios and the crowds. He sent Celia a warm, newsy postcard, unaware that American intelligence operators had been monitoring his trip and adding more fabrications to his dossier—including rumors that Elias had been flashing a large roll of US currency around the streets of Nairobi, allegedly a payment from the Americans, and showing off "his American passport" to reporters with the offer of special discounts for those who wanted their own.[12] These baseless lies, he later scoffed, were designed to hamper his ability to gather news.

·

Elias returned to the Greek capital on April 16, 1957, taking a different plane than the archbishop's. He arrived in time to watch Makarios's triumphant motorcade from the airport into the city.[13] But he was distracted by some devastating news. His mother was in the hospital and had been there since just after he'd left. She had advanced cancer and only a short time to live. There was no person in the world he loved more. He anxiously discussed finding new doctors and moving her to another hospital where care might be better. It was too late for surgery. He reached out to Celia, asking her to write to his mother as soon as possible, without mentioning the gravity of the diagnosis.[14] On May 14, 1957, he telegrammed his ex-wife: "Mother passed away today. Many thanks for letter. God bless you." His mother was dead at 59, less than a month after his return. She had said nothing about her health before he left for Nairobi, and nor had his father. Elias berated himself for not knowing of her condition sooner, for going on the Makarios trip instead of spending every possible remaining day with her.

In the following weeks, Makarios asked Elias for private briefings during which he asked the reporter to tell the American ambassador, George Allen, with whom Elias had a good relationship, that the archbishop was worried about threats on his life and wanted Americans at the highest levels to know that they should not try to scare Greeks into making concessions on Cyprus. Allen was noncommittal and urged that Makarios go to London to negotiate.[15]

In the Greek Orthodox religion, the most important memorial service is *ta saranta,* marking the ascent of the soul into heaven and held on the Saturday or Sunday closest to the fortieth day after the death. Arrangements were made with the priest at the venerable Proto Nekrotafeio, the First Cemetery in Athens, for a mid-June memorial. When the day arrived, the Bokolas and Demetracopoulos families and their friends walked along a park-like pathway of monuments shaded by pine, cypress, and olive trees. They lit candles as they entered the chapel, moving toward the large photograph of Panagiota on an easel at the front. To the surprise of all, especially Elias, the unannounced officiant was Archbishop Makarios. That the archbishop had cleared his calendar to perform this role touched Elias greatly, and would come to color his reportorial objectivity—though not, he believed, the fairness of his coverage of Makarios.

■

ELIAS'S SCOOPS AROUSED the envy of many colleagues in competing newspapers, who passed around scurrilous rumors, even to the point of telling outright lies to CIA investigators. Demetracopoulos, in turn, treated most of them with undiluted disdain. In September 1957, after months of individual complaints from a variety of publications, representatives of *Acropolis, Naftemboriki, To Vima*, and *Ta Nea* together protested to the embassy's public-affairs and press officers what they described as a pattern of USIS favoring *Kathimerini* on breaking news. According to their list of grievances, (1) the embassy and USIS were unethically discriminating; (2) their professional status was being impaired because of *Kathimerini*'s many scoops; (3) they had strictly followed the rules of channeling their requests through the press office, but Demetracopoulos did not; (4) they published many pro-American articles, while *Kathimerini* had been hard-hitting; and (5) Elias received invitations to embassy functions, and they didn't.

Press officer Robert Lawrence pointed out that none of Elias's stories had come from official American sources and told the newspapers that the embassy tried to be impartial to all, but that there were "times when an especially enterprising reporter like Demetrakopoulos [sic] will, by digging deeper, come up with exclusive stories."[16] In the case of a coveted exclusive interview with a Sixth Fleet admiral, the press officer said, the interview had been arranged without embassy knowledge, causing Lawrence some embarrassment when, while taking the assembled press corps aboard the *Salem* for the regular press conference, he "met Demetrakopoulos [sic] on the deck returning from [his] exclusive interview."[17]

Elias tried to work through his grief by throwing himself into his work. He spent time with his father, and for much of that year was uninterested in socializing. The exception was Persa Metaxas [no relation to the dictator], a statuesque brunette reminiscent of movie star Ava Gardner, whom he met aboard a visiting Sixth Fleet American warship later that year. Elias had come for interviews; Persa was there to visit some of the same officials, family friends she had come to know in London during the civil war. Her great-grandmother was English, and Persa had grown up bilingual.[18]

Persa's stepfather had been active in the resistance, hiding New Zealand and Australian soldiers in their home in Athens, then helping them escape. He did the same for Jews targeted by the Nazis. He became an important contact for the British in Cairo and London, evading German attempts to arrest him, and arriving safely in the Middle East at precisely the same time the Nazis were ransacking the family house in Athens. Before leaving, he had arranged false papers for his seventeen-year-old stepdaughter to connect with royalist insurgent groups in the mountains, where she served as an interpreter between allied officials and *antartes*. On one of her trips a British colonel, fearful for her safety, helped her flee to London, where she reunited with her family. She spent the civil-war years there, became a nurse, and later continued her nursing studies in the United States.

Elias wanted to date her, but was disappointed to learn she was married, had a young son, and was not one to play around. Three years older than he, Persa Metaxas would become his dearest and longest-standing friend.

■

DURING THE SPRING and summer of 1957, Cyprus policy disagreements caused major problems for Prime Minister Karamanlis's fractious governing majority in Parliament. That fall, the Russian launch of Sputnik made things even worse for his conservative government. The October space shot triggered widespread anxiety among Americans and Europeans that Soviet missile technology now credibly threatened both Europe and the American mainland with nuclear annihilation. Some grassroots groups, in Greece and elsewhere, advocated nuclear disarmament or neutralist political positions. But in major NATO capitals, discussions turned in earnest to strategic responses, including plans for placing missiles in countries well-positioned to counter Russian nuclear capabilities.

The Russians, eager to weaken Greek ties to NATO, amplified rumors that NATO was planning on placing nuclear missiles in Greek Macedonia, Prime Minister Karamanlis's home region. To head off political damage from this issue and allay public concerns regarding intermediate-range Jupiter and Thor missiles with nuclear warheads on Greek soil, the Karamanlis government denied the reports.

Demetracopoulos, however, had been following the issue for months and had a different story to tell. Contrary to Karamanlis's denials, Italy, Britain, Turkey, and Greece were indeed all under serious consideration as bases from which to point warheads toward the Soviet Union.[19] Among the sources from which Elias had learned this was General Konstantinos Dovas, the chief of the Hellenic National Defense General Staff, upon his return from NATO's November meetings in Malta, where alliance members showed a preference toward Greece as a nuclear missile facility. Dovas added that he saw no point in resisting the NATO plans, which would be formally made during the alliance's December summit.[20]

Elias prepared what he thought was a restrained, yet blockbuster, story for the front page of *Kathimerini*'s widely read Sunday paper. Then things got ugly. His two-column article was placed on the back-news page of the Saturday edition, and without a byline. As the paper's chief political reporter, he was insulted. He submitted the same article to *Makedonia*, which printed it the same day on its front page. Headlined "Training Center for Missiles to be Installed in Southern Crete?" the November 23 story described NATO's plans for a guided-missile testing site on Greek soil, to be reviewed by the Greek government with the goal of installing "special" nuclear weapons and training Greek, Italian, and Turkish personnel how to fire them.

Karamanlis was furious about this disclosure. Public opposition to nuclear weapons on Greek soil was widespread, and an election was coming up.[21] He demanded that Eleni Vlachou fire Demetracopoulos. Vlachou asked Elias for his sources. Elias refused. The two had words. Demetracopoulos agreed to take a month off from the paper and Vlachou asked another political reporter to write an article that, using other sources, effectively criticized the points Elias had made. Demetracopoulos was embarrassed to have been suspended from his beat, but not quite ready to move on. He told others that the paper was wavering between pro-West and anti-West stands and was being pressured politically to become neutralist on the nuclear-missiles issue. He claimed he had been targeted because he was too pro-American, and he reportedly said to an American official that he was preparing a resignation letter that would say, in effect, that "even if Sputniks and Bulgarian letters had frightened *Kathimerini* into a neutral stance, they hadn't frightened him."[22]

When his month-long suspension ended, he still hadn't decided what he would do. Elias felt he could easily go to work for any of the three leading liberal newspapers, *Ethnos*, *To Vima*, or *Eleftheria*, but he was reluctant to do so because, at least to start with, he wouldn't have as much say over their editorial policies as he had until recently as *Kathimerini*'s chief political reporter. But he leaned toward resignation.

The gossip mill was rife with contradictory reasons for why Elias was not writing. He was out because he was too close to "Communist elements," or had double-crossed his KYP paymaster.[23] The American Embassy passed these canards on to the CIA and other intelligence services without seeking corroboration.

George Anastasopoulos, who shared a similar beat at *Kathimerini*, recalled that even before the blow-up Elias's stories had been causing "quite a stir," creating "political problems" for "cautious" editors. Increasingly, he said, important stories that Elias solidly reported never got published.[24]

Elias decided he had lost too much face at the paper to stay, and resigned in early 1958. Eleni Vlachou never said publicly that he had been fired, and privately only that his employment had ended because he was "such a lone wolf that he could not get along with other people in the office."[25] According to a confidential State Department memorandum, Vlachou promised the Americans that "if you people are not satisfied with [Elias's replacement], let me know and I'll put someone else on the job."[26]

Elias's plan was to build a journalistic career weaving together his established contributor roles with *Makedonia* and the North American News Association (NANA) with new representation at other publications. He discussed augmenting his role with *Makedonia* to include that of full-time Athens correspondent, but publisher Ioannis Vellidis said such a decision should wait until liberals controlled the government. He had discussions with several newspapers, but they went nowhere. Demetracopoulos heard back that he was too independent, not a team player, and too controversial. He was also told that Karamanlis's allies, as well as sources at the CIA and the American Embassy, had discouraged papers from hiring him. Then Elias received an offer to supplement his income and audience by creating a newspaper of his own.

George Skouras published a French-language paper in Athens that was failing. He thought he'd do better with an English-language daily that could take advantage of the growing American community. One major hurdle: Skouras himself didn't speak English and had difficulty reading it. He approached Elias with an offer that he become a partner and that together they would hire a bilingual staff. Skouras would be first in both ownership and management. Elias agreed and, even though the start-up struggled to attract advertising, within a year papers like the *Times* of London were running news items crediting the *Athens Daily Post* as its source.[27] In addition to the *Athens Daily Post*, Elias still had his relationship with *Makedonia*. That summer, he started negotiating arrangements to become a full-time diplomatic and political correspondent for *Ethnos*, a non-Communist, center-left newspaper, which he regarded as a "serious" publication, his highest praise. Already working well with Vellidis and his Venizelist *Makedonia* and irked by Karamanlis and some of his conservative zealots, Elias, who at the time regarded himself as a political centrist, felt no discomfort in moving to respectable papers on the moderate left.

■

AS EXPECTED, THE Greek government's alleged acceptance of US missiles and its failures regarding Cyprus were the leading issues in the May 1958 election. The revised, "reinforced" proportional representation system, which disfavored smaller parties, assured Karamanlis's conservative National Radical Union Party (ERE) a comfortable majority of seats with 41.2 percent of the vote. However, voter concerns and the fragmentation of centrist and liberal parties enabled a unified Communist-dominated EDA, which ran a successful anti-NATO, anti-Western campaign, to come in second with nearly a quarter of the vote. The results sent chills through the political establishment in Greece and its benefactors in Washington.[28] By the end of the year, the CIA had established a covert operation to discredit EDA and its candidates in future elections.

At the American Embassy's annual Fourth of July reception in 1958, Demetracopoulos's independent reporting brought serious consequences. It was a warm evening and the throng spilled out onto the lawn, with cool drinks, tasty food, and geniality the order of the day. Elias, dressed in a light-colored silk-and-linen suit, was chatting with a group of diplomats and guests when the prime minister arrived. The usually austere and aloof Karamanlis started with social pleasantries, but when he saw Demetracopoulos he moved quickly toward his nemesis.

The prime minister, who prided himself on his physical fitness and strength, grabbed Elias by the lapels, ripping his suit, and, with his face inches away, snarled in Greek: "Don't mess with me! Don't mess with my foreign policy." Startled, Elias pushed away his country's highest-ranking political leader. Journalist Mario Modiano remembered that Karamanlis then raised his fist in escalation.[29]

According to another eyewitness account printed in the conservative newspaper *Estia*, a group of officials managed to get between the two men, stopping further hostilities. Elias reportedly "maintained his calmness and with a straight face said to Karamanlis that his sources were trustworthy."[30] A CIA report on the confrontation said: "Ilias [*sic*] was given unshirted hell by Karamanlis at the ambassador's party for a recent article in which [Elias] quoted NATO Commander Norstad expressing outrage at being uninformed about important matters in Greece: 'How can they expect me to know what's going on behind the Iron Curtain when such things occur right under my nose.' At the party Ambassador Riddleberger confirmed . . . the fact that the Norstad quote was accurate."[31] *Estia* said that almost everybody was astonished at Karamanlis's behavior. The US Embassy was completely silent on this incident in all its contemporaneous transmissions to Washington.

■

DESPITE GREEK QUEASINESS about the stationing of nuclear missiles, American influence was still at its height. Greeks tended to assume that Americans were the most important people to know and that nothing happened without them. Elias cultivated his image of being close to Americans as a strategy for newsgathering. He permitted wild rumors to spread, even to the point of being characterized as America's "boy" whose articles and statements should be viewed as an accurate portrayal of American plans and policies.[32]

In exasperation, the CIA prepared a memorandum called "Perpetuation of the Dimitrakopoulos [sic] Myth by the American Element." The heavily redacted document noted that, Elias "is still very much in evidence at their official functions, witness the ambassador's Fourth of July party. Wherever prominent Americans congregate, there is Ilias [sic] . . . Thus the myth of Dimitrakopoulos and his fantastic American connections."[33]

The CIA criticism, presumably prepared by its station chief John Richardson, was sent to the ambassador, who shared it with his staff. In response, press officer Robert Lawrence sent a memorandum to the ambassador with an opposite viewpoint. Enclosing a series of clippings on a Demetracopoulos front page article concerning US military aid to Greece, Lawrence compared the positive coverage "on this one story [as probably amounting] to a normal six months of output of USIS on this sheltered subject," and pointed "out the many services he has rendered us in the past":

These have ranged all the way from being the trusted [US and Makarios] go-between . . . to spearheading the local drive for Greek donations when our library was destroyed. He has suggested ideas which have resulted in USIS projects, like the "open skies" photography of the Acropolis which helped our local publicity on Eisenhower's disarmament program. He has been a confidant of embassy officials and his letters of credence from Americans in high office are very impressive.

Although at times his persistence has been somewhat time consuming, I have admired his way of digging hard for news which is in the best traditions of American newspaper reporting. I have never known him to violate a confidence "off the record," either directly or through leaking to colleagues . . . I have known only one instance when they were "uncomfortable." . . . This is the first time I have written a tribute about one of our press contacts, but Mr. Demetracopoulos has been outstanding and I thought it would be helpful to pass this information along.[34]

THE CIA'S OFFICE in Athens responded by asking the Agency's director, Allen Dulles, to prepare a full "trace" of Elias Demetracopoulos, starting from "his birth 1 Dec 1918"—a decade before he was actually born.[35]

10.

"I Don't Sit at My Desk"

IF THE FALLOUT FROM THE May election results loomed as Greece's biggest domestic political issue of 1958, continued turmoil concerning Cyprus was the most important international concern. To break the Greek-UK diplomatic impasse, Britain proposed to internationalize the island, providing a tripartite arrangement that gave Turkey, which had earlier ceded all its claims, an equal voice in decisions. In September, Makarios, furious with this drastic British move, concluded that independence for Cyprus was preferable to union with Greece. With the help of the United Nations, he believed, both Greece and Turkey could be sidelined. This incensed Greek generals who were unalterably committed to *enosis*. General Grivas, furious with what he characterized as incompetent governments in Athens and Nicosia, stepped up violence on the island.

On the evening of October 21, 1958, Elias attended an Athens reception given by the Italian counselor for a delegation of visiting Yugoslav generals. During the event, Veselin Martinovic, the Yugoslav counselor, informed Elias that some Greek generals had told him that the only solution for the Cyprus problem was a military dictatorship in Greece that would also maintain its membership in NATO. Elias learned that the possible leaders of the plan included the Greek ambassador to Yugoslavia (retired General Thrasyvoulos Tsakalotos), the minister of public works (retired General Solon Gkikas), and the present head of the Athens military command (Major General Ioannis

Pipilis). Gkikas and Pipilis, longtime plotters, were active in IDEA (The Sacred Band of Greek Officers).

Coup speculation in Greece was almost as common as the sound of clicking *komboloi* (worry beads). Elias didn't follow every alleged plot, but IDEA and its highly conspiratorial, deeply conservative, nationalist, royalist, and virulently anti-Communist right-wing army officers, who deemed themselves to be the true guardians of the Greek state, were different. IDEA was an expanded version of a secret society formed in 1944 by Greek officers serving in the Middle East. Apparently co-opted by the Papagos government and inactive under Karamanlis, it surfaced in the wake of the May 1958 elections during which EDA, the Communist-front party, made its shockingly strong showing.

Demetracopoulos was sufficiently concerned to have a conversation the next day with the US Army military attaché, Colonel Joseph McChristian. Elias thought it important that the Americans, who were indirectly engaged in the Cyprus negotiations, be aware of the "keen pessimism and dissatisfaction" within the Greek government over Cyprus that could encourage sympathy for a military dictatorship.[1] However critical he was of Karamanlis, Elias was infinitely more troubled by the specter of a military dictatorship. A passionate democrat since his days studying Periclean Greece, Demetracopoulos believed that anti-democratic activities should be monitored and scotched before they festered or went underground. Colonel McChristian had a long career in military intelligence, and he passed along Elias's information confidentially to the political section of the US Embassy. They shared it with the Athens CIA station, which dismissed it as valueless.[2]

■

FROM PARIS TO Zurich and London, negotiations to resolve the situation in Cyprus proceeded during 1958 and 1959, with outside pressure from Britain and the United States. In February 1959, settlement talks finally led to an agreement to form an independent republic. The complex constitution called for a Greek Cypriot president and a Turkish Cypriot vice president, and allowed Turkish Cypriots disproportionately powerful representation given their minority status. A Treaty of Guarantee prohibited either *enosis* or *taksim* (partition) and, if common action proved ineffective, permitted each of the three Guaranteeing Powers (Greece, Turkey, and the UK) to take unilateral action to reestablish the state of affairs. Elias thought the terms were inherently unworkable and would inevitably lead to more conflict.

Makarios returned to Cyprus on March 1 to a hero's welcome and prepared for elections. Elias remained troubled. General Grivas had come out of the shadows to be toasted in Athens. Elias disagreed with those who characterized IDEA as a quiescent relic and was especially concerned that IDEA had expanded its outreach to junior officers with their own clandestine cadre, the National Union of Young Greek Officers (EENA).

He increased his tracking of IDEA adherents, such as the Greek ambassador to Yugoslavia, obtaining a Greek Third Army Corps secret memorandum that discussed an IDEA plot to overthrow the Karamanlis government and replace it with one that was "more efficient and less corrupt" and would reduce the King to "a puppet."

Elias viewed the plot as more than just talk. Rather than writing about it, he quietly showed his copy of the memo to the American political-affairs counselor. Embassy personnel were often the last to know about intelligence matters, but Elias felt they were more committed to democratic norms than the local CIA staff—especially the Greek-Americans, who were very protective of KYP leaders and their confederates. The embassy filed away Demetracopoulos's tip without action. The CIA and KYP, hearing about Elias's report, disregarded it. Instead, they used Elias's tip as evidence that he was secretly working for the Yugoslavs.[3]

■

DEMETRACOPOULOS WAS ALSO a debonair man about town. Nearly thirty, impeccably dressed in conservative British attire, wearing a splash of cologne, his now-thinning well-trimmed black hair parted and combed back, he developed a personal brand of sophisticated politesse, charming others by paying attention to their opinions. He was simultaneously a proud egotist and an inveterate name-dropper, giving the impression that he had contacts everywhere in the world—though he carefully cultivated an air of mystery by withholding specifics. Wherever people went—from cocktail parties to diplomatic receptions to national days and commemorative events, to airport arrivals and departures involving notables, there was Elias Demetracopoulos, often the center of attention.

To admirers he was a highly intelligent, well-informed man of influence, generous in doing favors, and a loyal friend. To critics he was an unctuous and opportunistic courtier who would play his role at whatever court presented itself. To still others, especially some women, his suave mannerisms were a sign of cultured refinement. Elias had a reputation for being a ladies' man whose little black book contained telephone numbers of starlets, cabaret singers, airline stewardesses, and daughters of shipping magnates.

In February 1958, not long after Ambassador James Riddleberger assumed his post, Elias invited to dinner his beautiful daughter Antonia, in Athens on an after-college holiday. Before she went out, Toni recalled, her father warned her that Demetracopoulos was a clever journalist who would pump her for information. The two went to a taverna and she sat there, extra-careful not to blab about anything important.

"I needn't have worried," she remembered. "Elias spent the whole evening telling me about his fascinating life, starting from being a teenage resistance fighter."[4] At one point during the meal, he offered to open his shirt to show his scars from the whippings and raised his pant leg to show the bullet hole. Toni, a sophisticated observer who married Monteagle Stearns (later a highly regarded ambassador to Greece), thought Elias's approach was to worm his way into the listener's confidence with spellbinding personal stories, then ferret out whatever intelligence he could use, though perhaps he did that more with women than men. Asked about the episode decades later, Elias acknowledged with a smile that Toni's recollection was correct. He remembered her as radiant and recalled being more interested in impressing than interrogating her.

■

ELIAS WAS SO ardent in his anti-Communism that he reportedly once told an American official that, given a choice of living under Communism or fascism, he'd choose fascism, because fascists "only took people's freedom but left their souls alone, whereas Communism took freedom and souls too."[5] This attitude never translated into an actual sympathy for fascism. He carried with him the physical and emotional scars of his years in the resistance and fervidly denounced the behavior of Greeks who used their anti-Communism as an excuse for having collaborated with the Nazis.

Elias understood the American rationale for supporting the reintegration of wartime collaborationists into the police agencies to help battle the Communist insurgency and the international politics behind Karamanlis's 1959 decision to put an end to Greek trials of Germans involved in war crimes in Greece by transferring to the West German government any responsibility for such prosecutions.[6] But it offended his sense of justice. He told Greeks and Americans, including CIA officials, that the Nazi utilization program shaped by CIA director Allen Dulles and Frank Wisner, Chief of CIA Clandestine Operations, that involved falsifying war records to cover up loathsome pasts could have serious unintended consequences.[7] One person whose collaboration with the Germans during World War II disturbed Demetracopoulos was George Papadopoulos, a right-wing field officer who had helped form the Nazi-armed Greek Security Battalions that fought against the Communist-led resistance. Papadopoulos, a longtime IDEA leader, worked assiduously to whitewash members' collaborationist activities.

■

OVER THE NEARLY ten years that Elias Demetracopoulos had been a journalist, embassy officials, CIA agents, Greek ministers, politicians, and other journalists frequently discussed what made him run. He seemed to have no identifiable partisan fervor and was difficult to pigeonhole. Some press colleagues dismissed him for having no goal larger than self-promotion but were astonished that he was so successful in getting stories that others didn't. Intelligence services repeatedly alleged that he must be in the pay of some foreign power, though they could never confirm which one.

Demetracopoulos seemed to have well-placed sources everywhere. They shared sensitive information with him because they knew their identities would be protected. He tried to confirm his scoops with second- and third-source corroboration but was not reticent about using unnamed single sources if the story was juicy and he thought his informant trustworthy. Elias believed in his own instinct to quickly size up a person's truthfulness, a skill honed during his teenage years in the resistance.

Elias made clear that in addition to knowing "a great many people," he was always out making contacts, asking questions, "always working hard . . . I don't sit at my desk."[8] He said he didn't measure himself against other reporters but delighted in scooping them. His own standards prized unrelenting persistence. His happiness came from making the extra phone calls that yielded disparate nuggets of information that he could connect, from ferreting out classified documents to rushing to the airport in the wee hours of the morning to meet people departing for flights who would give him the material for exclusive stories.

Well-informed, he could usually calculate what an official might do in a given situation. He would go to that person directly or a reliable source nearby and get confirmation or denial of his hunches. Either response could make a "scoop."[9]

On occasion, Demetracopoulos would grudgingly concede his mistakes, but overall, he was proud of the quality of the information he gathered and re-ported. He once took exception when the wife of a diplomat complimented him on his writing style. "What about the content of the story, that's much more im-portant than style," he asserted.[10] Elias was a terrible typist, but he always turned in clean copy to both his English-language and Greek-language publications. This led to a churlish rumor that in lieu of writing his own material he was sub-mitting articles provided by mysterious sources with nefarious agendas.

One widely circulated tale was that he had once been forced by *Kathimerini* to sit down and type a story in front of suspicious editors and that what he pro-duced wasn't as polished as the story he'd turned in previously. This so-called test never happened, snorted Elias. "It was a complete fabrication." The truth was, he never wanted to take the time to learn how to type, and therefore paid a one-woman secretarial service to type his longhand drafts. Eleni Vlachou her-self repeatedly asserted that the anecdote was false, and no witness ever publicly confirmed it. This didn't stop US agencies from repeating the rumor as fact for more than two decades in their burgeoning classified summary profiles on Elias.

■

IN 1959, AFTER not having been in the United States for close to five years, Elias decided it was time for another visit. By then, building a case against Demetra-copoulos strong enough to deny him entry had become a cottage industry for more than a few federal agencies. The US Embassy began the year with a "Secret" request to reinvestigate why Elias had never applied for a visa in 1957 after hav-ing been put on an approved Exchange Visitor program list: it seems that even when he *didn't* do something, Demetracopoulos attracted attention.[11] In 1959, he had no trouble securing a visa, but noticed that there were unusual delays in scheduling many of his interviews. In the end, however, he managed to meet with most of his targets.

During his stay in Washington, he became a regular at the Old New Orle-ans, a popular restaurant and jazz club run by Nick Gaston, a gregarious Greek-American. There he met a tall, attractive blonde with a beehive hairstyle and a hearty laugh who seemed to know everybody. Self-confidant, smartly dressed, and big-boned, she reminded him of high-society screen actress Con-stance Bennett. Her name was Louise Gore, and she was the manager of the Fair-fax on Embassy Row, the residence hotel that her family owned.

Louise's father was Colonel H. Grady Gore, from the Republican side of that illustrious Tennessee family. Born in Leesburg, Virginia, in 1925, she grew up at the family's thirty-three-room Marwood chateau in Maryland, started college at Bennington, and finished at George Washington University, majoring in international relations. She had a love of fashion and was about to begin work at *Vogue* in New York in 1950 when her father asked her to drive him to a candidate event in Baltimore. There she caught the political bug. Before long she became the national coordinator of Ladies Clubs for Ike, hosting fundraisers for state and national Republican candidates and giving speeches. In 1959, she planned to be active supporting Richard Nixon's 1960 presidential campaign.

Louise and Elias had instant chemistry, and over his weeks in Washington they formed a romantic relationship. She introduced him to her family and brought him to Marwood. They discussed her visiting Athens soon. She insisted that on his return he stay at the Fairfax. After he left, they exchanged transatlantic phone calls and she wrote him love letters, telling him how much she and her family missed him. Louise said she yearned to hear him call her "sweet pie."[12] All this passion cooled abruptly when someone told her that Elias not only played around but was still married. Louise had once had a loving relationship with a married man that ended badly. Long distance, Elias explained the "still married" part was not true, and she offered to bribe him with chocolate milkshakes to hear the full story.[13] She accepted his explanation and welcomed him back warmly, but their relationship had lost its lust.

Asked decades later why he and Louise never got married, Elias explained simply that "she was Maryland aristocracy." Those closer to Louise speculate that the two might have been best buddies and confidants but never a successfully married couple. Where Elias's lifestyle was restrained and abstemious, Louise, who never married, cultivated a robust informality and enjoyed a good drink and a well-played poker hand. And there were other realities. For Louise, being married to Elias Demetracopoulos would have been a drag on her political career. Elias, for his part, had become unwilling to commit to one woman after his short-lived marriage with Celia. From their first encounter in 1959 until her death in 2005, Elias and Louise remained cherished, plain-speaking friends, but led largely separate lives.

In her letters and telephone calls to Elias, Louise Gore shared stories about her travelling the United States in late 1959 and 1960 campaigning for the election of Richard Nixon and the GOP ticket. She sent her Greek friend a copy of Barry Goldwater's *Conscience of a Conservative* that expressed her political philosophy. For his part, Elias did not have a comprehensive political ideology. He was wary of partisan true believers. He had experienced first-hand both the abuse of state power and the possibilities of responsible leadership in trying times. He hated communism and fascism and preferred republicanism to monarchical rule. He believed in the promise of a well-constructed constitutional framework to guide a flourishing representative democracy. But he observed with cynicism the gaps between the normative claims of Western political thought and its actual practice, especially in Greece. Questions of political theory mattered less to him than reporting empirical realities. To do his job well required cultivating sources on all sides, and forgoing allegiances to any single leader, faction, or philosophy. A favorite aphorism was that he never put all his eggs in one basket.

Although lacking an identifiable political ideology, Elias at this time could have been justifiably characterized as a moderate centrist. In American terms, his political philosophy might have made him a Cold War Democrat such as Senator Henry Jackson. He never told Louise that, if participating in the 1960 American election, he probably would have voted for apparent foreign policy hawk Jack Kennedy.

Without asking Louise for help, Elias tried once more to interview Nixon, as he had five years earlier, but again was unsuccessful. In later years, Elias would sometimes look with bitter irony at the 1954 picture of him and Nixon shaking hands.

Also, in 1959, with years having elapsed since the Time-Life fiasco and both Peurifoy and Karamessines long gone, Demetracopoulos decided to check on becoming a stringer or special correspondent for the international edition of the *New York Herald Tribune*. The "*Trib*" had a prestigious cachet, similar to *Kathimerini* under Chourmouzios. And it meant writing for a much larger international audience for serious news. He consulted his friend Barrett McGurn, the *Tribune*'s Mediterranean Bureau chief, who favored the idea. Others wrote letters on his behalf. One described him as "an energetic, intelligent and ambitious reporter who works hard and has a wide circle of contacts in government and other important fields."[14] The director of the US Operations Mission in Greece said: "Mr. Demetracopoulos is considered one of the best . . . [whose] hard hitting, intelligent . . . exclusive 'scoops' . . . have gained him a world-wide reputation."[15]

Elias also told George Allen, recently departed as US Ambassador to Greece and then director of the United States Information Agency, about his interest. Allen promptly replied that "the *Herald Tribune* needs an energetic correspondent in Greece," and wrote to *Tribune* publisher Ogden Reid, recommending "thoughtful consideration" of Demetracopoulos.[16]

In September 1959, Elias scheduled a series of job interviews in New York with editors and other newspaper officials, including Reid. On October 7, the *Tribune* hired Elias as a special correspondent for Greece. This affiliation was a career highlight. And his enemies took notice.

II.

Blowback

AMBASSADOR ELLIS ORMSBEE BRIGGS CAME to Greece with an understandable chip on his shoulder. Over more than three decades he had completed six ambassadorships in Latin America. In 1956, he had been appointed Ambassador to Brazil with assurance from Secretary of State John Foster Dulles that he could remain there for the duration of the Eisenhower Administration. It was a plum diplomatic assignment, and would be the capstone of his career. On February 1, 1959, however, he was informed that Clare Boothe Luce, the powerful wife of Time-Life publisher Henry Luce and the US ambassador to Italy, coveted his post, and Briggs was reassigned. Uprooting his family again, he went to Greece, where he thought serving as ambassador "ought to have been 80 percent picnic and 20 percent work." Instead, he found Greece to be "one of the most arduous assignments" of his life, because of "the Greek character and the hordes of supernumerary [American] official personnel."[1]

Briggs took up his Athens post on July 15, his top priority to rein in the rapidly growing American presence. Elias, whose beat had been the American community in Greece and who was always eager to uncover a good story, could have helped the new ambassador make his views known. He had played that role, to varying degrees, with the previous three ambassadors. But, other than sharing a December 1 birthdate, the two men had little in common.

Elias was gregarious. Briggs, nearly twenty years his senior, was known as a curmudgeon. The new ambassador resisted all forms of unconventional behavior and did not believe it was his role to be popular in the host country.

At first Briggs treated Elias no differently than other reporters who found Briggs insular and remote. Briggs was even helpful when Demetracopoulos applied for a US visa in 1959 to report on the impact of Khrushchev's American visit and latest developments on Greek-American relations, writing to the secretary of state that he saw no legal grounds for excludability and that refusing him a visa "would react to our disadvantage."[2]

This attitude changed after Elias returned from his early autumn trip and wrote a series of articles that displeased Briggs. The ambassador objected to Elias's gathering stories from State Department and military officials without prior embassy clearance. Elias also returned with press credentials from the New York Herald Tribune News Service, which put Briggs on notice that Demetracopoulos's stories would be reaching a far wider audience—notably Briggs's superiors in Washington. And if Briggs thought Demetracopoulos was beyond his control, the first state visit to Greece of a sitting US president confirmed it. Briggs, who didn't have much respect for Eisenhower or his staff, opposed the December 1959 trip, and was irked to see Demetracopoulos repeatedly included in presidential ceremonies.

The frustrated ambassador also resented Sixth Fleet admirals for making political speeches involving Greece without embassy clearance. He seemed to think himself at war with the US Navy, accusing the admirals of operating with "the pomp of a viceroy of India in the days of Queen Victoria."[3] Whenever Elias had access troubles with State Department personnel, he turned to his friends in the military for stories. In doing so, he stepped directly into the line of fire between the Pentagon and Briggs's colleagues in Foggy Bottom.

In January 1960, shortly after Eisenhower's visit, Elias asked for an on-the-record interview with Vice Admiral Charles B. Brown, Commander in Chief, Allied Forces Southern Europe and former commander of the Sixth Fleet. The admiral agreed to answer two pages of questions Elias sent him and routed his responses by diplomatic pouch to the naval attaché in Athens. The attaché then showed the text to Briggs, who killed the entire interview, claiming that the publicity would benefit Demetracopoulos more than "our broad objectives."[4] Admiral Brown did not work for Briggs, and felt the embassy had no authority to intercept, edit, or veto his remarks. He was so incensed that he went straight to his superior Admiral Arleigh Burke, then Chief of Naval Operations. Burke protested to both acting Secretary of State Christian Herter and President Eisenhower. Although there is no apparent record of a response, in Pentagon–Foggy Bottom confrontations during that era, the Pentagon usually came out on top.

Briggs, however, was not finished. Believing that Demetracopoulos should never have tried to circumvent the embassy in arranging his interview but hesitant to intervene with Elias's Greek newspaper affiliations, he instead attacked the journalist's new relationship with the *Herald Tribune*. When Briggs turned to the CIA station chief and his recently arrived public-affairs officer, Leonard Greenup, to forward his concerns to CIA headquarters, he found willing attack dogs. Heretofore Demetracopoulos had been able to rely on the positive attitude of embassy press officers as a counterbalance to the CIA. During a dinner with visiting *Washington Post* executive editor Jim Wiggins sometime after his return from the US, Elias criticized the current performance of the USIS under Greenup, without realizing that Wiggins was on the Washington-based USIA Oversight Board. Word of Elias's critique made its way back to Greenup.[5]

The immediate consequence was a summons to CIA headquarters of the *Tribune*'s Washington bureau chief, Robert J. Donovan. After this meeting Donovan wrote a letter to his boss in New York, managing editor Fendall W. Yerxa, including an unsigned, unsourced blind memo that repeated defamatory falsehoods about Demetracopoulos. According to Donovan, this screed had been handed him "by a C.I.A. man in the presence of Allen Dulles," director of the CIA, whom Donovan described as "a great friend of the paper" who "wouldn't pass anything like this on to us frivolously."[6] He added that the CIA man—who, Elias later learned, was Dulles's chief press aide Stanley Grogan—had characterized Demetracopoulos as "vicious." The memo warned he would use his role with the *Herald Tribune* as an international forum from which to embarrass the US, ominously adding "he . . . seems to live well beyond his income from writing activities."[7] Though clearly the CIA wanted Elias fired, nothing in Donovan's letter implies that Grogan had made that explicit request. Initially, Yerxa did nothing but file the memo.

■

IN 1960, ELIAS broke more exclusive stories. In March, he reported from Paris on NATO-Greek negotiations regarding placement of nuclear missiles. In May, he angered the CIA by publishing in *Ethnos* classified information on Soviet activity in the Balkans, despite the article's accuracy and what American officials described as its "pro-Western" tone.[8] A day later, he embarrassed the Greek government by publishing information on NATO defense plans for Greece, triggering "an investigation in the highest levels of the Greek armed forces to determine the source of the leak."[9] Athens and Washington became concerned that Demetracopoulos would soon make another Washington trip. The embassy plotted with the Greek Desk at State and the USIA about how to "head him off."[10] Embassy counselor Sam Berger objected that "they perpetuate the myth that he has carefully cultivated here that he has a special 'in' with the Americans. No matter how often we deny this to the Prime Minister, Foreign Minister, [head of KYP] General [Alexandros] Natsinas, and dozens of others, they persist in stating to me that he is 'our man,' and we must do something to curb him."[11] Elias, however, did not go to the United States in 1960. He was too busy elsewhere.

On May 20, Demetracopoulos exposed in *Ethnos* a classified document the Italian government had submitted to NATO that depicted Greek Epirus as part of Albania.[12] Disclosure of this document roiled already-troubled waters, since Greece entertained territorial claims to Northern Epirus that included Albanian land. The article enraged parts of the Greek public, who saw the Italians as still having greedy designs on a Greek province and it prompted a lengthy debate in Parliament as well as anti-Italian street protests in Athens and Thessaloniki. Once again, Karamanlis exploded and, on June 8, 1960, sent a secret order to all Greek embassies instructing them to "avoid any communication whatsoever" with Elias because he is officially deemed a "persona non grata."[13]

Despite efforts by both Greeks and Americans to stymie him, Elias astonished both skeptics and critics by conducting an exclusive interview with Raoul Castro, who had been sent abroad by his brother Fidel to build support for the Cuban revolution in the wake of growing conflict with the United States. Between conferring with Egyptian President Gamal Abdel Nasser in Cairo and returning to Havana, Castro and a party of about twenty stopped in Athens for four and a half hours to hold a meeting at the Cuban Embassy and take a tour of the Acropolis. There were no official Greek welcomers, and only one journalist learned of the visit and managed to speak with Castro. As Ambassador Briggs wrote the secretary of state, "Newspaperman Demetracopoulos on his toes as usual obtained question-and-answer interview. Full text being pouched."[14]

Elias managed to get his exclusive interview transcribed by the Cubans, with Castro signing each page. Afterward, proud of his scoop and believing some context could be useful, Elias called the USIS reporting officer to pass along some "inside information."[15] Demetracopoulos disclosed that Castro spoke "only very bad English" and the interview was carried on through Castro's wife. Elias added that he "was not impressed with the whole group," that "others in the group were afraid of Castro, including the Chief of Police," and that he sensed that the Cubans were less than fully satisfied with their visit to Moscow.[16]

Meanwhile, as part of his wide cultivation of sources, Elias befriended the Israeli legates in Athens, who held the lowest level ("de facto") of any diplomatic representation in the country and had to contend with an undercurrent of Greek anti-Semitism.[17] As part of their role, the representatives tried to arrange familiarization trips for Greeks to learn about Israel, especially journalists and other opinion makers. They found it a tough sell, as several reporters, when invited, explained they were afraid of the personal consequences of visiting a country Greece had not fully recognized. For reasons of state—including needing Arab votes at the UN on Cyprus, and still trying to secure compensation for the expropriation of Greek property in Egypt—Greece did not want to alienate Arab support by elevating Israel's diplomatic status.[18]

The Israeli representative who approached Elias in 1960 had been told by his superiors in Jerusalem that Demetracopoulos—who had been decorated by the Egyptian government and had met with Nasser—was unlikely to accept an invitation. Elias, however, accepted without hesitation, saying that "no one is going to deprive me of the right to go where I want to go and when." The trip was arranged to take place just before Demetracopoulos was scheduled to attend the swearing-in ceremony for Archbishop Makarios on Cyprus's Independence Day.

Elias became the first Greek journalist to visit Israel. For ten days he traveled the country from north to south, from Haifa and Tel Aviv to Jerusalem, focusing mostly on strategic places near borders. He attended briefings, stayed on a kibbutz in the Negev, and went to the Holocaust memorial at Yad Vashem, the Church of the Holy Sepulcher, and other Christian sites. He met with both Prime Minister David Ben Gurion and Foreign Minister Golda Meir. Knowing his next stop would be Cyprus, the Israelis discussed with him their interest in active relations with this new, independent, non-Arab state that lay a mere 140 miles from Haifa.

When Elias arrived in Cyprus, he was met at the airport by Greek Ambassador Konstantinos Tranos, who insisted they go first to the Greek Embassy to send to Athens information on Israel's Cyprus recognition plans. Afterward, Elias participated as Makarios and Tranos devised a successful diplomatic solution concerning Cypriot-Israeli recognition. Elias never returned to Israel, but that did not stop his critics from adding Israel to the growing list of countries alleged to have hired Elias to spy for them—a list that would include Egypt, Yugoslavia, Bulgaria, Czechoslovakia, the Soviet Union, France, Great Britain, and the United States, as well as his native Greece.

■

IN SEPTEMBER, AFTER his trips to Israel and Cyprus, Demetracopoulos broke an "exclusive" on the Eastern Mediterranean maneuvers of fifteen units of the Soviet Black Sea fleet. Karamanlis and security chiefs at Naval Headquarters were "shaken" to notice how closely Elias's story "paralleled" a secret report disseminated to the Greek military community. The American Embassy again complained to the CIA. Grogan approached the *Tribune*'s Donovan for a second time to warn about Demetracopoulos, but once more nothing came of it.[19]

Briggs blocked Elias's appointments when he could, but because of his ongoing gripe over the frequency of US naval visits to Greek ports, he "took to staging trips out of Athens, when what [he] regarded as a superfluous naval visitation loomed,"[20] leaving his naval attaché in charge. Thus, Briggs was away in late September when Vice Admiral George W. Anderson, Commander of the Sixth Fleet, invited Elias on board his flagship, the *Des Moines*, for lunch in the harbor at Piraeus. Elias used the opportunity to brief him on the details of what had happened earlier with Admiral Brown. Otherwise, it was a routine visit and the two posed for a photo, which Anderson inscribed "with warm personal regards and high esteem for your professional excellence."[21] Anderson started to give what Elias described as "a rather fiery interview" on Soviet activities, the Black Sea, and other matters. When time cut short their face-to-face interview, Anderson took with him the written questions Elias had prepared. This time, remembering the lesson of Admiral Brown, Anderson bypassed the diplomatic pouch and sent the answers by regular mail directly to Elias. The full Q & A text was published on October 2, 1960. Anderson, incensed by Briggs's "shabby" treatment of the Sixth Fleet and reports of Briggs's censorship, complained to Admiral Burke in Washington, who passed it up the chain of command to the secretary of state and eventually the President.[22] There was immediate blowback.

Two days later, on October 4, the CIA's Grogan again approached the *Tribune*'s Robert J. Donovan. This time the "ask" was explicit:

Dear Bob,

1. You will recall our conversations in January and in May 1960 regarding Dimitrakopoulos [sic]. This man continues to represent himself as the Athens Stringer of the New York Herald Tribune and carries a letter of accreditation from the Tribune, dated 7 October 1959. He is listed by the foreign press division of the under ministry of press and by the Foreign Press Association in Athens as the representative of the New York Herald Tribune. If the information furnished previously regarding this individual was not sufficient, I can when you return to Washington give you a fill-in.

2. It would be helpful all around, in view of the information I have on this man, if the Herald Tribune would send a letter stating that he is no longer in their employ to the following:

(1) Foreign Press Association;

(2) Foreign Press Division of the Underministry of Press; and

(3) Protocol section of the Greek Ministry of Foreign Affairs.

3. We hope you will be able to cooperate in this request which would not be made except of the most compelling reasons.

Stanley [Grogan][23]

To make it easier to comply, Grogan attached a draft letter dated ten days later, October 14, to each of the three entities, all with managing editor Fendall W. Yerxa's name and title typed in as the signatory. Donovan sent the Grogan correspondence to Yerxa, and this time Yerxa sent a letter to Elias advising him that "that the working agreement . . . with the Herald Tribune News Service . . . is hereby canceled. The letter of accreditation to you . . . is on my authority voided."[24] No explanation was given, although the letter also informed him that "notice to this effect" would be mailed to the three press organizations. Thereafter Yerxa sent the exact text submitted by the CIA, on *Herald Tribune* stationery and over his signature, to the three offices named by Grogan. The only difference between Gorgan's draft and Yerxa's letter was one corrected typo.

Trying to connect the dots some years later, Elias said it "is very unlikely Grogan would know of these organizations. That type of detail would have to come from the CIA and the embassy in Athens. Briggs's fingerprints are all over the letter." He continued:

I found it extraordinary then, and today, that one of the world's premier dailies would take a draft submitted by the CIA—by any outside organization or individual, for that matter—and use it intact . . . More significant, the letter levels accusations against my character and was mailed to people with whom I had to interact. I was incensed . . . Professionally I had to respond. If the letter simply had withdrawn my accreditation, the matter would have ended. I had no right to accreditation, and the *Herald Tribune* had every right to withdraw it whenever and for whatever reason it wished. But neither Grogan nor anyone at the newspaper seem to have thought through the draft and to have realized it was asking for more trouble than it gave.

Before he received his termination letter, Elias had submitted a story to the *Herald Tribune*'s Paris office revealing that Greece and the United States had formally agreed to place nuclear weapons on Greek soil several weeks after the Greek government officially denied that "any such weapons" were based in Greece. The story could not be used, however, on account of Yerxa's order.[25]

The Foreign Press Association of Greece letter was sent to its president, A.C. Sedgwick, the Athens Bureau chief of the *New York Times* and son-in-law of *Times* heavyweight columnist C. L. Sulzberger. Though Sedgwick competed with Elias for stories, he was so angry at the letter's tone and content that he wrote a blistering reply to Yerxa on 29 November, reading in part:

Insofar as this letter was addressed to the Foreign Press Association I felt free, indeed compelled, to permit the members to read it. A number of them, myself included, felt that both the tone and language employed suggest defamation and positive harm to our colleague's reputation as a journalist and to his prestige . . .

Mr. Demetracopoulos is known here to be an enterprising newspaperman, held in high esteem. He has been able to produce letters from the Herald Tribune News Service editors showing that those editors placed confidence in him. That suddenly, and that for no reason we know of, the accepted estimate of the man was thrown into reverse has left many of us wondering if some character assassin has not found his mark for personal gain.

Ultimately, Yerxa's libels hurt Elias more than the unexpected termination. Elias contacted a lawyer in New York with the thought of suing the *Herald Tribune* to "rescind the aspersions cast."[26] He did not expect to get his job back, but he wanted a retraction and an apology.

12.

A Dark Side of Camelot

THE CIA ATTACK ON ELIAS through the *Herald Tribune* was but one shot in a fusillade. Half a century later, many documents have been destroyed or are still heavily redacted; the full scope of this nefarious campaign may never be known.[1] At the end of November 1960, after telling other agencies it "would like derogative information," CIA deputy director Richard Helms prepared a four-page memorandum to US Naval Intelligence, the Department of the Army, the State Department, and the USIA, claiming that Demetracopoulos, "regardless of whether or not he was the witting instrument of hostile interests . . . is a trouble-maker who has misused any contact with US officials or institutions, and the such contact should be avoided wherever possible."[2]

Nevertheless, in early January 1961, Elias flew to the United States to cover the presidential inauguration of John Fitzgerald Kennedy and report on what the change of administrations might mean for Greece. He also wanted to conduct a series of high-profile interviews that he could place in his different papers upon his return.

He found Washington more festive than on past visits and was delighted to be back with Louise Gore, now his Fairfax Hotel landlady. Although a Republican Party stalwart who had worked hard for Nixon, she now graciously welcomed guests from around the world to the inauguration of a Democratic president.

In the weeks leading up to the inauguration, Elias was all business. Members of the State Department were apoplectic that, despite their objections, he repeatedly scored interviews with top American officials. Demetracopoulos even arranged a brief meeting with vice president–elect Lyndon Johnson at his Senate office and received a written response to previously submitted questions.[3]

When Demetracopoulos interviewed Admiral Arleigh Burke, Chief of Naval Operations and member of the Joint Chiefs of Staff, Burke was in the last months of an unprecedented third term, one which Kennedy had asked him to complete.[4] Dwight D. Eisenhower was still President, but the interview would not appear until after the change in administration, and this timing "put a whole new complexion on a relatively minor event," Elias later wrote.[5]

Elias's acquaintance with Burke went back to the mid-1950s. As a Cold War strategic planner and programmer, the 59-year-old admiral was a celebrated war hero and anti-Soviet hawk, unafraid to speak his mind.[6] The two men had had many discussions about the requirements of modern navies in a nuclear age and the degree to which a calibrated "flexible response" involving non-nuclear weapons was better than "massive retaliation." They had some political differences, especially regarding the Greek royal family, but they respected each other.

At two o'clock sharp on January 12, 1961, Elias entered the admiral's imposing Pentagon office. Before beginning the interview, Elias updated Burke on his ongoing battle with the US Embassy in Athens over his interviews with Navy brass. He also told him of his suspicious firing by the *Herald Tribune*. Off the record, the admiral offered to help. In the formal interview, Burke provocatively said he didn't think Russia would "dare start a general nuclear war, because she will be destroyed."[7] And in response to a question about Soviet Communist Party First Secretary Nikita Khrushchev's threats that the Soviet Union would not tolerate Sixth Fleet exercises in the Black Sea, Burke forcefully asserted that the "Black Sea is an international body of water . . . and in international waters, we will go anywhere we please and [the Soviet Union] won't stop us—neither will anyone else."[8]

Elias knew immediately Admiral Burke had given him great material. He recalled that "to insure no complaints about the text, Admiral Burke and I agreed to have the transcript approved by the Department of the Navy. Several days later the Navy returned it to me, with the upper right corner stamped: 'No objection to publication on grounds of national security.'" Someone had written by hand, "Courtesy Review."[9] In the middle of the stamped block was the date: JAN 16, 1961.

INAUGURATION DAY, JANUARY 20, was bitterly cold and snowy, and Elias didn't even try to brave the weather and the crowds to get a good vantage point along the parade route. He watched Kennedy's address and other pageantry on television from the warmth of the Fairfax Hotel, near a crackling fireplace, with Louise Gore and a bipartisan group of onlookers. After the inauguration, Elias completed his remaining interviews and returned to Athens, via New York.

The day after the Burke interview, outgoing President Eisenhower went on national television and radio and delivered his Farewell Address to the American People, warning about the dangers of a growing military industrial complex. The tone of the valedictory speech contributed to the incoming administration's eagerness to make sure it was viewed as not only strong on defense, but that substantively and symbolically the military was under its civilian control. Desiring better relations with the Soviet Union, the Kennedy Administration did not want any loose-lipped generals or admirals saying things that would inflame tempers in Moscow. It would strictly enforce a longstanding rule that no military official could make a public statement without formal clearance.

Burke accepted the concept of civilian control of the military. Although he didn't have the same personal relationship with the new president as he had had with his predecessor, he respected the office and, initially, Kennedy himself. He also told Elias he admired the intelligence of the new Secretary of Defense Robert McNamara but was troubled by his inexperience. Burke was greatly displeased by the arrogant attitude of junior officials at the Pentagon who projected the sense that "any civilian was superior to any military officer."[10]

Later in January, Admiral Burke, as instructed, submitted to the Defense Secretary the draft of a speech prepared for his January 27 acceptance of the Silver Quill Award. In the draft, he said the Russians could not be trusted. Around January 23 he was informed that the text was unacceptable. Burke and his speechwriter prepared a new draft, which passed muster. Word of this wrist-slap soon leaked out. As he suggested in later testimony to Congress, Burke was more miffed at the public disclosure than the initial rejection. He suspected the leak came from Arthur Sylvester, the new Assistant Secretary of Defense for Public Affairs, and was meant to embarrass him.

Before departing Washington, Elias had given the English version of his January 12 interview to his NANA editor Sid Goldberg, with the understanding it would be embargoed until he could translate it into Greek for *Ethnos* and *Make-*

donia and prepare an English version for the *Athens Daily Post*.[11] It took him until February 15 to get everything ready for the interview's release. The syndicated story, featuring Burke's provocative language, was widely headlined in papers in Greece, Britain, and the United States.[12] "I enjoyed writing that article," Elias remembered, "but I never dreamed it would be a bombshell."

Explode it did. The Kennedy White House and the Defense Department were furious. In his February 1 and February 8 press conferences, President Kennedy had put his personal stamp of approval on the policy of military personnel pre-clearing any public pronouncements.[13] The simultaneous international publication of Elias's February 15 front-page stories looked to Burke's superiors as if the admiral was purposely challenging the young president. Rumors spread quickly that some in the new administration wanted the Eisenhower holdover fired for disrespect. At the same time, administration opponents jumped quickly to Burke's defense. Barry Goldwater led other senators in attacking the White House for "muzzling" military leaders.[14]

In his defense, Burke clarified that he had consulted his log and that the interview had been conducted before the inauguration, while Eisenhower was still president. The Kennedy Administration did not believe him. An anti-Burke campaign was organized by Arthur Sylvester and Pierre Salinger, the new White House press secretary. Asked by candidate Kennedy in early 1960 what would be the first thing he'd do if elected president, a drunken Arthur Sylvester, then a reporter for the *Newark Evening News*, had replied that he'd "shut the mouths of every General and Admiral . . . [who] seem to speak with more authority than elected . . . officeholders."[15] Kennedy and Salinger remembered this and had him appointed Assistant Secretary of Defense. Now, as Salinger's designated "armpit nuzzler," Sylvester warned that military control required that Burke be brought to heel.[16]

President Kennedy was asked about the Burke interview during his February 15 press conference at the State Department, the same day the article appeared. He replied: "I have been informed . . . that the interview was given on January 12, which was before the Administration took over on January 20 and before we gave any indication that we would like all statements dealing with national security to be coordinated." The President went on to joke that "I would say that this makes me happier than ever that such a directive has gone out."[17]

The press corps tittered, but it was no laughing matter for the White House.[18] Privately Kennedy was livid, and members of his staff knew it. The White House viewed Burke's blunt remarks as a right-wing assault and remained unconvinced that the interview had been conducted before Kennedy took office. Sylvester held a press briefing in which he told reporters that neither Burke nor Elias should be believed.[19] In its lead story the next day, the *New York Post* asked: "Now where were you Mr. Demetracopoulos on the day of January 12?"[20]

■

ON THE DAY after the presidential press conference, Pierre Salinger summoned the CIA to the White House for a briefing. "Lucky Pierre" was a tough, inside-politics player whom Jack Kennedy had picked to run his presidential campaign press operation after watching him help Bobby Kennedy during the Estes Kefauver hearings on racketeering. However, Salinger was originally kept out of the loop on sensitive matters of state. For example, he knew nothing about the Bay of Pigs planning. Shut out of real policy-making decisions, Salinger welcomed any attention from agents and desk officers elsewhere in the administration, and they in turn were only too pleased to feed him their anti-Demetracopoulos misinformation. Gregarious and jovial as he could be, Salinger had a peculiar fondness for conspiracy theories—so much so that decades later the term "Pierre Salinger Syndrome" was coined to describe "the condition of thinking that everything one reads on the Internet is true."[21] Sitting in his White House office the day after the interview broke, Salinger fingered a white business card someone had given him: "Elias Demetracopoulos, Political Editor, Ethnos, Makedonia, Athens Post, Omonia Street, Athens." He started immediately to coordinate a search for the whereabouts of Elias and any and all intelligence "traces" about his background.[22]

From Athens, Ambassador Briggs expressed outrage at the Burke interview, characterizing it as Elias's "zooming up and down the Mediterranean (and Black Sea to boot) with US Sixth Fleet, hand-in-hand with Admiral Burke; with every funnel belching sparks and missiles guided and unguided spinning in all directions."[23] The CIA's Stanley Grogan sent the White House a "Secret" CIA follow-up titled "Restored Prestige of Ilias Dimitrakopoulos [*sic*] Since His Trip to US," in which he reported that, despite the attacks from Karamanlis and his "lost status" after being "dropped" by the *Herald Tribune*, Demetracopoulos was:

> getting back nearly all of his former prestige. He has, in the face of
> known opposition of the Greek government, contrived to achieve a
> status which compels many within his profession and without (e.g. the
> military) to conclude with some reluctance that Dimitrakopoulos has
> in fact very close relations with high-standing people in the United

States. Regardless of whether he is an American agent or not, Ilias Dimitrakopoulos [sic] has the stories which appeal to Greek nationalist readers, since the stories deal in many cases with American foreign and military policy in the Eastern Mediterranean.

... Since Dimitrakopoulos' return and subsequent to his journalistic success, the atmosphere toward him in the Greek Parliament has changed. Opposition politicians and ERE (National Radical Union) deputies alike seek him out in an effort to assure that their views on every imaginable subject are conveyed to high American circles.[24]

Soon after, State Department security officers started to build a case to block Elias's further travel to the United States. They re-circulated reports from the early 1950s that claimed he had lied on his visa application, was "not a recognized journalist," and was considered by an earlier US ambassador to be a "mental case."[25] Meanwhile, a choleric CIA complained that Elias's articles "continue to have a damaging effect upon US prestige in Greece and NATO harmony" and asserted he had "probable ties with an unknown group or organization."[26] Of particular concern to the CIA's deputy director of plans was a "substantially accurate but incomplete account of a forthcoming NATO practice exercise, CHECKMATE."[27] A befuddled Briggs concluded that Demetracopoulos obviously had access to classified information given him by "person or persons unknown," a conclusion perhaps bolstered in March when a high-level Greek government official, outraged by a Demetracopoulos-bylined newspaper article, characterized the journalist as "as an American agent not subject to the control of the embassy or State Department."[28]

Pierre Salinger remained furious at Elias after the events of February 1961, becoming one of the most incessant drumbeaters bent on destroying the Greek journalist.[29] For years, and long after the Kennedy White House era, Salinger rarely missed an opportunity to pass on unfounded rumors regarding Demetracopoulos, even calling the Greek's high-profile friends and business associates to warn them that this "charmer" was really a fraud, a Communist, a double agent, and worse.[30]

■

WHEN ELIAS, BACK in Greece, got word of the controversy in Washington, he confirmed Burke's recollection that the interview had indeed taken place more than a week before the inauguration. He explained that, as was his custom, the interview had been transcribed and returned to Burke for corrections and confirmation and that he had in his possession the Navy copy stamped January 16, 1961. To his surprise, Ambassador Briggs called him shortly thereafter and for the first time invited him to a private dinner at his residence. As a seeming afterthought, he asked Elias to bring with him the original copy of the Burke interview. Elias, sensing something amiss, brought with him a copy, not the original. During the meal, the ambassador asked for the transcript. Elias said he'd brought a copy and that Briggs was welcome to it.

Briggs was displeased not to receive the original and said that others would be displeased as well. Pointedly, he warned Elias that the President's brother and ruthless enforcer, Attorney General Robert Kennedy, was personally looking into this matter, and that Elias's non-cooperation could cause him "big trouble." Elias still declined to produce the original. Later that evening he discovered that his office on Omonia Street had been broken into and ransacked.[31] His files had been searched, but it appeared that nothing was taken. Luckily, before going to dinner, he had taken the precaution of placing the original interview transcript in a bank safety deposit box in downtown Athens.

The following day, Demetracopoulos received several transatlantic telephone calls from people at the State Department urging that he not support Burke.[32] They, as well as embassy officials in Athens, noted that "it's a new administration" and that, if he cooperated, his past problems would disappear, and he'd enjoy increased access to exclusive interviews. As a sweetener, arrangements could be made to have his relationship with the *Herald Tribune* reinstated. Elias's response was quick and unequivocal. He asked his editors to arrange to have his story reprinted, this time with a photostat of the interview cover sheet containing the Navy "approval" box and the January 16, 1961 date highlighted in boldface. On February 19, *Makedonia* ran the interview and article again on its front page, with an introductory note and the Navy stamp.

An embarrassed Kennedy Administration stepped up its harassment of Elias and his sources. A World Bank executive who'd given Elias an interview was told by the FBI not to do it again. At the same time, Elias gained entry to a network of right-wing congressional conservatives who were furious at the shabby treatment of their beloved Admiral Burke. The confrontation with Burke was the first salvo in a partisan battle. New Hampshire Republican Senator Styles Bridges called for hearings on Kennedy's treatment of the military. Mississippi Senator John Stennis convened his Armed Services Special Preparedness Subcommittee and later issued a report critical of the administration. Elias joined the fray, preparing a pro–Sixth Fleet editorial that was inserted into the Congressional Record.[33] Later, he editorialized against the muzzling of the US military.[34]

The White House distrust of Burke and his Pentagon allies may have contributed to the President's decision to give the CIA broad leeway and leave the military relatively in the dark in the run-up to the Bay of Pigs. Late in the evening of April 16, at the conclusion of the annual congressional reception in the East Room of the White House, President Kennedy, Vice President Johnson, Secretary of State Dean Rusk, in white tie and tails, along with General Lyman Lemnitzer, Chairman of the Joint Chiefs of Staff, and Admiral Burke, in dress uniforms and medals, gathered in the Oval Office to monitor the invasion that was to begin at midnight.

According to Burke's biographer, E. B. Potter, Richard M. Bissel of the CIA informed Kennedy that although the situation was bad, it "could still take a favorable turn if the President would authorize sending in aircraft from the carrier."[35] Burke concurred, arguing for American naval intervention. "Let me take two jets and shoot down the enemy aircraft," he urged. But President Kennedy said "No," reminding them that he had said "over and over" that he would not commit US forces to combat, knowing that this would broadcast to the world the truth that the whole expedition had been conceived, planned, and armed by the United States. Burke then suggested sending in a destroyer. Whereupon Kennedy exploded. "Burke," he snapped, "I don't want the United States involved in this."[36]

"Hell, Mr. President," Burke snapped back, "but we are involved." One can reasonably assume that the dust-up between the two men two months before colored this unpleasant exchange.[37]

Burke's August retirement hardly meant a diminution of Demetracopoulos's high-level access to Navy sources, since his successor was none other than Admiral George W. Anderson, who had provided the September 1960 interview that had provoked the CIA to demand Elias's firing. Just a few weeks before he assumed his new position, Admiral Anderson wrote to Elias, thanking him for an *Athens Post* editorial supportive of the US Navy and warmly inviting him to come see him on his next visit. [38]

■

ON THE DAY before the Bay of Pigs invasion, President Kennedy, keeping up a façade of normalcy, held his first meeting with a head of government since his inauguration. There were toasts and photos aplenty at the Greek Embassy, where Prime Minister Kostantinos Karamanlis greeted him and the American First Lady cordially accepted an invitation to visit Greece.[39]

Kennedy also held a private meeting with Karamanlis. The Americans wanted to cut back their foreign aid spending and planned to encourage allies, notably Germany, to pick up the slack with countries like Greece as part of "burden sharing."[40] On the table were other matters as well. An agreement on terms of Greek repayment of prewar claims to American bondholders was still unresolved. And Greece's plans to establish a tariff union with the European Economic Community were thwarting American efforts to open up another market for its tobacco growers.

Given the electoral scare from the left in the Greek elections of 1958, Kennedy felt that Karamanlis, however flawed, was still the best option to secure American interests, although some advisors preferred a more liberal alternative.[41] With the Berlin crisis escalating, the President reassured the prime minister of Greece's importance to the NATO shield against Soviet aggression. And Karamanlis used American concerns about Communism spreading in Laos and Vietnam to retain an acceptable amount of military aid.

With fallout from the Burke interview hurting his access to top American Embassy officials, Elias cultivated a friendship with the American in charge of negotiating the bond debt issue, and worked lower-level officials, whose leaks helped him explore angles for covering the coming cutbacks in American aid.[42] Much later, reviewing Kennedy's unsuccessful June 1961 confrontation with Khrushchev in Vienna, Elias wondered why the young president had not spent more effort planning and weighing the risks involved.[43] With a blend of sorrow and exasperation, he later chided: "With all the important decisions facing the President in the Oval Office, why was he, or his press secretary, wasting any of their important time trying to punish me for being right? I had expected something more from him."

■

GREECE HELD ITS own election in October 1961, with the rules again altered to reduce the strength of the left-wing EDA in favor of a centrist coalition.[44] To further facilitate the result, the CIA engaged in covert funding of both the center-right ERE and center-left EC (*Enosis Kentrou*), George Papandreou's party.[45] EC moderates fared better than they had in 1958, but still came in second to Karamanlis's conservatives. Ambassador Briggs privately admitted that the

Greek crony capitalist government and its ham-handed patronage system was corrupt and had lost touch with the people. Nonetheless, he openly supported Karamanlis and his right-wing victory.[46]

EC leader Papandreou, believing the system had been rigged to relegate his party to the role of token opposition, thundered that the election had been stolen, notably by machinations of the right. He pledged to engage in *anendotos* or *anendotos agon,* an "unyielding struggle" to overturn the results with new elections. The CIA pigeonholed Elias as a Papandreou partisan and Karamanlis opponent, but the journalist denied having a political ax to grind. "Few reporters want to beat to death an office holder or institution," he explained. "I got my kicks from scooping other reporters. It is often hard for people in public life to understand that this is what drives most reporters."[47] Demetracopoulos acknowledged widespread fraud in the 1961 election, including intimidation, violence, and double voting, but believed the absence of these factors would not have changed the outcome. To him the ERE was not the main threat to Greek democracy. He was more concerned about the growing political role of the IDEA faction in the Greek army and its offshoot, EENA (the Union of Young Greek Officers).

Elias's primary military sources were leading pro-Western, pro-monarchist admirals and generals, some of them senior IDEA members or sympathizers. Through them he heard about a group of several dozen junior officers who seemed to admire Egyptian President Gamal Abdel Nasser for his authoritarian personality and strongman nationalism, while eschewing his Cold War neutralism. However, he had trouble figuring out this group's specific agenda. Some of their names—Papadopoulos (nicknamed by his cohorts "Nasser"), Ioannidis, Ladas, and Roufogalis—would eventually become quite familiar, unalterably changing Elias's life.

Elias was not alone in being happy to see Ambassador Briggs leave in February 1962. The outgoing diplomat was seen as so partisan that Greek opposition leaders refused to attend his farewell ceremonies. He was replaced in January 1962 by the more liberal Henry Labouisse, husband of Eve Curie, the daughter of Nobel Prize winners Marie and Pierre Curie. They came to Athens as a power couple, said to be close to the Kennedys. Elias's sources, however, told him that Labouisse was in fact damaged goods—dumped in Greece to get him out of an embarrassing situation in Washington after the American president realized that Labouisse was out of his league trying to restructure the US AID program; Jackie Kennedy had endorsed the soft landing.[48]

While some embassy personnel described the new ambassador as a sweet, calm, laid-back Louisiana gentleman, Elias's assessment was closer to that of the former embassy senior staffer who recalled: "I'm not sure that Henry knew a lot about what was going on, or even worried about it."[49] Elias thought Labouisse's well-organized wife would have made the better ambassador. He longed for the days of ambassadors Grady, Allen, and Riddleberger—engaged professionals whose postings in Greece weren't consolation prizes.

·

MEANWHILE, DEMETRACOPOULOS HAD not abandoned his resolve to rectify his suspicious 1960 firing from the New York Herald Tribune, which he thought might have been connected to Ambassador Briggs. During the preparation for Kennedy's inauguration, Elias had met with American attorneys to discuss how to proceed in a lawsuit. His New York lawyers agreed that he had been "badly treated" by the newspaper but told him that this did not mean he could win a long and expensive libel action.[50] They were troubled by technical questions involving venue and jurisdiction and whether, if "publication" of the letters took place in Greece, the Greek law of defamation should apply. His attorneys recommended negotiations with the Herald Tribune to obtain a face-saving letter of apology to the newspaper groups that had received the offending letters. Only if no such letter could be obtained should he consider filing suit. Even then, prosecuting a lawsuit from Greece would be difficult, take years, and be a huge drain on his resources.

Demetracopoulos had taken a step toward this goal during his Kennedy inauguration trip by calling Robert White, former president and editor-in-chief of the Herald Tribune, who had recently left the paper over management issues. Elias had talked to White over the phone during his hiring process but had never met him face-to-face. Elias informed White that he was planning to sue the newspaper over managing editor Yerxa's letter to the Foreign Press Association. White invited Elias to his suburban Westchester home to discuss the matter. Demetracopoulos took a cab from the train and arrived at White's 200-year-old house in Rye after a harrowing trip through a torrential, tree-snapping winter thunderstorm. The former Tribune executive, who had hired Yerxa, listened attentively to Elias's side of the story. As Elias was leaving, White said: "Anyone who braved such weather to make his case must be telling the truth."

White acted quickly. He arranged for the Greek journalist and his attorney to meet with Yerxa and himself in Manhattan. It was agreed that the libel action would be dropped if a letter were sent to the reporter and the others involved—the Foreign Press Association, the Protocol Section of the Greek Ministry of Foreign Affairs, and the Foreign Press Division of the Greek Ministry of the Press—retracting Yerxa's allegation that Demetracopoulos had misrepresented himself as a correspondent for the *Herald Tribune*.[51] It was understood that the paper would not reinstate Elias.

Yerxa agreed to be responsible for sending out the retractions. The letters, however, were never sent. Perhaps, with White's returning to the hinterlands of Mexico, Missouri, later that month, Yerxa felt no pressure to follow through. On April 29, 1961, almost three months after the letter was to have been sent, Demetracopoulos cabled Yerxa, noting that he had in his possession "sufficient documentary evidence" to prove that the US Embassy in Athens had "acted in a manner contrary to the basic principles of freedom of the press" and that this interference caused "the severance" of his "working arrangement" with the newspaper.

Demetracopoulos never received a reply to his cable, and when Elias returned to the US in the summer of 1962, the *Herald Tribune* matter was still unresolved. Elias was impatient to remove the stain on his reputation which he felt prevented him from moving forward on other employment opportunities. It was also a matter of *philotimo* (personal honor). Elias told his attorneys that he was not seeking monetary damages. He simply wanted his reputation back, unbesmirched.

At the time, he was unaware of the extent to which the *Herald Tribune* and other US news organizations were eager servants of US intelligence agencies. Half a century later, Yerxa would admit to his participation in the nation's Cold War agenda, notably as the *Herald Tribune*–paid ghostwriter for Herbert Philbrick's McCarthy-era agitprop *I Led Three Lives*. Yerxa said he knew Philbrick was a "phony," but still took the $20,000 to complete the project.[52] He also had regrets for being "pushed" by his publisher into preparing a series of articles of virulent anti-Communist propaganda. "It wasn't a very good piece of work," he recalled. "It wasn't responsible journalism." He remembered the Demetracopoulos firing, in contrast, as a mere "administrative detail."[53]

■

IN WASHINGTON THAT summer of 1962, Elias met with Robert Donovan, the *Tribune*'s Washington bureau chief, who had congratulated him on his hiring in 1959, but had since acted as the CIA's anti-Elias middleman, a fact he didn't disclose during their lunch. Donovan's message was clear. "These things happen," he said. "Just suck it up and move on quietly. Making waves will cause repercussions."

Elias responded: "So, there may be repercussions, because I'm not going to back down."

Donovan replied: "Well, you must remember that these people in power have many ways to come back against you."

"Obviously you know things that I don't know," Elias interrupted, "but they have not yet met Demetracopoulos. I'm going to follow through with the *Herald Tribune*."

"Don't. Let it alone," Donovan advised. "The people in the bureaucracy will try to destroy you."

"Bob, who will try to destroy me?" Elias asked, his voice getting louder. "I will destroy them first." The men parted and never talked again.[54]

In July, word passed around the White House that Elias was looking for top-level interviews. Robert Komer, National Security Council advisor and former CIA operative, sent a memo to Malcolm "Mac" Kilduff, Deputy White House Press Secretary, with copies to McGeorge Bundy, Pierre Salinger, and others:

> State tells me that a smart and pushy Greek journalist named Demetrakopoulos [*sic*] . . . is in town and says he's going to try to see the President, or, at least someone in the White House.
>
> He is legitimate, so we don't want to give him a complete brush-off, but State is worried lest he write troublesome stories. He is no supporter of Karamanlis, and apparently wants to write that the US is not backing the Greek defense effort because it doesn't like the current government. He apparently saw Reston the last time."

In a handwritten note "to all," he added: "I strongly urge he not be received at a high level—I know him too well."[55] Two years later, Robert Komer would make an offer he thought Elias would not refuse.

13.

Moving Left

U PON RETIREMENT FROM THE NAVY, Arleigh Burke became the first head of
the Center for Strategic and International Studies (CSIS) at Georgetown
University. When Elias met him in his new offices on July 16, 1962, Burke
asked the status of the lawsuit against the *Trib*. Hearing that the promised letters
of retraction had never materialized, Burke fired off a letter the next day to *Herald Tribune* publisher John Hay Whitney in which he warned of a possible "injustice done to Mr. Demetracopoulos," given "his excellent reputation, his staunch
anti-Communist attitude over the years, and his support for the United States."[1]

Three weeks later, Elias also spoke about his problems with his old pal from
a decade earlier, retired General William W. Quinn, then deputy director of the
Defense Intelligence Agency. Quinn suggested that the firing had not been
Yerxa's initiative but done at the behest of the CIA. Rather than asking Quinn to
take an action that might further strain relations between Defense Intelligence
and the CIA, Elias took the general's advice to involve Richard Russell, Senate
Armed Services Committee Chairman, who had as much oversight of intelligence budgets as anyone in Congress. Elias used Senator Strom Thurmond,
who'd praised Elias effusively for standing up for Admiral Burke, as a conduit to
Russell.

Too impatient to wait for responses to Burke's letter or his own message to
Thurmond, Elias made a cold call to William Hill, the managing editor of the

Washington Star. It may have been the slow summer schedule, but Hill agreed to see him without delay. At their August 3 meeting, Hill appointed Demetracopoulos the paper's Mediterranean correspondent.[2]

Soon after, Senator Russell's response to Thurmond's overture exceeded Elias's expectations. Instead of merely writing to the CIA on his behalf, the Georgia lawmaker summoned John McCone, Allen Dulles's successor as head of the CIA, to his hideaway Senate office in the Capitol to meet Elias personally on the afternoon of August 13, 1962. Russell had instructed McCone to come alone, not telling him the meeting's purpose. McCone, who had frequent private meetings with Russell on intelligence matters, saw the request as nothing out of the ordinary. The only other person present was Senator Strom Thurmond, along with Russell, one of the most hawkish, anti-Communist legislators on Capitol Hill.

Russell went straight to the matter. McCone was taken aback at being confronted by a case he said he knew nothing about. He was forced to take his own notes during the hour-plus meeting, most of which consisted of Elias's lengthy description of his *Trib* discharge and was at an unfair advantage asking questions.[3] "I frankly felt sorry for the man," Elias recalled. "I slowed my pace while he visibly sweated over his notes—the supreme commander of American intelligence reduced to the role of stenographer all because of me. It was all very embarrassing."

The day after the confrontation with McCone, the CIA's congressional liaison met with Senator Thurmond and his chief of staff Harry Dent to try to undo the damage. According to a "SECRET" CIA report, Thurmond, "listened politely" to the attack against Elias, "but stated he had received very good reports about [Demetracopoulos] from people whom he respects" and asked for "the evidence on which we have reached our conclusions."[4] Because the CIA's dossier on Demetracopoulos was replete with uncorroborated rumors and disinformation, the CIA liaison concluded that "providing trustworthy evidence . . . could prove a difficult case." He told Director McCone, "We have not fully satisfied Thurmond," but that he would try again. He did, and again Thurmond and Dent dismissed the Agency's personal attacks as not credible.

A few days later, Elias received a telephone call from Everett Walker, director of the *Herald Tribune* Syndicate & News Service, inviting him to come to New York to accept a "to whom it may concern" letter reinstating him as the service's Athens correspondent.

Elias was euphoric and raced to the train to pick up the letter that expressed the paper's "highest esteem for his professional ability and personal integrity."[5] This was far more than he had expected. He had sought an apology, not "reinstatement." He was also given copies of registered letters sent to the recipients of Yerxa's earlier screed, basically identical to the letter of apology agreed upon in the meeting with Yerxa and Robert White eighteen months earlier. Elias called Celia in Connecticut to share the news. She, perhaps more than anyone, understood what Elias had been through. They met in Manhattan for a celebratory dinner.[6]

Could it be that the battle that had begun with Ambassador Peurifoy and CIA Station Chief Karamessines was now over? Elias's victory was more bittersweet than that. In fact, this public reversal transformed what had been a highly personal vendetta on the part of some CIA personnel into an institutional crusade. Within days of Elias's "reinstatement" at the *Herald Tribune,* the CIA, furious at McCone's humiliation in front of Russell, discussed targeting his former wife—providing it could be "definitely ascertained" she was "angry" with him.[7] They then proceeded to identify Elias as a permanent "security risk."

The first signs of this retribution came in September 1962, when Elias was back in Greece. Shortly after publishing some of his controversial Washington interviews, he received a letter reminiscent of those he'd received from *Time* in 1952 and the *Herald Tribune* in 1960. This time it came from *Washington Star* managing editor William "Bill" Hill, who had just hired him, terminating their less than two-month agreement. Unlike the earlier notices, which had directly or indirectly called into question the reporter's effectiveness or integrity, Hill's letter explained only that "coverage as we will need . . . can best be handled by one of our full-time employees operating out of Washington."[8]

To Elias, this seemed more than coincidental, as he was able to confirm a year later. Managing editor Hill told Elias that the order—not suggestion—to fire him had arrived from Richard Helms, then the CIA director of plans, and editor Newbold Noyes "had had no choice."[9]

After the August 1962 confrontation in Senator Russell's office, the CIA returned to the White House to make sure Pierre Salinger and the President took the Demetracopoulos threat seriously.[10] McCone's representatives stressed that the Agency had information supporting much more incendiary charges and discussed efforts to get the damaging material to all government agencies and "seal off" Demetracopoulos from sources of interviews. The problem, observed the

CIA memorandum writer, was that State Department opinion was split. Those handling press relations were generally in agreement with the CIA, but those on the political side continued to regard Demetracopoulos as "an asset and friend of the Americans and are more reluctant to take action against him."[11]

In Washington in late August, Elias had interviewed each of the military chiefs of staff: General Curtis LeMay of the Air Force, the Army's General Earle Wheeler, and Admiral George Anderson of the Navy. Generals LeMay and Wheeler dutifully submitted their transcripts to the press office under Defense Secretary Robert McNamara, as required by the Kennedy Administration edict, and the transcripts from both interviews were promptly killed. Since Admiral Anderson had a prior positive relationship with Demetracopoulos, he directed that the text be transcribed and sent directly to Elias without first obtaining a stamp of approval from the office of the Secretary of Defense. Elias duly published it in Athens on September 13.

In the published text the admiral said no changes were planned in the size of the Sixth Fleet, sidestepped a question about bringing Polaris submarines into the Mediterranean, and gave a non-provocative response to Elias's question about Soviet naval buildup. "It is difficult to see how these words could irritate anyone," recalled Elias. "But they did. McNamara was livid with Anderson for violating the standing order that interviews be cleared with his staff."[12]

A few weeks later, the Cuban Missile Crisis erupted. Because the Kennedy Administration decided to impose a naval blockade, Admiral Anderson was at the center of activity. On October 24, the Navy spent hours assessing all the data about Russian ships steaming toward Cuba with missiles on board. Just before noon, the Office of Naval Intelligence and Admiral Anderson's tactical and navigational control room in the Pentagon became convinced that information provided earlier in the day by the National Security Agency was correct: sixteen of eighteen Russian vessels headed for Cuba were dead in the water or had turned back. This was key information. The Russians had blinked and would not challenge the naval blockade.

According to Dino A. Brugioni's history of the crisis, McNamara learned later that day that some of the information about the Russian ships had been available hours before he was told. He "stormed" into the naval control room and began chewing out the officers on duty.[13] The officer in charge notified Anderson, who also rushed in. In the first of a series of confrontations, the Secretary of Defense accosted the Admiral, who just weeks before had refused to submit his

Demetracopoulos interview for clearance. As Elias later pieced it together from Anderson and others, "It was not a pretty scene." The stories of the October confrontation and the earlier interview were shared with Pierre Salinger and others at the White House, further contributing to the anti-Demetracopoulos animus.

■

THE UNITED STATES had been making overtures toward softening Cold War tensions with Yugoslavia. At the same time, Yugoslav radio was propagandizing on behalf of what it said was the plight of the Slav minority living in Greek Macedonia, which some Yugoslavs claimed as its own. Greece was not pleased by either of these developments.

Before returning to Greece in anticipation of Vice President Johnson's early September 1962 trip there, Demetracopoulos had added two exclusive interviews to his calendar: with Assistant Secretary of State Robert J. Manning and with Edward M. Kennedy, the President's youngest brother, who was then running for the US Senate seat formerly held by his brother. In the interviews, Elias asked about American attitudes toward totalitarian dictatorships, Greek elections, the continuation of US aid, American policies in southeastern Europe, and the "Macedonian Question," all items that could reasonably be raised on the Johnson trip. Both men gave essentially the same answers, urging calm and hoping the Macedonia issue would not be "exacerbated" or "inflamed."[14]

The Greek press and Karamanlis government picked up on the Demetracopoulos interviews and suggested that the United States was showing "excessive friendliness to Yugoslavia."[15] Recognizing the similarity of the two responses, Greek officials protested that official US policy apparently failed to side with its ally Greece against Yugoslavia. When Johnson arrived, according to an American reporter travelling with him, the vice president had to assert repeatedly that in the face of Yugoslav claims "the United States will tolerate no compromise of the territorial integrity or domestic tranquility of our ally and friend."[16]

Johnson was furious that his goodwill visit had been subverted. He had wanted to be portrayed as the face of American generosity and charm while visiting "slums, villages, depressed areas, etc."[17] He complained to Ambassador Labouisse about the interview Ted Kennedy had given Elias, published in the *Athens Daily Post* only days before his arrival.[18] Johnson saw this as one more part of a plot orchestrated by Bobby Kennedy to undermine him as Vice President and dump him from the ticket in 1964.[19]

Johnson grossly overreacted. Elias had been looking for good stories that would contribute to his journalistic celebrity, not to embarrass Johnson. If any-thing, given Ambassador Briggs's dark warning about the attorney general's hos-tility toward him in the Arleigh Burke incident, Elias was predisposed toward Johnson in his feud with Bobby Kennedy. But facts did not get in the way of Johnson's pique. He refused to meet with any opposition leaders, permitting Karamanlis to have Johnson's ear without challenge. The Vice President re-turned to Washington, telling the President: "We cannot allow ... Karamanlis to fall before an irresponsible opposition because of our termination of defense support."[20] Elias's request to interview the Vice President during his Athens visit was denied.

Elias continued to stir the pot of Greek-American relations. On the day Johnson left for Rome, he published another interview he'd conducted in Washington over the summer with the conservative presidential hopeful, Sen-ator Barry Goldwater.[21] He'd asked the Arizona Republican about rumors that the US had interfered in the last Greek election. Goldwater replied, "A careful investigation should be carried out on those accusations against our embassy role in Athens. I would certainly hope," he continued, "that free elections would prevail and no country, including my own, should stick its nose into the business of whom the Greek people want to be their leaders."[22] Labouisse chas-tised Elias for having asked a loaded question of a man "who was unaware of the possible repercussions."[23]

To American intelligence Demetracopoulos was an enigma. He worked for major center-left papers, which supported George Papandreou of the Center Union, but was held in high esteem by leading conservatives.[24] They repeatedly claimed he was taking secret funds from mysterious interests but couldn't find credible evidence to prove anything.

On the troublesome issue of Cyprus, he wasn't pro-*enosis* or anti-*enosis*, but supported "what's best for Cyprus." He sympathized with Greek Cypriots, but wasn't viscerally anti-Turk, and thought the minority should be treated fairly.

Demetracopoulos eschewed partisan labels. He wasn't right of center or left of center, just Elias-centered. And on October 26, Elias P. Demetracopoulos won an Athens press award for the best reporting of 1962.[25]

Elias took full advantage of his membership in the Foreign Press Associa-tion and, according to American public affairs officers, often asked the high-level guest speakers the most trenchant and difficult questions.[26] He delighted in ver-bal combat and showing up his less aggressive colleagues. In Greece in the early

1960s there was much to cover: tensions rising with Cyprus and the Western alliance, signs of a slowing economy, the ending of American economic aid, neglected social services and education—all with about one-third of the national budget committed to defense. Papandreou's uncompromising attacks against the Karamanlis government escalated and eventually included the Crown, which was spending lavishly and getting involved in politics, criticizing Karamanlis yet refusing to dismiss him. The Queen told the CIA station chief it was time for a new government—but not with Papandreou.[27] Meanwhile she grumbled that Karamanlis exhibited bad judgment, was difficult to get along with, and failed to protect the Crown from the opprobrium of the press, which she chastised as "venal and disruptive."

In April 1963, after months of parliamentary debate over tax hikes needed to cover the royal family's ostentatious living expenses and their frequent trips abroad, Queen Frederika decided to make a private visit to London with her daughter Irene for the wedding of her third cousin, Britain's Princess Alexandra. Karamanlis advised her not to go, warning that expected protests would prejudice the more important Greek royal state visit there in July.[28] Although the civil war had ended fourteen years before, there were still about a thousand political prisoners in Greek jails and a similar number in exile.

In London on April 20, Frederika and Irene faced noisy demonstrators outside Claridge's, their swank Mayfair hotel.[29] Trying to leave by a side door, the Queen encountered Betty Bartlett Ampatielos, the Welsh wife of prisoner Antonios Ampatielos, who had been leading a sixteen-year international campaign to free her husband. She tried to present the Queen a petition calling for his release and that of other political prisoners. The royal duo bolted, running into a cul-de-sac where they took refuge and called for help.

The next day, a drizzly Sunday in Athens, was to have featured the First Pacifist Rally, a peace march from Marathon to Athens, echoing the massive four-day international anti-imperialist, anti-capitalist nuclear disarmament protest from Aldermaston to London the week before. But the Greek government banned the demonstration. Protected by his parliamentary immunity, the charismatic doctor Grigorios Lamprakis, a fifty-one-year-old gynecologist, medical professor, celebrated track and field athlete, and Independent-EDA peace activist, marched alone with the same black banner he'd carried at Aldermaston.[30] On April 26, Lamprakis reacted to the international coverage of the Claridge's confrontation by flying to London in the hope of getting Betty Ampatielos an audience with the Queen.[31] He failed, but, on his return, he took the fight to Parliament, raising his profile as one unafraid to champion democratic principles against the Crown and its allies.

Elias knew of Lamprakis's activities and had met him before. He regarded him as a man of accomplishment, strong principles, and integrity, but hopelessly naïve on the issues of nuclear disarmament and the effectiveness of a non-aligned world peace movement. He respected Lamprakis's record of fighting the Axis in World War II, but thought his current battle was even riskier. While Elias doubted the Queen actually said the words attributed to her—"Who will help me to get rid of this man?"[32]—he gathered from his sources that some kind of revenge was on her agenda and that of others who deemed Lamprakis dangerous. After one of the Parliament debates, Elias approached Lamprakis and advised him to be very careful. Lamprakis, who'd been receiving anonymous, menacing telephone calls and letters since London, took the warning in stride.

Elias had spent much of April on trips to France and Germany with five other Greek political editors. When he returned, he focused on preparing articles for the *Herald Tribune* and Greek papers on the coming visit of French President Charles de Gaulle, probing government anxieties that the French leader's remarks could drag Greece into current inter-Allied antagonisms.[33] Several days after de Gaulle left Greece, Elias learned that Lamprakis would be speaking at a major peace rally in Thessaloniki. Lacking any hard evidence, but picking up on rumors, he darkly intuited that Lamprakis might soon be killed. Indeed, as a biographer of Lamprakis later wrote, all the preparations for the event "smelled of a trap, a perfidious attack in the making."[34] The original venue was changed unexpectedly. Hostile crowds outside greeted Lamprakis. En route from his hotel on May 22 at 10:20 p.m., he was smashed on the forehead. In great pain, he delivered his humanistic and idealistic speech, rich in "guileless optimism," warning of the dangers of thermonuclear war, extolling the promise of disarmament, lauding the Aldermaston marchers, claiming portentously peace was something "beautiful to live for . . . and noble to die for."[35]

After Lamprakis left the rally hall on foot, the assassination plot unfolded while police stood by passively.[36] Two right-wing thugs attacked the parliamentarian, one driving a careening three-wheeled delivery van next to him while the other, standing in the back, delivered a devastating blow with an iron bar. Lamprakis never recovered from his coma and died five days later. More than half a million mourners, some carrying placards with the first letter of the Greek word *Zei* ("He lives!"), came to his funeral in Athens. This was the real-life incident fictionalized by Costa-Gavras in his 1969 Oscar-winning movie *Z*.

For the next three years, Thessaloniki's chief examining magistrate Christos Sartzetakis and four prosecutors tried to get at the truth, to expose the conspiracy—the connections between local police and a military cabal—and punish those responsible for the assassination. However, they were stymied by more powerful authorities who blocked their efforts, restricted their resources, erected a wall of silence, and protected the masterminds.[37] The trial ended on December 30, 1966, with the conspirators largely unscathed and the murderers treated as if involved only in a random traffic accident. After the junta took over in 1967, Sartzetakis and his prosecutors were jailed. Those implicated in the murder were exonerated.[38]

Elias was not one of the three reporters who doggedly investigated the Lamprakis assassination, disclosing sinister facts.[39] It wasn't his beat. But the gruesome murder prompted him to deepen his resolve in piecing together fragmentary details about right-wing military members of IDEA and EENA and their alleged plots. Sometimes he'd privately share his concerns with American and Greek officials, but he never used his information as part of a published article. It's unclear whether he knew anything specifically about the Lamprakis conspiracy or shared it with the frustrated prosecutors. Late in life, Elias said he believed that IDEA/EENA and their paramilitary accomplices bore ultimate responsibility for the parliamentarian's death. Undoubtedly, the assassination and failure to prosecute spotlighted the fragility of Greek democracy and animated Elias's emerging center-left sentiments.

■

IN LATE MAY, the newspaper *Thessaloniki* carried another Elias exclusive interview with an American military official that enraged Secretary of State Dean Rusk.[40] He fired off a "Confidential Message" advising all NATO diplomatic posts and military branches to boycott Demetracopoulos and copied "P. Salinger/ White House." Like others during the Kennedy years, Rusk was making sure that Salinger spread the CIA misinformation to other members of the Kennedy White House and its political team, including Kenny O'Donnell, Joe Napolitan, Malcolm Kilduff, and Larry O'Brien. Demetracopoulos had been warned about how skilled the Kennedys were at getting even.

Rosemary Rorick, a top staffer for freshman Indiana senator Vance Hartke, was an important conduit. Her boss, interested in Greece and NATO, had befriended Elias and sought ways to help him. The wife of Assistant White House Press Secretary Kilduff, Rorick alerted Elias to Salinger's personal attacks. She repeatedly told Elias about White House comments disparaging him, including after the Admiral Anderson–McNamara confrontation and Rusk's NATO-wide boycott message. Elias appreciated the intel, but was stubborn and self-confident enough to believe that trouble went with the territory of being an aggressive, independent journalist.

Anticipating his return to the United States in the late summer of 1963, Demetracopoulos wrote to Edward R. Murrow, then director of the USIA, for help in setting up interviews through the submission of written questions to Defense Secretary Robert McNamara, assistant secretary of state for Near Eastern and South Asian Affairs Phillips Talbot and, most ironically, Assistant Defense Secretary Arthur Sylvester. Murrow's executive assistant, Reed Harris, gave Elias a discouraging response, but at the same time sent a sharp rebuke to the State Department for its anti-Demetracopoulos messages.[41] Harris, who had personally felt the sting of Senator Joseph McCarthy's red-baiting tactics in the 1950s,[42] chided his colleagues for being outplayed by "an astute journalist, very skillful in asking penetrating and often embarrassing questions." To him, occasional political uproars because Elias "chooses times when his articles will sell widely" were not legitimate grounds for discrimination. Harris explained:

> Demetracopoulos writes a series of penetrating questions, submits them to the official concerned several days in advance, then receives the answers orally or in writing. When he obtains the answers orally, he asks that a stenographer be present. In the end, he always obtains the answers in written form signed by the official or the stenographer. This is certainly a careful and ethical way to proceed. If our officials are not careful enough or well enough informed to answer in accordance with U.S. policy, they need not answer; but when they do answer, there is hardly a legitimate reason for complaint when the journalist publishes the interview at [a] time when it will sell best.
>
> [State] has been unable to supply me with any examples of use of the question and answers "out of context" . . . [O]ur State Department people especially seem to be rather afraid of him and they fall back on exaggerations to support their requests that he be denied the kind of access to officials which he seeks.[43]

Harris's, however, was a lonely voice. More typical reaction to gripes about Demetracopoulos was the classified message CIA director McCone sent to unidentified recipients on November 13, 1963: "State pressing for any substantive derog[atory] data which c[a]n be utilized to deny subj[ect] any subsequent entry to the US."[44]

■

ELIAS INTERVIEWED ADMIRAL Burke again in August 1963. As Jack Anderson observed, the retired admiral was "emerging as the most articulate conservative critic of the Kennedy Administration's military policies," and many Republicans were urging him to run for the 1964 presidential nomination.[45] Burke had served with Robert Kennedy and General Maxwell Taylor on the investigation of the 1961 Cuba debacle, and, contrary to his earlier opinions of them, "had nothing but disdain for President Kennedy and his 'bagman' at the Department of Defense, McNamara."[46] In the interview, Burke declared bluntly that the armed forces had had nothing to do with the disastrous Bay of Pigs invasion, and implied that the CIA was solely to blame.[47] This was still major news because, despite disclosures, the CIA wanted to downplay its extensive role in covert operations, and Kennedy was probably nervous about the incident becoming a campaign issue.

In late August, responding to Elias's comments to him about the *Washington Star* firing, Admiral Burke arranged for Elias to have a one-on-one talk with former CIA director Allen Dulles—the original source of his problems—at Dulles's Washington, D.C. home. The early September conversation was brief and cordial, with Elias recounting the suspicious trail of perceived CIA abuses and Dulles confirming the Agency's role, but not his own involvement, in the *Time* and *Herald Tribune* affairs. Dulles promised to "look into" the *Star* matter, about which he claimed to have no knowledge.

A few days later, upon *Washington Post* editor Russell Wiggins's strong recommendation, Managing Editor Fred Friendly named Elias the *Post*'s special correspondent in Greece—only to have *Post* foreign editor Philip Foisie, brother-in-law of Secretary of State Dean Rusk, revoke the agreement on September 17, 1963.[48] Friendly later told Elias that pressure from the White House and his "alleged problems" with the CIA had cost him this job. On September 18, Elias phoned Dulles, who told him: "Look, you got your *Herald Tribune* job back. That's enough. Don't be greedy. It's too greedy to want to represent two US papers."

That summer, Elias stayed again at the Fairfax and complained to Louise Gore about intelligence-community surveillance and his belief that someone had accessed his room without permission and gone through some of his stacked files. Louise thought her friend was unnecessarily anxious but agreed to help test for wiretaps that may have been placed on his phone. He made prearranged calls to her at certain times, making cryptic references. Afterward, Louise told Elias that a friend, Frank Sheridan of the CIA, mentioned he'd heard from sources (presumably the FBI) disclosing the "planted" information. Sheridan warned her to stay away.

■

IN THE WAKE of the Lamprakis assassination, Karamanlis advised King Paul that the planned royal state visit to London in July 1963 should be postponed. The prime minister feared more attacks like the ones the Queen had faced in April, and further trouble from the British Parliament. Not wanting to appear pressured by the left, the royal couple rebuffed the recommendation. Karamanlis resigned, anticipating that the King would call new elections and confident that he would be victorious. A State Department assessment, believing Karamanlis's resignation had increased his appeal, concurred in this forecast.[49]

The monarchs went to London and the expected demonstrations took place. Most were protesting the continued incarceration of civil war political prisoners. Some demonstrators came with philosopher Bertrand Russell and his ban-the-bomb peace activist followers. Labour Party leader Harold Wilson and Deputy Leader George Brown boycotted the welcoming banquet. Queen Elizabeth was booed for associating with her cousin, Queen Frederika, who was also castigated by some for her past membership in a branch of the Hitler Youth movement.[50]

The King had set November 3, 1963, as the date for new elections. Center Union party leader George Papandreou, who hadn't stopped running since his 1961 defeat, was ready with his attacks. After time away in Zurich and Paris, Karamanlis returned to Athens on September 29 to resume his electoral campaign as the head of ERE. That season, Elias published two major stories that had a significant impact on the election.

The first was a relaxed interview he had conducted with Barry Goldwater in mid-August during his Washington trip, a follow-up to the interview from a year earlier. The conversation, transcribed by Goldwater's office, covered a wide range of international and domestic issues, including Goldwater's apprehension over the Test Ban Treaty, skepticism over a NATO multilateral nuclear force, unconcern over the treatment of Negroes affecting the US image abroad, and high praise for "one of my closest friends" Tom Pappas, a leading Republican Party fundraiser, who, after success in the food business, was trying to build a second fortune as a Greek industrialist.[51]

Elias held publication until the Greek campaign was on full boil. Then, on October 13, the *Athens Daily Post* published the interview as a full front-page story, along with a photograph of the two men talking under the headline: "The Next American President?" In the ten-page transcript were the senator's answers to some questions on Greek affairs, which might have seemed benign to an American audience. In one section, Goldwater responded forcefully to a question asking if a dictatorship might solve Greece's problems by declaring: "I am against the establishment of a dictatorship anyplace . . . Oh, Lord, no. Greece is the most sophisticated civilized country in the world. Our democratic way of government came from Greece . . . It would be tragic if Greece, where democracy itself was first founded, were to go back to dictatorship. I can't even imagine the Greeks thinking about it."[52] So close to an election, these remarks took on a different tone, and within the Greek political arena, this answer could be interpreted as veiled criticism of Karamanlis.

The interview included a follow-up to a question Elias had asked Goldwater the year before. "What has been the result of your US investigation into accusations by the Greek nationalistic parties against the role of the American Embassy in Athens during the last elections, and generally how do you feel about the question of free elections in a democratic society?" Though allowing how he hadn't seen the "final results of the investigation about alleged US favoritism shown in the 1961 election," Goldwater added, "We must take all necessary steps that this will not happen again . . . I certainly hope that the next elections will be absolutely free and that our embassy over there this time will stay completely neutral and out of them."[53]

Elias had drawn blood. Publication of this and Elias's other exclusive interviews, according to the State Department, had the net effect of raising the troublesome issue of American intervention in Greek politics. Elias had also injected questions regarding possible Yugoslav and Bulgarian designs on Macedonia, the answers to which exacerbated the long-festering Macedonia issue. Other Center Union–slanted newspapers used Elias's articles to imply that the Karamanlis government had mishandled the country's foreign affairs.

For his second blockbuster, on Sunday, October 20, 1963, Elias disclosed in all three of his publications the full text of a confidential aide-memoire on US assistance matters sent to the Greek government on August 7. It outlined Washington's thinking on the scope and nature of military and economic assistance the US proposed to offer Greece after 1964 and had been personally approved by the President. Coupled with it was a "top secret" report prepared by American economist Richard Westebbe, who was serving as executive director of the Foreign Trade Administration of the Greek Ministry of Commerce, a vestige of the Marshall Plan that exercised great influence over major government procurements. Entitled "Background notes for discussion in Washington," it had been prepared for the Greek minister of coordination's recent visit.

Elias received his copy, in Greek, from a source in the Greek government and prepared an English-language version for the *Athens Daily Post*. Concerned that such a report be both authentic and translated correctly, he called a surprised Westebbe and told him what he was planning to publish, but that he first wanted Westebbe to verify the documents and his translation. Westebbe was a longtime friend of Andreas Papandreou and a fellow Harvard economist. He willingly complied, over dinner at now-divorced Persa Metaxas's place.[54]

Ambassador Labouisse called it a "further bombshell."[55] Even competing papers gave the news front-page coverage, with *Eleftheria* headlining: "Americans discontinue all aid and demand increase of defense expenditures at expense of budget, fruits of Papaligouras mission to Washington."[56] The Center Union candidates and their supporting press hammered away at the idea that the Karamanlis government had failed to represent Greece adequately in negotiations and that the "discontinuance" of aid was the result of ERE consistently boasting about Greece's prosperity. As Ambassador Labouisse scrambled to prepare a response, he worried in a confidential memorandum to the secretary of state about what else Elias might publish: "This series of mischievous and irresponsible articles . . . may well influence election results."[57] On November 3, Papandreou's liberal Center Union party won a narrow victory, earning a 42 percent plurality and 138 seats. The ERE conservatives won 132 seats. The far-left EDA, with 28 seats, held the balance of power. This was not the ERE victory predicted by the CIA in its "top secret" analysis.[58] A November 10 article in the *Los Angeles Times* declared "Goldwater Linked to Greek Premier's Fall."[59] The *Washington Post* amplified this the next day on page one: "Taped Goldwater Interview Proves Factor in Upsetting Caramanlis [sic]," explaining that the senator had "unwittingly" helped change the expected outcome of "one of NATO's most right-wing regimes."[60] An American observer commented, "Beware Greeks bearing tape recorders."[61]

The Center Union victory, while personally pleasing, was a secondary matter to Elias. He was ecstatic that, in such a close election, his work might have tipped the result. Papandreou, not wanting to form a minority government dependent on Communist and far left support, resigned, gambling on a new election. On February 16, 1964, his party won a decisive victory—an absolute majority with 171 seats.[62] A new era in Greek politics had arrived. But, Elias wondered, how long could it last?

■

ELIAS'S GOLDWATER INTERVIEW had also provoked a sarcastic remark at Kennedy's last press conference before Dallas. On October 31, in response to a reporter's question about the undeclared candidacy of GOP frontrunner Barry Goldwater, Kennedy jested that it would be "unfair" to assess the Arizona senator's presidential prospects because he "has had a busy week selling TVA . . . suggesting that military commanders overseas be permitted to use nuclear weapons . . . [and] involving himself in the Greek elections."[63] The room erupted in laughter, but a week later many in Athens found the quip anything but funny.

News of Kennedy's assassination shocked Elias. He reacted "sadly and horribly" and waited in the long line to sign the memorial book at the US Embassy. But he had never embraced the Camelot myth: if he had had to give Kennedy a grade as President, it would have been a charitable "incomplete." Elias believed that "JFK was convinced, until the day he died in Dallas, that Burke and I were involved in a conspiracy against the Kennedys. In no way was that ever true."

The day after the Greek election, Phillips Talbot, the head the State Department's Bureau of Near East Affairs, circulated a confidential memorandum with secret attachments seeking to deny Demetracopoulos future entry into the United States.[64] Among the recipients was Pierre Salinger.

14.

The Koumparos and the Star Reporter

I N THE GREEK ORTHODOX FAITH, a *koumparos* is the best man at the wedding who becomes the godfather to the first-born or all the children of the marriage. In business and politics, he is the leader who cements and wields his power through the provision of patronage and favors. Tom Pappas was proud to be a koumparos. To some he was a benevolent godfather figure, opening doors of opportunity to fellow Greeks and Greek-Americans. He was the civic-minded, public-spirited, generous philanthropist. He was the fixer providing much needed cash, advice, and connections to an expansive network of beneficiaries, reaching well beyond his ethnic or village kin to the highest reaches of political power in Greece and America. To others he was a manipulative, ruthless, and cunning operator, a braggart, robber baron, an amoral or immoral power-hungry narcissist.

Born Antonios Papadopoulos on October 24, 1899 in the village of Filiatra, in the Western Peloponnesian region of Messinia, near the Ionian coast, Thomas Anthony Pappas emigrated to Boston with his parents in 1903. The family, which later included a brother and two sisters, lived in an apartment in working-class Somerville, Massachusetts.

He first worked for nothing in the corner grocery store his father, Konstantinos, ran in Boston's gritty North End, where poor immigrants from Eastern and Southern Europe lived in a world of congested tenements, coarse coal soot, and manure-pocked streets. His first job was selling newspapers for pennies. Later his father paid him fifty cents a week.

Little is known of Tom Pappas's childhood other than his driving ambition, eager participation in all parts of the family business, and steadfast devotion to his church. While his younger brother John attended public and private schools, college and law school, Tom was tutored privately by a neighbor, then took night classes at Northeastern and Boston Universities to hone his business skills. In 1916, after taking over C. Pappas Co. Inc., his father's import-export operation and a small grocery, he steadily grew the business into a chain of thirty neighborhood food stores, then forty-nine supermarkets, which he sold in 1954. Along the way he converted the operation from one servicing retail stores into a leading food- and liquor-importing and distribution business.[1]

The interlocking businesses, operating under the names of C. Pappas Company, Gloria Food Stores, and Suffolk Grocery Company, did well from the start. But the accelerant for his early success was the cache of alcoholic beverages he stockpiled before Prohibition, along with his skill at securing additional inventory during the dry years. The brothers reportedly lost nearly $2,000,000 (more than $27 million in today's dollars) in the Wall Street crash, and saw much of their fortune destroyed, but they treated it as merely a "temporary annoyance."[2] Embracing the attitude that they "always get what [they] want," their business recovered and flourished better than ever.[3]

Pappas kept his Greek citizenship when he became an American citizen in 1924. This dual connection proved invaluable when he diversified into shipping and built an empire in overseas investments during the 1950s and 1960s. The brothers Pappas saw community and political participation as essential ingredients to successfully growing their core business before branching into real estate and horse racing. In politics, Tom Pappas cultivated relationships with Republicans. His brother John became an active and quite conservative Democrat, rewarded in his twenties with a part-time political appointment that allowed him the lifetime honor of being called "judge."[4] For decades the brothers hosted weekly private luncheons in a back room at their company warehouse in South Boston.[5] Later their expanded Summer Street corporate headquarters included a dining room that could accommodate two dozen politicians, public officials, lobbyists, and favored journalists for good fellowship and lavish two-to-three-hour midday meals of Greek food and alcoholic beverages. Smoke from fine cigars hung in the air. Political gossip and insider business information were always on the menu.

Participants came from both political parties. Republican President Dwight Eisenhower was probably the top draw. But the place was also a favorite hangout for Democrat John McCormack, Speaker of the US House of Representatives, whenever he returned to Boston. Wisconsin Senator Joseph McCarthy visited several times during his spectacular rise and fall, as did Senators Leverett Saltonstall from Massachusetts and Styles Bridges from New Hampshire. In the 1960s and 1970s, the Nixon crowd came too.

The brothers served on for-profit boards that furthered their strategic business interests. Tom also joined non-profits, serving not only as board member, but also as trustee, chairman, president, and fund-drive leader for a diverse group of organizations, especially the Greek Orthodox Church. To some organizations, Tom Pappas was known as a "ten-percenter." This meant he would typically pledge large amounts at big public charitable events, get his photo taken for the accompanying newspaper story praising his generosity. Then, when the organization tried to collect, he would play hard to get, finally donating only 10 percent of his original pledge. A business partner recalled another trick Pappas would pull at fundraising events: forcefully advocating a particular cause and immediately writing a large check on its behalf. Announcing his contribution with great fanfare, he would then publicly pressure others to do the same. At the end of the evening, while the organizers were tallying their haul, Pappas would quietly take back his check.[6]

Tom worked his way up the ranks of the Massachusetts Republican Party and attended his first national convention as a delegate to the 1944 Republican Convention in Chicago. At the 1948 Convention in Philadelphia he met and bonded with thirty-five-year-old freshman California congressman Richard Nixon, sharing stories of growing up with fathers who operated small grocery stores. Moving to a national stage in 1952, Pappas became a state chairman of Citizens for Eisenhower and joined the Republican National Finance Committee. Tom worked hard, and during the next eight years was rewarded for his fundraising successes. Soon Vice President Richard M. Nixon became simply "Dick."

Not long after the inauguration in 1953, Pappas arranged to bring business associates to the White House and federal agencies, demonstrating his access and clout. He also met during the day, privately, with the President for "off the record" meetings and in evenings at White House stag parties.[7] He was a guest at state dinners, providing Eisenhower a steady stream of personal gifts, solicitous notes and telegrams, and fundraising opportunities.[8]

Just as brother John was known as "The Judge," Tom was deferentially referred to as "The Ambassador," often erroneously thought of as having served as United States Ambassador to Greece.[9] The reality is something else. Shortly after the Eisenhower inauguration, Tom Pappas's friends in the new administration sought to make him ambassador to Greece, but FBI background checks revealed some unsavory aspects of his past, including tax delinquencies and underworld gambling connections.[10] The most odious revelations concerned Pappas's time as the chairman of the World War II Greek War Relief campaign, from which he funneled charitable funds to pet Republican causes.[11] Pappas probably would have had enough White House support to overcome these damaging FBI reports except that, during the frenzied anti-Communist atmosphere of the time, other uncorroborated misinformation found its way into his FBI file that confused him with a same-named supporter of a Greek umbrella group monitored by Senator Joe McCarthy's committee for its Communist activities.[12] That was enough to derail his nomination.

Pappas continued to be a White House presence, and in February 1955, Eisenhower aides wrote to Secretary of State John Foster Dulles that the President would appreciate the Secretary's "willingness to consider Pappas for some embassy."[13] Within days, Pappas was appointed "special ambassador" to Uruguay in connection with the second-term inaugural ceremonies of President Luis Batlle Berres, scheduled for two weeks later in Montevideo. This brief March trip gave him the right to be called "ambassador" for the rest of his life, although Uruguay was hardly an area of business interest to him.

Eisenhower's heart attack in late September 1955 shocked the nation and caused the convalescing President to consider replacing Nixon on his reelection ticket with someone he believed had the gravitas to be Commander in Chief.[14] Tom Pappas joined a group of Republican regulars who appreciated Nixon's red-meat rhetoric and were outraged at the idea of Eisenhower distancing himself from his vice president. When Eisenhower ran unopposed in the New Hampshire presidential primary of 1956, Pappas and his allies organized and funded a stealth write-in campaign for Richard Nixon instead.[15] Pappas continued to block various efforts to "Dump Nixon," even one at the convention that would have replaced him with a longtime Pappas ally, Massachusetts governor Chris-tian Herter.[16] He also convinced his brother to work for a Democrats-for-Nixon group.

■

THE PRESIDENTIAL ELECTION year of 1960 dawned optimistically for Tom Pappas and Richard Nixon. "Dick" sent "Tom" a note thanking him for his expression of friendship and gushing over the "generous supply of pistachio nuts."[17] Pappas offered to do all he could to ensure victory and underwrote the cost of sending copies of Nixon's book, *The Challenges We Face*, to all delegates at the Republi-can National Convention.[18] He involved his friend Spyros Skouras, president of 20th Century Fox, in the production of a flattering campaign film biography. He hosted a major fundraiser. But in November his candidate lost to John F. Kennedy.

At the beginning of 1961, Pappas was invited to join the series of meetings concerning Nixon's future.[19] He supported his move to New York and plans to practice law. Pappas stayed in regular communication with Nixon during his wilderness years, urging him, for example, to defend his movie mogul buddy Skouras against the Hollywood 10 blacklisting lawsuit brought by "those 10 Communist lawyers."[20]

Throughout Richard Nixon's career, he made use of clandestine contribu-tions, though when exposed, they would plague him. Eisenhower almost dropped Nixon from the ticket in 1952 because of his history of cultivating sleazy financial connections.[21] Disclosure of a deceptive $205,000 loan from ty-coon Howard Hughes in 1956 played a decisive role in Nixon's 1960 defeat.

Over the years, Nixon acquired many wealthy patrons, but few proved as longstanding, powerful, and steadfast as Thomas Anthony Pappas. In the early 1960s, however, Pappas's primary focus was his own investment opportunities in Greece. Recent changes in Greek law designed to attract foreign investment provided Pappas with an opening. The Greek economy was booming. At the time, Shell and Mobil were the dominant oil-producing multinationals in the country, with BP, Fina, and Caltex lagging behind, and the otherwise mighty Standard Oil of New Jersey (Esso) on the outside looking in. According to a for-mer Esso executive, his company "never could develop the government relations that were essential to the issuance of the permits that were required."[22] That all changed in 1962, when Esso Executive Vice President Bill Stott turned to his fellow Republican and friend Tom Pappas. Aware of Pappas's frustrated goals,

Stott proposed a strategic alliance, asserting: "You're going to get us into Greece."[23] Pappas took the $166-million challenge, pulled the necessary strings, and made the right payoffs. His reward was an equity interest in a new venture called Esso-Pappas—the first time an individual had received equal billing with Esso.

It was not a simple transaction. Prime Minister Karamanlis wanted Serres, his hometown prefecture, in the Macedonian region of northern Greece, to be a substantial beneficiary of the investment. In exchange for his approval, he demanded that Pappas build not only a large-scale oil refinery, but a chemical plant and a company to promote local interests. He also wanted a fertilizer plant and a mill to produce rolling steel, all located in Thessaloniki. It was this ambitious overreach that had caused other potential refinery developers, such as Aristotle Onassis and Stavros Niarchos, to back out of the competition.

While working on the Esso deal, Pappas was also developing parallel interests in shipping, a tomato-paste plant, and the establishment of a Greek Coca-Cola operation. To him, if not Esso, these different deals were mutually reinforcing.

In return for accepting Prime Minister Karamanlis's conditions, Pappas demanded sweetheart contracts heavily weighted in the company's favor. Karamanlis readily acceded, but for years the deal was hotly debated in Parliament and in the Greek press. Its supporters trumpeted what was described as a $200-million investment that would create as many as 7,000 jobs. At the same time George Papandreou excoriated the transaction as "colonialist exploitation," giving Pappas exclusive monopoly rights to twenty-nine products plus the right to supply oil to Greece at prices well above market value.[24]

When Papandreou and his Center Union Party mounted their challenge to Karamanlis in 1963, they made this "colonial treaty" giveaway a leading issue and pledged to revise the agreements as a campaign promise. It helped Papandreou win the election. Taking charge in 1964, the new prime minister brought in a foreign consulting firm that confirmed the grossly inflated price of the crude oil Pappas was selling and a long list of monopolies he controlled on synthetic products.[25] The next step was assembling a renegotiation team of Andreas Papandreou, his father's chief economic advisor; George Mavros, a moderate member of the Center Union Party (and longtime Demetracopoulos friend); and Richard Westebbe, the American head of the Greek Foreign Trade Administration (and a reliable Demetracopoulos source).[26]

The negotiating triumvirate sought five revisions, all of which reduced the power of Pappas in the Greek economy.[27] The Greek-American tycoon tried to parry the government demands, dragging out the conversation as he sought ways to avoid giving in, recalled Westebbe. But in the end Pappas blinked. Mavros had used Pappas's desire to have the King and Queen participate in his highly publicized cornerstone-laying celebration as a "lever to get the last concessions from Pappas in the revised contract. He paid a heavy price," Westebbe reflected.[28]

Pappas was delighted by the large turnout and all the praise heaped on him at the ceremony but quietly seethed at the outcome of the negotiations. Shortly thereafter, he stepped up his hiring of personnel with American Embassy experience, including former covert CIA operatives. He also added employees from his ancestral village and took a closer look at Greek politics. He didn't sweat the political details himself, instead hiring those who did. He was always ready to make generous cash payments to smooth his way. This Esso setback, he made clear, was only one battle in an ongoing war, which he intended to win.

●

THERE WAS NO question on which side Elias Demetracopoulos stood in the struggle between Tom Pappas and the Papandreou regime. Elias thought George Papandreou's two-year "relentless struggle" campaign had been melodramatic, but politically effective. Now the elder statesman had to deliver, not just give stirring speeches. Elias looked favorably on the Center Union's Keynesian reformist economic agenda and the reorientation of domestic policies to further education and public health and increase social services, even if the agenda risked being inflationary. The new government programs were shaped in no small part by the prime minister's son Andreas, whose years in American academia brought him personally close to New Frontier insiders in Washington and, like them, advocated a "liberal awakening."[29] He entered politics in 1964, first winning his father's old seat in parliament and then getting appointed by his father as "minister to the prime minister." Elias was not close to Andreas, but regarded George Papandreou with fondness and respect, unlike many US Embassy officials, who snickered that he was a an old "fool."[30]

Elias's positive sentiments toward George were reciprocated. On March 18, 1964, the Papandreou government cancelled Karamanlis's 1960 order declaring Elias persona non grata, calling it a "violation of press freedom and our democratic regime."[31] Greek ambassadors around the world were instructed to provide the journalist "every possible assistance."[32] Elias took advantage of these courtesies to travel more broadly, taking trips underwritten by non-Communist foreign governments and corporations. At home, the Papandreou team granted him access, even as the American Embassy did not. It gave him clout, which he didn't hesitate to use to his advantage.

Demetracopoulos boasted that he was one of the journalists who had brought about the fall of the Karamanlis government and now had appreciative high-level connections. Modesty was not his strong suit, and he had an exasperating habit of overselling himself, even to friends: talking with notables at a cocktail reception over canapés might become "dining together," for instance. Nevertheless, all of Elias's exaggerations had a credible basis in fact, which greatly annoyed his enemies. Privately, American officials refused to call him a "phoney [sic]," especially compared to his "generally irresponsible" press colleagues, and described him as "one of the most able newspapermen of this area" who relied on a network of "excellent sources."[33]

Elias's three newspapers each provided him different benefits. Liberal *Makedonia*, his longest-standing relationship, extended his national reputation to the north and provided him his largest expense account. At his center-left English-language *Athens Daily Post*, with the smallest general circulation, he could write whatever he wanted and knew it would be read regularly by embassy officials and others in the American community. The widely read and respected *Ethnos* (Nation), founded in 1913 to be the leading republican voice, was his primary journalistic outlet. All three papers had endorsed the Center Union, and Demetracopoulos's pieces were frequently supportive of government policies. When Papandreou opponents tried to undermine his economic plans by claiming that only buying gold and hoarding sovereigns could save their life savings from disaster, Elias wrote lengthy articles designed to calm the fears of panicked bank depositors and help stabilize the drachma.[34]

In April 1964, when the visiting Greek-American publishers of *Greek Heritage* requested an interview with the prime minister to discuss the Cyprus issue, Papandreou's office asked Elias to handle it, telling the publishers that Demetracopoulos was an "official political counselor of the prime minister."[35] A bitter CIA accused him of having used unexplained "devious means" to "work his way into the good graces of Prime Minister Papandreou."[36]

Elias often sparred with the American Embassy about its perceived hostility to the Papandreous, especially Andreas. In May, he was instrumental in publicizing a confrontation between Andreas and Vincent Joyce, the US public-affairs officer, over Voice of America broadcasts.[37] Joyce also had had several clashes with Elias. However, when *Ethnos* published a harsh editorial that included a gratuitous attack on Joyce's Turkish wife, Elias sharply opposed the provocation, earning Joyce's thanks.[38] Nevertheless, after Joyce was told by the Greek government to leave the country, word passed on the street that Elias had the clout to "get" anyone. Elias, who continually refined his knack of working all sides, never publicly clarified the facts of the Joyce episode, encouraging an air of mystery, even danger.

Demetracopoulos was not, however, a Papandreou government toady. He made headlines when he disclosed efforts of Lockheed and Northrop to bribe Greek officials to win military sales contracts. In the face of planned cuts in Greek military spending and renewed communal violence in Cyprus, he urged increased support for the navy, arguing that any Turkish invasion of the island would come by sea.

Elias would often say that Andreas's self-centered approach to building his own political base put the Center Union Party's reformist agenda at risk. He also acknowledged the effectiveness of opposition charges against Andreas's personal integrity and did not defend Andreas when he became involved in a sex and financial scandal.[39]

Elias's primary commitment was getting good stories with less concern for partisan consequences. In November, 1964 a mine exploded, killing thirteen and wounding fifty-one, during an anniversary picnic honoring Greek resistance veterans of the 1942 ELAS-British commando operation who blew up the Gorgopotamos railroad bridge to interdict German supply lines.[40] Although it seemed to be just a tragic accident involving ordnance left over from that war or the civil war, Greek leftists wanted to make it into something sinister. The next August, *Ethnos* called Elias early one morning to tell him they'd received a copy of a letter purportedly sent by US Army attaché O. K. Marshall to Washington, taking credit for the success of the American-led secret operation.

Other papers also had copies of the same document, and Elias did not want to be scooped. It was an obvious forgery, and both Greek and US governments did not want the press to grab the bait and make more of it than it was. Other papers hesitated. Elias, believing the forgery itself newsworthy, pushed the US Embassy to issue a formal statement denouncing the forgery, which *Ethnos* printed in a special edition, along with the forged letter.

The government denounced the *Ethnos* publication as a "deliberate effort to disturb Greek-American relations."[41] Rightist newspapers speculated that the bomb had been set off by Communists, and leftist publications bruited CIA involvement. Radio Free Greece in Bulgaria also got involved, using Elias's reporting for its propaganda. With Elias developing new angles to replay the story, the controversy continued for months, boosting *Ethnos*'s circulation and management praise for their star reporter.

■

PAPANDREOU'S VICTORY IN 1964 was not the only dramatic change that year. King Paul died in March, shortly after swearing in the new prime minister. His charming 23-year-old son, known more for his convertible sports car and 1960 Olympics yachting gold medal, assumed the throne as King Constantine II, and moved up his marriage to Princess Anne-Marie of Denmark. When Elias flew to Copenhagen to cover pre-nuptial ceremonies, he warned Danish officials about the Queen Mother and her influence over her son. Demetracopoulos also criticized the US Embassy's policy of letting the CIA be the prime interlocutor with the Palace. A majority of Greeks were republican, he said, and siding with the royal family put the United States on the wrong side of history. The embassy shot back, chastising *Ethnos* for its "anti-American policy."

That same year, Elias returned to Washington. Admiral Burke and General Quinn had successfully convinced CIA director John McCone to meet with the journalist privately. It was an unsatisfactory encounter in which Elias angrily complained about the CIA being "out to get him."[42] Naturally, McCone denied there was any evidence to support the charges. Afterward, at a black-tie Georgetown dinner given on December 10, 1964, by Greek ambassador Alexandros Matsas, Robert Komer, then Deputy National Security Advisor and former CIA liaison officer with the White House, approached Demetracopoulos and asked: "What's your price? Everybody has a price." Demetracopoulos, not knowing whether this might be a reference to the McCone meeting, a cryptic second offer to work with the CIA, or something else, tersely replied: "The truth."

Komer told Elias, "Go fuck yourself," and walked away.

■

INITIALLY, THE PAPANDREOU government reform agenda created an atmosphere of national optimism. Political prisoners were released. The hated certificates of national probity were no longer impediments to getting jobs or benefits. Efforts were made to curtail the unbridled influence of the CIA.[43] Those in the military who'd been identified as being involved in recent right-wing coup plots were not arrested but were scattered to more remote postings.[44]

For a while it seemed that George Papandreou might have effectively co-opted the Palace.[45] After years of criticizing the Queen's overspending, the prime minister increased the royal budget. And for the sensitive post of defense minister he selected General Petros Garoufalias, a wealthy beer baron popular with the King, though of uncertain loyalty to the prime minister.[46]

Each of Papandreou's liberalizing actions disrupted entrenched relationships. Cutting the military budget 10 percent to provide social funding and planning to replace Army officers committed to the old regime with those loyal to the Papandreou government met fierce resistance from the military and its conservative allies.

One of those who sought to exploit these fissures for his own ends was dual citizen Tom Pappas, always seeking a business advantage. Described by his former managers as "a chameleon, with a keen instinct for survival and, ultimately, dominance," who could "play the side that he thought was best suited to the situation," he delighted in being known as the "the inside fixer." However, his public persona as generous paterfamilias clashed with the ugly realities of his private life. The devout church lay leader fought often with his wife and his only child. He acted abusively toward Bessie, his spouse of more than three decades, and mercilessly hectored Charles for not demonstrating the academic prowess or business ambition that he demanded.[47]

During the early 1960s, Pappas spent increasing time away from Boston, setting up opulent residences in Athens at the Grand Bretagne and the Hilton, with an escape villa in suburban Kiffisia. He cultivated the image of a hard-driving bon vivant, a perpetual-motion machine making deals by day and entertaining beautiful women at night. He was not discreet in his extramarital relationships. As his businesses flourished and blue-and-white Esso-Pappas service station signs spread throughout the country, some Greeks faulted Pappas for being an overbearing "Ugly American" and sarcastically mispronounced Esso-Pappas as "Hesso-Pappas," slang for "shitty-Pappas." When the joke crossed the pond, one who took to using the expression with her friends was his wife, the refined but beleaguered Bessie Pappas.

Pappas was omnivorous in his political largesse. To assure his success, he boasted about funding competing candidates to make sure he would maintain his influence no matter the winner. Travelling in a big American car with cash in hand, he was a regular visitor to Peloponnesian villages and other strongholds, identified by his minions as worthwhile targets. With an assortment of hugs, kisses, backslaps, and playful pinches, he bestowed *koumparos* blessings and sowed the seeds of *rousfeti*, expensive political favors that must be repaid.[48]

Pappas's patronage found fertile ground among the old-line forces who bitterly opposed the Papandreou center-left agenda. According to a secret CIA intelligence cable, King Constantine began plotting a coup to get rid of Papandreou as early as January 1965.[49] He planned to "exert pressure on, but not flatly ask" for the prime minister's resignation as early as the end of February. The tipping point, according to Constantine, was the new law requesting the resignation of about 60 percent of the captains and majors in the gendarmerie. Constantine feared that if he waited beyond the winter of 1965, Papandreou would have attained sufficient strength in the military, police, and government to resist a demand for his resignation. The King planned to force the prime minister's hand by attacking his son with a press campaign to "destroy" Andreas's image, while distancing himself from any blame if the attack failed.[50]

In February, before the King acted, Papandreou presented to Parliament the findings of an official inquiry into allegations of fraud in the 1961 elections and misuse of a NATO defense program, the "Pericles Plan." Striking back, the rightist opposition attacked the government for weakening the nation's defense and aiding Communists, then advanced a conspiracy theory that targeted Andreas. Driving the right's attack were allegations that a cabal of Greek intelligence officers stationed in Cyprus, led by Andreas Papandreou, were plotting to take over the army, jettison the constitution, and create a Nasserite or Communist dictatorship. The group in question was Aspida ("Shield"), an acronym for "Officers, Save the Fatherland, Ideals, Democracy and Meritocracy." This small group of about two dozen reform-minded army officers and politicians was politically sympathetic to Andreas. Defense minister Garoufalias endorsed the conspiracy theory and took it to the King.

The charges were absurd, as was demonstrated when the case eventually came to trial.[51] The Palace and Parliament presented no credible evidence that Andreas was the mastermind of Aspida, but targeting Andreas served the King's purpose well. George, with a parliamentary majority and popular support, had reckoned that the King and his advisors would not want to raise the specter of a constitutional crisis or the "national schism" that had torn the country apart half a century earlier, as this would put the monarchy itself at risk. But he misjudged the depth of animosity he'd stirred among longtime members of his own coalition who were jealous that their own desire for power was being thwarted by a father's desire to promote his ambitious son.

In May, the prime minister told the King to dismiss Garoufalias and a list of officers. The King refused, and Garoufalias would not leave voluntarily. George Papandreou then named himself defense minister, an appointment the King rejected, claiming it would interfere with the investigation of Aspida and Andreas.

On July 15 Papandreou announced he would resign, in anticipation of new elections. Constantine accepted the resignation without even waiting for it to be formally tendered. Instead of calling for new balloting, which Papandreou was expected to win, the King meddled directly, cobbling together a coalition government from the existing parliament, trying to unite ERE conservatives and Center Union defectors who became known as "Apostates" or renegades. Enough new ministerial posts were created to provide one for every defector.[52] An outraged George Papandreou accused the monarch of unconstitutional interference and prepared to lead another "unrelenting struggle." Massive crowds of demonstrators took to the streets shouting, "The King reigns, but the People rule."[53]

The showdown between the King and George Papandreou gave Tom Pappas openings for revenge and a route back to greater power. Richard Barham, a controversial State Department diplomat thought to be a covert CIA agent, went to work at Esso-Pappas, where he allegedly played an important role.[54] After several failed attempts, enough politicians eager to be "purchased pure and simple," often with funds from Pappas, gave the Apostate-infused coalition a tiny governing majority.[55]

Over the next year and beyond, would-be prime ministers attempted to form viable coalitions and struggled to govern. Pappas was especially frustrated with the instability. "I had to buy four governments in five years to get the [Esso-Pappas] deal going," he later complained.[56]

During the rule of the Apostates, Elias did not write about Pappas's activities but criticized the United States in a variety of articles, notably for its role in the resignation of Papandreou. He distinguished between the State Department, which he said was "opposed to a coup d'etat," and the CIA, which supported political intervention by Greek military officers and whose views "hold sway."[57] The American Embassy objected that Elias's articles were an attempt to make the United States the scapegoat. The embassy explained to Washington that *Ethnos* was considered a house organ of Andreas Papandreou and that Elias's articles paralleled the position of Margaret Papandreou, Andreas's wife, with whom Elias reportedly met frequently.[58]

■

THOUGH HE COMPLAINED about the instability of the Greek government, Tom Pappas took full advantage of the political chaos. He returned to Washington as needed to nurture contacts and make sure that the pipeline of federal support for his projects remained open. With his brother John working their Democratic connections, the Pappases did not suffer while Republicans remained out of power. John Pappas was made part of the US delegation to the funeral of King Paul. Tom was a regular at diplomatic receptions and big events in Athens, especially when prominent visiting Americans such as Jackie Kennedy arrived. Fellow Bostonian John McCormack arranged an "off-record" private meeting in March 1966 at the White House for Tom with President Johnson.[59]

Construction of the $200,000,000 Esso-Pappas oil refinery and steel and chemical industrial complex was completed in early 1966, using mostly American funds. Thousands, including leading politicians and other notables, attended the opening ceremony, described as "the largest public-relations event in modern Greek history."[60] The royal family came, this time without the impediment of a liberal Greek government, to sit under a canopy on two gold thrones.

Pappas, however, was the true center of attention. His easy access to the movers and shakers on both sides of the Atlantic enhanced his image, and he was never shy about letting Greeks know how high his connections ran, although some dismissed his intimations as braggadocio. He indicated that some of his executives were or had been on the CIA payroll, and said he planned to recruit more. At least one of his non-profit foundations was used as a CIA front, and he explained his CIA relationships to a Greek newspaper as part of his pride "to do all I can for my country."[61] Rumors of a military takeover didn't disturb Tom Pappas. To the contrary, he welcomed one, expecting it to be orchestrated by the King and his generals.

The political stalemate in Greece worried Elias. After reporting trips to European capitals and visits to Lisbon, Angola, and other parts of Southern Africa as a guest of the Portuguese government, he wanted to return to Washington to explore American attitudes toward the changing situation in Greece. He also thought he should expand his trip on account of the US escalation in Vietnam, which he had not yet experienced first-hand.

His papers liked the idea of a world trip by their star reporter but didn't want him to run up travel expenses where he couldn't confirm advance appointments. So, he accepted a long-standing invitation from the Japanese government to visit Tokyo as its guest and interview economic and political leaders. He arranged to have meetings in Hong Kong en route. But when he tried to schedule meetings in Vietnam with Ambassador Henry Cabot Lodge as well as US and South Vietnamese generals, the State Department blocked him.[62] They also blocked meetings he tried to set up in Bangkok and elsewhere and closely monitored his travels, although careful surveillance did not prevent the CIA from reporting erroneously on his schedule.

Interest in Elias was as strong as ever. On March 14, 1966, Elias's old nemesis Tom Karamessines, then deputy director of plans at the CIA, sent a memorandum to the CIA director warning about Elias's planned stay in Washington. A SECRET March 17 message from the US Embassy's public-affairs officer to USIA headquarters in Washington offered strategies on how best to handle Elias on the upcoming trip to Washington and fretted that he might not leave by June 1 "but ... stay ... indefinitely."[63]

Elias's four-month American trip of 1966 involved more than just business. In some circles, he was becoming a celebrity. When he arrived from Asia in April, friends in Los Angeles honored him with a black-tie dinner attended by Hollywood stars and entertainers like Dinah Shore and Ed Sullivan, actresses Virna Lisi and Mona Freeman, and actor Hugh O'Brien.[64] But a dark shadow continued to follow him.

A Los Angeles attorney with connections to US intelligence warned Elias that Pierre Salinger was spreading vicious lies about him. After leaving the West Coast, Elias also heard from one of his hosts, Nancy Jackson, that her friend Pierre had not only been aghast that she was going to visit Elias on her upcoming trip to Greece but claimed that Demetracopoulos "works for the other side."[65] When Jackson protested, Salinger promised to show her intelligence reports (which never materialized). Why, Elias wondered, was Salinger continuing to traduce him, even now, long after he was out of the White House? Was there no statute of limitations to Kennedy vendettas?

In D.C., much of Elias's time involved "wining, dining, and interviewing" a score of American senators, cabinet members, high-ranking US policymakers, and other important personalities, despite efforts to block him from exclusives. Some of the common themes in the interviews provoked sharp commentary back home: American notables expressing the wish that Queen Mother Frederika would lend her influence to come up with a democratic solution to the domestic political crisis, criticism of the Greek government's non-settlement of pre-war debt, references to the CIA being an invisible government, and warnings about the dangers of a dictatorship in Greece. Washington sent an urgent request to Athens to get copies of the *Athens Daily Post* series "as soon as possible." According to the State Department, the deprecations of the Queen Mother raised a "storm of protest" and caused her and King Constantine "considerable embarrassment [*sic*]."

·

ACCORDING TO AMERICAN intelligence reports, tracking his US visit, Demetracopoulos this year "had some of his finest hours."[66] Elias would have agreed. He enjoyed summertime in Washington, staying at the Fairfax, expanding his Georgetown circle of friends and news sources, and spending hours with Louise Gore. They dined regularly at local restaurants, and she invited him to black-tie parties and informal family gatherings at her Marwood estate.[67] In 1966, Elias's Republican Party friend was deeply involved in the hotly contested governor's race in Maryland. Louise Gore knew Spiro Agnew from his early years as Baltimore County commissioner and later rise in Maryland politics. He sought her out when considering his run for the state's top job, and she encouraged his fellow Greek-American Tom Pappas to become his leading contributor.

Louise took Elias to fundraisers to meet and talk with Agnew. Her candidate was running in a three-man race. When contrasted with the others, especially the Democrat George Mahoney, who was campaigning as a dog-whistle racist, Agnew came across as moderate, even liberal, in spite of using tough law-and-order rhetoric after riots in Baltimore. Given the alternatives, Agnew was the clear progressive choice, and both the *Baltimore Sun* and the *New York Times* endorsed him.

At six-foot-two and over 200 pounds, bullet-headed, with a stiff posture exaggerated by inserting extra-large shoulder pads into his suit jackets, Agnew stood out at gatherings. Elias remembered the candidate's ready smile, firm handshake, and distinctive cologne, choosing not to probe behind the affable exterior. He paid small attention to rumors about Agnew's being a wheeler-dealer in the world of Baltimore County public contracts. Compared to other political figures he had known, Agnew's transgressions sounded penny-ante.

After meeting the gubernatorial candidate, Elias spoke positively about his fellow ethnic Greek, albeit one who couldn't speak the mother tongue and was an Episcopalian to boot. When he returned to Athens, he talked up the promise of Agnew's candidacy. When he heard that Agnew had won the governorship, Elias was happiest most for his friend Louise, who had worked hard and long for the victory.

Elias didn't see Pappas at any Agnew campaign events, but in conversations he often heard the name. When Elias interviewed John McCormack that summer about "the prospects of future United States–Greek economic cooperation," the House Speaker repeatedly cited the Esso-Pappas project and "the great contribution" and "leadership" of his friend and "former Ambassador."[68] The new refinery "would create a virtuous circle," McCormack said, "which would avoid any anti-democratic dictatorship."[69] Elias, who knew the backstory about the Pappas contract, said nothing.

Later in the year, when the American Embassy contacted Senate Foreign Affairs Committee member Vance Hartke to discuss his fact-finding Athens itinerary, they learned that all of Hartke's arrangements were being made by Elias Demetracopoulos. And when Hartke and his traveling companion, columnist Eliot Janeway, arrived in October, Demetracopoulos greeted them at the airport "in conspicuously cordial fashion, attached himself to them and stayed with them throughout virtually all of their Athens visit."

Janeway's articles harshly criticized Johnson Administration policies in Greece and praised Elias for warning about the growing risks of an antidemocratic putsch,[70] prompting Vice President Hubert Humphrey to mediate a dispute between Janeway and President Johnson. In less than a year, these players would engage again over the fate of Elias Demetracopoulos.

15.

From Reporter to Activist

AT THE END OF 1966, Elias watched the Apostates-controlled government fall apart. King Constantine appointed a caretaker government under the deputy governor of the National Bank of Greece to last until Spring elections, but, faced with partisan gridlock, the governor resigned.

The right wanted to bring charges of high treason against Andreas Papandreou for his alleged role in Aspida once the dissolution of parliament removed his immunity as deputy. Kanellopoulos, who considered the attack on Andreas baseless, nevertheless opposed extending the protective immunity period. With no one willing to compromise, the stalemate continued, as did sporadic strikes and demonstrations. On April 3, the King appointed Kanellopoulos to form a coalition government. Unable to do so, he dissolved parliament and called for elections on May 28, 1967.

Athens was awash in Stygian rumors. From the chic cafés of Kolonaki to boisterous tavernas outside Athens, citizens angrily debated the preferred direction for their country. Provocative newspaper headlines and outrageous editorials inflamed passions; some supported—or were resigned to—a military intervention. As if scripted by classical Greek playwrights, the principal actors assumed roles that would lead inexorably to tragedy. The often-ill-advised King was aware that free and fair elections would likely restore the Center Union to power with an even stronger role for Andreas, whom he feared as a gateway to

Communist control and the destruction of the monarchy. He told *New York Times* columnist C. L. Sulzberger that "he would act by any means to save the nation from disaster."[1]

Constantine discussed with his generals the implementation of a NATO contingency plan, code-named Prometheus, designed to repel Communist aggression, reassert control, and eliminate leftist subversives in the event of an invasion from one of Greece's northern Balkan neighbors. National Defense Chief General Grigorios Spantidakis and his high-ranking officers prepared a plan but decided to wait for the May election results before acting.

Constantine, meanwhile, vacillated. As winter turned into spring, he seemed more inclined to try to influence the electoral outcome so as to produce a "unity coalition" that would include more conservative members of the Center Union. Constantine talked with Philips Talbot, who had become US Ambassador to Greece in October 1965. Talbot approved a CIA plan for a "limited covert action" to achieve the desired political outcome and sent it to Washington.[2] There, on two occasions in March, the 303 Committee, in charge of overseeing covert actions, discussed intelligence reports on pro-dictatorship coup planning and the electoral alternative.[3]

The 303 Committee included representatives of the National Security Council, CIA, State Department, Defense Department, and White House. It had been set up to stop the spread of Communism outside the Communist bloc, and had supported American intervention in Chile in 1964 and in Brazil and the Dominican Republic in 1965. It would approve more than 300 covert operations during the Kennedy and Johnson administrations. In Greece, however, they took a pass, fearing that the political risks outweighed the security benefits. According to one recollection, a high administration official said: "Maybe we should let the Greeks try a military dictatorship; nothing else seems to work over there."[4] Secretary of State Dean Rusk likely had Tom and John Pappas in mind when he suggested: "If the dual national Greek-Americans are concerned about the prospects and if 200 to 300 thousand dollars will make the difference, they should have no trouble raising that sum themselves."[5] Johnson's national security advisor, Walt Rostow observed: "I hope you understand, gentlemen, that what we have concluded here, or rather have failed to conclude, makes the future course of events in Greece inevitable."[6]

In March, Ambassador Talbot confirmed to Washington the existence of an inchoate "junta" involving Queen Mother Frederika, dismissed defense chief

General Garoufalias, former ERE foreign minister Panagiotis Pipinelis, and retired General Dovas, who were all urging Constantine to suspend the constitution and impose a royal dictatorship.[7] The American ambassador downplayed its
significance as well as that of reports of another and more potentially serious
army cabal that would later be known as the unexecuted Generals' Coup. Constantine asked Talbot about Washington's attitude to an extra-parliamentary
solution. The ambassador hedged, replying that it would be negative in principle,
"but would depend on circumstances at the time."[8] Washington was more concerned about Vietnam.

ERE's Kanellopoulos was in a difficult position. A principled conservative,
he believed in an enduring parliamentary democracy, even if that meant a Center Union victory in May. Unable to control the army, having only tepid support
from the Palace and the conservative press, he was resigned to Karamanlis controlling their party from his self-exile in Paris.

Karamanlis got into the act. After advising the King that he would not return to Greece unless Constantine imposed martial law, Karamanlis flew to
New York to lobby retired Supreme Allied Commander General Lauris Norstad
to push for US support for a coup d'état that would put Karamanlis in charge of
a conservative government. Norstad declined to help.[9]

George Papandreou had other problems. In March, CIA polling pointed to
further ERE erosion and a Center Union victory, with an even larger majority
than in 1964 as long as Andreas attracted support from EDA left-wing candidates. But the Center Union coalition was deeply divided, with more-moderate
members furious at Andreas's increasingly divisive rhetoric and afraid of his
"evil influence" in a new government. Outside observers feared an inconclusive
outcome that would only prolong Greece's instability.

Greek political leaders muddled on, apparently unconcerned that their in-
transigence could have dangerous consequences. Andreas publicly "ridiculed"
the idea of a military takeover.[10] Margaret, his American-born wife, believed that,
if the King could not prevent a coup, the US would intervene to stop it.[11] Some
party leaders, though publicly dismissive of conspiratorial gossip, betrayed their
discomfort with the charged atmosphere in private. Andreas, for all his bravado,
was sufficiently concerned about his safety to start sleeping away from his house.[12]

■

ELIAS TOOK ON a role as a self-appointed guardian of democracy. He assembled
the articles he had prepared from Washington interviews the year before into a

slim compilation, *The Threat of Dictatorship.* In the book's preface, prepared in March 1967, he explained that the authoritarian threat had always been present in Greek politics, more so since the July 1965 removal of Papandreou, and that unscrupulous politicians had used such fears to blackmail voters into supporting them to prevent an anti-democratic alternative. Speculation in Greece that the United States secretly backed a military coup and dictatorship had prompted him to interview a variety of high-ranking American officials across the political spectrum in summer 1966 on the subject of Greece. From Republican presidential nominee Senator Barry Goldwater to Democratic House Speaker John McCormack to top generals and admirals, he found all strongly and unequivocally supportive of free elections and opposed to a military junta. Elias, friendly with both Panagiotis Kanellopoulos and George Papandreou, hoped to squelch rumors.

Notwithstanding these reassuring statements, Demetracopoulos continued to track new indicators of brewing conspiracies. Most serious speculation saw the driving force for a possible coup coming from the Palace and high-echelon generals. Elias, however, was also looking in a different direction. In his effort to reform the army, George Papandreou had scattered some former targets of Elias's concern to posts in Cyprus and northern Greece. By mid-1966, Elias learned from his army sources that some of these conspiratorial EENA true believers, having completed their outside tours, had been assigned to command positions back in Athens. He didn't have access to the detailed intelligence gathered by the Americans, but he learned that a group of officers including Ioannidis, Ladas, Roufogalis, and Papadopoulos, people he had heard of since his early investigations into IDEA, were soon to be well-placed within the KYP, the military police, and battalion commands.[13]

His information came confidentially, on deep background, and since he could not get confirmation elsewhere he didn't write about it. Instead he suggested to friends like Mavros and Kanellopoulos that the source of real trouble might not be connected to the Palace or the generals, but an alternative lower-level military group. He tried doing the same with Norbert Anschutz, the second in command at the American Embassy, but embassy attitudes toward him were so negative that it was useless. Anschutz would later discuss receiving similar information from a right-wing parliamentarian and former member of "X," Nick Farmakis. He, however, was deemed so unreliable that the tip was never passed on to Washington.[14]

The only serious discussion Elias had on this with any American was in

Washington during a summer 1966 lunch with Charlios "Charlie" Lagoudakis, a veteran Greek-American analyst in the Department of Intelligence and Research within the State Department. Lagoudakis was privy to all the reports prepared by State, Defense, the CIA, and NSA, and he wasn't about to share classified secrets with Elias. But the two men discussed the difficulties of sifting legitimate intelligence from unverifiable rumor. They agreed that sometimes the coup that occurs is "the one you don't know about," and he reassured Demetracopoulos that the reporter's EENA tracking was a legitimate focus.

Lagoudakis, unbeknownst to Elias, had been doing the same thing. For two years, he'd monitored and distilled CIA field reports about the band of lieutenant-colonel conspirators, called "Rightist Greek Military Conspiratorial Group."[15] He'd identified individuals, their histories, and coup chatter. George Papadopoulos, for example, had said in December 1966 that once a dictatorship was established it would seek US support in order to implement social and economic measures that could sway the present tendency toward the left. But after January 19, 1967, Lagoudakis's information about the group dried up. It was as if they'd gone off the grid. On February 6, Lagoudakis sent an urgent request to the CIA and the embassy's political section for "discreet inquiries." He wrote again but received no reply.

It was a warning sign, like the dog that didn't bark in the night. Elias telephoned Lagoudakis several times long-distance in early 1967, but the analyst didn't return the calls, perhaps because of State Department anti-Elias warnings. When Demetracopoulos tried to probe his EENA colonels' coup theory with others in Greece, they largely dismissed it.

Elias was in regular contact with several of the King's advisors, Greek intelligence, and IDEA-connected military officers, and retired KYP director Natsinas. Natsinas told him nothing of value. He also talked often to his longstanding and usually reliable source, retired General Dovas, who was a member of the Queen Mother's "junta" and perhaps knew about any Papadopoulos connection to the Palace.[16] Dovas considered Andreas an outright Communist and told Elias that if he were looking at lowly colonels he was looking in the wrong direction. Any extra-parliamentary action, he maintained, would come from higher up.

■

ON THURSDAY MORNING, April 20, 1967, Elias arose even earlier than usual, unable to sleep. Almost twenty-six years earlier to the day, German tanks had rolled into Athens as the Axis completed its invasion of Greece and the occupation began. Fresh and disturbing childhood images of that time interrupted his sleep and felt like a premonition.

For a busy journalist, it was a normal day. While foreign tourists, the city's cosmopolitan elite, and the King and Queen sought refuge from that afternoon's heat at the Hilton's swimming pool, Elias read some reports, made telephone calls, listened to radio news, had a business luncheon, and met some contacts for upcoming stories. His publisher called to tell him that *The Threat of Dictatorship* was being readied for distribution to local bookstores. In the afternoon he received a call from one of his unnamed sources, telling him "There's movement." No details, just an intimation that something significant might be underway.

Early that evening, Elias dressed for a cocktail reception at the stately Kolonaki home of Virginia Tsouderou, daughter of a former governor of the Bank of Greece and late prime minister who had led the Greek government in exile during the World War II. It was a lovely soirée, with drinks and hors d'oeuvres passed among the Athens intelligentsia and high society. Amid the genial chatter, someone asked Elias, who was nursing a ginger ale, to predict the outcome of the balloting scheduled for May 28. Others turned around to hear the reply. Elias said, with a touch of sadness, "Not only do I see the election not happening, but something very bad will happen very soon . . ."

There was stunned silence. George Papandreou was scheduled to open his campaign with a large rally in Thessaloniki in a couple of days, and Kanellopoulos's kickoff was also the coming weekend. Elias was known to have access to all significant players. Pressed to clarify his ominous pronouncement, he indicated with a slight wave of the hand that he didn't want to go any further. The evening continued, but his remark left a perceptible chill in the air.

Nearing midnight, Elias departed to join friends at his uncle's popular Café Bokolas on Voulis Street in the heart of Athens. He was to meet Persa Metaxas, along with Mario Modiano, Athens bureau chief for the *Times* of London, and Modiano's wife, Inci. The two women were there already, but Mario was working on deadline to finish a long article and would come later.

As he arrived, Demetracopoulos was accosted by friends who challenged him to do more to assure that fair elections would take place. John Pesmazoglou, deputy governor of the Central Bank of Greece, and his elegant wife, Miranda, had been at the same party earlier. They told him that he should stop his jeremiads and become an engaged reformer. He thanked them for their advice. However, he still believed that activism was not the proper role for a serious journalist.

As his group talked and slowly ordered food, the mysterious telephone tip from that afternoon weighed on him.

Elias registered what he imagined were changes in normal street sounds and the late-night traffic flow, but nothing seemed to justify his anxiety. Nevertheless, some form of sixth sense had kicked in. He told the others that they should not wait for Mario, should not even finish their meals. He feared that something was about to happen, and they should all leave immediately.

The trio scattered.[17] Persa went directly home. Inci Modiano left for the news bureau to join her husband, where they would be well placed to report on the unfolding story. As for Elias, he reasoned that, if there were to be some kind of coup, he might be targeted. It would not be wise to go home or to his father's place or to any of his newspaper offices. But where to hide? It was after 1 a.m. Nearby, people chattered, laughed, and licked ice cream cones.

At about 1:30 a.m., tanks rolled into Athens following the same route that the Germans used in 1941, passing the dark and silent US Embassy on the way to the Parliament building. At *Kathimerini*, Eleni Vlachou and her late shift were closing for the night when "the first phone calls came, asking what was happening; why so many tanks were around; why officers were stopping cars, ordering pedestrians about, taking over from the police. No one had any answers . . ."[18] The military started arresting people about 2 a.m., the prearranged hour for the strike, and cut phones an hour later.

The dragnet targeted thousands, including editors connected to centrist and leftist publications. Later that night—decades after the Nazis had invaded the house on Dafnomili Street—soldiers again searched Elias's childhood home. They achieved nothing other than scaring his father. For some unknown reason, they did not proceed to his current apartment on nearby Dimokritou Street, where Elias had returned from the restaurant, but went off to look for others in their haphazard roundup. Elias didn't hear the rumbling of tanks in the night. His phone was dead. Martial music and announcements blaring from the radio were his first signs that something had happened.

Early in the morning, Persa rushed over in a panic, fearful that they had taken Elias away. With a touch of swagger, he assured her that he was fine and wouldn't be intimidated by a dictatorship, the leadership and goals of which were as yet unknown. He told her that he might go into hiding and be gone for some time, but he would not give her any details. She needed to have absolute deniability.

In late morning, with phones still down, Elias took a less than ten-minute walk from his apartment to the German Embassy on Loukianou Street, where he was to have a long-scheduled lunch with German Ambassador Oscar Schlitter. The streets around Kolonaki Square were uncomfortably quiet.

Oskar Schlitter was a sixty-two-year-old career diplomat who had begun his foreign service in 1929. To advance his career, he joined the Nazi Party in 1934, served under Ambassador Joachim von Ribbentrop in London, and during the war worked mainly as a counselor at headquarters in Berlin. After the war, he was interrogated at Nuremburg, cleared, and then retired to his farm. He returned to the Foreign Service in 1952, posted to Madrid and then London. In 1964, he was appointed Ambassador to Greece. Elias claimed that if the Bonn government was prepared to send Schlitter to Athens as its representative, knowing all Greece had suffered, he was prepared to give him the benefit of the doubt. He found the ambassador a "serious" professional not given to pretentions, pettiness, and gossip. He met with him often. Over time, Schlitter became one of his closest friends in the diplomatic corps, as well as a reliable source. The friendship extended to Schlitter's whole family, including his wife, Daisy, and their two children.

Over a long luncheon in Schlitter's dark-paneled office decorated with family heirlooms, they discussed the implications of the coup, and the likely crackdown on the press, which could limit, if not stop, Elias from earning a livelihood. Leaning forward, the tall, heavyset ambassador paused and quietly said, "If you ever need to get out of the country, to a place of asylum, I would make the necessary arrangements." Elias thanked him for the unsolicited offer.

After leaving the German Embassy, Elias had second thoughts about the safety of staying in his own apartment. The Papandreous, he'd been told, had been arrested, and some people claimed that Elias was their "mouthpiece." His old friend Kanellopoulos had been arrested as well. Elias's book critical of a dictatorship had just been published, and he'd spent years making enemies. Most importantly, if the coup leaders were part of EENA, his repeated alerts about the danger they posed might put a target on his back. In any event, he was sure he could reduce his risks by staying with a remote friend or relative. He decided to go unannounced to his older cousin, Spyros Handrinos, whom he had saved from the Communists in December 1944.

Spyros lived in Koliatsou Square, about twenty minutes from Elias's normal sphere of activity. He readily took in Elias, saying he could stay as long as needed.

But Spyros was not master of his household. By the next morning his wife, Maritsa, expressed her discomfort at having Elias around. But with rumors of more than 10,000 arrests, Elias feared returning home. He largely kept to his room.

Over several days, Maritsa made clear that she thought Elias was putting the family in danger. She was particularly concerned that Spyros might lose his job as a hospital administrator. Both were afraid that their neighbors would say something, and she convinced him that their house was being watched. By midweek his cousin told Elias that Maritsa wanted him gone immediately. Spyros confessed that he had acceded to her wishes, though he did not want to dump his cousin out on the street. Elias did not argue, and Spyros arranged to have someone drive Elias north to the suburb of Kiffisia before the weekend. It was the last time the cousins would see each other.

Elias's next safe house had been arranged by Daisy Schlitter, the wife of the German ambassador. It was an exquisite mansion on an old tree-lined street, owned by the family of Mary-Louise Karayannopoulou, the Swiss-born proprietress of Delicieux, perhaps the finest confectionery and chocolatier in the country. Her Kolonaki shop had a small restaurant on top that was a gathering place for the city's social and business elites. It was unlikely that the house, home to Mary Louise's parents, would be targeted by the junta. Elias stayed for about a month, while Mary Louise and a few of her friends discreetly dropped by to bring journals, newspapers, mail, and updates on the real and imagined happenings. Censorship of the press had begun. Persa was told he was safe, but he refused to contact her or let her visit, for her own protection.

Daisy was his most regular visitor. Her husband had been careful to remain diplomatically correct in his dealings with the new regime—so much so that it seemed he had no reservations about what had taken place—but Daisy was not at all restrained. Born a baroness in Potsdam in 1913, she had been discovered by movie director G. W. Pabst and featured as "Daisy D'Ora" in several of his silent films. Later she became a celebrated Miss Universe contestant, the toast of Berlin. As such, she was used as the model for blond, blue-eyed, Nordic-Aryan beauty, and uncomfortably required to attend an intimate piano recital featuring Adolf Hitler.[19] Some of Elias's colleagues would later gossip that Demetracopoulos carried on a torrid affair with the older, still strikingly attractive Daisy, using the Kiffisia safehouse as a convenient love nest. Elias angrily denied such charges. To have done so would have violated one of his cardinal rules of chivalry: "Never have an affair with a woman whose husband is your friend."

During his weeks in hiding, Elias learned who was behind the coup, their agenda, and the uncertain prospects ahead. He thought the junta's justification for intervention—allegedly to prevent an imminent Communist takeover—deceitful, their overblown metaphor of Greek democracy as a sick patient needing medical intervention stupid, and their claim to be trustees of morality and Christianity fraudulent. He heard disdainful comments about the small-mindedness and unsophisticated personal histories of the leaders, but Elias wouldn't laugh along with those who ridiculed their apparent incompetence.

The Americans may have initially struggled to identify the players actually in charge, but Elias knew many of them from his earlier investigations, notably colonels Georgios Papadopoulos and Stylianos Pattakos. He was reluctant to admit that he had underestimated their cunning and feared they would use their anti-Communist bona fides to win American support and box in their NATO partners. Elias believed that top leaders in the US Embassy and CIA station may have been genuinely surprised by the coup,[20] but that mid- and lower-level Greek-American intelligence agents were not. For many years it had been US policy not to assign ethnic personnel to sensitive postings in countries of their heritage, but an exception had been made for Greece because of the difficult language. Since World War II, Greek-American intelligence officers had dominated the Athens CIA station and, as oral histories later described, they brought with them or quickly assumed the extreme right-wing values of their KYP counterparts.[21] Elias thought that, at a minimum, these individuals conveniently overlooked what they knew about the conspiring colonels, most of whom didn't speak English.

As the days ticked by without any signs of international pressure on the new government to stand down—no landing of American marines, no counter-move by troops loyal to the King, no reports of any public resistance toward the dictatorship—Elias feared the worst.

Eleven articles of the Constitution had been suspended, but the Greek economy was in good enough shape to weather the initial shock. No immediate price would be paid for the populist measures that had just been announced. They would balloon public debt, but that reckoning lay some years in the future. Meanwhile, Thomas Pappas and others were quick to take advantage of the new government. Immediately after the coup, Pappas told his friends in America about the "stability and efficiency" of the new regime in Athens. According to an Esso-Pappas employee, on the day of the coup, Pappas "didn't know anyone in charge. Within days he was on the first name basis with all of them."[22] His personnel director, Paul Totomis, was appointed minister of public order.[23]

■

CENSORSHIP WAS THE first order of the dictatorship. There was an immediate news blackout. For the first couple of days, no newspaper was published. Three days after the coup, only three of the thirteen political dailies printed editions. When papers appeared on Sunday, April 23, they were "pathetic specimens," all only four pages long, with identical texts announcing government policies, the names of new cabinet members, and the prime minister's message.[24] The regime proclaimed: "We prohibit any announcement, publication of information, or comment that, in any manner, opposes directly or indirectly the regime." The next day the regime printed its fictionalized account of the manifest threat to public order that constitutionally justified imposing a "state of siege." Readers were told that Communist disturbances in Thessaloniki in advance of Papandreou's opening campaign rally had made the coup necessary.

Papers on the left were banned and their files seized. Some editors and journalists were arrested. Others went into hiding. When the authorities couldn't find the publisher of *Eleftheria*, they took his seventy-six-year-old father hostage.[25] Foreign correspondents tried to get their stories out, but often had their cables home interrupted or deleted. Foreign broadcasts provided what passed for local news; foreign newspapers and magazines appeared with stories clipped out. Then foreign editors shifted their attention to the run-up to June's Arab-Israeli Six Day War. Regional correspondents left.

Several days after the coup, Georgios Papadopoulos was appointed minister of the presidency. Over the coming months he consolidated his leadership, becoming minister of national defense and prime minister in December 1967. He ordered Elias's book banned and copies already in bookstores confiscated and destroyed.

After more than a month in hiding and learning that for now he wouldn't be arrested, Elias returned to his flat. It had been broken into, his files and other personal property ransacked. Staying hidden in Kiffisia had likely saved Elias from interrogation, arrest, and possible imprisonment.

Press censorship affected principal as well as principle. *Kathimerini* owner and publisher Eleni Vlachou surprised the junta by asserting that she would not publish her newspapers under a dictatorship that abrogated press freedoms. Decades later, her obituary would call this her "finest hour . . . delivering a devastating blow to any hopes the junta may have entertained of co-opting the constitutional Right."[26] But as she told visiting *New York Times* publisher C. L. Sulzberger days after the coup, "she would lose more money by publishing now than by not publishing. She would get very little advertising as things are, and she [had] no reserve cash. On the other hand, she [had] a large payroll."[27]

Other papers tried to continue, but there were few profiles in courage. Accepting censorship was safer than dealing with the vicissitudes of self-censorship. Elias knew that his editors were palpably afraid of what the junta could do to them and responded accordingly. It was clear what stories wouldn't be accepted.

Briefly, and with difficulty, Elias tried submitting some copy that wouldn't be immediately rejected. He refused to rewrite releases and "notes" provided by the government's Press Control Service. He tried to get an exclusive interview with Richard Nixon when he stopped briefly in Athens on June 21 as part of a larger tour, but he wasn't even permitted to attend the airport press conference. He had better luck providing tips to foreign journalists, like visiting columnist Robert Novak.

Elias's income was immediately hurt. With his book banned, his publisher was unable to pay the promised book advance and royalties on sales. *Ethnos* cut staff and wages. The paper still hadn't paid his expenses for his 1966 articles from Washington and said it would also not be able to pay him for salary arrears owed at the time of the coup. *Ethnos* had been a popular liberal publication, but since it was "politically unwise" to be seen reading it, its circulation dropped more than 50 percent between April and May.[28] By August the paper was bleeding so badly that it decided to declare bankruptcy, but the military regime would not permit it. Instead, it forced the publishers to accept a four-million-drachma loan from the National Bank of Greece to keep publishing and ordered it to accept a government nominee to run things and a right-wing junior reporter as editor. To Elias this meant that an "unethical, sycophantic incompetent" had replaced an editor whom he had considered merely irascible.

Makedonia had more resources but struggled to survive in a difficult environment. Stories were carefully selected to avoid confrontations with the government, which controlled editorials and opinion columns, photographs, headlines, other news copy, and layout. Vellidis, the publisher, continued to pay Elias for articles and maintained much of his expense account, but said he would be cutting back on editorial content and would take far fewer of his stories.

At the *Athens Post*, where Elias had an ownership stake and management interest, the situation soured quickly. His relationship with erstwhile business partner George Skouras, already strained, broke down. Skouras held up monies he owed Elias and, with spineless opportunism, insisted that their centrist-left paper move hard right and embrace the new regime.

Between April and July, Greek newspaper circulation fell 40 percent. There wasn't much difference in the content from one publication to another, and the same news was available on government-controlled radio. Demetracopoulos was largely living off his savings, and some support from his uncle. It was a dispiriting time. His self-image as an independent, fearless newspaperman was challenged by the new realities. The regime made clear that it saw the press as an extension of government. To people who suggested that draconian rules of the junta were only temporary, he replied that he feared that Greece could become another Portugal, where Salazar had ruled unchecked for nearly forty years.

Quite apart from being a journalist, Elias Demetracopoulos was a zealous democrat who supported political freedoms and human rights. He favored an "open society" capable of evolving and adapting to changing circumstances. He believed in robust public debate, compromise, and incremental reform.

He agreed with Churchill's observation that "democracy is the worst form of government, except for all the other forms." Greek democracy in early 1967 was not working well, but neither had fifth-century Athenian democracy. For Elias the essential elements of a functioning democracy were simple: majority rule, with free and fair elections; respect for minority rights; an independent judiciary; and a free press able to investigate and criticize its government. The new regime failed all four tests.

Elias chafed under the restrictive rules.[29] He knew he was being watched and assumed his phone was tapped. When former California governor Edmund G. "Pat" Brown inquired about making a first-hand assessment and publicizing his findings, Elias was noncommittal, telling him "do whatever you think God would tell you to do." Brown came and met openly one evening early in his visit with Elias and Margaret Papandreou in the lounge at the Grand Bretagne Hotel. An eavesdropper, ineffectively hiding behind a newspaper, monitored them.

As Margaret described in her *Nightmare in Athens*:

> I hadn't seen Elias since before the coup, and I was happy to see him
> out and free. He was one of Greece's best liberal writers . . . and had
> important contacts in the United States . . . I pegged him as nobody's
> agent but his own . . .

I wanted desperately to talk to Elias . . . We made a date at the
Hilton bar for the next week, agreeing ahead of time that that if he
didn't show up, I would try again the following week at the same time.
Arrangements for seeing people had become complicated, along with
every phase of daily living. No one wanted to use the telephone, and no
one knew what his personal situation would be in the future.[30]

THIS WAS NOT an environment in which Elias wanted to work. He wanted to
escape but wasn't sure how to do it. In the days that followed, word went around
Athens that Elias wasn't keeping his mouth shut, and that those associating with
him could also be in trouble. Greek officials spied on his meetings with visiting
journalists, friends, and sources. The American Embassy and the Athens CIA
station also monitored his words and activities.[31]

The challenge put to him the night of the coup by the Pesmazoglous rang in
his ears: that he be a positive agent for change, not just a reporter of society's
failings; that he summon the spirit of his teenage self, the one that had led him to
risk his life to fight fascism in his homeland. Now that foreign demon had been
replaced by a homegrown evil. It was time to join the resistance. This time, however, whether driven by hubris or his own brand of *philotimo*, he did not want
merely to follow others. He wanted to lead.

Over the summer, Elias confided in his friend Jean Back, the UN's representative in Athens, that he was trying to find a way to get out of Greece. He wanted
to fight to restore democracy from outside his country. Back suggested that a
good exit strategy might be through a United Nations invitation to an international conference. He asked Elias, "Do you want us to get you an invitation to
represent the Greek press at a meeting in Warsaw this September?" He was
talking about that year's UN's Editors' Roundtable.[32]

"The conference itself is not the important part," he told Elias, and on August 5 the anxious Greek journalist received a formal invitation from United Nations headquarters in New York. The UN would pay participants round-trip air
travel, economy class, and $12 per diem. That was the easy part. Now, how to
obtain the necessary "special security exit" permit? He turned to his lawyer, who
made an appointment to see Colonel Georgios Papadopoulos, now firmly in
charge, to try to get permission for Elias to leave. The meeting was brief. The
answer: "Absolutely not."

Elias's lawyer next approached Colonel Nikolaos Makarezos, the third horseman of the troika responsible for the coup and regarded as the most reasonable of the group. Formerly in military intelligence and now minister for economic coordination, he handled the country's finances. In his office, Makarezos took the carrot approach. He said they'd let Elias go to the conference if he agreed to say positive things about the junta or at least stayed neutral at the Warsaw conference; if he played nice, he could even be rewarded with an ambassadorship to West Germany. The attorney took the offer to Elias, who refused the bargain on the spot.

Elias asked and received from the American Embassy in Athens a letter of introduction to the American Embassy in Warsaw. But beyond that he decided not to ask for any assistance from the US Embassy in either city, because he thought that Ambassador Talbot would be unhelpful. As his situation became more complex, he also became increasingly guarded in speaking to people from the larger American community in Greece.

He quietly settled his affairs. Elias told his attorney that he didn't want the overdue money from *Ethnos* that the attorney had finally obtained by exploiting a provision in the junta's new laws, because acceptance would imply loyalty to the regime.

The most emotionally difficult part of his escape strategy involved saying goodbye to his aging, ill, and blind father. An only child whose mother had died a decade earlier, Elias knew that, if he left Greece, he might never see his father again. He raised the subject at first obliquely, then directly, and, on his father's name day in mid-August, told his father that he was planning to use the UN invitation to get out of the country, and that he did not know what his next step would be. The two men had a long and emotional conversation, more deeply personal than they'd ever had before. His father didn't want him to go but understood that his son had no choice. The only other people he confided in were Persa Metaxas and Daisy Schlitter.

On September 5, the UN publicly announced the Warsaw Roundtable. Elias was listed along with the other regional representatives, journalists from Turkey and Cyprus.[33] On September 7, he received confirmation of his hotel booking. On September 9, he received a letter from a United Nations official regretting "very much" to inform him that "earlier this morning I was notified by the Greek government of their decision to refuse your exit from Greece to Poland."[34]

The news of Elias's blocked exit spread from Athens to Geneva to UN Secretary General U Thant in New York, then back down the pipeline. The UN in

Geneva telegrammed the UN in Athens to "suggest you immediately request Colonel Papadopoulos to intervene, stressing importance granting exit."

When it looked as if the government would let him leave after all, he booked a flight on September 11 to Warsaw. But, after an internal squabble, the dictatorship said no. The UN again intervened, letting the colonels know that this Editor's Roundtable had originally been scheduled for Athens, but had been moved after the coup. Jean Back, who had been furiously cabling his colleagues in Geneva and New York, warned Colonel Makarezos that if Elias weren't permitted to go to Warsaw for another UN conference, its First International Symposium on Industrial Development, scheduled to run from November 29 through December 20, 1967 in Athens, could also be relocated. One hundred thirty-one governments had been invited, and about 800 persons were expected to attend, including representatives from the private sector. The Greek government was seeking foreign investment and public relations benefits from hosting the event and had already invested time and money in providing installations and facilities. The not-so-veiled threat hit a nerve with the Greek official most responsible for the event, and may have tipped the balance between the KYP, which had been adamantly opposed to letting Elias go, and the colonels, who had been vacillating.[35]

Despite ultimately granting permission, the government placed tough restrictions on Elias including a limit of US$200 on money he could take with him and making it difficult even to get through the airport. There, the authorities confiscated his passport (which had a valid US visa stamped in it) and exchanged it for what was in effect a three-day pass to go to Poland and return. It looked as if he'd miss the entire first-day program. As he raced to get to his flight, customs officials and other security forces intentionally and repeatedly delayed him with questions and engaged in debates with each other. It seemed as if the battle between the KYP and the junta continued to the boarding staircase of the plane.

Daisy, who had driven him to the airport, parked and came inside. She didn't want to hide her presence from Greek officials, or her connection to Elias. She wanted to see him off for moral support and also bear witness in the event the government blocked him again. Coincidentally, Colonel Oliver K. Marshall, military attaché to the American Embassy was there too. He later testified: "I observed him for protracted minutes arguing his way past the customs. If ever you saw a man in flight when he got by, it was Mr. Elias Demetracopoulos."[36]

On the plane at last, his mind was a jumble of thoughts. "I'm now out of Greece, but what to do next? Whom to call? And when?" He had no plan.

16.

Escape

ELIAS ARRIVED LATE ON THE first day of the UN Editor's Roundtable conference, carrying a briefcase, a suitcase, and the two hundred dollars he was allowed to take out of the country. The weather was Indian-summer warm, what the Poles call *zlota polska jesien* (the golden Polish autumn), but Elias felt none of its spirit. Warsaw was gray, drab, and impoverished, but at least it wasn't Athens.

The large Grand Hotel in the center of the city was newer than other buildings but fit in with the surrounding Stalinist architecture. The military was less than omnipresent, as it was in Greece, but in his first pass through the hotel lobby he thought he saw a Greek security officer. In the coming days, he spotted no fewer than three plainclothes Greek agents watching him from different vantages and talking to Polish police. They never spoke to him, but each day they locked eyes with him menacingly.

The first night he joined some friends from Cyprus, the BBC, and Italian newspapers in the busy hotel lounge. The bar was reminiscent of something in a Le Carré novel. Run by the Polish police, it offered access to prostitution rings and black-market exchanges to separate foreigners from their coveted hard currency. Elias's mind was elsewhere.

When Demetracopoulos walked into the large conference room the second day of the program, he received a round of applause. Putting on the oversized translation headphones, he considered his next step. The sessions were a blur, the poor sound system making it difficult to follow what was said. It was good to see old friends and meet journalists from around the world who wanted his views on Greece, but Elias was careful to steer conversations away from the personal. During lunch on the last day of the conference, he walked silently past the Greek agents watching him and went to his room. It was time to act.

He didn't want to stay in Poland. His goal was to get to the United States to assume his place in the resistance against the junta. The best stepping-stone might be London, Paris, Rome, or Copenhagen. The more he thought about it, the more he became convinced his "Danish Connection" was worth trying.

Five years earlier, Demetracopoulos had become friends with the Danish Deputy Head of Mission, Hans Severin Moeller. When Cuban stowaways were found aboard a Danish ship en route to Copenhagen from Havana via Athens, Demetracopoulos had written a story at Moeller's request presenting fairly the Danish government's position.[1] After Moeller left, they continued to communicate. At the announcement of the 1963 royal engagement between Danish Princess Anne-Marie and Greek Prince Constantine, Demetracopoulos went to Copenhagen to cover the diplomatic angle. Moeller arranged a private interview with both the foreign minister and prime minister, during which Elias asked about the role of the royal family under Denmark's constitutional monarchy, giving himself an opportunity to discuss candidly the meddlesome role of the Greek Palace and indirectly criticize Queen Frederika in print.

When Prime Minister Jens Otto Krag next visited Athens, he met with Demetracopoulos, telling him he appreciated his candor. The prime minister made a point of suggesting that Elias be in touch "if there is ever anything we can do for you." Remembering this while sitting in his Warsaw hotel room with the conference nearly over, he thought, "What do I have to lose?" He called Copenhagen.

Krag's chief of staff told him that the prime minister was in the middle of an important cabinet meeting. Elias insisted: "The matter cannot wait. Please interrupt him now. It's important that the cabinet meeting is taking place right now because what I'm calling about will probably need cabinet approval." The aide interrupted the meeting, and the PM came to the phone. Elias reminded him of their meeting and said, "I'm in Warsaw. Papadopoulos has confiscated my passport. I want to go to America, and I'm having difficulty because I don't have a visa or a legal Greek passport."

Jens Otto Krag had a visceral antipathy to the Greek dictatorship, a distaste that aligned with Danish public opinion.[2] Without hesitation, he told Elias: "Give me the name of the hotel you are staying in and the telephone number. I will call you back . . . and don't leave the hotel until you hear from me." As Elias recalled, "He didn't say what he was going to do. One hour passes. Nothing. Then two hours. It was the longest wait in my life. I was getting extremely nervous. About three or maybe four hours went by. Then, late in the afternoon, there was a knock on my door. 'Who's there?' I asked. From outside a voice replied, 'The Ambassador of Denmark. I've come to take you.'"

The Danish Embassy in Warsaw was tiny and had responsibility for all of Poland, Hungary, and Bulgaria. Its new ambassador, Svend Sandager Jeppesen, had arrived only four months earlier. But Elias was fortunate. Sandager Jeppesen was a battle-tested diplomat, a large man with a strong personality who knew how "to act quickly and decisively without being hamstrung by bureaucratic considerations."[3] Elias opened the door, and the Ambassador continued: "I have personnel with me. We will go as a convoy from the Danish Embassy, including the political consul and other attachés. The secret service of Poland will not dare arrest you if you're protected by the Danish government. And the Greek government has no authority here."

They positioned Elias, briefcase, and suitcase in the middle of a seven-person cluster, with the imposing ambassador in the lead. Together they walked him through the hotel lobby full of departing delegates and seated him in the protocol-honored right rear of the ambassador's car. Danish flags fluttering, the black Mercedes took off, followed by two Volvos: the embassy's white one and a red one driven by the consul. No one stopped them.

Traffic at dusk was relatively light, and for the next twenty to thirty minutes Elias glanced out the window, looking for signs that they'd been followed. They drove down Krucza Street, turned and passed the monstrous Palace of Culture, then turned again near the headquarters of the Warsaw Pact and its military guards. Elias thought fleetingly of Greece. Near their destination, they turned from a broad avenue onto what seemed like a country lane, paved with cobblestones. This led to the ramshackle terminal building at the small Warsaw airport. The ambassador's driver carried Demetracopoulos's luggage inside.

Polish border control was usually a time-consuming affair, as border guards meticulously tried to block any unauthorized Polish citizen from leaving the country. The presence of the Danish diplomats sped things up, but the process still took time. The Danish group had provided his ticket, and stayed with him in the nearly empty terminal, watching carefully during the hour or two before the Scandinavian Airlines flight was to depart. Greek government agents responsible for making sure he returned to Athens were nowhere to be seen. Elias arranged to settle his hotel bill, profusely thanked the ambassador and his diplomatic convoy, climbed the passenger staircase to the aircraft, and took his seat.

Everything about the escape had been carefully arranged.[4] At the Copenhagen airport late that evening he was met by Hans Moeller, then Chief of Protocol of the Foreign Ministry. Moeller took his tired Greek guest to his house in Frederiksberg. Elias exhaled a great sigh of relief, thinking, "A new life is now beginning, because I am really free."

But the next day, as he strolled with his friend in a nearby neighborhood, he reflected on the kaleidoscope of autumn colors on the leafy branches that had looked so drab the night before. They reminded Elias how first impressions could be misleading. His challenges would be complex; the next steps not simple. He had never asked for assistance from Ambassador Talbot in Athens as he felt sure that Talbot would not have helped him. Still, he couldn't imagine that the freedom-loving United States would turn away a self-exiled political refugee trying to escape an oppressive regime. His initial plan was to attend a World Bank meeting in Rio de Janeiro as an invited guest whose expenses would be covered, then proceed to the annual International Monetary Fund–World Bank meetings in Washington. For that he would need both Brazilian and US visas.

Brazil, ruled by a military dictatorship since 1964, quickly approved his visa. When he applied to the American Embassy in Copenhagen, however, the response was not helpful. The junta, furious that Elias had eluded its grasp in Warsaw and now fearful that he would use the United States as a stage from which to attack it, had implored the American Embassy in Athens to prevent his landing on American soil.

To comply with the junta's request, Ambassador Talbot threw gasoline on the anti-Elias sentiments already smoldering on the Greek Desk at Foggy Bottom. On September 19 Talbot sent a telegram to the State Department restating KYP's forceful opposition to Elias's leaving Greece, discouraging the issuance of a visa, and recommending that the Department consult the CIA for data on Demetracopoulos.[5] This was an open invitation to cherry-pick from all the spurious material in his growing dossier. In Washington, the chief of the Greek Desk at the State Department was Daniel Brewster, who, according to columnist Robert Novak, "had tangled with Elias over the years and seemed to enjoy disparaging him." Further, noted Novak, Brewster was "an unabashed friend of the [Greek] colonels"[6] As Brewster would admit years later, the CIA "loved to send in material; . . . it was not vetted, it came back to Washington raw."[7] This meant that all the years of unsubstantiated rumors and outright lies in Elias's files could be weaponized without any quality control.

On September 23, 1967, the telegram to Elias in Copenhagen formally denying his visa application arrived. Hans Moeller commiserated with his friend and told him he could stay with him indefinitely. But Elias did not want to take advantage of his friend's hospitality, and his meager exit money was mostly gone. Whatever his affection for Copenhagen and the Danes, he knew he could be more effective opposing the Greek dictatorship from Washington than from anywhere else in the world.

Preparing to win or go down fighting, he took a yellow legal pad and made a three-page handwritten list of names. The next day he began systematically calling and sending telegrams, seeking help through his more than a decade and a half of American friendships. At first, he did not announce that the State Department had already rejected his application. Typical was the telegram he sent to archconservative Mississippi congressman Mendel Rivers, who had appreciated Elias's staunch defense of Admiral Arleigh Burke.[8]

Urgently request your assistance obtaining immediately entry visa.
Greek regime confiscated regular passport with valid US visa for
attending United Nations Editors Roundtable. Ask State Department.
Advise accordingly. Thanks. Elias Demetracopoulos. Political Editor
Athens Daily Post.

The same message was sent to all shades of Democrats and Republicans, including Speaker of the House John McCormack; liberal New York congressman Emanuel Celler, chairman of the House Judiciary Committee, responsible for immigration matters; and Dixiecrat Strom Thurmond, who had changed from Democrat to staunch Republican.

Telegrams went to businessmen, Wall Street money managers, and representatives of the Federal Reserve and the World Bank, who had invited him to their meetings. He sent other cables and made calls to admirals and generals, friends in the press (including Robert Novak, who had recently met him in Athens), and Frances Howard Humphrey, the younger sister of Vice President Hubert Humphrey, whom Elias had hosted on her trips to Greece. Also included, of course, was Louise Gore.

Return telegrams and telephone calls conveyed offers of help and requests for more clarification, spurring Elias to provide additional details and background. Responses divided roughly into three groups: those who expressed concern and made generalized offers of help; those who offered to help on specifics of his appeal; and those who reported on their efforts to target soft spots susceptible to political pressure. California industrialist, philanthropist, and Democratic Party fundraiser Nat Dumont cabled: "Have contacted Assistant Secretary of State familiar with your situation. Governor Brown extremely helpful among others."[9]

Eliot Janeway's son, Michael, told Elias that his father had received Elias's message while travelling in France, had shown the Demetracopoulos cable to Charles "Chip" Bohlen, the American Ambassador in Paris, and warned Bohlen of the "repercussions" that would follow if the decision were not reversed.[10] Another message indicated that Janeway had also spoken to Vice President Humphrey on Elias's behalf. Eliot Janeway later said that he had also talked directly with President Johnson.

Emanuel Celler helped to fine-tune Elias's non-immigrant visa application. He cabled Elias on September 26 to say: "State Department requires proof you are bona fide non-immigrant. Do you intend return after visit?"[11] Elias's reply: "Intend return Europe after this visit. Can go either Denmark or Germany. Intend to go Denmark where already officially admitted. Since 1951 have visited USA nine times. Although married once to American citizen never tried to obtain US citizenship or residence. Plan return to Greece where my professional, family and economic interests are as soon as it would be safe. Thanks."

Robert Brimberg, head of an eponymous Wall Street brokerage firm, had been hosted by Elias in Athens the year before while accompanying Indiana senator Vance Hartke, telegrammed: "Hartke is working hard on it" and asking on September 27: "Do you need any money?"[12]

The collective pressures worked. Elias believed that, aside from Janeway, his most persuasive advocates were Chairman Celler and former California Governor Pat Brown, two men who knew the President well and could speak his language effectively, regardless of the Demetracopoulos file or who sat on the Greek Desk. President Johnson told Secretary of State Rusk to lift the barrier and let Demetracopoulos in.

On September 28, five days after his official denial, Elias was granted a nonimmigrant visitor's visa. On October 1, 1967, he took a flight to Hamburg and then on to New York. In Hamburg, he met with Marion Schlitter von Cramm, Oskar and Daisy's daughter, who was brokenhearted after a recent divorce. Elias consoled her and told her to call or write him any time. He arrived in the United States, well-groomed and well-dressed, toting leather briefcase and suitcase. He had $67 in his pocket.

It was clear that Demetracopoulos could no longer work as political editor for any of his Greek publications, which would be reluctant to print any stories he might send them. Furthermore, it was highly unrealistic that non-Greek publications would want to hire a Greece-focused correspondent with seriously curtailed access to sources at home. He had an ongoing relationship with the North American Newspaper Alliance (NANA) listed on his visa application, but per-article-pay from them could not provide a sustainable income. Without any means of support beyond the kindness of friends, he needed to find steady work, and quickly.

Of all of his friends during this time who had helped in large and small ways, Eliot Janeway opened the most doors. Understanding the magnitude of the problems facing Elias and all their subtle complexities, Janeway suggested how to turn Wall Street broker Bob Brimberg's generalized offer of help into a real job. On his first full day of self-exile in America, Elias sat down with Janeway and Brimberg in the latter's Lower Manhattan office to discuss how they could help one another. Bob Brimberg headed a small and aggressive firm that was constantly seeking a competitive advantage over its larger competitors. Nicknamed "Scarsdale Fats" for his hometown and Falstaffian build, Brimberg was the "corned beef and pickles Perle Mesta of Wall Street."[13] He had developed a reputation for hosting popular informal luncheons for representatives of big investment institutions like Fidelity, Wellington, Keystone, and Chemical Bank. These gatherings included "no-nonsense," off-the-record discussions of what the companies were buying and selling. At other times Brimberg would invite guests to speak on relevant topics or provide executive briefings for his clients.

Brimberg needed an internationally savvy advisor who could provide his investment clients sophisticated economic and political briefings on developments abroad. He also wanted a well-connected Washington representative who could attract marquee names to give speeches at his popular events. In Elias, he found both.

Elias knew he could do the job and do it well, but he also knew he hadn't come all this way just to make money. His priority was to connect with anti-junta interests in America and do everything possible to rid his country of its dictatorship. Understanding this, Brimberg offered an arrangement whereby Elias would be tasked to organize certain client events in New York and Washington and attend once-a-week meetings in New York. The rest of the time Elias would be on his own. It would be full-time pay for less than full-time work. And the firm would cover his "business development" expenses. Elias immediately agreed. Both men knew that before Elias could do any serious work, he would have to establish himself anew and get into a routine. So Brimberg started him out with a generous bonus. For the first month, he had no specific responsibilities, just get settled and make plans.

Elias left for Washington several days later. He decided to make his base of operations the Fairfax Hotel because of its prime location and ambience, its Jockey Club restaurant that could serve as his private club office, the friendly responsiveness of the staff, and the feeling that, of all the places he'd lived recently, especially with Louise Gore nearby, it felt like home. Louise was delighted to welcome him, this time as a long-term tenant.

Despite his jump in salary, Elias carefully watched his personal expenses. He chose to live in one of the smallest, shabbiest residential apartments in the building, and resisted repainting and remodeling offers in order to avoid rent increases. Instead, he poured much of his new income into long-distance telephone calls, photocopying documents, and other expenses that advanced his anti-junta activities.

As he settled himself into the fifth-floor unit, listening to the muffled noises of yet another city on the street below, Elias saw his life as renewed. Instead of being exhausted, he was energized. He reflected on the concept of friendship and the lessons he had learned, or had reinforced, during the past eventful month. Friendships formed at a time of crisis, he observed, are deeper and more enduring than those deriving from shared ideology or commitment to a particular cause. "I have very conservative people who came to help even though they knew that I was liberal. There were liberals who refused to help because they felt that I was going to cause them trouble. It was the same experience I had in the Arleigh Burke thing. You often never know who your real friends are until a crisis comes."

One of the downsides of living at the Fairfax, with all its celebrity tenants and prime location, was that he already knew his phones would be tapped, as they had been in the past. Indeed, within days, as records later released under FOIA would show, the FBI acted on orders to put Elias under "extensive surveillance."

17.

Exiled in America

BEFORE ENGAGING IN ANY RESISTANCE efforts, Elias wanted to understand what was already being done to block American support for the junta. Whom could he rely on, in Washington and elsewhere? Who shouldn't be trusted? Who were new players and what resources could they bring? He didn't want to rehash the activities of others and didn't want others to be blindsided by his plans. His approach was non-ideological. He wanted allies from across the political spectrum. Organizing a powerful opposition force, then mobilizing it would take hard work, beginning with hundreds of phone calls, letters, and personal visits.

Elias first contacted influential Greek-American business and civic leaders in Chicago. Unanimously they told him that they identified as good Americans and, if the US government wasn't seriously opposed to the junta, then neither were they. If the United States wanted to support the dictatorship outright, so would they. Although there were notable exceptions, voices from Greek-American communities, from New York to San Francisco, echoed these sentiments. The responses from Boston, Tom Pappas's hometown, were even more strident, asserting that the political change had made visiting Greece more comfortable, and that those arrested, and perhaps tortured, probably deserved it. Known junta opponents were hissed at when attending Sunday services.[1] These reactions were especially dispiriting because they stood in stark contrast to the overwhelming anti-junta sentiment among Greeks living throughout Europe, Canada, Argentina, and Australia. It was an inauspicious beginning.

After he arrived in Washington in October 1967, friends from Elias's past visits eagerly invited him into a swirl of seasonal Georgetown cocktail receptions and dinner parties. A few who knew the story of his escape and difficult entry cautioned him to be careful. "There are people who are quite angry that you managed to get into the country. They will do anything to get rid of you," warned Colonel Walter Bryte, after taking him aside at a gathering. "Don't fall into a trap. Don't do anything that will give them ammunition to deport you." The German Embassy alerted Elias that the Greek Embassy wanted him sent back, also cautioning him that his D.C. activities would cause trouble for his friend Ambassador Schlitter.

One of the bright spots of those early months was his renewed relationship with A-list power couple Blake and Deena Clark, who welcomed him and his cause. Born Ruby Constandina Speliakos in La Jolla, California in 1913, Deena was a popular television personality who hosted award-winning celebrity interview programs and also had moderated *Meet the Press*.[2] Although growing up with her mother despising her father's Greek ethnicity, Deena proudly embraced her Hellenic heritage and "venerated" Elias and his strong personality.[3] They made him a regular at events at their Kalorama Road mansion "Arcadia," opening up important connections.

·

IN DECEMBER 1967, King Constantine attempted a counter-coup, relying on close advisors and royalist generals whom he expected to help him establish an alternative government in Thessaloniki that would then overthrow the colonels. On December 13 he flew north, only to be faced with mid-level pro-junta officers who had learned of the disorganized scheme and arrested the loyalist generals. The King was forced to flee to Rome the next day with his royal entourage.[4]

That same month, Elias was asked by a dinner party hostess to escort an attractive divorcee who lived nearby. The woman, Ingrid Rodenberg, had an alluring combination of a pretty face, stylishly coiffed dark hair, and a lithe, athletic body from spending hours on tennis courts. Elias knew this was someone he wanted to see again. And so, he was happy to accept her invitation to join her and her children for dinner at their Massachusetts Avenue home on December 22.

Earlier that day, Eleni Vlachou, the exiled publisher of *Kathimerini*, had telephoned Elias from London to tell him that she had been interviewed by American television about her own harrowing escape from Greece in the wake of King Constantine's failed counter-coup. The story would be on the news in the United States that evening and Elias did not want to miss the broadcast. After dinner, Rodenberg told him he could go watch the news on the second-floor master-bedroom television, while she bathed the children on the third floor and got them ready for bed.

While watching the news, he heard a great commotion outside the bedroom.[5] Fearful that someone sent by the junta had come to assault or kill him, he locked the door and tried to call the Washington office of the FBI. The phone was dead. Suddenly, the door was broken open and three men barged in. "Who are you?" Elias shouted, "What do you want?"

"A friend of Mr. Rodenberg, the woman's husband," replied one.

"She doesn't have a husband," Elias snapped back, believing Mrs. Rodenberg's divorce was ancient history.

One man reached for Elias's neck and grabbed at his tie. They scuffled. Punches were thrown. Someone kicked him. Another man pulled a gun, held it close to Elias's head and ordered him to undress. Obediently, he removed his tie and shirt. Even with a gun pointed at him, he balked at going further. He had on a truss and corset he wore to deal with the slipped disc he suffered from his imprisonment tortures. Removing it meant pain and limited mobility. When he refused to move, they roughly pushed him into a chair and forcibly tore off his pants, shoes, socks, and undergarments.

When Elias was completely stripped, he started to laugh to himself. "In a way I was relieved," he recalled, "because here I was expecting a political attack, and I found myself naked." This wasn't the junta. These men were not there to kill or kidnap him. He was in the middle of a domestic squabble, not a life-threatening confrontation with the Greek dictatorship.

Elias broke away, ran onto a sleet-covered balcony, but it was too high to jump from safely, especially with his bad back. His screams for help in the near freezing winter night went unanswered. When he tried to go inside one man pushed his full weight against the door and another took photos of a shivering, naked Elias.

After about ten minutes, they let him in. They took more photos, including some of Ingrid Rodenberg, who was fighting another man trying to disrobe her after she had rushed downstairs. A man, later identified as her estranged husband Robert Rodenberg, took Elias's trousers and wallet from the floor. The wallet contained about $400 in twenties, identification, and some personal papers. Then the group departed into the night with camera and gun.

Furious, Elias wanted to go to the police immediately to press charges. They talked with Ingrid's attorney, who recommended that Elias first talk to his own counsel. In the wee hours of Saturday morning, December 23, Elias Demetracopoulos, distinguished journalist and a self-appointed leader of the opposition to the Greek dictatorship, walked from the Rodenberg residence to the Fairfax Hotel, wearing an overcoat but no pants, trying to avoid the yellow glow of the sodium street lamps and traffic headlights.

Elias spent Christmas Eve and Christmas at Doctors Hospital, where his physician and lawyer insisted he go to be checked out for assorted contusions, scrapes, hematomas, and piercing back pain that radiated down his leg. The day after Christmas, Elias met with his attorney, and together they went to the Third Precinct police station.

Between the holidays, Elias was contacted separately by John Richardson, former CIA Athens station chief, and Norbert Anschutz, who'd been political officer at the Athens embassy and served on the State Department's Greek Desk. A coincidence? He thought not. They advised him to let the matter drop. Elias would not.

Rodenberg's lawyer arranged with Elias's lawyer to return his trousers and wallet. When the billfold arrived, most of the cash was missing. Demetracopoulos met with Assistant US Attorney Robert S. Bennett, who said it was an office policy to steer clear of domestic disputes. Elias would later learn that Robert Ridgway Rodenberg was a powerful Washington-area real estate developer and a founder of the original Baltimore Colts football team. Elias fully expected that Rodenberg could muscle his way around the Washington legal system, but he refused to be a "patsy." Concerned that the incident could have an adverse effect on Elias's yet-unfiled petition to stay in the United States, Ingrid Rodenberg went to the district director of the INS on December 28 to disclaim any wrongdoing on the part of Elias.

Elias learned that the Rodenbergs had started squabbling shortly after their 1961 marriage, filed for divorce in 1964, and since then had been engaged in protracted and bitter separation, support, and custody proceedings.[6] Robert Rodenberg, having stopped all payments and filing for full custody just prior to

Elias's fateful visit, was now seeking fresh examples to strengthen earlier evidence of his wife's adultery.[7]

Rodenberg and his hirelings' account of the December confrontation was quite different from the reality experienced by Elias. Rodenberg claimed that he had broken into his own house with private detectives after returning early from a European business trip to find his unclothed wife blocking their marital bedroom door in order to protect a naked man hiding on their balcony. When they pushed into the bedroom, they found the bedding in disarray, male and female clothing and underwear scattered about, and two glasses of amber liquid on the night table. They took some photos of Mrs. Rodenberg and the naked strange man and left, taking with them his pants and identification. Their account made no mention of anyone with a gun or any scuffle with Elias.

It seems clear that Rodenberg's group had come to catch Ingrid in bed in the middle of a tryst. They had been staking out the house, waiting for the bedroom light to go on, which it did when Elias went to watch television. Upon breaking in and finding no *flagrante delicto*, Robert Rodenberg decided to fabricate a scenario and document it.

Elias berated himself for getting entangled in such a smarmy marital mess. This could be a major distraction from his purpose in Washington. He was even more outraged to learn that, in early January 1968, Mr. Rodenberg had amended his divorce counterclaim, listing Elias as another co-respondent who had committed adultery with Ingrid.

Since the days of the false diagnosis in his Eginition medical record, he had refused to allow erroneous reports to populate official documents about him. A conviction for either the underlying crime or for perjuring himself in sworn testimony could adversely affect his immigrant visa standing. He directed his attorney to challenge the allegation. In an unlikely move for an alleged adulterer, he went on the attack, publicly calling for a full police investigation and demanding that charges be brought against the mysterious man with a gun—who turned out to be an off-duty D.C. policeman who was later investigated and found to be "a self-confessed liar."[8]

Compromising photographs are an essential ingredient of a successful private-investigation divorce raid. Yet Rodenberg never produced any of the photographs taken that night, claiming they had been "lost" while being developed. This lack of photos did not vindicate Elias, however. Until the case was heard and adjudicated, the record would consist only of Rodenberg's allegations and Demetracopoulos's sworn denial. Those provided ammunition for his enemies at a time when the FBI was conducting investigations for the Immigration and Naturalization Service.

Among the interviews it conducted was one with Ymelda Dixon, the society reporter for the *Washington Star*. Although she was not the dinner-party hostess who had asked Elias to pick up Ingrid, Dixon nevertheless claimed to be the person "responsible for introducing SUBJECT and Mrs. RODENBERG."[9] According to the FBI report, prepared more than a year after the incident, Dixon "stated that SUBJECT was aware Mrs. RODENBERG was married" and she was "of the opinion that the relationship between subject and Mrs. RODENBERG still exists."[10] Dixon piled it on. Elias, she said, is "a single and attractive male" who "has charmed several prominent married women . . . and has had affairs with them . . . That he more or less operates as a 'gigolo,'" adding that no one had told her of any incidents where money was borrowed, but that "by conversations she had formed this opinion."[11] Was Ymelda Dixon part of the hostile web Colonel Bryte had warned him about, Elias later speculated?

■

ELIAS HAD SECURED his B-1 "temporary visitor for business" visa on September 28, 1967, by claiming he was a working journalist. Sid Goldberg of the North American Newspaper Alliance, referencing Elias's years of connection to the syndicate, provided the necessary employment letter for his entry. But he was never a salaried employee of NANA, and clearly his annual freelance income was not enough to live on. According to the terms of his visa, he was admitted only until February 3, 1968, and required to notify the district Immigration and Naturalization Service office on or before January 25, 1968, of the arrangements he had made for his voluntary departure, including the date, place, and manner.

Elias knew he would never leave the US voluntarily. To him, there was no better place than Washington from which to organize an anti-junta campaign. But what to do? Elias's enemies were real, and more than a few wanted to get him out as quickly as possible. From the moment of his arrival in October, negative reports and out-of-context information had been forwarded to INS from the CIA, State, and FBI.

Robert Brimberg was Elias's angel. The federal agencies knew from shortly after Elias's arrival that he was working on the Brimberg & Company payroll. But in accepting that additional employment, he was also violating the terms of his entry visa. Since well before Elias's escape, his plan had been to quickly adjust his non–US citizen arrival status to that of a legal permanent resident, so he could get a "green card" and stay indefinitely. On January 10, 1968, Brimberg petitioned on Elias's behalf for a so-called Sixth Preference classification—an immigration exception that provided for a change in status if a job were deemed essential and the quota for applicants from a particular country had not been exceeded.

Brimberg & Company's petition maintained that Elias was uniquely quali-fied for the "economist and consultant" job Brimberg needed to fill—one that, not incidentally, required someone who had "at least three years as a foreign cor-respondent." Unfortunately, no immigrant visa for natives of Greece was imme-diately available, and Elias was forced to turn to friends in Congress for help. The first to act was Emanuel Celler, the powerful and respected chairman of the House Judiciary Committee, who had represented Brooklyn in Congress for nearly half a century. He was a passionate advocate for immigration reform, the leading architect of major civil rights legislation, and a fierce opponent of civ-il-liberties abuses.

On January 30, Celler called Lewis Barton, the INS district director, to ex-press his concern for Elias's life and personal safety if he were forced to return to Greece during the dictatorship.[12] Oregon senator Wayne Morse and Indiana senator Vance Hartke made similar appeals.[13] Responding to their concerns, Barton extended Elias's stay first to April 3 and then July 3, 1968, but warned that, even if the Greek visa quota were solved, the background reports needed for prompt action had not yet been prepared.

In early May, Celler wrote to US Ambassador Phillips Talbot in Athens not-ing that the documentation originally requested in January needed for process-ing Demetracopoulos's immigration case was still missing. He asked that Talbot provide "expeditious consideration."[14] Talbot had tried to block Elias's entry into the US and eight months later was still in no mood to help. He told Celler offi-ciously that his embassy had received the application on March 18 and "it would carry out, as promptly as possible, the functions required by law . . . [which] may require 2 to 4 months."[15]

On June 17, 1968, to overcome the delays, Senator Hartke proposed trump-ing the quota problem by introducing Private Bill S3650 in the United States Senate, "for the relief of Elias P. Demetracopoulos." The bill was assigned to the Senate Judiciary Committee headed by James Eastland of Mississippi, a cigar-chomping, scotch-drinking arch-segregationist. Although Elias counted a number of prominent Southern conservative legislators as friends, Eastland was not one of them. Eastland requested that the INS prepare a full investigation and report in twenty days, but, when it did not, made no further push.[16]

Over the summer, the INS gathered information from various federal agencies. The CIA, after admitting it had "no confirmed derogatory information" in its voluminous dossier, still fanned rumors, distorted facts, omitted evidence, and flagged areas to be investigated that could lead to deportation-worthy evidence.[17] Tom Karamessines, the former CIA Station Chief in Athens, had since Elias's arrival tried planting seeds of doubt that could overturn approval of the Greek exile's visa. Promoted to deputy director of plans in charge of CIA dirty tricks worldwide, Karamessines sent a SECRET eight-page, single-spaced report to the INS, the FBI, the State Department's Security Secretary, as well as the White House Situation Room. The essence of his case opposing Elias was that "the subject" had "been inimical to United States interests," and "had numerous contacts with Soviet Bloc officials, many of whom are known intelligence types."[18] In response to Hartke's private bill inquiry, Karamessines also resubmitted to the INS a vicious error-filled summary of Elias's background that the Agency had prepared for Ambassador Talbot the month before Elias's escape.

Karamessines's strategy was apparently designed to convince a hyperventilating anti-Communist like Senator Eastland that Demetracopoulos should be denied special legislation benefits and deported. To further his case, Karamessines resurrected false information about Celia's activities in Moscow and pushed Elias-as-Soviet-agent speculation, even when J. Edgar Hoover himself reported there was no supporting evidence.[19] He pressured the INS to use raw CIA data, which it did, and to open a wider investigation to include the Rodenberg matter.[20]

■

1968 WAS A tumultuous year, a year of demonstrations, assassinations, and urban violence. Martin Luther King was gunned down in Memphis. Cities erupted in flames and riots. From college campuses to the streets of Paris and beyond, from the Miss America beauty pageant to the Mexico City Olympics, social unrest rocked the nation and the world. Saddam Hussein usurped power in Iraq. And in August Soviet and Warsaw Pact troops marched into Czechoslovakia to crush the blossoming liberal reforms of the Prague Spring. American casualties in Vietnam jumped dramatically, and public support for the war declined. Senator Eugene McCarthy, running as a peace candidate, challenged President

Johnson in the early Democratic primaries. Robert Kennedy entered the race in mid-March and less than three months later was shot to death. At the end of March, President Johnson surprised the nation by announcing he would not seek re-election. In April, Vice President Humphrey became the candidate of the Democratic Party establishment.

Elias Demetracopoulos followed these stories but was much more focused on news from Greece and his own immigration status. There was nothing to cheer on either front.

In Athens, the dictatorship entered its second year, with a dismal "illusion of normalcy."[21] Americans officially recognized the military regime on January 23. Others, from Britain to the Soviet Union, followed. Purges of Greek civil servants and senior military officers continued.

Riding a boom in the world economy, the junta incentivized foreign investment and introduced ultimately inflationary measures. People traded their ancestral homes for residences in new concrete apartment buildings. Tourism was promoted heavily to soften the junta's international image.[22] Holiday visitors came, including George Harrison of the Beatles, despite appeals from junta opponents for a boycott. Greek-American vacationers praised the country's new leadership for stopping strikes and making trains run on time.[23] Tom Pappas was in the ascendancy, with former employees and friends well-positioned in the regime.

Behind closed doors, the military security police continued its campaign of torture and extracted confessions. Staged international inspections of prisoner conditions led to whitewashed reports, but independent European investigators were hearing horror stories. Elias received phone calls, smuggled tapes, and journals, all asking for help.

The opposition, however, was scattered and disorganized. George Papandreou and Panagiotis Kanellopoulos were under house arrest in Athens. Andreas Papandreou was in Sweden; Konstantinos Karamanlis in Paris; Eleni Vlachou in London; and Elias in Washington. The King was in Rome, his failed December 1967 coup attempt already a faded memory. An army deserter and poet, Alekos Panagoulis, attempted to assassinate Papadopoulos by bombing the dictator's moving car. He missed, and was caught, imprisoned, and brutally tortured. The regime talked about restoring parliamentary democracy when conditions were ready, but few believed them. Some agreed with the sentiment that "every few decades the Greeks need a Metaxas or a Papadopoulos to bring order and get everybody moving in the same direction."[24]

■

ONE OF THE first calls Elias made when he arrived in self-exile was to Spiro Agnew. The appointment was easily arranged. He visited the Maryland governor's office in Annapolis in November 1967 to urge him to commit to the cause of Greek democracy, and especially to oppose resumption of US arms shipments to the dictatorship. Agnew was cordial, but balked, telling him that for political reasons he could not publicly oppose the junta. He did, however, promise to be neutral.

A couple of months later, Louise Gore brought Agnew to a Republican Women's Club dinner in New York, and invited Richard Nixon to stop by her postprandial reception to meet the governor, who was then a leading supporter of Nelson Rockefeller's incipient candidacy. After the men talked for two hours, Louise walked Nixon to the elevator, and he said: "Your governor—make him speak out more. He's got a lot to say."[25] Back in Washington, she shared with Elias her observations from the evening.

For months, Agnew had been making clandestine trips to New York to meet with Rockefeller to plot the latter's presidential candidacy. When Agnew's benefactor Tom Pappas urged him to back Nixon instead, Agnew demurred, forming instead a Committee to Draft Rockefeller for the Republican nomination, with headquarters in Annapolis. Unexpectedly, on March 21, Rockefeller announced that he would drop out of the race, without ever having alerted Agnew—a crushing embarrassment.

After President Johnson announced on March 30 that he would not run for reelection, Rockefeller reconsidered, and by the end of April he had formally reannounced his candidacy. By then the jilted Agnew had met again in New York with Nixon, embraced his candidacy, and enthusiastically worked to beat back the Rockefeller challenge.

After he was nominated, Nixon had still not chosen his running mate, though it was clear he wanted a low-profile, ideological centrist willing to play second fiddle.[26] After three rounds of meetings, polarizing figures like Illinois senator Charles Percy, New York mayor John Lindsay, and California governor Ronald Reagan were eliminated, leaving under consideration Tennessee Senator Howard Baker, Maryland congressman Rogers Morton, Massachusetts governor John Volpe, California lieutenant governor Robert Finch, and Maryland's "favorite son," Agnew. Over the years much has been made of Tom Pappas's intimations and boasts that his opinion was decisive in Agnew's getting Nixon's nod, but there's no evidence that his voice was considered more important than the hundreds of letters and recommendations Nixon solicited from party leaders. Pappas also told reporters he had urged Nixon to pick Percy or Volpe.[27] At a meeting with the vice-presidential selection deadline fast approaching, Nixon and his closest advisors concluded that everyone on the final list had flaws. Agnew won by default.[28]

Instantly, Agnew became the highest-profile Greek political figure in the world. It didn't matter that he couldn't speak Greek, didn't follow the Greek Orthodox religion, refused to give his children Greek names, had married a non-Greek, had a non-Greek mother, preferred to be called "Ted," and had only a rudimentary understanding of Greek history, culture, and current politics. His nomination became a source of pride for Greeks everywhere, and his views of Greece were already a matter of great importance.

Elias watched the Republican Convention in Miami Beach, with VIP tickets provided courtesy of South Carolina senator and Nixon insider Strom Thurmond. Although Thurmond had become an unabashed supporter of the junta, his personal relationship with Elias, which dated back to the Admiral Burke interview days, was amicable. Even if Elias had a low opinion of Thurmond's intellect and hard-right views, he remained grateful for Thurmond's help in his reinstatement at the *Herald Tribune* and was friendly with his top staffers Harry Dent and Fred Buzhardt.

As he watched Agnew's selection and acceptance speech, Elias experienced a touch of ethnic pride in Agnew's ascent. He liked being on a first-name basis with political leaders, and he was particularly happy for Louise Gore. This feeling was quickly replaced by a feeling of discomfort once he realized that the man sitting next to Pat Nixon in the presidential box at the convention was Tom Pappas.

Elias viewed the world through the prism of Greek democracy, and thus saw Pappas as a symbol of those reaping rewards from championing the military regime. As long as Agnew was at least neutral regarding the Greek junta, Elias was comfortable overlooking stories about Agnew's seamy scandals while county commissioner. Garden variety US political corruption was not Elias's focus. But rumors that influential businessmen in Greece and some Greek-Americans with financial interests in both countries—including Pappas—had given Agnew large amounts of cash and encouraged him to defend the military dictatorship troubled him. Elias suggested to some reporters that they explore links between Pappas, Agnew, and Nixon, but, lacking easy corroboration, no news publication did any serious follow-up. [29]

Demetracopoulos wanted Agnew to reconfirm his neutrality because any change in his position could undermine opposition to the dictators' plebiscite, scheduled for the end of September. He asked Louise Gore, now working on "practical politics" for the Agnew campaign, to arrange a face-to-face meeting with the candidate. At the early September gathering, Agnew promised Gore and Demetracopoulos, for at least a third time, that he would remain neutral. His eye contact was direct; his hand gestures demonstrative, and he even used language that hinted he was sympathetic to the movement to "restore democracy."

It was therefore with great pleasure that Elias accepted an invitation to sit with Louise at the head table at the National Press Club less than a week later, on Friday September 27, when Agnew would be the featured speaker. Agnew's speech consisted mainly of predictable Republican talking points. As he droned on, Elias found himself drifting off. Suddenly, the *Washington Star*'s Mary Mc-Grory asked the vice-presidential candidate if he were "for or against the Greek junta."[30] Elias sat up straight. Agnew paused, perhaps for effect, before answering. He then pulled out a typewritten sheet from his inside jacket pocket, squinted his eyes, and read from a prepared statement.

> I think the Greek military government that took over in 1967 has not
> proven itself to be as horrendous a spectre to contemplate as most
> people thought it would. I think as long as they are seriously living up
> to their obligations . . . There's supposed to be a referendum this Sunday
> on the Constitution and I think they have promised free elections
> thereafter . . . [T]his particular military government has done a bit to
> stabilize the Communist threat in Greece.[31]

Agnew went on to criticize "the Communist forces under Andreas Papandreou," and blamed him for "stimulating attempts of an uprising."[32] Asked whether that made him a Communist, the governor said: "a person who advocates the violent overthrow of a government . . . makes him undesirable."

Sitting only feet away, Elias and Gore looked at each other speechless, stunned by the sudden change. At the end of the luncheon, Elias departed immediately for an appointment. Returning home, Gore rushed off to another

Elias P. Demetracopoulos, 1950.
(Elias P. Demetracopoulos Collection / James H. Barron)

Ceremony celebrating Elias's WWII heroism, 1950. Top row: OAG leader Ioannis Bobotinos (4th from the left) and Dr. Kostas Giannatos (6th from left, next to Elias). Elias stands behind his seated mother and Celia. (Elias P. Demetracopoulos Collection / James H. Barron)

Elias with President Truman, 1951. (Elias P. Demetracopoulos Collection / James H. Barron © Benjamin E. Forte)

Tom Pappas arm in arm with George Papadopoulos during the Greek military dictatorship. (Photograph by Costas Megalokonomou © Benaki Museum/Photographic Archives [FA.26_566.35_103])

President Nixon with Tom Pappas in the Oval Office. (The Richard Nixon Presidential Library and Museum)

Elias with Celia in Rome, 1952.
(Elias P. Demetracopoulos Collection
/ James H. Barron)

Elias (R) with Prime Minister George
Papandreou after his 1964 election victory.
(Elias P. Demetracopoulos Collection / James
H. Barron)

Sen John F. Kennedy talking on the phone surrounded by aides during the 1960 Wisconsin
primary election. From Left to Right: Pierre Salinger, Kenny O'Donnell, Larry O'Brien, Malcolm
"Mac" Kilduff, Robert F. Kennedy (© Stan Wayman / Life Picture Collection / Getty)

Elias (R) with Prime Minister Konstantinos Karamanlis. (Elias P. Demetracopoulos Collection / James H. Barron)

Persa Metaxas and Elias in Athens on New Year's Day, 1964. (Elias P. Demetracopoulos Collection / James H. Barron)

Elias with Louise Gore, 1975. (Elias P. Demetracopoulos Collection / James H. Barron © Dorsey C. Patrick)

Jeanne Oates Angulo, 1987. (Elias P. Demetracopoulos Collection / James H. Barron)

Poster announcing Elias's speech on the 4th anniversary of the military coup, 1971. (Elias P. Demetracopoulos Collection / James H. Barron)

Anti-Elias cartoon distributed by Greek Proclamation Committee, a Greek-American pro-junta group, 1971. (Elias P. Demetracopoulos Collection / James H. Barron)

```
   7024513   DOCUMENT=      5 OF      5   PAGE =    1 OF    1
KEYWORDS   ACKNOWLEDGING SENS MOSS BURDICK GRAVEL RE MR DEMETRACOPOULOS DEATH IN
           ATHENS PRISON
DATE       701219
STATUS     C
SOURCES    BURDICK, QUENTIN N   GRAVEL, MIKE        MOSS, FRANK E
           TIMMONS, W
DISPATCH   ELIOT                TIMMONS, W
FILE/OC    WH

***** LAST DOCUMENT IN OUTPUT *****
(DOCUMENT SELECT: D= / TERMINATE: T / 3284 PRINT: P)
```

Mysterious December 18, 1970 NSC file index title referring to Elias's death in an Athens prison. File entirely redacted. (Elias P. Demetracopoulos Collection / James H. Barron)

Torture victim Spyros Moustaklis in Washington DC for medical treatment, Christmas 1974. Seated L–R: Elias, Persa, Spyros Moustaklis, Christina Moustaklis; standing: Cliff and Bea Hackett. (Hackett Family Collection / James H. Barron)

Elias arranges a congressional briefing about Cyprus with Greek Foreign Minister George Mavros, 1974. (Elias P. Demetracopoulos Collection / James H. Barron © Dev O'Neill)

Elias (C) introduces Andreas Papandreou (L) to Congressman Ben Rosenthal (R). (Elias P. Demetracopoulos Collection / James H. Barron © Florou bros. (Athens press photojournalism))

Greek Ambassador Alexandros Mallias bestows upon Elias Greece's prestigious Order of the Phoenix for his "constant fight to preserve democracy." January 7, 2008. (Elias P. Demetracopoulos Collection / James H. Barron)

Christopher Hitchens lauds Elias at the Order of the Phoenix ceremony. (Elias P. Demetracopoulos Collection / James H. Barron)

Former FBI and CIA director William Webster congratulates Elias at the Order of the Phoenix ceremony. (Elias P. Demetracopoulos Collection / James H. Barron)

meeting, but left Elias a handwritten note in his hotel mailbox expressing her dismay. Given her prominence in the Nixon-Agnew campaign, it was a remarkable document:

> Elias I have been trying to call you—I am shocked!! What happened at the Press Club? That certainly wasn't what I thought I was going to hear!!!!
>
> You must be indignate [sic] and I can't blame you. Why did Agnew tell us one thing one day and say something else the next??
>
> It was bad enough that he told us he was going to be neutral. But then to turn around and support the regime. I can't believe it!" she continued "What made him change his mind—or rather Who!"[33]

SHE CONCLUDED WITH: "What are you going to do? . . . You have every right to blast him. I'm really very sorry—damn!"

Demetracopoulos, acutely aware that worldwide publication of Agnew's position would give aid and comfort to the colonels in the run-up to the Greek plebiscite, hastily organized a press conference for the next day. The purpose: to criticize Agnew's comments, and warn that "Even a partial resumption of any kind of heavy military equipment . . . would be . . . throwing away the main leverage left to the U.S. Government to pressure the junta to move toward a real restoration of constitutional democracy."[34]

The proposed Greek constitution, to be voted on the following day, had never been published fully in advance, and Elias attacked the "sham" plebiscite, designed to make the Greek people "accept the indefinite abolition of democratic government, individual freedom, and the rule of law." Elias especially criticized draft provisions curtailing press freedoms for nine ambiguously defined offenses and a final article stating that provisions pertaining to individual freedoms of the press, parliament, and elections, as well as to guarantees against arbitrary arrest and judicial due process, "are not to be applied except as and when the military government decides." Elias ended the conference by saying that Agnew's "astounding" remarks at the National Press Club luncheon revealed the vice-presidential candidate's "surprising ignorance of the Greek situation."[35]

Despite scheduling the press conference on a Saturday morning, his plea and the Greek-against-Greek angle attracted coverage from wire services and foreign newspapers.[36] Le Monde's diplomatic correspondent included Elias's appeal in his weekend column. Demetracopoulos also called friends at the *Times* of London to urge they explore the dark side of Agnew's connections with Pappas and the Greek dictators. But, as his CIA monitors clucked happily in their report on Elias's activities, neither the *New York Times* nor *Washington Post* picked up the story.[37]

The eleventh-hour appeal and the articles weren't enough to make a difference. In Athens, Agnew's ringing endorsement of the junta was given prominent play in the state-controlled press and made part of its election-eve propaganda. The referendum took place on Sunday, September 29. Voting was mandatory, with failure to vote a punishable offense. At some voting stations, ballots clearly marked "NO" were intentionally strewn on the floor in advance to intimidate voters. The result was a foregone conclusion: 92 percent were said to have voted yes, although a remarkable 22 percent of the electorate abstained.[38]

The military was now firmly in charge of the state, free from any governmental or parliamentary oversight. Without even a symbolic gesture toward civil liberties, a special Constitutional Court was created to be the junta's watchdog over everyday life. This "referendum" provided the requisite fig leaf for the partial resumption of US military aid.

■

TO HELP THE INS make a deportation case against Demetracopoulos, the CIA sought additional damaging information from the Greek dictatorship. The regime responded by sending a fabricated military record that described Elias's profession as "electrician," reported that he received multiple medical military deferments, and claimed he was permitted to go to the US in 1952 "for health reasons." The deferrable maladies listed had nothing to do with his real health issues. Finally, the junta claimed he paid to get out of military service, ignoring the documentary evidence that his wartime record and time spent incarcerated by the enemy in World War II had exempted him from further service.[39]

Supporters of Elias actively lobbied the immigration authorities on his behalf, vouching for his character and integrity, his love for America, his heroic record against the Nazis and Communists, and the serious problems he would likely face because of his frontline opposition to the military regime in power. Among these were New York's Republican senators Jacob Javits and Charles Goodell and Oregon Democratic senator Wayne Morse, retired General William Quinn, and William F. Kann, executive vice president of Bache & Co. After Labor Day, with no quota number yet available for natives of Greece and with

Senate Bill S3650, Hartke's private bill, languishing in committee and due to expire with the end of the legislative session, the INS commenced formal deportation proceedings. On September 18, Elias received a registered letter charging him with violating his non-immigrant status and was ordered to appear before a special inquiry officer on October 3 to "show cause why you should not be deported."[40]

A few days later, he received a letter changing the date for his hearing to October 23. It seemed that the Rodenberg adultery charges that had been bubbling for much of the year had broken through the surface, and the INS investigators wanted that additional information to become part of the record. Under the law at the time, a finding of adultery by itself could not have been used against Elias in an immigration proceeding, but lying about it under oath could. Elias had given repeated accounts of the evening on pain and penalty of perjury. To the great disappointment of INS investigators, when the judge refused to refer any of Elias's statements for prosecution, given the contradictory testimony from Rodenberg, Elias was cleared.

On October 23, Elias appeared before the special inquiry officer and admitted the fact of his Brimberg employment and therefore his deportability. Then, through his attorney, he requested a stay of deportation under the section of the immigration law that requires the attorney general to withhold deportation of an alien who demonstrates that his "life or freedom would be threatened" thereby. In a supporting affidavit, Elias included his September 28 press conference statement, inserted in the Congressional Record by Utah senator Frank Moss, demonstrating his outspoken denunciation of the military regime and his active resistance to its leaders. He told the hearing officer he feared that if he returned to Greece, he would be killed.[41]

The hearing was suspended "until further notice."[42]

18.

Junta-gate and the O'Brien Gambit

1968 PROVED A YEAR OF missed opportunity for Elias Demetracopoulos, but it was not for lack of trying. In the final weeks of the campaign, Hubert Humphrey was rapidly closing a 15-point gap, and opinion polling the weekend before election day indicated a statistical dead heat.[1] Nixon won by just 0.7 percent of the popular vote, receiving more than three million fewer votes than when he lost in 1960. The contest turned out to be the second-closest presidential election in the twentieth century. Had Nixon lost just 153,573 of his 35 million votes (0.21 percent of his national total) to his Democratic opponent in four battleground states (Missouri, Ohio, Illinois, and New Jersey), Humphrey would have won the electoral vote outright.

And there were other potential scenarios. A change from Nixon to Humphrey of only 41,971 votes (0.06 percent of national total) in three states (Missouri, New Jersey, and Arkansas) would have resulted in no Electoral College majority. So too if only California, while ousting its incumbent Republican US senator, had flipped. Either outcome would have resulted in the US House of Representatives deciding the election, and there the Democrats held a clear majority. In the closing days, Nixon was so concerned about the election being thrown into the House that, despite his strong frontrunner advantage and refusal to debate Humphrey, he nevertheless reached out to his grossly underfunded opponent to try to get him to agree that, if there were no Electoral College victor, the House should abide by the popular vote.[2]

Nixon had good reason to be worried as his once-titanic lead slipped away. Humphrey's September 30 televised address in Salt Lake City, in which the vice president awkwardly and ambiguously tried to distance himself from President Johnson's policies in Vietnam without alienating the President, won praise for its fresh and conciliatory tone. Some alienated Democrats returned to the fold. Meanwhile, a well-organized labor campaign relentlessly chipped away at third-party nominee George Wallace's union support in the North.

While Humphrey was rising, private candidate polls showed Nixon support plateauing at about 40 percent. Polling data from the last month of the campaign indicated that Nixon was still particularly vulnerable on the trust issue.[3] His support was soft—wide, but not deep. Notwithstanding an expensive and slick public-relations campaign, well chronicled in Joe McGinnis's *The Selling of the President*, many people still did not like or trust Nixon and were uneasy voting for him. The Humphrey campaign sensed this weakness and focused their late campaign rhetoric on the "trust" issue. "In October, everyone suddenly got scared," recalled McGinnis. "The bubble had burst. The months of staleness were catching up . . . fear [was] starting to creep up from deep inside."[4] On the Election Day cross-country flight to New York aboard the campaign plane *Tricia*, Nixon's advisors anxiously picked at the reasons their candidate would lose.[5]

The third-party candidacy of the populist Alabama governor George Wallace, which eviscerated historic white Southern support for the Democratic Party, weakened during the year, but remained attractive enough to siphon anti-Humphrey votes and deprive Nixon of the full fruits of his Southern Strategy. In the end, Dixie gave Wallace forty-six electoral votes from six states. Democrats may have begun to lose the South, but Republican ascendancy had not yet fully kicked in. Fortunately for Nixon, this problem was more than offset by millions of disaffected Democrats who, upset by the administration's handling of the Vietnam War and not sufficiently hostile to Nixon, decided to stay home. Total eligible voter turnout in 1968 was down to 60.8 percent, a drop of 2.3 percent from 1960. According to the University of Michigan Survey Research Center, more than a few Eugene McCarthy and Robert Kennedy supporters even voted for Nixon as a protest vote.[6]

Ironically, Nixon was helped by many who in the past had been sharply critical of "Tricky Dick" and now wrote admiringly about a "new Nixon." The week before the election, *New York* magazine featured as its cover story "Gloria Steinem on Learning to Live with Nixon." Dismissing reported links between Tom Pappas, CIA money, and the junta, she wrote: "There's little doubt that Nixon learned a great deal from his 1952 fund scandal, and is making every effort to be honest and/or circumspect . . . Humphrey's staff doing "negative research" . . . hasn't turned up anything unusual about financing; and . . . front-running candidates, rarely need to be dishonest . . ."[7] Theodore White effusively explained that his chronicle—*The Making of the President 1968*—was designed to describe "the campaign of a man of courage and of conscience; and the respect it wrung from me."[8] An October Surprise in 1968—one in which Elias Demetracopoulos would have been a major player—could have changed the electoral outcome.

■

DEMETRACOPOULOS COULD NOT believe that Agnew's late-September endorsement of the Greek junta had been made for above-board reasons. Immediately, he drew on his contacts in high and low places. Knowing that his phone might be tapped by both Greek and US intelligence services, Elias avoided using his own room whenever possible. Louise Gore shared Elias's views on the restoration of Greek democracy and knew that investigating the whys and whos of Agnew's volte-face could be dangerous. Despite her prominent role in the Nixon-Agnew campaign, Louise was a loyal friend. She set Elias up in an unoccupied hotel room with what she thought would be a clean phone line.

At private dinners Louise joined Elias in hunting for the facts. She told him she'd heard that Nixon campaign officials John Mitchell and Maurice Stans had been in regular contact with Tom Pappas as he traveled back and forth among his corporate headquarters in Athens, his suburban Boston home, and his Washington office. As vice chairman of the Nixon finance committee, he had a private office at Nixon campaign headquarters. Elias knew that Pappas had been a driving force behind efforts to get Greek-Americans to open their wallets. Louise told Elias that Stans and Mitchell had also been urging Pappas to bring in more donors from Greece. And the *Times* of London article, prompted by Elias's tips, had noted that Pappas's non-profit charity had "been named as one of the 'conduits' used by the CIA for distributing secret funds in Greece."[9]

Elias's first break came in an early-October call to Athens. He reached at home a well-placed, lower-level operative who worked at KYP headquarters, a man who had been a reliable source in the past. The informant reported there had been heavy pressure on KYP to come up with a lot of cash fast for the Nixon campaign—more than half a million US dollars. The cash had to be in large-denomination US currency, preferably $1,000 bills that could be easily transported. The man behind this aggressive demand was said to be Tom Pappas.

The CIA had shaped KYP and trained many of its agents. The two organizations shared space in the same building. Their personnel worked together, socialized together, and shared common values and worldviews. Papadopoulos had been part of this group. American funding "came directly . . . bypassing the standard budgetary channels of the Greek government."[10]

When George Papandreou took power in 1964, he began "restructuring" KYP, imposing some government controls on the clandestine CIA-to-KYP relationship and making the funding process more transparent.[11] The arrangement reverted to its old pattern after the military takeover. It is highly likely that, in 1968, US taxpayer funds sent to Greece through annual authorized, unvouchered CIA black budget operations ended up amongst the money secured by Pappas for Nixon.[12]

The KYP point person identified by Elias's informant was Michael Roufogalis, then deputy director and acting head of KYP, a close friend of Papadopoulos from their days in military school, an EENA conspirator, and one of the original 1967 coup plotters. Elias knew Roufogalis's reputation for tawdry sexcapades and unbridled corruption. During an earlier stint when he was in charge of KYP personnel, tales of supplicants streaming to his house with cash-filled bags were commonplace. Elias learned that Roufogalis had presided over the meetings at Greek intelligence agency headquarters. KYP had loads of drachmas on hand, but it lacked the foreign exchange necessary to provide the requested US currency.

Elias was told that KYP turned to the treasurer and fiscal agent of the Greek government itself, the Central Bank of Greece. It was the only institution in the country that had enough foreign exchange on hand to produce more than half a million US dollars in high-denomination bills. It also had a reputation for secrecy and, if the right levers were pushed, could be made to act quickly.

Roufogalis had Pappas's requested funds, but in drachmas. All he wanted to do was make a legal currency exchange. But it didn't work out as smoothly as he and his confederates expected. Although the Central Bank had much more foreign exchange on hand than did KYP, it said it didn't have enough to give Pappas all the large-denomination cash he wanted at once. Because the bank would need to replenish its resources, Pappas was told he would have to make several trips back and forth between the USA and Athens to collect and deliver the full contribution.

Roufogalis checked with his military-regime colleagues. Involving members of the junta turned a semi-clandestine caper into an open secret. In an effort to trace the money Pappas was bringing to the US, Elias called his friend John Pesmazoglou, scion of a distinguished banking family whose Greek roots extended back before the War of Independence. Pesmazoglou had been a high-ranking official at the Central Bank until he resigned to protest the junta takeover. It was Pesmazoglou who had challenged Elias to do more than just air his suspicions of a coming coup. In a scene recalled years later by Pesmazoglou's widow, Elias asked Pesmazoglou if he could confirm the KYP story. Assuming his phone was tapped, Pesmazoglou was noncommittal, stating only that "nothing the junta did would surprise him."[13]

Next Elias called Xenophon Zolotas, the former head of the Central Bank who had resigned at the same time as Pesmazoglou. Zolotas was a man with an international reputation for probity. Had he still been in office, he would surely have resisted the overture from KYP, compelling a frustrated and angry Roufogalis to turn to members of the ruling government to intervene. But Zolotas was gone from the bank. In response to Elias's question, he confirmed that he had second-hand knowledge that a demand on the bank had been made by Roufogalis, acting on behalf of Pappas. If Demetracopoulos wanted direct confirmation, however, Zolotas said he should talk to the current Central Bank governor.

Dimitrios Galanis had been a deputy governor of the Central Bank since 1955, in charge of the administrative wheels and levers. When the junta took over and his superiors resigned, he was promoted to governor. A short, sixty-nine-year-old, balding man with bushy dark eyebrows and round plastic eyeglasses, he sat on chair-cushions so he could see visitors over his desk.[14] Elias considered Galanis a loyal cog in the junta machinery and delayed making the call. Then a big break came serendipitously, when he called Daisy Schlitter—not to explore the money-transfer story, but to check up on how the family was faring under the dictatorship, and how Daisy's daughter Marion was doing after her difficult divorce.

Daisy told Elias that Marion had found someone new—an older man who was besotted with her daughter and lavished gifts on her and her children. The man's name: Dimitrios Galanis. And Galanis, according to Daisy, had talked in general terms to her daughter about the Roufogalis overture being made on behalf of Pappas.

At first Elias couldn't reach Marion, so he called his well-informed friend and journalist Mario Modiano, who told him the Marion Schlitter–Galanis relationship was anything but a secret. Modiano said he had gone to a cocktail party hosted at Marion's place at which the head of the Central Bank of Greece was wearing an apron and tending bar.[15] When Elias talked to Marion, she updated Elias excitedly on her relationship and offered to speak to Galanis in advance of a telephone call from Demetracopoulos.

Elias's conversation with Galanis was brief but frank. Off the record, the head of the Central Bank described the $549,000 drachmas-to-dollars request and its breakdown into three tranches, which had been completed. According to Elias's later account, which he said included three different credible sources on the United States side, three tranches of money went directly from Pappas: once to Mitchell and twice to campaign treasurer Maurice Stans.[16] Galanis confirmed Roufogalis's role as a go-between, adding that Tom Pappas had been the *meson* (fixer), and the person who Galanis said personally transported the cash to the Nixon campaign. Galanis, however, would not provide Elias with copies of any documents involved. Years later, after the junta fell, Elias asked Kostas Tsimas, then director of EYP, KYP's re-named agency, for documentation of the money transfer. Tsimas was unable to do so but told Elias that longtime agency staff had orally confirmed it.[17] Pavlos Apostolides, former head of the EYP and author of a leading history of Greek intelligence services, wrote later:

> Having gone through most of the outgoing documents, my conclusion
> is that anything important has been destroyed . . . , there was probably
> never any written account of the role of KYP in the affair.[18]

The Greek government viewed the Nixon campaign contribution as a good investment. According to Ambassador Henry Tasca's 1975 statement to a House investigator, the colonels' campaign "gift" was the apparent reason for Agnew's endorsement of the junta in late September 1968.[19] The Greek leaders had decided that Nixon-Agnew would be much more sympathetic to their cause than the Democrats. The junta had already spent $250,000 hiring Thomas Deegan's New York public relations agency, which also represented Tom Pappas's business interests, for the first year of an image-building campaign. Deegan had promised progress on getting the arms embargo lifted, but Elias and his anti-junta allies had succeeded in blocking that campaign. If Nixon-Agnew won, the colonels reasoned, much of their image-management work would be done for free.[20] A European PR consultant who was preparing to take over the Deegan account said that his contract negotiations stopped cold in the fall of 1968, presumably after Pappas made the money transfers.

Had any of the money transferred to the KYP from the CIA for Greek security activities then been laundered back to influence a US presidential campaign been US taxpayer money—as Demetracopoulos and others believed—it would have been a clear violation of the CIA charter against getting involved in domestic politics. Federal campaign-finance laws about foreign contributions, designed to protect the integrity of the American political process, were largely nonexistent or toothless at the time. Nevertheless, the untested 1966 amendments to the 1938 Foreign Agents Registration Act, particularly 18 USC Section 613 concerning political activities on behalf of a foreign principal, provided fines of $5,000 and five years of jail time for each offense. This legislation clearly applied to the KYP-Pappas-Nixon money connection. Even if the $549,000—the rough equivalent of $4,000,000 today—were not ultimately adjudicated as a violation of federal law, public revelation of it, handled correctly, would have been an explosive October Surprise and a potential game-changer for the Humphrey campaign.

While the Nixon campaign was unfolding its well-lubricated campaign, the Democratic Party was desperately worried about money. Contributions, especially since the riots at the Chicago Democratic Convention, had all but dried up, and the campaign was on track to being outspent by Nixon 5 to 1. Political scientists like Kathleen Hall Jamieson and longtime political analysts like Mark Shields have asserted that the 1968 race was definitely "decided by money."[21] The idea that US taxpayer dollars had been laundered by the Greek junta with CIA complicity could have been a major blow to Nixon.

Demetracopoulos could have fed such a big story to several reporters and urged them to follow up. He was a reliable source for scoop-hungry columnists like Rowland Evans and Bob Novak, and muckrakers like Jack Anderson and Drew Pearson. He also could turn to his friends on Capitol Hill for statements of outrage and calls for investigations. But none of that happened.

With less than three weeks until the election, Elias decided the most efficient approach with the strongest payoff was to get the story directly to President Johnson and have the President ask his CIA director to confirm or deny it. Afterward, assuming it were true, Johnson could then leak the story, along with high-level confirmation of its veracity. Richard Helms, Elias reasoned, had been appointed to the top CIA job by Johnson himself and would not lie if asked directly because he was afraid of the President's vindictive streak. At the time, Elias was unaware of the extent to which he was known to and disliked by Helms.[22]

Demetracopoulos pondered how best to reach Johnson. His first choice was Larry O'Brien, Democratic Party Chairman and Humphrey campaign manager. O'Brien would surely have the necessary incentive and access. But how likely was it that the campaign manager would ever make himself available to a foreign journalist from a small country during the last weeks of a heated campaign?

Demetracopoulos telephoned longtime friend and former California governor Pat Brown. Although defeated by Ronald Reagan in November 1966 in his bid for a third term, Brown was still a highly regarded Democratic Party elder who could open doors quickly. When he called early in the week of October 14, 1968, Elias was so cryptic in his message and opaque about the supporting evidence that at first Brown didn't understand what Elias was talking about. Finally piecing together enough to convince himself of Elias's seriousness, he agreed to call O'Brien. O'Brien, appearing not to understand the importance of the message, tried to beg off the idea of a meeting and advised Brown to have Elias prepare a thorough memorandum and send it to his office. "Please tell him it's so late and I'm so busy it will be difficult to find time," he said. Brown urged his friend not to give up hope, telling him he would be in Washington in a couple of days and they could discuss the matter in person.

On Thursday, October 17, over lunch at the Madison Hotel, Elias gave Brown the full story. He also showed him an article from Tuesday's *New York Times* with an October 14 Athens dateline, referring to a press statement from the Greek junta dismissing as "ludicrous" rumors that it was financing the Nixon campaign. The regime said it had an "impartial attitude" toward the American election and blamed Andreas Papandreou, the "well-known roving former politician and country abnegator," for spreading the allegations.[23] Elias did not tell Brown that he was a source behind the article, having shared the information with Papandreou in Sweden, who had in turn talked to the Swedish press.[24] Brown thought that Elias's scoop was a blockbuster. As someone then representing Indonesian interests in Washington, he knew how an orchestrated exposé of foreign money in an American election could be exploited to the detriment of both donor and recipient.

Brown agreed that the best strategy was to go through O'Brien to Johnson. O'Brien, after all, had worked as White House congressional liaison during both the Kennedy and Johnson administrations and had been LBJ's Postmaster General. Running the President's campaign in Wisconsin in March, O'Brien was the one who had warned his candidate of his looming defeat there, which prompted Johnson to announce that he would not stand for reelection. Armed with additional information from the Demetracopoulos luncheon and believing that the story could be a game-changer for beleaguered Democrats, Brown called O'Brien again and insisted that he sit down with Elias. O'Brien agreed to a Saturday appointment.[25]

■

LARRY O'BRIEN WAS also on the mind of reclusive business magnate Howard Hughes, who was seeking to buy himself presidential access by donating to Humphrey, Bobby Kennedy, and Nixon, his favorite.[26] Hughes was in awe of the entire Kennedy campaign staff, especially campaign manager O'Brien, and viewed the RFK assassination as an "opportunity" to hire him.[27] When Hughes's consigliere Robert Maheu contacted O'Brien on June 28, he found "a man without a job . . . quite available to discuss the possibility of involvement with Hughes" and happy to have the tycoon as his first client in a new consulting business.[28]

Hubert Humphrey was also eager to have Larry O'Brien take charge of his presidential campaign. O'Brien agreed to design the first draft of a strategic plan and to help only through the convention. He brought with him political consultant Joe Napolitan, often dubbed the father of modern campaign professionals.

In Chicago with demonstrators chanting "Dump the Hump, Dump the Hump" and much worse in the streets below his hotel window, Humphrey, according to O'Brien, asked, "Larry do you hear those people down there? . . . Don't leave me naked. How can I pull all the pieces together in so short a time?"[29]

O'Brien did not think Humphrey could win but agreed to continue with the campaign through election day, putting off going full-time with Hughes until after the election. To avoid any seeming conflict of interest, Maheu wrote, "we eventually worked out an arrangement in which we paid $15,000 a month to the public relations firm of Joseph Napolitan Associates in Washington, D.C. with O'Brien overseeing the company's work . . . that arrangement continued until

October 1969, when O'Brien opened his own consulting firm . . . and went officially on the Hughes payroll."[30]

·

WANTING TO BE prompt and fresh for his Saturday, October 19, meeting with
Larry O'Brien, Elias asked his longtime friend from his days in Greece, economics advisor Dick Westebbe, to drive him the short distance from the Fairfax to
the Democratic headquarters in the Watergate complex.[31] While waiting, he was
surprised to see across the street an Air Force colonel, who had been a US intelligence officer in Athens, walking toward him. The two men exchanged silent
nods. Coincidence, Elias wondered?

Inside the capacious and crenelated Watergate complex, Demetracopoulos
rode an empty elevator to the sixth-floor executive offices of the DNC and pushed
open the glass doors to the brain trust of the Humphrey campaign. Larry O'Brien
greeted Elias with his storied Irish charm. After sharing warm words about Pat
Brown, O'Brien ushered him into his office and introduced him to staffers he had
invited to hear Demetracopoulos's hot news. They included O'Brien's principal
assistant Ira Kapenstein, a former *Milwaukee Journal* reporter who had been
O'Brien's right hand at the Postmaster General's office; Claude Desautels, assistant to the chairman, who would later go into business with O'Brien and Howard
Hughes; and Andrew Valuchek, Assistant for Ethnic Groups.

When Elias looked across the table from him, he saw a Democratic Party
power broker, someone with direct access to the President of the United States,
a trusted friend of the current candidate who would likely jump at his report, and
veteran campaign staffers, highly skilled at vetting information and getting the
word out. Elias told his story slowly and carefully. He explained the chain of
events, from the junta leaders' fears of a Humphrey presidency and Agnew's
changed position to the involvement of the KYP, probably while using CIA
funds. He told them about Tom Pappas as personal instigator and bagman, from
start to finish.

Several times they interrupted Elias to ask: "How can you prove it?" Elias
first told the group that he had corroborating witnesses both in KYP and the
Bank of Greece, as well as American sources who claimed to know about the
Pappas transfer of funds to John Mitchell and Maurice Stans. He said that it was
possible, with O'Brien's help, to establish a full audit trail.

He recommended that O'Brien ask Johnson to call in Helms and ask him
directly for corroboration, using his CIA sources. If that didn't work, Elias told

the DNC group, he had two backup solutions. O'Brien, he said, could send a couple of staffers or trusted friends of the campaign to Greece and meet Elias's sources. If they went, he added, he could probably get others to confirm links in the chain. Demetracopoulos said he could make the arrangements for O'Brien's representatives to meet his Greek sources in relatively secure locations. And if O'Brien didn't want to do that, Elias offered to personally pay the airfare and interim accommodations for his sources and their immediate families to come to the United States and tell their stories. This third scenario, however, would require a provision for long-term funding for the sources, because after speaking out they could not return home.

The meeting lasted more than an hour. O'Brien wrote down the information about the names, connections, and payments, and told Elias he would explore the feasibility of the first proposal. He then instructed his staff to meet with Elias outside the office to discuss the other two approaches. The DNC chairman also asked that Elias not discuss this matter with anyone else, warning him that if he did and word leaked out, it could irreparably upset communications with the President and the CIA, which were delicate. Elias left the meeting feeling that a good-faith effort would be made.

Over the next week Kapenstein, both alone and with another aide, came to Demetracopoulos's apartment at the Fairfax Hotel and to the Jockey Club to discuss the logistics of alternative scenarios. At first, Elias thought it strange that they agreed to meet so publicly. But if they chose to use him as such, he had no trouble promoting himself as a player in a national presidential campaign. The group was, indeed, watched.

He had a further talk with Daisy's daughter, Marion, who earlier had said she was eager to relocate to the United States and wondered if Elias could help her get a job with an antiques store. She told him that Galanis was so in love with her that he would leave Greece, and his job, and follow her to Washington.[32] She added that he had ample resources to provide for both their passage and indefinite living expenses for them and her children. Safely out of Athens, she said, Galanis would agree to speak to O'Brien's investigators. As a result, resources would be needed only for one or two KYP contacts and their immediate families.

■

OTHER EVENTS THAT week were sober reminders of the difficulties Elias faced in his fight against the junta. On Sunday, the day after the O'Brien meeting, news reports circulated widely about a picturesque wedding in a tiny chapel, nestled among cypress trees on the Greek island of Skorpios. Earlier Elias had tried, through Ted Kennedy's confidential secretary Angelique Voutselas, to get the senator to urge the widowed Jacqueline Kennedy to choose a different venue for her nuptials with Aristotle Onassis. Elias knew that publicity from the event would be used by the dictatorship as a propaganda tool. Although Voutselas was sympathetic, she knew well it was not her place to ask her boss to get his sister-in-law to move her wedding "anywhere other than in Greece."[33] Even if she had, it would likely have had no effect. Jackie Kennedy appeared indifferent to being used, and other Kennedy intimates preferred a Kennedy-Onassis wedding as far as possible from paparazzi-prone venues.[34]

Then, on Monday, October 21, Elias was surprised to receive a letter instructing him to come in two days to a hearing concerning his deportation. The timing appeared more than coincidental, coming in the same week it seemed the US would resume sending heavy military equipment to Greece (which would be seen as a reward for the rigged September vote) and the Greek Supreme Court had dismissed appeals challenging the lawfulness of the plebiscite.

■

THE FINAL WATERGATE meeting with O'Brien, on Saturday, October 26, was a lot shorter than the first. Apologizing for being the bearer of bad news, O'Brien said he had approached the President, but that Johnson said he would not ask Helms about the Greek money transfer. Furthermore, O'Brien had concluded that, although the story was "compelling," every solution proposed by Elias "had a lot of pluses and a lot of minuses, with more minuses." He said that sending any of his staff to Greece to interview sources was far too risky. They could get arrested or entrapped in some embarrassing exposé that would reflect badly on the Humphrey campaign and turn off Greek-American voters.

He then returned to the proposal to bring one or more of the sources and their families to the US to corroborate the story publicly. O'Brien told him, "Elias, if we win the election we'll not have any problems, but if we lose the election I cannot guarantee that we could cover their living expenses." Laughing, he continued, "If we lose, I don't know how I'll cover my own living expenses."

Reflecting on those words more than four decades later, Elias bristled at the apparent disingenuousness of the comment. "If I knew then what I know now about O'Brien's dealings with Howard Hughes before, during, and after his chairmanship, that he would be fine financially regardless of the outcome, the meetings with O'Brien would have been far different. I still would have tried to get Johnson to question Helms, but I wouldn't have agreed to keep quiet."

He definitely would not have violated his longstanding principle of not over-relying on one source or outlet. Instead, he would have turned elsewhere to get the story out, particularly to his highly respected friends in Congress. Although Congress was in recess and members had scattered to their districts to campaign, more than a few, he thought, would have been willing to issue statements decrying the illegal money transfer. Once Johnson declined to help, Demetracopoulos also would have given the story to syndicated columnists Evans, Novak, Pearson, and Anderson, and to the main wire services. He himself would have held a major press conference, disclosing everything he knew. Not doing so was a fatal miscalculation.

■

PUBLICATION OF THE Greek money story could have had a major impact on the 1968 election. Public opinion on the rapidly narrowing race was volatile. Pollsters said pre-election measurements could be further from accurate than at any time since 1948, when they had predicted the wrong winner. The three-person race made screening non-voters and "undecideds" more difficult. In mid-October, a Gallup poll reported that 29 percent of voters were not certain they'd vote for their preferred choice on election day.[35]

As Eileen Shanahan reported in the *New York Times* on October 16, three days before the first Demetracopoulos-O'Brien meeting, predicting an outcome is made more difficult because of "what appears to be a widespread lack of enthusiasm for any of this year's candidates [which] may mean a higher-than-usual possibility of last minute switches if there is a last minute campaign issue or disclosure."

Nixon's team, relying on their internal tracking polls, saw the same developments. Campaign aides Herb Klein and Len Garment worried they were one bad story away from blowing the race. Harry Dent, architect of the Southern Strategy, told Elias years later he believed the Pappas story could have changed the outcome of the race.[36]

It's not as if such a thing had not happened before. Drew Pearson's late-October 1960 exposure of a mysterious $205,000 (almost $1.5 million in current dollars) non-recourse loan made in 1956 from tycoon Howard Hughes to Richard Nixon's mother, allegedly to save the vice president's brother Donald's "Nixonburger" enterprise, was decisive in providing JFK's razor-thin margin of victory that year—perhaps more so than voting-machine irregularities in Chicago or paper-ballot problems in Texas, or the first-ever televised presidential debates. It was rationalized by Hughes as the "chance to cement a relationship" with the Nixons.[37] Shortly after the loan was processed, Hughes's various businesses overcame multiple roadblocks involving US regulations and won a major defense contract.

The 1960 Hughes loan story was first exposed thirteen days before election day in Drew Pearson's column. As expected, it evoked "semi-sleeping perceptions of Nixon . . . the huckster whose personal ethics were less than presidential."[38] By providing the public enough but not all of the story two weeks before the election, Pearson meant to tempt a Nixon denial and then rebut the denial with follow-up articles disclosing the most damning specifics. The stratagem worked.[39] In the face of six syndicated stories, the Nixon camp lied, tried to cover up, challenged the critics' motives, played the victim, stonewalled, and at last grudgingly conceded the truth. The Kennedy campaign amplified the stories, encouraging doubts of Nixon's trustworthiness. Voters drew their own conclusions. It was the October Surprise of the 1960 presidential campaign.

Like Nixon's 1968 campaign managers, Humphrey's had similar internal polling data indicating the same softness in Nixon's support. Napolitan, sensing an opportunity, shared this information with O'Brien. "If the story had come out publicly about Greek CIA money going to Mitchell, you bet your ass it could have been woven effectively into ads," Napolitan recalled years later. "Just having that accusation and being able to determine its veracity would have given us a good weapon."[40] He urged O'Brien to go on the attack, but the campaign manager told Napolitan "not to say anything to anyone." Napolitan added, "I wasn't calling the shots then; Larry was." Even after the second Demetracopoulos meeting, Napolitan felt "we still had time" to turn the election by making statements and creating powerful ads. But "Larry was running the show . . . and asked that we not do it."[41]

Respected *Washington Post* columnist David Broder, dean of the Washington press corps, observed that if the payoff story had been released in mid-October 1968, it would have been "explosive."[42] The "New Nixon" myth would have quickly evaporated, he surmised, inviting "others to come forward with similar reports, which cumulatively could have changed the outcome of such a close election." It could also have created an atmosphere in which Humphrey or LBJ released intelligence reports about the even more sensational Nixon Paris Peace talks sabotage.[43]

■

CRESTFALLEN, ELIAS LEFT the Watergate Hotel that beautiful autumn afternoon and slowly walked back to his apartment at the Fairfax Hotel. In the privacy of his room, emotionally exhausted, he briefly shed tears. He cried for the wounded cause of Greek democracy and the lost chance to prevent the pernicious effects of an ascendant Agnew. He cried in frustration at his failure to achieve the anti-junta objectives he'd sought, after months of sleepless effort. He cried in fear for himself. Then he coldly assessed his situation and wondered what he, with an uncertain immigration status, under wiretap and other government surveillance, should do next.

He knew that if he were denied legal permanent resident status, he would have to leave the country, and briefly considered carrying his self-exile to Copenhagen, London, or Rome and picking up the fight there. But those capitals paled as a base from which to mount a serious, sustained campaign against the junta. To be effective, he needed to stay in Washington and fight harder.

He decided to file the Pappas-KYP money story away and not discuss it further. If, in such a close campaign, O'Brien and the Democrats didn't think his "scoop" was of great value, worth confirming and promoting, then maybe someday a serious congressional committee would investigate what happened and expose the truth. History would provide answers. But the Pappas payoff could not remain his priority issue. Johnson-Humphrey had not been great for Greek democracy either; Eugene McCarthy and Robert Kennedy had been much more forceful in criticizing American support of the military dictatorship. How much worse could Nixon-Agnew be, especially if the Democrats held control of Congress? The fight would go on, he rationalized.

He dried his eyes and called his lawyer to discuss the deportation risks he faced and plan the next steps. And then, in classic Elias Demetracopoulos compartmentalizing fashion, he walled off the week's events and went to a square dance to which he'd been invited. But rather than wearing cowboy boots, Stetson hat, and a colorful bandanna as did others, he wore wingtips, navy suit, white shirt, and carefully knotted tie.

■

AT THE LAST meeting with O'Brien, Ira Kapenstein held out the promise of a critical story on Tom Pappas. Robert Healy, *Boston Globe* political columnist, reporter, executive editor, and later chief of the *Globe*'s Washington bureau, had Pappas on his radar for years. Covering the Eisenhower Administration, Healy had watched as Pappas came and left the White House as he pleased, often securing decisions favorable to his business interests.

Healy was also a regular at Washington Sunday-evening pot-luck suppers where reporters dined informally with sources, including CIA officers. The rules were that all conversation was "off the record," definitely not for attribution, but the information exchanged could be developed. And the information, Healy said, was usually reliable. It was there that he picked up fragments of stories of Pappas and Agnew leaning hard on Greek-Americans, Greek nationals, and members of the Greek government for serious cash to help the Nixon campaign.[44] So Healy was primed when, about the time of Brown's call to O'Brien, Kenny O'Donnell, former appointments secretary in the Kennedy White House, raised the issue of Pappas and channeling possibly illegal Greek money to the Nixon campaign.

Healy passed the tip on to the *Globe*'s editor Tom Winship, a stalwart liberal who had long been interested in profiling the Pappas brothers' roles in Boston and Washington politics.[45] Winship disliked Tom Pappas, and relished an opportunity to knock him down, or, better yet, nail him in a breakthrough article that could influence the campaign. He assigned a large feature story to Christopher Lydon, a young, well-regarded, Boston-based political reporter and ardent admirer of Hubert Humphrey. Sensing a big story, Winship pushed Lydon to "dig deep."[46]

The day before Demetracopoulos's first meeting with O'Brien, Lydon met Tom Pappas for breakfast at the Boston Ritz Carlton Hotel. Pappas turned on the charm, denying the negative allegations as baseless rumors. That Friday, October 18, was a memorable day for Lydon. His wife was about to give birth to their first child, and he was conducting the early-morning interview before going to the hospital. When he got to Mass General, he found in his wife's room an enormous basket of fruit, a gift from Tom Pappas, with a note of congratulations and best wishes.

In the course of his research, Lydon talked with Larry O'Brien, who gave him the gist of what Demetracopoulos had told him, without disclosing his source, but indicating that the story couldn't be corroborated. O'Brien's assistant Kapenstein, focusing on feeding the press allegations of Agnew's corruption, also failed to push the Demetracopoulos disclosures.[47] Although he continually monitored the development of the *Globe* story, Kapenstein said nothing to Lydon about Demetracopoulos or to indicate that the Pappas charges were anything but "unsubstantiable [sic] rumors." It might not have mattered. With a new baby, Lydon was not going to fly to Athens to check out the details, and the Globe wasn't going to pick up the unlimited tab for any sources moving to the States.

Some who knew Winship well, however, believe that the Globe editor, given the opportunity to help, would have sought out benefactors who could have provided living expenses for the corroborators.[48] As it was, Winship was disappointed that no smoking gun had been uncovered, but nevertheless gave Lydon's profile big play. The article came out on Thursday morning, October 31, and highlighted Pappas's "near-legendary reputation as a Midas among party money men," who always made sure he got full credit for his fundraising prowess. It quoted an economist who called Pappas a modern-day "robber baron" and "monopolist," and described the Greek-American fundraiser as a salesman for the junta who was planning to lead a series of meetings after the American election on "Greece: Business Opportunities in a Developing Economy." Asked about being a power broker on both sides of the Atlantic, Pappas "dismissed the question" with a "tsk, tsk," responding "I am an American citizen" and denying "any more than a civic interest in the American election."

About the dramatic headlines in the New York Daily News and London Sunday Times instigated by Elias's tips and late-September news conference, headlines "which inspired new legends about Pappas the wonder worker," Lydon wrote: "Few of those original suggestions about Pappas and Agnew seem credible now."[49] The section dealing with the KYP money was buried in the piece. It said only: "In the rumor mills of Boston and Washington it is being whispered that Pappas is the conduit of campaign funds from the Greek junta to the Nixon-Agnew treasury—an unsubstantiable charge. Yet the government in Athens was sufficiently concerned about it to issue an official statement branding the rumor a 'ludicrous fabrication of enemies of Greece.'"[50]

The article was enough of a news hook for the Democratic National Committee to issue a press release later the same day, blandly headlined: "O'BRIEN ASKS EXPLANATION OF NIXON-AGNEW RELATIONSHIPS WITH PAPPAS," and including a call on Nixon and Agnew to "explain their relationships." It had no impact on the race. The Nixon campaign was silent. No reporter picked up the story. And, even if one had, there was little that could have been done to penetrate the noise of the final days of the campaign.

October 31 was the day that President Johnson announced the halt to bombing in Vietnam. That story, the so-called "breakthrough to peace," led the news. Even the normally voluble Elias Demetracopoulos thought the *Globe* piece was too little, too late. That evening he issued a simple anticlimactic press release of his own, criticizing Agnew's "surprising ignorance of the Greek situation" and stating that he preferred "to make no comment whatsoever, under the present circumstances" about "the relationship between the Greek military junta, . . . Mr. Thomas A. Pappas and the Republican vice-presidential candidate, Governor Spiro Agnew."[51]

On November 1, the day after O'Brien issued his Pappas release and Johnson announced the bombing halt, a Pearson-Anderson column appeared under the headline: "Agnew's Junta Ties Disturb NATO."[52] Trying to do a takedown article on Nixon with the impact of his 1960 Howard Hughes exposé, Pearson focused on Agnew and his alleged Geppetto, Tom Pappas. Like their earlier 1968 Nixon exposés, this one also failed to draw blood, only nibbling at parts of the big story.[53] Kapenstein was one of Pearson's anonymous sources for this article, but never told him about the Demetracopoulos disclosure. When Pearson, who had extensive contacts in Greece dating back to his covering the Greek Civil War, found out that Elias had withheld information that could have helped him write a blockbuster CIA/Pappas/Nixon/Agnew exposé, he was furious and, until his death the following year, refused to talk to him.[54]

Jack Anderson's biographer, Mark Feldstein, said that, while it is impossible to say with certainty, he believed that had Pearson and Anderson been able to confirm Elias's allegations with other "tangible evidence," they would have run with it hard, in their nationally syndicated column and daily radio program, probably using the same approach they successfully used with the Hughes loan in 1960.[55] Les Whitten, then a junior member of the same muckraking team, also felt that Pearson and Anderson, each for different reasons, would have gone with the information, even before they'd pinned everything down, because of Elias's reliability as a source and the importance of stopping Nixon.[56] Awareness of the *Boston Globe*'s contemporaneous investigation of Pappas would also have fueled their competitive juices.

What would have happened had they published the exposé? "Think about it," Feldstein asked. "[I]f this story had cost Nixon the election, there would have been no Watergate . . . Instead of Woodward and Bernstein, Pearson and Anderson might have become journalistic icons for a generation of budding investigative reporters. And Elias Demetracopoulos, not Daniel Ellsberg, would have become the international poster boy for whistleblowers . . ."[57]

■

YEARS LATER, IT is still not entirely clear why O'Brien did virtually nothing with the information, or why he appears to have lied to, or at least misled, Demetracopoulos on several key issues. Historian Robert Dallek developed plausible reasons why Johnson might have said no.[58] But information in the archives of the LBJ and JFK libraries, not previously available, now points to the president never having been asked to intervene by either O'Brien or Humphrey.[59] Indeed, Johnson may not have known anything about the Pappas money transfer.

According to Demetracopoulos, when he inquired if Johnson personally refused him, O'Brien said he never went directly to LBJ, but sent the request through Humphrey, who had received the refusal from Johnson. O'Brien did have a few conversations with his candidate during this period, but there is no evidence that he ever mentioned Elias's revelations to Humphrey, let alone indicate they should be treated seriously. Johnson's autobiography and other leading biographies are silent on the issue, as are those of Humphrey. Surviving members of Humphrey's top campaign staff have no recollection that LBJ and Humphrey ever discussed the matter during the single exchange between the two in this period, an "off-the-record" meeting at the White House the day after Elias met O'Brien. Likewise, there is no record of O'Brien's talking to Humphrey before he met with the President. Humphrey's press secretary, Norman Sherman, who helped prepare the vice president's memoirs and was thus privy to his detailed recollections, has stated that he would have known about any Humphrey conversation with O'Brien or the President about the Demetracopoulos charges, had such a conversation happened.[60]

In later years, when challenged by reporters to explain why he never used the Demetracopoulos information, O'Brien said the story was "impressive . . . but not subject to absolute proof."[61] This was clearly not true. Elias had names, dollar amounts, and witnesses. Any of his three options could have led at least to clear and convincing evidence. Obviously, asking Helms directly could have been dispositive, but most likely Helms would have resorted to plausible deniability. To a question posed by historian Stanley Kutler on a CIA-KYP-Pappas-Nixon-Agnew connection, Helms responded:

> There are certain things, Dr. Kutler, that we learned through hard
> experience and one of them was that you don't get yourself involved at
> any time in any way in allowing foreign money to come into American

elections . . . Even if somebody suggests they would like to do it, I would insist that they don't tell <u>me</u> about it because that is dynamite."[62]

Given Helms's long history monitoring Elias and contributing to his negative dossier, it seems unlikely he would have told the President that Demetracopoulos was a credible source for anything. But even without Helms, Robert Healy's usually reliable CIA dinner companions had given him the story of Pappas's transferring the Greek money to Nixon.[63] The *Globe* and *New York Times* need not have stopped their coverage with the junta's perfunctory denial. Kapenstein could have spent as much time following up on this as he did gathering dirt on Agnew's unlawful fundraising practices while he was governor.[64] Congressman Don Fraser, co-chair of the Democracy in Greece Committee, said that, if he had known, he would have talked to colleagues who knew about CIA funding of Greece and urged the Justice Department to conduct an immediate inquiry.[65]

It is interesting that O'Brien used the qualified language "absolute proof" as his standard. O'Brien and the Humphrey campaign could have readily obtained contemporaneous corroborative proof, if they had cared enough to do so. No one ever questioned Phillips Talbot, then US ambassador to Greece, or others connected with the embassy or the Athens CIA station. Former Ambassador Thomas Boyatt, who was then a political officer in Cyprus, said he heard about the KYP money transfer and believed that the facts could have been nailed down at the time. A former American ambassador told Sy Hersh he learned about Pappas's conduit role in 1968 at the State Department, asserting: "We were carrying out a policy to support 'a Greek bearing gifts.'"[66]

There are several possible reasons why O'Brien never used the information. The first is an overabundance of caution. To say, as O'Brien did, that he was concerned about the possible embarrassment of having DNC staffers arrested in Athens is disingenuous. An arrest of DNC staffers at the hands of the Greek dictatorship would have increased news coverage of the issue. Furthermore, he knew that, with Agnew on the ticket, many traditionally Democratic Greek-Americans were already planning to desert their party.

O'Brien may have thought there was nothing of substance in the Demetracopoulos information and that, even if what was done by Pappas and his Nixon confederates was reprehensible, nothing involved was illegal or worth pursuing. But this sounds like a strange reaction from someone known to exploit all types of opposition research. Joe Napolitan waited in vain for the signal to prepare ads on this issue. Had O'Brien instructed him, Kapenstein would likely have been more aggressive urging his high-level press contacts to follow the CIA-Greek money trail.

Even if O'Brien harbored a fear that exposing the 1968 Greek money transfer could open the Democrats up to charges of foreign-money payments coming to them from the likes of the Shah of Iran and Philippine president Ferdinand Marcos, it shouldn't have chilled him. Big-ticket foreign donors traditionally gave to the Republicans in equal or greater amounts, and 1968 was no exception.[67] To be sure, the threat of mutually assured destruction had led to a bipartisan tradition of not disclosing illegal foreign contributions. However, circumstances around this one-sided Greek money transfer presented extraordinary political potential.

It is plausible that O'Brien thought the allegations were too complicated and came too late in the campaign. Experience may have taught him that voters would probably dismiss the charges as an unfair last-minute smear and, even if thousands were swayed, it would not move any votes in the Electoral College. If this were the case, he could have said so directly to Elias, but he failed to do so in either of their two meetings.

A second possible reason for O'Brien's lack of initiative is that he wanted the information for his own purposes. The 1968 Demetracopoulos file on Nixon-Pappas was still in Larry O'Brien's possession, unused, at the time of the 1972 Watergate break-in. But, according to Napolitan, the file on Pappas and the Greek junta money was not kept in the office because O'Brien removed the 1968 Demetracopoulos information to his private residence. This action might imply that, like Johnson's withholding disclosure of the incriminating Paris Peace Talks sabotage as insurance against Nixon, the information could have been more valuable to him personally than politically. Did O'Brien believe that Demetracopoulos's information would be more useful in a Nixon Administration than in a Humphrey one? Unlikely: the thought that O'Brien might be willing to sacrifice his candidate in order to serve his own future private interests seems outrageously conspiratorial.

A third theory, that O'Brien discounted the message because of the messenger, seems most likely and logical. Elias did not know O'Brien personally when he walked into the Watergate, but O'Brien may have remembered Elias then, or had his mind refreshed shortly thereafter. As a member of the White House staff, O'Brien would have been well aware of the fallout from Demetracopoulos's 1961

Arleigh Burke interview. O'Brien, Kenny O'Donnell, and Pierre Salinger were all close, and O'Brien may have talked to one or both after the first meeting. Healy believed that his tip from O'Donnell came from O'Brien. If O'Brien was not at first aware of Elias's infamous intelligence dossier, he would definitely have heard about it after talking to Salinger. Did O'Brien think that Demetraco-poulos might be laying a trap for the Humphrey campaign? If O'Brien were in touch with Salinger about this, as he was with him and O'Donnell about other campaign matters, he would clearly feel that Demetracopoulos should not be trusted. It is probably no coincidence that on Tuesday, October 22, three days after his first meeting with O'Brien, Elias received a call from Nancy Jackson, his Los Angeles friend who sent him the 1966 letter telling him how Salinger had tried to smear him by claiming Demetracopoulos worked for the "other side." This time, she told Elias, Salinger had called her to say her friend [Elias] was "causing trouble again . . . telling lies." Maybe it was better, as O'Brien told Na-politan, just to gather Elias's information and file it away.

In *Camelot's Court*, Robert Dallek pointed out that O'Brien's "affinity for negative thinking" and "impulse to emphasize impediments" had initially made President Kennedy reluctant to appoint him White House liaison with Con-gress.[68] Jim King, for decades a celebrated advance man of Kennedy and other Democratic campaigns, knew O'Brien and his father from the 1950s when they operated a Springfield tavern serving and organizing working-class Irish Demo-crats. King concurred with the description of O'Brien's proclivity for negative thinking. He surmised that, even in 1968, "the McCarthy that would strike deepest fears into O'Brien's Irish Catholic heart was not Gene but Joe." O'Brien came of age in the era of Joe McCarthy witch hunts and still believed that it was a political third rail to deal with anyone tainted with so much as a suspicion of Communist connections. The disinformation campaign against Elias had been anything but subtle. The problem O'Brien had with Demetracopoulos was not his message, but the messenger himself. Blowback from years of inflammatory anti-Elias attacks fanned by Kennedy insiders may well have cost Humphrey the election and given the country Richard Nixon.

■

DEEMING HIS FORAY into the presidential campaign a wasteful distraction, Deme-tracopoulos refocused on Greece even before Americans voted. He renewed his criticism of September's sham plebiscite and attacked American plans to resume partial shipments of heavy military equipment to Greece. Meanwhile George

Papandreou, who had fallen critically ill, died on November 1—the day after the O'Brien press release. His November 3 funeral in Athens attracted some 300,000 demonstrators. Chanting anti-regime slogans, they turned the private service into a paean for democracy. Arrests followed. Heavy sentences were imposed on some, and Alekos Panagoulis was sentenced to death for his earlier assassination attempt on George Papadopoulos. The junta decided never again to let such a crowd gather in Athens. By year's end, with opposition in disarray and tolerance of the dictatorship rising, the junta had "little cause for anxiety either at home or abroad."

O'Brien may have used the Demetracopoulos information fecklessly, but it was still potentially damaging. During the presidential transition, John Mitchell discussed Demetracopoulos's Pappas disclosure privately with J. Edgar Hoover.[69] Afterward, the Attorney-General designate told Louise Gore that her Greek friend was worse than a troublemaker and that it would be better if she stayed away from him. This would not be a one-time warning. As Watergate historian Stanley Kutler later observed, the matter of Pappas's 1968 Greek money transfer, the Greek Connection, "caused the most anxiety for the longest period of time for the Nixon Administration, and the agencies that served it."[70]

19.

Fighting the Dictatorship

FOR ELIAS, 1969 DAWNED MUCH as the previous year had ended. He monitored the situation in Greece, exchanged messages with exiles in Europe, prepared a revised list of congressional opponents and targets in the new administration, attended holiday parties, returned to Capitol Hill to push his anti-junta agenda, extended his Wall Street business networks, and consulted with his attorneys regarding the best way to secure legal permanent-resident status. Although federal agencies repeatedly tried to make an illegal-foreign-agent deportation case against him, the FBI steadfastly reported that its "established sources" could not confirm any Soviet contact since his 1967 arrival, and US senators wrote to the INS director urging swift approval of his immigration petition, praising Elias's strong moral character.[1]

That January, Nixon and his chief foreign-policy advisor Henry Kissinger assumed office with grand plans. They wanted to take bold and dramatic steps to transform US relations with China and the Soviet Union. But, notwithstanding their intellectual recognition of a multipolar, interconnected world, their attitudes toward much of the globe were frozen in Cold War stereotypes. Developing and "intermediate" countries were largely regarded as pawns on a global chessboard, significant only insofar as they served the larger geopolitical agenda. Despite Greece's self-important view of its standing among nations, it was consigned to the lesser category.[2]

Kissinger began his tenure trying to prevent any leaks that he did not himself orchestrate, privately denigrating Secretary of State William P. Rogers as unqualified and serving as an interlocutor between the State Department and the President on foreign-policy issues raised by key supporters. Nixon assured Tom Pappas of his continued role as "unofficial middleman" between the White House and the junta.[3]

United States Ambassador Talbot had resigned his post effective at the end of the Johnson Administration, rather than wait until his replacement was named, but other officials at the embassy described the situation in Greece as being better than before the 1967 coup. While characterizing the new government as cartoonishly anti-intellectual, prone to making foolish pronouncements, and generally inept at public relations, they dismissed as "socialist agitation" signs of international opposition, noting that the "economic oligarchy" (including by name Aristotle Onassis) had "unmistakably cast its lot" with the regime and that serious internal opposition was nonexistent. They looked forward to a Nixon Administration "less inclined to badger the [Greek government]." Its message was to "keep our 'cool,'" be realistic, and delink military aid from "internal political performance," adding that "there's not very much that the liberal minority in Congress can do about it other than make noise."[4]

■

FRIENDS SAID THAT Elias worked six hours a day for Brimberg and fourteen hours a day toward the overthrow of the Greek dictatorship. Demetracopoulos's paying job involved gathering useful investor intelligence on legislative and regulatory developments, making client presentations, and identifying, inviting, and escorting notables who would be draws for Brimberg's business luncheons.

Elias's evenings were spent at political and diplomatic receptions and dinners, where he would be one of the first to arrive. For the first hour or two, he fulfilled Brimberg-related tasks. Then, for the remainder of the evening, he'd switch gears, becoming an unabashed advocate for a free Greece. He was usually the last to leave. Sipping his preferred ginger ale or Coca-Cola instead of alcoholic beverages meant he could make his case while stone-cold sober and remember the information he'd gathered without taking notes. Then, before going to bed, he would use the five- to seven-hour time differences to brief and get reports from his European sources. He usually slept no more than four hours a night.

Elias needed to demonstrate to Brimberg his value as a serious player at the intersection of business and politics. He also liked doing favors for friends like Elmer Staude, who had organized a large Los Angeles dinner in his honor after his 1967 escape. President of the Brunswig Drug Company, a growing West Coast pharmaceutical enterprise eager to merge with the East Coast firm of Bergen Drug, Staude wanted antitrust approval and high-level networking. So, on February 26, Elias hosted a posh reception and dinner for Staude at which the guest list included a Brimberg & Co. partner, Democratic and Republican senators, Treasury Under-Secretary Paul Volcker, officials from the World Bank and State Department, business leaders, journalists, former CIA Athens station chief John Richardson, and a variety of diplomats from missions not including Greece. Staude, Brimberg, and Elias deemed the event a great success.[5]

It was not considered a success, however, by CIA director Richard Helms, Deputy Director Tom Karamessines, and their intelligence colleagues who, after reviewing the VIP guest list, reported in exasperation that "Demetracopoulos is flying high around town."[6] The CIA memorandum recommended that senators who sounded "like the straight Demetracopoulos" be given "a low-key warning about [him] . . . [and] the embarrassment he might create for anyone becoming involved with him." To that end, Karamessines authorized the preparation of a report to recycle past false claims and generate fresh calumnies about Elias. Their pursuit was relentless.

·

ELIAS FELT HE did his best anti-junta work alone, nurturing a network of sympathetic congressmen and administration officials, and serving the needs of journalists looking for new and interesting copy, connecting with other groups only on an as-needed basis. To him, the anti-junta efforts outside Washington had been largely ineffective. He found that many on the left were passionate in their opposition, but in their ideological purity often failed to make common cause with moderates and conservatives who could be allies for different reasons.

Elias believed in a broad-based coalition that could animate world opinion, sustain pressure on political leaders, and guide the inchoate opposition groups emerging in Greece. He believed that no one should try to organize it rigidly, because the strong and diverse personalities would never defer to a single leader. Engaging Greek-Americans in the fight might be a worthwhile goal, but, after the hard rejection he received in 1967, he decided that dealing with them was a task best left to others.[7]

Sometimes graphic portrayals of what was happening in Greece followed by a soft appeal to human rights, political idealism, and the restoration of cherished democratic symbols were sufficient to win support. With others, however, especially conservatives, it was often necessary to appeal to American self-interest. Customizing his approaches and selectively invoking the names of different allies made him mysterious to some, but he believed it helped his effectiveness. Jim Pyrros, longtime legislative aide to Democratic Michigan congressman Lucien Nedzi, and a key player in the Don Fraser/Don Edwards–led United States Committee for Democracy in Greece (USCDG), had grudging respect for Elias as a "lone wolf" who outworked everyone else.[8]

Demetracopoulos, true to his strategy of diversifying his approaches, kept up with the different anti-junta factions but seldom joined in their activities. He believed that Karamanlis, Andreas Papandreou, the King, Eleni Vlachou, and others could be important players in different ways, but was unconvinced of the usefulness of a so-called Greek government in exile. Determined not to carry baggage from earlier relationships into this battle, he tried to work with and not publicly criticize potential allies.

Andreas Papandreou was a case in point. After he was freed from prison in a 1967 Christmas Eve amnesty, he went into exile, first to various European cities, then briefly in Sweden where he taught economics and formed his own Pan-Hellenic Liberation Movement (known by its acronym PAK). Andreas became the self-styled leading international anti-junta figure on the left, enjoying rock-star status as he travelled to college campuses and other venues promoting PAK's agenda. In 1969, having moved to Toronto to teach at York University, Andreas wanted to visit Washington as part of a "Crusade to the American People." With less than a month's lead time, his wife Margaret contacted Elias asking him to take Andreas "under your wing."[9]

Elias had been close to George Papandreou but had reservations about his son. They were never friends and were mutually suspicious. Yet they often had shared interests, especially their desire to oust the dictatorship. Elias never doubted Andreas's intelligence and charisma but found him irresponsible, undisciplined, and untrustworthy. He was troubled by Andreas's sweeping New Left rhetoric and lack of judgment. Reports that Andreas was consorting with a revised Greek Communist party still "sentimentally attached to the Soviet Union,"[10] as well as perceptions of his increasing anti-Americanism, created persistent public-relations problems. Elias worried that Andreas's repeating EAM/

ELAS's Civil War mistakes could be used by an emboldened Moscow. He was also disturbed by reports that Andreas, after founding PAK, "set about assiduously undermining other anti-junta groups," entering alliances but then working to "discredit his supposed colleagues."[11]

Nevertheless, without hesitation Elias arranged a trip, including a pseudonymous hotel registration. Painstakingly, he created a schedule that connected Andreas with influential individuals who were either actively or potentially sympathetic, avoiding settings where Andreas might say something untoward.[12] An ungrateful Andreas left Washington without settling some bills, which Elias quietly paid.

Shortly thereafter, Eleni Vlachou ("Helen Vlachos" when abroad) arrived in the US. Elias, who had stayed in regular contact with his former *Kathimerini* publisher, now based in London, did advance work for her meetings and publicity as well. Eleni's husband had remained in Athens. After the junta took him into custody, Eleni, a former voice of the pro-American Greek establishment, wrote Elias about having come to recognize the "new reality":

> Don't expect the militaries and the merchants who rule America to help you back to freedom. You have to BECOME A PROBLEM . . .
>
> The Americans—and the English, and the French that have power dont [sic] care, and those who care can do very little," she added, "Journalists, politicians, diplomats, intellectuals . . . they say the right things but the Juntas, the fat Pentagon mother Junta or the lean Athens one, don't take any notice.
>
> . . . IF Greeks want freedom, they will have to fight for it. In any way they can.[13]

ELIAS WAS SURPRISED by the intensity of her language, viewing it as a sign of growing outrage across the political spectrum. He hoped she would carry the spirit forward in *Greek Report*, the newsletter she was now publishing in London.

The August 1968 assassination attempt on Papadopoulos had led to more large-scale arrests and more people in detention or exile. Elias became an interlocutor of choice for people trapped in Greece wanting to get the word out that the rosy portrayals by the Greek Embassy in Washington were misleading. Sometimes letters and packages came addressed to his fake name, "Robert Speer," at the Fairfax Hotel. Sometimes senders used only "Elias," and some communications were mailed simply to "Elias Demetracopoulos, Washington D.C., USA." The post office knew where to find him. He was most affected by pleas for help from torture victims and their families.

Elias believed that the opposition had to be relentless in its approach to Washington decision-makers. He asked sympathetic congressmen to insert his remarks and articles about him into the *Congressional Record* as a means of legitimizing his words and activities. He ran off hundreds of reprints with congressional letterhead to use in his lobbying packets. From retail politicking to background briefings, he proselytized constantly. He prepared articles under his own name and ghost-wrote others, appeared on talk shows, held press conferences, engaged in formal debates, and gave speeches to groups large and small. He was always competing for attention against bigger stories: Nixon's Cambodian bombing and the resulting anti-war Moratorium, the Apollo 11 moon landing, Chappaquiddick and Woodstock in 1969. A dictatorship in Greece was no longer fresh or pressing news. Elias, however, refused to let the "Greek problem" fall under the radar.

Demetracopoulos spoke to an assortment of business groups, women's organizations, and college assemblies, encouraging his audiences to become activists and recruiting some as volunteer researchers. On April 29, 1969, he gave a speech at George Washington University titled: "Greece: A New Vietnam?" warning that misreading signs and taking wrong actions could lead the United States into another disastrous quagmire. He asserted as demonstrably false the contention that the dictatorship would help American strategic interests. "Purging the cream of the Greek officer corps" and a "preoccupation" with internal security had instead put at risk the stability and combat capabilities of the Greek armed forces, jeopardizing Greece's NATO responsibilities. Citing inflationary spending and declines in foreign investment, GDP, and consumer confidence, he also noted the rise of corrupt business dealings, despite junta claims of purity. Moreover, he criticized the double standard of expressing outrage at left-wing coups while condoning right-wing ones, a practice that fostered a pernicious anti-Americanism and created a fertile breeding ground for Soviet exploitation. The speech gained traction with members of Congress, who sent copies of his "pertinent warning" to Secretary of Defense Melvin Laird, NSC director Henry Kissinger, and Vice President Agnew, and asked for their responses.[14]

GRATIFIED BY THE favorable reaction from junta opponents on the left to the circulated copies of his GWU speech, Demetracopoulos wanted to present his argument to potential allies on the American right who might have more influence with the Nixon Administration. Senator Fulbright recommended he contact Herman Kahn, who had left his longtime position as a physicist and mathematician at the Rand Corporation to create the Hudson Institute think tank.

Kahn was a 300-pound bespectacled intellectual giant most famous for his Strangelovian views on how to win, or at least survive, a thermonuclear war.[15] He asked Elias to submit a reworked version of his speech as a formal Hudson Institute paper that challenged US policy regarding Greece as weakening NATO's southern flank and running counter to "America's own national interests." In his commentary on the piece, Kahn, while conceding disagreement on some issues, emphasized other points—chances of a renewed civil war and a weaker Greek military—that were "worth serious study."[16] He directed that the paper be sent to the Institute's full mailing list.

The State Department, the Nixon White House, and the Greek Embassy were not pleased. The Greek Desk at the State Department prepared a confidential memorandum, summarizing the paper and describing Demetracopoulos snarkily as "a correspondent and public relations man who considers himself as the coordinator of anti-regime activities in the United States." The CIA expressed surprise that Kahn would publish it.[17]

.

TOWARD THE END of May, bombs went off in Athens at Syntagma Square and the Ministry of Finance. There were reports of more than a dozen generals involved in an attempted coup, all were arrested, and the regime cast a dragnet to round up sympathizers. Then on May 27, LOOK magazine published a damning article titled "Greece: Government by Torture."[18] Its author, senior editor Christopher S. Wren, said that until he visited Greece he had not believed torture reports. After a series of businessmen, priests, army officers, lawyers, and housewives, all former political prisoners, described their ordeals in detail and let him "see, and touch, the scars," he concluded that "torture has taken place in Greece on victims who number into the thousands. Under a frightened, unpopular military regime, torture goes on today."[19]

After reviewing nearly 200 cases, Wren portrayed gleeful torturers beating their victims to unconsciousness, jamming urine-soaked rags into their mouths and detergent into their throats, forcing them to lick up their own vomit, smashing their heads into walls, poking eyeballs, sticking hot peppers into their mouths, noses, and eyes, slugging testicles with iron bars, then shoving the bars into rectums, and tearing skin or violating women with broomsticks. Family members were sometimes beaten in front of those being interrogated. Doctors risked having their telephone service cut if they treated victims. Questioning America's role in all this, Wren warned that American aid had become identified with the tortures, provoking anti-Americanism among "once loyal friends." "The reckoning," he wrote, "has yet to come."[20]

Two days after publication of the *LOOK* article, Elias was interviewed on the syndicated Washington television program *Panorama*. The hosts wanted a debate, but the Greek Embassy declined to send anyone, so Elias presented the coup's origins and the horrors revealed in the *LOOK* article unchallenged.[21] Asked about his politics, Elias described himself "as a man with liberal views who favored conservative approaches" and as not belonging to any political party. He dodged singling out the CIA for blame, talking instead about a widespread belief in Europe that the United States was "involved" in Greece "by commission or omission." "It would be a good thing all around," he recommended, for the Nixon Administration to support a congressional investigation of US policies and activities in Greece over "the last few years."[22]

Listening to testimony before the House Committee on Foreign Affairs, Demetracopoulos smirked at Under-Secretary of State Joseph Sisco's use of the phrase "our need for friends in the region" as a rationale for sending military aid to the junta, and laughed audibly when Deputy Assistant Secretary of State Rodger Davies predicted the junta would fully implement its new constitution "by [the] end of [the] year."[23] He fed reporters information on the lack of combat readiness of Greek armed forces and conferred regularly with USCDG leaders Congressmen Edwards and Fraser, who tried hard to get the administration to develop a new agenda toward Greece, only to be faced by Nixon officials pushing ahead in a different direction.

While Britain and France debated internally on how best to take a moral stand without adversely affecting their commercial interests, other European nations, especially those from Scandinavia, were much more forceful in their opposition to the junta. The Council of Europe, founded in the aftermath of World War II and dedicated to the protection of fundamental freedoms, became the crucible for member states to decide whether they had the stomach to dele-gitimize one of their own for mishandling its "internal affairs."[24]

For the USCDG and other American-led groups opposed to the junta, the highest priority was blocking Greek demands to restore full military aid, partly suspended after the April 1967 coup. The arms restriction dealt only with major military items not yet in the weapons pipeline, like aircraft, naval vessels, mis-siles, and tanks. Though important symbolically, the list of banned items did not include small arms, ammunition, communications equipment, or trucks, all of which could be used against citizens of a police state.[25] Demetracopoulos be-lieved that the administration would use the pretext of the Soviet invasion of Czechoslovakia the previous summer to mount a powerful counteroffensive. As early as October 1968, the United States announced that, in response to Soviet moves, it was resuming delivery of some heavy arms. It was clear that US mili-tary aid would soon return at least to pre-1967 levels. By February 1969, F-104 Starfighters, HU-16 maritime patrol aircraft, and self-propelled artillery had started to arrive. Elias assumed that Colonel Gaddafi's overthrow of the Libyan monarchy in September, with the attendant expulsion of the American Air Force base and the British naval station at Tobruk, would provide a further US ratio-nale for accepting the situation in Greece. Delegitimizing the Greek dictator-ship in the eyes of the world would not be easily or speedily achieved.

The only anti-junta option thought to be possibly acceptable to the Ameri-cans was the "Karamanlis solution," some compromise government led by the conservative former prime minister. But Karamanlis had been publicly silent and privately ambiguous. On October 1, 1969, the first anniversary of the new constitution, Karamanlis made his strongest attack yet on the junta. Calling the regime a "tyrannical and illegitimate institution," he charged, "they had never intended . . . to restore democracy . . ." By their blunders, he said, they had caused the disintegration of the armed forces, undermined the economic future of the country, and isolated Greece politically and morally. Now they were resorting to "terrorization of the Greek people and deception of international public opin-ion."[26] He offered himself to convince government leaders that their downfall was inevitable, either peacefully or by being overthrown. Then he followed up with a private letter to the retired chief of the general staff that "could have been read as an invitation to a military counter revolution."[27] The *New York Times* ed-itorialized that it was a "moment of truth for Nixon's State Department; time "to face up to the fact that their policy in Greece is bankrupt."[28]

■

FOR NEARLY TWO years, Bob Brimberg had been patiently waiting for Elias's immigration problems to be cleared up so Elias could travel abroad to help enhance the firm's presence in Europe. In early September, Demetracopoulos was finally told that he was eligible for permanent residence as the recipient of a Sixth Preference immigrant visa, but had to leave the county to have it processed. On the morning of September 23, 1969, with his immigration attorney at his side, he flew to the American Embassy in Montreal and returned that afternoon, landing first in New York, where he was readmitted to the United States by INS. Less than a week later, as he was preparing to leave for Europe for the first time since his 1967 escape, his lawyer took precautionary steps to make sure that he could get back into the US.

Meeting clients and associates, Elias stayed with Brimberg at the poshest European hotels and dined at the finest restaurants. When travelling alone, he worked both to develop a network of sources and business prospects for his employer and coordinate anti-junta strategies with leading Greek exiles in Europe. Friends of Elias, from the diplomatic corps to Governor Pat Brown, had written effusive letters to embassies and business executives asking for full courtesies. Elias was intent on gathering intelligence on European economies not fully captured in published reports. He met with OECD officials and research firms conducting proprietary research. Brimberg wanted to assess the direction of the British pound and the interplay of fluctuating exchange rates of other currencies. A typical telegram Elias sent to New York from Brussels reads, "Belgian Franc strongly pressed STOP . . . Dealers here expect . . . Franc to backwash on Dutch guilder."[29]

When his official work was done, he was free to crisscross the same towns with a different agenda. Using his Brimberg expense account, he scheduled back-to-back meetings with other Greek exiles and strategized the best way to free their homeland from the dictatorship. His first appointment was with Karamanlis at his apartment in the historic Marais district of Paris. Any bad blood between them was put aside, and their conversation focused largely on the implications of the former prime minister's recent statements. Karamanlis described exchanges he had had with former leaders of the center and right, and the two discussed the recent cutback by Litton Industries in their Greek investments, other looming economic issues, and Tom Pappas. Elias contributed carefully selective perspectives gleaned from his center-left contacts.

Karamanlis was extremely upset by the reaction in Greece to his statement. That Papadopoulos and Makarezos would accuse him of encouraging "terroristic activity" was expected, but silence from others at home—except for Mavros and Kanellopoulos, who had responded positively—was a great disappointment.[30] With the exception of a retired general, no one in the military spoke out. Only one newspaper, *Vradyni*, "was bold enough" to express support. Afterward, Elias telephoned Andreas Papandreou to keep him informed and solicit his views.

Elias visited Jules Dassin and Melina Mercouri in their Left Bank flat and urged them to mobilize a network of international celebrities. He travelled later to meet with the self-exiled King in Rome, German officials in Bonn, and Paul Henri Spaak, architect of the European Union and former socialist prime minister of Belgium, outside Brussels. In London, he met with Eleni Vlachou and other Greek exiles, including Melina's brother, Spyros Mercouris, active in the opposition group Democratic Defense. He also spent a couple of days lobbying UK Parliament members, updating Liberal and Labour junta opponents, and pitching Conservatives identified as persuadable.

At all hours he met with journalists, including old friends from the London bureaus of the *New York Times*, *Washington Post*, and *Christian Science Monitor*. He was especially pleased that the Greek Desk of the BBC World Service served as an information-exchange clearinghouse, setting up meetings, including with an intelligence officer from the State Department. Elias was so focused on Greece that he gave possible news scoops (such as Soviet submarine activities off Sicily during NATO exercises) to colleagues without asking for public credit.

His whirlwind trip was not all work. Demetracopoulos made time to have dinners with Louise Gore in Paris, where she was just finishing her first session as the new American ambassador to UNESCO. He took great pleasure responding to her request to provide her with lists of books that would help her grow into her role as a diplomat. She worried about Elias. She knew personally some of those in the US who were after him and could only imagine what forces were at play on the Greek side. After Louise returned to Washington, Elias met Persa Metaxas, who flew from Athens to join him briefly. Afterward, in other cities, he visited some of the attractive eligible ladies recommended to him by women friends in Washington and identified sponsors to help Deena Clark in her NBC negotiations for a European television syndication deal.[31] Before leaving, he purchased bottles of perfume to take back as gifts.

While Elias was away, his enemies in Washington were busy. Jack Caulfield had spent more than a decade at the New York City Police Department's Bureau of Special Service and Investigations, providing security for visiting public figures such as Fidel Castro, Nikita Khrushchev, and Richard Nixon and investigating groups including the American Nazi Party and the Fair Play for Cuba Committee. In 1968 he went to work as chief of security for the Nixon campaign staff, and in April 1969 he was hired by the White House with the special assignment of creating an in-house unit to gather sensitive information and investigate political opponents. He set up a 24/7 surveillance of Edward Kennedy, initiated illegal wiretaps on the press, and recruited his friend from the New York police, Tony Ulascewitz—who was later arrested and convicted for his role in the Watergate break-in—to help with the surveillance.

On October 3, 1969, Caulfield sent a confidential memo to White House counsel John Ehrlichman titled "Greek Inquiry."[32] Several days later, Agnew foreign-policy advisor Kent Crane, who had been involved the year before in the secret Anna Chennault Vietnam communications, prepared a confidential memorandum for State Department internal security asking for material on Demetracopoulos "both in the US and abroad."[33] Al Vigderman at the Greek Desk, one of Elias's harshest critics, replied that he would provide only an "oral briefing," nothing in writing.[34] As investigators focused on Demetracopoulos's criticism of Tom Pappas, State, INS, and CIA continued to build their phony case against Elias, making sure that congressmen, White House staffers, and political operatives got the most damning information that they could supply. However, the FBI, which would have been on the front lines in bringing an actual case against Elias, recommended closing the investigation without taking any action.[35]

■

AMIDST ALL OF this, Elias turned to Celia for a serious conversation. In recent years, they'd exchanged postcards and letters but spent little time together. Recently she'd visited Washington "with mixed emotions" but "not wanting to interfere with his life."[36] She was pleased that he was doing well and had so many friends, but worried about his developing ulcers and the attacks on him. He scheduled a time to talk after she'd returned home. She waited by the phone, but he got busy and never called. When they finally connected, the two spoke frankly about their past and enduring ties. She invited him to come to Connecticut, to see her and her nieces, who remembered him fondly. He declined.

Afterward, Celia told him that when she left in 1954 she loved him, but felt they needed to separate. "I suppose the greatest surprise to me during the past years has been the fact that you never did marry one of the shipowner's daughters you were always talking about," she said. She later wrote that after years of not dating, she had met a man she really liked, who had proposed to her, but that she'd ended the relationship. "One of the reasons for my refusal," she explained "was that I felt that I had an obligation to you. God alone knows how I come by this quixotic notion—but there it is. If you had remarried then I would no longer have felt concern about your welfare."[37]

Celia ended the letter with "God bless you and good-bye. Best wishes." It was not the end between them. Elias fleetingly imagined what might have been, but quickly turned to the business at hand.

■

ELIAS NEVER FORGAVE US ambassador Phillips Talbot for mishandling the 1967 coup but thought well of his decision to resign his post at the end of the Johnson Administration.[38] The gap in official American representation and the selection of a successor were both opportunities. Working with friends in the Senate, Elias aimed to delay the new appointment as long as possible as a way of symbolizing American reservations about the dictatorship. He also wanted an ambassador strong enough to withhold gestures that could be construed as an embrace of Greek leadership. Many in the Greek-American community wanted Nixon to select one of their own, but there was no consensus choice. The State Department preferred a more traditional career diplomat, such as Henry Tasca, then ambassador to Morocco. Nixon had been acquainted with Tasca since 1947, and never forgot having been entertained royally by him while on a visit to North Africa during his post-1962 wilderness years. However, an impediment to Tasca's nomination arose that would prove ironic: Tasca's post-doctoral training at the London School of Economics and work as economics advisor to Democratic grandee W. Averill Harriman on NATO matters had branded him as a "liberal" and prompted many Republicans to question his candidacy.[39]

Demetracopoulos's choice was retired Lieutenant General William W. "Buffalo Bill" Quinn, his buddy from early-1950s Greece and a leader in the transformation of the OSS into the CIA. At the time, Quinn was the vice president of the Aerospace Group of the Martin Marietta Corporation. Elias socialized frequently with Quinn and his wife in Washington. And Quinn's daughter Sally, the future wife of Washington Post editor Ben Bradlee, had asked Elias for help in finding her suitable employment. Early in the year, General Quinn gave Elias a package of materials and approval to test the waters.

Some of Elias's liberal friends had an immediate negative reaction to Quinn and made their opposition public.[40] They assumed that as a military man he would be biased toward the colonels. Elias's attitude was: to hell with bad optics—Quinn was the best person for the job. For months, Elias met quietly with Barry Goldwater, using the Arizona senator as the point of his spear in a lobbying campaign. They avoided any discussion of Elias's tendentious use of the 1963 interview with Goldwater or the senator's long friendship with Tom Pappas. Both men jokingly agreed that Pappas, a runner-up in earlier diplomatic posting sweepstakes, had so much power with the new Greek government that an ambassadorship would have been a step backward. On March 5, Goldwater met privately with the President in the living room on the second floor of the White House to make the case for Quinn and followed up by asking Tom Pappas to support Quinn as well.[41] Pappas immediately agreed, adding: "Any friend of yours is a friend of mine." However, two months later, in an Oval Office exchange about the ambassadorship, Pappas offered no endorsement of General Quinn. While Elias strategized regularly with Quinn and Goldwater, reporting success in winning the backing of US senators across the spectrum, others in Nixon's circle pushed their own choices. John Mitchell had promised the job to a scandal-embroiled Greek-American friend in Chicago, and Senate Minority Leader Everett Dirksen tried to secure the appointment for a suburban Virginia neighbor and banker. In mid-August, *The Chicago Tribune* said the choice of ambassador to Greece had become "an Achilles heel" for the Nixon Administration. According to unnamed administration officials, "whoever is chosen by the White House will have to be first cleared by Thomas Anthony Pappas."[42] Nixon told Goldwater that Quinn was out.[43] The military regime in Athens made known its anger at the delay. Elias considered every day that passed without an ambassador being appointed a small victory.

Finally, in late August, Nixon nominated Henry Tasca. Although disappointed that Quinn had lost, Demetracopoulos was pleased that delays had kept the post empty for much of the year, during which time the Council of Europe had gathered mounting evidence of human rights violations by the Greek junta and was considering a vote to expel Greece. Fulbright did not schedule a hearing on Tasca with the Senate Foreign Relations Committee until November 4. When they finally convened, Rhode Island Senator Claiborne Pell led hours of tough questioning, greatly displeasing the nominee.[44] Although the committee approved confirming Tasca, Senate opposition loomed.

Tasca asked to meet with Demetracopoulos, who invited him for what became a more-than-three-hour dinner at the Jockey Club on November 28. It was a cordial meeting during which each man took the measure of the other. Tasca drank. Elias didn't. At evening's end, Elias told the nominee that, while he wasn't his first choice, it was time to have an ambassador in place. The next night, at another black-tie dinner party at the Clarks's, this time honoring Secretary of State William Rogers and his wife, he told the secretary of state that if he were a senator, he would vote for Tasca.[45]

Nevertheless Demetracopoulos, while not saying it publicly, had requested that Fulbright delay the Senate confirmation vote until after the expulsion vote at the Council of Europe. On November 18, the European Commission on Human Rights presented a scathing 1,200-page report to the Council of Europe, detailing its findings that the regime allowed torture to be used against its political opponents "as an administrative practice."[46] Commission representatives had received 941 documents and taken oral testimony from fifty-eight witnesses, investigated torture chambers, and verified five executions. Doctors had examined 213 cases of torture.

Meanwhile, Elias had enlisted a group of senators, led by New York Republican Charles E. Goodell and including Democrats Frank Moss of Utah, Quentin Burdick of North Dakota, and George McGovern of South Dakota, to hold up the nomination.[47] They feared that confirmation a few days before the Council's expulsion or suspension of Greece would be misconstrued in Europe as a gesture of support for the junta.

On December 12, in Strasbourg, as members met to consider whether to expel or suspend Greece, Foreign Minister Panagiotis Pipinelis denounced the Council of Europe and the European Convention on Human Rights and Fundamental Freedoms. Before suffering the humiliation of being kicked out, Greece resigned from the body. No vote was taken.[48] Elias was pleased with the news, although later that day the US Senate voted against a Foreign Relations Committee proposal to ban full military assistance to Greece until the regime had taken "meaningful steps" toward democratization.

Regime leader Colonel Pattakos dismissed the European Council confrontation as "a mosquito on the horns of a bull."[49] More ominously, Prime Minister Papadopoulos delivered an unyielding speech three days later to an audience of about 500, including Aristotle Onassis, in what had been the parliament chamber, announcing a further delay in the implementation of the still-suspended guarantees and principles of the 1968 constitution.[50]

On Friday, December 19, 1969, Goodell withdrew his hold, and the Senate confirmed Henry J. Tasca as Ambassador to Greece by a 79-to-4 roll-call vote—only after a harsh debate on American policy in Greece.[51] Attacking American hypocrisy, George McGovern compared the situations in Vietnam and Greece, where applying military aid to right-wing governments was not an investment in freedom, but a setback for it.[52]

Ted Kennedy, in the wake of Chappaquiddick, had been absent from the debate and other recent congressional anti-junta activities, but returned to fault "America's coddling of the junta," and its "cold and calculated indifference . . . to the plight of the Greek people."[53]

Unlike his troubled dealings with Jack and Bobby, Elias had developed a positive relationship with the senior senator from Massachusetts and sometimes referred to him as "the good Kennedy." Appreciative of the strong help he'd received from him and his staff in support of human rights issues in Greece, Elias wanted to help Kennedy with his reentry to public activities. He arranged a December luncheon event in Boston with Fidelity Investments, one of Brimberg's clients, which featured Kennedy as speaker. Kennedy was gracious in his thanks. Never could Elias have imagined that a year later Kennedy would play a part in saving his life.

20.

"Senator, are you telling me it's a trap?"

U S AMBASSADOR HENRY TASCA ARRIVED in Athens in early January 1970. Keeping with assurances he'd given during his confirmation, Tasca initially objected to a scheduled visit by US Apollo 12 astronauts, the second crew to land on the moon, arguing that such an appearance would undercut US efforts to encourage a return to constitutional government. Kissinger promptly overrode Tasca's objection.[1] Nixon's final instructions to his new ambassador to Greece were to tell Papadopoulos that the US was ready to resume all normal military-aid shipments but would like some atmospheric gestures—"insofar as possible"—"toward a constitutional situation" that "would ease our problems in speeding the release of the suspended equipment."[2]

At the end of March, Tasca sent Washington a whitewashing "Report on Greece." Providing the on-the-ground justification for the administration's already-made decision to restore full military aid, the ambassador made clear that the dictatorship was "here to stay."[3] Not only had the American arms embargo failed to positively influence the colonels' behavior, he reported; now they were preparing to turn instead to France for weapons.

To give cover against congressional criticism, Papadopoulos had offered Nixon an unspecific promise for "normalization." Tasca told Washington that he was "satisfied that the Greek government does indeed intend to move forward, albeit at its own often reluctant pace...to implement the constitution [of 1968]."[4]

Meanwhile, Papadopoulos made clear to the ambassador that there would be no linkage between Greece's NATO role and its internal affairs. The colonels would determine if, when, and at what speed any move was taken toward constitutional change.[5]

■

THE DIFFERENT STRANDS of Elias Demetracopoulos's life converged in his mailbox at the Fairfax: dozens of invitations to Georgetown parties, private dinners, charity galas, and diplomatic receptions; international and federal agency reports and copies of draft documents from Senate staffs; warm acknowledgments from Republican and Democratic legislators for his year-end political contributions; letters and smuggled tape recordings from families seeking help for relatives imprisoned or missing or victims of torture; thank-you notes from Perle Mesta and Anna Chennault for his floral gifts. Also included: clippings from the *Hellenic Chronicle* (Boston's Greek newspaper) from Ted Kennedy's confidential secretary Angelique Voutselas, who was "shocked" to see what they were saying about "the Senator" and wondering if the paper is "run by the Colonels."[6]

In her letters, Persa Metaxas provided affectionate concern and a steady stream of news from home. Executives from insurance companies, banks, and brokerage houses sent investment prospectuses and business information. Friends worried about his health, safety, and the situation in Greece. Female admirers, from California to Zurich, sent billets-doux, eager to have him come visit or to meet somewhere. Opposition groups and individuals sent him proposed manifestos and letters, asking for his review.

At 41, he had slowed down little. He subscribed to the *New York Times, Washington Post, Wall Street Journal, Christian Science Monitor*, news magazines, and business publications, and read them. He ordered European and American anti-junta journals and newsletters and, from Athens, censored newspapers. To make sure he hadn't missed anything, he'd hired Press Intelligence, Inc. to mail him thick packages of national news clippings related to Greece and anything mentioning him. These were all scattered and stacked high on the floor or on his couch, table, and chairs, organized according to a system only he could decipher. To would-be burglars and spies, it appeared that someone had already ransacked the place. He would live like that for decades.

The Greek exile continued assiduously to keep the different parts of his life separate. To meet all his various responsibilities, self-defined and imposed by others, Elias projected a public persona of passionate advocacy, business efficiency, charming sociability, and fearlessness. He slept little, but in the predawn quiet of his bedroom, he stewed over upsetting family issues in Athens and uncertainty about his father's welfare. He had not communicated with his cousin Spyros Handrinos since just after the coup, when Spyros's fearful wife kicked Elias out of the house. In the years since Elias's escape, his cousin, like many other small-property owners, angled to cash in on the building boom by tearing down small ancestral homes and putting up concrete multi-family residences.

Handrinos owned his parents' place on Dafnomili Street, which was next door to that of Panagiotis Demetracopoulos. He wanted to package the two parcels together and make a real-estate killing, removing Elias's aging, infirm, and legally blind father from his home of nearly fifty years. He also tried, apparently in collusion with local officials, to deceive Elias over the size and value of the Demetracopoulos parcel. Handrinos never contacted Elias directly, but for a year he used Elias's business representative and Persa as middlemen, sending architectural plans and real-estate contracts.[7]

Further punishing the father for the political sins of the son, the government increased already unfair taxes on the Demetracopoulos property. Mysteriously, Elias's father also received a dramatically enlarged insurance bill. Attorneys were reluctant to file for abatements, fearing they too would be targeted. Elias responded by ignoring Handrinos's requests, objecting to proposals, and telling his father to refuse any negotiation. This tumult upset the old man. He started to close himself off from others, refusing even the visits of friends. The oppression of the dictatorship had become personal.

Then, in early 1970, Elias heard that Spyros Handrinos had been arrested for embezzlement and would be going to jail. His wife turned to relatives to shamelessly pressure Elias, telling him that he needed to help pay back the embezzled money in order to preserve the family's honor. Reflecting on this period years later, Persa said that Elias's family treated him outrageously and selfishly, totally unsympathetic to the pressures he was under. At one time, Elias had risked his life to save his cousin and uncle. This time, inaction seemed a just response. But Elias continued to worry about his father.

None of his Washington world knew anything of this.

■

THE INTERNATIONAL OPPOSITION was in disarray. Karamanlis was smarting because his public statement the year before had been ignored or dismissed as premature. The King was still licking his wounds from his treatment at Eisenhower's funeral at the end of March 1969, when Nixon had warmly received Colonel Sty-lianos Pattakos, but fobbed Constantine off to others.[8] Andreas Papandreou was operating in his own orbit as he moved from ADA progressive to champion of Third World liberation.[9]

Elias had mixed feelings about the involvement of celebrities in anti-junta activities. Some, like composer Mikis Theodorakis, he regarded as illiberal Communists with an ulterior political agenda. Others, like Melina Mercouri, he thought well-meaning, but politically unsophisticated and potentially risky if let loose in unscripted interviews. Still, their star quality attracted publicity that could never have been achieved by ordinary activists. *Melina Mercouri: I Was Born Greek*, a television documentary blending Melina's vivacious "Zor-ba-like dancing" and melodramatic acting with her international crusade to rally support for her beleaguered homeland, was a huge success.[10] In a simu-lated interrogation, she admitted her sense of shame at having failed to resist the German occupation, and now urged others to avoid such feelings by join-ing the resistance. After the broadcast, Corporation for Public Broadcasting president Bill Duke wrote: "Elias, if only you looked like Melina—see what could be done!"[11]

Meanwhile in Athens, Democratic Defense had plateaued. Comprised mostly of Greek academics and Center Union intellectuals who'd studied abroad, it began by producing anti-junta propaganda and "talking" refrigera-tors—exploding devices designed to blast leaflets out and not hurt anyone—then turned to planting real bombs targeting major businesses supportive of the junta.[12] After some DD members were caught and put on trial in March, their protests petered out at home, although as exiles scattered abroad they continued to be resources for sympathetic European publications.

It was a bleak time. Oral histories later revealed some dissenting voices at both the American Embassy and the State Department, but they had little ef-fect.[13] In mid-January, Elias had been invited to give a talk after a screening of the movie Z, a fictionalized version of the 1963 assassination of activist Grigoris Lamprakis and the contorted investigation that followed. The movie's epilogue portrayed an ascendant dictatorship under which all hopes of eventual justice were dashed. Whereas American audiences had been applying the movie's uni-versal message of not trusting the official version of events to such US experi-ences as My Lai, the Bay of Pigs, and the Kennedy assassinations, Elias kept his spotlight on Greece, telling the largely student crowd to transform their feelings into action, learn the facts about Greece today, then contact congressmen, especially those who still vocally supported the junta.[14]

■

ON THE THIRD anniversary of the dictatorship, Athenian streets and highways were lined with signs proclaiming: "Long Live the 21 of April," "Long Live the Army," and "Long Live the National Government."[15] Some oblivious visitors had difficulty distinguishing life there from that in the country's democratic neighbors. An amended press code lifted strict "preventive" press censorship, substituting instead an insidious form of self-censorship. Papers were free to publish factual accounts so long as neither the subject matter nor related commentary were deemed derogatory. The junta also used its power to inflict economic punishment on publications that strayed, selectively applying newsprint taxes, restricting provincial circulation, withholding government advertising, and conducting random inspections for alleged irregularities. The regime had forced *Ethnos* to take a multi-million-drachma loan from the National Bank and install a government nominee to oversee operations. When the historically liberal paper decided to test the limits of censorship, the government called in its loan, forcing *Ethnos* into bankruptcy.[16]

■

IN THE UNITED States, center-right opponents of the junta bemoaned how "counterproductive" decentralized efforts had been and tried to assemble a new group of "prominent citizens and middle of the road personalities." Led by exiled General Orestis Vidalis, close to the King, and including at one point the brother of Nixon aide Daniel Patrick Moynihan, it met with US officials and struggled to create a magazine, *Common Heritage*, and a radio program in Greek and English.[17]

On the left, the principal organization was the US Committee for Democracy in Greece (USCDG). It was largely driven by House staffers Jim Pyrros and LaVerne Conway and given credibility by the sustained commitment of Congressmen Edwards and Fraser. The group's principal anti-junta work was House-centered, whereas Demetracopoulos took the lead in educating and pressuring the Senate. During the junta years, USCDG members were often encouraged by outsiders to become better organized, but that "suggestion got nowhere, and properly so," concluded Pyrros. "It was not practical, not wise, and probably not possible to form one group, headed by one person . . . Better to have . . . the junta . . . receiving incoming fire from all sides than to waste time in a futile effort to speak with one voice."[18]

Elias was his own boss. He was indefatigable and omnivorous in his relations. He was in regular contact with Pyrros, Vidalis, exiles in Europe, and opposition leaders at home. He stayed in touch with former Greek government
decision-makers and "all anti-Communist elements" concerned with the Greek
problem.[19] "It can be fairly said that nobody worked harder in the anti-junta
cause," wrote Pyrros in his memoir. "Demetracopoulos was committed, tireless
and knowledgeable, which attributes outbalanced a seemingly chronic need to
see his name in the newspapers."[20]

Reporters who used Elias's information knew he was a one-sided advocate,
with a "single purpose . . . [to bring] down the dictatorship." "He's not objective,"
said Bob Novak, "but his data is meticulously accurate. I find him a triple-A
source."[21] Les Whitten echoed the praise, noting that many of Jack Anderson's
columns "have been jewels because of Elias' industry."[22] And Sy Hersh, who
found he could "take to the bank" the "pure gold" Elias gave him, criticized his
colleagues, including at the New York Times, for making "a big mistake not listening to him more carefully."[23]

It was clear by early 1970 that the Nixon Administration would remove limits on military equipment deliveries to the colonels. Prior to preparing a Senate
briefing, Elias met with his sometime adversaries at State, Joseph Sisco and Alfred Vigderman. Instead of asking questions, he sternly lectured them. After
enumerating the many ways the Pentagon had eluded the embargo by listing
"new" military equipment as "old," undervaluing it, and shipping it to the colonels as "surplus," he faulted American military officers for "providing fulsome
praise" that was "then published as evidence of American love and support."[24]

Shortly after third anniversary celebrations had concluded in Athens, the
US arms-ban deception became clear. Using information Elias had assembled
with the help of congressional staffers, he told the Christian Science Monitor that
the value of current military aid was nearly double what Congress had approved.[25]

Senator Fulbright used the Foreign Relations Subcommittee on Security
Arrangements to excoriate the surplus heavy arms ploy and other misbehavior.[26]
The subcommittee approved an amendment to the 1971 Military Sales Act to
prevent all future US military aid to Greece unless later authorized. Elias worked
intensively on this issue, providing background materials, lobbying reluctant
and opposed senators, and writing talking points and floor speeches for supporters.[27] He called on friends to assist, getting the out-of-state family of his then–

principal girlfriend to lobby their senators in Missouri and Kansas and asking Celia to write to her Connecticut senators.[28] Even if they lost on the vote, he reckoned, news coverage of the debate could be helpful.

The amendment provided a momentary diversion from major public attention on the war in Southeast Asia. When it came up for a Senate vote, there was an hour's debate, but it was overshadowed by the Cooper-Church Amendment fight to cut off support for US activities in Cambodia. Elias listened in the Senate press gallery, with two press releases ready, one for either outcome. The Administration had lobbied hard, threatening both Democrats and Republicans with fierce negative campaigns against them in the November elections if they failed to vote against the amendment. The final vote on June 29 was relatively close. Fifty senators rejected the amendment. Forty-two supported it. The *New York Times* editorialized that Nixon would be making a serious mistake to interpret the "narrow rejection" of the arms ban as a green light for unchecked restoration of military aid, and Elias's press statement tried to put the best face on the defeat.[29]

News from Greece was confusing. The junta had failed to make the substantive reform changes promised, was unpopular both at home and abroad, and was said to be in "disarray," "divided," and suffering from "stagnation and inertia."[30] Nevertheless, its leaders appeared firmly in control. To those who hoped the colonels would cede their powers voluntarily, Demetracopoulos could be scathing. People might laugh at the colonels for their unsophisticated behavior and small village origins, he observed, but they displayed the cunning savvy of peasants skilled at taking advantage of city-slickers.[31] He suspected that, after the embargo was lifted and American attention turned to basing its fleet in Greece, the junta would again try to drive a hard bargain to sustain its power.

After the death of Foreign Minister Pipinelis in July 1970, Papadopoulos added that role to his portfolio that already included prime minister and defense minister. The power grab animated long-simmering junta rivalries and jealousies that spilled into public view. Whenever Papadopoulos's statements hinted at liberalization, the hard-liners, who were the majority, became upset, but their criticism was contradictory, blaming him simultaneously for weakening the dictatorship and seeking to maintain it forever. When Papadopoulos surprised his colleagues by threatening to resign, the internal crisis was settled relatively quickly in his favor. Papadopoulos knew he needed to court international public opinion, especially from the Americans, but without alienating other junta leaders. So, when he talked about reforming the government, he allayed his confederates' concerns by indicating that his words to the world were merely "cosmetic." Revising his earlier pledge to hold elections, he cryptically said: "Elections are not a theme of the present moment but of the immediate future." Junta supporters may have twisted logic explaining what this meant, but Greek exiles were not distracted by talk. Watching Papadopoulos feint left and right, making gestures toward both Washington and even the Soviet bloc, Elias concluded that for now the prime minister only wanted to stay in power.[32]

Luckily for the Greek leader, statements from Ambassador Tasca, Secretary of State Rogers, and businessmen from NATO countries lusting after big contracts made clear that "allied officials" were "easily satisfied."[33] On June 3, 1970, Tom Pappas hosted a widely publicized Athens dinner for Nixon's younger brother Donald in celebration of an in-flight-catering deal for his employer Marriott Corporation with Onassis's Olympic Airways. Donald sat next to Interior Minister Pattakos, with Onassis and Tasca seated nearby.[34]

■

SEVERAL HOURS AFTER midnight on September 19, 1970, in Genoa's Matteotti Square, a twenty-two-year old Greek student named Kostas Georgakis committed suicide by self-immolation.[35] His motive: to protest against the dictatorship in his homeland. Two months earlier, Georgakis had given an anonymous interview to a local magazine, disclosing that the regime had infiltrated the Greek student movement in Italy and had discovered his identity and his association with Andreas Papandreou's PAK. The junta had then cancelled his military exemption, harshly pressured his parents in Corfu, and blocked his family's financial stipend.

Georgakis hoped that by dousing himself with gasoline and setting himself ablaze he could shock the West into action against the Greek regime. But, unlike the monks in Vietnam, or Czech self-immolators who sought to protest the demoralization of their country the year before, Georgakis took his stand alone, in the middle of the night, with no organization behind him, and virtually no one to witness or photograph the event. Street cleaners at a nearby palazzo, attracted by the flash of light and the smell of burning flesh, tried to save him. He ran away shouting: "Down with tyrants," and "Long live Greece."

Melina Mercouri led a banner-waving, anti-junta funeral procession in Italy. Andreas sent PAK representatives to speak at a press conference. The colonels, who directed their secret police to monitor activities, made sure that Georgakis's remains were not returned home until January, well after the tourist season.

In a letter to his father, Georgakis asked for forgiveness. "Kiss our land for me," he wrote. "After three years of violence I cannot suffer any longer . . . I write to you in Italian so that I can raise the interest of everyone for our problem. Long Live Democracy . . . Our land which gave birth to Freedom will annihilate tyranny . . ."[36] Elias viewed Georgakis's death as a tragic example of the profound pain inflicted by the dictatorship, though he thought it unlikely to awaken those not already sympathetic.[37]

■

DEMETRACOPOULOS WAS PUSHING for a House investigation of the Pentagon's providing Greece with twice as much weaponry as approved by Congress when the junta announced on September 13, 1970, that the issue of full restoration of all US military aid was "considered settled."[38] Nine days later, Washington made it official: $56 million in tanks, planes, artillery, and military services would go to Greece over two years. Nixon liked the strategy of hiding controversial decisions "under the mantle of the Middle Eastern crisis."[39] A failed assassination attempt on Jordanian King Hussein and several Palestinian hijackings, which prompted the US to move its Sixth Fleet into the region to protect American interests, provided a convenient cover. The State Department proclaimed Greece's importance to NATO's eastern Mediterranean flank. In response to critics of the resumption of aid, State Department officials wrapped themselves around junta statements that conditions were being established to "restore normal democratic life" and that they had "taken steps to resume constitutional government by the end of this year."[40]

Demetracopoulos was at once cynical and optimistic. He had predicted the return to full arms shipments since the plebiscite in 1968. It's not the end, he told friends, but time to redouble our efforts. Besides lobbying Congress, he pressed new lines of attack by publicizing Greece's economic woes. Learning from sources at the International Monetary Fund of confidential reports about Greece's heavy short-term borrowing, he tipped off fellow journalists about the junta's efforts to stave off a balance-of-payments crisis. And when the Greek consulate in New York tried to use a World Bank loan for propaganda purposes, Elias turned a routine transaction into an international embarrassment by pressuring the bank to criticize the regime for playing politics with the payment.[41]

But his most ingenious move was to use the alleged importance of Greece to NATO security against itself by questioning the safety of its management of nuclear weapons.[42] The US had never publicly acknowledged that it had placed nuclear missiles on Greek soil. Elias had known about the weapons decisions since the 1950s, though he had never published his January 12, 1961 interview with Army Secretary General Wilbur Brucker confirming the fact. In one of his private conversations with Senator Fulbright in his hideaway Senate office, Elias shared a story heard from reliable sources that at the time of the 1967 coup, the junta had ordered Greek troops with a personal allegiance only to the colonels to surround two US nuclear missile sites. They had portrayed the move as part of "Operation Prometheus," a NATO contingency plan designed to protect the arms from possible Communist treachery. The real reason, Elias maintained, was not to safeguard the weapons from Communists, but to pressure the US not to interfere with the takeover. When the Americans stood by silently without objection, the troops withdrew.

Fulbright wanted to consider publicly the risks of US-supplied weapons falling into the wrong hands as part of his Foreign Relations hearings on US security commitments, but he was frustrated by State and Pentagon redactions of testimony transcripts and an order to witnesses not to discuss the nuclear weapons issue even in executive session. Fulbright complained to reporters that he did not know why they were still trying to keep it secret, since he was "sure the other side knows."[43]

Demetracopoulos made his move, sharing with a wire-service reporter the transcript of his 1961 interview confirming the presence of nuclear warheads in Greece and other European locations.[44] He issued a press statement quoting Senator Stuart Symington, the subcommittee chairman, as expressing "deep concern . . . over the security of . . . warheads stationed in Greece." Then he followed up by disclosing publicly "reliable reports" that in 1967 officials at the US Embassy were fearful that "the relatively few American military men stationed at the sites of nuclear warheads could probably be overwhelmed by Greek troops without firing a shot if they moved swiftly enough." Reporters jumped on the story and confirmed it. UPI sent an article worldwide describing "H-Bomb Blackmail in the Greek Coup."[45]

The reports provided anti-junta senators with a new angle. On the eve of the NATO ministerial meeting in Brussels, Senator Vance Hartke of Indiana declared that the "disclosures . . . reveal a direct threat to all members of the Atlantic Alliance and justifies" efforts to halt all US military aid to Greece.[46] It had already been expected that northern European members would try to inject political repression in Greece onto the NATO agenda. This enlarged the debate, though it did not immediately affect NATO policy or result in any official chastisement of Greece.

Elias's behavior continued to outrage officials, still trying to nail him on something from the CIA's growing dossier.[47] The Greek Desk at State served as a clipping service for the Athens embassy, documenting the exploits of the peripatetic exile, while American embassies elsewhere in Europe shared rumors of Elias's alleged anti-American activities, including a journalistic career that they characterized as hostile to NATO since 1947—two years before NATO was created, and while Elias was a teenager in a TB sanitarium.

Meanwhile, from Athens Elias heard uncorroborated reports that the minister of the interior had recently stripped him of his Greek citizenship because of his "anti-national activity." He'd been expecting this news for some time and planning to treat it as a badge of honor if it happened.[48] Still, it gave him a strange and hollow feeling.

■

ELIAS WORKED HARD to keep the different aspects of his life carefully compartmentalized. If he had to change an appointment, he never explained why, even to friends. Professional colleagues said they never knew Elias's sources or friends, and his friends never knew his business associates. He held fast to his pledge to protect sources, even after the sources died. Former girlfriends insisted he didn't drop his guard in pillow talk. An ideal extra man at social events, he would never reveal secrets whispered to him by his tablemates.

As a journalist, he believed that by closely guarding confidences he could maintain sources in sometimes-opposing camps, giving him better opportunities to ferret out underlying truths. Friends and colleagues could only speculate on what he did in the other spheres of his life. Persa, who didn't know many facets of his American life, was his eyes and ears concerning the personal world he left behind. Telephoning and writing, sometimes daily, in loving prose, always addressing her envelopes to his "Robert Speer" alias, she was his foremost cheerleader, worrywart, and trusted advisor, and his best friend.

A November letter from Persa was the first sign that something was wrong with Elias's father. Panagiotis had been hospitalized after running a high fever;

the diagnosis was pneumonia. Persa had known Panagiotis for more than a decade, and since Elias's exile she had monitored his health, visiting him more often than his own relatives and friends did. A skilled nurse, she tried to be calming in her communications with Elias but did not disguise the serious situation.

Letters changed to phone calls as Panagiotis's fever spiked. His father said he wanted to see his son. Through Persa, Elias told him to hold on, that he would come as quickly as he could. Elias was shaken and desperately wanted to see his father before he died. The promise that he was coming itself had a beneficial effect. The eighty-one-year-old man rallied, and his fever temporarily dropped.

Although he suspected that the rumors of his being stripped of Greek citizenship were true, he had received no official confirmation of the fact. Fortunately, he now held an American green card, so he wasn't stateless. Knowing that his father did not have long to live, Elias called the Greek Embassy, explained the circumstances, and requested a "laissez-passer"—an unusual diplomatic authorization customarily granted for emergency travel for humanitarian-aid workers that is not normally provided to private persons. Such a pass would allow him to visit Greece for no more than a couple of days. The request was treated with unhelpful coolness and no suggestions of a timetable.

Elias then informed his Senate friends of his father's illness and his travel request. Democratic Senators Burdick, Gravel, Hartke, Fulbright, Kennedy, and Moss sprang into action, individually calling and sending telegrams to the Greek ambassador and addressing an "urgent request" to Prime Minister Papadopoulos through the American secretary of state.[49] Would he allow Demetracopoulos, an only child, to complete a forty-eight-hour safe passage to visit his dying, blind, widowed father and leave "without hindrance of any kind?" They received no response for nine days.

Still, Elias started packing. Early on a Saturday morning his phone rang, and a familiar voice said: "Elias, this is Ted Kennedy . . . I know my colleagues are trying hard to get you a safe conduct pass. I'm calling to tell you, if they do offer a pass, I don't think you should take it. I don't think you should go to Greece. I'm hearing things that make me very uncomfortable."

Elias replied: "What is it? Senator, are you telling me it's a trap?"

Kennedy: "I can't go into details, but I've done some checking. Elias, I'm saying that I fear that, if you go, you may never come back."

Elias thanked him. It was sobering news, but the promise to honor his father's dying request weighed heavily.

The same day, Secretary Rogers sent copies of the senators' communications to Tasca, with "confidential" instructions, that in delivering the messages to the Greek government, the embassy "should be clear [they are] acting only as a routine transmitter and not as advocate."[50] However, Rogers did emphasize the "subject's very influential connections in Congress" and that the embassy might "point out obvious public relations benefits to GOG [government of Greece]."[51] State Department staff debated the matter internally and with the embassy staff over the weekend. Ambassador Tasca, like Briggs before him when confronted with an unwelcome task, took the weekend off. Rogers noted that "Demetracopoulos [is] in position to do far more damage to regime within the US if denied a visa than anything he might write on return from visit."[52]

Three days after the State Department's "priority" communication, Tasca had taken no action. On Tuesday, conveying no sense of urgency, Tasca asked someone in his office to ask someone in the prime minister's office "about possibility of [an] answer." He was later told the matter had been referred to its foreign office. Five days after the request was received, Tasca wrote to Rogers, telling him the Greek government had instructed its Washington ambassador to get in touch with Demetracopoulos to tell him he should apply for "Greek laisserpasser [sic]."[53]

The State Department and the embassy knew that Elias was without Greek citizenship and that simply appearing there in person could put him at risk for detention or kidnapping. Rogers and Tasca were clear with each other that they could not guarantee Greek government assurances that Demetracopoulos would be allowed to depart Greece since "someone in security affairs might attempt to have Demetracopoulos detained."[54] Tasca also speculated that the Greek government "may be willing to consider some deal for Demetracopoulos' return," bizarrely adding "knowing Demetracopoulos' past history, Greek government may have decided he wishes come to Greece to discuss some such deal."[55]

Meanwhile, nobody from the Greek Embassy ever contacted Elias. No one from the State Department told him he should initiate an application, and that same day—Wednesday, December 16, 1970—his father died.

Persa called. The funeral was set for Friday. Services would be held in the same chapel at the First Cemetery as they were for his mother. Because of the son's notoriety, Greek newspapers, she said, had refused to accept the customary death notice. Elias asked that the funeral be moved to Saturday, to give him a chance to come. She promised to do so. Alone in his small, cluttered apartment, Elias wept.

Condolence calls and telegrams came from Athens, other European cities, and across the US. He discussed just flying home for the funeral, consequences be damned, but friends urged him not to. Alaska senator Mike Gravel told Elias he would travel to Athens as his stand-in. Clearly someone was listening in to these phone calls. Before the next day's dawn in Washington, Tasca had sent an anxious confidential telegram to Secretary of State Rogers wanting to know "all the circumstances relative to Senator Gravel's attendance at funeral."[56]

Tasca's first concern was that the government would regard the senator's attendance as a "provocative political gesture, particularly if arrangements have been made by Demetracopoulos" for him to meet with members of the opposition. Tasca dreaded the idea of a Gravel press conference, or even Gravel's just talking with foreign correspondents or trying to meet with the Greek prime minister.

Of even greater concern was the possibility that Gravel might bring Demetracopoulos with him, "in which case problems could become even more delicate." Deputy Foreign Minister Christos Palamas had reportedly assured Tasca that the government would not "move against" Demetracopoulos provided he "did not violate any laws."[57] But it was quite easy to violate laws inadvertently under the dictatorship. If the government had taken away his citizenship, it was because he was by definition a lawbreaker. Tasca assumed that if Elias came he might not get beyond the airport before being grabbed for interrogation.

The ambassador's most wild-eyed fear was that Elias would prove to be some kind of proxy terrorist, arranging through his contacts "some manifestation of violence, such as a small bomb."[58] This might provoke a heavy-handed government response, thus "demonstrating that conditions here are as repressive as he has been representing them to be." In the end, an important Senate cloture vote scheduled for Saturday prevented Gravel's Athens trip, but the Alaska senator asked that Tasca convey to the Greek government his "personal displeasure" over its handling of the situation.[59]

The day of the funeral was appropriately lugubrious, gray and chilly, with intermittent drizzle. Elias hoped that in his absence there would be a respectfully large turnout, but mourners filled fewer than forty seats. Regime-spread rumors of a violent disruption scared away some family and friends; the colonels still suspected that even without proper papers Elias would somehow appear, perhaps with a "small bomb." According to Persa, mourners represented "a small but choice crowd," including some journalist friends, a strong sample of junta opposition, from center-right to left, past and future ministers, ambassadors, Center Union loyalists, Apostates, and Alekos Panagoulis's mother.[60] The Bokolas family came, but cousin Spyros Handrinos and his wife did not.

Police appeared to outnumber mourners at the cemetery, and some participants, sensing danger, departed immediately after the church service. Plainclothes secret police from the chapel and a fierce cordon of gendarmes in blue trench coats, armed and ready, surrounded the two dozen mourners at the tomb. Some watched the ceremony while displaying their machine guns, while others faced outward, apparently on the lookout for Elias.

Legendary newsman George Androulidakis turned to Elias's nephew, Dimitrios Tsalapatis, who worked for a "semi-outlawed" weekly journal, and said, "You don't have to be here until the end. We don't know what will happen."[61] The burial, however, ended without incident.

Afterward, in a long-distance call with Persa, Elias let down his guard, "I'm dying every day alone," he confided, sharing his anguish with words that "crushed" her.[62] She reminded him that he had "loyal friends" and needed to take care of himself so he "may be able to enjoy in full the better days that are sure to come." His dearest friend described the funeral as "beautiful and dignified . . . just the way you would have liked it," airbrushing the intrusive police presence. Persa tenderly told him, "Your father has left this world peacefully and with the hope that his son would soon arrive."[63]

Senator Gravel and other senators protested to President Nixon, requesting he conduct a "personal and thorough" investigation of the lack of "humanitarianism" by the State Department and the Greek government to their request for safe passage.[64] Asked about the senators' request, a State Department official conceded to the *New York Times* that they had received no assurances that Demetracopoulos "would have been permitted to leave Greece after his visit."[65] For two days at daily news briefings, State Department spokesman Robert McCloskey fielded questions concerning the failure to grant Elias safe passage, finally acknowledging that American communications to the regime had not been as prompt as first stated.[66]

Tasca also confessed that he'd advised against pushing the Greek government to respond to the congressional entreaties. He reminded Washington that Demetracopoulos had been the junta's "most aggressive and most effective critic abroad," and the leader behind much of the negative editorial comment that pro-longed congressional support for the arms embargo. "It would be imprudent to expect" that the Greek government "would be willing to turn their back on his activities," he warned, and not seek to take some revenge. Humanitarian con-cerns, he explicitly recommended, should take a back seat to American strategic interests.[67]

Backing away in stages from earlier statements blaming Demetracopoulos for failing to apply for a laissez-passer that would have been readily granted, the State Department admitted that there had been risks involved: that Elias might indeed have been detained, tortured, imprisoned, or killed, and that the United States knew much more on this point than it was revealing. When William Tim-mons, Assistant to the President, promised the senators that Nixon would look into the matter immediately, he blind-copied "Dr. Kissinger" for "URGENT ACTION."[68]

Years later, asked what he would have done had the laissez-passer been granted, Elias said he would have risked a visit to Athens, despite what he learned after gaining access to his US government files through Freedom of Information Act requests. Disclosure revealed one of the most mysterious items in the entire Demetracopoulos saga: a National Security Council entry, without accompany-ing text, dated December 18, 1970 titled "ACKNOWLEDGING SENS MOSS BURDICK GRAVEL RE MR DEMETRACOPOULOS DEATH IN ATHENS PRISON DATE 70 18 12." If the word "prison" were eliminated, the index title would probably be a simple reference to correspondence to the named senators concerning their entreaties. The word "death" could be an understandable refer-ence to Elias's father. But the inclusion of the word "prison" clearly conveys a sinister connotation, hinting at the content of the missing file. It lends credence to the rumors of Greek scenarios to kidnap and kill Elias and validates Ted Ken-nedy's early-morning telephone call of warning.[69]

Demetracopoulos's battle to restore democracy in his homeland had clearly unnerved the military rulers and their American counterparts. Syndi-cated columnists Evans and Novak wrote a blistering account of what they characterized as "A Modern Greek Tragedy," excoriating both the junta and the Tasca-run American Embassy for "the squalid handling of the affair," which "casts doubt on the wisdom . . . of the United States in restoring military aid to Athens," and raised questions in the Senate about continued American support for the regime.[70]

Undersecretary Joseph Sisco sent a confidential memorandum to Secretary Rogers that ended: "the Greek government has missed an opportunity to improve its image and perhaps even to disarm its most severe critic in the United States."[71] He then wrote to Tasca commiserating about the "brickbats" thrown in his direction," predicting that "the 'Demetracopoulos Affair' will quickly recede into the wings."[72]

The Demetracopoulos Affair wasn't receding quickly, however. The Evans and Novak column was published abroad. Syndication and wire services extended its life. Letters to the editor decried the "callous ineffectiveness of our representatives in Athens." The BBC and Deutsche Welle broadcast their own stories on the topic. In reaction to adverse media coverage, the State Department claimed reservations about Elias's motivations and credentials as "a resistance leader." It requested that the FBI and INS provide material to buttress an updated CIA profile, saying they were "particularly interested in the sources of his funds." Two versions of their reports were prepared: a "sanitized" one for use with senators, and a full compilation of uncorroborated smears for the White House.[73]

In a December 30 news story, the *New York Times* reported that the press office of the military-backed regime challenged Demetracopoulos's motives. It claimed "This gentleman was not interested in seeing his dying father. He was interested in creating a noise to the detriment of his country."[74]

A month earlier, the dictatorship had announced that, before the end of the year, it would tell the people when elections could take place. But on December 19, Papadopoulos proclaimed that "as far as the question of the regime and the constitution are concerned, there would be no change in the coming year."[75]

21.

Pushing Congress

WITH THE ARRIVAL OF 1971, Elias persisted in arranging and escorting former Greek political leaders of different stripes to meet with US government officials, despite the secretary of state's exasperated dismissal of these visits as "obviously stage-managed." He brought former minister of justice Dimitrios Papaspyrou, the last president of parliament, and former minister Emmanouil Kothris to the State Department to meet with Near East Affairs Deputy Assistant Secretary Rodger Davies, who was in charge of the Greek Desk. Afterward, Davies prepared a memorandum mocking the visitors and their concerns about the regime's continuing censorship and the embassy's lack of a balanced view of the "true situation."[1]

In early February, Elias was given an opportunity to take the measure of one of Tom Pappas's closest confidants. Socialites "Pyma" and John Pell, cousins of anti-junta Rhode Island senator Claiborne Pell, had invited Elias to dinner with opera singer Maria Callas and Spyros Skouras, who would be in New York briefly on separate business. With all the dinner guests knowing the clear differences between the two Greek men, conversation generally steered clear of politics. Elias made reference to his friend Daisy Schlitter, whom Callas remembered when she was known as "Daisy D'Ora," an ingénue movie star.

Elias was pleased to see the diva in such good form, especially after her mysterious overdose on medications following tabloid tales about her torrid relationship with Aristotle Onassis. He was touched when at the end of the meal she patted his arm and told him she'd like to hear from him privately about the situation in Greece. Skouras was more direct, inviting him to lunch the next day. Skouras was late, and Demetracopoulos left his office, snapping in a loud, exasperated voice: "No one is worth waiting a half hour." Later that afternoon he received a call from Skouras, furious that Elias would "act that way in front of my people." After Elias shot back with a reminder about the rules of simple courtesy, Skouras calmed down, apologized, and asked: "Can you come again?" Elias replied that he had no time left that trip but would be pleased to do so at some later date. They never met again. Skouras died of a heart attack six months later.

That fall, Elias reminisced with John Pell, who told him it was Skouras, on short notice, who specifically requested that Elias be invited, because he wanted to talk to him privately about Pappas. Elias wondered if Skouras had been acting independently or as an emissary.

Early the following year, Elias received a surprise call from Aristotle Onassis, asking to meet. Was this something prompted by Maria Callas or someone else? Elias wondered. Demetracopoulos knew that Onassis had helicoptered to Athens days after his 1968 wedding to Jackie Kennedy to discuss a $400 million investment package designed to bolster the industrial prowess of the dictatorial regime, and that Papadopoulos was living in a villa provided by the tycoon. Despite being furious with Onassis for cavorting with the colonels, Elias invited him to lunch at the Jockey Club, a place first made popular by Jackie Kennedy's visits. Knowing Onassis's reputation for lavish spending, Elias paid for everything in advance, tipping everyone with explicit instructions not to take any of Onassis's money. And when Onassis opened his wallet, everybody, from waiters and busboys to Maître d' Jacques Scarelli, politely refused him.[2] Onassis told Elias nothing he didn't already know about Papadopoulos's shaky control of the government, but Elias used the opportunity to talk up the power and resolve of the opposition.

■

ELIAS FLEW TO Europe on business at the end of February 1971 with a heightened sense of urgency. Exiled leaders continued to operate apart, each looking at their homeland from a different angle. Interspersed with talks about international economic issues with IMF and World Bank officials, policymakers, and academics, and appointments with clients of Brimberg and other Wall Street firms, he spent hours in meetings with often-frustrating political allies. He also telephoned European military leaders and exhorted them to call their col-leagues in the States to exploit tiny cracks in Pentagon thinking.

For more than a year, Elias had been seeking ways to stage a large public debate on the situation in Greece. He contacted Harvard international law pro-fessor Roger Fisher, who was the moderator of the PBS public-affairs program *The Advocates,* which used as its television format a courtroom setting. Fisher was skeptical, but Elias persisted, insisting the military funding issue was not dead, and suggesting proponents and opponents who could make for lively tele-vision, including Melina Mercouri. For weeks in early 1971, Elias helped pro-ducer Susan Mayer prepare the program, from arranging witnesses to refining lines of argument.[3] Meanwhile, the pro–military aid side relied on the State De-partment to identify and vet their witnesses. When PBS announced the national TV debate in late February, it touted the participation of Mercouri, Elias Deme-tracopoulos, and Max Van Der Stoel, a Dutch political leader whose fact-finding trips to Greece had contributed to the country's withdrawal from the Council of Europe. The only potential witness named for the other side was Greek-Ameri-can Tom Pappas.

At the March taping in Cambridge, Elias's side remained the same, with the addition of columnist Robert Novak. Pappas was replaced by William Kitner from the Foreign Policy Research Institute in Philadelphia, Kenneth Young, for-eign policy advisor to Lord Beaverbrook's UK newspaper chain, and former Karamanlis foreign minister Efangelos Averof.

Elias made his usual points that the undemocratic government was a secu-rity liability for the US and NATO, and that opposition groups across the politi-cal spectrum viewed military aid as symbolizing support for the junta.[4] He swatted away his cross-examination and protected Melina from such an ordeal by pre-taping her appearance. (She nevertheless was attacked as coming from a Communist family and parroting the Communist line.) The other side said pre-vious Greek governments had been "cancerous" and it would take time to resolve "structural deficiencies," that the junta was Greece's "last and best hope," and that an arms embargo would turn Greece over to the Communists and make the Mediterranean a Russian lake. The national audience voted overwhelmingly for the arms-embargo side.

Elias's manifold activities continued to confound the junta apologists. When pressed to define himself politically in interviews, he said he was a center to center-left anti-Communist who believed in free enterprise, free elections, and a free press.⁵ Then he would turn the tables by asking the important, unanswerable question: If the Greek government had such widespread support, why was martial law still imposed, and no date established for elections? If the regime won truly free elections, he said, he would accept the results. But he doubted that would ever happen.

Undaunted by persistent vitriolic attacks, Elias also poked back at Kissinger and Nixon's foreign policy advisors with a series of speeches on college campuses and before civic groups, reworking his George Washington University and Hudson Institute material and provocatively questioning whether Greece could become "A New Vietnam."⁶ The State Department, which sent someone to follow him and take notes, expressed surprise to the embassy that not only was his presentation "a spiel designed for right-wing audiences," but that he would deliver it to "leftists."⁷

■

IN HIS ROLE as Wall Street consultant, Elias would occasionally invite members of Congress to New York to give paid speeches to different firms' clients and business associates. In spring of 1971, at the request of Brimberg and the firm of Sartorius & Co., Elias arranged for Congressman J. Wright Patman (D-TX), chairman of the House Banking Committee, to make a well-publicized dinner speech to the New York financial community at Club 21. In June, he escorted him to and from the event.

While on the trip to New York, Elias told Patman about Republican fundraiser and tycoon Tom Pappas's illegal campaign financing activities for Nixon in 1968, behavior Demetracopoulos planned to describe in testimony he would deliver to Ben Rosenthal's House Foreign Affairs subcommittee a few weeks later. The evening was a success. Afterward, believing the plausibility of the illegal campaign-financing information, which reinforced Patman's suspicions and doubts about the President, Patman urged Al Hunt, the *Wall Street Journal*'s national political correspondent, to check out Demetracopoulos's story. Hunt, however, failed to do so.⁸

Meanwhile, Associated Press investigative reporter James Polk, looking for an angle to discuss troublesome aspects of money in politics, decided to focus on speaking fees paid to powerful members of Congress to address groups with an interest in legislation coming before their committees.⁹ Interviewing congressional staffers looking for some good examples, he hit pay dirt with Jim Pyrros, Detroit congressman Lucien Nedzi's legislative aide, who told Polk about the

Patman trip to New York. On June 29, the AP reported about the $1,500 fee and dinner. The payment wasn't illegal, but Elias was angry because Pyrros's tip to Polk had turned into a news item that made Elias's behavior look unseemly. Pyrros apologized and thought that was the end of the matter.[10] It would surface again in ways neither could have expected.

■

STILL FURIOUS ABOUT Ambassador Tasca's role in blocking Elias's Athens trip a few months earlier, Senators Moss, Gravel, and Burdick asked Senator William Fulbright to demand the ambassador testify before the Foreign Relations Committee. They then made public their letter that charged the White House and the State Department, and particularly Tasca, with whitewashing their ugly behavior in "The Demetracopoulos Affair."[11] For days the State Department's spokesman was besieged at his press conferences with questions he couldn't answer. Henry Kissinger decided the President should be briefed on "The Demetracopoulos Affair," and provided his own "Secret" memorandum concerning the "recent flap over a request by Greek 'journalist' and resistance leader, Elias Demetracopoulos, to return to Greece to see his sick father."[12] After the Greek press published critical wire-service stories, Tasca demanded a counterattack.[13]

The State Department believed "it would be inadvisable to openly discuss Demetracopoulos's personal background with people on the Hill because "we would run the risk of exposure to charges of character assassination."[14] It decided instead to smear Elias surreptitiously, using Republican senator Hugh Scott of Pennsylvania and "key staff members" of the Senate Foreign Relations and House Foreign Affairs committees to do their dirty work. State hand-delivered a one-page, unsourced account of the laissez-passer history, which claimed that Elias had failed to contact the Greek Embassy in Washington for a temporary pass.[15]

Fulbright and other members of his committee had become increasingly concerned that Tasca was too close to the colonels, who had failed to undertake promised political reforms. "The Demetracopoulos Affair" reportedly played "a significant part" in the chairman's decision to dispatch in February two senior investigators from his committee to Greece to report back on the situation there.[16] To Tasca's dismay, they came with voluminous notes and extensive lists of persons to see. Greek officials bluntly refused to meet with them because of the "inadmissible character" of their mission, and according to an embassy report, the "Greek government's heavy-handed surveillance of the visitors did not help the situation."[17]

The sixteen-page investigators' report noted the gap between regime rhetoric and the actual progress toward restoring parliamentary government and other freedoms. To counter reports that political prisoners had been released, it pointed out the new arrests that had followed. To refute government denial of torture, it described contrary reports from victims and their families and noted the government's non-renewal of the agreement for International Red Cross inspections. Opposition groups described a "vicious circle" in which, because the Greek people believed that the United States supported the regime, opposition was deemed futile, and Americans then interpreted this absence of public opposition as evidence of public support. The investigators concluded that the regime "is able to exert more leverage on us with regard to military assistance than we have been willing to exert on the regime with regard to political reform. We see no evidence that this will not continue to be the case."[18]

■

IN 1971, "NEW Politics" congressional-rules reformers succeeded in opening up House subcommittee chairmanships and providing the staff resources to conduct investigations. Benjamin Rosenthal, a liberal New York congressman from Queens who was known for his consumer-rights advocacy and Vietnam War opposition, had been appointed the new chair of the Subcommittee on Europe. Several years earlier, Rosenthal had hired Clifford Hackett, an experienced Foreign Service officer who'd been a USIA congressional fellow in Congressman Don Fraser's office, where he had become sensitized to the situation in Greece. In the days following his appointment, Rosenthal was regularly accosted in the House gym by his handball regulars, USCDG co-chairmen Fraser and Don Edwards, who urged him to make the situation in Greece a subcommittee priority.[19]

Hackett proposed to Rosenthal a series of comprehensive hearings on American policy on Greece. When Elias heard about the House inquiry, he eagerly offered to help. But, because Hackett knew his chairman came with a clear viewpoint, he insisted on making the hearings as balanced as possible.

Demetracopoulos was aware of some dissenting voices in the State Department and at the NSC who were recommending that Tasca meet opposition leaders and nudge the junta into lifting martial law, even if Nixon's honoring of junta representatives in Washington and sending high-level officials to Athens provided a more forceful expression of American policy. One of these was Assistant Secretary and veteran State Department troubleshooter Joseph Sisco. Knowing that Demetracopoulos would be on the witness list for upcoming congressional hearings on Greece and probably quite frustrated in his recent dealings with some in the State Department, Sisco invited the exiled journalist to share his views in a one-on-one meeting.

Elias told Sisco that the administration was mistaken in asserting that the regime was moving toward parliamentary democracy.[20] According to Elias, the problem wasn't Papadopoulos per se, because Papadopoulos was a prisoner controlled by the military machine. "He's not a demagogue like Nasser or Hitler," Elias said. "He can't arouse the population; he has no charisma. If he thought he had 51 percent of the popular vote he would hold free elections. If he had 35 percent he would go to rigged elections. But he has much less than 35-percent support and finds himself locked in."

He warned about the already-strong anti-American trend in Greece. The United States was losing its traditional friends and allies. "When Kanellopoulos, Karamanlis, and King Constantine speak to me as they do, something is wrong," he said, adding that he believed 80 percent of the Greek people were against the junta, though they were not yet prepared to die to overthrow it. Demetracopoulos advised that the State Department "double-check" the information it was getting from Athens, because Ambassador Tasca "has identified himself so completely with the regime and isolated himself so much from the former politicians that he can see things only in one way." He described the ambassador as a stubborn man who had decided on a course of action and would not accept information that did not support it. He recommended that Sisco send someone he trusted to Athens, to make "an unhurried report on what is actually going on." The essential thing, Demetracopoulos said, was for the US to protect its 20-year investment in Greece by reestablishing its bona fides with a wide spectrum of the Greek populace.

At the end of the meeting, Sisco told Elias he appreciated his candor and "would always be very glad to see him." He added that he knew Elias cared deeply about the situation in Greece and had the interests of his country at heart.

Following the Demetracopoulos-Sisco meeting, Secretary Rogers sent a SECRET memorandum to Nixon cabinet officials and Kissinger asking to be informed in advance before accepting invitations to Greece, considering it "desirable to limit visits . . . to those cases where overriding need clearly exists."[21] Instructions were also sent to Tasca about the possibility of making contacts with the opposition. Not surprisingly, Tasca was livid. He worried that some, including the regime, might think State had begun to accept Elias's appraisal of the Greek situation.[22] The ambassador sent Kissinger a response headed "TOP SECRET SENSITIVE EYES ONLY," advising Kissinger that there were "hazards to our interests" in meeting with the opposition and warned Rogers that prioritizing a return to parliamentary government was "fraught with great risks to security interests, with quite doubtful chances of success."[23] He directed his political counselor to compose and send to everyone on Sisco's wide distribution list a SECRET four-page letter, challenging Demetracopoulos's assessments as part of his "personal vendetta against the Ambassador," revisiting outright falsehoods from Elias's earlier dossiers, and describing Elias as a selfish opportunist and a "con man."[24]

■

THE HOUSE FOREIGN Affairs Subcommittee on Europe opened the first of seven days of hearings on Greece on July 12, 1971.[25] Demetracopoulos strode into the spacious, high-ceilinged, brightly illuminated chamber impeccably attired, his thinning black hair combed straight back, his baldness and white teeth gleaming under the chandeliers. He chatted easily with committee members, witnesses, and reporters. This was a moment he'd been waiting for. Scheduled to respond to Rodger Davies's State Department presentation, Elias was the third out of twenty-two witnesses. The selection of American University professor Theodore Couloumbis to open the hearings with an overview rankled him. He might be a decent academic, Elias thought, but he was a "moral eunuch" for standing on the sidelines during the past four-plus years.

Accompanied by a twenty-four-page prepared statement, Demetracopoulos began his testimony decrying the influence of Tom Pappas in Greek political and economic affairs.[26] Rosenthal asked Elias, who agreed, to provide documentation to support his charges. Elias then summarized his analysis, including his warning that the dramatic drop in Greek military preparedness put NATO and American security interests at risk, along with a more recent alert about the risks of mishandling nuclear arms now stockpiled in Greece.

Elias forced the committee into executive session by offering to insert into the record a translation of a top-secret 1964 document from the chief of the

Greek National Defense Staff.[27] It concerned Defense Secretary McNamara's response to Greek requests for aid, discounting the military threat to Greece from Bulgaria, despite its military superiority over Greece. Elias pointed out that alleged threats from a non-threatening Communist Bulgaria, hyped by both the Johnson and Nixon Administrations as part of their justification for lifting the heavy military–equipment embargo, was even more wrongheaded in 1971, when the Greek military regime was expanding its contacts with the entire Communist world, "notably Bulgaria."

In the second half of July and into August and September, Defense and State Department officials as well as regime supporters and opponents provided more testimony. Reviewing the lengthy hearings transcript, historian James Miller concluded: "The most incisive testimony came from Tasca's personal bête noire, exiled journalist Elias Demetracopoulos, who underlined the unreliability of Greek Armed Forces."[28]

Tasca did not wait to testify himself before attempting to limit the reverberations from Elias's assertions. Eight days after Demetracopoulos's appearance, he sent an urgent telegram to Secretary of State Rogers and Attorney General Mitchell warning, in all capital letters:

DEMETRACOPOULOS IS PART OF A WELL-ORGANIZED CONSPIRACY WHICH DESERVES SERIOUS INVESTIGATION. WE HAVE SEEN HOW EFFECTIVE HE HAS BEEN IN COMBATING OUR PRESENT POLICY IN GREECE. HIS AIM IS TO DAMAGE OUR RELATIONS WITH GREECE, LOOSEN OUR NATO ALLIANCE AND WEAKEN THE US SECURITY POSITION IN THE EASTERN MEDITERRANEAN.[29]

TASCA COMPLAINED THAT those who regarded Demetracopoulos as simply an aggressive newsman-lobbyist concerned about Greek democracy or a "light-weight rascal" without any substantial following were seriously wrong. He maintained that while "smooth operator" Demetracopoulos "has always been mysteriously financed," new evidence indicated his financial expenditures now exceeded previous lavish estimates and he was "giving financial assistance to various congressmen. "This suggests," the ambassador wrote, that "he is . . . a subsidized agent" running a well-financed campaign that has "international ramifications." He then implored Rogers and Mitchell to step up their investigations,

TO IDENTIFY HIS SPONSORS, HIS SOURCES OF FUNDS, HIS
INTENTIONS, HIS METHODS OF WORK AND HIS FELLOW
CONSPIRATORS.

WE SHOULD NOT BE MISLEAD [sic] BY DEMETRACOPOULOS'
PROTESTATIONS AS TO HIS PRO-AMERICAN SENTIMENTS ... WE
MUST LOOK AT WHAT HE IS DOING AND HAS DONE.[30]

AT THE JUSTICE Department, John Mitchell saw Tasca's request as an opportunity to nail Elias for the crime of failing to register under the revised Foreign Agents Registration Act. Indicting Elias could sully his reputation, impede his attacks, and perhaps finally build a case to deport him.

Elias had never registered as a foreign lobbyist because he never represented anyone but himself. He was not on the payroll of any agent of Greece or its opposition. His lawyers told him that legally he didn't meet the statutory definition of someone who should register. That did not stop the US government. James C. Hise, chief of the Justice Department's Registration Section, was told by his superiors to get the as-yet-uncorrected transcript of Demetracopoulos's July 12 testimony to help determine if any activities of the subject would obligate him to register.[31]

Despite SECRET memoranda—and hush-hush meetings held in person "because ... the delicacy of the matter [made] it ... advisable not to discuss it over the telephone,"—officials could not point to any direct evidence of a relationship between Elias and a foreign principal.[32] Nevertheless, they declared their belief, based on an extensive knowledge of Greek affairs, that the subject must be acting for someone or some organization. State was eager that Justice "do everything possible to see if we can make a Foreign Agents case," while simultaneously warning that any FBI investigation should proceed carefully so as not to alert the "very clever" Elias or any of his "powerful friends on the Hill (Congressmen and Senators) to whom he might turn with charges of persecution and harrassment [sic] by the Government."[33] When State asked the FBI to do another check, John Edgar Hoover personally resisted, telling his intelligence-community colleagues: "No information was developed from our [prior] investigation indicating him to be engaged in intelligence or subversive activities ... In the absence of specific information indicating subject is engaged in activities which could be considered inimical to the internal security of the

United States, no additional inquiries by this Bureau are contemplated."[34]

Angry State Department security officials, unwilling to accept "not guilty" for an answer, continued to explore ways to strike back at Elias. Admitting in SECRET memoranda that there was "nothing in the FBI file that would be very useful in dealing with Demetracopoulos' supporters," they discussed how best to investigate his tax returns.[35]

On August 6, with his anodyne testimony before the House Foreign Affairs Committee behind him, Ambassador Tasca paid courtesy calls on Capitol Hill and at the Pentagon. Later that same day he had a heated exchange at the White House with Henry Kissinger and NSC staffer Harold Saunders.[36] Kissinger, piqued, said he couldn't understand why, if he could go to China, there was such a "fuss about not letting people go to Greece." While he could "understand the necessity for some cosmetics to keep our allies happy," he believed it was "none of our business how they run their government."

Tasca griped: "You ought to see some of the instructions I get," complaining that he'd been asked to meet with opposition members and let the press know it. Kissinger, his voice rising, snapped, "How the hell would we like it if the Greek ambassador here started running around with Senator Fulbright?" Then Kissinger trashed Joe Sisco, saying, "that Sisco operation is the worst disaster I've seen."

Beyond Sisco, Tasca's greatest concern was the ubiquitous Demetracopoulos, who, he said, was not only "orchestrating a campaign against him," but trying to run him out of his job. Kissinger told Tasca there was no chance that he would be "pulled out of Greece," saying it was "not the US policy to give the Greek government a hard time." Kissinger assured Tasca that whenever he received instructions he felt were not in keeping with the President's policy, he should "send a message to the White House by the back channel."[37] It was not clear to which back channel he was referring. Kissinger? John Mitchell? Tom Pappas?

■

ROSENTHAL DECIDED IT would be useful to send Cliff Hackett to Greece during the August recess for a first-hand assessment from a diversity of Greek voices. In the late-summer heat of Athens, Hackett met with embassy staff, opposition leaders, and a government representative. Discontent was widespread not only among the opposition. Hackett also found low morale within the embassy, some of whose staff claimed that political reporting was being "subordinated to the exigencies of rescuing the ambassador and his career."[38] The Greek government representative told Hackett that internal Greek politics were not a "proper" US concern, and the Greek secret police followed him to his appointments, presumably to intimidate those he was interviewing. Hackett estimated that public support of the government was at 15 percent. He concluded: "nothing can change truly [in embassy reporting] so long as the ambassador remains."[39]

Elias spent much of the rest of the summer on the Pappas memorandum he had promised Rosenthal, unaware that on August 25 the FBI, in coordination with the State Department and CIA, had commenced a new round in their search for actionable dirt. He wasn't secretive about his work and, on August 29, a nationally syndicated column disclosed that on September 8, Tom Pappas, "a rich Greek-American friend and backer of President Nixon will . . . be the target of a 50-page blast before a House [F]oreign [A]ffairs subcommittee" delivered by Elias Demetracopoulos. He would charge Pappas with "misusing his high connections" and "urge a Justice Department probe of Pappas' contacts with the White House, Cabinet, and Congress to 'talk up' the Greek junta."[40]

In early September 1971, Murray Chotiner called Elias and asked to have lunch with him at the Jockey Club. For years, Chotiner, though dogged by a history of links to organized crime, had been Nixon's consigliere in charge of malicious tactics.[41] He had managed Nixon's red-baiting Senate race in 1950 and worked with John Mitchell on the 1968 presidential campaign. In 1970, Chotiner directed Agnew's campaign to savage so-called "radic-lib" candidates for the Senate, helping to defeat one of Elias's better congressional friends, New York Republican Senator Charles Goodell. At the time of the Demetracopoulos invitation, Chotiner had left the administration for private practice, but located his law offices on the floor above the Committee to Reelect the President. He still had a White House phone.

Elias remembered being "flabbergasted" when he received Chotiner's call. Elias had met Chotiner at social gatherings in the past, and had even once invited him to participate in one of Brimberg's financial briefings in New York, an invitation Chotiner had graciously declined.[42] What did he want now, Elias wondered. Whatever it was, he thought it might be prudent to have a witness to the meeting and so suggested to Rowley Evans that he come sit at a nearby table. Evans laughed off the request: "You're joking. What would Chotiner want to do with you?" he asked.

Nevertheless, on September 7, shortly after Elias entered the Jockey Club and took a seat at his regular table—positioned inside the entrance to the right and against a wall, so he could see people coming in before they saw him—he noticed Evans seated alone at a nearby table. He rose to greet Chotiner, and at first the conversation was light and amicable, with Chotiner displaying an uncharacteristic sense of humor. They touched on topics from life in general to domestic and international politics, past and future. Then Chotiner became specific. He wanted to know why Elias was so upset with Pappas. Before his guest could give him a straight answer, Chotiner cut him off.

"Lay off Pappas," Chotiner advised, deadly serious. "You can catch a lot of trouble. You can be deported. It's not smart politics. You know Tom Pappas is a friend of the President." Chotiner glared. His tone became increasingly menacing, and he repeated: "You know Tom Pappas is a friend of the President. You know what that means?"

The message was clear: You're playing over your head. Pappas and the President will crush you. If you think things are difficult now for you, submitting the memorandum will only make matters worse. You may think your immigration troubles are behind you, but remember you've been stripped of your Greek citizenship. You have no country. If you don't play ball, you can be thrown out of America as well. If you're sent back to Greece it means torture, imprisonment, and probable death.

Elias kept calm, though discomfort and anger were welling up. After about an hour-and-a-half meal, Elias stood up and thanked Chotiner for lunch, but added that he still planned to submit the memo. Chotiner pursed his lips, slowly shook his head, and made his exit.

Evans was sitting too far away to hear any of the conversation but witnessed clearly the facial expressions and body language. He never again questioned the validity of a tip from Elias or thought his friend was "joking" about possible danger.

Back in his apartment, Elias remembered fleetingly the promise he had made to himself when he was recovering from torture in Averof Prison: that if he got out alive, he would not be brutalized or bullied by anyone, ever again. That certainly included Nixon's henchman. Years later, Chotiner's widow disputed the intensity of the encounter and claimed that Robert Mardian, the Nixon Administration official who had become close to John Mitchell during the 1968 campaign, was the one behind the strong-arming of Demetracopoulos.[43]

FRIDAY MORNING SEPTEMBER 17, 1971, was still warm, but summer was turn-ing into autumn. Elias took a cab up to the Rayburn Office Building on Capitol Hill and dropped off his "Memorandum Concerning Activities of Thomas Pap-pas" at the office of the House Foreign Affairs subcommittee on Europe. Elias had structured his report as an examination of Pappas's involvement in Greek economic and political affairs, followed by a description of the tycoon's role in American politics and policy toward Greece. He described, with citations, how Pappas "sought and secured . . . monopolistic control over large sectors of the Greek economy," and detailed the Pappas brothers' support for the dictatorship, their links to American politics and foreign policy, and the use of Pappas foun-dations as conduits to the CIA.[44]

Pappas's embrace of the junta, Elias wrote, had a "psychological impact causing incalculable damage" and constituted "meddling in the making of US foreign policy toward Greece" that furthered "simultaneously, their own finan-cial interests as well as the interests of a ruthless military dictatorship" all at the expense of long-range US interests in that crucial part of the world.

Surprisingly, when it came time tell the story of the 1968 Greek money in the Nixon campaign, he did so softly and indirectly. A congressional committee, he reasoned, could do a better job getting at Pappas's role in the laundering of what were presumably US taxpayer funds to aid Nixon's presidential campaign.[45] Nevertheless, he ended his submitted memorandum with a note of mystery:

> The analysis and conclusions of this memorandum are ascribed to
> by many major Greek and non-Greek personalities whom this writer
> has polled on the matter before submitting this memorandum to your
> subcommittee. Finally, I have submitted separately to the subcommittee
> items of documentary evidence, which I believe will be useful.[46]

BUT WHAT HAD he submitted? Nothing, in truth. Years later, he characterized this deliberately misleading maneuver of his as "the birth of Watergate." To him, the seeds of Watergate were sown in Pappas's behavior during the 1968 elec-tion, then germinated after the September 1971 memorandum. During the pres-idential transition, when Hoover told Mitchell about Elias's October meeting with O'Brien, the FBI director didn't know exactly what information had been shared. Afterward, Nixon's men fixated on finding out what damaging evidence Elias or others had on Pappas that could be linked to the President. "This is what made Mitchell and Nixon furious," he reckoned. "They saw the paragraph at the end and went ballistic." This September 1971 memorandum suggesting he had submitted likely incriminating evidence, but actually withholding submission of the documents, was, he believed, the accelerant that inflamed Administration "paranoia" about him and "set off their willingness to have me kidnapped and eliminated."

There was method behind his stratagem, even if at wasn't completely thought through. Audaciously, he assumed that dropping ominous hints of having secret, damaging documents, but not actually providing them, would make him a target for those who wanted the information. He was willing to play quarry with the expectation that his hunters would do something stupid in coming after him and could then be exposed in the press, in congressional hearings, and possibly in a court of law. He speculated that John Mitchell, pressured by Pappas and upset with Elias's close friendship with Louise Gore and his knowledge of Mitchell's romantic relationship with Louise's sister, might be the first to crack.

Elias didn't know what, if anything, Larry O'Brien had done with the 1968 Pappas information Elias had given him at his Watergate offices. Elias did not store his Fairfax hotel room files neatly in cabinets, but stacked them around his place according to a system only he understood. Although he was not aware of any recent break-in, he decided to move some documents to a safe deposit box and later gave his most sensitive materials to writer Christopher Hitchens to guard.[47] If Elias was afraid of serious risks to himself, he didn't acknowledge it, but he started carrying a heavy walking cane for protection.[48]

Rowland Evans and Robert Novak focused their attention on Pappas, believing that Elias's report "is certain to lead to a formal summons" for the mysterious Greek-American industrialist to testify before Congress.[49] After checking with their Administration sources, they wrote that Elias's referencing items of documentary evidence was causing "extreme nervousness in the Nixon White House."[50]

Elias made sure that other news outlets had the story too. Rosenthal confirmed he was considering holding hearings into Pappas's relationship with the Athens regime and whether he had violated laws covering private-citizen dealings with a foreign government. Headlines from Kansas City to London speculated that "US may probe financier's role in aid to Greece," and "Probe of Greek's Favor-Seeking."[51] Negative coverage included Pappas's hometown papers, especially unwelcome when he returned to Boston for his late wife's memorial service.

On October 20, Carl Marcy, the chief of staff to Chairman Fulbright, sent a letter to David Abshire, the State Department's assistant secretary for congressional relations, asking about stories implying that Tom Pappas "exerts undue influence on US policy toward Greece."[52] The State Department's November 3 reply, probably prepared by Greek desk officer George Churchill, praised Pappas as "a successful businessman with interests in Greece as well as the United States" who "has never exceeded the bounds of propriety or legality."[53]

■

IN ALL OF the years of following Pappas and his activities, Elias had met him face-to-face only rarely, in Athens in the early 1960s. During lunchtime on October 27, 1971, however, he was deep in conversation with Bob Novak at the Sans Souci, a chic French restaurant that was one of the popular "power dining" places in town, when suddenly he saw a well-dressed, bald, barrel-chested older man approach them quickly from several tables away. He was of average height, physically fit, and enraged, shaking clenched fists.

Elias realized immediately that it was Pappas. Temples pulsating, his face flush with amaranthine glower, the Greek-American tycoon ranted in English: "Stay away from me and shut up. You know who I am. Don't mess with me. I can make big trouble for anyone I want. I can have you investigated. I know all the Wall Street firms where you work, and I'll make sure they know all about you. You won't have a dime. I'll take away your livelihood."

All around them people stopped eating and talking to watch the unfolding drama. Pappas repeated his threats and added: "When I'm done with you, you'll be nothing." With that, he quickly pivoted and returned to his table, without giving Demetracopoulos or Novak a chance to respond.

Elias was about to get up and go to Pappas's table when Novak extended a calming arm and chuckled. He told Elias with a broad smile, "See, you're having an impact. You're doing your job." Then, gesturing toward Pappas and his White House dining companions, he added: "If he's that mad, you can be sure he's told the President and his people. Get ready for their response."

Shortly after the Pappas threats, the FBI visited Elias's employers in New York with a long list of leading questions. Under pressure, a couple of firms terminated their contracts with Elias. Others cut back his consulting work. At about the same time, the KYP and Greek secret police conducted similar inquiries of his friends and acquaintances in Athens in an effort to aid the State Department in building its case for his deportation.[54]

Elias refused to back down. In early November, he distributed copies of Hackett's confidential Athens-trip "internal memorandum," which he got not from Hackett but from a subcommittee member.[55] Headlines proclaimed: "A Bad Fitness Report for Envoy to Greece" and "US Embassy Morale Held Low in Greece."[56] This episode was too much for the embassy in Athens and the Greek Desk in Washington. Tasca, vacationing in Switzerland, was called back to Athens and threatened to resign. In late November, Kay Folger, a member of the State Department's congressional relations staff, provided Roy Bullock, House Foreign Affairs Committee staff administrator, an anonymous memorandum that contained serious and unsubstantiated allegations against Demetracopoulos. Bullock was told it had been prepared in the State Department at the behest of Speaker Carl Albert's office, which also received an identical copy. The plan was to have each office spread the scurrilous information.

When Elias got a leaked copy, he wrote immediately to William Macomber, head of State's congressional relations, about the libelous falsehoods. Two days later, on December 5, Assistant Secretary of State David Abshire tracked Elias down in New York on a Sunday to apologize, assuring him that he had ordered an immediate recall of the memo. Rosenthal, who judged the memorandum "deplorable both in content and manner of distribution," confirmed to Elias that he'd been contacted by Abshire, who had said the "blind" memorandum had not been authorized by him and "should be considered withdrawn."[57] In fact, there was a firestorm at State, with some wanting to double down on the attacks, whereas Abshire, who knew Elias from his days working with Arleigh Burke, doubted the allegations and demanded that the State Department claims be carefully verified. Preparing for a December 27 meeting between Abshire and Rodger Davies, the head of the Near Eastern Affairs (NEA) bureau, George Churchill was forced to admit "our files on Demetracopoulos contain mostly secondary material—compilations of information and the like. We simply don't have the primary source material to do the kind of 'Ph.D. research' that Mr. Abshire has urged us to do."[58]

Nevertheless, State continued to leak negative material, especially references to Elias's alleged relationships with Andreas Papandreou and Melina Mercouri, and asked J. Edgar Hoover, personally, to direct a full FBI investigation.[59] Rodger Davies, head of NEA, took steps to break Elias's support in Congress and sent copies of his confidential note to Ambassador Tasca and Jim Potts, the CIA station chief in Athens.

■

ALTHOUGH GREECE WAS not high on Nixon's agenda, Vice President Agnew yearned to make a triumphal entrance into the land of his father as the highest-ranking Greek-American in the Nixon Administration. For much of the year, he had talked up his going to Greece only to have Administration officials quash the Agnew-generated press accounts.[60] Instead of Greece, Nixon and Kissinger kept sending him on goodwill trips anywhere he could play golf, have his photo taken, and do no harm. Foreign policy was Nixon's strength, and not to be shared with his vice president. Further, Nixon was considering dropping Agnew from the ticket in 1972.[61]

Agnew's hometown columnist observed that with each new public disclosure linking Tom Pappas to the junta, the possibility of an Agnew Hellenic stop on his upcoming Mideast trip grew "dimmer."[62] Indeed, no first-tier leader of any Western nation had visited Athens since the coup. However, when Nixon changed his mind about representing the United States at the Shah's lavish festivities celebrating the 2,500th year of the Persian Empire and designated Agnew to attend in his stead, Agnew beseeched the President to permit him to visit Greece as part of the trip.[63] State Department staff attempted to convince him to give up this dream, but failed.

Elias viewed the announcement with forboding and cringed to read accounts of Agnew's trip. He was not pleased to see television broadcasts of Papadopoulos and Tom Pappas alighting from the vice president's helicopter when they traveled to Agnew's ancestral village. Normally, Gargalianoi had a population of 6,200, but when he arrived there, according to *Time*, "the streets were lined with some 60,000 cheering peasants who had come on foot and by donkey and by chartered bus from miles around."[64]

As the vice president arrived in Athens, Elias called press attention to Agnew's 1968 endorsement of the junta, and his missteps since. Concern for the regime's victims was not on Agnew's agenda, nor did he make any attempt to meet with the opposition. He met Papadopoulos on October 16 and toasted him at a US Embassy reception. Tom Pappas took both men out on a yacht and hosted a "sumptuous" dinner in Agnew's honor. The vice president praised "the achievements that are going forward under the present Greek government."[65]

The British ambassador cabled his foreign office. While Papadopoulos's warm words about the Western alliance made it less likely that Greece would opt for Cold War neutrality, he reported, the Agnew visit "strengthened the regime's standing internationally," which could make the colonels "more difficult and demanding in their relations with other allies, including the United Kingdom."[66]

Press accounts noted that Agnew's "unreserved support" for the Greek regime went far beyond the polite demands of protocol. Upon his return, Agnew told the President proudly how he had resisted embassy entreaties to invite some token opposition figures to the reception for him in Athens. Nixon gave his nod of approval.[67]

Three days later, after senators deleted a House provision to ban military aid to Greece, the US Senate defeated, at least temporarily, the entire US Foreign Aid bill—a signal of disapproval of the junta. Democratic Senator Quentin Burdick and Republican Senator Mark Hatfield each wrote Elias afterward to thank him for his "persuasive" testimony before the Foreign Relations committee, which they credited for affecting the final vote.[68]

22.

Campaign 1972

FROM THE TIME THAT NIXON assumed the presidency, he was committed to assuring that his 1972 re-election victory would be sufficiently grand to obliterate memories of his razor-thin contests in 1960 and 1968. As early as January 1969, he met with campaign advisors in the Oval Office to design a strategy to win at any cost. The President approved a privately funded political-intelligence network in which loyalists would aggressively plug any embarrassing leaks and conduct sustained espionage—ranging from surveillance to wiretaps to infiltration—against real and imagined opponents. Soon, the Special Investigations Unit, aka "the Plumbers," formed by the White House as a reaction to the release of the Pentagon Papers, escalated the range of operations to theft and sabotage. The Watergate planning and break-in was but a small part of a larger enterprise that included vindictive tax audits, attacks on the press, expanded domestic espionage, mail intercepts, and burglaries.

On January 27, 1972, in the attorney general's office, Committee to Reelect the President (CREEP) counsel G. Gordon Liddy presented the first of his elaborate "Operation Gemstone" covert operations to deputy campaign director Jeb S. Magruder, John Dean, and John Mitchell, who was preparing to leave Justice to become head of CREEP. By the March 7 New Hampshire primary, the Nixon campaign's dirty-tricks unit had effectively crippled the candidacy of Maine senator Edmund Muskie, Humphrey's 1968 running mate, widely considered the strongest Democratic candidate. Attention turned to the reform-wing campaign of Democratic senator George McGovern. Demetracopoulos's close relationship with the long-shot candidate was well known to Nixon operatives.

Going into the race, Nixon was confident that the disproportionate Republican money advantage could overwhelm the cash-poor Democrats. The prolific fundraising of Tom Pappas, co-chair of CREEP's finance committee, was one of the President's best weapons; any disclosures that would implicate Tom Pappas as the bagman for an illegal funds transfer from Greece in 1968 could be explosive. Mitchell and Maurice Stans suspected that Larry O'Brien might still have in his files documentary evidence supporting such charges. Three days before the Operation Gemstone meeting, Elias received a concerned letter from Louise Gore.

> I went to Perle's [Perle Mesta's] luncheon for Martha Mitchell yesterday and sat next to John [Mitchell]. He is furious at you—and your testimony against Pappas. He kept threatening to have you deported!! At first I tried to ask him if he had any reason to think you could be deported and he didn't have any answer—But then tried to counter by asking me what I knew about you and why we were friends. It really got out of hand. It was all he'd talk about during lunch and everyone at the table was listening ... If there is anything I can do—not that I know what—let me know.[1]

IN THE WEEKS before Mitchell's outburst, fallout continued from the State Department's botched attempt to undermine Elias with their blind memo to Speaker Carl Albert. Forwarding Abshire's third reply to Demetracopoulos to his boss, John Dean, Deputy White House counsel Fred Fielding noted that State had given Congress "bad info that it will not stand behind if info becomes public," adding "What a grande screwup!"[2]

Distancing himself from Mitchell, Dean tried to take charge, telling Abshire that "before I pass judgment on this beauty I want to know what was fact vs. fiction in the document."[3] A meeting was held at the CIA to decide who would conduct a time-consuming "exhaustive review" of Demetracopoulos files, because his dossier contained "sensitive correspondence."[4]

While Dean and Abshire urged restraint, others in the US government were directed to attack. The State Department's Intelligence and Research Bureau sent a SECRET memorandum to the FBI's Domestic Intelligence Division enclosing a January 20 airgram from the Athens embassy. An FBI SECRET airtel purported that Demetracopoulos might be collaborating with Andreas Papandreou, perhaps in some violent anti-junta action.[5] A CIA report depicted efforts to implicate Elias in Archbishop Makarios's efforts to secure Czech arms for Cyprus.[6] All the while, Mitchell's Justice Department was attempting to confirm the existence and identity of some foreign principal behind Elias and thus nail him for violating the Foreign Agents Registration Act.[7]

On January 29, Elias attracted the administration's attention for a different matter, when he became the first to disclose to the press confidential negotiations to home port the Sixth Fleet in the Athens port city of Piraeus. Elias opposed the "shocking and ill timed" Pentagon plans to use Greece as a permanent naval base on moral, political, and military grounds.[8] Within a month, the House Foreign Affairs subcommittees on Europe and the Near East were preparing to hold joint hearings on the decision.

The idea for a home port in Greece had originated with the new Chief of Naval Operations, Admiral Elmo R. Zumwalt. The admiral had fond memories of his times in Greece and thought that tripling the current level of navy personnel by moving some 10,000 sailors and their families there would be good for morale, personnel retention, and budgetary efficiency. Foreign policy and strategic considerations were not his primary concerns.

American officials would claim that anti-Americanism in Greece was essentially nonexistent; that the addition of a huge American colony would have little adverse impact on Greece and no implications for current relations with the junta. For its part, the Greek government lusted after the deal, believing that in exchange for a few thousand homes, new docks, and ancillary facilities, it could strengthen its role as an indispensable American ally.[9]

By the time the House hearings convened in March, President Nixon had invoked national security and exercised his authority to waive the Hays amendment blocking the supply of arms to the Greek dictatorship. Angry junta critics blasted Nixon's decision and the selection of Greece over other Mediterranean homeporting sites.

State Department officials blamed Elias for submitting a polemical memorandum and orchestrating negative testimony from others. Demetracopoulos argued that the homeporting proposal violated the essential purpose of the Navy's "Mobility Doctrine," which called for an armada able to operate independent of any shore facilities. Such land dependence, he warned, could jeopardize its flexibility. He pointed out the political risks of implementing a program without giving either the US Senate or the Greek people a vote on the matter.[10]

The Defense Department bulled ahead, refusing to supply important witnesses or provide documentation regarding other possible facilities. The State Department had opposed homeporting in Greece until Admiral Zumwalt invited Joseph Sisco to play golf with him at the exclusive Burning Tree Country Club.[11] Afterward, Sisco and his Foggy Bottom colleagues flipped and began supporting Zumwalt's fiction that Athens had been selected only after carefully examining fifteen other ports in the Mediterranean. State went so far as to backdate a hastily prepared analysis describing the disadvantages of every place except Piraeus, while Near East Affairs director Rodger Davies claimed that a home port in Piraeus would facilitate settlement of the Arab-Israeli dispute.[12]

In response to pressure from other intelligence agencies, the FBI expressed frustration that they had so much information on Demetracopoulos "it was frequently not possible to tell what information in the files related to variations of previously reported incidents or to incidents merely similar in nature to those previously reported."[13]

Elias knew he was viewed negatively by American officials but was unaware of the extent to which some people he thought were his friends, or at least not his enemies, would undermine him. Mary Gore Dean, Louise's sister and John Mitchell's paramour, with whom he'd socialized for more than a decade, told the FBI that because Elias held liberal views he might be a Communist. [14]

More significantly, for decades Elias had submitted stories to the North American Newspaper Alliance and thought he had a good relationship with its president/executive editor Sid Goldberg, his staff, and his family. He knew that Goldberg was a former American intelligence officer and a conservative Republican, friendly with the likes of Murray Chotiner and opposed to McGovern. But Goldberg had vouched for his NANA employment at the time of his 1967 escape and stood by him in the ensuing immigration battles, fully aware of his anti-junta activities. Elias couldn't have foreseen that NANA's manager and Goldberg's right arm, Vera Glaser, would inform the FBI that Demetracopoulos had no substantial relationship with the news service and volunteer that because Elias was "single, intelligent and a good mixer," he'd been asked to escort "very prominent" married women to functions and "taken advantage of the situation."[15] She did not disclose the names of his victims, she said, because she could not prove any of the allegations. At the time he was similarly unaware of the activities of

Goldberg's wife, Lucianne, whom he knew socially and who would later achieve notoriety as the literary agent who advised Linda Tripp to tape her conversations with Monica Lewinsky about Bill Clinton. In 1972 she was embedded by Murray Chotiner into the press team covering George McGovern's presidential campaign to conduct political espionage and help produce "Democrats for Nixon" propaganda.[16] While she pretended to be working for the Women's News Service—part of her husband's organization—she was in fact being paid by Chotiner to provide salacious personal gossip, private poll results, and schedule changes. Chotiner sent her reports directly to Haldeman on the Nixon campaign plane.

SHORTLY AFTER MIDNIGHT on Sunday June 17, 1972, five men broke into offices of the Democratic National Committee at the Watergate complex and were arrested for attempted burglary and wiretapping. What would later become a great national scandal involving White House connections, cover-ups, and congressional investigations began as a minor crime story. At the time, Elias gave limited thought to what the burglars might have been looking for in the offices of DNC chairman Larry O'Brien. He did not know if any of the notes on his charges taken by O'Brien's staff in October 1968 in that same suite had been kept in the office. News of Howard Hunt's involvement brought back recollections of Hunt's work with the CIA in Athens in the 1950s, but nothing more. Elias remained disappointed that O'Brien had not only failed to use his evidence in 1968 but had done nothing with that intelligence over the past three and a half years. What kind of opposition research were Democrats conducting on Pappas, Elias wondered. Little to none, he assumed.

In early summer 1972, Elias was most focused on convincing the Democrats to include a ban on military aid to Greece in their party platform. He had once been hopeful that Secretary of State Rogers might try to balance the administration's clear support of the junta with gestures of support for regime opponents during a Fourth of July visit to Athens, but he soon discovered that no such pressure would be put on the junta.[17] Even student demonstrations, scattered small bombing incidents, and a hit-and-run attack on the American embassy did nothing to deter the US government from its support for the Greek regime.

Elias's critics maintained that he was such a publicity hound he wouldn't give tips to reporters and columnists unless they featured or quoted him. In truth, Elias repeatedly found ways to pass along information with the explicit understanding that he would not be identified. He ghost-wrote correspondence, speeches, testimony, articles, and letters to the editor on behalf of United States senators and congressmen, and he used the role of anonymous "special correspondent" as a favorite stratagem, including with the *New York Times*.[18] State Department and embassy officials lost track of how many articles in a variety of publications they believed were secretly supplied by the indefatigable exile.

As censorship rules changed, many Greek newspapers still hesitated to editorialize, but published their partisan views under the guise of straight reporting from their special correspondents abroad.[19] Demetracopoulos's old paper *Makedonia/Thessaloniki* used this approach, relying on their special correspondent, "L. Costis," in London. When an American consular official asked *Makedonia* publisher Ioannis "John" Vellidis whether L. Costis was a nom de plume used by Demetracopoulos, he explained that Costis was a Greek graduate student at the London School of Economics working for the *Times* of London who had "a good connection in Washington."[20] Neither the school nor the *Times* has any record of an L. Costis being a student or employee during that time. When Elias was asked about the mystery years later, he smiled and said, "No comment."

■

BY LATE JUNE 1972, believing that Nixon would not change his policy toward Greece in the foreseeable future, Elias focused his presidential-election energies fully on the Democrats. The so-called Greek plank in the Democratic Party Platform on which he and the Committee for Democracy in Greece had lobbied heavily pledged that a Democratic administration would cease all support for the "repressive Greek government."[21] Elias carefully worked the raucous Democratic National Convention in Miami Beach that was dominated by "New Politics" reformers at the expense of party regulars. Demetracopoulos had friends in both camps and knew that Greece would not be the center of attention. Nevertheless, he personally delivered packets of information to all of the presidential candidates, asking for written support of the anti-junta cause.

Separately, he held discussions with McGovern and his staff regarding the importance of making American policy toward Greece part of the senator's campaign. He wrote a public letter to the presidential nominee, praising his support of the platform plank and asking about "the specific ways" of implementing it if McGovern was elected.[22] Two days later, McGovern and his aide John Holum, working with Elias on precise language, crafted a detailed response, also in the form of a public letter. McGovern said that as President he would terminate all aid to the Greek dictatorship, notify NATO of the United States' "strict adherence" to NATO's democratic preamble, and order a full review of the Nixon agreement regarding the establishment of homeporting facilities in Greece. He added that the number of US military personnel stationed in Greece would be reduced "to an absolute minimum." Finally, McGovern would "sharply curtail" the number of visits to Greece of high-ranking US civilian and military officials and cooperate with NATO, the EEC, and the Council of Europe regarding their decisions on "participation by the Greek dictatorship."[23]

McGovern's candidacy may have been a long shot, but Elias believed that the senator was principled and, if elected, would become a leader in the fight to restore Greek democracy. The widespread attention to his involvement in the McGovern statement nourished Demetracopoulos's large ego, but also made him a more valuable target for his Greek and American enemies.

Elias's reaction to news of more special treatment from the junta for Tom Pappas stirred up new troubles. Demetracopoulos had blown the whistle years before when learning of the sweetheart deal Pappas negotiated in 1968 to become the first to bring Coca-Cola to Greece. To placate local fruit growers' fears of competition from the soft-drink giant, Pappas had agreed to invest $20 million in local fruit-canning facilities. Quietly, on May 23, 1972, the regime enacted Royal Decree 72 A, scaling back Pappas's earlier commitment to only $2.5 million. The reason: "lack of raw materials with which to construct the canning plants." *To Vima*, one of the Athens papers for which Elias served as an anonymous correspondent, asked rhetorically how the raw materials unavailable to build canning plants for the citrus industry were in such plentiful supply to build plants for Coca-Cola.[24]

Over a June dinner, Louise Gore told Elias she had heard separately from a retired CIA friend and from John Mitchell that his criticism of Pappas had again been a topic of discussion in both the White House and the Nixon campaign. She also revealed that both had asked her to help stop Elias.

On July 20, Evans and Novak's syndicated column mentioned that: "the facts in the Pappas–Coca-Cola case have now been submitted by Elias Demetracopoulos . . . to the House Foreign Affairs Committee," and that Pappas's lobbying for the dictatorship seemed "certain to swing tens of thousands of Greek-American votes, normally Democratic, into the Nixon column on Nov. 7."[25] The day after the column appeared, the FBI outlined for the CIA and State ways to depict Elias as having violated the Foreign Agents Registration

Act. It also reported that, in cooperation with the IRS, it had started to look at Elias's tax records.[26]

The American relationship with Greece was not high on the list of issues most voters cared about in 1972. Nixon nevertheless tried to spin McGovern's anti–military aid position into a wedge issue for American Jews, long a loyal part of the Democratic coalition, by claiming that American aid to Greece and home-porting were indispensable for the protection of Israel. Elias quickly pointed out the absurdity of this claim, noting the Greek regime's refusal to help the US aid Israel during the 1970 Jordanian crisis, its dependence on Arab oil and UN support for Cyprus, and its deserved reputation for being the most anti-Israeli government outside the Arab world and the Soviet bloc. Elias did not have to wait long before Greece, Arab countries, and even some European governments protested. The White House walked back the president's remarks.[27]

The colonels' regime made no official comment on McGovern's letter, which was widely covered in the Greek press, but government spokesman Byron Stamatopoulos described it as "unacceptable" interference in Greek affairs.[28] In late July he amplified his attack in the conservative newspaper *Estia*, characterizing Elias as "an agent of more than one foreign power," who during World War II collaborated with the occupying Fascist authorities and received "considerable financial benefits" for his services.[29] Justifiably angry, Elias engaged the legal services of Dimitrios Papaspyrou, the pre-junta president of the Greek parliament, to demand a correction from Stamatopoulos and *Estia*, but neither responded to his demand, and no Greek newspapers other than the *Athens News* would print Elias's formal rebuttal.[30] Stamatopoulos continued his vindictive campaign using the regime's mouthpiece, *Eleftheros Kosmos*, to lambaste Elias and publish misinformation about him.

Meanwhile, the McGovern letter angered many in the Greek-American community. Editorials and commentary in US Hellenic papers asserted that "nearly all Greek-Americans . . . say that the people in Greece are happy with the regime in power." Some criticized "prejudiced Greek exiled resistance leaders" who advocated "ultra-liberal policies." Singling out Elias by name, they urged McGovern to investigate who was supplying junta critics with the "monies necessary for their large expenditures and lavish parties."[31]

Conservative syndicated columnist James J. Kilpatrick made the case against McGovern's Greece policy, characterizing the letter as "foolish" and McGovern as a "prize sucker," naïve and inexperienced in foreign affairs. He warned that if the Greek government fell, Andreas Papandreou and his gang would install an East German–style version of communism. Kilpatrick reserved his harshest vilification for Elias, whom he described as a "one time political writer and minor journalist in Athens" who "never was a major figure in the Greek press ... [and] is remembered in Athens as the author of a story in August of 1965 based upon a forged letter that gave currency to vicious anti-American propaganda."[32] State Department officials in Washington, who may have helped source the article, exchanged sniggering messages about Kilpatrick's portrait of their target.

After an outraged Elias asked his right-wing and military friends, who had phoned to commiserate, to call Kilpatrick in protest, he and Kilpatrick met at the Sheraton Park Hotel. Only days later, Kilpatrick devoted his entire column to making "amends and amplifications," under headlines such as "Columnist Eats Crow in Three Great Gulps."[33] In this retraction, Kilpatrick described Elias as a "handsome ... personable bachelor" and "remarkable fellow." Correcting all of his earlier criticisms point by point, he apologized for calling him a "minor journalist," noting that the conservative weekly *Human Events* had described him as "the foremost political editor in Greece" and Herman Kahn identified him as "the distinguished political editor in exile." He said Demetracopoulos's "sensational" 1965 news story was a legitimate scoop. And he corrected his description of Elias as a left-wing hustler, noting his work for Brimberg and the diverse group of congressmen he'd successfully cultivated, including Senators Byrd, Javits, and Thurmond, who had "warmly inscribed" a photograph. "In the annals of high level lobbying, he holds a respected place," Kilpatrick concluded.

This retraction so stupefied Elizabeth Brown, the political affairs counselor in Athens, that she asked the Greek Desk in Washington to investigate why Kilpatrick changed his mind. Exasperated by Demetracopoulos's "remarkable talent for landing feet first," Ambassador Tasca confidentially contacted Jim Potts, former CIA Station chief in Athens, to urge him to help dig up actionable dirt that would show that Elias "is not what he says he is." And while Elias's enemies were "nosing about" in Washington, the embassy passed on an uncorroborated rumor that Elias was in negotiations with Papadopoulos to get a "well-paying" job in Athens in exchange for his support for the regime and "disclosure of many secrets about communist endeavors to subvert Greece."[34]

■

OUTSIDE THE BELTWAY, Kilpatrick's correction often failed to catch up to his original diatribe. Sam Nakis, the supreme president of Ahepa, the largest

Greek-American organization, took on McGovern, contending that a clear majority of Greek-descent voters supported the regime. In a public letter to McGovern, Nakis wrote of his distress over the Democratic nominee's reliance on "the self-proclaimed expatriate ... whose profession of idealistic motivation is extremely suspect."[35] Shortly thereafter, Nakis stepped down from Ahepa to become vice chairman of Democrats for Nixon at the behest of its chairman, Nixon treasury secretary John Connally. This shell organization was largely designed to funnel campaign funds into opposition research and anti-McGovern dirty tricks. Connally directed Nakis to find and work with another highly visible Greek-American Democrat to attack McGovern and smear Demetracopoulos. Nakis chose John Rousakis, the Democratic mayor of Savannah. Using language that Nakis fed him, Rousakis prepared a letter to McGovern dated August 18, 1972, in which he claimed he was "shocked and appalled" not only by McGovern's position on Greece, but by his using as his mouthpiece "an obscure Greek communist journalist." Distributing it in late August with no one around would have been a waste. Instead, just weeks before the election, when there was little time left to respond, Connally, Nakis, and Lucianne Goldberg arranged to publish the Rousakis letter by circulating it nationally to Greek-American newspapers and clergy on Democrats-for-Nixon letterhead, as well as including it in a targeted mass mailing. Many months after the election, after the provenance of the letter text had been determined, Rousakis apologized publicly for making false charges.[36]

Other Greek-American groups and newspapers not directly involved in the Nixon campaign attacked Demetracopoulos as well, but none as virulently as Tom Pappas's local Boston paper, *The Hellenic Chronicle*, and The Greek Proclamation Committee, an ad hoc group led by Pappas acolyte Constance Booras Roche and Nicholas Cassavetes, father of the Greek-American actor and film director. At the Fairfax, Elias received anonymous phone calls and letters threatening him with physical harm—these in addition to the death warnings that friends in the US and abroad learned about and reported to him. It is not clear whether a mysterious letter was spontaneous or part of the anti-Demetracopoulos disinformation plan, but a female reader in Muskegon, Michigan wrote to the FBI to say that the "obscure and suspicious" Demetracopoulos had played a role in the George Wallace assassination attempt and would now try to assassinate Nixon. Acting FBI director L. Patrick Gray forwarded her warning to the Secret Service, which had the primary responsibility for protecting the President.[37] The episode was added to other fresh "Secret" Elias intelligence information, including a memorandum from A. Russell Ash of the National Security Council, FBI field agent interviews with allegedly "reliable" informants, and a new report drawing on the State Department's Security Office.[38] An even more invasive investigation of Elias Demetracopoulos's personal life was about to begin.

■

WHEN NEWS OF the Watergate break-in arrests hit Capitol Hill, the first member to pounce on the story was J. Wright Patman, the seventy-nine-year-old Texas Democrat and chairman of the House Banking and Currency Committee, whose New York speaking engagement had been arranged by Elias a year earlier. An old-style populist from the hardscrabble northeast Texas town of Texarkana, he was known for exposing miscreants who had engaged in what he deemed abusive behavior and economic injustice. His 1932 legislation for an immediate World War I veterans' bonus had led to the Bonus Army march on Washington, and in 1970 he blew the whistle on the Nixon Administration's taxpayer bailout of the "scandalously mismanaged" Penn Central Railroad.

Reading about the Watergate arrests, Patman recalled what Elias had told him on their train trip a year before. Sensing a connection, he recounted the 1968 Pappas money-laundering story to his staff and instructed them to conduct their own investigation by "following the money." Within five days of the Watergate arrests, members of Patman's staff were vigorously tracing the new and numbered $100 bills found in the burglars' possession from Texas through Mexico and back to Washington. Working diligently, they identified the source of the four checks totaling $89,000 found in the Florida bank account of one of the burglars, Bernard Barker, a CIA operative who had been at the Bay of Pigs invasion. By August, they were preparing a preliminary report that alleged the involvement of Maurice Stans, the Nixon reelection committee's treasurer, in a widespread money-laundering scheme. Patman surmised that establishing the burglars' connection to the Nixon campaign could lead to the top of the administration.

At the time, the Patman probe was the only official investigation of the Watergate break-in. Patman's staff, experienced in the way organized crime used secret, numbered, foreign bank accounts to launder money, was well-qualified to carry out this work. They prepared a list of witnesses to be interviewed. But on September 14, the first of them declined to appear. So, Chairman Patman decided to get from Congress the power to subpoena witnesses and documents, scheduling an authorization vote for his next committee meeting on October 3,

1972. The White House immediately launched a furious, multi-pronged attack on the Patman investigation. First, they challenged the committee venue as improper, insisting that any hearing would be unfair to the defendants' civil rights given pending criminal proceedings. Patman countered that the committee's planned investigation was "aimed at information far beyond the activities of the defendants . . ."[39]

The second approach was to portray the investigation as a baseless, partisan attack. The President's men believed they could convince the Republicans on the committee, but given the Democratic majority, they would lose if it came down to a straight party-line vote. House Minority Leader Gerald Ford was directed by Nixon to quarterback the campaign.[40] After firming up some wavering Republicans, he targeted several pro-Nixon Southern Democrats, aided by White House operatives who warned that the administration would expose any violation of election law or other misbehavior, no matter how trivial or technical. The Nixon team did its homework well. Kentucky Democratic congressman William Curlin, Jr. remembered: "Certain members of the committee were reminded of various past political indiscretions, or of relatives who might suffer as a result of [a] pro-subpoena vote." The White House also smeared Patman himself by associating him with the "known Communist agent," Elias Demetracopoulos.[41]

In early 1972, as part of the administration's effort to blunt Demetracopoulos's activities, the FBI had gone to the Dupont Circle branch of the Riggs Bank, where the CIA had set up dummy accounts and regularly monitored legitimate customers. Elias had maintained an account there since his self-exile in 1967. The bank allowed the FBI to rummage through Elias's bank records, and readily turned over a copy of a $150 check Elias had deposited into his account.[42] The check was a reimbursement from Sartorius & Co. for advance payments Elias had made toward Patman's transportation and other incidental costs associated with the June 1971 trip.

In June 1972, a New York–based FBI agent presented a copy of the check to George Kendall, president of Sartorius & Co., who had asked Elias to invite and escort Patman to New York. After confirming the connection, the agent warned Elias's employer about Demetracopoulos, making his activities sound sinister, and invited Sartorius to reconsider the wisdom of employing him. Shaken, Kendall called Elias to terminate their relationship.

Then, in September 1972, as Patman sought to round up votes for subpoena power, Nixon's men shared a curated Demetracopoulos dossier of lies and disinformation and gave it to members of the committee "in confidence," including a secret cable from Ambassador Tasca charging Elias with being head of a "well organized conspiracy being paid by foreign power." Demetracopoulos, they were told, was a Communist or perhaps even a double agent. These lies were bundled with the fact that Demetracopoulos had arranged the Patman speech, the honorarium, and coverage of all related expenses—a relationship that was completely lawful.

A third line of attack was to explicitly threaten that any committee members' "yes" votes would be used against them in and after the fall election. Nixon had an ally on the committee in Democratic congressman Richard T. Hanna from California. Both John Mitchell and Henry Kissinger possessed FBI reports implicating Hanna in the receipt of illegal campaign contributions from the Korean Central Intelligence Agency. Hanna had been expected to vote "yes" for subpoenas, but, when he saw the Demetracopoulos dossier, he folded immediately. Hanna's vote switch provided cover for others to change position. When the committee met on October 3 to decide whether to convene hearings with subpoena powers, the vote was 20 to 15 against, with six Democrats on the committee joining with the unified Republican minority in opposition.[43] The failure to secure subpoena powers was enough to kill this first investigation into the Watergate break-in and any other political hearing until long after the election, even though the scandal was the only potential trump card available to the Democrats.[44]

In the last weeks of the presidential campaign, with heightened negative attention on Elias from the McGovern-letter reaction, the Patman Watergate inquiry, and the accelerating intelligence-community investigations, the State Department considered springing its own October Surprise in an effort to silence the troublesome Greek. Ambassador Tasca urged Washington to immediately declassify and release all of the summary reports compiled by four previous US ambassadors to brand Demetracopoulos as persona non grata. In a series of "Secret" oral and written exchanges debating the tradeoffs of such a release, State decided in the end to heed the observation of an unnamed Greek Desk staffer: "There are things mentioned in the correspondence that I'm sure we still don't want to remind people of . . . I'm afraid that releasing this kind of thing in an effort to nail Elias would likely cause us greater pain than it would him."[45]

23.

Fallout from a Mutiny

UNDER NO ILLUSIONS THAT MCGOVERN would be able to stage an upset, Elias took some solace that despite Nixon's landslide victory, Republicans lost seats in the Senate and didn't win the House. He knew, however, that continued Democratic control of Congress would not assure support for Greek democracy.

Well before November 7, Demetracopoulos had arranged to go to Europe for Brimberg and other business clients as a cover for his activist agenda. From his luxurious Le Bristol hotel room in Paris, he looked down at the chic boutiques of the Rue du Faubourg Saint-Honoré and reviewed a stack of telephone messages that awaited his arrival. Elias refined his crammed schedule and reached out to contacts representing different facets of his highly compartmentalized life. He prioritized a private dinner and a US Embassy reception with Louise Gore, now in her part-time role as UNESCO ambassador. His presence with her at the social gathering displeased some State Department officials, but Louise was a loyal friend and his most trusted pair of eyes and ears in Republican circles.

One of his more significant appointments was with Konstantinos Karamanlis at his tenth-floor apartment with a panoramic view of Paris. Less formally dressed than Elias, the former Greek prime minister said he would not return home to implement the so-called Karamanlis solution until there had been a strong transitional government in power for six months to a year. Elias also met with other Greek exiles in other European cities, exchanging intelligence on the growing weaknesses of Papadopoulos, the splits within the increasingly corrupt regime, and further troubles in the armed forces. Elias regarded Brigadier General Ioannidis as increasingly the real power behind the regime and predicted that his ascension would make matters worse.

•

ON THE CHILLY, gray, overcast morning of January 5, 1973, with snow forecast, an impressive gathering of notables, friends, and foes together, paid their last respects to Harry Truman at an invitation-only memorial service at Washington Cathedral. The Associated Press described those attending as "a dichotomy on the Truman Doctrine ... Sitting only four seats apart were the Greek Prime Minister [*sic*], Stylianos Pattakos, representing his government . . . and the leader of the Greek exiles in the US, Elias P. Demetracopoulos ... who sat next to Senator Edward M. Kennedy."[1]

Three days later, the Nixon Administration signed a five-year agreement to move ahead with the plan to expand facilities in Piraeus and create "the American navy's largest home port in Europe."[2] Sensitive to public opposition to the plan, the Greek government told the US it would decline the $15 million of military aid and pay cash for future armaments. Refusing to accept that his side had lost this battle, Demetracopoulos continued to inveigh against the deal. To buttress his argument, he shared widely an October 30, 1972, letter he'd received from Senator Frank Church, which described private meetings the Idaho senator had had with Israeli military intelligence. The Israelis were irritated at having been made a "shuttlecock" in a badminton game among Greeks, Arabs, and Americans. The "high military officials" clearly "did not consider US bases in Greece as essential to their security."[3]

Despite his position of authority, Henry Tasca viewed himself a victim. He felt frustrated by repeated political interference from Nixon, Agnew, Kissinger, the CIA's Jack Maury, and Pappas—all of whom played back-channel roles, cutting Tasca out of the loop and creating a constant stream of problems. Pappas was the worst. The Greek-American magnate was already part of the landscape when Tasca arrived, and the ambassador knew he had to deal with him, but, as he would confide later, Pappas was a constant irritant, working all the angles, cultivating the colonels, acting as an asset for the CIA and expanding his businesses in Greece. Tasca resented Pappas's blatant disrespect. To make matters worse,

Tasca often felt he had to keep quiet about the President's pal's wheeling and dealing.[4]

At different times Tasca discussed the untenable situation in which he found himself with Kissinger, Agnew, and Nixon, who indicated to him that he would receive his long-desired posting as US Ambassador to Italy. Tasca and his wife looked forward to the Rome-based ambassadorship and then a happy retirement in a villa in the Borghese Gardens, part of Tasca's wife's inheritance from her father's childhood friendship with Mussolini. He thought he had the President's firm commitment to make the change after the election. Elias's State Department sources told him that it was a done deal, even providing the name of Tasca's likely replacement.

Nixon, however, concerned about how to provide hush money for the Watergate burglars, had become more involved in the cover-up. When asking Bob Haldeman what Chuck Colson, White House special counsel and "hatchet man," was looking for during the break-in, his chief aide replied, "Two things": one financial, and the other evidence of a possible Democratic plot against them.[5] In March, Haldeman told Nixon that Mitchell had advised that the best way to provide money to "keep those people in place" was through Pappas, "the best source we've got for that kind of thing . . . and he's able to deal in cash." There was only one ask, Haldeman said: "Pappas is extremely anxious that Tasca stay in Greece . . . and the plan was, you know, to remove him and put someone else in Greece, but Mitchell says it would be a very useful thing to just not disrupt that." Nixon replied: "Good. I understand. No problem," and then cryptically added: "Pappas has raised the money for this other activity or whatever it is."[6]

Four days later, Nixon thanked Pappas personally in the Oval Office for money that was used to buy the silence of the Watergate burglars: "I am aware of what you're doing to help out on some of these things [Maurice Stans] and others are involved in. I won't say anything further, but it's very seldom you find a friend like that, believe me."[7]

∎

IN FEBRUARY AND March 1973, the regime in Athens was startled by previously dormant university students, the "sleeping giant" that Elias had long thought, if mobilized, could be a powerful catalyst for change. Since late 1972, there had been signs that students were unwilling to accept government interference in matters of academic freedom such as curriculum selection and the election of academic committees. When students at the prestigious Polytechnic Institute boycotted classes, the regime overreacted, beat demonstrators, and made arrests. Strikes and demonstrations, articulating these and other grievances, spread to other colleges.[8]

The government responded by reasserting martial-law provisions that had been slowly relaxed. Demonstrators were threatened with immediate revocation of their student deferments. Newspapers were ordered not to cover demonstrations. The editor and publisher of the independent right-wing *Vradyni*, who refused to comply, found his home and office ransacked by tax investigators and police. Six lawyers who stepped forward to serve as defense attorneys for the victimized students were also arrested, held incommunicado, and brutalized at the special interrogation branch of the Greek military police, located opposite the American Embassy.[9]

The dictatorship easily survived the protests. The old political guard cheered the resistance, but workers did not take to the streets in solidarity. The army held, although some officers expressed outrage. Portraying the government's overreaction as evidence of its instability, Elias used the *Vradyni* example to illustrate that the regime was increasingly being criticized from the right. He pressed for support from the American Newspaper Association and the Paris-based International Federation of Newspaper Publishers.[10]

The Greek government struck back, claiming that anti-junta New York congressman Benjamin Rosenthal had "incited" the recent student disorders at the behest of Demetracopoulos, a claim that even the State Department thought wildly "impossible."[11]

Demetracopoulos's reaction was to invite to Washington the celebrated exile Lady Amalia Fleming, the Greek widow of the creator of penicillin, to put a human face on regime brutalities through a series of congressional visits, press briefings, and fundraisers. The most memorable part of Fleming's presentations was her playing a tape recording of the mother of Alekos Panagoulis plaintively describing the malevolent treatment of her son in prison.[12] Elias followed up with a live rematch debate with Howard University professor Demetrios Kousoulas, broadcast to a national television audience.[13] Three years before, in their regional television confrontation, Elias had repeatedly put the contributing author of the 1968 constitution on the defensive. This time the two got personal, with Elias eviscerating the professor's apologia for the regime's failure to restore democracy.[14]

The State Department continued to push hard to "get" Demetracopoulos by pressuring the CIA and FBI to find his "foreign principal." A frustrated FBI complained that CIA information appeared to be contradictory and came from "less reliable sources" and that State had consistently failed to support its conspiratorial suspicions with any substantive information. Elias, it said, had been of interest to the US government for over twenty years but "to date, nothing has been developed through all available records to indicate that the subject poses a threat to the internal security of the US or is in violation of Federal laws under the jurisdiction of the FBI."[15] Acting director Patrick Gray recommended the FBI close its case, expressing concern that further action would result in allegations of harassment, intimidation, and infringement of constitutional rights.[16] State and CIA pushed back, claiming that Demetracopoulos was much more nefarious than the FBI believed, and directed the Bureau to focus on Elias's federal income tax returns from 1967 to 1971.

▪

IN LATE MARCH, the British Ambassador to Greece cabled London: "Real progress toward a restoration of democracy is clearly less likely now than ever." But a fresh shoot of resistance was emerging from among members of the armed forces who had either been sacked, arrested, or voluntarily retired. Some of the remaining dissident officers considered a variety of clandestine and largely impractical plots. One of these conspirators, Commander Nikolaos Pappas (no relation to Tom Pappas), had picked up new information on the bitter factions within the junta from a talkative and zealously pro-junta lieutenant colonel while studying at the NATO Defense College. He made contact with a few like-minded active-duty naval officers scattered throughout Europe. He also passed his intelligence on to key Greeks in exile, including Elias.[17]

By the spring of 1973, Nikolaos Pappas's Navy-led group believed that splits within the regime provided an opening for a revolt. They had a scheme that could succeed by working with Major Spyros Moustaklis, one of the few Army officers aligned with them. Moustaklis was a career soldier who had fought against the Nazis and Communists, then distinguished himself in the Korean War. Handsome, with deep blue eyes, a high forehead, wavy black hair, and the erect bearing of a proud officer, he was in charge of the small military garrison on the island of Syros.

The plan, scheduled to be implemented on May 23, involved taking over the island and setting up a military administration under the command of Moustaklis, who would then transfer power to a provisional Government of National Unity. Collaborating ships would blockade the Greek ports of Piraeus and Thessaloniki. If the dictatorship refused to resign voluntarily, the ships would isolate Athens from the rest of the country with gunfire and force a surrender. Previously scheduled NATO war-game exercises were to provide cover for the extra provisioning and movement of Greek ships prior to the onset of the rebellion.[18]

Two days before execution, leaks and betrayals alerted the regime, which moved to crush the resistance. Officers and politicians were rounded up and arrested. At home in Athens on May 20, Moustaklis waited in vain for the coded message that was to instruct him to go to Syros and put the plan in motion. He knew something had gone wrong. At dawn on the May 21 he drove west for more than four hours to Messolonghi, where he planned to hide at his sister's. Hearing that his five-month-old daughter had accidentally burned herself with boiling water, however, he returned home immediately and was grabbed by the infamous security police.

That same day, after Commander Pappas heard of the arrests, he decided to act on his own. He was already at sea aboard the HNS Velos. After starting the day's maneuvers as if nothing were wrong, Pappas explained to his crew his intention to carry out the plan, warning that those who chose to join this mutiny would face serious consequences and urging that most—even though they expressed their solidarity—plan instead to return home to their families. Then, on the morning of Thursday, May 24, after news broke that two Greek admirals had been arrested for plotting to incite the Hellenic armed forces to mutiny and as the squadron sailed between Sardinia and Genoa, Pappas astounded the commanders of other NATO vessels from Italy, Greece, Turkey, the UK, and the US by removing his destroyer from the exercises and sailing into the Italian fishing port of Fiumicino.[19]

En route, he wired a message pledging fidelity to NATO and to the Greek civilization founded on principles of democracy, liberty, and the rule of law, principles he and his mutineers wanted to reestablish. He implored the free world and NATO to recognize the corruption and illegitimacy of the hated regime.[20] Surrounded by Italian police boats, he asked for political asylum for himself and about thirty of his officers and crew. Two officers went ashore, indicating that Pappas would hold a press conference the next day. At the request of Italian police, they returned to the ship. An Italian tender and five Coast Guard cutters tried to block the Greek vessel from paparazzi-chartered boats and other civilian craft with Italian leftists aboard shouting support.[21]

The standoff continued for more than twelve hours as terms were negotiated among NATO officers, Greek diplomats, Italian officials, and the *Velos* insurgents. Pappas and his crew had to make sure that Italian prime minister Giulio Andreotti would deny the Greek Embassy's demand for extradition. After tense negotiations, the Italians recognized the special circumstances and granted Pappas and his coterie political asylum.

For days, the mutiny attracted positive international coverage. The Greek government claimed it was a royalist plot. But when Nikolaos Pappas spoke to the press, he made clear: "We are not royalists, or politically involved. We are Greek officers who can no longer tolerate military rule in our homeland."

After the publicity faded, the refugees were on their own. Some stayed in Italy, others sought asylum elsewhere. Many exiled political leaders, such as Karamanlis, quickly backed away from the failed venture. Andreas was silent. The King wrote that funds were available only to help the immediate needs of the political refugees.[22]

The father of one sailor in the *Velos* mutiny wrote to Elias for help to get his son to America. Elias's initial effort was unsuccessful because the American ambassador in Rome, former Massachusetts governor John Volpe, a longtime beneficiary of Tom Pappas's financing, was disinclined to provide visas for anti-junta Greeks. Demetracopoulos organized an international campaign to raise funds for the mutineers. In September, Commander Pappas sent him a progress report from Varese, Italy. Listed were names and amounts donated or committed by King Constantine, Nikitas Venizelos, Konstantinos Mitsotakis, Elias, and others, with a question mark by the name of Karamanlis, indicating to date his non-support. Andreas's name was entirely absent. Pappas thanked Elias effusively for being "the only Greek living abroad who provided such important financial assistance."[23] For all of the disparaging talk of his publicity-seeking self-centeredness, Demetracopoulos never disclosed this behind-the-scenes role.[24]

In Athens the rulers viewed the failed mutiny as an opportunity. For months, Papadopoulos, Makarezos, and Pattakos had been discussing the country's constitutional future without coming to any conclusion. Should it be a constitutional monarchy with Constantine as king, or someone else as regent, or a republic under the presidency of Papadopoulos? On Friday, June 1, Papadopoulos declared the monarchy abolished. Greece would become a republic. He ordered a plebiscite in two months to ratify these decisions and announced that parliamentary elections would be held in 1974.

At a NATO council meeting in Copenhagen in mid-June, there was growing support for a serious discussion about the alleged impairment of Greece's military capacity under the junta. While many delegates were reluctant to criticize the internal behavior of a member, several were prepared to do so directly, and all looked to the United States for leadership. Again, America shielded Greece from any negative action.[25]

Meanwhile in Washington, the Senate approved 46 to 41 a Pell amendment to the Foreign Assistance Act that would only authorize military aid to Greece when the US President, after a comprehensive review, reported to Congress that the Greek government was fulfilling its obligation under the North Atlantic Treaty. House hearings on homeporting provided another forum in which critics could question American policy toward Greece. The State Department's Bureau of Intelligence and Research predicted the imminent fall of Papadopoulos. Secretary of State Rogers, in the face of congressional pressure, suggested that the second phase of homeporting be postponed. Obdurately, Nixon ignored his recommendation.[26]

The President, increasingly obsessed with Watergate issues, ceded much control of foreign affairs to Henry Kissinger, who by late summer would replace Rogers as secretary of state. Greece was not high on Kissinger's agenda.

All of this was more unwelcome news for a frustrated Tasca, who by now realized he wasn't going to Rome. In a private meeting with Papadopoulos, the ambassador modestly observed that the Greek people deserved a fair vote, triggering from the Greek leader an outburst of complaints about the United States. A diplomatic colleague observed that "Henry, who used to be so positive about the Greek regime," had become "disillusioned," feeling he had been "deceived" personally by Papadopoulos.[27] However, when some in the State Department wanted to use the uncertainties in Greece as an opportunity to revisit American policy, Tasca allied himself with Kissinger in vetoing the suggestion.

Most believed that, if the Pell amendment became law, the President would invoke his congressionally provided authority to override the ban in the interest of national security, as he had done with the Hays amendment the year before.

When Greece held a plebiscite on a new constitution on July 29, the question was rigged so that a "yes" vote meant not just accepting a republic, but approving Papadopoulos as its first president. Some in the Nixon Administration were "worried that something might happen" and predicted that a clear majority would vote "no."[28] Elias, however, assumed there would be enough intimidation and falsification to ensure Papadopoulos's victory.

Some opponents urged a boycott, and abstentions ran high at 25 percent, but official results indicated that Greece as a whole had voted 78.4 "yes" for the referendum: over 80 percent in the countryside, 59.6 percent in Athens' periphery, and 51.1 percent in Athens proper. Papadopoulos had his mandate. He was empowered, for seven years, to reconstruct the government as a presidential parliamentary republic, a "guided" democracy that would still be under military control. Tasca declared admiringly that the Greek president had "outfoxed them all."[29]

After his formal accession, Papadopoulos broadcast decrees that included a general amnesty for crimes committed since April 21, 1967, and covering more than 300 known political prisoners. He abolished martial law and the military tribunals used to punish offenses against the state, and promised to hold elections in 1974 and to restore a freely elected parliament the following year. Some highly visible members of the opposition, such as Eleni Vlachou, Andreas Papandreou, Mikis Theodorakis, George Mylonas, Konstantinos Mitsotakis, Orestis Vidalis, and Melina Mercouri, were told they could return, even in cases where their citizenship had been stripped. The *Velos* conspirators were pardoned, but not restored to their military careers. Even Papadopoulos's would-be assassin, Alekos Panagoulis, had his own special pardon, which he refused to accept.[30]

Most Greeks received these pronouncements favorably. Secretary Rogers expressed pleasure at the announced restoration of "political freedoms" and the promise of elections. Tasca returned to his pro-Papadopoulos stance, even proposing to Nixon, with Tom Pappas's encouragement, that the beleaguered President pay a state visit to Greece. Kissinger vetoed the idea. Other US administration officials who'd urged pressures against the junta remarked that these liberalization gestures had tied their hands.[31]

Elias, however, saw through the rhetoric. Travelling in Europe, he said that although he was pleased for the released prisoners and their families, he remained "skeptical" of the government's "true intentions." He warned that "the junta still retains a very large repressive machinery which it can at any time apply again."[32] At best, the country was entering a "Portugalization" phase of modified dictatorship. Politicians were told that political parties, when they were permitted to return, would be monitored by a "special" Constitutional Court. The general amnesty covered only "crimes" committed within the jurisdiction of Greece. Individuals who had committed "crimes" against the Greek government from outside the country were not pardoned. Thus, although many who had lost their citizenship could safely return, others, like Elias, Karamanlis, and Lady Fleming, could not. Demetracopoulos wore being on the "unforgiven" list as a badge of honor. "Even if everybody returns to Greece, and only three persons remain outside," he insisted, "I will be one of them."[33]

■

AMONG THE RELATIVELY unexamined decrees issued by Papadopoulos in October, but flagged as dangerous by Elias, was one that absolved "any lawyer or state official of crimes committed during the exercise of their duties related to the defense, prosecution, interrogation and trial of any form of criminal activity or acts related to them." This was a move to block political prisoners from suing their jailers or interrogators for torture, illegal detention, or other maltreatment. The issuance of this decree was no accident, as the ordeal of Spyros Moustaklis and his family would eventually prove.

After the May 22 abduction and arrest of Major Moustaklis, his wife Christina went daily to the infamous Boumpoulinas Street headquarters of Asfaleia, the civilian security police, with food and clothes, but was repeatedly told that he wasn't there. Finally, on Wednesday June 4, someone from police headquarters called to say not to come again, for her husband had been transferred almost immediately after his arrest to ESA headquarters. She knew what that meant. ESA was the Greek Military Police, an internal security branch of the Greek Army, known for its aggressively repressive tactics. It was controlled by Dimitrios Ioannidis, recently promoted from colonel to brigadier general and considered the most fiendish member of the ruling junta. He ran ESA as his private army. Ironically, the dank, windowless underground rooms of ESA's Special Interrogation Section, where much of its torturing took place, was located at Freedom Park.

The paramilitary army officers at ESA believed that the treasonous behavior of a celebrated battalion commander deserved special attention. During the forty-seven days Moustaklis was kept incommunicado, he was mercilessly abused. All the while, he stoically ignored verbal assaults and psychological tortures and refused to provide names, plot details, or a confession. Day and night, music blared and motors roared outside to disguise from passersby the shrieks of other prisoners' pain. Inside, no cosmetic precautions were taken. When torturers took rest breaks, they played recorded tapes of the same screams and moans. Moustaklis was ordered to relieve himself during "standing ordeals" and not permitted to wash or change clothes. When they finally gave him a bucket to use, they went days without emptying it.

His handlers quickly realized that it would take much more than routine beatings to get him to break. So, under the watchful eyes of Ioannidis, they turned to harsher methods. They struck him hard with iron rods and used electric cattle prods to burn him on his back and neck. They went after his genitals, beating his testicles with a braided steel whip and thin sandbags. And they pushed a long metal probe deep into his penis then heated it with a cigarette lighter to increase the pain in his prostate and bladder. The ESA withheld nourishment, then gave him heavily salted food and offered only soapy water to drink. Still Moustaklis refused to divulge any information, instead spitting curses at his captors, triggering more beatings, especially to his upper body and head, causing concussions.

Many of the torturers were young recruits made to feel part of an elite unit and specially trained to inure them to the tasks at hand. They followed orders unquestioningly, working in groups of at least two, because those in charge believed that a single torturer would not be as brutal. Moustaklis endured at least two different daily shifts. The first focused on his lower body, beating him black and blue. The second moved higher, and others attacked his head.

On May 26, unable to break his resolve, the torturers broke his neck. A blow to his carotid artery was so strong that it created a clot that blocked blood to the brain, causing a stroke. Moustaklis was paralyzed and unable to speak. For about a day, he was left in a room without any medical attention. Later, guards wearing civilian clothes transferred Moustaklis to the neurology clinic at Military Hospital 401 under a pseudonym, "Michailidis," telling the admissions personnel that he had suffered a cerebral stroke connected with a traffic accident.

Not knowing he had been removed weeks before, Christina, a dentist with a busy practice, went daily to ESA headquarters, unsuccessfully imploring that she be allowed to see her husband. On July 7, she was finally told that he had fallen ill and been hospitalized. They gave no details, saying only that she could see him in ten days. When she returned, the ESA's army doctor—the "traffic controller" whose job it was to ensure that victims stayed alive for more interrogations and torture—explained that her "husband has suffered a thrombosis of the internal carotid. You understand how these things happen." Christina did not understand any such thing. The last time she saw Spyros he had been completely healthy. Driven in a private car to Military Hospital 401, Christina was horrified by her husband's medical record shown her by another military doctor: the date on one of the X-rays was May 27, more than a month earlier.

Armed guards patrolled the hospital floors. Spyros's room was in the hospital's psychiatric section. Seeing her husband again was "appalling," Christina vividly recalled forty years later. "I did not see a man but a ghost, a human vegetable with the dreadful mask of a stroke case. I tried to control myself." That he recognized her was the only positive sign. The military doctor, visibly uncomfortable, told her he was "not responsible," and took off some of the bandages to reveal two huge wounds on the right heel and right shoulder, which he called bedsores. After he left for a brief moment, Spyros gestured to his wife to uncover him and look. Christina saw that "besides the two wounds, his hips, thighs and genital organs were black." Moustaklis was communicating with nods since he could not speak.

Major Moustaklis remained at this military hospital, receiving minimal medical attention, until Papadopoulos declared amnesty for prisoners in July. Then Christina had him transferred to a better facility for injury, paralysis, and neurological deficits. The prognosis was bleak.

Christina knew of Elias Demetracopoulos by reputation as a well-connected journalist and the "soul and voice of Greece, beyond the Atlantic" and wrote him asking for assistance.[34] Elias replied that he had not been included in the government's amnesty list and could not come to Athens, but he wanted to help. After reaching out to medical specialists in the US and Europe, Demetracopoulos contacted a highly recommended neurosurgeon in London, Dr. Peter Schurr, who agreed to fly to Athens at Elias's expense to examine Spyros. After the examination, Dr. Schurr recommended, in lieu of surgery, "a rigorous program of physiotherapy and speech therapy."

Elias also contacted Harvard psychiatrist Dr. Leon Eisenberg, who had been in Athens earlier in the year to testify as a character witness for a Greek pediatrician sentenced to prison on charges of planting bombs as a protest. Elias asked him to fly again to Athens, at Elias's expense, to see Spyros and provide a second opinion about diagnosis and the best venue for treatment. His recommendation, like Schurr's, was for a carefully designed course of physical therapy. The best place for such treatment: Walter Reed Army Medical Center. But when Elias contacted the facility he was told that—for a variety of reasons—Major Moustaklis was ineligible.

24.

Watergate, Window Dressing, and a Counter-Coup

CONVICTIONS OF MEMBERS OF THE Plumbers' Unit were followed in April 1973 by suspicious White House resignations and firings. In May, Senator George McGovern gave Senate Watergate Committee investigators evidence linking Savannah mayor John Rousakis to John Connally's Democrats-for-Nixon smear campaign against Elias Demetracopoulos.[1] It was the first time Nixon's former treasury secretary was publicly connected to the Watergate scandal.

To avoid being sued for libel, Rousakis had already made a public apology for calling Elias a Communist, but on May 17—the afternoon the nationally televised hearings of the Senate Select Committee on Presidential Elections began—the Savannah mayor, worried about being drawn into the larger Watergate investigation, called Elias's attorney Warren Woods to "confess" that "the drafting and circulation of the anti-McGovern letter was orchestrated by the Democrats for Nixon," specifically Murray Chotiner and Lucianne Goldberg.[2] The Senate Watergate investigation became a riveting national soap opera, feeding speculation as to how high the criminal behavior went.

This attempt to turn Greek-American voters against McGovern's candidacy quickly became a topic in confidential State Department–Athens embassy correspondence. "Elias is still riding high around here," wrote a Greek Desk official. "Last I heard he was green with envy that the whole Watergate scandal should take place without his participation," and was trying hard to "cut himself in."[3]

Far from trying to "cut himself in," Elias in fact made sure to avoid efforts to drag him into the middle of Nixon's Watergate defense. Not long after the public hearings opened, the *Washington Post* reported that John Dean had told investigators that he'd discussed the cover-up with President Nixon at least thirty-five times. And in early June, Watergate prosecutors found a memo addressed to John Ehrlichman detailing plans to burglarize the office of Pentagon Papers defendant Daniel Ellsberg's psychiatrist. In response, Nixon discussed with his team the idea of trying to change the story by exposing similar behavior in previous Democratic administrations.

About a month before, on May 17, after John Dean was fired and started leaking stories, Joseph Fred Buzhardt was appointed White House counsel to deal with Watergate. Buzhardt had once been on the staff of Senator Strom Thurmond, and in his recent position as general counsel to the Pentagon, he had dealt with such troubling matters as the My Lai massacre and the Pentagon Papers. Nonetheless, he found the difficulties of his new job staggering as incriminating evidence against the President seemed to accumulate daily.[4]

According to the President, surreptitious entries and wiretaps were commonplace during the Kennedy and Johnson administrations. "This has been going on for twenty years," Nixon said. "It is the worst kind of hypocrisy for the Democrats to make so much of it."[5] Others had also heard Capitol Hill rumors of FBI wiretaps on congressmen and reporters. But how to prove it? Buzhardt, known for his intellect, honesty, and Christian rectitude, agreed with Nixon's desire to mount a counter-offensive documenting that break-ins did not start with Watergate. He pressured Eliot Richardson to compile a list of questionable "national security wiretaps" authorized by previous attorneys general. However, the FBI apparently did not keep written records of its illegal break-ins. John Dean had also been asked to prepare such a list and came up with nothing. With the televised Watergate hearings underway, Nixon rode Buzhardt hard to find something usable.

Under great stress, Buzhardt had an idea that Demetracopoulos could help. He had known Elias since his time with Thurmond, and he remembered his Greek friend's story about the Kennedy Administration authorizing a break-in at his office in Athens following the 1961 Arleigh Burke interview. As general counsel to the Defense Department, Buzhardt had access to federal-agency classified information about Demetracopoulos and may well have had prior knowledge of records of pre-Nixon wiretaps and break-ins at Elias's Washington residence that could have helped the President's case. As Nixon's counsel, his access to information had accelerated exponentially. Contained in one of Elias's Defense Department files, prepared by the Naval Investigative Service, was a photocopy of the rough draft of a 1963 Burke interview. This showed clearly the first typed draft of the Q & As and Burke's handwritten corrections.[6] On the first page, in handwriting different from Burke's, were notations reporting that copies were provided to two naval officers including one assigned to intelligence. As Burke would say later: "My secretary certainly wouldn't have sent a rough draft out."[7]

In the summer of 1973, Elias was completely unaware of the 1963 Burke break-in. Buzhardt deduced that if Elias had only a clean copy of the 1963 interview, the target of the break-in must have been Burke, not the controversial reporter, and, given the admiral's stature, that made the transgression all the more outrageous. It might have been directed by a White House eager for opposition research concerning a possible Kennedy challenger in 1964. This was something Nixon defenders could use.

So, late on a sultry June evening, instead of going home after a long day, the President's Watergate counsel went to the Fairfax Hotel without telling anyone in the West Wing or recording it in his daily diary. After flashing his White House card at the desk clerk, he took the elevator to the fifth floor. It was about 10 p.m. when Buzhardt knocked on Elias's door unannounced. Buzhardt looked ashen and exhausted, and Elias invited him in without hesitation. His friend declined, requesting instead that Demetracopoulos leave his air-conditioned apartment and take a little stroll in the breezeless, muggy night.

Still wide-awake and working in shirtsleeves and tie, Elias put on his suit jacket. As they rode down the elevator together, he wondered what this was all about. Elias speculated that Buzhardt's not wanting to come in meant he probably knew not only that Elias's phone was bugged, but that other listening devices were planted in his room.

As they walked, Buzhardt came right to the point. He knew Elias retained extensive records of his work. Could Elias give him the Arleigh Burke files connected with the 1963 interview? It was a matter of national security. The President needed and wanted it. So did Buzhardt. He would explain more later.

Elias felt no need to help Nixon with anything, but "Fred Buzhardt was my friend, and, if I could have helped him, I would have." He stopped walking and faced his beleaguered companion. He regarded his raw work product as confidential, he began, but even if he had not, he feared that anything he gave Buzhardt would go to Nixon and Colson, who would likely twist the information. Most importantly, he explained, "providing the files would involve Admiral Burke in the Watergate morass, something I'm sure he would want to avoid ... To help you I'd have to hurt Arleigh Burke and that is something I cannot and will not do. My friendship with him is transcendent."

Buzhardt said he understood, shook hands with Elias, and walked off into the night. Years later, Harry Dent told Elias that when Buzhardt recounted the incident to him, both men were touched by Demetracopoulos's sense of loyalty. Not long before his death from a second heart attack in 1978, Buzhardt talked with Elias by phone, and the former White House counsel confirmed the stratagem. When Admiral Burke learned the details, he expressed his gratitude for having been kept clear of Watergate.

·

ELIAS LEFT WASHINGTON in mid-August 1973 for a month-long European trip, ostensibly to cultivate business clients and consulting prospects, but really to confer directly with exiled Greek leaders in a half-dozen cities about Papadopoulos's liberalization gestures.

American news was never far away. In Rome, the front page of *Corriere della Sera* carried a story with a photo of a smiling Lucianne Goldberg captioned "Spia per Nixon." Agnew's dramatic fall from power was also widely covered. When Elias read reports about the Maryland US attorney investigating Agnew for possible violations of federal laws on bribery, extortion, conspiracy, and income taxes, he was prepared to believe the worst.[8] Maybe Agnew's lying to him about Greece was just a small part of a corrupt and mendacious persona. Elias now thought of Agnew as a crypto-Greek who'd discovered his ethnicity only at election time and had revealed himself to represent the essence of shallowness and bombast. The willingness of so many Greek-Americans, even lifelong Democrats, to lionize Agnew dismayed him. When the vice president resigned, Elias wondered what not having Agnew in the White House might mean for the Greek regime.

Back in Washington, Elias uncovered in a stack of correspondence a small pale-blue envelope postmarked "New Britain, Connecticut, September 11, 1973," from Celia's sister, Helen Varhol. The letter said simply: "I thought you might like to have the enclosed newspaper clippings. Until we see you again, our very best to you." The clippings were from Hartford newspapers dated September 1, announcing that Celia Was had died at 55, "after a brief illness." Elias found the obituaries a sterile portrait of the beautiful and vivacious woman he had fallen in love with twenty-three years before.[9] Images of their courtship, marriage, divorce, and years of enduring friendship flashed through his mind. He also thought of the excruciating post-Moscow pressures she had endured in Athens and how the once-wide world of this strong and proudly independent woman had become so small. In the privacy of his room, he cried.

When he reached Helen, she told him Celia had been diagnosed with lymphoma sometime in 1972 and over a period of months her health had slowly declined. When Celia had last seen Elias, earlier that year, she had said nothing about what her doctors had agreed was an early death sentence. Chemotherapy treatments made her violently ill. She retired from her job and spent the summer riveted to the televised Watergate hearings, her mind still sharp. Celia died in the hospital in the early hours of August 31, in the company of her sister and a niece. The family tried in vain to reach Elias. Her funeral had been on September 4.

Elias briefly berated himself for not knowing and being unable to comfort her or say goodbye. He thought of his own mother's terminal illness, which she had hidden from him when he went to meet Makarios. He remembered Celia, then divorced from Elias for several years, writing beautiful words of comfort to her dying former mother-in-law. Helen Varhol responded to Elias's heartfelt request to arrange with the Catholic priest at Sacred Heart Church in New Britain a small graveside memorial service for him to attend. Several weeks later, on a lovely early-autumn afternoon, the three of them gathered in the cemetery so Elias could pay his final respects. It was a work day; no other family was around, and Elias, with business in Hartford, did not linger.

■

AS WINDOW DRESSING for his new rule, Papadopoulos gave up one of his titles and appointed as prime minister a member of the old political establishment, Spyros Markezinis. Opponents at home and abroad were not fooled, but Tasca was smitten. According to a confidential message British ambassador Robert Hooper sent to his home office, his "rather volatile colleague seems to have gone overboard for . . . Markezinis . . . [accepting him as] the only alternative to a takeover by left or right."[10] Tasca recommended that the US government fully support the new Greek government.

In fact, Markezinis's days were numbered. His fate had been sealed in August 1973 when Ioannidis and senior generals in the army reacted negatively, not to the abolition of the monarchy, but to the move by Papadopoulos to assume supreme power. Dismissing from office all members of the original junta, save for Ioannidis, and creating a civilian government with merely a vague promise of free elections was too much for the regime hardliners. Starting in August, Ioannidis began plotting a coup against the recently declared "president" of Greece.[11]

ONCE THE JULY 1973 Watergate investigation uncovered the White House secret taping system, demands to release the tapes escalated. Talk of impeachment became louder. Nixon demonstrated a facile willingness to abandon loyalists to try to save his presidency, but seemed remarkably protective toward Tom Pappas, no longer treating the tycoon merely as his political piggy-bank. Worried about the potential criminal liability of his benefactor, Nixon asked Buzhardt to "tell me about Pappas. I don't want him to get hurt . . . [T]hat loveable guy, Tom Pappas . . . it's clear . . . that Pappas was raising money for Mitchell. Now that wouldn't make him guilty, would it?"[12]

In a March conversation, Nixon and Dean had discussed elements of the cover-up, ascertaining who'd talked to Pappas about what and when. Looking for a million dollars in cash as hush money for the burglars was proving to be "a very difficult problem." After Mitchell had talked to Pappas, Dean called him and asked: "Did you talk to the Greek?" And he said, "Uh. Yes, I have." Dean asked: "Is the Greek bearing gifts?" Mitchell, with his wife Martha sitting nearby, replied: "Well, I want to call you tomorrow on that."[13]

Nixon's interest in Pappas telling the right story if questioned by investigators is shown clearly in the May 23 and June 6 recordings of the President's conversations with his secretary Rose Mary Woods:

PRESIDENT NIXON: Good old Tom Pappas, . . . He came up to see me
   on March 7, . . . about the ambassador to Greece, that . . . he wanted to
   keep [Henry] Tasca there. We did not discuss Watergate at that point.
   It's very important that he remembers that . . .
PRESIDENT NIXON: I'm not asking him to lie . . . but . . . I thanked him
   for all his fundraising activities, you know.
ROSE MARY WOODS: Well, he worked over there almost alone . . .
NIXON: Things are very much in his interests, and it's very much in
   ours . . . I'm piecing this together now[14] . . . Mitchell got Pappas into the
   act, you know, to help them raise money. Mitchell needed Pappas.[15]

IT'S NOT CLEAR to what extent Nixon was thinking only of 1972, or also re-membering the 1968 Mitchell-Pappas fundraising relationship. When a Pappas friend, visiting him in his CREEP office in Washington in 1972, asked what he was doing in the campaign, the tycoon moved his right index finger to his lips, then mimed stuffing money into his vest pockets. Pappas also privately boasted of playing a similar role in 1968.

·

SCATTERED GREEK STUDENT protests that started in February 1973 re-emerged at different times during that year but were promptly suppressed. Tasca dismissed the student actions as a seasonal "dissidence sparked by academic and intra-pro-fessional woes."[16] Not so easy to dismiss was the follow-up to violent clashes with police at a large demonstration on November 4 commemorating the fifth anni-versary of George Papandreou's funeral. On November 14, the day after the trial of arrestees, Polytechnic Institute students went on strike, staged a sit-in, and created a makeshift radio station to broadcast their messages. Increasingly large crowds, running into the thousands, gathered in and around the Polytechnic courtyard, stretching for blocks. As a three-day siege began, the regime at first held back.[17]

What began as a focused criticism of education restrictions soon morphed into a generalized protest against the dictatorship and for the restoration of de-mocracy. Hand-painted banners and signs demanded "Bread, Education, Free-dom," "Today Fascism dies," and "1-1-4," a reference to the last article of the 1952 Constitution, abrogated by the Colonels. Article 114 said the "safeguarding of the Constitution is entrusted to the patriotism of the Hellenes"—that the ulti-mate source of power and authority lay in the hands of the people. This had been the cry in 1965 after the King forced out George Papandreou.

During the day, sympathizers came with bread and other provisions. Curi-osity-seekers came too. By nightfall the Polytechnic was packed. The surround-ing crowds shouted anti-junta and anti-American slogans. Parodying the junta's ubiquitous motto: "Greece for Christian Greeks," demonstrators chanted: "Greece for tortured Greeks" and "Greece for Imprisoned Greeks."

A great majority of the demonstrators were idealistic students buoyed by spontaneous camaraderie and hopes for revolutionary change in their lives, but they were not the only ones inside the buildings and on the streets. Anarchists and left-wing extremists eagerly inflamed the situation. Even more pernicious were agents of the junta, embedded to monitor activities and, as false flags, create conditions to justify a violent military intervention. They reportedly were behind some of the most incendiary chants and posted signs. Student broadcasters announced: "We totally reject these slogans as having no connection with the student movement."[18]

On November 16, street barricades went up, and mass protests spread. Construction workers, entertainers, a farmers' committee from Megara protesting land expropriation, and thousands of other workers, some carrying aloft the banners of their professional groups, joined the demonstrations. Students from universities in Salonica and Patras demonstrated their support. Euphoric protestors sang the Greek national anthem. Others sang the Cretan revolutionary song "Pote Tha Kanei Xasteria" (When will the sky be clear). The pirate radio station of the "free fighting students" proclaimed, "Down with the junta, down with Papadopoulos, Americans out, down with fascism, the junta will fall to the people."

Street traffic had stopped. The military police, wearing ESA bands on their left arms, were remarkably quiet. One confessed to onlookers "It isn't my fault; they put me in this job; I'm just doing my military service." People nearby cheered him, opening a clear path. One demonstrator observed that "with just a little kindness Greeks can be won over to do almost anything." Participants remarked how un-Greek the demonstrators were in their extraordinary politeness, saying "excuse me" as they jostled their way around. But there was a wariness as well as they looked out for "police stooges" in plainclothes. Some students stood atop the stone pillars of the Polytechnic gates twisting large sheets of shiny metal to produce blinding flashes to prevent cameras visible in upper balconies across the street from recording the identities of their compatriots.

That evening, armored cars arrived and police clashed with demonstrators. Shots were fired in street battles. Rounds of tear-gas canisters exploded, enveloping the area in a choking fog. Shooters fired from fourth-story windows in the once genteel Acropole Palace Hotel and other buildings, hitting people in the eyes, throat, legs, and stomach. One helper remembers: "The sidewalk was thick and oily with blood." Tear gas was thrown at real ambulances carting away the wounded. Other fake "ambulances" were driven by male "nurses" wearing white smocks over their uniforms who took the wounded not to first-aid stations but to the interrogation chambers of the military police. Dead and wounded were taken to an improvised hospital/morgue at the Polytechnic and nearby apartments. A curfew was imposed. The city went black.

Between midnight and 1 a.m. on Saturday, November 17, fear-inspiring American M40 tanks rolled in, with enormous floodlights "turning the darkness into an aurora borealis," sweeping slowly up and down, back and forth. They easily tossed aside a bus used as a barricade. Helmeted and club-wielding special forces followed on foot, bruising bodies and cracking bones on outside streets.

Efforts to negotiate a safe exit for the students inside Polytechnic failed. Before a ten-minute grace period expired, an AMX 30 tank smashed through the main gate to which students had been clinging and didn't stop until it reached the steps of the university's Averof Building. Amid gunfire, some soldiers tried to help students escape, but policemen, cadets, and other troops were waiting at the exits with truncheons and idling vehicles. By 3:20 a.m. everyone was gone. A second pirate station, elsewhere in Athens, played melancholy songs of Theodorakis followed by an "utterly drained and broken" young voice announcing: "we say good-bye to you for the last time."

Some survivors ignored the risks of tapped phones and tried to call foreign correspondents from kiosks, restaurants, and strangers' apartments to share their eyewitness accounts. The message board at the Fairfax was filled with messages for Elias. In the following days he received mailed packages of live tape recordings from inside the Polytechnic, contemporaneous interviews, emotional handwritten letters, and a thirty-three-page personal account typed on onion-skin paper. He shared their contents with friends, opposition allies, members of Congress, and trusted reporters.

Papadopoulos blamed old-guard politicians and put some under house arrest. At noon on November 17, Chief of the Armed Forces General Dimitrios Zagorianakos announced a state of siege, the re-imposition of censorship, martial law throughout the land, and a curfew from 4 p.m. until 5 a.m. the next day. Nonetheless, smaller demonstrations, hit-and-run encounters, shootings, and killings continued for several days. Student organizations nationwide were shut down and their bank accounts confiscated.

Accurate totals of those killed and wounded were never compiled. At the time, the regime said that fourteen died, the American Embassy "unofficially" counted twenty-three, *To Vima* wrote forty-three, a team of doctors estimated 204, and demonstrators claimed it was more than 400. Estimates of the injured ranged from fewer than 200 to about 3,000. Many victims were afraid to get professional medical assistance, and some families of the dead were said to have buried their loved ones in ways that avoided attention. The count of arrests ranged from 2,473 to 9,000. Police injuries, none due to firearms, were fewer than twelve.[19]

The American Embassy's Elizabeth Brown, political counselor and persistent Demetracopoulos critic, tried to mislead a small congressional delegation coincidentally visiting Athens, assuring them that the gunshots they were hearing were only "a small disturbance . . . taking place over curriculum issues."[20] In a secret telegram, Greek Foreign Minister Christos Xanthopoulos-Palamas sought to dissociate himself from another Greek diplomat who had framed the essential American "choice as between Greece and Demetracopoulos."[21] Sensitive to the opinions of their Washington benefactors, the Greek government singled out anti-American anarchists and Communists as the primary evildoers in the Polytechnic troubles. These extremists, it said, were against NATO and American involvement in Greece, including homeporting. Papadopoulos explained that martial law had been re-imposed because a "subversive plot had developed." Tasca similarly blamed "subversive elements" for undermining the Papadopoulos reform efforts. He wrote to Kissinger that "available intelligence just prior to demonstrations" indicated strong support for the Markezinis government from the "old political world . . . a fact which could not fail to disturb Andreas Papandreou (and his stooge in Washington Demetracopoulos), as well as other extremist elements." At the same time, Tasca expressed concern about widespread anti-American sentiments.[22]

Early in the morning of November 25, eight days after the student uprising, tanks rolled again into central Athens. Brigadier Ioannidis and coup leaders of "The Revolutionary Committee" took over the police station, closed the international airport, and cut telecommunications, A separate armored army convoy travelled to Papadopoulos's Onassis-provided residence in Lagonisi. There, an army officer handed the Greek president a message:

> At the request of the armed forces, you have submitted your resignation; so have the Vice President and the Markezinis government. You will follow further developments on television. Your credit and that of your family will be respected.[23]

A STUNNED PAPADOPOULOS meekly accepted the bloodless coup.

At first, there was an air of public optimism; the uprising at Polytechnic seemed to have yielded positive results. Politicians under house arrest and those arrested around the November 17 attacks were released. Censorship was abolished. Criminal actions were commenced against some corrupt junta officials. Other popular-sounding reforms were announced. A short time later, however, it became apparent that reality was quite the opposite. The newspaper *Vradyni* was shut down without explanation. The weekly magazine *Political Subjects* was ordered closed because it had praised the students' demands. A German television cameraman disappeared while filming the Army assault at the Polytechnic, and other journalists were harassed or arrested. Martial law was extended indefinitely; an island concentration camp was reopened. The court that was to oversee political parties and promised elections was abolished before it began work.

Those selected to lead the civilian government were essentially puppets. Behind the scenes, Brigadier Dimitrios Ioannidis, the head of the feared military police, was pulling all the strings. A military communiqué proclaimed the coup necessary to continue the revolution of 1967. Papadopoulos was accused of "straying" from the founding ideals and "pushing the country too quickly" toward parliamentary rule. Far from being on its last legs, the dictatorship in Greece had been revitalized.

The decision to overthrow Papadopoulos had been made in August; the November 25 coup date had been selected in October. The Polytechnic events were a distraction but had not upset the plotters' timetable.[24] The idealistic students and their supporters, the wounded and those who lost their lives, who had thought their actions would be a catalyst for positive change, had been collateral damage in a battle waged by forces beyond their reach.

News stories describing post-coup Greece painted a depressing picture. Editorials were overwhelmingly critical of the new leadership and political cartoons unsparingly sardonic. American students protested developments, waving signs reading: "US tanks kill Greek students" and "US out of Greece."[25] Congressman Don Edwards wrote to Kissinger urging the US to speak out for a return to representative government. Silence, he said, was viewed by the Greek people as a sign of approval, and the country's vulnerability provided a "moment of opportunity" for a new US policy that might "prove decisive . . . and be morally and politically right."[26] Nixon Administration policymakers debated how to respond to the events. Some urged distancing the US or pressing the government to restore democracy. Kissinger, effectively America's chief foreign-policy executive, overruled them.[27]

As he had in earlier crises, Demetracopoulos responded to the events of November by gathering intelligence, discussing strategy with opposition leaders, giving interviews and speeches, hosting lunches, and working with members of Congress to change American policy. Well before the Polytechnic confrontation and the coup, he had concluded that Karamanlis was the only person who could lead the country back to parliamentary government, though he believed that even this would require a lot of painstaking advance work. In a November 2 meeting with a State Department official, he warned that anti-American sentiments in Greece had replaced earlier anti-Communist paranoia, that the US was losing many of its longtime friends, particularly on the right, and that "someday the US will find it cannot protect its interests there." John Day, the country officer for Greece, scoffed that Demetracopoulos "has probably been repeating this line so long that he actually believes it."[28]

In and outside Greece, anti-American paranoia was growing. Many Greeks suspected that the unexpected downfall of Markezinis and Papadopoulos had been precipitated by the US. Andreas Papandreou, then in Stockholm, insisted it was "entirely a work of the United States," and charged that Chicago-trained Adamantios Androutsopoulos, the new prime minister and former interior minister, was on the CIA's payroll.[29] Other Greeks believed that the US had turned on their previous leaders because of Greece's neutrality during the October 1973 Yom Kippur War between Egypt and Israel.

Elias told the press that the United States had not engineered the latest coup, but "did not lift a finger" to save the ousted Papadopoulos. Publicly, he deflected Andreas's charges, saying that whether Androutsopoulos was on the CIA's payroll was "immaterial," adding: "It is no secret that the new premier had a close relationship with the CIA in recent years."[30] Privately he told Andreas that whatever the truth to the Androutsopoulos connection, Papandreou's overall analysis was simplistic and counterproductive.

Demetracopoulos claimed that the US gave up on Papadopoulos because he would not permit the use of Greek airspace by US planes for delivery of weapons to Israel, while at the same time he allowed Soviet planes to fly war material over Greece to the Arab countries.[31]

Elias acknowledged that the recent coup was engineered by right-wing extremists opposed to pledges of democratic reform but added that it was not a coincidence that Ioannidis first met with his co-conspirators in August, when news from Washington about Nixon and Watergate was compounded by news disclosing the Agnew criminal investigation. Agnew's resignation in October had "kicked [another] crutch out from under Papadopoulos."[32]

25.

Crisis on Cyprus

DEMETRACOPOULOS HEARD THAT AT THE Athens embassy and the Greek Desk in Washington there was more dissension regarding the proper approach to take toward the new leaders. Some worried that the Ioannidis government was so weak it would soon implode. Even Tom Pappas and the shipping magnates wavered in their support for the regime. Yet, after an internal discussion about formal recognition, the US accepted the leadership change without fanfare.

Elias's take on Ioannidis was that he was "a brutal man" and a "fanatic nationalist," but the only incorruptible member of the original junta. However, he was surrounded by largely incompetent ministers. Despite Ioannidis's proclaimed anti-Communism, his extreme nationalism, including designs on Cyprus, would, Elias believed, eventually place US security interests in jeopardy. He reckoned that even if Ioannidis tried to establish a government of national unity by calling for the return of Karamanlis, no such collaboration was possible. And if Ioannidis tried to hold on to power indefinitely, it might lead to yet another coup by even more ultra-nationalistic officers. In November 1973, Elias lectured John Day, the Greek Desk officer at the State Department, that the US needed to try to influence events before Ioannidis had fully consolidated his power.

After six years of battling, Elias was still cautiously optimistic that his strategy of blending realpolitik arguments with softer appeals to values, sweating organizational details, and assiduously courting international public opinion could pay off.

Elias reminded anyone who would listen that the only one who mattered in Greece was the pernicious Ioannidis, and that the regime's ability to provide stability and security for American interests was illusory. Purges of well-trained senior Army officers continued, he warned, leaving in their wake fissures and a growing anti-NATO, neutralist, ultra-Qaddafist faction. To make matters worse, he added, the Polytechnic demonstrators had revealed "almost as much hostility toward the United States as toward the Athens regime."

Demetracopoulos also lost no opportunity to point out Greece's drop in economic growth, tourism receipts, and foreign investment. He mocked the underwhelming capabilities of the regime's leaders, singling out in particular Prime Minister and Finance Minister Adamantios Androutsopoulos, who had been touted by the Greek Embassy in Washington for his stellar credentials as an economist. Androutsopoulos, they claimed, had received his degree from the University of Chicago and taught in its prestigious economics department "for many years." Tips provided to reporters by Elias revealed that not only was most of Androutsopoulos's résumé fraudulent, but the owner of a Greek restaurant in Chicago said that he had to fire the erstwhile manager of Greece's economy from a job as night cashier "because he couldn't keep the [cash] register straight."[1]

In public, Nixon Administration officials continued to fault Demetracopoulos for being inaccurate, wrongheaded, and intentionally deceptive. But privately, a National Security Council action memorandum, prepared by a multi-agency drafting group for Secretary of State Kissinger, confirmed Elias's assessments. The NSC report criticized the Greek regime for being "reactionary" and showing "no promise of moving toward representative government." It described the leaders as "political nonentities," with "less technical capability" of dealing with the country's serious economic, political, and social problems than the previous one. Portrayed as "narrowly nationalistic" and fanatically anti-Communist, "the new regime is not a group of 'Atlanticists' who see their relationship with the US and NATO based on shared values." The Army, it said, was divided, upset about its close identification with the regime, worried about its military capabilities, and concerned about the "Qaddafites." The report also acknowledged "an element of anti-Americanism . . . that would have been unthinkable a few years ago" and worried about Tasca and Kissinger being called to testify before tenacious critics in Congress.[2]

Although aligned with Elias's analysis, the report diverged from his and his allies' positions in its recommendations. Afraid that "moralist/interventionist" pressures would make matters worse, the NSC memorandum gave the Ioannidis regime a life expectancy of less than a year and advocated a "substantially hands-off" approach modified by a "nose holding public posture." The regime's likely successor, it suggested, would be a series of coups varying only "in degree rather than in kind." No actionable decision was to be made because Kissinger was busy elsewhere and his staff deemed there were "no pressing issues" in Greek-US relations.

·

IN FEBRUARY 1974, Tom Pappas, after months of jockeying among attorneys, was finally scheduled to testify behind closed doors before the Watergate committee to tell what he knew about the cover-up of fundraising for the original Watergate defendants. Elias had hoped that the Watergate investigators would look at Pappas's long history as a Nixon fundraiser and not limit its probe to his fundraising in 1972. The Pappas connection, however, was regarded by Watergate investigators as a Committee "loose end."[3]

To try to influence the process, Elias had encouraged Seth Kantor, Washington correspondent for the *Detroit News*, to look at Pappas's earlier activities. Kantor was a dogged investigative reporter who'd been with President Kennedy in Dallas on the day he was assassinated and would spend more than a decade investigating the background of Jack Ruby, the killer of Lee Harvey Oswald. In January, he published an article noting that Watergate probers had started showing interest in a so-called Greek Connection, and the role of foreign nationals illegally funding American campaigns. He spotlighted the mysterious fundraising role of Tom Pappas in the 1968 election, Agnew's surprise endorsement of the junta, and charges that the Greek military regime had funded the 1968 Nixon campaign.[4]

Despite Kantor's story, Roger M. Witten, a member of the Justice Department's Watergate Special Prosecutor Force, intentionally limited the possible charges against Nixon's moneyman. When Witten and his colleagues met with Pappas and his attorney on February 2 for a voluntary interview, Pappas denied doing anything knowingly illegal or improper during the 1972 campaign. No one asked him about 1968.[5]

The fix was apparently in to protect Pappas. In his prosecutorial memorandum on February 22, 1974, Witten wrote that by accepting and receiving a $15,000 political donation in Greece from a Greek citizen residing in Greece and delivering it for him to Maurice Stans at Nixon finance headquarters in Washington, Pappas technically broke the law. Nevertheless, he recommended "we do not prosecute Pappas, unless further evidence of venality or corruption develops."[6] The task force never considered any such evidence of "venality or corruption," though it was readily available in Pappas's FBI file and other records. Other Watergate staff claimed later to have had no knowledge of Pappas's alleged role in Nixon's 1968 campaign and maintained they would have considered it had it been brought to their attention.[7] Years later, Witten refused to discuss the apparently willful exclusion of Pappas's pre-1972 criminal behavior.

Demetracopoulos was not surprised that Pappas escaped prosecution, let alone conviction, for his financial crimes. After witnessing years of corruption on both sides of the ocean, he'd seldom seen anyone punished or even deterred from similar behavior. Skimming had been common during the US aid programs of the 1950s, CIA money had been used to influence outcomes in Greek elections, and the outright bribery of the apostates in 1965 and 1966 was well known to the informed public. Such behavior in Greece disgusted him, but he didn't see the United States as appreciably better. American politicians who needed substantial financial support weren't about to bite the hands that fed them. He didn't regard his own friends in Congress as corrupt, but he could cite examples of others, such as New Jersey senator Harrison Williams, who had tried to shake Elias down for cash.[8] The law about campaign contributions by foreign nationals was toothless, and probably would not be used even if it were tougher, Elias believed. The only real hope was an aggressive press allied with bipartisan congressional investigations that exposed bad behavior—especially before an election.

Even if he had wanted to, Elias was too busy lobbying against the junta to be an investigative journalist on American campaign finances. He was pleased with the 1971 reporting that James Polk of the Associated Press had done about thousands of dollars of mysterious campaign money sent in the names of Greek-Americans to the Nixon campaign in 1968. The alleged donors said they never made such contributions.[9] This, Elias thought, could have been part of the web of Pappas fundraising stories Drew Pearson had been trying to uncover back in 1968. Years later he regretted how, in honoring his pledge to Larry O'Brien, he had failed to help Pearson.

IN JANUARY 1974, Congressman Don Fraser, chairman of the subcommittee on international organizations, with staff consultant Clifford Hackett, went to Athens to ask tough questions about the current situation. Elias helped arrange appointments for them with opposition leaders and others beyond the embassy's control. Tasca was furious to read their critical twenty-seven-page assessment portraying a government on its last legs, unable to resolve its political and economic problems, which were only aggravated by America's "faulty policy" of acquiescence.[10]

The Fraser report recommended immediate suspension of the next phase of homeporting, along with an announcement that any further strengthening of ties would await "unequivocal and irreversible steps" toward free elections and civilian democratic rule. It also suggested that Tasca be replaced by "a new American ambassador who comes free of identification with past American policies." Elias made sure that American and Greek audiences were well aware of Fraser's "timely warning," using it to blunt Tasca's anticipated testimony of "qualified assurances." Congressional opposition to the most recent incarnation of the Greek junta was on the rise.

Tasca's most important appointment during his early 1974 trip to D.C. was not a closed-door appearance before the House Foreign Affairs subcommittee, but a March 20 Regional Staff meeting at the State Department, led by Henry Kissinger, to discuss American policy toward Greece after the November coup.[11] Tasca maintained that the current US policy had been "reasonably successful," but difficult to implement because of, among other things, Demetracopoulos's meddling and Greece's historical and cultural "singularity." He warned that "sooner or later, with the repression that's going on in Greece, we're going to lose" congressional support and with it military credits and military supplies, and then Greece will "turn to France or 'go Arab,' with Qaddafi."

Kissinger, supporting the current policy, asked, "Why is it in the American interest to do in Greece what we apparently don't do anywhere else—[require] a commitment . . . to move to representative government?"

> MR. TASCA: Well, I think because Greece and the Greek people—in
> terms of their position and public opinion in Western Europe—are
> quite unique. You can go back to the constitutional Greece or the
> Greek lobby—whatever you want to call it—and they've got a position
> in Western Europe and the United States that . . . these other countries

don't . . . None . . . has a Demetracopoulos who for four years has been leading a very vigorous fight on our policy in Greece.

SECRETARY KISSINGER: But that just means we're letting Demetracopoulos' particular group make policy.

MR. TASCA: How do you stop it?

UNSATISFIED WITH KISSINGER'S generic response, Tasca went on to explain the foreign factor that had figured so exceptionally in Greece since the 1821 revolution, noting that, like it or not, the Americans had become part of the country's value system and political process. The US should get out, he said, but it would take time. When Kissinger advocated announcing that we "don't influence things," Tasca countered that that was tantamount to intervening in favor of Ioannides.

Coming into the meeting, Kissinger had demonstrated his unawareness of the internal dynamics in Greece by not even knowing who Ioannidis was. And, when Tasca raised his concerns that the debate between Greece and Turkey over oil exploration could escalate and drag Cyprus into the dispute, Kissinger dismissed the comment as a "foreign policy problem" not germane to their discussion of publicly confronting the Ioannidis regime over democracy for Greece. Kissinger brushed off the senior staff debate as "hopelessly abstract," claiming that the issue wasn't "between democracy and non-democracy," and declaring, "[w]e don't muck around with other countries . . . as long as they're not anti-American."[12] A few months after this meeting, far from challenging Ioannidis, Kissinger endorsed providing the Greek dictator $400 million worth of military aircraft.

■

ELIAS TRAVELLED BACK and forth from Washington to New York regularly, with side trips to Boston and Hartford to service his paying clients. His mind was always on the changing situation in Athens.

On one New York trip, he visited a makeshift soundstage in a warehouse on West 19th Street in Manhattan. He had been invited by Jules Dassin, who was directing a docudrama he wrote in collaboration with Melina Mercouri, titled *The Rehearsal*.[13] The film, shot in less than a month on a tiny budget using donated services, sought to portray the November events at the Polytechnic Institute as a rehearsal for democracy. The day Elias visited, most of the cast, which included Melina Mercouri, Olympia Dukakis, Laurence Olivier, Arthur Miller, Lillian Hellman, and Maximilian Schell were on hand. Stathis Giallelis, star of Elia Kazan's award-winning *Amerika, Amerika*, played the lead student. Melina narrated and starred. The dictators were lampooned, and the celebrities had cameo roles reading letters and poems. Mikis Theodorakis and Giannis Marko-poulos contributed the music.

Elias endorsed the "melodramatic" production as a way to tell the world of Greece's suffering and enduring spirit, and he was pleased to learn that some of the extras were Greek-American students whose parents still backed the junta. After seven long years, Elias saw public opinion mounting against the regime.

■

IOANNIDIS, FACED WITH rising economic problems, a dysfunctional administra-tion, simmering political unrest, and factionalism in the armed forces, compen-sated by calling for unification with Cyprus and manufacturing a crisis on the island. Both American and British intelligence reports indicated that the Greek leader was preparing to move against Cypriot president Makarios, but the re-ports were belittled by Nixon Administration officials.

Elias too heard reports about plots against the Cypriot president. Ioannidis supposedly had turned to his CIA contacts in Washington to do "something" about the archbishop. The most chilling account placed the former CIA station chief in Nicosia, who had been known as openly anti-Makarios, in a February meeting in Athens with Nikos Sampson, the most notorious terrorist in EO-KA-B, the pro-*enosis* underground Cypriot paramilitary organization. Sampson, who reviled Makarios, had built his reputation in the 1950s as a photojournalist who fiendishly murdered British soldiers and civilians, then took pictures of their bloody corpses and put them in his newspaper.

After the State Department told Demetracopoulos that his concerns were exaggerated, he approached Senator Fulbright in late June to share his sense of urgency. He warned that Tasca apparently had no direct communication with Ioannidis, and that Ioannidis communicated to Washington via his Athens CIA contacts. Kissinger and his team appeared to have accepted this protocol.

■

HISTORIANS HAVE NOTED how outwardly calm the Greek and Cypriot principals were as the crisis came to a head. All actors performed as if they were parts of a charade in which players carried out their historically assigned roles, expecting that at the end of the day the Americans would intervene to prevent a major conflict, as they had in 1964 and 1967. But Makarios fatally misjudged Ioannidis, Ioannidis fatally misjudged the Turks, and both fatally misjudged the Americans.

In early July, American attention was focused on the House Judiciary Committee's release of the transcripts of the Nixon tape recording, while the President closeted himself. Kissinger, now essentially running American foreign policy, was also under attack from both left and right at home and unsure whether he'd survive politically if Ford became President.

In response to Elias's urgent warning, Senator Fulbright had tried to talk Kissinger into pressuring Ioannidis not to move against Makarios, but Kissinger refused to do so. The secretary of state was oblivious to the tinderbox ready to explode. In early May, Cyprus was not even on Kissinger's radar screen, except perhaps as the place he told people he'd recently eaten the best wiener schnitzel of his life.[14]

On Saturday morning, July 6, Elias read in the *Washington Post* that President Makarios had accused the Greek government of supporting a movement to overthrow him. Demetracopoulos called contacts in Cyprus and Greece to confirm the story. The plots and protest, he was told, were quite real. Makarios made the mistake of assuming that publicly claiming that the junta sought to "liquidate" him, and detailing steps the regime had already taken toward that end, would prevent it. He revealed details about the guidance, financing, propaganda, and weapons being supplied to the EOKA-B terrorists by the Greek regime, and demanded that Greek officers then staffing the Cypriot National Guard leave the island. Makarios would personally take over Cypriot military forces.

In Athens, leaders of the façade government's cabinet met until the wee hours of the morning. The top three Greek foreign-ministry officials resigned, probably anticipating the incipient catastrophe. In Washington, a "high State Department official" described the resignations as "routine developments." "As of now, there's no civilian government in Greece," Elias told Jim Pyrros, the US-CDG workhorse. "They don't want to be scapegoats and have their necks in a noose when the Greek government falls."

At about 2 a.m. Washington time on Monday, July 15, Elias was brushing his teeth, readying himself for his usual four-hour catnap, when the switchboard at the Fairfax patched through a transatlantic call. Heavy gunfire had just been heard at the presidential palace in Nicosia. Was this the start of the feared coup? Demetracopoulos started calling his sources. The chiefs of staff had met in the

Greek Pentagon and were told the action against Makarios had begun, but no one at the US State Department claimed to know anything. Phone lines to Cyprus were down. Sources in Europe were scrambling to get information.[15]

Minutes after 4 a.m., Elias received a call from General Orestis Vidalis in Toledo, Ohio, telling him that he'd just heard from Europe that there had been a coup on Cyprus and Makarios was dead. The news had been announced at 11 a.m. Greek time. More calls came in. The wire services were reporting that the Cyprus Broadcasting Corporation had announced Makarios's death. In his place, "the armed forces" had installed a government of "National Salvation" with the hated Nikos Sampson as president. Memories of his 1957 meetings with Makarios off Madagascar and in Nairobi flashed through Elias's mind, then an image of the archbishop officiating at his mother's memorial service. He felt a profound sadness.

At 5:30 a.m., Pyrros called the State Department, which still had no information. Foggy Bottom officials, told that his sources were Demetracopoulos and Vidalis, concluded that the reports were likely true.

In the hours that followed, Elias's anti-junta sources shared scraps of news and shards of hope. CBS television reported that the coup leaders were Greek army officers. Cyprus Radio had been the sole outlet to announce the death. There had been no independent verification. Wire services provided conflicting reports. By 10:40 a.m., Elias, after hearing from UN sources who told him that Makarios had sought safety at a UN outpost near the Green Line, which separated Cyprus into two regions, surmised Makarios may have survived. At 11:41 a.m. the State Department said it had "no definitive information," but was inclined to believe Makarios was dead.

At 12:44 p.m., UPI issued two conflicting reports. But no one other than Elias seemed to have received information that Makarios had been seen alive and had reached out to the UN. Even the UN and the British foreign minister denied the reports.

As for US reaction to the Cyprus/Greece showdown, a member of the State Department Greek Desk confessed: "Kissinger is indifferent. Nobody gives a damn."[16] On the day of the coup, the Cypriot ambassador, Nikos Dimitriou, told the US secretary of state the new Cypriot president was a "paranoid" and an "egomaniac." Kissinger jested dismissively that he too had been called an egomaniac. The ambassador replied sharply that Sampson was no joking matter.[17]

At 1:45 p.m. Washington time, Elias was unsurprised that the State Department was still in the dark but wondered why the CIA was still unable to confirm whether Makarios was dead or alive.

At 4:15 p.m., Elias told Pyrros "I'm more optimistic than I was three hours ago. I'm getting [favorable information] from a lot of quarters." A half-hour later, Elias said: "I just finished talking with the British Embassy on a very high level. They have plenty of rumors that he has escaped, but nothing that puts him physically on a British base."

By 9:10 p.m., Elias had been operating for nearly seventeen hours nonstop on the three telephone lines in his Fairfax apartment. Persa, who had moved to Washington in 1971 to do pediatric nursing work and be close to Elias, came by to make sure he ate something other than chocolate milkshakes and chocolate candy bars. News was still coming in. He made a final round of calls asserting: "I am satisfied for the first time that he is alive."

Later, he was able to reconstruct what had happened. At 8:30 a.m., Cyprus time, Makarios, having returned from a weekend at his mountain retreat, heard gunfire outside the presidential palace. Armored cars and two tanks were in the courtyard. Heavy mortar shelling began. While his palace guard held off would-be assassins, Makarios removed his headgear, pectoral cross, and formal garb and escaped through a French window in his study.

He and an aide scrambled down to a road where they flagged down motorists to take them to the Kykkos monastery in Paphos, where the monks were surprised to see him alive. With UN help, he was taken by British helicopter to the UK base at Akrotiri, then flown to Malta. The next day, Makarios went to London where Elias talked to him by phone.

■

DESPITE THE WATERGATE distraction and other world crises, the United States, given its powerful relationships with all the key players, was in a good position to resolve the Cyprus crisis. "What it lacked was a statesman," observed diplomatic historian James Miller, explaining how Henry Kissinger, through "incompetence, not malice," had instead doubled down on the mistakes that America had repeatedly made in its Greek policy.[18] During the entire emotional day of July 15, Kissinger never once expressed concern for the fate of Makarios or the future of Cyprus without him. When told the archbishop had survived, a State Department official responded: "How inconvenient."[19] While the US stayed mum, a Turkish diplomat remarked that the installation of Sampson was "an unbelievably stupid move by the Greeks, giving us the opportunity to solve our problems once and for all."[20] Hearing nothing from the US that might hold them back, the Turks readied their invasion plans.

Kissinger's recent State Department administrative reorganization, splitting the Turkey Desk from the Greek and Cypriot one, made matters worse by depriving him of coordinated and knowledgeable staff leadership and support, should he have wanted it. He rejected Tasca's advice to condemn the Makarios coup publicly and demand restoration of Greek democracy. He told the British he opposed an emergency meeting at the UN because it would likely "internationalize the situation in an undesirable manner."[21] He preferred to talk to a narrow group, including the Russians, and find a compromise "third guy," neither Makarios nor Sampson, who would be acceptable to both Turkey and Greece.[22] Ioannidis, meanwhile, still wanted to kill Makarios, fearful that the archbishop could expel non-Cypriot Greeks from the island and then come for the regime in Athens.

Still smarting from his earlier attempts to warn American officials who could have prevented the coup against Makarios, Elias wondered how to stop a Turkish invasion. He believed the best means was to go through Fulbright. The Arkansas senator, who had been courted heavily by the secretary of state, promptly agreed to meet Elias. Demetracopoulos prioritized his list of objectives, with fallback requests that could be accepted, including support for the British request that Greek troops be removed from the island, not just rotated.

At 12:15 p.m. on July 17, he met Senator Fulbright alone, in his private office. "Ask Kissinger how he would react to an invitation from Archbishop Makarios to have the Sixth Fleet pay a goodwill visit to the ports of Cyprus," he recommended. American warships, he suggested, were already in the region and could serve as a buffer between Cyprus and the two hostile NATO members. Interposing Sixth Fleet ships between Turkey and Cyprus had been used successfully in the 1964 confrontation. In accepting the Makarios invitation, he added, US action could also effectively repudiate Ioannidis's aggression and make unnecessary a Turkish military invasion. This could all be done, he said, without any cost to US security interests. Additionally, he wanted Kissinger to invite Makarios, as president of Cyprus, to meet with him immediately.

With Demetracopoulos sitting nearby, Fulbright called the secretary of state to express concern about the volatile situation in Cyprus. Kissinger rejected the Sixth Fleet invitation suggestion without discussion. But he said he'd be willing to receive Makarios in Washington, while avoiding specifying "in what capacity." Kissinger's State Department was still refusing to acknowledge that the archbishop remained president. Asked later whether Makarios would be received as a private citizen, archbishop, or president of Cyprus, Kissinger's spokesman replied, "Archbishop."[23] That was unacceptable to Elias. Makarios would be coming to the United Nations to plead his country's case, and it was important that he visit Washington as the recognized head of the Cypriot government.

Fulbright agreed to invite Makarios to the Senate Foreign Relations Committee as president. Demetracopoulos spoke to the House Foreign Affairs Committee, which agreed to do the same. Eight anti-junta House members sent a telegram to the secretary of state asking that he "take whatever steps are needed, including a request for an immediate Security Council meeting, to ensure that appropriate international action deny success to this illegal military threat to Cyprus and its government." Elias also arranged a letter from Senators Pell, McGovern, McGee, and Humphrey calling for Kissinger to suspend diplomatic recognition of the Sampson regime, restore the Makarios government peacefully, expel those who participated in the coup, and engage the Foreign Relations Committee on diplomatic moves concerning Cyprus.

On Friday, July 19, Makarios, recognized as a head of state, made a forceful case at the United Nations Security Council, blaming the military regime of Greece for extending its dictatorship to an independent Cyprus. To Greek assertions that they had not been involved, he asked why the bodies of the dead and wounded were being evacuated to Athens. He requested that the Security Council restore without delay the constitutional order on the island.[24]

Considering it a waste of his own time, Kissinger sent Joseph Sisco from the State Department on a last-minute shuttle-diplomacy mission. Visiting Nixon in San Clemente, California, Kissinger had already decided a modest Turkish invasion would be the most acceptable option. He also probably saw it in his own interest to stay close to Nixon as the pressures from Watergate mounted. Kissinger assured the increasingly out-of-touch President that his smart diplomatic moves, tilting toward Turkey, had neutralized their liberal opponents.[25] In reality, a once-divided and -reserved Greek-American community would soon join the liberal opposition in Congress, academics of all stripes, Greek clergy, and the news media in support of Cyprus, against the Greek junta and Turkish "invaders."

Early on Saturday morning, July 20, Turkey attacked Cyprus's north coast, ostensibly to fulfill its responsibilities as a treaty guarantor of peace. The Security Council called for cease-fire negotiations to restore peace and constitutional order. Instead, Ioannidis prepared a declaration of war and ordered a full mobilization of the Greek armed forces. Turkey's military was much larger, and better-trained and -equipped. They were also closer to the island. Seven years of Greek military purges had taken a toll. The Greek mobilization was described by military observers as "a fiasco," "a shambles," and a "dramatic failure," and the Greek chiefs of staff quickly decided that following through with a war was impossible.[26]

On Cyprus, the EOKA-B–led National Guard, weakened by infighting and defections, was not at full strength. Many guardsmen took their guns and went home. Those who were left, fewer than 5,000 Cypriots and Greek officers, took horrific casualties as they tried to hold off a Turkish force that grew to 30,000, not counting air support. Two submarines sent from Greece were called back. Thousands of Greek Cypriots became refugees in their homeland as Turkish forces pushed them southward.[27]

While Sisco was meeting with Tasca and Greek officials to try to stop the escalation, Ioannidis was secretly preparing submarine and aerial attacks on Turkish forces. He ordered 300 commandos to seize Nicosia airport. Some of the planes he sent were downed by friendly fire. On Sunday morning, Ioannidis's aide-de-camp told the heads of the Hellenic armed services that the General wanted to attack Turkey on all fronts. They balked, telling him they were unprepared to go to war and quietly discussed among themselves the need to remove Ioannidis.[28]

Around 2 a.m. Athens time on Monday, July 22, negotiator Sisco, shuttling between Athens and Ankara and communicating with Kissinger in Washington, was able to gain Turkish prime minister Ecevit's consent to a cease-fire. On the Greek side, however, no one was available to concur. Sisco woke Admiral Petros Arapakis, chief of naval operations, the only leader fluent in English, who said he didn't have the authority to agree. The admiral spoke to Prime Minister Androutsopoulos, who according to Greek and American reports had suffered a nervous breakdown, was incoherent, and could do nothing but ask Arapakis to stall for time. Other Greek officials were likewise afraid of taking responsibility.

Sometime later, Arapakis called Sisco and asserted that he had his government's approval. Sisco specifically asked: "Did you get the concurrence of General Ioannides?"

"Yes," the audacious admiral lied, telling himself "the national interest comes first." The cease-fire went into effect later that afternoon, averting more bloodshed.[29]

On Monday, Athens was rife with rumors, which quickly spread around the world. One speculated that Third Corps commander General Ioannis "John" Davos was leading his armored units from Macedonia to Athens to arrest Ioannidis. Another, inadvertently triggered by Kissinger, suggested that Ioannidis had been overthrown in a counter-coup.[30]

In truth, the Greek chiefs of staff, though resolute the day before against going to war, had dithered through the day, unclear as to how to remove Ioannidis. If Ioannidis were politically wounded but retained control of the ESA security police and loyal units in the army, might he reassert his powers? Although details of what exactly happened over Tuesday, July 23, are a Rashomon tale, there was a common thread. The chiefs reaffirmed that Ioannidis must be removed and conveyed that message to General Gizikis, made president by Ioannidis after the Papadopoulos ouster. They agreed that authentic civilian rule must be restored. The chiefs and Gizikis either summoned Ioannidis, or he walked in uninvited. He disagreed with their characterization of the disastrous state of affairs but accepted their decision to dismiss him since it was unanimous. Ioannidis went free, technically still controlling ESA for a few weeks, but promising that his officers would be obedient to the government.[31]

The Chiefs then urgently invited some former prime ministers, senior ministers, and economic leaders, including Kanellopoulos, Mavros, Markezinis, Averof, Zolotas, and Pesmazoglou to a conference. For more than an hour the assembled group debated whether the composition of a civilian government should be "all-embracing," "political," "service," or "transitional." They next considered who should be prime minister—at first suggesting a coalition of the two major parties headed by Kanellopoulos, the prime minister from 1967, with Center Union's George Mavros as his deputy prime minister. Then, anxious about a resurgent Ioannidis undermining a return to civilian rule, the group recommended Karamanlis as the strongest leader. Kanellopoulos graciously bowed out, and Mavros was reaffirmed as deputy prime minister in a government of national unity.[32]

Reached in Paris, Karamanlis hesitated. The Athens group told him he had to decide immediately. He agreed, but then could not get a direct flight to Athens until French president Giscard d'Estaing provided his plane. Even after Karamanlis landed, there were fears that forces loyal to Ioannidis might interfere with the transition. Anxieties abated somewhat when an announcement was made to a cheering crowd that Karamanlis was on his way and would arrive at 2 a.m. on Wednesday, July 24, as arrival on the superstitiously unlucky day of Tuesday had to be avoided.

The euphoria of Karamanlis's arrival was comparable to the jubilation that greeted the end of World War II. Horns blared, church bells pealed, and celebrations continued throughout the night.[33] The revelers also demonstrated a somber side: thousands marching with candles and singing Easter hymns paused for a moment of silence in memory of the fallen dissidents as they passed the Polytechnic.

So insecure was Karamanlis in his new role that for several weeks he slept on a yacht outside Glyfada, guarded by a naval vessel, instead of using accommodations at the Grande Bretagne Hotel. Afraid to go after the ringleaders of the coup, he prepared a general amnesty. After seven years, three months, and two days, the dictatorship had imploded.

The dictatorship had failed to achieve its primary objectives. More Greeks likely identified as Communists in 1974 than had in 1967. Greece had sullied its reputation abroad, sown distrust between the Greek people and their allies, and demoralized its armed forces.

It brought devastation upon Cyprus and at home left behind an economy in shambles and the highest rate of inflation in Europe.

26.

After the Junta

WITH THE APPARENT END OF military hostilities on Cyprus, Washington refocused on Nixon's final days. Ankara took advantage of the distraction to restock supplies and prepare to strike again. Peace talks toward a political solution proceeded inconclusively in Geneva. Turkey moved to dismantle the 1959 Zurich-London Agreement that had created a Republic of Cyprus, arguing that Makarios's alleged violations had destroyed it.

On July 29, for the second Monday in a row, Makarios met with Kissinger. Elias had been upset that the archbishop had missed opportunities to make his case before American audiences to help build pressure on the secretary of state. He'd set up a *Today Show* morning television interview and arranged to have the archbishop be the featured newsmaker on *Meet the Press*, only to have the Cypriot leader's people in New York cancel.

Makarios sought "clear and decisive" evidence that American "silent diplomacy" in Geneva was more than just words. He wanted Turkey to start pulling its invading troops off the island. Kissinger was evasive in the meeting and afterward dodged press questions about American willingness to pressure the Turks. Makarios warned that the situation on Cyprus was deteriorating and an American "wait and see" attitude would only make matters worse.

According to State Department oral histories, Kissinger despised Makarios. To the secretary of state, Makarios was a "Castro of the Mediterranean" with

Nasserite tendencies and likely to tilt toward Moscow. Disdainfully approaching his meetings with Makarios, he ignored staff who knew the archbishop well and understood his history of complex relations with the United States. An old Cyprus hand, William Crawford, remembered:

> I went up to talk to the Secretary before Makarios' arrival, and
> Dr. Kissinger said, "Bill, what do I call him?" I said, "Your Beatitude."
> So we went downstairs to the front entrance. Dripping with cynicism
> and dislike, Dr. Kissinger greeted the archbishop when the limousine
> pulled up at the door. "Your Beatitude, I'm so glad to welcome you to
> Washington, your Beatitude."[1]

A USELESS MEETING and a dozen or more saccharine "Your Beatitudes" later, Crawford—crushed in a small elevator with the archbishop, Secretary Kissinger, and their bodyguards—heard the secretary of state tell the archbishop, "Your Beatitude, when I'm with you, I really quite feel that I like you." The archbishop looked at him benignly and said, "Dr. Kissinger, it lasts for just about five minutes after we've parted, doesn't it?"[2]

WITH THE FALL of the junta and early reports of a cease-fire accord on Cyprus, opposition exiles talked about going home. The new government published a list of those who officially had their Greek citizenship restored. This time the names of Amalia Fleming and Elias Demetracopoulos were included. Television captured the emotional returns of Melina Mercouri and Mikis Theodorakis. Leading anti-junta members of Congress wryly described warm overtures made to them by Greek-American members of Congress who'd either been silent during the past seven years or had actively opposed their pro-democracy efforts.

An article in the Metro section of the *Washington Post* at the end of July was headlined: "Two Greeks Consider the Future," accompanied by photographs of Elias along with Stavros Dimas, a young World Bank attorney who was planning to return and join the army. Elias, more prominently featured than Dimas, who later became a distinguished Greek and EU politician, was described as "more circumspect about returning home."[3]

Asked if he would accept the role of Greek ambassador to Washington if offered, Elias listed reasons why he'd say no. The Karamanlis unity government offered Demetracopoulos the ambassadorship anyway, largely as a gesture to acknowledge Elias's years of heroic service. As expected, he declined. All parties were aware that "lone wolf" Demetracopoulos lacked the temperament to handle the tedium of administrative duties and would not be able to function as an unquestioning public servant. The title might have been nice, but as Elias told others, it came with "little power."[4] Declining the offer meant Elias could still enjoy the busy social life of a diplomat, without the bureaucratic responsibilities.

With the fall of the junta, some financial firms that had rejected his calls because they did not want to upset their relationship with the Nixon Administration telephoned to discuss consulting work. The World Bank and the Ford Foundation asked him to teach their employees about shoestring lobbying. Immodestly, he reminded friends that he'd been a star journalist with "influence" since the age of twenty and had, despite obstacles, successfully "established a new career in the banking community," where his horizons now could be unlimited. Half-jokingly, he suggested returning to Greece and starting a powerful news publication or building a media empire with the backing of moneyed friends.[5]

In Greece, it seemed Elias's persona non grata days were gone. He considered 80 percent of the recently announced cabinet to be friends. But in Washington, State Department Javerts remained hostile, nagging the CIA for help in repackaging anti-Demetracopoulos intelligence and trying to enlist the FBI in digging up fresh evidence to support a case for civil or criminal violations.

■

WHILE CYPRUS NEGOTIATIONS were falling apart in Geneva, Nixon, facing almost certain impeachment and removal from office for his cover-up activities in the Watergate scandal, resigned. Kissinger stayed, assuring allies abroad of continuity in American foreign policy. On August 9, four hours after Vice President Gerald Ford was sworn in as President, Assistant Secretary of State of Inter-American Affairs Jack Kubisch was sworn in at the White House as Henry Tasca's replacement. Kubisch had never been an ambassador and had no experience in the region, but his appointment was praised in Greece because it meant Tasca would be gone. Others sourly noted that all along the real American ambassador had been Tom Pappas, who was still active in both Athens and Washington.

The United States could have played an honest broker role at the Geneva Cyprus talks, urging inter-communal deliberations that led to serious reforms. Instead it looked the other way as Turkey flouted the cease-fire. The US would not cut off Turkish arms. Most significantly, it supported Turkey's desires to create, in effect, two distinct states with separate administrations. The "enclaves" or "cantons" plan that Kissinger endorsed would provide Turkish Cypriots with more than one-third of the land area.

Talks broke down on August 14. Turkish troops attacked Nicosia from two sides, looting, raping, and turning longtime residents into refugees in their homeland. The second invasion was simply a land grab.

By the next day, the Turks, having taken Famagusta (Ammoxostos) in the east and divided Nicosia, now controlled the entire northern part of the island. Conceding Turkish military superiority, a weakened Athens hesitantly prepared for war. Unable to help Greek Cypriots, the new Greek government withdrew from the military side of NATO, which had failed to stop the conflict.

Previously, a State Department staff recommendation that NATO Supreme Allied Commander General Andrew Goodpaster become involved went nowhere. Goodpaster had the respect of both sides.[6] Kissinger, however, preferred to deal with the heads of state directly, even alone. This proved especially disadvantageous to the Greeks. Kissinger remembered Prime Minister Ecevit from the time the Turkish diplomat had been a participant at one of Kissinger's Harvard seminars for emerging leaders. Ecevit leveraged that prior relationship. By contrast, Karamanlis had no prior personal history, and had difficulty even speaking English.

Deputy Prime Minister and Foreign Minister George Mavros called Elias to ask for his help. Elias immediately flew to Geneva and for about two weeks assisted him "from morning to night."[7] Elias told Jim Pyrros to call him collect at the Intercontinental Hotel with news from the US, but he was seldom there. Demetracopoulos sat with Mavros during much of the conference, breaking away to brief the press, because, Elias said, there was no one else. He visited London to see Makarios, who expressed disappointment at repeated Turkish violations of the cease-fire and persistent squabbling among the old politicians in Greece. Returning to Washington from Geneva late on Saturday, August 17, Elias recounted to Pyrros Turkish negotiating tactics that augmented their overwhelming military and diplomatic advantages. He criticized the Greek Foreign Service's complete disorganization and its inability to frame consistent messages to garner favorable news coverage.

En route home, Demetracopoulos also visited with Eleni Vlachou in London, who said, after much hesitation, that she would be returning to Greece to reopen *Kathimerini*. He also talked with Andreas Papandreou, who said he had postponed his return to Athens at least three times. Elias advised him to delay a while longer, because he "can only raise the temperature while being unable to contribute anything."[8] Andreas disagreed and ended his exile of nearly seven years with 15,000 supporters turning his airport arrival into a rhetorically hot political rally. An interview Andreas gave to the *New York Times* a week later calmed Elias some. Andreas, claiming he'd matured, said he did not intend to organize large public demonstrations, not because he'd changed his positions, but out of fear they could provoke the military's return.[9] This sounded responsible, Elias said, but added that Andreas was always unpredictable, often changing direction completely within a couple of hours.[10]

Even without Andreas stoking anti-American sentiment, demonstrators took to the streets of Athens for days. And in Nicosia, on the morning of August 19, an angry crowd of more than 1,000 Greek Cypriots, shouting anti-American epithets, marched on the American Embassy to protest the failure of the United States to stop the Turkish invasion. Women shouted "kill them, kill them" from nearby balconies. American cars were set ablaze. Tear gas didn't stop the surging crowd. High-powered rifles targeted shuttered windows. Rodger Davies, a career foreign service officer and the former director of Near Eastern Affairs, who had often tangled with Elias, had recently been appointed ambassador to Cyprus. He sheltered his tiny embassy staff in a second-floor hallway, where a bullet killed him almost instantly.

A day later in Washington, on a hot and sunny Sunday, the once-reticent Greek-American community, reluctant for generations to call attention to themselves, poured into the streets and surrounded the White House in an unprecedented demonstration. Elias and others couldn't believe their eyes. Messages had circulated quickly in Hellenic ethnic neighborhoods, and soon—arriving in buses, cars, and planes from New York, New Jersey, Greater Boston, Chicago, Detroit, St. Louis, San Francisco, and elsewhere—more than 20,000 Greek-Americans of all ages spilled out of Washington, D.C.'s Lafayette Park, snaked down Pennsylvania Avenue, around the Ellipse, and back. The rally turned into a peaceful walk. Some carried banners—"Greece offered friendship, Turkey offers opium"—and signs depicting Kissinger as a killer. Marchers chanted "El-las" and sang the Greek national anthem.[11]

Although many were angry at Kissinger and America's role, the demonstrators' mood was largely festive. Elias asked waspily: "Where were they during the seven long years of the dictatorship?" Pyrros replied that the second Turkish offensive, imposing a humiliating defeat on Hellenism and creating a heartbreaking wave of refugees, had touched a nerve. "Virtually every person of Greek blood has deep in his or her psyche a memory, a family tale, a personal experience of Turkish wrongdoing," he explained. "And now, even among those persons who believe themselves immune from such feelings, the passions are aroused, the ancient sense of being wronged rekindled."[12]

At Cyprus hearings before the House Foreign Affairs Committee, anti-junta stalwarts shared puzzled looks when they were joined by former junta apologists. Elias remembered well the post–World War II period when Greeks who'd collaborated or failed to resist were the first to embrace the calls for freedom and democracy. Pyrros saw a similar phenomenon in Washington. "Many of those who curried favor for the junta," he wrote in his journal, "are now scrambling to position themselves as 'Greek-American leaders' and anti-Turkish, of course."

Eugene Rossides, a former Nixon official not known for ever speaking out against the junta, reacted to events in Cyprus by founding the American Hellenic Institute as a DC-based lobbying, research, and communications think tank. With a paid staff; a restricted, high-dues-paying membership; and largely non-American funders, he became an imposing lobbyist, but he turned off some would-be supporters who saw the organization primarily as a Rossides-controlled piggy bank designed to help him recover family property in Turkish-occupied Cyprus.[13]

Demetracopoulos had promoted and lobbied the pro-democracy cause for seven years, using his own income to cover expenses. Fighting for Greek freedom and Cypriot independence, he believed, should be done out of patriotic love and pride, not as a money-seeking business. In coming years, the loose band of Washington-based anti-junta activists continued to work to change American policies toward Turkey and Cyprus but did so out of the limelight. In sheer numbers and volume, they were overshadowed by the newcomers. Elias was quoted less in news stories, though his behind-the-scenes work was still noticed by his opponents.

After the second Turkish invasion, some Greek-American congressmen, who'd been loath to speak up against the Athens dictatorship, became more vocal, but didn't replace the legislators and their staffs who skillfully led the earlier battles. When in September the House of Representatives voted 307–90 to ban all military aid to Turkey until the President deemed "substantial progress toward agreement . . . in Cyprus," it did so "without great involvement of the Greek-American community."[14] Congressman Ben Rosenthal and Senator Tom Eagleton, who sponsored the companion Senate resolution, were the legislative drivers.

Without regard to the island's complex history, Greek-Americans often reduced the situation in Cyprus to good Greeks versus bad Turks. They prematurely celebrated congressional resolutions forbidding the aggressive use of American equipment, without understanding the legislative labyrinth still ahead to change provisions in US military-aid law or the diplomacy needed to achieve a sustainable solution.[15] Kissinger viewed congressional action as antithetical to the flexibility he claimed he needed. The Ford Administration fought aggressively to rescind congressional legislation and scrambled to reassure Turkey of America's overall commitment and prevent it from turning to the USSR.

As the Greek-American community stepped up its lobbying pressures, the White House tried to divide and conquer, attacking troublemakers like Elias and courting Greek-American leaders like Archbishop Iakovos. On the afternoon of October 7, the Greek Orthodox spiritual leader met Secretary of State Kissinger, NSC head Brent Scowcroft, and the President in the Oval Office and attempted to convince the Ford Administration to show support to the Greek-American community. "I can't reason with my people," Iakovos told them. "They are demonstrating against me."[16] Although Ford was willing to make a brief statement about the more than 200,000 Greek Cypriot refugees displaced by the Turks, Kissinger rejected the idea, telling Iakovos that Karamanlis and Mavros had asked him not to get any concessions from Turkey before the November 17 Greek elections.[17]

An Iakovos assistant provided Elias with a summary of the forty-five-minute Oval Office exchange that emphasized the Greek government's fear that any announcement from Ford before the election would portray the US as Greece's patron. The document described Iakovos, unpersuaded by their arguments, insisting that the President do something about Turkish forces on Cyprus. Elias passed the memorandum on to Evans and Novak, who confirmed its accuracy with the archbishop, then published an article noting Iakovos's assessment that Ford had good intentions but was "too weak to take a position by himself."[18]

In response, Kissinger sent a confidential telegram to the new American ambassador decrying the article as "malicious" and "totally inaccurate," and instructed him to tell the Greek government that "there were no 'backstage deals.'"[19] With the election less than a week away, Mavros and Karamanlis loudly claimed that they had never said such things to Kissinger, while the politically right-centrist newspaper *Akropolis* editorialized that Kissinger could act without presidential approval and was motivated by his "hatred toward Greeks."[20]

The first free election in more than a decade went relatively smoothly. Karamanlis's New Democracy, which replaced his old ERE as the right-center party, was largely a cult of personality. The voters' choice, as campaign ads proclaimed, was simple: "Karamanlis or Tanks." Oriented toward the West and especially committed to closer economic ties with Europe, Karamanlis also appealed to anti-American sentiment by questioning if American bases should be in Greece.

George Mavros, heading the traditional Center Union, joined in alliance with John Pesmazoglou's small party of liberal intellectuals, New Forces. Save for its clear opposition to reinstating the monarchy and a greater emphasis on social welfare, their agenda was remarkably similar to that of Karamanlis. Both leaders were trusted friends of Elias. Many of their candidates had been harassed and imprisoned during the junta years. Had Demetracopoulos voted in this election, this group would have been his choice.

Andreas Papandreou's party, Panhellenic Socialist Movement or PASOK, embraced a socialist manifesto, called for a complete break with NATO, and held the United States, notably the CIA and Pentagon, largely responsible for Greece's problems. He used the Iakovos memorandum at one of his rallies.[21] Three parties also ran in an electoral alliance of the United Left, with Communists campaigning openly and legally for office for the first time since 1936. The far-right party, National Democratic Union, supported the discredited dictatorship.

Karamanlis received 54.4 percent of the vote, which, based on reinforced proportional representation, meant 73.3 percent of the seats in parliament.[22] Nearly 20 percent abstained, even though voting was compulsory.[23]

∎

SINCE SEPTEMBER 1973, Elias had spearheaded a campaign to get torture victim Spyros Moustaklis the best medical attention possible. The specialists Elias had flown in from London and Boston agreed that despite permanent damage to his flesh and internal systems, which meant he would never again read, write, or speak, his spirit was strong. They believed he could benefit from special therapy available at the Walter Reed Army Medical Center in Washington. But the highly regarded hospital for wounded veterans turned Elias's requests down several times because Spyros was neither a US veteran nor a citizen.

Elias provided examples of past exceptions. He asked sympathetic senators and congressmen to intervene on Major Moustaklis's behalf, but they too could not budge the bureaucracy, even though the request was only for a few tests, a thorough medical evaluation that could be done in a day, and design of a preliminary physical-therapy protocol. An Army official tentatively allowed the admission but was overruled. Even Elias's offer of cash up front—his own— didn't help.

When the junta was still in place, the Nixon Administration had considered it politically unwise to invite such a high-profile victim to the United States—especially after Ioannidis, personal orchestrator of Moustaklis's torture and mistreatment, became de facto head of the Greek government. Once the junta fell, however, requests by Elias and others were rejected again. Not even the new American ambassador, Jack Kubisch, responding favorably to Christina Moustaklis's plea, was successful in getting Kissinger to reconsider.[24] Eventually though, pressure from Kennedy, Fraser, and Rosenthal and the intervention of State's Joseph Sisco persuaded the number-two person in the Defense Department, William Clements Jr., to cut the red tape.

On December 22, Spyros and Christina arrived at Dulles Airport, with Persa Metaxas serving as nurse and interpreter. Walter Reed provided three weeks of outpatient therapy, during which Moustaklis received medications, physiotherapy, and speech therapy. The staff trained Persa and Christina to continue his treatment back in Athens. Doctors who examined him said the only hope for any recovery of function would be long-term physical therapy.

Elias ensured that the news media covered the trio's arrival, visit, and departure, but he guarded the Moustaklises' privacy and time. Uncharacteristically, he refused most television coverage and requests for interviews, aware that they could prove exhausting, and arranged just a few direct press interactions. Even so, feature articles provided an account of the major's heroic military career and the torture he'd suffered.[25]

On January 15, 1975, hours before President Ford delivered his State of the Union address to a joint session of Congress, Senator Ted Kennedy hosted a luncheon in Moustasklis's honor in a private dining room at the Senate. Christina thought Spyros was "living proof" to Americans that there were indeed people tortured by the Greek junta. Looking at the faces of the legislators, she knew he'd removed all doubts.

Back in Greece at the first court-martial trial of the torturers, which began on August 7 at Korydallos Prison outside Athens, nearly one hundred former prisoners and thirty former ESA soldiers gave testimony.[26] Others provided written depositions or declined to appear because they'd been threatened or paid to keep silent. Spyros was the fourth to testify. Mute, semi-paralyzed, and brain-damaged, he walked into the courtroom with difficulty, on the arm of resistance comrade Tasos Minis. Sitting on a wooden chair in front of the panel of judges, with thirty-one defendants nearby, he struggled to identify his torturers among the defendants. Glaring at them, he clumsily tore open his shirt and with grunts, groans, and gestures beat himself with his fist, pointing to the clearly visible scars that marked his body. Agitated, he shouted obscenities, and police were asked to calm him down.

In a hushed courtroom the prosecutor asked: "They beat you?" Moustaklis replied by gesturing to his neck: Pat, pat, pat. The prosecutor stopped his questioning. Christina made a statement on his behalf, providing graphic and damning evidence of his ordeal. She said that when, after three months, she was finally allowed to see her husband, he was "a living corpse, a body with no brain, a human plant . . . The horror lives on with us," she explained. "We have a little girl who has never heard her father's voice, who will never feel the warmth of his hand's caress."[27]

More harrowing details of his torture were revealed during cross-examination. After a series of defendants claimed to know nothing and passed responsibility for the torture onto others, one of the tribunal members interrupted: "I have heard a lot from all of you [officers] about bravery and manliness, but so far—and the trial is nearing its end—there has not been a man to come forward and accept his responsibility. For me this is a stigma which attaches to us all . . ."[28]

Years later, Christina recalled the smug rudeness of the defendants, so arrogant that it made her feel as if she and her husband were on trial. Some even assaulted a reporter, previously victimized by the junta, who was covering the proceedings. None of Moustaklis's torturers was executed. Only one received a lengthy sentence. Most received modest fines or no punishment.

According to Amnesty International, none of the junta's torture victims received any direct compensation for their suffering. Major Moustaklis received some small benefits provided for all disabled war veterans, and survived for another eleven years, until April 28, 1986. His rank was raised to colonel, a step adjustment provided all dismissed officers, nothing more. Elias was disappointed by the government's failure to compensate all of the junta's victims, and especially Spyros Moustaklis. Although he acknowledged how rare it was for a country to punish its own for wantonly brutal behavior, he was nevertheless furious that the Karamanlis administration never properly stood up to the torturers and for their victims.

27.

"The Plot to Snatch Demetracopoulos"

AS ONE OF A MUCH larger group of lobbyists, Elias worked in the fall of 1974 with Senator Thomas Eagleton and Representatives John Brademas, Paul Sarbanes, and Benjamin Rosenthal to cut off all government-financed and guaranteed sales of arms to Turkey, plus all cash sales, whether from public or private sources. After a series of fierce legislative battles, from resolutions to presidential vetoes, the embargo went into effect on February 5, 1975, as a requirement of the 1974 foreign-aid bill. It was a major defeat for Secretary of State Kissinger, and the day after the law went into effect, "Demetracopoulos" was the only Washington lobbyist mentioned by name at an Oval Office meeting among Ford, Kissinger, and some supportive members of Congress called to strategize a way around the bill's provisions.[1]

■

WITH HIS CITIZENSHIP restored, client obligations under control, and the Turkey vote behind him, Demetracopoulos decided that, after more than seven and a half years, he was ready to visit Greece. He told his friends, including columnists Jack Anderson and Les Whitten. They thought it was a good time to write a "valedictory" profile.

For years, Elias had kept under wraps handwritten letters from Louise Gore that he could have used to his advantage against Nixon and his henchmen. His deep friendship and sense of honor prevented him from doing anything that could hurt Louise or impede her career. When he told her that he'd been talking to Jack Anderson and Les Whitten about the column they were preparing that would describe his years of being harassed, loyal Republican Gore, who had been her party's 1974 candidate for governor of Maryland, told him he could use her letter from 1972 that mentioned Mitchell's deportation threat. "Despite the risk to her political career," Gore told Whitten, "she would warn Demetracopoulos again if she had it to do over."[2]

Whitten was especially eager to do the article. He'd recently confirmed evidence about the FBI's aggressive June 1972 inquiry to Sartorious & Company pressuring the employer to terminate Elias's contract. Then he received information from a reliable source who had overheard John Mitchell and Murray Chotiner discuss "getting" Demetracopoulos at a cocktail party; Tom Pappas's name had been part of the conversation.[3] On February 12, 1975, the syndicated column was headlined in different papers: "US Officials Harassed Greek Exile," "Nixon Crowd Sought Greek Exile's Ouster," and "Greek Newsman Fought Odds and Won Out."[4] The article recounted the highlights of Elias's ordeal, the efforts of politically motivated White House, Justice Department, FBI, CIA, and Nixon-campaign officials to have him fired and worse, including John Mitchell's public threat to have him sent "home to certain torture and possible death." The piece concluded with the idea that after eight years in exile, "Demetracopoulos is returning to his beloved Greece, not as a deportee facing torture, but as a patriot." Wire services, including Reuters, Agence France Presse, and the *New York Times*, carried the story worldwide.

The Anderson-Whitten column had an impact far beyond its purported valedictory intent. Senator McGovern wrote to Senate Intelligence Committee chairman Frank Church calling the allegations "grave" and deserving "full and careful . . . priority" consideration during his Select Committee's forthcoming hearings. Elias gave the McGovern letter to the *Washington Post*, which ran a story the next day and included an interview with Elias, who said that, after the junta's collapse, he had heard from friends in Greece that they were visited by the KYP on behalf of the CIA seeking compromising information about him. A spokesman for Senator Church said his committee would consider the McGovern information carefully.[5]

Press attention to government harassment of Demetracopoulos forced the various intelligence agencies to respond publicly. The FBI made efforts to convince Whitten to disassociate its responsible behavior from more questionable practices by other federal agencies, saying it had kept alive a Foreign Agents inquiry from 1971 until 1974 only at the direction of the State Department, and had played only "a limited role . . . related in no way to inquiries by the White House or Attorney General."[6] New FBI director Clarence M. Kelly tried to further minimize the agency's record, in the process also overlooking entirely its intrusive investigations of Demetracopoulos during the 1950s and early 1960s (the Bureau's "bad old days").[7]

Prompted by calls from congressmen to CIA director William Colby, the agency worked for more than two weeks on its public response, apparently skittish after Colby had been taken to the woodshed by Kissinger for being too open and cooperative with Congress. After assembling a compilation of some of the more egregious falsehoods in its "Dimitrakopoulos" dossier, the CIA produced a restrained memorandum that described "Dimitakopoulos [sic]" as "an annoyance" who while he has "made a number of enemies, many of them senior American officials . . . there are no hard facts in the record to show that he has worked for any foreign government against the interests of Greece (or for that matter the United States), that he is in the pay of any national government, that he has ever been a member of a foreign intelligence service or has ever been involved in criminal activities."

It concluded:

In hindsight, the Agency may have overreacted to the provocations of Dimitakopoulos [sic] . . . As far as we can tell we have not taken any action against Dimitakopoulos which may have contravened American law . . .

Since he has been a controversial figure and the subject of many suspicions as well as antagonisms, we inevitably have had a reporting responsibility but do not know at what point this could begin to be considered "harassment." [A large text redaction follows.][8]

■

Elias delayed his return to Greece after these stories about his persecution expanded the Church Committee's growing investigation into US intelligence-agency abuses.[9] But when Senate staff told him in early April that he would not be asked to testify until late May, he used the interlude to visit his homeland.

On Sunday, April 13, 1975, Elias, now forty-six years old, returned to Athens in triumph. A crowd of several hundred was waiting for him when he arrived at Ellinikon International Airport, many waving newspapers that heralded his return. They cheered enthusiastically when he stood atop the mobile staircase wearing a dark three-piece suit, a crisp white shirt, a perfectly knotted tie, and highly shined black balmorals, and carrying a leather briefcase. He waved back, blinking his eyes in the bright Athenian sunlight. The first person to greet him was Colonel Spyros Moustaklis, smiling and gesturing welcome from his wheelchair. Elias teared up at the outpouring of support. Friends embraced and kissed him, some presenting bouquets of flowers. After retrieving his luggage, the entourage piled into a caravan of cars, honking all the way into the city.[10]

The month that followed was a whirlwind of emotion and business. Elias went first to the Proto Nekrotafeio Cemetery to pay his respects at his father's grave. He met with Karamanlis, to whom he gave messages from members of Congress he had generated. He conferred with opposition leaders. There was time for Persa Metaxas and other old friends. It seemed that every night involved another celebratory dinner or a long, intense briefing to discuss a myriad of domestic and international issues.

The *Athens News* covered Elias's visit at several stages and published letters of warm praise from Senators McGovern and Hartke.[11] Correspondent David Tonge covered his arrival for the BBC and published a profile on Elias in the *Guardian*, later expanded in the Greek press, dubbing him "the emigré eminence." "For seven years," Tonge wrote, Demetracopoulos "had managed to keep the Greek issue alive" and recently "played a large part in undermining Dr. Kissinger's pro-Turkish policies."[12]

On May 10, Efangelos Androulidakis, the one-time *Kathimerini* reporter whose writing in the 1940s had inspired Elias's initial interest in journalism, hosted a cocktail party at the Grand Bretagne Hotel in Elias's honor. Among more than 200 guests were several ministers from the Karamanlis government, other deputies, opposition leader George Mavros, and former Bank of Greece governors Xenophon Zolotas and John Pesmazoglou, who had quit their posts rather than serve under the junta. The American Embassy continued to disparage Elias, downplaying his contacts, the reception attendees, and his coverage in the Greek press in a SECRET communiqué to Washington.[13]

After the dictatorship's implosion, the Greek government had embarked on a "de-juntification" process, dismissing or replacing some military personnel and bureaucrats. There were promises that junta leaders would be put on trial for their crimes. Hearing that KYP chief Michael Roufogalis was to be deposed, Demetracopoulos hoped that secrets from the seven-year reign might come to light. Maybe he could find out the details behind his near miss of an escape, his blocked return to visit his dying father, and the intermittent warnings he had heard since 1967 that the colonels were out to "get" him and interrogate him. He did not yet know the full scope and intensity of their plots and the names of those involved.

But after the government announced it would limit its investigation and trials to those responsible for the most egregious tortures, Elias assumed that his concerns for justice were unlikely to be vindicated. After all, Greece had no laws providing a right of access to government records. Getting answers would take hard digging, and relevant files might have already been destroyed.

Beginning with confidential meetings in Athens with Greek intelligence contacts and conversations with the head of the Greek government press office, Panagiotis Lamprias, Elias received confirmation of a long-rumored scheme of junta strongman Papadopoulos and KYP chief Roufogalis to kidnap him. He shared this information with Christopher Hitchens, who did his own complementary research. According to the most complete published account of the coded cables, Athens was prepared to dispatch a special team to the United States to carry out the plot, which was planned in cooperation with the Greek military mission in D.C. Elias was especially outraged by the revelation he found included in a Greek cable marked "COSMIC Eyes Only," the highest security classification: "We can rely on the cooperation of the various agencies of the US Government, but estimate the congressional reaction to be fierce."[14]

Elias fixated on ascertaining which of the "various agencies of the US government" could have been "relied on" to cooperate in his proposed abduction, torture, and murder. Who were the players, and what did they know and do?

He also wanted additional credible authentication of the kidnapping plot or plots. He called Jack Anderson, who assigned Les Whitten to research the story on both sides of the ocean. Working independently of Elias, Whitten discovered that Brigadier General Floros Astrinidis, head of the military mission in Washington, had been ordered by Papadopoulos in 1971 to look into ways of kidnapping Elias. Astrinidis, who successfully arranged the 1972 US arms deal, was well connected to many in the Nixon Administration.[15]

According to Whitten, junta leaders—especially Papadopoulos, Roufoga-lis, Astrinidis, and their allies—deeply loathed Demetracopoulos and sensed that "President Nixon and his aides hated" him as well. At first, the conspirators thought they would not have to do anything: Nixon Administration officials in-dicated that they were building a case to deport Elias. But when John Mitchell made his threat public in February 1972 and then failed to act, the conspirators "took up the cudgel."[16]

For months, Papadopoulos and Roufogalis "burned up the back channel" cable traffic from Athens to the Greek military mission in D.C. with demands to carry out the plot. It is not clear to what extent Tom Pappas was used as a back channel, but, in his handwritten notes, Whitten wrote the name "Tom Pappas" in large capital letters next to a giant asterisk and, in an interview years later, as-serted that Pappas was intimately involved. Americans, especially those in the CIA, were apparently aware of the Greek plans. CIA Station Chief Jim Potts met so often and openly with junta leaders that even Tasca was upset. Highly classi-fied Greek cables indicated that American advice and help was sought, although it was not clear "who, if anyone, in the U.S. approved the kidnapping." As laid out in the coded cables and in secret messages sent by diplomatic pouch, Athens "drew up at least three operations to get him back."[17]

The easiest of the contemplated schemes was to "snatch" the exile from the District of Columbia and take him by force in a car to New York and then put him on a (preferably empty) Olympic Airways jet that could be flown nonstop to Athens. The second plan involved transporting the abducted Elias on a Greek military plane, but that had to be abandoned because of the need for refueling stops. The third alternative was to "subdue Demetracopoulos in Washington" and somehow get him into a waiting Greek submarine. This plan, though ini-tially deemed too logistically difficult for success, was revived later by others.

According to the secret messages, these scenarios all had a common objec-tive and conclusion: "Once kidnapped, the exile, Elias Demetracopoulos, was to be interrogated about his American and Greek contacts and presumably tor-tured if he did not reveal them. This done, there would have been little other course but to kill him to conceal the kidnapping."[18]

In their April 26, 1975 column, headlined "The Plot to Snatch Demetraco-poulos," Anderson and Whitten described the three abduction schemes and highlighted the plotters' confidence that they could "rely on the cooperation of the various agencies of the US government." Whitten said he and Anderson held back some of his most explosive findings, including interviews attesting that Elias would ultimately be murdered. They also left out any reference to Tom Pappas's involvement. According to Whitten, junta files disclosed that the kidnapping idea was initially "dropped" in 1972 because the risks were thought too great on account of Elias's strong congressional network. Responding to "U.S. security officials," who swore they knew absolutely nothing about the plots against Demetracopoulos, Whitten said later, "They were lying . . . They knew and did nothing to stop it."[19]

Earlier that year, President Ford, Henry Kissinger, and some congressional leaders had met in the White House to discuss their efforts to maneuver around the Turkish arms shutoff. Someone asked, "Can't we get to the Greek-Americans?" Kissinger replied; "We tried. They are being used by Papandreou and his supporters—like Demetracopoulos." According to the once-confidential February 6, 1975, "Memorandum of Conversation," Kissinger, after mentioning Elias's name, made the following cryptic aside: "Bitsios asked. Couldn't we get rid of him?" During the discussion, Kissinger never provided any context for this request from anti-Elias Greek foreign minister Dimitrios Bitsios's request. He never clarified when it was asked nor indicated what he said in response. But those in the group all knew Elias, and no one at the meeting asked what "get rid of him" really meant. Coupling this remark with the 1970 NSC document that contains the skeletal index heading "Mr. Demetracopoulos death in Athens prison"—prepared while Kissinger was NSA director—it is reasonable to infer that Kissinger and others knew about at least some of the different Greek plots to "get" Elias, a legal permanent resident of the United States, and did nothing about it.

In response to doubters in the American and Greek communities who claimed that the kidnapping planning documents were forgeries, Constantine Panagiotakos, who served as ambassador in Washington during the junta's last months, later wrote Elias a notarized letter in which he affirmed that, from the time he arrived, he had direct knowledge of a plan to kidnap him. He knew the junta's henchman and would-be assassin was a "protégé" of Greek foreign minister Dimitrios Bitsios, a career diplomat whose hatred for Elias was so profound that he felt comfortable trying to enlist the support of Kissinger in the plot.[20] In his memoirs, Ambassador Panagiotakos also implicated others:

On 29 May a document was transmitted to me from Angelos Vlachos, Secretary General of the Foreign Ministry, giving the views of the United States Ambassador Henry Tasca, which he agreed with, about the most efficient means of dealing with the conspiracies and the whole activity of Demetracopoulos. Tasca's views are included in a memorandum of conversation with Foreign Minister Spyridon Tetenes of 27 May.[21]

On June 12, 1974 the Foreign Ministry in Athens had asked Panagiotakos to "seek useful advice on the extermination of Elias Demetracopoulos from George Churchill, director of the Greek desk at the State Department, who was one of his most vitriolic enemies."[22]

Panagiotakos's political counselor, Charalampos "Babis" Papadopoulos, number three at the embassy, similarly swore in an affidavit that he attended a luncheon at the Jockey Club (downstairs from Elias's apartment) between late May and early June 1974, at which assistant military attaché Lieutenant Colonel Sotiris Yiounis discussed kidnapping Demetracopoulos with the help of a submarine at harbor in Virginia. The political counselor affirmed that at least two other named officials at the embassy were aware of such plans.[23] Papadopoulos said later that he "was assured that Henry Kissinger was fully aware of the proposed operation, and 'most probably willing to act as its umbrella.'"[24] This testimony gives added weight to Ted Kennedy's earlier warning to Elias not to visit his dying father.

After meeting with Prime Minister Karamanlis during his homecoming, Demetracopoulos suggested that the 1972 abduction plan may have been dropped because of fear that public indignation in the US would help Democratic nominee McGovern and the anti-junta cause. According to the documents provided to Whitten, "Greek officials were still grumbling about Demetracopoulos right up until the junta left office last July."[25]

News about the kidnapping conspiracy soon became an "affair" all its own. South Dakota Senator Jim Abourezk, a member of the Senate Judiciary Committee, wrote to Senator Church on April 28, 1975, expressing his outrage that the Greek junta could have planned to kidnap Demetracopoulos with the sympathetic understanding, or even direct help, of the United States intelligence agencies.

If it is true that the CIA and other United States agencies were involved in this affair, or even that they knew of the plans by the junta and did not actively seek to stop them, then this fact should be revealed by your committee and legislative action should be recommended to insure that this sort of plotting with a foreign government can never happen again.[26]

Abourezk told the press he hoped "the Demetracopoulos affair" will lead to "a detailed investigation of the persistent allegations" of CIA involvement in the military coup of April 21, 1967. McGovern followed up with Church, who told him that he had assigned both matters to the "appropriate staff members . . . for further action." The Greek press picked up the story, reporting "US Senate Committee to Investigate Alleged CIA involvement in Demetracopoulos kidnap plot."[27]

Meanwhile, on the other side of Capitol Hill, Congressman Don Edwards told the press that the allegations of a kidnapping conspiracy "will be investigated in depth, I am sure, by the House Select Committee on Intelligence."[28] About two months later, Edwards said the matter had been referred to Searle Field, the committee's staff director, for "follow up," and the Associated Press reported that Demetracopoulos "is expected to appear before the committee as a witness in their investigations."[29]

■

ELIAS'S RETURN TO Greece was bittersweet. For all his busyness, he felt a sense of loss, a kind of *kaimos*, the residue left in the heart after a love affair had ended. His world there had changed, and so had he. It wasn't just the uglification of Athens, with new concrete apartment buildings having replaced stately homes, increased traffic cacophony, and the spreading air pollution that clouded cherished vistas and blue skies. He found Athens less interesting than Washington. Having made it in fast-paced America, where he moved freely in the corridors of power and around a relatively efficient, modern city, he was reluctant to return to Greece's frustrating quotidian realities. If he returned permanently, his life would be decidedly different and more difficult. He wasn't recognized on the streets of Athens the way he was in Washington. His heart was in Greece, but his home was now in the United States. Elias told the *Athens News* he had a job to do in America. He had promised the Senate Intelligence Committee that he'd provide testimony and evidence detailing the close relationship of Tom Pappas and the colonels as well as the junta's plans for his own abduction, with possible American complicity.

Meanwhile, the Greek unity government's limited exposure of dark truths about the junta years left him dissatisfied. The official Greek investigation of his abduction concluded on Friday, June 13, 1975, in a hearing room at the Greek Parliament, with testimony that Dimitrios Petrounakos, part of a special committee to attack Greek journalists, had been "assigned a special mission to deal with the reactionist Elias Demetracopoulos, who was active in the USA." His mission, never completed, had been the "*exoudeterosi* (elimination)" of Elias.[30]

After learning of the kidnapping and assassination reference in the parliament debate, Les Whitten thought the public catharsis (cleansing) process, including trials, then underway might also apply to exposing Greek involvement in the 1968 money transfer. He called Panagiotis Lamprias, deputy minister in charge of intelligence, to find out what the new government had found out about the KYP passing CIA funds to the 1968 Nixon campaign. Lamprias told Whitten that the government "planned to investigate," promised "more information" in two days, but never replied to repeated requests. Whitten and Anderson later learned that the CIA station chief in Athens, Stacy Hulse, had "made a quiet, subtle request that the government lay off the 1968 fund mystery. Hulse passed the word, according to our sources, to the new KYP chief, Maj. Gen. Konstantinos Fetsis, who informed his civilian boss, George Rallis . . . At a hectic meeting it was decided to ignore our calls rather than risk worsening relations with the United States."[31]

Whitten said he was later told that Karamanlis was also involved in this decision not to respond. Given the prime minister's agenda, the CIA station chief need not have pushed hard. The new government had decided early on that, in the interest of not reigniting the country's history of political polarization and revenge, it would limit its investigation of evildoers to top junta leaders during narrow time periods, and then only to the persons held responsible for the most egregious tortures. Thousands of legitimate claims were ignored. Permitting the disclosure of the Demetracopoulos kidnapping plots was a relatively low-cost activity that would only hurt already-discredited junta miscreants. However, allowing this to trigger a thorough investigation of real and imagined CIA–KYP collusion and skulduggery, before and after the coup, was a different matter altogether. With the Cyprus confrontation still unresolved, a clear increase in anti-American sentiment in the country, and Greece having pulled out of the military wing of NATO, there was no reason to make relations with Washington any more difficult. The Greek people were already acutely susceptible to conspiracy theories. Why give them a justifiable reason to get whipped up?

■

A DOOR MAY have closed in Athens, but Demetracopoulos saw an opening in Washington. After he discussed the developments in Greece with Louise Gore, she told him he could now also go public with her 1968 letter expressing shock at Agnew's about-face on Greece. Elias gave copies to the staffs of both the Senate and House intelligence committees and Evans and Novak. They speculated that the private letter "may prove indispensable to the committee's probe of long-standing charges that the junta funneled Greek government money into the Nixon-Agnew campaign in return for Nixon-Agnew support." Congressional sources told them that Tom Pappas "is certain to be summoned when the Church committee ends the assassination phase of its probe and moves into the explosive area of covert CIA operations abroad."[32]

The CIA claimed: "there is no truth to these allegacions [sic]," but withheld in their entirety—then and now, more than fifty years later—the contents of top-priority memoranda concerning Thomas Pappas's "connections with CIA."[33] Spiro Agnew claimed to be outraged by the column, denied any personal involvement, but did not exonerate or even mention Pappas in his statement.[34] Although Agnew said he wanted to testify before the Senate Intelligence Committee to "clear the air," some Republicans feared that the disgraced former vice president would use a closed-door session for payback against Nixon. In that spirit, the Republican vice chairman, Texas senator John Tower, made sure that Agnew was never formally asked to appear.

■

GIVEN THE NEW Greek administration's "general amnesty" and reluctance to initiate prosecutions, it's not surprising that questions about the extent of American government and CIA support for the dictatorship went unanswered. On August 9, 1975, the eleventh day of the Athens trial of the twenty coup protagonists, lawyer Alexandros Lykourezos tried to give evidence of coup leaders' contacts with US "secret services." He referred to a statement by then–CIA director William Colby, who said in his 1972 Senate confirmation hearings that the CIA had "for some time . . . cooperated with Mr. Papadopoulos."[35]

When the presiding judge, John Degiannis, commented that American military and political leaders were not being tried in the current case, Lykourezos responded, "Perhaps they are, indirectly." He expressed regret that the current trial was not heading in that direction. He then recommended that Elias Demetracopoulos be invited to appear before the court as a person "who would be able to prove . . . the pre-April meddling and support of the defendants by foreign powers." Judge Degiannis turned down the request as not "feasible." When Elias then cabled Degiannis to state that he could "return to Athens within twenty-four hours," his telegram was returned "with the excuse that the person who was to receive it refused to do so."[36]

Undeterred, Elias prepared materials for a possible Washington deposition that could be used in Athens, but, in the perpetrators' trial that ended on August 23, he was never invited to give testimony.[37] After less than a month of deliberations, Papadopoulos, Makarezos, and Pattakos were sentenced to death by firing squad for insurrection. Fifteen others, including Ioannidis, received life sentences and lesser terms.

On principle, Elias did not believe in the death penalty, but in this case he believed that a harsh decision would have served the cause of justice. He bristled at Karamanlis's eventual decision to commute the junta trio's death sentences to life imprisonment. He understood Karamanlis's desire not to create martyrs by execution and feed political polarization and revanchism, but he did not like it.

■

BY SEPTEMBER 1975, the case for full congressional investigations of CIA activities in Greece before and during the junta years was growing stronger. The Senate Intelligence Committee had heard some testimony on the issue but had not released its findings.[38] Several of those interviewed by staff acknowledged that before the 1967 coup they had been aware of Greek and American discussions, even including Karamanlis, considering a military solution to the Greek political chaos. The AP reported that a list of American witnesses identified by Demetracopoulos would be asked to tell what they knew about such plotting.[39] However, for much of the year the White House, notably Deputy Assistant to the President Richard "Dick" Cheney, had worked to deter congressional intelligence committee investigations. Disclosures, the CIA warned, would be "disastrous." All the while appearing cooperative, the Ford Administration effectively shielded essential information by invoking national security. The Church Committee was reduced to "appealing, cajoling, negotiating or begging for data," and in the end essentially let the administration set the agenda.[40]

Elias knew that the Senate hearings had been delayed, but still expected to be given a new time to testify. Months passed, and no calls came. Eventually John Holum, McGovern's lead staffer, informed Elias that he had been told that Kissinger had warned Church specifically against pursuing the CIA-Greece angle, using danger to national security as his justification. An angry Elias gave the tip to syndicated columnist Nick Thimmesch, who confirmed publicly Kissinger's intervention.[41]

Seymour Hersh, in his Kissinger book, *The Price of Power*, dug more deeply into the larger issues and confirmed that the Church committee investigation of the 1968 Pappas-to-Nixon money transfer was also "abruptly cancelled at Kissinger's direct request."[42] Church, ignoring the commitment he had made to members of the Senate when assuming the select-committee chairmanship, was at the time actively considering running for President. The committee proceedings were being wrapped up; the final report being prepared. For Church, who had never been in the forefront of congressional opposition to the junta, there were more important issues.

House Select Committee on Intelligence Chairman Otis Pike was not as deferential as Church, and not afraid to investigate the Pappas-CIA matter. Even dire warnings from Kissinger and Defense Secretary James Schlesinger would not dissuade him. In September 1975, Pike sent committee counsel Jack Boos to Rome to get a sworn statement from Henry Tasca on his recollections of CIA activities in Greece and Cyprus during his tenure.

The retired ambassador was relaxed and affable, exhibiting none of the dyspeptic acerbity of his years in Athens. As part of a more general conversation, outside the sworn formal interview, Boos asked Tasca what he knew about the CIA and Pappas's roles during and after the Nixon campaigns.[43] Tasca wasn't there in 1968 but said that some of the colonels and others had told him stories confirming the Demetracopoulos allegations. The junta, Tasca added, "leaked like a colander," and the Pappas financial skulduggery was widely known to others outside. He thought former Ambassador Talbot probably knew about it, but in his view Talbot was a "see-no-evil guy." CIA officials, noted Tasca, were tight-lipped about their own roles, but he felt the station "would have been clearly aware of the fundraising stuff." As for the recycling of CIA money, he said it wasn't as if someone wrote initials on the CIA money and then those bills came back to the US, even if "it was functionally the same thing."

As Tasca understood the process, the request for Greek money was advertised to the colonels as being urgently needed by the Nixon campaign, with Tom

Pappas the one shaking them down. If Nixon-Agnew won, Pappas predicted, "you've got great 'ins,' but if they lose you're really out in the cold." He stressed that the race would be extremely close, and money was tight. "If you want to get maximum credit," he said, "now's the time!" According to Tasca's account, the CIA chief of station, Jack Maury, met with the colonels separately and backed up Pappas's sales pitch. Tasca may not have trusted the CIA, but he admired how deeply they had penetrated the junta. Maury "knew when Papadopoulos went to the bathroom and would definitely have known about the Pappas money transfer," Tasca recalled. CIA antennae were acutely sensitive at the station level when American partisan politics came into play. Operatives in Athens would have been very cautious about formally apprising their superiors. According to Tasca, CIA director Richard Helms was a "smooth, slippery guy" and wouldn't want to know about a lot of things.

Pappas was back at his Nixon fundraising in Greece for 1972, Tasca said, but Tasca claimed to know nothing about the scope and details of that campaign. Pappas often made it clear to him that important things were happening of which the ambassador would be kept unaware.

When Boos returned to Washington, he turned in the sworn statement from Tasca and presented to the committee his findings on the 1974 coup and Cyprus.[44] Privately, he briefed his chairman on the confidential details he had learned about the 1968 money transfer and the role Pappas had played. Pike was inquisitive and followed up, asking Congressman Ben Rosenthal for the memorandum on Pappas that Demetracopoulos had submitted to Rosenthal's subcommittee in September 1971.[45] The 1968 money transfer was clearly illegal, and, if it involved recycled US taxpayer funds subsidizing candidate Nixon, a legitimate scandal. But Tasca's story was second-hand and occurred before he was on the scene. He could never say, "I saw the money being transferred." Former Central Bank head Galanis, who had confirmed to Elias the cash transfer, was dead. Tom Pappas had effectively lawyered up to beat any Watergate rap, and would likely use his age (seventy-six), health, or some other excuse to avoid ever appearing before Congress. Roufogalis and the other junta leaders were en route to jail. The Pike committee wasn't going to get them to come to Washington and testify. Sure, Pike could call former CIA director Richard Helms to testify. But Helms had walled himself off, as he later confirmed. If, in the unlikely event someone in the Athens station had passed the information to headquarters, he would have been told by someone lower than the director to "sit on it."

The Pike Committee was already fractious and highly partisan, and its Democratic chairman wanted to complete the committee's work without the Republicans bolting. Pike was not one to waste political capital, and the Pappas contribution in 1968 was ancient history. Nixon was gone. Simply raising the issue of the 1968 election would be explosive, even before requesting testimony from Mitchell and Stans. Pike and some other members were considering running for the Senate. They had hoped that favorable reviews of their work on the committee could help launch their campaigns. But, by late fall of 1975, many had begun to have second thoughts.

Pressure from the White House may well have played a role. Dave Peterson, President Ford's intelligence briefing advisor, had provided a special report to Ford about Elias, detailing "derogatory traces from our files."[46] Afterward, according to the meeting transcript, the President exclaimed: "Boy, he's a no goodnik isn't he?"[47] To drive the point home, Peterson left a "negative blind memo" along with a "long Kissinger memo on Elias" with Ford's National Security advisor, Brent Scowcroft. Elias was branded a problem for a sixth successive American administration.

Elias was relentless. Seeing the Greece-CIA part of the Church Committee hearings faltering, he had looked to the House side to expose Pappas's ongoing influence and the story of his own years of being victimized by US government agencies. When it appeared that Pike was also slow-walking his investigation, Elias asked individual members to pressure the chairman. He gave Warren Nelson, an aide to Wisconsin Congressman Les Aspin, some of what he would have given the Church committee. On December 15, Nelson wrote a four-page memo to his boss, summarizing highlights of US government attacks on Elias and making it clear that there was "somebody in the system who really has it in personally for EPD."[48] He pointed out that Demetracopoulos had "substantial documentation, including the names of many living and prominent persons he says were witnesses to or participants in parts of the story."

Nelson concluded:

I think there's something here demonstrating CIA abuse in the form of personal harassment . . . He wants to go public now and quite frankly is shopping around for a means . . . so that when it comes out it's not just his allegations, but an independent body saying it. [49]

Aspin, a congressional workhorse and serious Pentagon reformer who would later become defense secretary, thought an investigation was still warranted and told chairman Pike as much. At Elias's request, Congressman Don Edwards did the same.[50] On December 18, 1975, American newspaper stories identified Tom Pappas as a "Probe Target" who'd joined President Ford's camp as a fundraiser for 1976. A former member of the Watergate special-prosecution task force said it would be "an outrage" if Pappas were raising money for Ford.[51]

In the Greek press the next day, Elias read that Pappas, in exchange for his legendary financial support, had asked President Ford to intervene with the Greek government to prevent him from losing his Coca-Cola franchise.[52] Senator McGovern observed that Pappas had repeatedly escaped "a direct accounting for his activities . . . because investigators have been preoccupied with other bigger targets."[53] Demetracopoulos hoped that, with Aspin and Edwards pushing Pike, this time would be different.

His hopes would not be fulfilled. On December 23, Athens CIA station chief Richard Welch, returning from a Christmas party, was assassinated at close range, in front of his wife, in his suburban Psychiko driveway. The CIA blamed sensationalist anti-Americanism in the Greek press, worldwide publicity of Washington investigations of Agency "black" operations, and public disclosures of Welch's identity.[54] Within days of the murder, CIA defenders effectively charged Congress and liberal media with having Welch's blood on their hands. Crusading zeal against the CIA ceased to be good domestic politics. Some blamed Elias. In one ugly scene at the Fairfax, John Mitchell screamed at Louise Gore about her friend's responsibility, as if he had pulled the trigger.

The congressional committees backed off. On the intelligence committee, CIA hunters became the hunted, and members ran scared. In such an atmosphere, nobody wanted to consider Pappas's 1968 money-laundering. Nobody wanted to pursue the CIA's and others' attacks against Demetracopoulos.

By year's end, Elias had not achieved the objectives for which in May he had claimed to be returning to the US. He had received confirmation of plots against him. Louise Gore's letters were now public. But his many FOIA requests into his own records had not borne fruit. Soon he and others would learn there was far more than a single "somebody in the system" gunning for him.

28.

Fighting for Vindication

A DECEMBER 1974 *WASHINGTONIAN MAGAZINE* EXPOSÉ of foreign lobbying in the United States featured Elias, calling him "mysterious" and "powerful." But it also mischaracterized him as a paid lobbyist.[1] This offended his great pride in the fact that whatever he did for the restoration of democracy in Greece had been at his own expense. He'd insisted for years that he was nobody's agent, on nobody's payroll, least of all that of a foreign state.[2] The story, by freelancer Russell Warren Howe, a former Reuters journalist and *Penthouse* magazine contributor, was the type of publicity he did not covet, especially after Howe, in 1975 and 1976, reworked defamatory claims about him into a book critical of foreign lobbyists.[3] Elias considered legal action against the writer, though he ultimately decided against it, in part because it would require probing for the identities of the author's confidential sources.[4] As a journalist who had spent a lifetime protecting his own sources, he found such a prospect distasteful.

Such ethical niceties escaped Howe, who falsely claimed to be a foreign-affairs correspondent for US newspapers while in the paid employ of the Turkish government-controlled news service and its service academy. He wrote tendentious articles and taught his employers public-relations skills. Howe was a willing tool for Elias's adversaries; he later admitted he'd also worked for a CIA false-front news organization.[5]

With Elias's help, McGovern and his key staffer John Holum discovered that the primary source for Russell Howe's "dirt" on Elias was George Churchill, the State Department Greek Desk official named by the Greek Foreign Ministry as an asset in their Demetracopoulos elimination plans. Churchill had repurposed smears from the defamatory 1971 memorandum generated by State, disclosed additional CIA disinformation, and lied to Howe that Elias had falsely claimed to have worked for the CIA as a ruse to overcome his difficulties in gaining entry to the US in 1967. When McGovern asked Churchill direct questions about providing anonymous and defamatory information to Howe, he responded with a cloud of obfuscation.[6]

Then, in January 1977, when McGovern saw Churchill's name on a State Department list of 558 Foreign Service officers nominated for promotion by President Ford, he exercised his Senate prerogative and delayed consideration of all the promotions for three months, until he received more responsive replies.[7] Slowly a picture emerged of Churchill as a dissembler and active participant in a Nixon Administration scheme to get back at Elias and his congressional support by circulating the malicious 1971 memorandum as payback for Elias's filing of the anti-Pappas report. Churchill's story that his anonymous attack letter was merely something prepared at the request of the Speaker of the House was diametrically contradicted by Carl Albert, who said he'd known Demetracopoulos for years and had never requested a "blind" memorandum.

George McGovern was well aware of the post-Welch assassination firestorm that caused many of his colleagues to back away from investigating the CIA's misdeeds in Greece and its harassment of Demetracopoulos. He was sensitive to the need to protect identities of intelligence personnel and supported reasonable security classification restrictions. But with Church's investigation of Greece blocked by Kissinger and the House Intelligence committee under siege by the White House, McGovern considered using his chairmanship of the Senate's Subcommittee on Near Eastern and South Asian Affairs, which then included Greece, to undertake a formal review of US policy toward that country during the years of the military dictatorship.

On October 29, 1976, before deciding to hold committee hearings of his own, McGovern asked Senator Daniel Inouye, Church's successor as chairman of the Senate Select Committee on Intelligence, to investigate American intelligence activities in Greece over the previous eight years. He reasoned that the Inouye-led Intelligence Committee would have more resources and flexibility to do a thorough investigation than would a stand-alone McGovern-led inquiry.

McGovern summarized four areas that deserved careful inquiry: (1) expanding and publicizing the Church Committee's case study of intelligence-agency covert action in Greece; (2) investigating the role of former vice president Agnew in the 1968 presidential campaign as regards Greece and the funneling of secret CIA funds back to the United States for use in Nixon's 1968 campaign; (3) examining the efforts directed against Elias Demetracopoulos between 1967 and 1974 by American and Greek governments, including kidnap plans; and (4) investigating the role of Tom Pappas, his business interests, and his American and Greek political fundraising connections and possible involvement with "our intelligence agencies."[8]

The memorandum was prepared for the senator by John Holum, who'd worked on Greek democracy issues with Elias for years. While other congressmen and their staff had shifted to other issues post-junta, Holum was tenacious and easily convinced McGovern that this was critically important unfinished business.[9]

Elias couldn't have been more pleased if he'd drafted the memorandum himself. Some of them were questions he'd asked to be explored since 1967. If the investigations were done well, people on both sides of the Atlantic would finally have facts from which to move forward, and not be hobbled by unsubstantiated claims and rumors.

Indeed, suspicions about connivance between US intelligence agencies and right-wing dictators had been heightened by the September 21, 1976, car-bombing that killed Salvador Allende's exiled former foreign minister Orlando Letelier and his aide Ronni Moffitt on the streets of Washington. The assassination was carried out at the behest of Chilean dictator Augusto Pinochet.[10] Speculation that Kissinger and the CIA had advance knowledge of the plot made CIA awareness of Greek junta plots to kidnap Demetracopoulos seem less bizarre.[11]

■

THE NIGHT JIMMY Carter was elected, bells rang out at Greek-American churches because of a widespread belief that he and his administration, unlike those of Richard Nixon and Gerald Ford, would not favor Turkey in disputes with Greece. They would be disappointed.

It took Inouye more than four months to respond to McGovern's October letter.[12] Privately, Inouye noted problems with pursuing the investigation. When Elias heard of the foot-dragging, he provided a copy of McGovern's letter to Jack Anderson and Les Whitten. They wrote that McGovern's secret letter urging a probe of "unresolved questions" about CIA dirty tricks in support of the now-fallen Greek dictatorship suggested a "scenario of intrigue at the highest levels," and "could start more fireworks in the already volatile US-Greek-Turkish situation."[13] It could also prompt, they said, official interrogation of "such former Washington stalwarts" as Nixon, Agnew, Kissinger, Mitchell, Pappas, and CIA director William Colby.

Inouye, likely furious with Elias's leak, authorized Holum to tell the press that although all of the four areas defined by McGovern were "certainly worth an investigation," only the harassment of Demetracopoulos would be investigated because it involved "new allegations." Inouye, he said, would not take up the other three because they were "old cases that had already been gone over" and the committee lacked resources to delve into the past.[14]

At the time, Holum didn't know that Senator Goldwater had discouraged Inouye from continuing the larger investigation in much the same way Kissinger had derailed the Church inquiry. This time, instead of using national security as the excuse to stop digging, the rationale was personal. Tom Pappas had learned of the McGovern letter and was furious. Three of the areas of recommended inquiry directly involved him. Arguably, he was also indirectly involved in the Demetracopoulos harassment. He went to Goldwater and told him the investigations must be stopped immediately. As a decades-long major financial supporter of the Arizona senator, Pappas had leverage. On the scales of power, Goldwater's years of cordial relations with Elias did not count. Goldwater directed his chief of staff, Earl Eisenhower, the late President's nephew, to talk to Inouye.

Bending under Goldwater's entreaty, Inouye never released his committee's investigation of the CIA in Greece. However, on August 3, 1977, claiming a desire to "clear up this matter once and for all," he told McGovern he was pursuing leads related to intelligence-agency "discrediting" of Elias. From August to October 1977, Inouye and McGovern sporadically followed up, with Inouye dealing with the CIA and McGovern the State Department, to ascertain the roots of anti-Demetracopoulos attacks in 1971 and 1974.

The State Department reported that most of the questionable content on Elias "was taken from CIA and FBI reports which appear in our files."[15] The CIA and FBI instructed State not to forward the records. As the senators pushed for more information, the CIA resisted. A CIA spokesman told a reporter that the new Demetracopoulos-inspired congressional investigation "is causing us a lot of problems." Elias heard the same thing from his Capitol Hill sources. It appeared that the CIA, recovering from the past siege by congressional critics and emboldened by fresh support from the Carter Administration, was getting ready to strike back. Elias was still an attractive target.

Meanwhile, Elias's lawyers were aggressively pursuing his Freedom of Information Act (FOIA) requests at State, the CIA, the NSC, the FBI, the INS, and other divisions of the Defense, Justice, and State Departments.[16] It was frustrating and tedious work. Some of these requests had been pending since 1974 and 1975. Long delays, arbitrary bureaucratic decisions, and high fees undermined the law's idealistic goal of an informed citizenry. Elias's attorneys explained that the flood of requests following disclosures about domestic spying had overwhelmed FOIA staffs. Even when responses came, restrictive disclosure procedures, with broadly interpreted exemptions, meant that documents would likely arrive with much of the requested material redacted. Trying to extract information from the National Security Council was particularly exasperating. For years the NSC said it was exempt from disclosure requirements, that it had no records relating to Elias, or that the documents it had could be found elsewhere in the bowels of the federal bureaucracy. Kissinger claimed thousands of documents as his personal papers.[17] At Justice, Mitchell did the same. Throughout 1977, Elias's lead attorney, William Dobrovir, engaged in contentious exchanges with the CIA over the simple release of information and, when it was finally disclosed, the unavailability of documents without sweeping redactions. Demetracopoulos continued to press for records. For months his legal team went through the ritual of filing requests, getting denials, filing more appeals followed by more denials, or maybe a few documents with major redactions. After multiple letters, phone calls, and personal meetings, lawyers and officials tasked with responding to requests were on a first-name basis, but even that didn't speed up the process or shake loose more information. Statutory deadlines for responding to appeals were routinely missed, allegedly due to a substantial backlog and a shortage of attorneys.

Typical determinations made in response to requests for specific documents were: "denied in its entirety," "released with portions deleted," or unavailable because being "currently coordinated" within the agency or other agencies or the White House. Even with Dobrovir discounting his fees, Elias's legal costs steadily grew. He adjusted his living expenses to prioritize this pursuit.

Despite the obstructionism, dozens, then hundreds, and eventually considerably more than 1,000 pages of Demetracopoulos files (including duplicates), were released to him. Most had been stamped "SECRET" or "CONFIDENTIAL." Bit by bit he assembled the elements of the more-than-two-decade campaign to discredit and defame him as punishment for what American officials deemed his having "caused friction in Greek-American relations." Suspicious American intelligence agents had wasted countless hours and resources trying to identify the source of his allegedly nefarious funding.

The truth about Elias's finances was much simpler: hard work, a parsimonious lifestyle, and generous employers, family, and friends. From almost the beginning of his career, Elias worked at multiple publications, cobbling together a basic income. His wealthy maternal uncle, Costas Bokolas, had further helped him financially. After the 1957 death of Panagiota, his favorite sibling, Costas provided his nephew a variable allowance that enabled Elias to keep up appearances of living beyond the means of a lowly journalist.[18] For a brief while, in addition to his father's home, Elias also owned a house in Phaleron he inherited from his mother, which provided rental income.

Throughout his life, Elias was never acquisitive and never lived extravagantly. He was a renter, never owned a vehicle, and never took luxurious or extended vacations. He didn't even own a bathing suit. His living accommodations were modest, their furnishings shabby. When he dined out, he preferred simple fare to fancy meals. He didn't smoke, drink alcoholic beverages, gamble, or use illicit drugs. He kept a tight rein on his expenses, and when owed money, he usually insisted on being paid back in full. Unlike Tom Pappas, who used politics and his political connections as a means to amass his fortune, building personal wealth didn't matter to Elias. Money was never his yardstick. He wanted only enough to be a successful player in the worlds of politics and business.

He spent money on his personal appearance and was often described as the best-dressed person in whatever place he went. Ever eager to pick up the tab for meals or drinks with sources, he was usually the one who grabbed the check at dinners with friends. He wanted money to be able to bring beautiful flowers or houseplants to hostesses, surprise congressional secretaries with bottles of perfume, and provide lovely experiences for his lady friends. The generous expense account from *Makedonia* publisher Vellidis, provided in part because Elias gave him a steady stream of unpublished reliable under-the-radar news, helped him do this in Greece. A large expense account from Brimberg, even when his base salary was low, similarly helped him in America.

During the junta years, when his business income was curtailed and expenses for European travel, long-distance telephone calls, and photocopying were staggeringly high, Deena Clark and her husband occasionally gave him cash as a gift, which he treated as a loan and tried later to repay in full. Louise Gore kept his small apartment "rent-controlled" at about $300 per month and waived some of his Jockey Club tab.

■

DESPITE HIS GROWING portfolio of Wall Street consulting, Elias still identified as a journalist, and his primary reportorial project in the mid-1970s was aggressively investigating himself as he appeared in government files.[19] Nonetheless, he could not resist the call to break news that could have consequences. When, in July 1977, the Senate Foreign Relations Committee considered the new President's nomination of William Schaufele to be the ambassador to Greece, Elias was in the audience. Responding to a question about conflicting territorial claims over Aegean islands, Schaufele, an old Africa hand without Greece experience, thoughtlessly described the islands as "essentially [a] bilateral dispute between Greece and Turkey" caused by "unusual arrangements" that had resulted in Greece's owning territory close to the Turkish coast.[20]

To an American audience the language was anodyne, but Elias knew that describing Greek sovereignty over its islands as the product of "unusual arrangements" would be explosive. He contacted friends in the Athens press. Demonstrations in Athens and angry editorials provoked problems for the Karamanlis government. The State Department went into damage control, issuing a statement that described Greek ownership of the islands as "based on longstanding international agreements which the United States fully supports." However, when the State Department released the official transcript of the statement, Elias noted that those last six words had been deleted.

This, to Elias, was an even bigger story. It could mean that the United States had made the change to signal to Ankara that the Carter Administration would continue the Ford Administration's tilt toward Turkey on Cyprus and other matters. Sharing this analysis with American and Greek columnists resulted in more editorials and demands that Schaufele's nomination be withdrawn.[21] The appointment was postponed until September, then cancelled. The State Department blamed Elias. Elias countered that it was State's own obtuse handling of the episode that had created the problem. Demetracopoulos hadn't lost his touch for the controversial scoop.[22] But, again, there would be a heavy price.

Early in September, after the Schaufele dispute, David Binder of the *New York Times* called Elias for an interview. Demetracopoulos knew Binder from the early 1960s, when Binder had covered the Balkans and was assumed to have close CIA connections. The two journalists had never clicked. Binder had suggested to colleagues that Elias was a Communist, warned the Greek ambassador he was "dangerous," and told Demetracopoulos directly that in his life he'd known only two honest Greeks, and Elias wasn't one of them. Debating whether he should do the interview, attorney Dobrovir advised: "If you don't do it, they'll write the same negative story they were planning to all along and just add that you refused to comment."

Afraid that Binder might take liberties in quoting him, Elias took the precaution of taping the September 30 session. In his cramped apartment, he told his story, answering all of Binder's questions, first about Schaufele and then about his life story and the CIA's long history of discrediting him. He handed Binder news articles, hearing transcripts, and other documents to supplement the interview. Included in the packet was the 1975 CIA memorandum asserting that there were no "hard facts" showing he'd ever worked for any national government or foreign intelligence service. A couple of weeks after the interview, Elias sent the unedited, typed transcript of the interview to Binder along with additional documents.

Nothing appeared in mid-October. One month passed, then two, and no article. Puzzled by the delay, Elias thought at first that the paper might have been engaged in careful fact-checking. He remembered the *Times* editorial from December 30, 1970, praising his work against the military dictatorship and describing him as "a respected self-exiled Greek journalist."[23] He began to relax and think his suspicions about Binder and the CIA were unfair.

On December 2, 1977, responding to Demetracopoulos's frustration with months of Senate inaction, McGovern complained to Inouye that the information he'd received from State was "entirely unsatisfactory" in establishing how the anonymous 1971 memorandum concerning Demetracopoulos had been "devised and circulated" to congressional offices. McGovern said, publicly, that it was time to demand that State Department personnel be questioned "on the record."

Four days later—by coincidence?—the *Times*'s silence ended. On Monday evening, December 5, 1977, after getting a bulldog copy of the next day's edition, a friend telephoned Elias from New York and said excitedly, "Elias, my friend, there is grave news."[24] Swallowing hard, Elias said, "Read it."

Elias seethed quietly as he listened. Binder essentially called Demetraco-poulos's entire life a lie.[25] He dismissed Elias's journalistic career as "self-styled." Using what he claimed were CIA and State Department records, to some of which Elias had been denied access, Binder passed on prevarications and mali-cious gossip, challenging his wartime service and asserting he'd repeatedly tried to become an American intelligence agent. "CIA records," he wrote, "further allege that in the 1950s he was associated with both the Yugoslav and Israeli in-telligence services." Many of Binder's questions had related to Elias's role in the Schaufele episode, so Elias had asked him to check back if others contradicted his account of any matter. They did, and Binder didn't.

For Elias, the indication that a "secret hand" guided Binder's piece was the spelling of his name. Instead of spelling it the way he did, the way it appeared in Elias's publications, in the *Times*'s own pages, and even in State Department re-cords, Binder referred to him throughout as "Ilias P. Dimitracopoulos"—one of the spellings regularly used by the CIA.

What to do? Elias had always regarded the *New York Times* as one of the world's great newspapers, though he readily acknowledged that it was far from perfect. He'd heard many inside stories about the arrogance and petty behavior of some personnel. But he believed that the *Times*, if presented with documents that refuted what the CIA records allegedly revealed, would promptly print a correction. He did not anticipate that, in fighting back against the *Times*, he was taking on another institution as proud, secretive, and unyielding as the CIA.

Elias had met Executive Editor A. M. Rosenthal on several occasions and felt it unlikely the irascible newspaperman would be responsive to his demand for a correction or apology.[26] Managing Editor Seymour Topping, on the other hand, was someone he knew socially and had even escorted to a Brimberg din-ner. Topping, however, refused to speak to him. His secretary instructed Elias to call a deputy foreign editor, who in turn told him to call the Washington bureau. Finally, traveling farther and farther down the *Times* masthead, he was told to "write a letter to the editor and we will consider it."

Elias wrote a four-page letter, refuting the article's many gross inaccuracies. The *Times* published a heavily edited version of the letter, diminishing the arti-cle's falsehoods and misrepresentations.[27] Friends rallied around. With sardonic humor, Bob Novak told him that getting that kind of feature news story in the *Times* meant he had finally "arrived." But some of his employers fretted that the news was not good for business, and a few cancelled scheduled executive briefings to their clients. Others postponed his presentations on investor implications of foreign events. His income suffered.[28]

Outraged but unwilling to play the victim, Demetracopoulos instructed Dobrovir to submit new FOIA requests asking the CIA and FBI for "all documents referred to or reflected in" Binder's article. He also turned to his friends in Congress, urging that his mistreatment be made part of upcoming congressional hearings on CIA conduct. On December 14, 1977, McGovern wrote to Inouye, sharply criticizing the CIA's selective release to the American press of "demonstrably inaccurate" materials designed to discredit Demetracopoulos, made even worse because included were documents withheld from Elias's earlier FOIA requests.

The CIA told Dobrovir it could find no record of providing Binder any Demetracopoulos-related document or information "in writing or telephonically," but was silent as to whether there had been any "in person" contacts.[29] Evans and Novak attacked the CIA for "Harassing the Spy Who Never Was." They recounted their own experience of receiving defamatory information about Elias from the CIA, notably around the time of Elias's 1967 escape when a CIA officer had warned them "off the record" that Demetracopoulos had been a "double agent in Greece, for the Soviet KGB and Western intelligence services," charges refuted by the Agency's own files. They criticized the *Times*'s reporter for shoddy journalism, reporting that Binder "told us flatly that CIA officials supplied him with information years ago in Athens," and more recently was given new, unspecified information by CIA officials "past and present."[30]

In dueling letters-to-the-editor in the *Washington Post*, Binder denied he said he'd used any CIA information from his past in the Balkans. Incredibly, he wrote that he "didn't know anybody from the CIA when he was a correspondent and never received any information on Elias or anyone else." Evans and Novak responded, claiming that Binder was being untruthful.[31]

This exchange occurred against the backdrop of six congressional hearings between December 1977 and April 1978 on the relationship between the CIA and the news media. After the Senate Intelligence Committee backed away from the issue, the House Intelligence Committee took over. Committee chairman Congressman Edward Boland acknowledged the history of CIA contractual relationships, paid and unpaid, with individual journalists and news organizations, some American and others foreign. Describing Elias's world of the 1950s and '60s, in which some journalists routinely exchanged information and often faced enticements and other choices, Boland noted that, for different motives, some journalists "went further" than routine interactions: "They published stories both true and false for the CIA or they helped recruit agents. Sometimes the journalists weren't really journalists at all, but CIA agents under cover."[32]

Watergate veteran Carl Bernstein wrote a major piece in *Rolling Stone* that described how leading publishers and news executives had "allowed themselves and their organizations to become handmaidens to the intelligence services."[33] According to twenty-five years of available CIA records, more than 400 American journalists "secretly carried out assignments for the CIA." Some of the most prestigious and powerful organizations were involved, notably CBS; Time, Inc.; and the *New York Times*. As Elias could attest from painful personal experience, Allen Dulles was a good friend of *Time*'s Henry Luce. And he was not surprised to learn that *New York Times* columnist C. L. Sulzberger was deeply involved, and, according to several CIA officials, had at least once turned a background CIA briefing piece almost verbatim into a column.

Les Aspin, who had tried unsuccessfully to get the Pike Committee to deal with Elias's claims regarding Pappas, was now chairman of the Intelligence Subcommittee on Oversight and ran the hearings. On January 4, 1978, Morton Halperin, a national security expert and fierce critic of intelligence agency abuse of civil liberties, focused his testimony on two issues: the CIA's use of the news media to influence events in the US, and its background investigations of journalists without their permission. To illustrate his points, he used four "tip of the iceberg" examples: the CIA's efforts to (1) discredit studies critical of the Warren Commission Report, (2) present Salvador Allende as a threat to a free press in Chile, (3) exploit the murder of Richard Welch, its station chief in Greece, and (4) discredit Elias Demetracopoulos.[34]

The Demetracopoulos example, Aspin pointed out, involved current CIA leadership going after a lawful resident alien it didn't like. Halperin asked if this was "part of a deliberate CIA effort by the clandestine services to discredit a persistent critic." Deliberately providing information from an individual's files without that person's permission violated the CIA Charter, and may also have violated the Federal Privacy Act. The *New York Times*, rather than assigning its own reporter, as it had for other oversight hearings, used a UPI story in covering Halperin's testimony, edited to exclude any mention of Halperin's implication that the paper had been used as part of a CIA smear campaign.[35]

■

IN 1978 AND again in 1981, Congressman Aspin attempted to convince successive directors of the CIA to refute Binder's allegations—brandishing Greek Embassy–provided documents attesting to Elias's war record and awards—but to no avail.[36] Finally, on June 17, 1983, almost six years after the Binder interview, Georgia congressman Wyche Fowler, who had succeeded Aspin as subcommittee chairman, took a novel approach. He asked CIA head William Casey to read the *New York Times* article, then review the files in his possession dealing with Demetracopoulos, and write him "an unclassified letter that states flatly and clearly that, contrary to the *New York Times* article, the agency has concluded that there is no basis on which to impeach Mr. Demetracopoulos' honesty about his war record, or to suggest that he was a spy for the Israelis and or the Yugoslavs or anybody else."

Fowler's proposal made no demand on the CIA "to investigate its own people" or "the source of the information in the *New York Times* article," or "to address any issues of right or wrong." Rather, it simply asked the CIA to state: "that it could not have supplied the information because its files, taken as a whole, do not support the allegations in the article." Fowler then quoted from the 1975 CIA internal study sent to then-director Colby: that the Agency found "no hard facts" that Elias ever worked for any government against the interests of Greece or the United States or that he'd ever been in the pay of any national government or been a member of a foreign intelligence service or been involved in criminal activities. He continued:

> My impression is that nothing in the Agency's file on
> Mr. Demetracopoulos today would change that judgment . . . If you
> agree with the impressions I have formed as to the Demetracopoulos
> file, I would appreciate your confirming this fact.[37]

Acting CIA director John N. McMahon replied to Congressman Fowler on August 16, noting that nothing in CIA records dating from 1975 would require a revision of the CIA's 1975 conclusion.[38] This acknowledgment of Elias's integrity pulled the legs out from under the contentions made in the Binder article six years earlier. "The CIA's denial that it furnished any information to Mr. Binder casts serious doubt upon the credibility of his 1977 article," wrote Fowler to

Elias. "Hopefully the CIA's confirmation of the conclusion reached in the 1975 report to Director Colby will at last put this matter to rest."[39]

Pleased that he'd finally received corroboration from the CIA, Demetracopoulos returned to the *New York Times*. In early September, he hand-delivered to William Kovach, the *Times*'s Washington bureau chief, a photocopy of the recent CIA letter and memorandum, the Greek Embassy's report on his war record, and a stack of other supporting documents, including many given or offered to Binder in October 1977. Kovach, whom Elias trusted, appeared sympathetic and told him he would do something soon to respond to the new information.

Opening the *Times* on Sunday morning, September 25, 1983, Elias saw the listing: "CIA review backs Greek's denial of report on him, [page] 12." At last, he thought, there would be a full correction and perhaps even a *Times* apology. But there was no story on page 12. Thinking the printed index page reference wrong, he carefully searched through the entire paper. Still nothing. He telephoned Kovach and learned that executives in New York had killed his piece. On Thursday, September 29, an unbylined article in the *Times* began with a decidedly different tone:

A Greek journalist accused by American officials in 1977 of misrepresenting his war record and of working for foreign intelligence services, has made public a new Central Intelligence Agency review of his case that refutes the allegations against him.[40]

IT EXPLAINED THAT the dispute arose after the *Times* published an article using statements attributed to CIA officials. It then proceeded to repeat all the original smears, followed by the recent CIA statement that there were "no hard facts in the record" to support them.[41]

It was better than nothing, and the *Times* even spelled his name correctly, but it was still a backhanded retraction and a great disappointment.[42] Remaining unapologetic, *Times* assistant managing editor Craig Whitney said: "The source of the retraction is the CIA, not the *New York Times* . . . [The September 1983 story] is a routine article of little significance except to the man who claims his reputation has been harmed."[43] Others, however, celebrated Elias's vindication, including a major profile in the *Washington Post* that noted how for Demetracopoulos "there are no tasks. Only missions," and that it was "characteristic of

Demetracopoulos to wage a battle to clear his name long after most people have forgotten the incident."[44]

The following spring, Jack Anderson claimed to have assembled the missing pieces of the "jigsaw puzzle" explaining the motive behind the CIA's use of Binder to smear Elias. From sources other than Elias, Anderson said he had found evidence confirming that the CIA, fearful that Inouye's Senate Intelligence investigation would expose the 1968 CIA-KYP-Pappas-Nixon money scandal, arranged to blacken Demetracopoulos's reputation by leaking false information to Binder.[45]

.

ELIAS HAD ALSO received a qualified exoneration from the State Department. His congressional allies, particularly McGovern and Holum, had doggedly tried to identify those responsible for the malicious October 1971 blind memorandum used by the Nixon Administration to punish Elias for his report critical of Tom Pappas. They got no further than identifying the State Department personnel who drafted and circulated the original document. In 1981, after Speaker Albert's 1977 retirement, Joe Spear of Jack Anderson's office identified the instigator as Leonard Greenup, the retired Athens USIS official whom Elias had sharply criticized in 1960. Greenup had access to both Albert and officials at State's Greek Desk and apparently had never forgiven Elias for giving his USIS supervisors a bad performance review.

A year later, Senator McGovern's ceaseless efforts to get State to clear Elias's reputation, including threats to open a new congressional investigation, succeeded. Upon receiving a CIA request for updated biographic data on Elias P. Demetracopoulos, "AKA: Dimitrakopoulos," State's official reply of July 29, 1982, was simply a bold stamp of approval that read: "NO DEROGATORY INFORMATION."

When Elias got a copy of the document, he assumed they really meant no legitimate derogatory information, and immediately decided to test his new status by applying for a State Department press pass. The request didn't sit well with the head of State Department's security, Robert B. Bannerman, who prepared a memorandum for his legal department rehearsing the familiar State and CIA complaints about Demetracopoulos. Despite Bannerman's remonstrance, the legal department replied that "a careful review of the file reflects no disqualifying information which could serve as a basis for a successful denial of a press pass." State Security allowed the application "reluctantly."[46]

THE *WASHINGTON POST* profile had called the "vindication" after Demetracopoulos's six-year struggle "a fitting epilogue to the career of one of Washington's
more enigmatic figures."[47] But Elias was not ready to depart the stage. He'd won
against the State Department and CIA. But he had not yet won his battle with
the FBI.

Since 1975, Elias had been trying to access his complete FBI files, beginning
with the earliest reports of snooping in 1951, but kept running into slow responses and widespread denials. Some of the records eventually released on appeal included never-corroborated wild rumors and erroneous allegations that
were then shared with other US government agencies and departments. Elias
pressed on despite the loss of a 1978 federal civil suit against the Bureau and a
failed effort in early 1982 to gain access to withheld records by going though
Michigan Congressman John Conyers, a member of the Judiciary Committee
and the Freedom of Information Act oversight subcommittee.[48] In late 1982 he
persuaded Congressman Rosenthal to use his House Subcommittee on Commerce, Consumer, and Monetary Affairs to hold hearings and demand some unclassified answers as to when, how, and by what authority the FBI had gained
access to Demetracopoulos's financial records.[49]

The FBI admitted that it had also investigated a different Elias Demetracopoulos who did have Communist affiliations and that this report was erroneously included in the reports it passed on to other federal agencies. It also
acknowledged having shared his tax records and unlawfully accessed his bank
accounts. According to FBI director William Webster, Elias had been investigated during six periods: June 23, 1964, to November 23, 1964; December 8,
1964, to June 16, 1965; May 4, 1966, to July 15, 1966; November 9, 1967, to October 2, 1969; August 25, 1971, to March 14, 1973; and February 19, 1974, to
October 24, 1974.[50] Webster was silent on surveillance during the 1950s and the
years of the Kennedy Administration, save for admitting that Pierre Salinger had
made a "direct" White House demand for action in 1961. Also excluded were
unrecorded activities such as break-ins, apparently euphemistically disguised
(in its files) as "confidential informants." It was unclear how many of these
name-redacted informants in Elias's files reflected surreptitious entries to his
residence.

In October 1983, Elias's longtime ally Congressman Don Edwards intervened with Webster, asking him to have the FBI review its own files and provide

Elias "a statement such as the CIA gave him."[51] The FBI, however, was more ob-
durate than the CIA. On December 7, 1983, Webster replied that the Bureau
never provides subjects of their investigations statements regarding guilt or in-
nocence and to do so would establish a bad precedent.[52]

In his youth, Edwards had been an FBI agent in California, and he knew
well the Bureau's internal procedures, limitations, and flexibilities. After extensive discussions with Elias and his lawyer summarizing the record of bogus
claims, Edwards wrote to Webster, systematically detailing instances when the
FBI had conducted requested investigations of Elias "for the benefit of the CIA"
and the State Department. He then provided a history of FBI replies that it had
found "no information" to support any charges, and that in 1973, for the third
time since 1964, the FBI had concluded that their investigations should be
"closed for good." In conclusion, Edwards asked the Bureau to review his narra-
tive and the documents on which it was based, and "confirm to me, in writing,
that my description accurately reflects the contents of the FBI's files respecting
Mr. Demetracopoulos and its investigations on him."[53]

Webster did a full analysis of the statements contained in Edwards's letter
and amplified the record with nine pages of information reinforcing Edwards's
contention. He concluded: "I hope that the remarks set forth above and the attached analysis will assist you."[54] Edwards replied to "Judge Webster" on April 30:

> I believe that we can close this matter on the basis of the FBI's
> review of its own records which you attached to your letter—which
> plainly confirms the substance of my summary. Your summary of
> the FBI's file on Mr. Demetracopoulos shows that almost ten years
> of diligent investigation, conducted under the prodding of the
> CIA and State Department, resulted in a complete vindication of
> Mr. Demetracopoulos and the repeated conclusion that not a shred of
> evidence existed either of conduct even remotely approaching violation
> of any law, or supporting allegations of activities inimical to U.S.
> national security.

It was finally over. In his letter to Elias, Edwards called the FBI findings a
complete victory. Elias released documents to the press saying: "This vindicates
me from all the accusations thrown at me . . . I am happy that after all this effort
the truth comes out."[55]

The Associated Press announced: "FBI concedes ten-year probe found nothing on Greek journalist." Jack Anderson wrote that on the twelfth anniversary of Watergate, "the FBI has finally cleared the Greek journalist of spurious charges."[56] Elias thanked Edwards for championing his cause and praised the Freedom of Information Act.[57] After more than twenty years of harassment, loss of employment, and tens of thousands of dollars spent to clear his name, he had won. "This has been a life-and-death struggle for me," he told a reporter. "It's not only a question of my honour. It's a matter of not letting the sons of bitches destroy my professional career. They thought because I had a long Greek name that I wouldn't fight back, but I did."[58] Once more he remembered the pledge he had made to himself in Averof Prison in 1943. He thought his parents would be proud. *Philotimo*, his way.

■

ELIAS FOUGHT TENACIOUSLY but, afterward, with some notable exceptions, he tended not to nurture grudges. He lost track of Tom Pappas after the tycoon was fêted at the 1980 Republican National Convention in Detroit and paid little attention to stories during the 1980s reporting that Pappas was in retirement or unavailable to comment.

He knew nothing about Pappas's disruptive outburst on a flight from Palm Beach not long after the 1980 convention, and a diagnosis of rapid-onset Alzheimer's. Instead of living in comfortable retirement in Palm Beach, as the cover story had it, Pappas lived most of his remaining eight years alone in a Hellenic chronic-care nursing facility in suburban Canton, Massachusetts. His only regular visitor was Charles, the son Pappas had treated so shabbily. None of the big-name Republicans who benefitted from his fundraising attended his largely family funeral at the Greek Cathedral in Boston in 1988. A former Pappas employee claimed that the only politician he saw at the ceremony was John McCormack, but in 1988 McCormack had already been dead eight years. When Elias first heard of Pappas's death, his only comment was to say "Life goes on" and "I'm a survivor." Told the details of Pappas's last years, decades later, he commented that it was a sad story, but that he did not want to revisit those wars.

Elias had, however, no forgiveness for those who had directly destroyed Greek democracy, especially the ones connected with the torture of Spyros Moustaklis. He was also pleased to learn that disclosures concerning John Connally's dirty-tricks campaign against him in 1972 had helped prevent his becoming Gerald Ford's running mate in 1976 and hurt the Texan's presidential candidacy in 1980.[59] And he decried as "shameful" Hillary Clinton's public admiration of Henry Kissinger, whom he held responsible for exacerbating the Cyprus debacle and for sitting by when others talked about having Elias exterminated. Referring to the Watergate gang, he said: "Nixon resigned, Mitchell, Dean and others went to jail. Meanwhile, Kissinger makes millions of dollars at his consulting firm. He has never paid any price, financially, legally or morally."[60]

29.

Later Years

THE GORES SOLD THE FAIRFAX Hotel in late 1977, prompting Elias to move to a nearby apartment building the following year. He continued to use the Jockey Club for meetings. Sitting by himself, near the large windows in the high-ceilinged living room of his second-floor apartment on 21st Street, NW, surrounded by stacks of newspapers, government reports, books, photocopies, and notebooks, he would click on his small black boombox and play cassette tapes of *rembetiko*—urban Greek folk music, songs of love and joy and sorrow, plucked out on bouzoukis and guitars. Greek singers Fleuri Dandonaki, who had used her popularity as a platform for Greek democracy, and Nana Mouskouri remained his favorite performers.

The 1980s were relatively good years for Elias. After he was cleared from decades of charges that he was a nefarious agent of some evil power, his consulting business flourished. His base salary jumped to well over $100,000. "People who once shunned me called me for advice," he recalled. He was a regular at briefings for financial and insurance firm executives in New York, Boston, and Hartford. His specialty was providing insights and prognostications, drawn from his private network, on the potential impact of world political and economic events on markets and investment portfolios. In addition to Fidelity and The Hartford, Citibank became an important client. Two-term Federal Reserve chairman Arthur Burns was one of his better confidential resources.

Making good money, he tried paying back Deena Clark in full. He had earlier stopped resisting Louise Gore's desire to repaint and refurbish his Fairfax apartment, which also entailed a long-postponed rent increase. Elias also tried to reimburse Louise for his Jockey Club tab discounts, insisting he didn't want to owe anybody money.

Remembering his World War II days, when mistaken trust could lead to death, he continued to compartmentalize his life masterfully and remained strict about confidential information, taking to his death the identities of many sources. Even friends of long standing knew little about his past or his personal relationships. Those who claimed they did often didn't. Renowned Greek journalist Mario Modiano, who talked frequently with Elias for almost seventy years and treasured their closeness, said late in his life: "We operated in different worlds. I knew . . . not to probe" about his life or ask about his sources.

Cliff Hackett worked with Elias on Greek causes before Congress and interacted with him for over forty years yet knew little about his activities as a Wall Street consultant, his girlfriends other than Persa, or his Georgetown social life. From time to time, Elias would show Hackett articles describing his activities in these other worlds, but he seldom inquired about Hackett's professional life unrelated to Greece. Nevertheless, Demetracopoulos trusted Hackett, cherished their friendship, and with no family of his own, was nourished by his involvement with Hackett's family and the lives of his children. Theodore "Ted" Kariotis, one of Elias's dedicated college-student assistants during the junta years, was pigeonholed in that role for life, even after receiving his PhD in economics and becoming a popular college professor. Using the honorific "Mr. Kariotis," Elias would call him from time to time to run errands and drive him to the airport. Kariotis so admired and respected Elias that he rarely said no.

Descriptions of Elias's unremittingly intense and humorless persona befuddled those who experienced his playful and self-deprecating wit. Speaking for many from her community, a Georgetown admirer cooed: "Oh, Elias, nobody knows the real story about you. All we know is you're fun!" While many chronicled and critiqued his apparent lack of interest in anyone beside himself, others readily documented multiple instances of his empathy and solicitude. As Admiral Burke grew old and frail and was forgotten by many, Elias travelled frequently to his country home in Virginia to encourage and listen to his reminiscences. He was there to comfort Louise Gore after she lost her races for Maryland governor. And when sixty-four-year-old Deena Clark wanted him to accompany her as she fulfilled a childhood dream to swim the Dardanelles, he dropped everything to be with her.

"He chose carefully to whom he would reveal his soft side," recalled Jeanne Oates Angulo, who, aside from Persa, was perhaps his closest companion in Washington during the nearly two decades that followed the junta. "He showed only certain people his humanity, . . . and many more his harder side," she said. "He did that to protect himself. He had no fear, but he wanted others to fear him, and he didn't want his soft side to show."

The closest he had ever come to getting remarried was in the 1960s with Persa Metaxas, after her divorce. But issues at that time concerning her son prevented her from joining Elias abroad. Later, she would meet Elias in Europe, and she worked for long stretches in Washington to be close to him. They clearly loved each other, and shared activities as a couple, but he pushed her away. He explained he didn't want to be tied down. One wonders if a man who worked incessantly, slept only four hours a night, lived alone in a cramped apartment, and never learned to drive from fear that his constant thinking about other things would make him dangerous on a roadway, could ever be domesticated.

To the outside world, he presented the sartorial elegance, courtly manners, and studied charm of an Edwardian gentleman. He could cross effortlessly from the refined salons of the city's multi-generational first families who preferred to see their names in the social register, not the newspaper, to the festive dinners of the *arrivistes*, the self-promoting lobbyists and cabinet secretaries who established themselves in town with every new administration.

To Deborah Gore Dean, Louise Gore's niece who also lived at the Fairfax during the 1970s, Elias in his black tie and tux "looked like a movie star." To hostesses arranging dinner parties at a time when formal seating was required and ladies whose husbands were otherwise occupied needed table companions, urbane Elias was the "extra man" of choice. In its November 1976 issue, *Washington Dossier* voted him one of "Washington's Ten Perfect Gentlemen," citing his "masculine mystique" that went beyond "toothy smiles and wavy hair." The glossy magazine's profile praised him for his "dependability," adding: [M]en and women alike admire Elias's ability to keep a tightly buttoned lip . . . He carries more confidences than any other man in D.C."[1]

Paradoxically, Elias could often monopolize conversations talking about himself and world events and somehow leave his dinner companions feeling he cared about them too. The little boy from Dafnomili Street who took little girls seriously grew up to become what one woman described as "a man's man who really respected women." He was a strong supporter of women's rights and furious at any descriptions of workplace sexual abuse, and those who knew him well said he could never be mean to a woman. Relishing his bachelorhood, he genuinely loved women of all types, and was nourished by their attention.

Criticized by some men for being a "womanizer" and *un chaud lapin*, who jumped from bed to bed with amoral abandon and "tried every type of woman in the city," Elias was no Don Giovanni libertine, nor a social-climbing suitor. More Casanova than Don Juan, he lived by a personal code of conduct. Women came second to work, but, when he found time, he dated omnivorously. Most were unattached and unmarried. He was discreet, engaging in illicit sexual relations only with women who knew they stood to lose more than he if their secrets went public. Many past lovers would seek to stay friends. For decades, Greek and American intelligence agents tried to pressure women in his life, particularly former girlfriends, for adverse information, but none ever betrayed him.

For all Elias's dalliances, his deepest and most enduring relationships were with a handful of strong women who did not need Elias Demetracopoulos to feel complete, including Celia Was, Louise Gore, Deena Clark, and Persa Metaxas. Each played a different role in his life.

Jeanne Oates was another. Tall, radiantly beautiful, blond, and—quite unusual for Elias—sixteen years his junior, Jeanne Oates came into his life in 1975, after the fall of the junta. An independently successful Washington radio station general manager who was not engaged in the power-seeking political world, she was initially smitten with this refined and mysterious man. But, when she realized she was sharing him with others, she broke off the romance. He respected her decision, but the two decided they still greatly enjoyed each other's company, so they developed a different kind of loving relationship as dearest friends.

Over the years, he opened up with Jeanne in ways he did with few others in his life. They trusted each other and relaxed together, watching public-television programs, from the *McNeil-Lehrer Report* to *Great Performances* to the New Year's Day Vienna Philharmonic concerts. She would drive them to the country for visits with Arleigh Burke and others or to concerts and restaurants, sometimes taking along the widows of his deceased friends. Insisting on wearing a suit and tie on their weekend drives, he would sit back, look at the unfolding bucolic rolling hills, smile and, with classical music often playing on the radio, calmly hum. One of their special pleasures was driving peacefully around Washington's beautifully lit neoclassical monuments late at night, outings that reminded Elias of freedom, democracy, and home.

Jeanne had a demanding career and often went days without seeing him. She chauffeured him whenever she could—to Deena Clark's surprise birthday party at the Mexican Embassy, for example, picking him up later since she wasn't invited. They went together to socialize with Christopher Hitchens, Stanley Kutler, and General Bill Quinn and their wives. She even drove him to Connecticut to visit Celia's grave, where she saw him more emotional than ever before.

Jeanne knew he could be self-centered, demanding, agenda-driven, and taciturn, but she knew that, if she ever needed him, he'd be there for her completely. She believed his captivity during World War II had engendered a compassion for others hurt by the hard knocks of life. She told stories from his post-junta years that illustrated acts of unselfish kindness and pure *philotimo*. She was with him in the late 1980s after he received a diagnosis of slowly progressing Parkinson's disease and tenderly helped him navigate the life-limiting symptoms that followed.

■

SEVERAL WATERGATE-RELATED NARRATIVES published during the 1980s and '90s assembled the fragments of the 1968 and 1972 election histories—involving, in shifting combinations, Elias, Pappas, and the Nixon team—into a theory loosely called "the Greek Connection." In varying degrees, Elias was both an informed source and a center of attention for these stories.

In June 1982, as the tenth anniversary of Watergate approached, Jack Anderson employed the term "Greek Connection," to mean the Demetracopoulos-as-a-dangerous-Communist device used by Nixon aides to scare a majority of Patman's committee into voting against subpoenaing key Watergate participants, thereby abruptly stopping the first serious investigation.[2]

In his 1983 book *The Price of Power*, Seymour Hersh presented and confirmed the Demetracopoulos allegations about Tom Pappas serving as a financial conduit in 1968. Although Kissinger, appearing on Ted Koppel's *Nightline*, called Hersh's description of his role in halting the 1968 investigation "a slimy lie," Jack Anderson called Hersh's revelations about the Pappas scheme the "smoking gun in the Greek connection."[3]

Christopher Hitchens found in the Hersh book a convincing explanation of the Watergate break-in. In 1986, Hitchens published a major essay in *The Nation* titled "Watergate: The Greek Connection," in which he highlighted blocked efforts to mount congressional investigations of Pappas's activities.[4]

Stanley Kutler's 1990 book *The Wars of Watergate* brought the Greek Connection theory front and center. He tracked down players in the Patman story and received independent confirmation of Pappas's 1968 illegal transfer of Greek money to Nixon. Former CIA director Richard Helms told a London friend that Kutler's was "by far the best book" on the topic.[5]

At gatherings marking the fortieth and following anniversaries of Watergate, and in other events, scholars, journalists, and Watergate aficionados have not agreed on exactly what the burglars were looking for.[6] Collecting intelligence on whatever "shit file" O'Brien had on Pappas's role in the 1968 Nixon campaign was surely not the sole motive for the 1972 break-in, but the Greek Connection endures as at least a plausible partial explanation.[7] Certainly, the anxiety that Elias caused people in the Nixon White House was real and had important consequences.

·

THE FALL OF the Berlin Wall and its aftermath in the 1990s had ripple effects as Greece, the United States, and much of the world focused more on domestic concerns. It was also a transitional period for Elias. He missed the adrenaline rush of getting news before it broke and influencing history. He was no longer a ubiquitous presence on Capitol Hill. Eventually, many of his best contacts moved on to other jobs, retired, or died.

After Bob Brimberg's fatal heart attack in 1993, disagreements with the firm's successors led to the end of that association. For a while, Elias kept up his Wall Street consulting work for other companies and made trips abroad on their behalf. But his business clients were changing their strategic focus from fundamental research to more quantitative approaches. In 1995, Citibank Global Asset Management ended their long relationship with Elias in an effusive letter praising his "exceptionally perceptive analyses" of the complex interaction of economic and political dynamics during the Cold War and post-Communism eras.[8]

Elias would continue to monitor international political and economic news, but only as an interested observer. He still read the *New York Times* and the *Washington Post* daily, and supplemented them with Greek newspapers and television newscasts. He never learned to use a computer, so he was unable to research topics of interest on the Internet or exchange emails. Always the old "scooper," he would feed his insights, tips, and outrages via telephone to friendly journalists, editors, and historians on both sides of the Atlantic.

He continued to attend Washington dinner parties and receptions, but more as another guest, not a man with a special agenda. While he was still often tapped as the desirable extra man, he was increasingly seen attending events with boon companions like Louise Gore, Deena Clark, and Jeanne Oates. He found great pleasure spending quiet time with close friends, and talked nearly daily with Persa, who, after 1988, largely stayed in Athens.

Instead of reinventing himself, retooling his skills and engaging with new players and their issues, Elias turned inward and looked back. He focused on burnishing his legacy, intent, as always, on setting the record straight. He tried to get federal agencies and authors to correct their erroneous or incomplete accounts and identify him properly. He was particularly incensed when the State Department's long-delayed official history of the controversial junta period in Greece (*Foreign Relations of the United States, 1969–1976, Vol. XXX, Greece, Cyprus, Turkey, 1973–1976*) misidentified a key reference to him as "Androutsopoulos."[9]

Similarly, although Demetracopoulos liked Tim Weiner's 2007 history of the CIA, *Legacy of Ashes*, he took sharp exception to the author's attributing the disclosure of Pappas's 1968 delivery of Nixon cash not to Elias but to a House speech by Congressman Don Edwards.[10] The June 17, 1993 speech, "Watergate and the Greek Connection," made on the twenty-first anniversary of the break-in, was a tribute to Demetracopoulos and directly credits Elias with being the one providing "proof" of the 1968 illegal money transfer.[11]

■

AS HE ENTERED his final years, Demetracopoulos repurposed the hundreds of once-secret government files he'd painstakingly uncovered. In the past, he had sometimes quietly assisted friends like Christopher Hitchens and *Washington Post* reporter Larry Stern as they wrote their Cyprus books, respectively *Hostage to History* and *The Wrong Horse*. Now Elias made it widely known that he was available as an informed source. He distributed a three-page list of topics and people he'd be glad to talk about. Describing himself as one who "speaks with documents," Elias prepared packets of articles featuring himself and his exploits. Being named as a source in nearly three dozen books pleased him immensely.

From time to time, Demetracopoulos wrote articles that usually concerned great moments in his life. In the *Washington Post*, for example, he challenged Newt Gingrich's assertion that Bill Clinton's taking Chinese money was the first case of foreign money in American politics.[12]

His critics found Elias's self-promotion excessive. Others saw it as a needed cathartic release after dealing with a lifetime of false rumors and malicious disinformation. Several psychiatrists and psychotherapists observed that Elias's compulsive compartmentalization and somewhat narcissistic behavior was consistent with that of Holocaust survivors and other abuse victims, suggesting that these tendencies might have been rooted in his World War II experiences, adaptive behavior that contributed to his survival.[13]

Elias made no apologies for his behavior. When asked years later what he thought was the most overrated virtue, he replied without hesitation: "Modesty." He shrugged off criticism, insisting flamboyance is proper if you have underlying substance. He felt he lived up to what he said about himself. He was also stubbornly reluctant to admit mistakes beyond the hackneyed observation that "everyone makes mistakes." Pushed to admit to some error of judgment, Elias mentioned only one.

In 1978, *Washington Post* national editor Larry Stern told Elias he wanted to write a feature on Demetracopoulos's CIA-driven troubles with *Time*, the *Herald Tribune*, the *Washington Star*, and the *Washington Post*, believing that it was a compelling tale of a compromised free press. He said editor Ben Bradlee, whom Elias had first met in Paris in the 1950s, agreed. When he was finished, Stern called Elias to ask him where in the paper he'd like the article featured but added that Bradlee didn't believe the *Post*'s part of the story was strong enough to be included.

Elias replied: "Larry, we agreed to do the story including the *Post*. Now . . . you've taken away the *Post*. I thought we had an understanding . . ." He told Stern to "Forget the whole thing. Kill it. Don't run it."

"That was my biggest mistake," Elias recalled in 2010, "because what I should have done was to have the *Post* publish the article without mentioning itself and then call *the New York Times* a month later with the story the *Washington Post* left out. I've made other mistakes, . . . but this mistake goes to the heart of the newspaper business." The "scooper" was angry at himself for having reacted personally, not strategically.

Demetracopoulos treasured two letters. In 1993, former CIA and FBI director William Webster, who had confirmed reports of extensive agency surveillance and helped clear his name, wrote a "Dear Elias" letter reflecting on
Demetracopoulos's "long travail": "As I am sometimes given to saying, good
things are worth waiting for . . . I enjoyed our visit . . . I hope to see you again
soon . . . Bill." Three years later, during the election-year debate over the Clinton
scandals, former Wisconsin congressman Henry Reuss, retired chairman of the
House Banking Committee, wrote to tell him he thought the transfer of Greek
money in 1968 was of "more transcendent importance than Whitewater," the
Arkansas land deal that led to Clinton's impeachment. Reviewing Elias's leadership during the seven-year struggle against the junta, Reuss concluded, "Pericles
would have approved of you."[14]

Elias stayed in touch with his friends in Europe and the United States by
telephone and letters. Especially with Mario Modiano and childhood friend Antonis Drossopoulos, he dissected the never-ending crises of their homeland.
Elias viewed events in Greece with a blend of anger and sadness. "So many years
of missed opportunities to make reforms that could make life better for people,"
he reflected, "broken promises, wasted sacrifices, and lessons never learned."

From time to time he'd visit Greece, but he was put off by Athens's pollution
and pugnacious drivers who would drive and park anywhere—which he saw as a
metaphor for increased incivility in Greek political discourse. To a *Washington
Post* reporter who asked why he stayed in D.C. long after the junta was overthrown and his citizenship restored, Elias replied that he had no family or job in
Athens and because "Washington is a fascinating city."[15]

Some who had worked with him in Greece and the United States were upset
with him for not staying more involved, not continuing to be a forceful public
voice for reform. Elias's response was that he had done his part and it was time for
others to do theirs. He also sensed that there was a new generation of leaders who
didn't care what he might have to offer. Other friends wondered whether his deteriorating health had become a limiting factor.

■

MANY OF DEMETRACOPOULOS'S later years were lonely. More and more empty
dates appeared on his once-overflowing calendar. He comforted close friends
like Deena Clark and Louise Gore during their last illnesses and grieved
their deaths in 2003 and 2005. Others drifted or moved away. Jeanne Oates

got married, became Jeanne Oates Angulo, and later retired to Texas. Elias recalled the quotation attributed to Harry Truman: "If you want a friend in Washington, get a dog." But he also remembered his father's teaching him Aristotle's three kinds of friendship: utilitarian, pleasurable, and that based on long-lasting goodness. "Poor Elias," commented Stanley Kutler, "he really believes in serious friendship."[16]

He acknowledged wistful moments when he thought it would be nice to have the companionship of a wife or the personal attention of a child, but quickly and unsentimentally concluded he had made the correct decision. "If I had a family, I never could have done the things I did. It would have been a dangerous distraction. I always would have been afraid of the impact on their lives. I would never have wanted to risk their safety and peace of mind, the way I did in marrying Celia. And now I pay the price, but so be it."

Asked to reflect on mortality and on Nikos Kazantzakis's famous epitaph "I hope for nothing, I'm scared of nothing, I'm free," Elias insisted there was more to do, lots to fear, and that it was still too soon to consider any freedom that could come from death. One persistent fear was being forgotten.

In October 2007, after lunch with a Greek friend at the restaurant that had replaced the Jockey Club, the nearly seventy-nine-year-old Elias, too proud to use a cane or hold onto the rail as his Parkinson's disease became progressively worse, took a fall on the steps outside. He fractured his collarbone and hip, and never fully recovered. Jeanne Oates Angulo returned from Texas to arrange for his health care and new living arrangements.

After surgery and a long rehabilitation, the world of the once-intrepid journalist shrank to a modest two-room residence at the Georgetown Senior Living facility on Q Street. Slowly his new place took on the cluttered atmosphere of the old apartment only blocks away. Notwithstanding the negative prognosis and persistent pain he tried to hide, he slowly drained his resources, continuing to pay full rent on his document-filled apartment, in the hope that one day he would be well enough to return there.

▪

ON JUNE 19, 2007, the Botsis Foundation for the Promotion of Journalism gave him an award in Athens, described by some Greek journalists as a prestigious "lifetime achievement" prize. Elias could not attend the ceremony, but Persa Metaxas and Christina Moustaklis attended on his behalf.[17] Several months later, Greek president Karolos Papoulias announced he would decorate Elias as a Commander of the Order of the Phoenix, for "outstanding services rendered to Greece in his capacity as journalist" and his "history of opposing Greece's military dictatorship."[18] Nearly a decade before, when US ambassador Nicholas Burns and President Bill Clinton had offered apologies to the Greek people for American behavior during the junta years, Demetracopoulos regarded their words as important milestones, but largely anticlimactic.[19] By contrast, this Greek recognition—from a government that had hounded him into exile and taken away his citizenship—was deeply personal. Of all the official recognitions he ever received, this one meant the most.

On the evening of Monday, January 7, 2008, the Greek Embassy on Massachusetts Avenue was aglitter for a well-attended reception in recognition of this new honor. The crowd represented a cross-section of his life. Columnist Bob Novak came, along with Sy Hersh, other journalists, former congressional staffers, diplomats, Georgetown society ladies, and historians such as Robert Dallek. Senator George McGovern flew in from South Dakota and Jeanne Oates Angulo, with her husband, from Texas. Even former CIA and FBI director William Webster came to congratulate him. Ambassador Alexandros Mallias described Elias's successful career as journalist and "his constant fight to preserve democracy."[20] Christopher Hitchens followed, extolling Demetracopoulos's courage in the face of abuses of power and his relentless and selfless commitment to great causes.

Then Elias slowly rose, still in pain from his accident, expressed his thanks, and urged that the award be seen as recognition as well for the many others who had struggled and suffered during the junta years. He paid particular honor to "the two American leaders, Congressman Ben Rosenthal and Senator Bill Fulbright, [who] could not survive to see their resistance to the junta recognized." He continued:

> I see this award, therefore, as recognition that many people contributed to a victory over brutality and subversion of democracy in its historic homeland. Many young people of Greece who demonstrated at personal peril and often harsh treatment and the military officers like Colonel Spyros Moustaklis who were tortured for their resistance must never be forgotten. A few of my fellow journalists also suffered from their attempts to preserve and present the truth in those dark days.

THE *VOICE OF AMERICA*, with which he had sparred in the past, broadcast a glowing report of the ceremony, and the *Greek Herald*, bastion of a Greek-American community that often criticized Demetracopoulos, described the award and the list of notables "who spoke about Mr. Demetracopoulos' great contributions to democracy."[21]

∎

FROM AFAR, DEMETRACOPOULOS commented on his growing concerns about deteriorating conditions in his homeland. For years he had told American friends that the European Union was not treating Greece fairly. At the same time, he warned Greek friends about the lack of responsible leadership and their unsustainable political system. His homeland had been deceitful in its public accounting. He said that cooking the books, effectively lying to the EU about the scope of Greek borrowing and the size of its national deficit and debt, would have severe consequences. Of course, heavily export-dependent Germany was complicit in lending credit. He blamed both major Greek parties for padding public payrolls and agreed with those who railed against the cronyism of a political system dependent on *rousfeti* (expensive political favors), *fakelaki* ("little envelopes"), and *grigorossimo* (bribe-induced stamps of approval).[22] He also criticized those who avoided paying taxes and hid their money abroad. Political and business leaders who committed crimes should be brought to trial, he said, and, if found guilty, jailed. He was particularly troubled by the rise of the far-right Golden Dawn party, a disturbing manifestation of a larger authoritarian trend in Europe that he feared would grow.

In this troubled 2010 atmosphere, directors Robert Manthoulis and Angelos Kovotsos produced a documentary about Elias Demetracopoulos, portraying his "spiritual audacity" as an inspiration for their countrymen. Their film, *It's Time for Heroes*, sought to connect Demetracopoulos's own struggle for justice with Greece's current situation and was enthusiastically received at the 2014 Thessaloniki Documentary Festival.[23]

On his eighty-fifth birthday in December 2013, friends in Washington gathered at his senior-living place to celebrate. The eclectic group included Louise Gore's niece Deborah Gore Dean, Sy Hersh, Cliff Hackett, and Dick Westebbe. Messages of congratulations were sent from Greece, Ireland, and across the United States.[24] The guests were informally attired for the noontime Sunday gathering, but Elias came dressed in a dark navy suit, a white shirt, a red-and-blue-striped tie, and freshly shined shoes. The meal featured his childhood favorites: spaghetti and meatballs, followed by chocolate cake and chocolate ice cream.

■

PARKINSON'S DISEASE CONTINUED to limit his speech and dexterity. His mind was still sharp, but he had difficulty articulating his thoughts. He comprehended more than he could communicate. During 2014 he had expressed increasing concern that he was being victimized by unspecified persons. Some of his caregivers downplayed his worries as signs of his disease, but his anxiety was justified.

Reluctantly relaxing his intense concern for privacy, he gave Cliff Hackett power of attorney for banking matters. Hackett discovered money missing from Elias's Capital One bank account. Although Elias seldom left his room, ATM withdrawals had been made in Rockville, Maryland, over fifteen miles away, and elsewhere almost $20,000 had been stolen from his accounts.

The episode reminded Elias of the Watergate era behavior of Riggs Bank, which had allowed the FBI to rummage around his accounts to serve Nixon's interests and then denied for years it had done so. In a scene reminiscent of earlier battles, Hackett, as Elias's representative, turned to the D.C. police fraud squad for help, and one bank employee eventually went to jail. Capital One never fully apologized, and never provided a full accounting of what had happened. Ever the "scooper," Elias wanted someone to expose how the bank had let it happen and was pleased to learn that *Washington Post* editor Marty Baron considered his case possible "material for a broader story on weak security at banks."[25]

The Capital One experience may have sapped much of Elias's remaining energy. He was deemed a candidate for hospice care. In early Spring 2015, his Georgetown facility announced it was closing for renovations. All its residents would have to leave before May for at least eighteen months. Relocating a hospice patient would be problematic, and Elias and Cliff Hackett considered other options. Returning to Athens was appealing, even if Greece was in the middle of its bad-debt crisis. Remembering his father's return from the diaspora to fight in World War I, Elias liked the image of standing with Greece in its time of trouble. But Lufthansa made it difficult, imposing last-minute boarding restrictions that forced him to change airlines and delay his departure. For several days, he was the only resident left in the place, as it was readied for a major demolition. One of his last visitors was Barbara LaRosa, the niece of Elias's late wife Celia, who still cherished her childhood memories of the once-happy couple. [26]

The various compartments of Elias's life could be seen in the trio of desig-nated legal decision-makers needed for his health-care and travel arrangements. Cliff Hackett, in Washington, handled the complicated departure; Jeanne Oates Angulo, in Houston, controlled his heath-care proxy, and Persa Metaxas, in Ath-ens—his executrix and sole beneficiary—held his living will.

Accompanied by a nurse, Elias landed in Athens on May 4, 2015, and was driven about five miles to Paiania, east of Mt. Hymettus. Skepi Pronoias, a fifty-year-old elder-care facility, became his new home. [27] His spare, single room on the ground floor had a balcony overlooking a large garden. For several months, Elias rallied in his new environment, more animated and talkative than he had been in Washington. But he never ventured outside his room, and his television remained unwatched.

His most frequent visitors were Persa's son, Stefan Manuelides, and Kostas Loukopoulos, a former *Ethnos* reporter. Stefan, who had roomed at Amherst College with future prime ministers George Papandreou (Andreas's son) and Antonis Samaras, had known Elias all his life and took charge of his final finan-cial and administrative arrangements. Loukopoulos focused on responding to the dying man's emotional needs. He had interviewed Elias by telephone years before, admired his forceful efforts to bring down the dictatorship, and had writ-ten about him, but he had never met him until now. Their connection was per-sonal. Kostas's idealistic father, crippled at birth, had been exiled and imprisoned during the civil war largely because of a relative's political notoriety, and was tortured and exiled again at the hands of the colonels.

Others visited, but Persa did not. She had not been well, and even short travel was difficult. His dearest friend of longest standing was also embarrassed for him to see her as she had aged. And she was fearful of replacing her own mem-ory of a robust and articulate Elias with the frail, bedridden reality.

Elias died peacefully on Tuesday, February 16, 2016. His last words, the night before to Stefan, were the standard ones he gave to all inquiries about his health: "I'm surviving."

His funeral was held Friday in St. Denis Church in Kolonaki, where Elias had attended high school classes in 1941 after the occupying Germans took over the Peiramatikon building for administrative offices. The wooden coffin was closed for the service. A white cloth and large bouquet of white flowers were placed on top, with a white sash inscribed: "Have a nice trip, *Giakoulele*, Persa"—

using her affectionate nickname for him. Smaller bouquets from others were placed nearby.

Fewer than two dozen mourners came to the service in this capacious and celebrated church, each representing a different facet of Elias's life. The group included Kostas Loukopoulos, the first to arrive; Persa, her brother, and her son Stefan; Christina Moustaklis and her daughter Natalie; politicians from both New Democracy and PASOK; Peiramatikon classmate Antonis Drossopoulos, documentarian Angelos Kovotsos, journalists, and some other old friends. Elias wasn't a regular churchgoer and the officiating clergy never knew him, but the nearly hour-long service was beautiful. One mourner described as especially soulful the head priest's chanting the melodic Byzantine hymns of the Idiomela, during which he censed the deceased and the faithful.

Elias's cousin Dimitrios Tsalapatis, an elected board member of the journalists' union, gave a prepared speech highlighting the most important events in Elias's career. Then, Apostolos Kaklamanis, the longest-serving president of the Greek parliament in modern times, made some impromptu remarks.[28] After praising Elias's battle for democracy and against the junta, he urged the journalists and others present to stand up and fight for Greece in the best Demetracopoulos tradition. His voice trembling with emotion, he criticized Greek journalists for being manipulated by political and business interests. Elias's life should be an inspiration not only for young journalists who never knew him, he concluded, but for citizens everywhere.

It is not clear to what extent the priests knew that Elias's last will, prepared years before in the United States, stated that he wanted to be cremated. Cremation had not been legal in Greece until 2006 due to church opposition. Even in early 2016, there were no functional crematoria.[29] Nevertheless, at the conclusion of the service, the head priest accompanied Elias's body to a waiting vehicle and offered blessings until the black hearse carrying the coffin pulled away. The cremation took place in Sofia, Bulgaria. Elias's cremains were delivered to the Athens funeral home early the next week.

Elias's last will was clear on cremation but not in directions to Persa for final distribution. Several years before, Elias had smiled at the suggestion that his ashes be buried on the Acropolis, near where his father brought him as a young boy. But Greek authorities prohibited that. The solution was the Pnyka, an uninhabited hill less than a kilometer southwest of the Acropolis, revered as the official meeting place of the people in the earliest days of Greek democracy. What could be more fitting?

On Friday, February 26, Persa, Stefan, Christina Moustaklis and Kostas Loukopoulos gathered near the St. Dimitrios Loumpardiaris church. Gently cradling the five-pound ivory-colored clay urn with a simple beige cross on its side, they chose a grove of pine trees partway up the rocky path, toward the *bema*, the large flat stone that served as a speaker's platform where Pericles, Aristides, Alcibiades, Demosthenes, and ordinary citizens had debated matters of public policy. This Pnyx, site of the ancient *ekklisia*, was the wellspring of democracy. They picked out a tree that would not require ninety-year-old Persa to walk too far and tenderly spread the cremains around it. Kostas whispered to himself: "Goodbye, Elias."

Above the treeline, spectators could appreciate a spectacular panorama set against a bright cerulean sky with light puffy clouds and a gentle breeze. All Athens spread out below, the Parthenon close ahead and, towering in the distance, Mt. Lycabettos, next to where Elias had grown up. After the shared customary blessing of "May his memory be eternal," Kostas looked up the hill toward the Pnyx and remembered the challenge of Kaklamanis from the funeral the week before, to Greeks, and especially Greek journalists, to live up to Elias's model of fierce independence, audacity, integrity, civic responsibility, and commitment to democratic values. That, he thought, would be the most fitting legacy of all.

The four concluded their ceremony at a nearby restaurant with the traditional simple post-burial meal of broiled fish, salad, and coffee. Christina brought some fine French brandy for a toast. They finished with Elias's favorite dark chocolate and Persa's empathetic benediction: "Elias is with St. Peter now, and for sure he's already giving the poor saint and heaven a hard time. Poor St. Peter, he obviously won't know what to do with him."

AUTHOR'S NOTE

Transliterating Greek names of persons and geographic places into English is made difficult by different conventions used. There are historical academic renderings of ancient Greek. There are phonetical transliterations that seek to approximate the sound of words in modern Greek. And there are official standards, such as the 1987 approved UN/ELOT system, which established rules for reproducing specific letters. There is also an informal approach used by individuals, spelling their family names distinctively for generations and often using their English first-name equivalents (e.g., John for Ioannis). In CIA files, Elias Demetracopoulos's name is cross-indexed with at least ten different "aliases."

This book largely concerns a period before the ELOT system standardized modern Greek transliterations, so, for example, if Antonios Ambatielos were to apply for a passport today, his surname would be spelled "Ampatielos," using the "mp" letters as they are spelled in Greek, not as they are heard. The same adjustment would be made for Melina Mercouri and Elias Demetracopoulos regarding the "c" and "k" changes in their names. I have made the UN/ELOT adjustment for less-common names and places, but it looks strange on the page for American readers to deal with odd English spellings such as Kretans from Kriti, Periklis not Pericles, and Thoukididis not Thucydides. Accordingly, I have used a combination of approaches, adhering to classical spellings of well-established names such as Crete and Pericles, but using the modern ELOT system for others. In cases where well-known individuals consistently used a particular spelling during their lifetime, such as King Constantine II (not Konstantinos), I have followed their approach.

From 2010 to 2015, I talked with Elias frequently, in face-to-face interviews and in sometimes-daily telephone calls, during which he would reconstruct events and read and orally annotate documents and private papers. At different times he would repeat himself, with slight differences in language used. I have not listed the specific dates of each of my conversations with him, but he is a source throughout. Whether drawn from government documents, broadcast transcripts, or interviews, all conversations quoted were recounted by one or more of the participants or observers.

In researching Elias's US government files, I first used the more than 1,000 pages of personal records accessed by his attorney, William Dobrovir, from 1975 to 1986, most containing extensive redactions. In Elias's private papers I found some files, notably from the FBI, that came unredacted, which presumably he received from Senator Vance Hartke during the 1969 Private Bill effort to adjust his immigration status. In 2009, Elias gave me full rights to stand in his place to access all available records concerning him and waive any privacy rights he would have to prevent disclosure. My Freedom of Information Act (FOIA) requests and mandatory appeals to denials yielded similar material, often still with extensive redactions. Some files continue to be withheld in their entirety; others have been destroyed or are missing. Many documents, especially concerning CIA, FBI, and the State Department Security Office information, omit the names of sender and/or recipient and do not indicate the originating or recipient agency or the date. I have not distinguished from which FOIA request tranche a document came. Similarly, I have not created a standard format for referencing documents that come from formal compendiums such as the Foreign Relations of the United States (FRUS) series, miscellaneous documents identified in on-line Declassified Central Intelligence Records (CREST), National Archives Research Administration (NARA) searches, presidential library requests, the irregular identifications of government documents obtained through FOIA submissions and appeals, or the unorganized serendipity of EPD's private papers. This accounts for some of the unevenness in identifying source materials.

For Celia Was's records I used both Dobrovir's 1970s material and my 2010+ inquiries. For Tom Pappas, I made 2009+ requests and appeals, getting most from his files in presidential library archives, a lesser number from State Department and FBI records, and slight responses from the CIA. A majority of the Demetracopoulos information was originally deemed "Classified" or "Secret." In the endnote listings I have not identified all that were so denominated or characterized the extensiveness of redactions.

ACKNOWLEDGMENTS

It would take another manuscript to properly thank all who have helped me prepare this book over its long gestation, which in some ways began with the insights provided me by Louis Georgantas, Alec Tsoucatos, Catherine Fisk, and their families and friends, during my time in Athens over the chaotic summer of 1966.

As I've described in the Introduction, Elias Demetracopoulos was a difficult and enigmatic subject who opened up over years with great reluctance. In the end, even though he knew this would not be an authorized biography, his generous cooperation made this book possible.

Dennis Johnson and Valerie Merians, Melville House's proudly independent publishers, enthusiastically embraced a book proposal concerning Elias that would deal with a largely unknown source of the Watergate scandal. Kelly Burdick, my first editor, advised me to revisit Athens to explore Demetracopoulos and his world before his anti-junta leadership years in Washington. On my return, he urged me to expand the biography. Mark Krotov, Kelly's successor, praised early drafts while encouraging me to write an even bigger book, including more US-Greek history during the Cold War. When the manuscript became too large, Paul De Angelis skillfully guided my restructuring and revisions. Ryan Harrington knowledgably captained the voyage during its final years and brought the book home.

Three people were preeminent. They embraced the project from its infancy, energized me when my spirit flagged, and repeatedly discussed the work in progress and reviewed entire, often unwieldy, iterations, always enhancing the work by their incisive criticism and wise recommendations. Cliff Hackett, Jean Monnet biographer, former foreign-service officer, House and Senate consultant and Elias's closest male friend in Washington, never failed to respond to my repeated requests for help. My wife, Margie Arons-Barron, journalist and former editorial director to whom this book is lovingly dedicated, put much of our family life on hold for years, patiently listened to my Elias monologues, and unstintingly gave me the benefit of her professional expertise. Athens-based journalist Kostas Loukopoulos started as an interviewee and became a trusted friend. The book would not be what it is today if it weren't for his long years of great assistance, fact-checking, conducting supplementary Greek language research and interviews, translating documents, and deciphering nearly illegible handwritten Greek personal correspondence. His unselfish support rose from pure *philotimo* and respect for Elias's fight against the junta and for Greek democracy.

In nearly ten years of researching and writing, I benefitted greatly from the work and encouragement of others. Historians, journalists, former diplomats, and chroniclers of that period provided my grounding, and some generously opened their files, exchanged emails and phone calls, and suggested others to contact. Many shared their reminiscences generously; others with tactful restraint or reluctance. A partial list of those who provided valuable research and writing assistance includes: George Anastasopoulos, Jeanne Oates Angulo, Pavlos Apostolidis, Susan Margolis Winter Balk, David Barrett, Fred Barron, George Behrakis, Frank Bellotti, Richard Ben-Veniste, Costas Betinakis, Michael Binstein, Jack Boos,

Evagelia Bournova, Thomas Boyatt, Jim Boyd, David Broder, Carl Brown, John Capsis, Ronnie Caragianis, Elliot Cattarulla, Gia Cincone, Charles Claffey, Chuck Clayman, Julia Clones, Robert Dallek, Stavros Dimas, Athanassios Douzenis, Spyros ("Stan") Draenos, Antonios Drossopoulos, Michael Dukakis, George Enislides, Leslie Epstein, Nouvelot Eudes, Stathis Eustathiadis, Mark Feldstein, Merle Fisk, Barney Frank, Arvonne Fraser, Don Fraser, Michal Freedhoff, Rebecca Gabbai, Pitsa Galatsi, Morgan Gale, John Gamel, Maria Gentekou, Jack Germond, Evelyn Godwin, Av Goldberg, Michael Goldman, Dick Goodwin, Doris Kearns Goodwin, Mike Gravel, Geir Gundersen, Michael Harrington, Louis Harris, Carl Hartman, Robert Healy, Sy Hersh, James Herzog, Christopher Hitchens, John Holum, Thomas Hyphantis, Kathleen Hall Jamieson, Charlotte Sandager Jeppesen, Loch Johnson, Michael Kalafatas, Elliot Kantaroulas, Vassilis Kapetangiannis, Pantelis Kapsis, Maria Karagiannis, Theodore Kariotis, Andreas Kastanis, Pinelopi Katsigianni, Robert Keeley, Brady Kiesling, Jim King, Bill Kovach, Angelos Kovotsos, Stanley Kutler, Leonarda Lamprianidou, Barbara LaRosa, Nikia Leopold, Anthony Lewis, Gordon Liddy, Bo Lidegaard, Polly Logan, Evangelos Louizos, Chris Lydon, Lilly Makrakis, Roviros Manthoulis, Alexandros Mallias, Stefanos Manouelidis, Ed Markey, Mark Mazower, George McGovern, Jim McGovern, Jessica McQuade, Persa Metaxas, Nikos Michaelis, Nick Mitropoulos, Mario Modiano, Joanne Montouris, Dick Moose, Connie Mourtoupalas, Christina Moustaklis, Natalie Moustaklis, Chris Murphy, Joe Napolitan, Warren Nelson, Marty Nolan, Nick Nikitas, Anders Harris Nielsen, Nancy Nizel, Kathy Olmstead, Frini Papageorgiou, Nick Papandreou, Alexis Papahelas, Georgia Pappas, Marina Pariscou, Deborah Gore Dean Pawlik, Rikke Bang Petersen, Dimitrios Piknis, Ed Perry, Miranda Pesmazoglou, Stefanos Pesmazoglou, Dimitrios Ploumpidis, Jim Pyrros, Vassiliki Rapti, John Richardson, Jan Saragoni, Thaleia Schlesinger, Elizabeth Sherman, Mark Shields, Panayotis Soldatos, Steven Stamas, Nick Stavrou, Toni Stearns, Tom Stuckey, Anthony Summers, Robbyn Swann, Patrick Theros, John Tierney, Photini Tomai-Constantopoulou, Dimitrios Tsalapatis, Amalia Tsiantou, Litsa Tsitsera, Phoebe Tully, Lou Urenek, Guy Vanhaerverbeke, George Vlachos, Elias Vlanton, Angelique Voutselas, Alexander von Cramm, Tina von Cramm, Dick Westebbe, Les Whitten, Jules Witcover, John Xifaris, Christa Xydaki, Fendall Yerxa, Nick Zervas, and Thaleia Zervas. I leave unacknowledged those whose price for candor was my pledge to respect their confidentiality.

Reference staffs at national archives, university archives, and presidential libraries were, with few exceptions, extraordinarily accommodating. Congressmen Don Edwards and Don Fraser authorized me to access their closed archives. Jim Pyrros provided context for his published diary and archives collection. Particularly helpful were Bill Burr at George Washington University's National Security Archive; Elli Droulia and the librarians at the Parliament Library in Athens; Liza Talbot and Charlotte Anderson at the Lyndon B. Johnson Library in Austin, and David Paynter at the National Archives in College Park, MD.

I want to thank: Leandros Papathanasiou, publisher of Pella Publishing Company, for permission to use quotations from James Pyrros's *The Cyprus File: Washington, D.C.* and Orestes Vidalis's *Confronting the Greek Dictatorship in the U.S.*; Deborah Gore Dean for permission to quote from Louise Gore's letters to Elias; and Barbara LaRosa to quote from the letters of Celia Was.

Thanks also to others on the Melville team: Stephanie DeLuca, Marina Drukman, Tim McCall, and Amelia Stymacks for their help in preparing the book for launch, and the hardworking staff at Penguin Random House for distributing it far and wide.

ENDNOTES

Abbreviations used in the text and in notes:

ADP	*Athens Daily Post*
ADST	Association for Diplomatic Studies & Training, Oral History Project
AmEmb	American Embassy, Athens
AP	Associated Press
CREST	CIA (Declassified) Records Search Tool
CR	Congressional Record
CW	Celia Was
DCI	Director Central Intelligence
DCM	Deputy Chief of Mission
DDEL	Dwight D. Eisenhower Presidential Library
EPD	Elias P. Demetracopoulos
EPDP	Elias P. Demetracopoulos's Private Papers
GRFL	Gerald R. Ford Presidential Library
LG	Louise Gore
FRUS	Foreign Relations of the United States
FCO	Foreign Office and Commonwealth
FO	British Foreign Office
FOIA/PA	Freedom of Information Act/Privacy Act
LBJL	Lyndon B. Johnson Presidential Library
JFKL	John F. Kennedy Presidential Library
JHB	James H. Barron
INR	State Department Bureau of Intelligence and Research
LTE	Letter to Editor
NARA	National Archives and Records Administration
NEA/GRK	Office of Greek Affairs, State Department
NSC	National Security Council
PAO	Public Affairs Officer
PREM	Prime Minister's Records
PRO	Public Records Office, Great Britain
RMNL	Richard M. Nixon Presidential Library
SAC/WFO	FBI Special Agent in Charge/Washington Field Office
SecState	Secretary of State
HSTL	Harry S. Truman Presidential Library
NYT	*New York Times*
UPI	United Press International
USIS	United States Information Service
WP	*Washington Post*

Books, articles, and other references abbreviated in the Endnotes are fully described in the Selected Bibliography. Works by the same author are listed chronologically.

INTRODUCTION

1 https://www.washingtonpost.com/outlook/2019/10/07/founders-knew-first-hand-that-foreign-interference-us-elections-was-dangerous/; https://www.npr.org/2019/06/14/7325718 95/fear-of-foreign-interference-in-u-s-elections-dates-from-nations-founding
2 Roberts, *NYT*, 2/26/2016; Langer, *WP*, 2/26/2016
3 Margolis, 86 and Chapter 2
4 Ibid.

I: GROWING UP

1 Connie Mourtoupalas interviews, 12/30/2015, and 12/4/ 2016; Gounardes and Pyrgiotakis, *National Herald*, 8/8/ 2017; AHEPA, the leading Greek-American fraternal organization, was formed in Atlanta in 1922 in part to protect Greeks from the KKK.
2 Frangos, 3/12/2005
3 Apostolos Doxiades, interview, 5/28/2012; Amalia Tsiantou, interview, 5/29/2012
4 "Helleno-Romaic dilemma" in Leigh Fermor, 106ff; Holden, 30–6; Finlay, 12; Woodhouse (*Modern*), 11–12
5 Percy Bysshe Shelley trumpeted: "We are all Greeks" and called Athens "a divine work." Lord Byron, Goethe, and Victor Hugo were some of the leading philhellenes.
6 Mateos, 94, 162; Brewer, 5; Kalyvas, 44; J. E. Miller, 3, 13
7 Close (*Origins*), 3; Clogg (*Concise*), 87
8 Rummel, "Turkey's Genocidal Purges," 233
9 Pallis, A. A. "The Greek Census of 1928," *The Geographical Journal*, Vol. 73, No. 6 (June 1929), 543-548; Kayser, Bernard, *Geographie Humaine de la Grèce*. Paris: Presses Universitaires de France, 1964 in Holden, 135
10 Campbell, 127–133; Holden, 136–9; Woodhouse (*Modern*), 212–15
11 Campbell, 150–1
12 Clogg (*Parties*), 12; Holden, 142
13 George Enislides, interview, 4/2012
14 Antonis Drossopoulos, interview, 5/31/2012
15 https://www.youtube.com/watch?v=vyOIgzVKLT4; Christopher Xenopoulos Janus, "Filotimo: The most untranslatable and unique Greek virtue," https://www.helleniccomserve.com/filotimo.html
16 He also instilled a hatred for Thomas Bruce, the infamous Lord Elgin, who notoriously removed priceless friezes, statuary, and other precious artifacts.
17 Plato's Apology, https://oll.libertyfund.org/titles/plato-dialogues-vol-2#lf0131-02_div_137; In Plato's Apology, "gadfly" was the term Plato said Socrates used to describe himself. Being criticized in a CIA document as a "gadfly" and in other US government documents as a "dangerous gadfly" gave EPD great pleasure. CIA, 2/19/1972
18 Ancient Rome, more than Ancient Greece, shaped the ideological thinking of the American founding fathers. Bailyn, 24–6; as in Europe, private American citizens, not their government, took the lead in embracing the cause of Greek independence.
19 P.J. Vatikiotis, Ch. 15-6; John V. Kofas, Authoritarianism in Greece: The Metaxas Regime. Boulder: East European Monographs, 1983
20 Nalmpantis, 50; Woodhouse (*Modern*), 232–3

2: RESISTING THE GERMANS

1 Woodhouse (*Modern*), 237; Lawlor, 171; Hondros, 46
2 Ilias-Tembos, 306, http://etheses.whiterose.ac.uk/10846/2/288043_vol2.pdf
3 Prime minister's personal telegram to General Wavell, 5/1/1941: "We have paid our debt of honour with far less loss than I feared . . . " Churchill War Rooms, London
4 *AP*, Ottawa Citizen, 4/21/1941
5 Hondros, 50; Mazower (*Inside*), 15–19

6   Jenkins, 735, indicates "romantic monarchist." Churchill's commitment to King George was more "tentative."

7   Mazower (*Inside*), 16–18, DGFP, D, XII, no. 409, 946–947; Hondros, 264; Keegan, 157; Ilias-Tembos, op. cit., 387

8   "The Greeks are what we were: they are what we shall become again," Schiller, "On Naïve and Sentimental Poetry," 84, in *Germans and Greeks*, chapter 5. https://www.coursehero.com/file/24 291223/GoldenCH5-1doc/; Beiser, 186

9   Keegan, 156

10 Beiser, 186

11 Editorial, *Vradyni*, June 2, 1941

12 Mazowen, 86, citing fn 5

13 Gerolymatos (*Guerrilla*), 189; Gerolymatos (*Red*), 47; Rigopoulas, 25

14 Hondros, 101

15 Macveagh in Clogg ("Cousins"), 107; Hondros, 52–3; Iatrides (ed.) (MacVeigh), *passim*.

16 EAM (*Ethniko Apeleftherotikon Metopo*), National Liberation Front; ELAS (*Ellinikos Laikos Apeleftherotikos Stratos*), Greek People's Liberation Army); EDES (Ethnikos Dimokratikos Eleftherotikon Ellinikos Syndesmos), National Republican Greek League

17 MI6 (Secret Intelligence Service) and MI9 (Escape and Evasion)

18 EPD anecdotes are supplemented by examples in Bobotinos's book and interviews with Leonarda Lamprianidou (Ivanof's niece), 6/2012 and 12/2016.

19 Beaton, 169

20 Fleischer et al. (ed.), 3; Professor Panayotis Soldatos, interview and email, 9/2011; British Embassy Athens letter to J. Bobotinos, M.B.E, 2/26/1952, praising how OAG's "gallant work . . . contributed to the success of the Allied cause." Royal Decree of Greek government's official recognition of OAG, 3/18/1950

21 The 11th Day: Crete 1941

22 Drossopoulos interview, 5/31/2012 and Enislides interview, 5/30/2012

23 Drossopoulos and Enislides, interviews, ibid.

24 Rigopoulas, 24

25 Ibid.

26 Jeanne Oates Angulo, interview, 4/2/2016

27 Clogg (*Concise*),121; https://www.spiegel.de/international/germany/greek-study-provides-evidence-of-forced-loans-to-nazis-a-1024762.html; https://www.dw.com/en/nazis-stolen-loan-from-greek-bank-will-germany-pay-it-back/a-18224874

28 Mazower (*Inside*), discusses food rationing, 26–30; Hionidou, 196, notes nourishment dropped as low as 400 calories per capita in Athens, 190

29 Panourgia, 51–2, 14n notes lack of agreement on the numbers.

30 "an oka (nearly three pounds) of bread, which cost 10 drachmas at the time of the Italian invasion, had reached 34,000,000 by the time of the German withdrawal in October 1944." Clogg (*Concise*), 124

31 Drossopoulos, interview, 5/31/2012

32 Bernard O'Connor, *Sabotage in Greece*, Lulu.com, 103, 2/4/2016; http://en.interaffairs.ru /experts/340-ivanov-ainovi-the-russian-james-bond.html; http://akrokorinthos.blogspot.com /2011/07/jerzy-iwanow-szajnowicz.html; interviews with Leonarda Lamprianidou (Ivanof's niece); Kuzminski, Agent #1

33 The Special Operations Executive, an amalgam of three secret organizations formed in 1940, was tasked with coordinating subversion and sabotage in enemy-occupied countries. https://ww-2greekveterans.com/soe-in-greece/

34 Bobotinos, 24–5

35 Bobotinos, 13, 19; interview with Leonarda Lamprianidou, 12/2016

36 O'Connor, 103

3: LOCKED UP

1   Condit, 87; Koliopoulos, 294

2   "Though its leaders thought otherwise, EAM ultimately was a social movement second, a national

movement first and foremost." Nalmpantis, 77

3   Ole L. Smith, "'The First Round'- Civil War During the Occupation," in Close (ed.) [Civil War], 58–71; Hondros, 171–99 *passim*.

4   Mazower (*Inside*), 148; see fn 132.

5   Heer and Naumann, 161; Mazower (*Inside*), 157

6   "Greek and Foreign Spies in Greece," *Stavros* magazine, 10/8/1950

7   EPD preliminary draft memoir [undated], EPDP; supplemented by Amalia Tsiantou research, 6–7/2012

8   Ibid.

9   Ibid.

10 "Site of Historical Memory 1941–1944: 4, Korai Street Ethniki Insurance Mansion," Department of Historical Archives (undated) and interview with Frini Papageorgiou, 6/2012

11 Drossopoulos, interview, 5/31/2012

12 Op. cit., *Stavros* magazine, 10/8/1950

13 EPD, undated, unpublished report, supplemented by interviews with Evangelos Louizos, Antonis Drossopoulos, and Amalia Tsiantou

14 Ibid.

15 https://diatribe-column.blogspot.com/2007/11/damaskinos-righteous-among-nations.html; *TIME*, 10/1/1945

16 https://www.ushmm.org/information/exhibitions/online-exhibitions/special-focus/holocaust-in-greece/athens; TIME, 10/1/1945; Commander was German General Jurgen Stroop in charge of SS and police in Greece.

17 Douzenis, 6

18 Ibid., 7–8

19 Christina Politi 2, Tsoukalis, 91–2; "What the Germans Did to Greece," *LIFE*, 11/27/1944. http://www.elliniki-gnomi.eu/o-foveros-apologismos-ton-katastrofon-pou-proxenisan-i-germani-ke-i-simmachi-tous-stin-ellada-kata-tin-diarkia-tou-v-pagkosmiou-polemou-ke-tis-katochis/ (in Greek)

4: DECEMBER UPRISING

1   British Public Records Office, PREM 3/66/7(169)

2   Jordan Baev, "The Greek Civil War Viewed from the North," http://www.coldwar.hu/publications/greek_civil.html

3   Australian Red Cross letter to ARCS Bureau, Sydney, 9/24/1945, Hellenic Red Cross Archives, Athens.

4   Hondros, 240

5   Gerolymatos (*Red*), 100

6   Ibid., Chapter 3, 99–107; Hondros, 246

7   Gerolymatos (*Red*), 105; *Dekemriana 1944* (flv) (Television production). tvxs (*Reporters Without Frontiers*), Stelios Kouloglou. 5/12/2006; retrieved 12/26/2011

8   Evert interview, *Akropolis*, 12/12/1958

9   Death toll in dispute. From 16 per Close, *Greek Civil War*, 85, to 28 dead on 3 December and 100 dead on 4 December. Panourgia, 65–9 https://dangerouscitizens.columbia.edu/1944–1945/amputated-bodies-broken/all/index.html; see Gerolymatos https://www.thenationalherald.com/33375/athens-deadly-december-1944/

10 December 5, 1944 telegram to Gen. Scobie. Churchill, *The Second World War: The Tide of Victory* Vol. 11, 256–258

11 Churchill, *Triumph and Tragedy*, Vol. 6, 291

12 Gerolymatos (*Red*), 170

13 Drew Pearson, American syndicated columnist, criticized Churchill, linking his behavior to that of Nazi collaborators. Pearson's sensitivity to Greek democracy would continue for decades, through his opposition to the military junta in 1967. Gerolymatos (*Red*), 139–41; Holden 166–67; https://archive.org/stream/in.ernet.dli.2015.185579/2015.185579.The-Royal-House-Of-Greece_djvu.txt; Clogg, ("Cousins"), op. cit., Jenkins, 770

14 Clogg (*Concise*),134. https://medium.com/@AndreasXenachis/standing-up-to-the-nazis-even

-when-faced-with-the-noose-29cbe34f2d1d

15 12,000 to 17,000 casualties http://www.mixanitouxronou.gr/dekemvriana-ston-emfilio-tis-athinas-se-33-imeres-i-nekri-itan-perissoteri-apo-ekinous-tou-ellinoitalikou-polemou/

16 Scholars have debated for decades the so-called rounds of the Greek Civil War, with traditional-ists viewing the second round beginning in December 1944 and revisionists asserting that the left "never had any intention of taking power by force," but were simply responding to "needless prov-ocations from British imperialists and their local collaborators." A post-revisionist school views the December phase as a combination of coup, civil war, and revolution. Delis (*The British Inter-vention*) 211–237, 212

5: A TUBERCULAR EDUCATION

1 *FRUS*, 1945, Vol. 8, 868.00/3–645, Athens, 2/12/1945; G. Mavrogordatos, "The 1946 Election and Plebiscite: Prelude to Civil War," in J. O. Iatrides (ed.), *Greece in the 1940s*, 181–95

2 Close (*Origins*), 173; G. Mavrogordatos, "The 1946 Election and Plebiscite: Prelude to Civil War," in J. O. Iatrides (ed.), *Greece in the 1940s*, 181–95; Clogg (*Parties*), 18

3 "What the Germans Did to Greece," *LIFE*, 11/27/1944 http://www.ww2wrecks.com/portfolio/the-nazi-occupation-of-greece-1941-44-an-endless-list-of-crimes-atrocities-and-bloodbaths/

4 Paul Porter *Economic Report*, April 1947 in Tsoucalas, 98

5 McDougall, 112; Evangelos Louizos, email to JHB, 10/14/2013

6 Lincoln MacVeagh, "Memoirs" in McCullough, 540

7 McCullough, 547–8

8 Truman Doctrine, 1–5

9 MacNeill, 86

10 Joes, 40

11 See Vlanton; Keeley (*Salonica Bay*); Marton; MacPherson, 277–81; Sperber, 302–14, 369; Steel, 487; William Burr (ed.). "The George Polk Case" https://nsarchive2.gwu.edu/NSAEBB/NSAEBB226/index.htm; https://www.npr.org/sections/parallels/2013/10/27/240768937/an-americans-death-still-a-greek-mystery-65-years-later; EPD later learned more Polk details from George Seldes not included in Seldes autobiography, *Witness to a Century*, New York: Ballantine Books, 1987, 378-81

12 Sperber, quoting Polk, 311

13 Djilas, 181–3

14 Rossos ("Incompatible Allies"), 42–76

15 J. C. Murray. "The Anti-Bandit War: Part I." January 1954: 38 *Marine Corps Gazette*, 18, in Wit-tner (American Intervention), 243, 251, and n49; A. C. Sedgwick, "Greek Army Opens Grammos Assault: Advance to Albanian Border Is Made on North in Drive in Last Main Rebel Zone." *NYT*, 8/26/1949

16 Neer, *Napalm*, 1, 15; *To Vima*, 6/29/2003

6: THE YOUNG JOURNALIST

1 Kapsis, 144–6

2 John Rigas, interview, 6/1/2012

3 At the time EPD joined *Kathimerini*, journalism was in practice largely a closed profession, rooted in a literary tradition, whose members were part of a "self-educated elite who believed that one did not need any special education or training to become a journalist." "The conception of 'talent' or 'journalists are born and not made' was the dominant view, therefore no school was needed." Skamnakis, 136–7

4 Kapsis, op. cit., 51–2

5 Sid Goldberg, head of North American News Alliance, wrote that EPD became NANA's "chief Mediterranean correspondent" in August 1950. Letter, 11/22/1967. Later EPD became one of six masthead "foreign correspondents" to *Technology Week: Including Missiles and Rockets.*

6 Gold Cross of St. Mark: "Decoration of Greek Newspaperman," *Kathimerini*, 10/5/1950; "Patri-arch of Alexandria Honors Distinguished Wartime Hero," Empros, 10/5/50; "Decoration," *Eleft-heria*, 10/6/1950; Acropolis, 10/5/1950; details of EPD awards in letter from Greek Embassy in United States to Congressman Les Aspin, 12/18/1980

7   The USAF Attaché sent a letter congratulating him on his "exceptional bravery," adding he was "honored in being . . . present." Leigh Wade to EPD, 3/11/1950
8   Less than a month after EDP's first award ceremony, OAG leader John Bobotinos wrote to Peurifoy to condemn Greek police from the Ministry of Coordination who, presumably at the direction of the US Embassy, interrogated OAG members about EPD's "reliability." Wrote Bobotinos: " . . . our organization guarantees Mr. Demetrakopoulos' honesty and reliability; actually he was one of the most energetic and honest of our men during the occupation and served our common cause without personal benefice." Bobotinos to Peurifoy, 12/6/1950
9   Flora Lewis, "Ambassador Extraordinary: John Peurifoy," *NYT,* 7/18/1954; "Thailand. Smilin' Jack," *TIME,* 8/22/1955
10 https://www.state.gov/documents/organization/176702.pdf, The 'M' Unit, 128; Senate Appropriations Subcommittee Hearings on Departments of State, Justice, Commerce, and the Judiciary Appropriations for 1951, 1950, 603; Johnson (*Lavender*), 70–71; "The Administration. Housecleaning," *TIME,* 4/7/1952
11 Koliopoulos and Veremis, 296
12 Ben Franklin Dixon, ADST, 10/31/1990
13 Pavlos Apostolidis, "Intelligence Services in the National Security System: The Case of EYP"; John M. Nomikos, "Greek Intelligence Service (NIS-EYP): Past, Present and Future," National Security and the Future 1–2 (9), 2008
14 Alfred C. Ulmer, Jr., Weiner (*Legacy*), 35; "God we had fun," *NYT* obituary, 7/1/2000
15 Meyer, 147
16 Report in Barnet, 109; Blum (*Killing Hope*), 36
17 Stewart Alsop cable quoted in D. F. Fleming, 444 and Blum, 36
18 Major General Reuben E. Jenkins to Major General Floyd L. Parks, 5/1/1951
19 Brigadier General Leigh Wade, USAF Air Attaché to Brigadier General S. Smith, USAF, Pentagon, letter, 5/9/1951
20 https://vimeo.com/54300842
21 Draenos (*Andreas*), 15
22 CIA report was based on reports from US Army intelligence officers, July/August 1951.

7: CELIA

1   CW letter to EPD, 7/2/1969
2   CW's biographical information is drawn from EPD, her State Dept., FBI, CIA, etc. files, and interviews with and letters provided by her niece Barbara LaRosa, 2016–2017.
3   Smith [Moscow], 186–7; A "Secret" State Department document 8/6/1948, described Lapschin as a "tame Russian," "well-known to the American colony" and "the element of possible disloyalty was just not thought of in such connections."
4   Bucar, "The Truth about American Diplomats." Chargé in the Soviet Union (Kohler) to the secretary of state, "Confidential," FRUS, 1949, Vol. V, doc. 129, Eastern Europe, the Soviet Union, 3/4/1949
5   Report of Mr. Wilson and Mr. McKinnon, 6/23/1948; on 4/8/1948, State Dept. had sent a "Top Secret" request for "a complete reinvestigation of the case as expeditiously as possible." FBI, "Secret" Office memorandum, 6/23/1948, prepared by Wilson and McKinnon. On 8/1/1948 the investigators warned that "top secret" information revealed "disagreement" in the department regarding the significance of CW's failure to immediately disclose Bucar's "predicament." She was extensively interviewed again on 8/6/1948.
6   Nicholson to Peurifoy, Secret, 6/28/1948
7   Ibid.
8   "Top Secret" letter from Elbridge Durbrow, chargé d'affaires, Moscow, to SecState, 5/21/1948; others aware of personnel conflicts in the embassy and having direct knowledge of CW told investigators they would recommend her for work "anywhere behind the Iron Curtain." FBI investigation, 8/31/1948; Final Report, 10/4/1948 returned to the "Slavic soul" qualification.
9   The United States Information Service (USIS), under the US Information and Educational Exchange Act of 1948 (Smith-Mundt Act), disseminated abroad information about the US, its people and culture. After the United States Information Agency (USIA) was created in 1953 USIS posts abroad became the field offices of the new agency.

10 Interview, 8/14/1951; published *Kathimerini*, 8/22/1951
11 EPD to CW, 10/8/1951
12 CIA report, 11/15/1955
13 "Alleged Communist Connections of US State Dept and ECA Officials in Athens, Greece" [names redacted], 8/23/1951; Official Dispatch, 9/10/1951, State Dept. Foreign Service Security Office, 10/10/1951; CIA [names redacted] 11/15/1951; John Betts Regional Security Officer, 11/27/1951; State Dept. Foreign Service Security Office, 12/11/1951
14 State Dept. memorandum, 8/8/1951
15 State Department [names and reference number redacted], 9/24/1951
16 CIA [names and reference number redacted], 9/24/1951
17 CIA [names redacted], 9/24/1951; death sentence reference added in SAC communication 6/23/1952; long imprisonment, 7/30/1952
18 AmEmb, 12/11/1951
19 Department of Defense to William Truhart, special assistant State Dept. intelligence, Lyman Kirkpatrick, assistant director for special operations, CIA; director, FBI, "Greece," 8/7/1952
20 Chourmouzios letter (from "Mr. Hourmouzios") to Ambassador Peurifoy, 3/20/1952
21 Ibid.
22 " . . . all connections with him should be discouraged." State Dept. Security, 6/23/1952
23 EPD letter to CW, 4/29/1951
24 CW letter to SecState, 6/20/1952
25 Chief of FBI's Special Security Division to Deputy Security Officer, CIA, 7/11/1952; CIA, 7/9/1952
26 FBI, ibid.
27 Attached to the FBI memorandum are two calls deemed "noteworthy" and a "list of telephone calls made by Subject from his hotel during the period from 13 June through July 1952, seven pages with full redactions save for the dates. SAC [CIA] followed with a "blind memo" and report to Lyman B. Kirpatrick, CIA Assistant Director for Special Operations, concerning "identity of more than 100 persons and places called by Subject." 9/15/1952
28 After referencing the EDP secret agent gossip in Athens, the CIA station chief asked headquarters to "clip wings" of "this menace" for passing himself off as American agent "unless he actually is one in which case request we be advised immediately." CIA Operations to Washington, 6/10/1952
29 Boyle to EPD, 8/2/1952
30 George Papandreou letter, 10/25/52; Panayiotis Kanellopoulos letter, 10/22/1952
31 Boyle to EPD, 11/21/1952
32 11/30/1952 reception at Grande Bretagne Hotel, CIA report, SECRET 12/1952; CIA deputy director for plans to FBI, State Dept. Security, INS commissioner, White House Situation Room 2, 10/19/1967
33 CW letter to EPD, 1/16/1954
34 WP, 3/18/1954
35 Final Decree, Florida Office of Vital Statistics, Chan. 34, 305, 16203, 11/5/1955
36 "Life 'Too Fast' for Greek Hubby," *Palm Beach Post*, 7/19/1955

8: PERSONA NON GRATA

1 Stern, 13
2 Dulles, known as a "pathological womanizer" (Moran) and "skilled seducer" (Kinzer) reportedly began his relationship with Queen Frederica aboard one of Niarchos's yachts and continued at least through a famous episode in a private dressing room next to his CIA office. Grose, 451
3 *Kathimerini*, 11/6/1951; memorandum from Edward S. Berry to William C. Truehart, Special Assistant Intelligence, State Dept. (cc: Assistant Director for Special Operations CIA) 12/6/1951; King and Queen had their state visit 10/28/1953–12/3/1953
4 FRUS "Secret" 4367, SecState to AmEmb, 5/17/1951
5 Embassy memorandum [names redacted], 8/3/1951
6 Robert de T. Lawrence to Commander in Chief US Air Forces Europe, 3/18/1958
7 CIA "Notes on Soviet Activities in Greece during July 1955," 8/22/1955
8 Athens, December 1954
9 Col. David Fowler, CINFO memorandum/74482, 5/25/1954

10 Demetracopoulos questions submitted 4/1/1954; negative response (undated), RMNL
11 CIA memorandum [redacted] to director, 2/26/1954; the British were often more helpful to EPD. E. J. C. Hare in the British Embassy in Athens asked London to give him assistance in obtaining interviews there because he is a "very good friend of the Department and a well-known Athens journalist." Ref. Inf: 1674/20/1956
12 J. E. Miller, 44
13 The Tripartite Conference on the Eastern Mediterranean and Cyprus held by the Governments of the United Kingdom of Great Britain and Northern Ireland, Greece, and Turkey, London, August 29–September 7, 1955, with relevant documents, FO
14 Olson to Medville E. Nordense, Chief Public Affairs Officer, USIS, Rome, 5/2/1955
15 6/13/1955
16 CIA, Deputy Director Plans to Secretary of State, Army and Navy, 4/19/1954; also 12/3/1954
17 Confidential memorandum, 12/3/1954.
18 Hatzivassilou, 68
19 Abadi, "Constraints and Adjustments in Greece's Policy," 45 (www.scribd.com/doc/23018215/Greece-Israel); Sakkas, "Greece and the Mass Exodus of the Egyptian Greeks," 101–15; Konstantina Botsiou, "Who is afraid of the Americans?," 20–22, https://ecpr.eu/Filestore/PaperProposal/56c182eb-9ec2-4516-92bc-10d98f6187e6.pdf; paper included in Brendan O'Connor (ed.), Anti-Americanism, Chapter 10
20 *Kathimerini*, 9/22/1955
21 State Dept. memorandum, 1/21/1958
22 At least four books have revisited in depth the case of Polk's murder, detailing the miscarriage of justice and how respected journalists allowed themselves to be used in a two-government whitewash of the so-called independent investigation of the murder. Elias Vlanton provided the most recent comprehensive review in English and Anthanasios Kafiris in Greek.
23 MacPherson, 280–1; Sperber, 312–14; Steel, 487; Like Polk, EPD never became a journalistic "insider." Vlanton, 191

9: ELIAS AND ETHNARCH MAKARIOS

1 "To whom it may concern" letter (undated)
2 Hersh (*Price*), 137
3 Ray L. Thurston to Walworth Barbour, 6/22/1956
4 *Kathimerini*, 11/29/1956; AmEmb dispatch, 12/5/1956
5 Heurtley, 170; Woodhouse (*Modern Greece*), 276
6 Mario Modiano, interview, 5/31/2012
7 Reuters, *Glasgow Herald*, 4/8/1957; AP, *Lewiston Evening Journal*, 4/6/1957
8 British Labour M.P. also flew to Nairobi and provided some *Kathimerini* coverage. Chief Secretary, Office of the Director of Intelligence & Security, Colony and Protectorate of Kenya, File AA 56/6, FCO/41/7197, ref: 5988/E/57; Secret Registry, 4/18/1957
9 "Makarios Freed, But Britain Bars Him from Cyprus," *NYT*, 3/29/1957
10 "Bishop Kiprianos of Kyrenia . . . prepared inflammatory public statement in Nairobi" which EPD "did not transmit for publication and which Makarios quashed." Priority Classified Message to Director [names redacted], 4/18/1957
11 Ibid.
12 CIA "undated, blind memorandum" furnished to FBI and State Dept. by Deputy Director Richard Helms for Nationalities Intelligence Section, 6/20/1966. Helms had previously sent US Naval Intelligence, State Dept., Army, and USIA (November 1960) a four-page memorandum concluding EPD is "a troublemaker" and contact with him "should be avoided wherever possible."
13 A. C. Sedgwick, "Athens Hails Arrival of Makarios," *NYT*, 4/18/1957
14 letter EPD to CW, 5/2/1957
15 AmEmb (Allen) communique to SecState, 4/18/1957
16 Robert de T. Lawrence, Press Officer, via Clary Thompson, PAO to the ambassador, 9/18/1957
17 Ibid.
18 Persa Metaxas, interview, 1/2012; Stefan Manuelides, 10/2017 and 1/2018

19 Woodhouse (*Karamanlis*), 73
20 Pelt, 176, notes that NATO formally decided to station the missiles at its 12/16–19/1957 meetings. Evangelia Batsakoutsa, in "Soviet Military Power and Limited War: Greece and N.A.T.O's South East Flank," an undated NATO report, claimed "US deployed [elements of] tactical battlefield nuclear weapons in Greece . . . in 16 bases all over the Greek territory" as early as 1955–56. SecState Christian Herter later confirmed EPD's 1957 scoop. Decision made at meeting prior to 12/19/1957 NATO communique, State Department SECRET Telegram 10/25/1960.
21 Nash, 61; Botsiou, op. cit., 24
22 State Dept., Leonard Greenup, Memorandum of Conversation, 1/21/1958
23 SECRET Memorandum of Conversation, Efthimios Papageorgiou, *Eleftheria* political correspondent and Edward Mulcahy, First Secretary, AmEmb, 1/17/1958
24 George Anastasopoulos, interview, 3/2016
25 *State Dept.* memorandum of Vlachou meeting with Clary Thompson, Public Affairs Officer, 2/11/1958; cc's included CIA's John Richardson.
26 Ibid.
27 "Soviet Warships in Mediterranean," *Times* (London), 4/20/1959
28 CIA, Secret NSC Briefing, "Greek Elections," 5/27/1958
29 Interview, 5/31/2012
30 "The American Embassy Incident—Prime Minister's Nerves," *Estia*, 7/5/1958
31 [Redacted], Memorandum for Record, CIA, 7/19/1958
32 Ibid.
33 Ibid.
34 Robert de T. Lawrence to ambassador, 8/28/1958
35 CIA Letter to Director Allen Dulles, 9/6/1958; EDP intelligence files are studded with erroneous information, including one that reported EDP was "a lawyer in Kalamata, Greece and later practiced in Athens . . . [source] feels strongly that subject is a communist agent." HDQS to SAC, 4/19/1968. An FBI field report (NY) also reports his being a Kalamata lawyer who was "active in EAM from 1942–45 but is "not known to be a communist." Another FBI report, citing 4/29/1968 and 5/7/1968 interviews, adds he is married with "one or two children."

10: "I DON'T SIT AT MY DESK"

1 "EPD and US Army Military Attaché, Col. Joseph McChristian," 10/22/1958
2 CIA "SECRET" blind memo (undated) referred to EPD's "clandestine contact" with Yugoslav intelligence officers operating in Greece.
3 Brennan, Internal Security, 6/20/1966
4 Antonia "Toni" Stearns, interview, 12/14/2011
5 State Dept., Memorandum of Conversation, 7/17/1959
6 West German Authorities closed the Merten Case, 4/3/1961; Susanne Sophia Spiliotis, "An affair of politics, not justice: the Merten trial (1957–1959) and Greek-German relations" in Mazower (After), 293–302
7 Christopher Simpson, *Blowback: America's Recruitment of Nazi's and Its Effects on the Cold War* (book inscription praised Elias for his assistance)
8 Leonard R. Greenup, Deputy Public Affairs Officer, Memorandum of Conversation, 7/17/1959
9 After criticizing EPD for his "egocentricity," and "preoccupation" with his career, a State Dept. Biographic Data profile added "he works extremely hard at his job and has developed to a high degree the journalist's technique for ferreting out news." 1/22/1960
10 Ibid.
11 Secret AmEmb memorandum, 1/5/1959
12 LG to EPD, 10/12/1959
13 LG to EPD, 5/18/1960
14 Lawrence to Luke Carrel, foreign news editor, 4/1/1958
15 Frank Grismer to Ogden Reid, 4/7/1958
16 Allen to EPD, 5/12/1958; Allen to Ogden Reid, 5/12/1958

II: BLOWBACK

1 Briggs (*Proud Servant*), 365
2 Briggs to State Dept., Control no. 14655, 9/21/1959
3 Briggs, 378
4 Briggs letter to SecState, 1/30/1960
5 Wiggins to EPD, 3/9/1960
6 Donovan to Yerxa, 2/11/1960; undated,note from unidentified sender on US Senate stationery to EDP: "Re Everett Walker, *Herald Tribune* assistant managing editor and Robert Donovan, Washington manager: High official of CIA told these men to fire Demetracopoulos and they did."
7 Donovan to Yerxa, op. cit.
8 *Ethnos*, 5/17/1960; CIA memorandum to State Dept. Office of Personnel Security
9 *Ethnos*, 5/18/1960; US Naval Attaché, Office of Naval Intelligence, 3/27/1960
10 Thompson to Mandlay, 5/20/1960
11 S. Berger, AmEmb to Greek Desk, 5/19/1960
12 *Ethnos*, 5/20/1960
13 Order No. 26942, marked "Secret," Howe (*Power Peddlers*), 418 and 422
14 *Ethnos*, 7/30/1960; Briggs to SecState, 7/30/1960
15 Embassy memorandum of telephone conversation, Greenup, USIS, 7/30/1960
16 Ibid.
17 Yehonatan Prato opened discussions, but his successor, Rene Shmuel Kapel, whose World War II exploits with the French resistance reminded EPD of Ivanof, made the arrangements; int. Rebecca Gabbi, 8/2014
18 Amikam Nachmani, *Israel, Turkey and Greece: Uneasy Relations in the East Mediterranean*, London: Frank Cass, 1987, 115-6; Greece–Israel: 25 Years Since the De Jure Recognition of Israel, https://kis.gr/en/index.php?option=com_content&view=article&id=568:greece-israel-25-years-since-the-the-de-jure-recognition-of-israel&catid=12:2009&Itemid=41
19 Reference to May 1960 conversation about EPD in Grogan letter to Donovan, 10/4/1960, CIA Declass. Ref. Box 30, NARA, College Park, MD
20 Briggs, 379
21 EPDP
22 US Naval Institute *Proceedings*, 5/2001
23 CIA-RDP83-00764R000500110004-8
24 Yerxa to EPD, 10/14/1960
25 BJ Cutler to EPD, 10/18/1960; SecState Christian Herter, "SECRET" memorandum, 10/25/1960, noted "delicacy" of matter and reported progress re: implementation of plan.
26 Peter A. Damman, Wilson & McIlvaine to John L. O'Donnell, Olwine, Connelly, 2/3/1961

12: A DARK SIDE OF CAMELOT

1 Waves of Freedom of Information Act requests identified at least twenty relevant documents regarding this episode: three were blocked by other agencies; three were released with large portions redacted and access to fourteen documents was denied entirely. Some records apparently have been lost or destroyed.
2 "Would like derogatory information" request, 10/27/1960
3 LBJ Photo w/statement, *ADP*, 2/12/1961
4 Shaarda ("Admiral Burke"); http://www.dtic.mil/dtic/tr/fulltext/u2/a428986.pdf
5 EPD, "Muzzling Admiral Burke," US Naval Institute *Proceedings*, 1/2000, 64
6 See biographies E. R. Potter, *Admiral Arleigh Burke*; and Ken Jones and Hubert Kelly, Jr., *Admiral Arleigh (31-Knot) Burke*.
7 Burke interview published simultaneously in *ADP*, *Ethnos*, and *Makedonia*, 2/15/1961; *Philadelphia Bulletin*, 2/15/1961; *Daily Telegraph*, London, 2/16/1961; *Times* (London), 2/17/1961
8 Ibid.
9 EPD, "Muzzling Admiral Burke," op. cit., 64
10 Arleigh A. Burke Oral History interview 1/20/1967 JFKL; David Allen Rosenberg, "Arleigh Burke: The Last CNO" in James Bradford (ed.) (*Quarterdeck&Bridge*), 360–93, https://www.his-

tory.navy.mil/research/library/online-reading-room/title-list-alphabetically/a/arleigh-burke-the-last-cno.html

11 NANA's "hold for release" note to managing editors explained that the interview was given on January 12 and cleared for security on January 16, "several days before the so-called 'gag policy' was put through by the new Administration" and some papers referenced this fact; CIA memorandum, 2/17/1961: Salinger doubted the interview was held prior to 1/20/1961.

12 EPD (NANA) interview, "Surprise Attack? Impossible," *Philadelphia Bulletin*, 2/15/1961; "Sea Borne Missile Strength Holds Russia in Check, Burke Says," *St. Louis Globe-Democrat*, 2/16/1961; "America Power to Destroy Russia; Outspoken Remarks By Navy Chief," *Times* (London), 2/17/1961

13 *February 1*, https://www.jfklibrary.org/archives/other-resources/john-f-kennedy-press-conferences/news-conference-2; Feb 8, 1961 https://www.jfklibrary.org/archives/other-resources/john-f-kennedy-press-conferences/news-conference-3

14 EPD, "Muzzling Admiral Burke," 65; "Military Cold War Education and Speech Review Policies," Report by Special Preparedness Subcommittee of the Senate Armed Services Committee, 1962; "Investigations: The Muzzled Military," *TIME*, 2/2/1962; "Investigations: More Than an Accent," *TIME*, 2/9/1962

15 Col. Barney Oldfield, "After Elk Creek: Everything; Encounters with Arthur Sylvester, Assistant Secretary of Defense, Public Affairs" (undated)

16 Ibid.

17 NEWS CONFERENCE 4, 2/15/1961, JFKL; https://www.jfklibrary.org/archives/other-resources/john-f-kennedy-press-conferences/news-conference-4

18 *TIME*, 2/24/1961

19 "That's Burke's story," Sylvester quotation in "Admiral Burke's Views Disturb Pentagon Again," *Washington Star*, 2/16/1961

20 Stan Optowsky, "The Fuse Was on Delay," *New York Post*, 2/16/1961

21 "Pierre Salinger Syndrome," https://www.techopedia.com/definition/2451/pierre-salinger-syndrome; https://science.howstuffworks.com/science-vs-myth/everyday-myths/10-tips-for-telling-fact-from-fiction6.htm; *Times* (London), 10/18/2004, online. https://www.thetimes.co.uk/edition/news/pierre-salinger-0l763sh3g26

22 CIA provided Salinger a White House briefing "on the background of Mr. Ilias Dimitrakopoulos." 2/17/1961, Pierre Salinger file, JFKL; memorandum for [redacted], Discussion with Mr. Pierre Salinger Regarding Mr. Ilias Dimitrakopoulos, "At the end of briefing Mr. Salinger requested and received copies of the classified summary correspondence which related directly to his interest in this case." CIA, no. 147, 2/17/1961; Salinger on 2/16/1961 telephoned J. Edgar Hoover to accelerate an updated FBI check on the missing Greek journalist. Hoover immediately replied, sharing 1959 Naval intelligence information that "He writes reams on where other people stand but . . . no one connected with our embassy knows where he stands." FBI added information about his having been married to a woman who was investigated for having had a roommate who defected to the Russians. Hoover to Salinger, 2/16/1961. CIA updated Salinger on EPD, 4/5/1961

23 Amb. Briggs to SecState, Confidential, no. 1557, 2/16/1961; Briggs Airgram to SecState reviewing Greek press coverage of interview, 2/17/1961

24 Grogan, "Restored Prestige of Ilias Dimitrakopoulos" forwarding CIA memorandum and attachment, which expressed concern that, despite efforts to block exclusive interviews, EPD obtained and published high-level interviews with the vice president, Under-Secretary of State Chester Bowles, Admiral Burke, and the heads of the International Bank for Reconstruction and Development and Development Loan Fund, 2/14/1961; CIA's deputy director of plans report "Restored Prestige of Ilias Dimitrakopoulos Since His Trip to US," 3/10/1961, included with CIA letter to Salinger 4/5/1961.

25 USIS from Michael Listgarten, 4/13/1961.

26 [Redacted], 6/8/1961

27 [Redacted], 8/1961

28 [Redacted], CIA, May 1961

29 "CIA discussion with Pierre Salinger regarding Mr. Ilias Dimitrakopoulos," 2/17/1961

30 According to the CIA, the President and DCI met to discuss further EPD actions, including efforts

to "seal Dimitrakopoulos off from sources of 'exclusive interviews.'" On 8/30/1962, the CIA followed up earlier conversations with Salinger to impress on him that EPD was much more dangerous than "just a pest." Salinger requested and received more detailed derogatory (and false) information.

31 Years later, when Elias accused the CIA, at Kennedy's press secretary's instigation, of being responsible for the break-in caper, Salinger didn't deny his role but told a reporter "I just don't remember anything about that." Jeff Nesmith, "Did CIA Ransack Greek Journalist's Office," *Cox News Service*, 1/7/2000

32 Burke later told an author that EPD "saved my neck . . . This man stood by me and told the truth." Margolis, 80

33 "Tribute to the 6th Fleet—A Mighty and Trusted Friend," *ADP* editorial, 4/12/1961, inserted in *Congressional Record* by Cong. Porter Hardy, 6/26/1961

34 "Let Them Speak," *ADP* editorial, 9/26/1962

35 Potter, 437

36 Ibid., 437–8

37 Jack Anderson and Jan Moller, "Did Kennedy mistrust butcher Bay of Pigs?," *United Feature Syndicate*, 11/21/1997

38 Admiral Anderson letter to EPD, 7/18/1961

39 "Visit of Greek Prime Minister," JFKL, Greece, 61–3, April 1961, Box 117; Tapley Bennett, Jr., Deputy Chief of Mission, ADST; Woodhouse (*Karamanlis*), 108–9

40 "Caramanlis Visit, Washington, April 17–20, 1961, Briefing Book," Position Papers, Tabs A–I, JFKL

41 Ibid., Draenos (*Andreas*), 36–7; Draenos, "Liberal Awakening," 134–6

42 Richard Westebbe, Interview, 12/11/2011

43 Nathan Thrall and Jesse James Wilkins, "Kennedy Talked, Khrushchev Triumphed," *NYT*, 5/22/2008; Frederick Kempe, "The worst day of JFK's life," Reuters.com/berlin1961/2011/05/27/the-worst-day-of-jfks-life/

44 Clogg (*Parties*), 40–43

45 Clogg (*Concise History*), 152; Katris, 96–7; Roubatis, 156–7; Stern, 14, 26; Draenos (*Andreas*), 39–40; "Athenian" (*Rodis Rouphos*), 42; FRUS, 1964–68, XVI, xxxi–xxxii

46 Brewster ADST

47 EPD (US Naval Institute *Proceedings*,) 5/2001, 69

48 Jackie Kennedy told Arthur Schlesinger "It looked as if he'd been fired for incompetency or something . . . Jack so badly wanted to have it come that he was being promoted by being ambassador to Greece." Jacqueline Kennedy (*Historic Conversations*), 320

49 Walter J. Silva, ADST, 1/23/1995

50 Peter Dammann to John L. O'Donnell, op. cit., 2/3/1961

51 A. C. Sedgwick, as president of Foreign Press Association of Greece, sent a letter to EPD 1/6/1961 attesting that Elias had never described himself as a correspondent or representative of the *New York Herald Tribune* newspaper.

52 Yerxa, interviews, 1/26/2010 and 2/15/2010

53 Ibid., 2/15/2010

54 When *Village Voice* reporter Cynthia Cotts tried to interview the *Tribune*'s former D.C. bureau chief Donovan in 2001 about his role in this episode, "he did not respond to a request for comment."

55 Komer to Kilduff, 7/31/1962, with three copies to Pierre Salinger

13: MOVING LEFT

1 Burke to Whitney, 7/17/1962

2 Hill provided a "To Whom It May Concern" letter confirming EPD's appointment as "Mediterranean area" correspondent. 8/3/1962

3 CIA [redacted,] Memo to Files, 8/13/1962

4 CIA memorandum, 8/15/1962, 1691, 30112; John Warner, Journal Office of Legislative Counsel, SECRET, 8/14/1962, 1, CREST; ibid., 8/17/1962, "Secret," CREST

5 8/17/1962. Signed by Everett Walker, director, Syndicate & News Service

6 Shortly afterward, Admiral Burke sent EPD an autographed photo inscribed "To my good friend Elias . . . with appreciation for what he does for the Free World." 8/1962

7 CIA [redacted], Memorandum for the Record, 8/15/1962; CIA [redacted], memorandum,

8/18/1962; the CIA's deputy director of plans had earlier asked the USIA Assistant Director of Security to cherry-pick its "Top Secret" correspondence concerning Celia's time in Moscow in 1948, apparently to find something that could be used to pressure her. 11/13/1957. CIA also suggested consulting with Eleni Vlachou for confirmation of her firing EPD, 8/18/1962. There is no information that she ever complied. CIA [redacted] memorandum referring to conference to discuss "ferreting out sources" of EPD's income and contacting his "now divorced wife" to 8/20/1962.

8   Hill to EPD, *Washington Star*, 9/20/1963; About a week before, 9/11/1962, the CIA's assistant deputy director of plans had written to the deputy director of plans, expressing frustration that, "despite our repeated warnings" over a decade, too many consider EPD "a charming fellow." He concluded that EPD had become the exemplar of "problems we face with the Fourth Estate."

9   Hill letter to EPD, 9/19/1992

10   CIA memorandum, 8/31/1962

11   Ibid.

12   US Naval Institute *Proceedings*, 5/2001, 69

13   Brugioni, 399

14   Manning, interview, ADP, 8/25/1962; Kennedy, ADP, 8/29/1962

15   Athens to SecState, telegram, 9/2/1962

16   Peter Braestrup, "Johnson Assures Greeks on U.S. Aid," *NYT*, 9/4/1962

17   Robert Schott to Daniel Brewster, State Dept. Confidential Memorandum, "Secret Attachments," 8/22/1962

18   Dallek (*Flawed Giant*), 42

19   Dallek, ibid., 42; Shesol, 110

20   September 10,1962, NEA/GRK, RG59, NARA

21   "Senator Goldwater Lashes the 'Weakness' of U.S. Foreign Policy: Don't Placate the Reds," *ADP*, 11/4/1962

22   Ibid.

23   Labouisse to State Dept., Confidential, A-232, 9/22/1962, with copies to Kilduff (Salinger's assistant press secretary) and Komer

24   State Dept. Security, confidential airgram, 9/11/1962; CIA classified message, 8/7/1962; CIA classified message, 8/20/1962; "US Ties with Greece," Charleston SC, *News and Courier*, 11/12/1962

25   Agency of Newspapers for the Athens Press

26   Modiano, interview, 5/31/2012

27   Memorandum for Director of Central Intelligence McCone, 2/8/1963, FRUS, 1961–63, XVI, doc. 342; memorandum, "Greek Governmental Crisis," 6/17/1963; NARA; Woodhouse (Rise), 1; Woodhouse (*Karamanlis*), 148

28   Woodhouse (*Karamanlis*), Chapter 6; Genevoix, 161–70

29   Gkotzaridis (*Pacifist*), 174; Murtagh, 60

30   Gkotzaridis, ibid., 213

31   Ibid., 175–6

32   Attributed to Royal Secretary Gerasimos Gigantes (Philip Deane), *To Vima*, 6/4/1976 in Gkotzaridis, "Who . . .", 314; Murtagh, 63; see J. E. Miller for doubts about Deane's veracity, 18–19.

33   "Coming De Gaulle Visit Worries Officials in Greece," *New York Herald Tribune*, 5/14/1963

34   Gkotzaridis, *Pacifist's Life*, 251

35   Ibid., 253

36   Ibid., 257

37   Ibid., chapter 10

38   Ibid., 346–7

39   Georgios Romaios, Ioannis Voultepsis, and Georgios Bertsos were later punished for their reporting; ibid., 347.

40   On May 28, "Confidential Joint State-Defense–USIA Message" to "All NATO Capitals," telegram, 5/28/1963, no. 2034

41   Reed Harris to IOS, Mr. McNichol, 8/12/1963; Harris letter to EPD, 8/15/1963

42   "Reed Harris Quits as 'Voice' Official," *NYT*, 4/15/1953

43   Op. cit., Reed to McNichol

44   CS File no. 201-55006 Sig Cen, 82261, 11/13/1963

45 Anderson, Jack, "Government Burglaries," *United Feature Syndicate*, 2/2/1977
46 Brugioni, 60–61
47 *ADP*, 10/17/1963
48 Philip Foisie to EPD, 9/17/1963
49 FRUS, 35, 7/15/1963
50 *Daily Express*, 7/11/1963; *Madera Tribune*, 7/11/1963
51 "Budding Presidential Candidate Speaks to Post," *ADP*, 10/13/1963
52 Ibid.
53 Ibid.
54 Interviews, Westebbe, 12/11/2011, and Persa Metaxas, 5/30/2012
55 Confidential to SecState, 10/22/1963
56 Ibid.
57 Ibid.
58 CIA, Special Article of Current Intelligence: The Greek Political Crises, 10/11/1963
59 *Los Angeles Times*, 11/10/1963
60 11/11/1963
61 Robert Hartman, *Los Angeles Times*, 11/10/1963
62 Clogg (*Parties*), 45–53
63 JFK NEWS CONFERENCE 63, OCTOBER 31, 1963; https://www.jfklibrary.org/archives/
other-resources/john-f-kennedy-press-conferences/news-conference-63
64 Talbot to SecState, 11/4/1963

14: THE KOUMPAROS AND THE STAR REPORTER

1 Pappas biographical information is largely assembled from his FBI files, journalist accounts, and
confidential personal reminiscences.
2 *NYT*, 5/24/1959
3 Ibid.
4 Part-time district court judgeships were then available for political contributions of $500.
5 David Farrell, *Boston Globe*, 11/30/1980; David Farrell, "Politics Was Always on the Menu," *Boston Globe*, 8/7/1983
6 Hewitt, 148.
7 E.g. "off-the-record" dinner meeting, 7/27/1953; "off-the-record stag dinner" 4/1/1954; President's luncheon for Queen Frederika, 10/23/1958; luncheon, DDEL, Pappas file
8 Ibid., The President's Appointments, 6/1/1953; correspondence from Mamie Eisenhower to Pappas, different dates, for presents including "exquisite" birthday gift of rubies and sapphires in shape of "Evzon shoe" of Royal Guard of Greece, 11/14/1957, Presidential Appointment Files, WHCF President's Personal File, WHCF General File, DDEL
9 "T. A. Pappas, 89, Dies, Was Envoy to Greece," *NYT*, 1/17/1988
10 Director FBI, 11/27/57, Confidential, State Dept. 1/30/1957; 10/21/1957; WH memo, 2/21/1959, Greece: Pappas; WHCF 2/17/1959; Executive Order 10450—security requirements for Government Employment
11 In a surprise to the FBI, Pappas somehow obtained a copy of the FBI report and wrote a stinging rebuttal to the charges, "Analysis of points raised in Pappas memorandum (undated)." Because Pappas was a "close personal friend of the President," FBI rechecked its intelligence and found the damaging data "to be correct," Nichols to Jones, FBI memorandum, 2/14/1957; Nichols to Tolson, FBI, 2/20/1957; financial condition, 10/17/1929, other information updated in 3/24/1969 FBI report.
12 "Secret/No Foreign Distribution," 3/24/1969, FBI, describing erroneous 2/1950 information; Executive Order 10450-Security requirements for Government Employment
13 John Foster Dulles Papers, 1/1957; Maxwell Rabb Papers, DDEL
14 Pappas letter to President Eisenhower, 6/26/1956; described in 5/29/1953 Rawlins-to-Barrow memo as "one of the biggest money raisers in the Republican Party," Maxwell Rabb Papers, Box 35, DDEL
15 Pappas telegram to Nixon, 3/14/1956; Nixon letter to Pappas, 3/17/1956, RMNL
16 Pat Hillings memo to Rose Mary Woods, 7/25/1956; memorandum, RN to RLK, 8/6/1956, RMNL
17 Nixon to Pappas, 1/26/1960, RMNL
18 Leonard Hall to Pappas, 7/7/1960; Stanley E. McCaffrey to Spyros P. Skouras, 7/18/1960, RMNL

19 E.g. Pappas letter to Nixon, 4/27/1961; Nixon to Pappas 4/29/1961; Nixon to Pappas, 11/8/1961; Pappas to Nixon, 11/18/1961, RMNL

20 Pappas telephone call to Rose Mary Woods, 1/9/1961, RMNL

21 Summers (*Arrogance*), 46–9, 54–8; Hersh (*Camelot*), 157

22 James C. Warren, Jr., ADST, 3/22/2001

23 Ibid., 30

24 Draenos (*Andreas*), 78; Unger, *Boston After Dark*, 10/12/1971

25 As testimony before the US Senate's Antitrust and Monopoly Subcommittee would later expose (1968), "The Pappas interests account for fully 75 percent of the total United States private investment and 54 percent of the actual capital exports to Greece." And in the country itself, Pappas holdings (in assets) ranked second in the petroleum industry, third in coal, and fifth in basic both metals and chemicals. US Senate hearings on economic concentration, 1968, Part 7

26 Westebbe, interview, 12/11/2011

27 (1) reducing the number of monopolies; (2) increasing the Greek public's share of oil profits; (3) eliminating ESSO as Pappas's sole source of crude oil; (4) reducing the Pappas monopoly on the import of domestically consumed oil; (5) increasing the Greek bank security deposit requirement for Pappas's steel mill.

28 Ibid.; it was described as "the biggest single foreign investment ever made in Greece," "Greece: Americans Bearing Gifts," *TIME*, 5/22/1964.

29 Draenos, "Liberal Awakening," 135. Andreas returned from the United States in 1959. In the early 1960s he ran the Center of Economic Research, financed by both the Karamanlis government and the Ford and Rockefeller foundations. The Center was designed to complement Kennedy Administration soft power initiatives that promoted mixed-economy approaches.

30 Peter B. Swiers, ADST, 5/27/1994

31 Howe, *Power Peddlers*, 422

32 Ibid.

33 CONFIDENTIAL [redacted] Report, 1/22/1960

34 E.g. *ADP*, 2/8/1964; Tsoucalos, 182

35 CIA, SECRET [redacted] report, 4/1964

36 CIA [redacted], 6/23/1964; FBI, 6/23/1964

37 Draenos (*Andreas*), 82–3

38 Joyce to EPD, 3/4/1964

39 Draenos email to JHB, 3/3/2019. Elias considered Andreas's behavior unscrupulous. He was even more outraged when Andreas humiliated Margaret in 1987 by abandoning her for an Olympic Airways stewardess barely half his age. Cody, Edward, "Papandreou Embroiled in Love, Money," *WP*, 12/2/1988

40 Reuters, "Blast Kills 13 During Ceremony," *Fort Lauderdale News*, 11/30/1964

41 "US Embassy Denies Involvement in Gorgopotamos Bloody Incident," *Ethnos*, 8/5/1965; AmEmb speculated EDP "actually involved in fabrication of document," Confidential, AmEmb to SecState, 8/6/1965; "Embassy (Vigderman) to USIS (Taylor), Confidential Investigator's Query," 2/24/1966

42 12/15/1964 meeting, EPDP; In May 1966, McCone (no longer CIA director) unexpectedly met EPD when visiting Gov. Brown's California office. McCone "assured" EPD that his suspicions regarding persecution and discrimination by CIA were completely unfounded. [Redacted] CIA account of conversation, 6/9/1966; CIA memorandum, 8/30/1967

43 Roubatis, 197; Tsoucalas, 187

44 State Dept., Field Information Report, Athens, 3/7/1966; FRUS, 1961–1964, XVI, doc. 225

45 Tsoucalas, 186

46 Ibid.

47 Whether their recollections were favorable or unfavorable, those who knew Tom Pappas and his immediate family or worked with him (and those who learned stories second-hand) overwhelmingly asked that their names not be identified.

48 Lilly MacCrakis, interview, 4/1/2014

49 CIA Intelligence Information Cable, SECRET, Priority, "King Constantine's Plans to Force Resignation of Prime Minister Papandreou," LBJL, National Security Files, Komer, 1965 Cabinet Crisis, 1/21/1965; Lagoudakis, "The April Coup." Lagoudakis Papers, Boston University, Box 143, Box 216

50 Ibid.

51 John Owens, ADST

52 Tsoucalas, 193; "Athenian," *Inside the Colonels*, 54

53 The shorthand chant shouted was "Ena, ena tessera," a reference to Article 114 of the 1952 Greek constitution, entrusting its protection to "the patriotism of the Greeks," Clogg (*Elections*), 52

54 Ibid., 206 (Tsoucalas spells his name "Barnum"); Draenos, email to JHB, 11/25/2014

55 It was alleged that Pappas had earlier bribed Queen Frederika with $1 million, followed by $250,000 annual "retainers" to use her influence to help advance his business interests. Murtagh, 49; State Dept. intelligence specialist Charilaos Lagoudakis said "the Palace did buy Center Union deputies" and there is strong "circumstantial evidence" that the CIA's Maury helped the Palace make its purchases, presumably with the involvement of Tom Pappas. Pyrros, 190

56 *To Vima*, magazine supplement, 7/30/2012

57 EPD "Athens Cautioned on Dictatorship" (NANA), *The Press* (Jamaica, NY), 9/15/1965

58 Anschuetz memo, 7/27/1965

59 Pappas criticized Robert Kennedy and George Papandreou and praised LBJ, then asked the President to invite Prime Minister Stephanopoulos to the White House to bolster his standing against opponents; Pappas also asked the US to put a nuclear reactor in Greece. "For the record," 3/16/1966, LBJL; Pappas followed this with a request to LBJ through Joe Califano to send White House aide Mike Manatos to Greece to represent the President at the opening of his industrial complex; Pappas to Califano, 3/26/1966; Johnson's immediate response was to ask Larry O'Brien to call him, then Califano on 4/15/1966 warmly wrote Pappas saying Manatos could not be spared at the time. LBJL

60 Kubly, 350

61 In 1968, when asked about his involvement with the CIA, he would tell the pro-junta newspaper *Apogevmatini* "I'm very proud of it. I have worked for the CIA every time they asked me for help," 7/18/1968.

62 Karamessines to Director, "Memorandum for Director of Central intelligence via Deputy Director for Plans, Subject: Ilias Dimitrakopoulos," 3/14/1966

63 Victor Stier to Donald Taylor, 5/19/1966

64 Event-related materials in EPDP

65 Nancy Jackson to EPD, 4/11/1966; The Jackson letter reconstructed a 3/1965 conversation she had with Salinger in which he explicitly claimed EPD was a "Communist," adding "while I was at the White House, he wasn't even allowed to interview Sister Kenny [a leader in the fight against polio]." Shortly afterward, EPD angrily told Victor Stier at USIA headquarters that he'd heard from an unnamed male friend in LA that Salinger was smearing Elias, claiming that he was a "double agent." Victor Stier, Program and Policy Officer, D.C., to Donald Taylor, PAO, Athens, 5/19/1966

66 CIA [redacted] Report prepared 10/1/1966; 9/22–25/1966; CIA report on Senator Hartke's visit to Greece, 10/17/1966; CIA [redacted] memorandum, 10/14/1966

67 "No 'Turkeys' for Black Tie," *WP*, 5/23/1966

68 EPD, McCormack interview, *ADP*, 8/9/1966

69 Ibid.

70 Eliot Janeway (Prescriptions), 42–3; *The Janeway Service* (newsletter), Vol. 13, no. 644, 9/28/1966; Janeway, "Greece Feels Policy of U.S. Is One-Sided," *Chicago Tribune*, 7/28/1966

15: FROM REPORTER TO ACTIVIST

1 Sulzberger, C. L. *An Age of Mediocrity; Memoirs and Diaries 1963-1972*. New York: Macmillan, 1978, 284.

2 FRUS, 1964–68, XVI, doc. 255

3 FRUS, 1964–68, XVI, doc. 259, 3/8/1967 and doc. 261, 3/13/1967

4 Maury, *WP*, 5/1/1977

5 FRUS, 1964–68, 16:555, no. 261, LBJL, National Security File, Intelligence File, Greek Coup, 3/13/1967

6 FRUS, XVI, doc. 259–61; Meeting of 303 Committee, Memorandum for the Record, doc. 261 FRUS; Marquis Childs, "A Coup in Greece—A Bit of Blackmail," *WP*, 5/15/1967, inserted in Congressional Record by Senator Fulbright, 12572, 5/15/1967; The Greek Junta: A Retrospective," *National Herald*, 4/21/2007; Tsoucalos, 203; J. E. Miller, 130; Draenos (Andreas), 280–1

7   FRUS, XVI, doc. 264, 3/24/1967

8   FRUS 1961-1964, XVI, doc. 265, Secret Letter from Amb. Talbot to Country Director for Greece (Brewster), 3/30/1967; doc. 267, Secret telegram from Department of State (Rusk) to the Embassy in Greece (Talbot), 4/3/1967

9   CONFIDENTIAL Memorandum for the Files: "Conversation between General Norstad and Former Greek Prime Minister Karamanlis, 3/3/1967, NARA Greece Record Group 59; Sulzberger (Postscript), 274, 277; letters to EPD from Senators Frank Moss and Quentin Burdick (5/3/1990) confirming they and Senator Wayne Morse received similar information from a 1975 "executive branch" briefing

10 J. E. Miller, 133

11 M. Papandreou (Nightmare), 132-9

12 Draenos (Andreas), 299; Woodhouse (Rise), 23

13 FRUS, 1964-68, doc. 225, Field Information Report, 3/7/1966 and doc. 245, Field Information Report, 12/20/1966, noted the rightest conspiratorial group had been in existence since late 1963 and had met secretly on 12/13/1966.

14 Stern, 45-6 (DCM Norbert Anschuetz received the tip in early April); Keely (Colonels' Coup), 86; Draenos (Andreas), 302-3; Klarevas, 36

15 Lagoudakis, "The April Coup,"28-9, Lagoudakis collection, Boston University, Box 143; Charles M. Perkins, US Army Attaché, "Plans of idea for coup and military dictatorship in Greece," 8/7/1965 in Lagoudakis file

16 According to USIS, another EPD source was Gerasimos Tsigantes (aka Philip Dean) secretary to King Constantine. AmEmb to USIADC, 5/7/1964

17 Mario Modiano, Persa Metaxas, interviews, 6/2012

18 Vlachos, Helen. "The Colonels and the Press" in Clogg and Yannopoulos, 60

19 Hitler war kein gutter Klavierspieler," Der Tagesspiegel, 2/14/2010; "Die goldenen Brücken," Der Spiegel, 3/23/1955; "Great Britain: Just Daisy," TIME, 1/17/1955; "Daisy D'Ora 1916-1920," https://www.youtube.com/watch?v=QMfivG_DtNs

20 John M. Maury, "The Greek Coup: A Case of CIA Intervention? No, says our Man in Athens," WP, 5/1/1977

21 Douglas Hartley; Charles Stuart Kennedy, ASDT; see Robert Keeley, ADST, and Colonels' Coup.

22 James C. Warren, Jr., ADST, 3/22/2001, 31

23 Because of Totomis's sordid role in a tabloid sex scandal, Papadopoulos resisted, but the CIA and Pappas were adamant. Katris, 260; Estia 11/1/1951; Kriton Gregoriades (undated) account in EPDP

24 McDonald, 41-2; Zaharopoulos, 28

25 McDonald, ibid., 24

26 Vlachos obit, The Independent, 10/17/1995

27 Sulzberger (Mediocrity), 334

28 McDonald, 28

29 The embassy reported that after his time in hiding, EPD "has re-emerged with a vengeance." PAO Donald K. Taylor confidential memorandum to ambassador, 8/16/1967

30 Margaret Papandreou, 236-7

31 Talbot wrote SecState in a confidential telegram: EPD "has made no attempt since April 21 to hide at public functions his distaste for present regime." Ref: 1249, 9/12/1967

32 UN Information Centre (Athens), invitation letter Jean Back, Director, to EPD, 8/5/1967; Jose Rolz-Bennett, UN Undersecretary for Political Affairs, Office of Public Information (New York), 8/22/1967

33 UN Press Release, "Sixth UN Editors' Roundtable to Convene in Warsaw, 12 to 15 September 1967," 1967/348, 9/5/1967; "UN Editors' Roundtable," ADP, 9/6/1967; "Greek journalist invited to UN 'roundtable' meet," Athens News, 9/7/1967; Frankfurter Allgemeine Zeitung, 9/13/1967

34 V. Zafiropoulos, 9/9/1967

35 Talbot confidential telegram to SecState Dean Rusk, Ref: 1249, 9/12/1967; confidential follow-up, AmEmb Athens (McClelland) to SecState, Ref: 1294, 9/13/1967

36 1971 House Foreign Affairs Committee hearings, 115; EDP FOIA request for CIA cable 9/13/1967 "denied in its entirety."

16: ESCAPE

1 CIA classified message, 3/31/1962
2 Bo Lidegaard emails to JHB, 10/6/2010, 10/7/2010
3 Retired Danish diplomat Anders Harris Nielson emails to JHB, 2010–2015, are the main source of then-contemporaneous Warsaw and Danish Embassy descriptions.
4 Geoffrey Hollingsworth, BBC, to EPD, 9/18/1967
5 Ambassador Talbot, Confidential telegram #1356 to SecState "Although his friends in US may apply pressure [for visa], we believe his presence in US at this time could be embarrassing to US." 9/19/1967
6 Evans, Rowland & Novak, Robert. "State Official Aided Greek Junta in Trying to Bar Political Refugee," WP, 11/2/1967
7 Brewster, ASDT
8 EPD telegram to Cong. Mendel Rivers, 9/24/1967
9 Nat Dumont telegram 9/27/1967, EPDP.
10 Notes from Michael Janeway telephone call, EPDP
11 EPD telegram exchanges with Celler, 9/24/1967–9/26/1967
12 Brimberg telegram to EPD, 9/27/1967
13 Adam Smith, *The Money Game*, "Lunch at Scarsdale Fats," chapter 16

17: EXILED IN AMERICA

1 Hon. John Xifaris, interview, 4/2012
2 *Deena Clark* (obit) "Deena Clark, TV Personality," WP, 8/5/2003; Deena Clark Papers, University of Maryland Special Collections in Mass Media & Culture; EPDP; Clark was the second host of MTP http://eyesofageneration.com/saturday-november-6-1947-meet-the-press-debuts-nbc-as-youll-see-in-thi/
3 Interviews and email exchanges (6/2017) with Nikia Leopold (daughter) and Susan Margolis Balk (9/2014). Despite some gossip to the contrary, EPD and Deena Clark had an asexual abiding symbiotic friendship which strengthened in the years after her 1973 divorce.
4 Keely (Colonels' Coup), 151–7; Stern, 54–7; J. E. Miller, 153–4; FRUS, 1964–1968, Vol. 16, doc. 344, 12/13/1967, doc. 348, 12/14/1967
5 Reconstruction of these events was aided by contemporaneous affidavits, FOIA secured documents, and court documents, supplemented by EPD and Richard Westebbe interviews.
6 Ingrid Rodenberg v. Robert R. Rodenberg, Civil Action no. D 3741–67, District of Columbia Court of General Sessions, Domestic Relations Branch
7 EPD asked congressional investigators on 12/8/78, why, if the purpose was to catch Mrs. Rodenberg engaged in adulterous behavior, Mr. Rodenberg and his crew didn't break in the night before when "a man was in the house until 3:30 a.m."
8 Metropolitan Police Trial Board, 6/30/1969
9 Dept. of Justice, INS Investigation of EPD, A17 351 989, 4/22/1969. FBI interview with Ymelda Dixon, 2/10/1969; McLendon and Smith, 197
10 Ibid.
11 Ibid.
12 Barton to Celler, 1/31/1968
13 Celler, Morse, Hartke: Morse letter to Dean Rusk, 3/8/1968; INS exchanges: letter to Wayne Morse, 9/16/1968
14 Celler to Talbot, 5/3/1968; Hartke to Talbot, 3/29/1968
15 Talbot to Celler, 5/7/1968
16 Eastland to INS, 6/25/1968
17 CIA advising INS, 7/30/1968
18 Karamessines CIA report, 10/19/1967; FBI memorandum, 10/23/1968
19 FBI memorandum, 10/23/1968
20 Lewis Barton, District Director INS, memorandum, 12/28/1967
21 Petros Markaris, *"Greece: the other side of 1968: Memories and Legacies,"* 209
22 Tony Judt, 507

23 The former San Francisco mayor and powerful player in Greek-American politics told *AP* journalist James Polk in 1971 that he knew the three heads of the junta and that "90 percent of the Greek-Am community is in favor of the present gov't because it brought STABILITY to Greece. No more civil war; no war with Turkey; real anchor for US in NATO." Polk to JHB letter, 12/27/2011

24 "Rise of the Junta in Greece," Matt Barrett https://www.ahistoryofgreece.com/junta.htm

25 Witcover (*Very Strange*), 6

26 He definitely didn't want to repeat the experience of 1960, selecting Henry Cabot Lodge, a foreign policy equal.

27 UPI, "A Good Word' for Agnew," *NYT*, 8/10/1968, 12

28 Donald Rumsfeld, "Confidential Memo—1968 Meeting to Discuss Vice Presidential Nomination," 8/8/1968; 1968%20Meeting%20with%20Richard%20Nixon%20re%20Vice%20Presidential%20Pick%2008-08-1968%20(1).pdf

29 Theo Wilson, "Pappas, the Rich Mystery Man Behind Agnew" *New York Daily News*, 8/9/1968; "Agnew, the junta and the CIA link with Nixon camp," *Sunday Times* (London), 9/29/1968

30 National Press Club Transcript, Friday, 9/27/1968

31 "Remarks by Governor Spiro Agnew, National Press Club, Washington, D.C., 9/27/1968

32 Ibid.

33 Louise Gore letter to EPD, 9/27/1968; on 2/21/70 Agnew told a fundraiser in St. Paul, MN, "I have made no public statements on the Greek government." Charles E. Claffey, "Exiled Greek Claims Agnew Supports Junta," *Boston Globe*, 2/21/1970; in 1989, Agnew wrote historian Kutler: claiming to recall nothing about Greek money, the Gore note "and nothing about the Press Club . . . Louise Gore was pressuring me to support Demetracopoulos and my advisers were telling me that he was some sort of wild-eyed leftist who was to be avoided." Agnew letter to Kutler, 2/1/1989

34 "Statement Made by the Greek Political Editor in Exile, Mr. Elias P. Demetracopoulos on Saturday, September 28 at a News Conference in Washington, DC," *Congressional Record*, Wednesday, 10/9/1968

35 Ibid.

36 UPI, "Demetracopoulos," 9/28/1968; "Greek Exile," AP, 9/28/1968; Alain Clement, *Le Monde*, 9/29–30/1968; "Agnew, the junta and the CIA link with the Nixon camp," *Times* (London), 9/29/1968

37 CIA memorandum, 9/30/1968

38 Nohlen & Stover, 830

39 Embassy of Greece letter to Cong. Les Aspin, 12/15/1980

40 Edward A. Junghans, Assistant District Director, Investigations, to EDP, 9/19/1968

41 Supporting Affidavit for INS, 10/23/1968

42 SAC, WFO to FBI director noted that INS investigator was "endeavoring to develop" additional information concerning "subject's morals" that could overcome the evidence of likely physical persecution in Greece and lead to EPD's deportation. 11/14/1968 and 12/11/1968

18: JUNTA-GATE AND THE O'BRIEN GAMBIT

1 Louis Harris, interview, 7/28/2004

2 Robert B. Semple, Jr., "Electoral Pact Pushed by Nixon," *NYT*, 10/30/1968

3 Devries, 147; "Rising voter confidence in Democrats is found; Gallup Poll Registers Cut in GOP lead on Ability to Handle Major Issues, 10/30/1968; Kathleen Hall Jamieson, *Packaging the Presidency*, 256–7

4 McGinnis, 126

5 Garment, 140

6 Converse, Miller, Rusk, and Wolfe ("Continuity and Change"), 1083–105

7 Steinem, 10/28/1968. Steinem declined multiple email and telephone requests to discuss her 1968 assessment.

8 Teddy White letter to Nixon printed in Christopher Hitchens's column Minority Report, *The Nation*, 6/5/1989, 764

9 *Times* (London), 9/29/1968; *Boston After Dark*, 10/12/1971

10 Roubatis, *Tangled Webs*, 197; Yiannis P. Roubatis and Karen Wynn, "CIA Operations in Greece," in Phillip Agee and Louis Wolf (eds.), *Dirty Work* 147–56

11 Roubatis wrote that KYP was the only security agency "restructured" by Papandreou and that it "presented the American CIA with a host of problems." Roubatis, 197; Andreas Papandreou interview with William Buckley on "Firing Line," 4/30/1972 in *National Herald*'s "The Greek Junta: A Retrospective," 4/21/2007, 12

12 Weiner, *Blank Check*, "The CIA Act kept the Agency's budget secret . . . creating a clandestine treasury for the CIA . . . ", 120; https://www.washingtonpost.com/world/national-security/black-budget-summary-details-us-spy-networks-successes-failures-and-objectives/2013/08/29/7e57bb78-10ab-11e3-8cdd-bcdc09410972_story.html?utm_term=.d36c757150b2 ("Historical data on U.S. intelligence spending is largely nonexistent.")

13 Miranda Pesmazoglou, interview, 5/29/2012

14 Westebbe, interviews, 5/4/2012 and 4/8/2013; "Demetrios Galanis, Headed Greek Bank," *NYT*, 5/5/1973; Economist Westebbe speculated that Pappas may have also taken junta funds for Nixon from the National Bank of Greece, which, based on Pappas's being a major business client, would have been a relatively softer target. EDP's sources only mentioned Central Bank involvement.

15 Mario Modiano, interview, 5/31/2012

16 According to former San Francisco mayor George Christopher, Nixon's 1962 lieutenant-governor running mate and 1968 Nixon-Agnew fundraiser: Pappas "raised a lot of money . . . working closely with Stans in '68," but Christopher was surprised that "nothing listed on records for Pappas." James Polk, July 3, 1971, notes from Christopher interview, included in letter from Polk to JHB, 12/27/2011

17 Tsimas also confirmed it to Stanley I. Kutler in a 1/5/1987 telephone conversation, *Wars*, 651; Kutler letter to EPD, 1/5/1987

18 Apostolides, email to JHB, 2/1/2015. According to Murtagh, in August 1989 the Greek government transported 16.5 million secret files compiled by the police and KYP since 1944 to a steel mill northwest of Athens and incinerated the records. Murtagh, *Rape*, 267

19 Jack Boos, interview, 1/5/2011

20 Deegan subcontracted part of his work to Burson-Marsteller and a "hard-sell publicist," Carl Levin. After Deegan, the Greek Embassy relied on Harry Anestos, a suburban criminal defense attorney, because of a friendship he had with Greek Embassy military attaché and later ambassador Iannis Sorokos, but paid him only $18,000 annually, largely to "cultivate" Agnew and congressmen with large Greek-American constituencies. Howe, *Power Peddlers*, 408

21 Shields, interview, 11/18/2014

22 Helms furnished the harshly critical "undated blind memorandum," 6/14/1966 on EDP to FBI, which forwarded it to State Dept. for action by the Nationalities Intelligence Section. Memorandum from S. J. Papitch to D. J. Brennan, Jr. re: "Ilias P. Dimitrokopulos," 6/20/1966. Report included such false reports as OAG members having "disrupted" his award for heroism, *TIME* magazine dismissing him for "unreliability," flashing "his" American passport and offering to procure similar false passports for Greek journalists, offering bribes, planting propaganda for the Yugoslavs, and the ironic observation that EPD has been a *New York Herald Tribune* stringer "off and on" since 1959. Deputy Director CIA, Richard Helms, "SECRET" Blind Memo attachment, 6/14/1966

23 "Greek Regime Denies Rumor That It is Financing Nixon," *NYT*, 10/15/1968

24 Under the title "Fascist Junta in Greece Financing Nixon's Campaign," Andreas Papandreou's interview with *Tidsignal* in Stockholm was published on 10/1/1968. Spyros "Stan" Draenos said Andreas received the information from EPD, interview, 5/28/2012

25 October 18, 1968, telephone call from EPD to O'Brien's office, 12:25 p.m.; returned call from O'Brien to EPD, 3:55 p.m. (Liza Talbot, Digital Archivist, LBJL), email to JHB, 5/31/2013; O'Brien file, JFKL

26 Maheu, 79, 208–10

27 Ibid., 206–7

28 Ibid., 207

29 O'Brien, *No Final Victories*, 257; Witcover (*Dream Died*), chapter 9; White, *1968*, chapter 9; Blum, *Years of Discord*, 305–10.

30 Maheu, 210

31 Westebbe, interview, 3/13/2012

32 Marion von Cramm letter to EPD, 9/13/1968, followed by October phone calls

33 Voutselas, interview, 3/2011

34 Salinger, 208
35 Gallup Poll, October 1968; Carl Brown, Roper Center email to JHB, 11/2/2010
36 In penning his inscription to Elias in his 1986 Watergate book, *Cover Up*, Harry Dent followed up his earlier sentiment with: "your view re the break-in (i.e. looking for the 1968 Pappas money file) makes sense."
37 Feldstein 62; Dietrich and Thomas, 281–3; Summers, 155, 157
38 Feldstein, 66
39 Ibid., 67–74
40 Napolitan, interview, 11/27/2009
41 Ibid.
42 Broder interviews, 10/2/2009 and 4/12/2010; Mark Feldstein, memorandum to JHB: "Nixon advisor Herbert Klein wrote that Pearson's decision not to air [in 1968] the rumor of Nixon's psychiatric treatment probably saved the presidency for Nixon. It seems equally likely that exposing Nixon's "Greek Connection" would have been just as pivotal. For while financial impropriety may be more complicated to understand than mental illness, Nixon's previous "slush fund" and Howard Hughes scandals would have made yet another, similar pecuniary one seem more believable, reinforcing the worst of Nixon's image." Mark Feldstein, memorandum to JHB "Re: Nixon & Demetracopoulos," 8/29/2013. Klein's "would have changed the results" statement is from his book at 412 and discussed in Feldstein, 95–9; Karen Tumulty, "Obama struggles to get beyond a scandal trifecta," *WP*, 5/15/2013: "The most corrosive political scandals are the ones that feed a preexisting story line."
43 Aloysius Farrell, "Yes, Nixon Scuttled the Vietnamese Peace Talks," *Politico Magazine*, 6/9/2014; W. W. Rostow, "Memorandum for the Record," 5/14/1973, LBJL
44 Healy also credited Princeton political scientist and campaign finance specialist Herbert Alexander with providing him tips concerning Pappas fundraising from Greek and Greek-American sources in 1968. In 1971, Alexander provided then–Associated Press reporter James R. Polk with a similar tip on Greek-American donors who contributed to a 1968 Agnew dinner in a Chicago suburb and discovered their names "attached to identical amounts, which apparently they did not give to a separate Nixon-Agnew committee . . . " The source of those duplicate donations remains a mystery . . ." "False Campaign Money." Polk letter to JHB, 12/27/2011
45 Healy, interviews, 10/2/2009 and 11/2009; http://archive.boston.com/bostonglobe/obituaries/articles/2010/06/07/robert_l_healy_at_84_globe_editor_columnist_political_insider/
46 Lydon, interview, 9/28/2009
47 Kapenstein notebooks, JFKL
48 Charles Claffey, interview, 10/2009, Healy, interview, op. cit. Note also that less than a year before, *The Boston Globe*, in a 11/3/1967 editorial, had specifically championed the cause of "persecuted" exile EPD ("distinguished editor and foe of the present military government") and endorsed the call for a congressional investigation to ascertain "why the Greek junta has so much influence with our State Department and a staunchly pro-American refugee editor has so little." But in October 1968 no one told Winship that the source of the charges about Pappas injecting Greek money into the US election was the same EPD.
49 Christopher Lydon, "Thomas Pappas: Portrait of a Wealthy Immigrant, Political Kingmaker," *Boston Globe*, 10/31/1968, 21
50 Ibid.
51 "Statement Made by the Greek Political Editor in Exile, Mr. Elias P. Demetracopoulos, on Thursday, October 31, 1968, Washington, D.C. at 6 PM," EPDP
52 *WP*, 11/1/1968
53 Feldstein memorandum to Barron, op. cit., "In the fall of 1968, Pearson and Anderson tried desperately to prevent a Nixon victory by publishing one exposé after another but none of them hit their mark." Drew Pearson Papers (G281) LBJL; William G. Helis, Jr., letter to Pearson, October 18, 1968, re: Pappas denial of Greek shipowner involvement in Nixon campaign and other Greek-American fundraising activities; Kapenstein notebooks re: sending Agnew material to Pearson, 10/10/1968, JFKL
54 Westebbe, interview, 8/12/2014
55 Mark Feldstein, "Memorandum to Jim Barron re: Nixon & Demetracopoulos," 8/29/2013
56 Whitten, interviews, 2011–2012

57 Feldstein email to JHB, op. cit., 4. When reports surfaced in 1975 about Agnew's support for the junta and Greek money in the election, Robert B. Lin wrote LTE *Philadelphia Inquirer* (7/30/1975): "If these revelations had been revealed in 1968, we wouldn't have had a Vice President and President forced to resign their offices, because neither would have been elected."

58 Robert Dallek, "Three New Revelations About LBJ," *The Atlantic*, April 1998. "Johnson wanted something to use against Nixon if the Nixon Justice Department started to comb the Johnson Administration for scandal, and Nixon's Greek connection would serve that purpose handsomely." https://www.theatlantic.com/magazine/archive/1998/04/three-new-revelations-about-lbj/377094/

59 Lawrence O'Brien, papers in LBJL and JFKL

60 Norman Sherman, email and interviews, 1/22/2014

61 Jack Anderson with Les Whitten, footnote to United Feature Syndicate column, 6/24/1975; later, "O'Brien denied suppressing information, suggesting he lacked supporting evidence," Norman Kempster, "Break-in Held Effort to Hide Nixon's Money Link to Greece," *Los Angeles Times*, 8/1/1990

62 Richard Helms, corrected transcript of his Kutler interview in Stanley I. Kutler papers in Univ. of Wisconsin (Madison) archives. Pappas proudly told *Apogevmatini* in July 1968 that he "worked for the CIA anytime [his] help was requested." In 1983, EPD told an interviewer, "It would be inconceivable for Tom Pappas to have done this transaction and not to have notified his CIA contacts." W. Dale Nelson, AP, 6/2/1983. EPD later specifically referred to Greek-American CIA agents in Athens as Pappas's frequent local contacts.

63 Healy, interview, op. cit.

64 Kapenstein, 1968 campaign diary, JFKL

65 Fraser, interviews and emails, 9/2014

66 Hersh (*Price*), 138–9; Hersh interviews, including 12/1/2013

67 Robert Healy interviews with JHB discussing Healy's earlier conversations with campaign finance expert Herbert Alexander; https://www.washingtonpost.com/outlook/americas-laws-have-always-left-its-politics-vulnerable-to-foreign-influence/2019/10/18/3fb7db62-f0f3-11e9-89eb-ec56cd414732_story.html

68 Dallek, *Camelot's Court*, 113; Baker, 141, 254

69 According to EPD, Louise Gore gave this information to him.

70 Kutler (*Wars*), 208

19: FIGHTING THE DICTATORSHIP

1 FBI memorandum, 10/23/1968; letters from Republican New York senators Jacob Javits (1/24/1969) and Charles E. Goodell (4/1/1969) to INS district director Lewis Barton

2 Early in the Nixon Administration, EPD described its "encouraging start on the explosive issue of Greece's military dictatorship," praising Secretary of State Rogers for going "well beyond any comments of his predecessor" in expressing concern about junta tortures and violations of civil liberties. LTE, *NYT*, 4/27/1969

3 Memo from RN to Bob Haldeman re: Drew Pearson columns, 1/15/1969, RMNL, WH Special Files Collection, box 1, folder 43; memoranda, RN to Kissinger and Haldeman, 1/15/1969; Kissinger to Haldeman, 1/15/1969 re: scheduling early RN appointment with Tom Pappas; Draenos, "Exile Politics," 63

4 Letter from Deputy Chief of Mission in Greece (McClelland) to Country Director for Greek Affairs (Brewster), FRUS, XXIX, 1969–1976, doc. 239

5 Staude party, details EPDP

6 CIA 5/6/1969

7 Moskos, 108

8 "Pyrros, "Memories of the Anti-Junta Years," The Pyrros Papers, 6/19/1991, Special Collections Library, LaBadie Collection, Greek Junta, University of Michigan

9 Letter from Margaret Papandreou to EPD, 4/6/1969

10 Draenos, "Exile Politics," 57

11 Murtagh, *Rape*, 104, 207

12 Notes and schedule details re: visit in EPD private papers

13 Vlachou to EPD letter, 3/26/1969
14 Cong. Don Fraser inserted the "Greece: A New Vietnam?" speech into the *Congressional Record*, Vol. 115, no. 87, 5/27/1969; Senator Frank Moss, letter to Agnew 5/7/1969; Agnew response 6/12/1969; Senator Quentin Burdick sent letters to Defense Secretary Laird, SecState Rogers, and Kissinger twice, soliciting their views, once enclosing the GWU speech, the other with the Hudson Institute paper.
15 Louis Menand, "Fat Man," *New Yorker*, 6/27/2005
16 7/16/1969; Kahn sent the paper to Hudson's entire mailing list, including Kissinger. Republican Senator Charles Goodell put the Hudson paper in the *Congressional Record*, along with the earlier EPD *Wall Street Journal* article, 8/5/1969
17 State Dept., 8/20/1969; CIA 7/16/1969; CIA memorandum, 10/17/1969
18 *LOOK*, 5/27/1969, 19–21; oral histories later revealed that Ambassador Henry Tasca didn't like to receive "reports describing torture or severe punishment without trial" and when confronted with reports of torture from American diplomats the CIA would say "That's not true. We hear from our sources...," the sources being those who were doing the torturing. Charles Stuart Kennedy, ADST
19 Ibid.
20 Ibid.
21 Panorama WTTG TV, 5/29/1969 transcript
22 Ibid.
23 Testimony, 7/8/1969
24 "The Council of Europe Fights for Democracy in Greece, 1967–1969," Andreas G. Papandreou Foundation, Historical Series no. 1, May 1998. "The Greek Affair" in Council of Europe's European Yearbook, Vol. XVII, 1969, 272–335
25 Kofas, 101; FRUS, 1969–1976, XXIX, doc. 257, 10/7/1969
26 Karamanlis letter, EPDP; Woodhouse, *Karamanlis*, 192; Vidalis, 59; State Dept. Confidential memorandum, 10/30/1969 noted EPD supporting Karamanlis statement in telephone conversation with Andreas Papandreou in Toronto.
27 Woodhouse (*Karamanlis*), 193
28 Editorial, "Caramanlis fights the junta," *NYT*, 10/1/1969
29 EPD telegram to Robert Brimberg, 10/29/1969
30 Vidalis, 64
31 Deena Clark letter to EPD, 10/5/1969
32 Historian Stanley Kutler reviewed the document at the Nixon archives and described it as filled with pages of scurrilous information on Demetracopoulos, largely drawn from CIA files. The archives have since been relocated to Yorba Linda, California, and archivists there now say that that Caulfield memo is missing, perhaps misfiled among the thousands of other documents.
33 10/2/1969, State Dept.; Secret [CIA] memorandum regarding discussion about EDP, 10/17/1969; [CIA] heavily redacted review of meeting with [X] at 10:30 a.m., 10/16/1969
34 Vigderman note attached to Kent Crane, Office of Vice President, 10/6/1969 confidential request, confirming oral briefing, "nothing in writing," 10/7/1969
35 "No further action is warranted and is considering case closed." It sent its assessment to State, the CIA, and the INS, all three of which kept their investigations quite active.
36 CW to EPD, letter, 7/2/1969
37 Ibid.
38 "Demetracopoulos Responds to TNH Interview with US ambassador Philips Talbot," *National Herald*, 8/27/2010
39 For better understanding of Tasca background, see J. E. Miller, 161.
40 Evans & Novak, Inside Report, *Philadelphia Inquirer*, 3/31/1969
41 Goldwater (*With No Apologies*), 214–5; Memorandum for the President's File, Washington, 3/20/1969. SUBJECT Early-afternoon Meeting in the President's Office with Honorable Thomas A. Pappas (1:00–1:15 p.m.) 1 Source: National Archives, Nixon Presidential Materials, White House Special Files, President's Office Files, and Memoranda for the President
42 Evans & Novak, Inside Report, 3/31/1969 included the *Congressional Record*, CR, E6084, 7/17/1969; Philip Warden, "An Achilles Heel—The Greek Post," *Chicago Tribune*, 8/12/1969; Evans & Novak, "Greek junta cynicism," 11/16/1969

43 Nixon would eventually write to Quinn, indicating he had picked Tasca, whom he had known "since 1947" and considered "several cuts above the average foreign service officer." Letter, 12/20/1983

44 Senate Foreign Relations Committee, Nomination Hearings, 11/4/1969, 28

45 State Dept., informal State Dept. memorandum, 12/3/1969

46 Yearbook of the European Convention on Human Rights; the European Commission and European Court of Human Rights, "1969: The Greek Case," The Hague: Martinus Nijhoff, 1972; editorial, "Greek Junta on Trial," *NYT*, 12/11/1969

47 News Release, Moss Opposes Confirmation of New Ambassador to Greece," 12/17/1969, *Congressional Record* S17228-9; Paul Grimes, "Senators Stall on Envoy to Greece," *Philadelphia Bulletin*, 12/10/1969; *AP*, "Block of ambassador's approval planned to protest Greek policies," *Arizona Republic*, 12/11/1969

48 Pelt, 297–9; Nafpliotis, 61

49 Munn, 99-100

50 Earlier that year, junta organ *Eleftheros Kosmos* editorialized "A Return [to democracy] is Precluded," 4/23/1969, and at Salonica Trade Fair, Papadopoulos proclaimed: "Leaps forward are not achieved with a parliament." 9/9/1969

51 *AP*, "Goodell Ends Stall on Envoy," Wilmington (DE) *Evening Journal*, 12/16/1969

52 *Congressional Record*, 12/19/1969, S17227–32; "Tasca Given Senate OK as Greek Envoy," *Philadelphia Inquirer*, 12/20/1969

53 "Statement of Senator Edward M. Kennedy on the Military Junta in Greece," 12/19/1969

20: "SENATOR, ARE YOU TELLING ME IT'S A TRAP?"

1 J. E. Miller, 162

2 "Kissinger to Nixon, memorandum, FRUS, 1969–1976, Vol. XXIX, no. 265, 12/19/1969

3 Report by Ambassador to Greece (Tasca), "Report on Greece," ibid., no. 273, 3/31/1970

4 Memorandum from chairman of the National Security Council Undersecretaries Committee to President Nixon, ibid, no. 278, 5/21/1970

5 J. E. Miller, 161–4

6 Voutselis to EPD, 1/13/1970

7 Persa Metaxas, letters to EPD, 1/17/1970 and 2/5/1970; interview, 5/30/2012

8 Brewster, Memorandum for the Files, 4/4/1969 NARA, RG59, Central Files, 1967–69, Pol 15–1, Greece; FRUS, 1964–68, Vol. XVI, doc. 301; J. E. Miller, 159–60; Vidalis, 25–6

9 Dimitrakis, 135–6; Sulzberger (*Mediocrities*), 601; Draenos, "Exile Politics," *The Historical Review*, Vol. XI (2014) 31–65; see Papandreou, 5/18/1970 letter to John Deros in Vidalis, 83. According to *Newsweek*, Andreas's "association with far left groups and individuals . . . scared off a good deal of émigré support." 1/12/1970, 36; In Geneva, George Mylonas said opposition groups and individuals should coordinate their activities, but refused to work together with Andreas, Vidalis, 90; even the US Committee for Democracy in Greece, whose original purpose was to free him from prison, reluctantly concluded that "Andreas isn't helping." Pyrros, 1, 4

10 March 12, 1970, NET (Channel 13) documentary: Rex Polier, "Watching the Wandering Greek in Exile," *Philadelphia Bulletin*, 3/12/1970; "Melina Mercouri Stars on NET Network," *NYT*, 3/11/1970

11 Bill Duke, handwritten note to EPD (undated). Duke had been an assistant to Senator Jacob Javits (R-NY).

12 Murtagh, 132–3

13 Blood, Fritzlan, King, ADST; see J. E. Miller, 164, fn 26 re: Haig suppression of 10/1/70 State Dept.'s Bureau of Intelligence and Research report critical of US policy

14 Remarks to Foreign Student Service Council of Greater Washington Film Benefit Program, 1/20/1970

15 Pillar, 70

16 Ibid., 72

17 Vidalis, 73; *Christian Science Monitor*, 5/6/1970

18 Pyrros, 16–17

19 State Dept. memorandum, 3/19/1970

20 Pyrros, Archives, Memoir, 17

21 Howe, *Power Peddlers*, 434

22 Ibid., 433

23 Hersh, interview, 12/1/13; Kovotsos, "It's Time for Heroes" documentary, 2014

24 "Demetracopoulos' Proposals for the Greek Situation," Confidential State Dept. memorandum of conversation, 3/19/1970

25 Saville Davis, "Nixon Congress Collision: Back-door US Arms Aid to Greece Strikes Congress Sparks," *Christian Science Monitor*, 5/6/1970; Vidalis, 81–2

26 Hartke Address to Senate, 6/29/70; Hartke Amendment and debate, 116 *Congressional Record*, 21995–22016, 6/29/70; Woodhouse (*Rise*), 80; EPD Press Statement, 6/29/1970

27 Saville R. Davis, "US Cools toward Greece," *Christian Science Monitor*, 6/17/1970; EPDP; Hartke to Rogers, 6/16/1970

28 Letters and telegrams exchange between Bob Riss (via Louise Riss) with Missouri senators Stuart Symington and Tom Eagleton (replies 6/30/1970) and Kansas senators James Pearson and Robert Dole (replies 7/7/1970 and 7/1/1970); letter exchange from and to CW with Connecticut senators Abraham Ribicoff and Thomas Dodd (respective replies 7/17/1970 and 7/6/1970) with 7/13/1970 and 7/21/1970 letters from CW to EPD

29 Editorial, "Arms for the Colonels," *NYT*, 7/3/1970; EPD press statement, 6/29/1970

30 James A. Wechsler, "July 4 in Athens," *New York Post*, 7/3/1970; Woodhouse, (*Rise*), 80–2

31 Embassy diplomats would refer to the triumvirate as "The Three Stooges," and snicker at the homeliness of their wives. David Fritzlan, Charles Stuart Kennedy, ADST

32 Harsh criticism from some W. European countries prompted junta leaders to reach out in trade and diplomacy to East European countries as a "kind of blackmail . . . to silence their critics." Anne Treholt in Clogg and Yannopoulos, 222.

33 Woodhouse (*Rise*), 82

34 "Brother of Nixon and Onassis in Deal," *NYT*, 6/4/1970

35 UPI, "Student Sets Self Ablaze in Genoa," Newport News (VA) *Daily Press*, 9/20/1970; Reuters, "Greek Protest Death," *New York Daily News*, 9/20/70; *Miami News*, 9/24/1970

36 www.allcorfu.com/georgakis.html

37 A year later, working with Howard University professor Nikolaos Stavrou he tried unsuccessfully to get contemporaneous American news media coverage of the mysterious murder of British freelance journalist Ann Chapman in Athens in October 1971; Stavrou, "The Case of Dorothy Ann Chapman," undated, EPDP; "Case of Ann Chapman, murdered in Greece in 1971," National Archives, Kew, FCO 9/3565, 1982; Mario Modiano, "Cause of Journalist's Death Challenged," *The Times* (London), 5/24/1984; European Parliament, Working Documents, 1984-1985, 5/7/1984, Document 1-206/84; Richard Cotrell, *Blood on Their Hands*

38 *WP*, 9/14/1970

39 FRUS, 1969–1976, XXIV (Jordan), "Minutes of a National Security Council Meeting," doc. 318, 9/23/1970. A Spanish base agreement and South African military sales were announced along with the Greek arms decision.

40 Editorial, *WP*, 9/24/1970; AP report, 9/23/1970

41 William Clark, director, Information and Public Affairs, letter to B. J. Merketos, *National Herald*, 4/27/1970; EPD to Burke Knapp, 5/12/70; Burke Knapp to EPD, 5/15/1970; Evans & Novak, "World Bank Assails Greek Junta for Bid to Play Politics with Loan," *Financial Times*; *WP*, 5/21/1970; "Row Erupts against $20 Million Loan to Greek Company," 5/22/1970; "World Bank Protest at Greek Claim," *Times* (London), 5/23/1970; *Congressional Record*, Senate debate, 5/29/1970

42 David E. Anderson, "Strategic," UPI, 10/3/1970; Hearings before the Subcommittee on The United States Security Agreements and Commitments Abroad, Senate Committee on Foreign Relations, 91st Congress, Second Session, Part 7, June 9 and 11, 1970

43 Fulbright quotation in UPI, "U.S. A-Bombs Abroad in '61?", 10/11/1970

44 Transcript of 1/12/1961 interview with Army secretary Wilber M. Brucker, described in Warren Nelson, Exclusive/Urgent UPI wire, 10/10/1970; Walter Scott, *Parade*, 12/20/1970

45 "I colonnelli greci nel '67 minacciarono basi Usa?" *La Stampa*, 11/25/1970; "Athener Obristen lieBen Automwaffen der USA umstellen," *Die Welt*, 11/25/1970; "Le ogive americane in balia dei colonnelli," *Corriere della serra*, 11/25/1970

46 Hartke press statement, 12/1/1970; Saville R. Davis, "Greek nuclear incident points to risk in

Nato alliance," *Christian Science Monitor*, 12/7/1970

47 In reviewing EPD's State Dept. dossier, Barrington King sent a SECRET memorandum to Amb. Tasca, including an excerpt from a 11/1963 memo describing a State Dept. surprise that David Abshire, at the time an associate of Admiral Burke, planned to visit EPD in Greece. Abshire's reply: "Yes, we know that the State Department has a file on him, but it's only because he dares to write the truth." 12/18/1970

48 His first formal confirmation came from Senator Frank Moss after June 1, 1971, reporting EPD had been stripped of citizenship on June 10, 1970. Abshire to Moss, letter, 4/1/1971, replying to Moss letter, 3/11/1971; AmEmb notes it had confirmation at least as early as December 1970, Elizabeth Brown to Walter Silva, 3/22/1971

49 Senators called the Greek ambassador on 12/11/1970 and telegrammed messages to the Greek prime minister, State Dept. documents re: "Senators to Prime Minister on Demetracopoulos Case," 12/12/1970

50 "Messages from Various Senators to Prime Minister on Demetracopoulos Case," Rogers to AmEmb Athens IMMEDIATE, drafted 12/11/1970, delivered 12/12/1970; SECRET telegram, Tasca to SecState, 6722, "We cannot obtain safe conduct . . . and we should stay out of middle of this." 12/15/1970

51 Ibid., 12/11/1970

52 Rogers/Sisco to Tasca, 12/14/1970

53 Tasca to Rogers, "confidential" telegram, 12/15/1970; State Dept. later admitted internally: "Demetracopoulos would certainly be justified in claiming that the Greek Embassy had taken no initiative to inform him as to how to pursue his request." Harrison M. Symmes to NEA/GRK— Mr. Rowe, 1/19/1971

54 Earlier, Sisco wrote "we must avoid being put in a position of guaranteeing any assurances that he may have on being able to depart." 12/14/1970; Tasca agreed, noting the possibility of EPD being "detained" by Greek security because of the not-uncommon problem of "one agency of government [issuing] passport to individual who then discovers at airport that another agency will not permit his departure." Tasca to Sisco, 12/15/1970. Similarly, Harrison Symmes told Hartke staffer Rosemary Rorick that a laissez-passer was a "convenience," that wouldn't protect the bearer from arrest. Memorandum for the Record, 12/15/1970

55 Ibid. [Tasca to Sisco], Athens 6739, 12/15/1970. Copies of this confidential communication were sent to the White House, CIA, NSC, and other US intelligence agencies.

56 Tasca to SecState, Confidential Telegram, 12/18/1970

57 Ibid.

58 Ibid.

59 Rogers to Tasca regarding Gravel's message to the Greek government. Confidential telegram, 12/18/1970; "Gravel on Greek Incident," *WP*, 12/28/1970

60 Persa Metaxas, letter to EPD, 12/12/1970

61 Tsalapatis, interview, 6/2/2012

62 Persa Metaxas, letter to EPD, 12/24/1970

63 Ibid.; Persa Metaxas, interview, 5/30/2012

64 Senators Mike Gravel, Quentin Burdick, and Frank Moss to President Nixon, 12/16/1970; "3 Senators Assail State Department," *NYT*, 12/21/1970

65 Robert McCloskey in *NYT*, 12/21/1970; Sisco to Rogers, "The Elias Demetracopoulos Affair," 12/18/1970; Rogers to AmEmb, "Athens Subj: Demetracopoulos" 1/15/1971, 30-8035; memorandum to Ambassador from POL-Elizabeth Ann Brown, 1/28/1971

66 Press briefing transcript, 12/21/1970; State Dept. Transcript of Press, Radio and Television News Briefing, 12/22/1970

67 Confidential to SecState "Immediate," 12/14/1970

68 Timmons to Senator Gravel, 12/18/1970; "White House to Investigate Demetracopoulos Case," *Athens News*, 12/29/1970

69 "Well, it's not every day that you read about your death in a state document." Hitchens (*Kissinger*), 110

70 Evans & Novak, "Another Greek Tragedy," *WP*, 12/23/1970; inserting the column into the *Congressional Record*, E300, 1/29/1971, Cong. Don Edwards described the handing of the matter by

Tasca and the Greek generals as "sickening, to say the least." *WP*, 1/7/1971

71 "The Elias Demetracopoulos Affair," Sisco to Rogers, 12/18/1970 and 12/22/1970

72 Sisco to Tasca, 12/14/1970; AmEmb to SecState, confidential telegram, 12/29/1970; Sisco to Tasca, confidential letter, 12/24/1970

73 Assistant Secretary Sisco to Ambassador Tasca, "SECRET" telegram, 1/16/1971

74 *NYT*, 12/30/1970; on the same day, a forceful *NYT* editorial ("More Tyranny for Greece") asserted that "by its last actions of 1970, Greece's military dictatorship has rendered even more ludicrous the claims of its apologists in Washington that it has 'established a trend toward constitutional order.'"

75 Grigoriadis II, 169; Mario Modiano, "US concern over Greek relations," *Times* (London), 2/8/1971

21: PUSHING CONGRESS

1   Davies, confidential memorandum on "Visit of Emmanuel Kothris," 2/3/1971

2   Jeanne Oates Angulo, interview; Jacques Scarelli described to her the dynamics of the EPD-Onassis meeting

3   Susan Mayer to EPD, 3/26/1971

4   The Advocates, "Should the United States discontinue military aid to Greece?" WGBH/KCET, on PBS-TV, 3/23/1971

5   Jerry Williams Show, WBZ Radio (Boston), 4/21/1971 Louis Lyons News & Comment: Interview with Elias Demetracopoulos, WGBH, 4/20/1971

6   Speech at MIT, 4/21/1971, inserted in *Congressional Record* by Senator Edward Kennedy, 5/26/71, S7846-9

7   Walter John Silva to Elizabeth A. Brown, 5/5/1971

8   Jake Lewis to EPD, 10/12/1995

9   The Associated Press, under the headline "Bankers pay Patman $1500; Hear Him Assail Their Policies," told its readers about the dinner. (*Gettysburg Times* and *Freelance Star*), 6/29/1971

10 Pyrros, interview, 12/20/2010

11 Saunders to Kissinger, 3/19/1971 and 3/22/1971; Kofas, 279, fn 65

12 Hitchens observed that Kissinger put "journalist" in quote marks, but not "resistance leader."

13 UPI wire, 1/14/1971; State Dept. briefing excerpt, 1/15/1971; Tasca to SecState "Priority," 1/15/1971

14 Harrison M. "Harry" Symmes at the Greek Desk wrote a CONFIDENTIAL letter to Elizabeth Ann Brown, Political Counselor at the Athens Embassy, 2/2/1971

15 Ibid.

16 Greece: February 1971; A Staff Report Prepared for the use of the Committee on Foreign Relations, United States Senate, 3/4/1971 ("Moose/ Lowenstein report"), 9, 13; Barkman, 44–6; Rowland Evans and Robert Novak, "Sen. Fulbright v Junta," *WP*, 1/31/1971 A ("Secret; Priority; Exdis [Exclusive Distribution])." After reviewing the Lowenstein report, EPD wrote: "If such an on the spot investigation were conducted before April 21, 1967 the coup probably could have been stopped." EPD talking points, EPDP, 2/18/1971

17 FRUS, 1969–1976, XLI, doc. 303, 2/19/1971

18 Moose/Lowenstein, 16; Moose, interview, 11/26/2010

19 Clifford P. Hackett, interview, 3/2/2012

20 Joseph Sisco sent a Memorandum of Conversation to the secretary of state, the Bureau of Near Eastern Affairs, the Bureau of European Affairs, the Greek Desk, the Cyprus Desk, the Office of Congressional Relations, the National Security Council, and the American embassies in Athens, Rome, Paris, and London, and he sent ten copies to the State Department's Bureau of Intelligence and Research. 6/2/1971

21 6/25/1971

22 Tasca to Sisco, SECRET, 6/23/1971

23 Athens to White House, 6/25/1971

24 Secret telegram, 6/25/1971

25 Greece, Spain, and the Southern NATO Strategy; Hearings before the Committee on Foreign Affairs, House of Representatives, July 12, 14, 19, 21; August 3; September 9 and 15, 1971

26 Ibid., EPD testimony, 64–110; "Greek Exile Asks US to Stop Military Assistance to Regime,"

NYT, 7/13/1971

27 "House Lawmakers Bewildered by Classified Greek Document," *Chicago Tribune*, 7/14/1971; Fred Emery, "Warning of Vietnam in Greece," *Times* (London), 7/13/ 1971; "NATO Paper warns US of Greek danger," *Christian Science Monitor*, 7/13/1971

28 J. E. Miller, 167

29 "Personal Comments of US Ambassador to Greece Tasca," 7/20/1971

30 Ibid.

31 Hise to Homer H. Kirby, Jr., 146-1-10642, 8/10/1971

32 Ibid., 2

33 Ibid., 4

34 John Edgar Hoover to Director of Intelligence and Research, Department of State, Subject: Elias Demetracopoulos Internal Security-Greece (NI-105-131803-45), 1/5/1971

35 Memorandum from INR/RNA/NE Philip Stoddard to Mitchell Stanley, INR/RNA/NE re FBI Check, 1/27/1971, following up similar 12/24/1970 confidential memorandum; confidential memorandum, Stanley to W. Raymond Wannall, FBI Domestic Intelligence Division, 11/28/1970, Demetracopoulos v. FBI, C.A. no. 78-2209-Exhibit 2

36 FRUS 1969–1976, XXIX, doc. 321, 8/6/1971

37 Ibid.

38 "Hackett Report," Report of Staff Study by the House Subcommittee on Europe, Athens, August–September 1971

39 Ibid.

40 Vera Glaser and Malvina Stephenson, "Millionaire Nixon Pal Pappas Faces Capitol Hill Fire," *Knight Newspapers, Miami Herald*, 8/29/1971

41 Ambrose (Nixon), 201; Summers, 54

42 Chotiner to EPD, 9/28/1970

43 Howe, *Power Peddlers*, 425

44 Craig Unger, "Tom Pappas: The Bostonian Behind the Greek Junta," *Boston After Dark*, 10/12/1971; Disclosure of Pappas Foundations as "Conduit" for CIA Activities in Africa, *Sunday Times* (London), extended conduit to Greece, 9/29/1968; Richard Harwood, "Probe of CIA to Go Well Beyond Student Groups," *Boston Globe*, 2/19/1967

45 He told the BBC in 1975 that, in order to assist the efforts of congressional committees with full investigatory and subpoena powers and "to diffuse any excuse which some in power would like to raise in order to avoid investigating the Greek question, I have carefully avoided making public my views and my material." Edited version of BBC interview in *Athens News*, 8/30/1975

46 EPD, "Memorandum Concerning Activities of Thomas A. Pappas," 9/17/1971, included in HCFA 1971 hearings, 459

47 Theodore Kariotis, interview, 1/16/2016

48 Ibid.

49 Rowland Evans and Robert Novak, "The Greek Colonels' Friend," *WP*, 9/19/1971; picking up on Elias's reference to Pappas's clandestine influence, they concluded that Congress wants to "put Pappas on the stand under oath." AP, Nixon's Donor's Ties to Greek Junta Eyed," *WP*, 9/21/1971; Lucia Mouat, "House report hints GOP-Greek junta ties," *Christian Science Monitor*, 9/20/1971; William Millinship, "US may probe financier's role in aid to Greece," *The Observer* (London), 9/26/1971

50 Evans & Novak, "Tycoon's Persuasive Powers Probed," (Appleton, WI) *The Post-Crescent*, 9/21/1971; "Pair Accused of Aiding Junta," *Philadelphia Inquirer*, 9/19/1971; Hitchens (*Kissinger*), 113

51 AP, "Nixon Backer Faces Probe on Ties with Greek Junta, Louisville (KY) *Times*, 9/20/1971; "Donor's Ties to Greek Juntas Eyed;" *WP*, 9/21/1971; Charles E. Claffey, "Pappas poses Nixon issue," *Boston Globe*, 11/13/1971; "Pappas Influence Cited," *Herald Traveler* (Boston) 9/20/1971; Marquis Childs, "Agnew plunges into the Greek tragedy," *Baltimore Sun*, 10/11/1971

52 Carl Marcy to David M. Abshire, 10/20/1971

53 George Churchill to Carl Marcy, 11/3/1971

54 They told their interviewees they were "just helping out the CIA." Anderson, 2/12/1975

55 Sherman P. Lloyd (R-UT)

56 Charles E. Claffey, "Study raps US envoy to Greece," *Boston Sunday Globe*, 11/14/1971; Jeremiah O'Leary, "Envoy to Greece Hit in House Study," *Washington Star*, 11/14/1971; AP, "Bad Fitness

Report for Envoy to Greece," *Honolulu Star- Bulletin*, 11/26/1971; Hedley Burrell, "House Consultant Hits Diplomacy in Greece," *WP*, 11/14/1971; Reuters, "Report Hits American Envoy to Greece," *Chicago Tribune*, 11/15/1971; "U.S. Envoy in Greece Criticized for Low Morale," *Atlanta Journal-Constitution*, 11/14/1971

57 EPD to Rosenthal, 12/8/1971; Abshire letters to EPD, 12/10/1971 and 1/31/1972

58 Churchill to Davies, 12/27/1971

59 References to EPD's alleged relationship with Andreas Papandreou and Mercouri in FBI report to Hoover, 11/4/1971, as part of a plan to turn around congressmen who have been taken in by "the charming and affable Demetracopoulos."

60 National Archives, Nixon Presidential Materials, White House Tapes, September 20, 1971, 3:01–4:40 p.m., Cabinet Room, Conversation no. 76–4; Earlier 6/4/1971 WH conversation between Nixon and Agnew recounted in *Strange Bedfellows*

61 Mark O. Hatfield, "Vice Presidents of the United States: Spiro Theodore Agnew (1969–1973), Senate Historical Office, Washington: US GPO, 1997

62 Lou Panos, "Greek Trip Dims for Agnew," *Baltimore Evening Sun*, 9/22/1971

63 Evans & Novak, 10/8/1971

64 "The vice presidency: Appointment in Gargalianoi," *TIME*, 11/1/1971; NBC News 10/19/1971, Vanderbilt Television News Archive, Archives Record: 454357

65 Telegram from the vice president's party to the Department of State, Athens, 10/18/1971, 2310Z, 36/5590. "Subject: Memorandum of Conversation Between Vice President and Prime Minister Papadopoulos," 10/16/1971, 5:30 p.m.

66 "[British] Foreign office releases more junta files," ekathimerini.com, 02/01/2002

67 Peter Grose, "Agnew, in his Farewell, Hails Greek Regime," *NYT*, 10/24/1971; White House tapes: 10/26/1971, President Richard Nixon and Vice President Spiro Agnew

68 Burdick to EPD, 11/1/1971; Hatfield to EDP, 11/2/1971

22: CAMPAIGN 1972

1 1/24/1972

2 Fred F. Fielding to "JWD," WHSF-Staff Member and Office Files-John Dean, Title: Elias Demetracopoulos, Box 21, RMNL

3 Dean note (to Fielding), 1/5/1972, RMNL

4 CIA memorandum, 1/5/1972; Laurence R. Houston, CIA, to Charles H. Brower, State Dept., 1/14/1972, RMNL

5 State Dept.'s Intelligence and Research Bureau to Raymond Mannall, FBI, Domestic Intelligence, Demetracopoulos, Elias, SECRET, 3/8/1972

6 CIA report re: Makarios, Secret, Central Intelligence Bulletin, 3/16/1972; Justice Dept, SAC, WFO to Director, FBI 3/16/1972 and 3/23/1972

7 A June FBI report to the acting director, with a copy sent to Kissinger's National Security Council, essentially confirmed their objective "to confirm the existence and identity of a foreign principal [behind Demetracopoulos]." SAC/WFO to acting director, 6/21/1972

8 EPD press statement, 1/22/1972

9 Woodhouse (*Rise*), 106

10 State Dept., "The Scooper and the Pols," 3/15/1972; letter to EPD from Congressmen Ben Rosenthal and Lee Hamilton, 3/15/1972; EPD, "Memorandum on Background of Homeporting," 7/28/1972, in Homeporting Joint Hearings, 253–60; EPD press statement against agreement to sell F-4 Phantom jets to dictatorship, 3/29/1972; UPI 4/2/1972; "US sells Greece two squadrons of F4s," *Boston Globe*, 3/31/1972

11 Walter J. Silva, ADST, 1/23/1995, 46

12 Davies, Homeporting testimony, 40–1

13 SAC/WFO to FBI acting director and 6/21/1972

14 Mary Gore Dean told the FBI: EDP "could go either way," adding "you know the way intellectuals are." Gore Dean was especially upset that EPD refused to support the Republicans in 1968, because Agnew supported the Greek military junta. FBI interview, 2/10/1969

15 Vera Glasser, FBI interview, 3/13/1969 report, 4/22/1969; "Washington Offbeat: Connally's Caribbean Hideaway," Newport News (VA) *Press*, 9/10/1972

16 Joe Conason & Gene Lyons, *Hunting the President*, 325–6
17 Vidalis, 191
18 "2 Foes of Greek Regime Get U.S. Legislators Greeting." *NYT*, 1/12/1972
19 *Makedonia/Thessaloniki*, using L. Costis as its source, was threatened with punishment for violating press law 253 of 11/22/1971 and 269 of 12/1/1971 for featuring 12/18/1971 front-page story on the US Senate's vote to cut aid to Greece and then reporting on BBC commentary on the event. State Dept. telegram, 1/7/1972
20 Edward T. Brennan, Consul General, Thessaloniki to George T. Churchill, NEA/GK, 1/11/1972
21 EPD letter to Hartke, 7/11/1972; Hartke letter to EPD, 7/12/1972
22 EPD letter to McGovern, 7/15/1972; McGovern letter to EPD, 7/17/1972
23 Ibid.; George Lardner, Jr., "McGovern Would End Greek Aid," *WP*, 7/23/1972; "McGovern letter on Greece," *Athens News*, 7/13–14/1972, JFKL
24 Evans & Novak, "Greek Gifts for President," *Boston Globe*, 7/20/1972
25 Ibid.
26 FBI memorandum re: Ilias P. Dimitropokulos, "Registration Act—Greece," 6/21/1972
27 Woodhouse 108, 180; "Scott Attacks McGovern on Greece," *Baltimore Sun*, 7/25/1972; "Greece denies US statements that bases help protect Israel," *Athens News*, 8/6/1972; editorial, "The Colonels Disagree," *Baltimore Sun*, 8/9/1972; AP, "Mideast," 8/7/1972; "White House disavows Greek aid as linked with Israel's defense," *Athens News*, 8/8/1972
28 In late July 1972 Papadopoulos told the Dutch ambassador that "he very much hoped, of course, that Nixon would be re-elected." Barkman, 81
29 "Stamatopoulos' indirect reference to Demetracopoulos," Tasca to SecState, Secret telegram, 7/25/1972; "Nazi charge refuted by journalist," *Athens News*, 7/25/1972
30 Declaration and Summons of EPD to Estia, 8/17/1962, EPDP; *Athens News*, 7/25/1972
31 "Aid Stand Questioned," *Hellenic Chronicle*, 8/17/1972
32 James J. Kilpatrick, "McGovern writes a foolish letter on Greece," *Washington Star*, 7/30/1972
33 "Columnist Eats Crow in Three Great Gulps," Saginaw (MI) *News*, 8/13/1972
34 Elizabeth Brown to Walter Silva, 8/21/1972; Tasca letter to Sisco 8/11/1972; Silva letter to Elizabeth Brown, 8/30/1972
35 Sam Nakis to McGovern, 8/10/1972
36 Bob Fort, "Smear Letter By Geogian Is Investigated," *Atlanta Constitution*, 5/15/1973
37 Acting FBI Director L. Patrick Gray thanked the [redacted] writer, 8/4/1972
38 Memorandum from A. Russell Ash of the National Security Council 1/6/1972; director FBI, 2/7/1972 and acting FBI director, 6/29/1972
39 Anderson, 5/13/1982
40 Kutler, 234
41 Ibid., 233
42 Jake Lewis, letter to EPD, 10/12/1995; Anderson, 12/21/1985; Powers, 110
43 Kutler, op. cit.
44 "After the Vote, the Election Was Lost." Mary McGrory's conclusion in her column "Getting Away with Dirty Stables," *Boston Globe*, 10/8/1972; LTE, *The Atlantic*, 11/1983
45 Memorandum from [redacted], Greek Desk to Davies, "Subject: Declassification: Demetracopoulos," 10/24/1972

23: FALLOUT FROM A MUTINY

1 Haynes Johnson, "Last Respects Paid Truman at Simple Cathedral Service," *WP*, 1/6/1973; "Truman-Greece-Turkey," *AP*, 1/5/1973; EPD statement, 1/5/1973
2 Graham Hovey, "Making Foreign Policy," *NYT*, 1/22/1973
3 Senator Frank Church to EPD, 10/30/1972; Evans & Novak, "Greek Aid and Israeli Safety: Scuttling the Nixon Connection," *WP*, 12/17/1972
4 Boos, interview, 1/2011
5 1/3/1973, Kutler, Watergate tapes, 196
6 Watergate Tapes, 5/23/1973; Kutler, Tapes, 218
7 Nixon White House Tapes, 3/7/1973; Kutler, Tapes, 225–6
8 *TIME*, 3/12/1973; Woodhouse (*Rise*), 128–9: Nafpliotis, 165

9   AAP-Reuters, "World News/ Greece: Arrest Sought after article," *Canberra Times*, 4/26/1973

10 "Concern for Vradyni publisher spreading," *Athens News*, 4/25/1973.

11 *Eleftheros Kosmos* editorial was picked up by another conservative publication, *Ellinikos Vorras*, which editorialized in greater depth on the alleged pervasive Demetracopoulos role, US Consul in Thessaloniki to SecState, 3/1/1973; "Rep. Rosenthal Incited Disorders, Greek Says," *NYT*, 3/5/1973; even the State Dept. thought the depiction wildly "impossible." State Dept. telegram, 3/14/1973

12 Couloumbis (*Junta Phenomenon*), March 3, 1973 entry, 190; A. Fleming, *Piece of Truth*, which described her personal encounter with imprisonment, trial, and forcible departure for her role in trying to help Panagoulis escape, *passim*.

13 On Martin Agronsky's "Evening Edition," the two sparred about whether the current Greek government was more a "tyranny" or a "democracy," WETA, Washington, D.C., 3/12/1973

14 In their earlier debate, Kousoulas predicted a partial return to democracy in 1970 and a full return by 1971. "Greece Today: Two Points of View," Professor Demetri Kousoulas, Howard University, co-author of the new Greek constitution, and E. P. Demetracopoulos, a leader of the Greek resistance in the United States, Passport, WMAR-TV (CBS), 9/27/1970, Radio-TV Monitoring Service, Inc. Washington, D.C.

15 SAC/WFO to acting director of FBI, 3/14/1973

16 Patrick Gray, acting director to SAC, WFO 3/14/1973; WFO 2/28/1973; Patrick concluded: "in view of the nebulous nature of the State Department's present suspicions about the subject, an active campaign of interviews could not be publicly justified and could possibly serve to increase criticism of the Bureau and also possibly offer the subject publicity which he would relish and be able to divert to his own benefit."

17 Woodhouse (*Rise*), 116; Vidalis, 130, 139

18 Woodhouse (*Karamanlis*), 198–99; Woodhouse (*Rise*),116–17; Christina Moustaklis interviews and EPDP

19 Christina Moustaklis, interviews and personal papers; EPDP; Woodhouse (*Karamanlis*), 198199; Woodhouse (*Rise*), 116–17

20 Cplakidas, transcript, 2013

21 *NYT*, 5/25/1973; 5/27/1973; 7/14/1973; 11/1/1973; Vidalis, 267

22 Woodhouse (*Karamanlis*), 199–200; Vidalis, 266

23 Nikos Pappas, letter to EPD from Rome, 9/30/1973; AP report in *NYT*, 5/28/1973; "Greece reports foiling plot by King's supporters," *NYT*, 7/14/1973

24 Letter discovered posthumously in EPDP

25 Woodhouse (*Rise*), 118

26 Amendment vote, 6/25/1973; Woodhouse (*Rise*), 118; Vidalis, 287–9

27 Carl Barkham, *Ambassador in Athens*, 107

28 "Greece: Papadocracy," *TIME*, 3/6/1973; "The Colonels" Referendum," Norfolk (VA) *Pilot*, 8/3/1973

29 Barkham, 116; Modiano, interview, 5/31/2012

30 "Greek Amnesty," *NYT*, 8/26/1973; Mario S. Modiano, "Amnesty is Given to 300 in Greece," *NYT*, 8/21/1973

31 J. E. Miller, 268

32 Reuters, "Amnesty," Rome, 8/20/1973

33 Couloumbis, 9/12/1973 (*Junta Phenomenon*), 208

34 Christina Moustaklis, memoir and personal papers; EPDP

24: WATERGATE, WINDOW DRESSING, AND A COUNTER-COUP

1   *UPI*, "McGovern Asks Probe of Letter," *Atlanta Constitution*, 5/14/1973; Bob Fort, "Smear Letter by Georgian is investigated," *Atlanta Constitution*, 5/15/1973; Transcript of Frank Mankiewicz Press Conference, 5/13/1973; Evans & Novak, "Election '72: Another Propaganda Letter," *WP*, 5/13/1973; AP, "Watergate Probers get McGovern's Greek file," *Syracuse Herald-Journal*, 5/17/1973

2   EPD attorney Warren Woods "Memo to Myself: Woods-Rousalkis conversation May 17, 1973"; exchange of letters, Woods to Rousalkis, 11/28/1972 and Rousalkis to Woods, 1/8/1972 [sic], EPDP

3   "Confidential" telegram [name redacted] Greek Desk to Robert M. Brandin, 6/8/1973

4   Woodward and Bernstein (*Final Days*), 33–4

5   Ibid., 51

6   Burke annotations to typed transcript, 8/28/1963, EPDP; Nesmith, 1/7/2000; Anderson and Blinstein, "Did JFK victimize an American hero?," Merry-Go-Round column, 1/14/1996

7   Norman Kempster, "Admiral: Government Burglarized Files," *Los Angeles Times*, 2/4/1977; statement made by Admiral Burke, 2/2/1977; letter, Mark Hatfield to Senator Robert Morgan, chairman, investigation subcommittee on intelligence, 2/9/1977; "Documents Believed Stolen from Office of Retired Admiral," *NYT*, 2/6/1977; "Theft at Admiral's Office? Senate Panel is Checking," *Washington Star*, 2/6/1977; Jack Anderson, "Government Burglaries," *WP*, 2/2/1977

8   "Spiro Agnew and the Golden Age of Corruption in Maryland Politics: An interview with Ben Bradlee and Richard Cohen of the *Washington Post*," Center for the Study of Democracy, Vol 2, no. 1, Fall 2006

9   "Celia Was Dies: Served in U.S. State Department," *Hartford Courant*, 9/1/1973; she was fifty-five. Her niece Barbara LaRosa provided context to CW's last days and EPD's last visit, interviews, 2016–2017

10 Hooper to Goodison, 10/18/1973, FCO 9/1712, PRO and 11/29/1973

11 Woodhouse (*Rise*), 142.

12 June 7, 1973: The President and Buzhardt, 3:53–5:30 p.m., Executive Office Building, Kutler (*Abuse*), 593

13 Transcript of a Recording of a Meeting Among the President, H. R. Haldeman, John Ehrlichman, Steve Bull, and Ronald Ziegler on April 26, 1973, from 3:59 to 9:03 p.m., RMNL, https://www.nixonlibrary.gov/sites/default/files/forresearchers/find/tapes/watergate/wspf/431-009.pdf

14 May 23, 1973: The President and Rose Mary Woods, 10:55–11:12 a.m., Oval Office, Kutler (*Abuse*), 549

15 June 6, 1973: The President and Rose Mary Woods, 8:25 8:53 a.m. Oval Office, Kutler (*Abuse*), 581

16 Airgram a-322, 11/9/1973

17 Tape recordings and private letters in EPDL

18 Circle of 13 website, November 17, 2008; Anonymous, "Athens: Black November—The Slaughter of the Innocents, by an eyewitness," November 1973. Letters and tape recordings made inside and outside the Polytechnic, EPDP; Tonge, "Athens Riots Crushed at Cost of Nine Lives," *The Guardian*, 11/19/1973; "A Demonstrator Narrates the Events As He Lived Them Outside the Polytechnic University," Tetradia Tia Democratias, Vol. 3, 2/1974, Stockholm, Sweden

19 Kiesling (Urban), 35, later confirmed twenty-four dead, including six students, and 1,100 wounded, including 300 students.

20 J. E. Miller, 269; see Nedzi to Kissinger letter, 11/27/1973, Pol 23–9 Greece, DSCF, RG59, NARA

21 State Dept. telegram, Control: 2917Q, 10/11/1973

22 FRUS, 1973–1976, Vol. XXX, doc. 7, telegram, AmEmb to State, 11/18/1973

23 Kakaounakis, 2650 Meronychta Synomosias (Athens 1976), Vol. 2, 48; Woodhouse, 144; *AP*, "Papadopoulos Safe in Villa; Believed Aware of Coup Plan," *Hartford Courant*, 12/10/1973

24 Woodhouse (*Rise*)

25 "Demonstrators protest Greek, British issues," *Salem News*, 11/19/1973. "Greek Façade Topples: Greece Steps Backward," Jasper (AL) *Daily Mountain Eagle*, 12/10/1973

26 "US Silence Approval of Greece Revolt," *Palo Alto Peninsula Bulletin*, 12/8/1973

27 J. E. Miller, 174

28 NEA/GRK, State Dept., "Comments of Elias Demetracopoulos," 11/2/1973

29 Draenos, "Papandreou's exile politics: the first phase, 1968–70," *The Historical Review/la revue historique*, Vol. 11, 201, 65, 435–66

30 Endre Marton, "US-Greece," *AP*, 11/28/1973

31 AP, "US-Greece (2)," 11/28/1973; Evans & Novak, "Policy on Greece Backfires on US," *Boston Globe*, 11/30/1973; Markezinis years later told *Kathimerini*, 2/21/1993, that he was "not overthrown by the Polytechnic, but by Kissinger because the Greek prime minister refused to provide bases in Crete to help supply Israel," cited in Vidalis, 322.

32 Warren L. Nelson, *UPI*, "Greek Coup is Connected to Watergate," *Denver Rocky Mountain News*, 12/11/1973

25: CRISIS ON CYPRUS

1   Charles Nicodemus, "Greek Premier Fibs about His Past Here," *Chicago News*, 2/9/1974
2   FRUS, Vol. XXX, Greece, Cyprus; Turkey, 1973–'76, Document 10; editorial, Louisville, Kentucky *Courier-Journal*, 1/10/1974
3   S. J. Micchiche, "Pappas to testify on funding for Watergate defendants," *Boston Globe*, 2/5/1974
4   Seth Kantor, "Greek Junta's Role in U.S Politics Questioned," *Detroit News*, 1/27/1974.; Roger M. Whitten to Pappas File, "Meeting with Seth Kantor," 1/11/1974
5   Watergate Special Prosecution Force, Department of Justice [WSPF], Memorandum to File No. 306 from Roger M. Witten, "Subject: Thomas A. Pappas," 12/13/1973; WSPF, from Thomas F. McBride to Philip Lacovara, "Subject: 18 U.S.C. section 613," 1/8/1974; WSPF, "Memorandum to File No. 306" from Roger M. Witten, "Interview of Thomas Pappas, February 2, 1974;" 2/7/1974, NARA, Record Group 460, Records of WSPF, CCTF# Pappas, Esso-Pappas Oil Refinery; WSPF, Kenneth S. Geller to Philip A. Lacovara, "Subject: 18 U.S.C. section 613 (Contributions by agents of foreign principals),"1/14/1974; reference was also made to investigation of Campaign Contributions Task Force concerning "possible violations" by Pappas of section 613 and related Internal Security Division "interpretation."
6   WSPF, Roger M. Witten to Thomas F. McBride, "Prosecutive Memoranda Re Thomas A. Pappas (18 U.S.C. sec. 613)," 2/24/1974 (with multiple redactions); WSPF, From Roger M. Witten to File No. 306-Pappas File, "Subject: Closing of Investigation," 1/5/1974; Robert Parry, Watergate Prosecutors Weighed Case Against Nixon Fund-Raiser," AP, 5/24/1986
7   Richard Ben-Veniste, email exchange and telephone interview with JHB, 5/13/2011
8   https://www.nytimes.com/2001/11/20/nyregion/ex-senator-harrison-a-williams-jr-81-dies-went- to-prison-over-abscam-scandal.html
9   Polk, "False Campaign Money," Polk, letter to JHB, 12/26/2011
10 UPI, "Controlling the Damage: US Policy Options for Greece," 2/26/1974
11 FRUS, 1973–1976, XXX, doc. 12, 47–60, 3/20/1974 (Secretary's analytical staff meeting, originally classified SECRET)
12 When the meeting transcript was finally declassified, Demetracopoulos, said: "This report will blacken forever the position of Henry Kissinger in history because it reveals the mentality of the former secretary of state," *National Herald*, 2/16–17/2002.
13 https://www.youtube.com/watch?v=Q4AJ_N3l7GA&t=213s
14 Pyrros, 296
15 We can reconstruct the day's events through Pyrros and Vidalis diaries; Makarios biographies; Stern, Miller, and Woodhouse histories; ADST oral histories; and EPD and Pyrros interviews.
16 Pyrros, 40
17 Stern, 111
18 J. E. Miller, 189
19 Stern, 111
20 Stern, 117
21 Nafpliotis, 235
22 Kissinger's preference was the post-coup acting president Glafcos Clerides; J. E. Miller, 192; ADST, Frederick Z. Brown, Cyprus DCM: "Kissinger was intensely concerned about his image in the media, everything we did was attuned to his personal whims."
23 Stern, 113
24 Makarios, Speech at the UN Security Council, S/PV 1780; 7/19/1974
25 J. E. Miller, 194
26 Vidalis, 375; Woodhouse (*Modern*), 305
27 Stern, 121
28 Woodhouse (*Rise*), 157–9
29 Ibid., 158; Colonel Frank Athanason, ADST, 6/10/2005
30 Ibid., 161
31 Ibid., 162–3
32 Ibid., 164–7
33 Charles Mohr, "Rejoicing Athenians Chant Demokratia," *NYT*, 7/24/1974; *Athens News*, 7/2/2004

26: AFTER THE JUNTA

1   William R. Crawford, Jr., ADST, 12/24/1988
2   Ibid.
3   *WP*, 7/31/1975
4   *Washington Star*, 8/31/1975; Lexington (KY) *Herald*, 9/8/1975
5   Pyrros, 176
6   Walter J. Silva, ADST
7   Pyrros, 260
8   Ibid., 268
9   Steven V. Roberts, "Papandreou Opposes Athens Protests," *NYT*, 8/21/1974
10   Pyrros, 280
11   Ibid., 262–5
12   Ibid., 263
13   Howe, 442–52; Pyrros, 269 and interviews; Elias Vlanton, interviews; Jack Anderson, "Reagan Aide was Suspected of Lobbying for Greek Junta," *WP*, 10/25/1980
14   Hackett, "Congress and Greek American Relations," 19
15   Ibid.
16   Kissinger classified the discussion minutes as "TOP SECRET." The only outside record of the meeting was a memorandum prepared by one of Iakovos's assistants. National Security Adviser's Memoranda of Conversation Collection, GRFL, 10/7/1974, 2
17   Ibid.
18   Evans & Novak, "Mr. Ford and the Archbishop," *WP*, 11/11/1974; State Dept. Press Briefing, 11/11/1974; Doran T. Howard (AP), "Greece," 10/23/1975; Kubisch to SecState, Confidential, 10/23/1975
19   SecState to AmEmb Athens, Confidential, Immediate, 11/13/1974
20   Kubisch to SecState, Limited Official Use, 11/14/1974
21   Draenos, interview, 5/28/2012
22   Center Union/New Forces received 20.4 percent of the vote, PASOK 13.6, United Left 9.5, and National Democratic Union 1 percent. Clogg (*Parties*), 61
23   Clogg, ibid.
24   AmEmb (Stearns) to SecState (Asst Sec Stabler) 9/5/1974; AmEmb to SecState, 10/25/1974; AmEmb to SecState, 11/18/1974
25   Anderson, "Greek Hero Seeks U.S. Aid," *WP*, 12/9/1974; UPI, "Tortured Greek Hero Arrives in US for Medical Treatment," *Las Vegas Sun*, 12/22/1974; AP, "Agony of a Greek War Hero,"*Oakland Tribune*, 1/27/1975; Ann Blackman, "Victim of Torture Going Home," *Miami Herald*, 1/28/1975; AP,"Partially Paralyzed Greek War Hero Going Home After Medical Treatment for Effects of Torture," *Sioux Falls Argus-Leader*, 1/28/1975; "Statement Made By Mrs. Spyridon Moustaklis, 1/27/1975, EPDP
26   "Greece: Answering to History," *Time*, 9/1/1975
27   Torture in Greece: The First Torturers' Trial, Amnesty International, 1967, 45 (http://www. Amnesty.org/en/library/asset/EUR25/007/1977/en/4e35f4ad-0257-42da-869d-873ea13c6c6d/eur250071977eng.pdf; Eleftherotypia (http:www.enet.gr/online_text/c=110,dt=16.11.2003,id=713 51500; TIME, 9/1/1975; http:news.kathimerini.gr/4dcgi/_w_articles_civ_1_21/11/ 2007_24 9686; Christina Moustaklis, interview, 5/30/2012, and Moustaklis private papers: e.g. "USA," and "Elias Demetrakopoulos,"EPDP
28   https://docplayer.net/amp/79206621-The-first-torturers-trial-1975.html

27: "THE PLOT TO SNATCH DEMETRACOPOULOS"

1   National Security Adviser, Memorandum of Conversation, Ford, Kissinger, Senators Case and Sparkman, Representatives Broomfield and Morgan, 2/6/1975, box 9
2   Anderson with Whitten, "Demetracopoulos Case," *WP*, 2/12/1975
3   Heim to McDermott, Secret FBI memo, 2/6/1975; Whitten interviews
4   Anderson and Whitten, "US Officials Harassed Greek Exile," *WP*, 2/12/1975
5   Letter from Senator George McGovern to Senator Frank Church, 2/12/1975; *WP* headlined the

McGovern letter: "Senate Probe Urged of Exile's Charges," George Lardner, Jr., 2/13/1975

6   Heim to McDermott re: Inquiry by Les Whitten re: FBI Investigation of Elias Demetracopoulos SECRET CONFIDENTIAL, 2/6/1975

7   Lardner, WP, 2/13/1975; FBI, 2/14/1975 (105-131803-83); Ret. FBI Special Agent John Gamel, interview, 4/24/2014; Kempster: FBI "Black bag" jobs to obtain intelligence information was routine until officially stopped in 1966, but some FBI burglaries continued, 2/4/1977

8   Chief, Security Analysis Group to [redacted], # 77 59 (C), 2/27/1975; separate memorandum, 2/19/1975; CIA [Blind] Memorandum, 2/19/1975; see Keeley [Colonels' Coup], 260–1

9   AP, "Junta-CIA link; Exile to Testify," 4/8/1975

10 Interviews, Persa Metaxas and Christina Moustaklis, 5/30/2012

11 "Exile returns to Democratic Greece: American Praise for Demetracopoulos," Athens News, 4/13/1975; "Exile Flies Home to Visit Father's Grave," Athens News, 4/23/1975; "Athens welcomes Demetracopoulos: Self-exiled Greek 'Voice of Democracy' in U.S. Returns," Athens News, 5/17/1975

12 David Tonge, "The émigré eminence," The Guardian, 4/18/1975; Tonge also reported on Greek government ordering check into junta's EPD kidnap plans, BBC 4/27/1975; The Guardian, 4/28/1975

13 AmEmb to SecState, Priority, Secret, NODIS, "British Report on US Emissary to Athens," 6/5/1975

14 Hitchens (Kissinger), 109

15 Les Whitten papers, Lehigh University, Folder 75.14, Demetracopoulos

16 Ibid.; presumably, Mitchell, who served on Kissinger's NSC's "40 Committee" that reviewed covert operations, was aware of Greek plots.

17 Jack Anderson with Les Anderson with Whitten, "The Plot to Snatch Demetracopoulos," WP, 4/26/1975; Jack Anderson and Les Whitten, "Plot to Kidnap Greek Exile Detailed," WP, 4/26/1975

18 Notes in Whitten's Lehigh archives; confirmed in Whitten telephone interviews.

19 Whitten, interview, 12/20/2010

20 "Panayotakos" to EDP, letter, 6/23/1987

21 Panagiotakos, memoirs, 175–6, 195–6

22 Ibid.

23 Papadopoulos added that also aware of the kidnapping plans were A. Nomikos, minister counselor of the Greek Embassy in Washington, and George Levidis, then director of the press office. Levidis was the person who called Christina Moustaklis the year before to discourage the Walter Reed Hospital trip. Papadopoulos later told Kathreftis (Mirror) magazine that he would be a prosecution witness against Kissinger if he were ever to be prosecuted for crimes against EPD, Political and Financial Mirror, 1/2007, 36; Affidavit prepared while Papadopoulos was Greek Ambassador to Pakistan, 6/20/1987, in EPDP; Hitchens (Kissinger), 118–19

24 Charalambos Papadopoulos, letter in EPDP

25 Whitten, archives

26 Abourezk to Church, 4/28/1975; AP wire, 4/28/1975

27 "US Senate Committee to Investigate Alleged CIA involvement in Demetracopoulos kidnap plot," Athens News, 5/2/1975

28 Edwards, press statement, 4/28/1975

29 AP, 6/3/1975; UPI, 6/25/1975

30 On that date, Greek legislators engaged in a detailed review of the activities of civil servants in the Department for Studying, Planning and Programming of the General Secretariat of Press and Information.

31 Anderson and Whitten, "Greek Probe of Funds Cancelled," syndicated column, 6/24/1975; Greek papers followed: To Vima, Ta Nea, 6/25/1975; Kathimerini 6/26/1975; AmEmb Athens to SecState, "Greek Government Denies Jack Anderson's story on CIA Pressure as Fiction." Ref: 4716, 6/26/1975

32 Evans & Novak, "Agnew's Turnaround on Greece," WP, 7/16/ 1975; "Miss Gore's Old Letter Leads CIA Probe to Agnew, Junta," Baltimore Sun, 7/16/1975
Lee Belser, "Gore Letter Seen Vital in Senate Probe of CIA," Baltimore News American, 7/17/1975

33 CIA Memorandum for the Record, 7/24/1975; Jack Anderson, WP, 6/24/1975; CIA, Review Staff no. 75/16, 7/16/1975

34 "Agnew's Response," Baltimore Sun, 7/16/1975; "Agnew denies funding from Greek Junta," NYT,

8/2/1975; Robert B. Ling, "Agnew's Money," *Philadelphia Inquirer*, 6/30/1975; "Hill Probers Eye Session with Nixon," *WP*, 7/29/1975; Agnew wrote Kutler that he was not involved in "raising funds from the Greek Colonels. I... had no part in Tom Pappas' fund raising efforts overseas..." Agnew to Kutler letter. 3/20/1989; Kutler thought Agnew to be "an incorrigible liar," Kutler interviews with JHB.

35 "AmEmb (Kubisch) to SecState CONFIDENTIAL "Coup Trial Witness asserts CIA-Papadopoulos Relationship," 8/9/1975; "George Gives Value," *The Nation*, 8/13/1973,101; Deane, 96; Winter (*American Intervention*), 305. This view has been contradicted by Woodhouse (*Rise*) and Klarevas, 37.

36 "Demetracopoulos," Athens News, 8/12/1975; "US Fears Revelations," *Athens News*, 8/15/1975; AP, "Greece Coup-CIA Probe," Bristol (CT) *Press*, 9/4/1975; *Ta Nea*, headline: "Prosecution of likely CIA agents in the April 21 coup" cited in AmEmb Athens to SecState, "Press coverage of the investigation of charges against former ambassador Tasca," Priority/limited official use Athens 6955, PR 111541Z, Confidential

37 EPD told the BBC he wanted US House and Senate intelligence committees to investigate the Greek question, particularly the relationship between US and Greek intelligence services. He said Congress had the power to "demand that the administration produce all the written materials which shed light on the case, and to demand sworn testimony of all the witnesses whom they consider necessary irrespective of the office they held or hold now." Paul Nathaniel, BBC Greek section, 8/25, 1975, edited in "Demetracopoulos—Outlook on Greece," *Athens News*, 8/30/1975

38 AP, "Greece, 9/25/1975; In 1978, EPD met with Senate staff several times and was told they would contact him later if they decided to pursue the matter, either with a report or with hearings. They never did.

39 Ben Rosenthal, chairman of the House Foreign Affairs Committee, subcommittee on Europe, had earlier commented on the Demetracopoulos book: "This book whose distribution was prevented in Greece after the 1967 coup, became thereby one of the very first victims of the Papadopoulos junta. It is also very significant that when these revealing interviews were first published in the Greek press, a number of their grave, timely and accurate warnings were ignored. If these insights had been taken into account the events which led to the night of April 21, 1967 might have been avoided." Rosenthal letter to EPD, 11/7/1974

40 John Prados and Arturo Jimenez-Bacardi (eds.), "White House Efforts to Blunt 1975 Church Committee Investigation into CIA Abuses Foreshadowed Executive-Congressional Battles after 9/11," National Security Archive, The George Washington University, National Security Archive Electronic Briefing Book no. 522, posted July 20, 2015; John Prados and Arturo Jimenez-Bacardi, "Fortieth Anniversary: The Church Committee, the White House and the CIA, Spring 1975," 4, 7; http://nsarchive.gwu.edu/NSAEBB522-Church-Committee-Faced-White-House-Attempts-to-Curb-CIA-Probe/; Digital Security Archive, "CIA Covert Operations II: The Year of Intelligence," 1975

41 Nick Thimmesch, "Birth of a Salesman," *New York Times Magazine*, 10/26/1975

42 Hersh (*Price*), 648

43 Boos, interviews, 1/2011, supplemented by information from files and interviews with Summers, Kutler, Pyrros, and Warren Nelson interviews

44 Appendix V—interview with Hon. Henry J. Tasca, former United States Ambassador to Greece, by Jack Boos, Committee Counsel, September 26, 1975, U.S. Intelligence Agencies and Activities: Committee Proceedings, Proceedings of the Select committee on Intelligence, US House of Representatives, 94th Congress, First Session, 1975

45 AP, "A Four Year Old Confidential Memorandum," 9/24/1975

46 "Memorandum for the Record, Dimitrakopoulos," 10/18/1974

47 Ibid.

48 Warren (Nelson) to Les Aspin, "Memo Re Alleged Harassment of Greek by CIA," 12/15/1975; James Pyrros archives; Special Collections, University of Michigan

49 Ibid.

50 Edwards request to House Intelligence Committee referred to in AmEmb telegram to SecState, 12/19/1975

51 "Probe Target Joins Ford's Fundraisers," *Florida Times-Union*, Jacksonville, 12/19/1975

52 Leonard Curry, UPI, "Industrialist Tied to Questionable Contributions: Pappas joins Ford fund-raising committee," *Dominion News*, Morgantown, WV, 12/19/1975; In Athens, *To Vima*

headlined, "Pappas Seeks Ford's Intervention for Coca-Cola! He is also collecting money for the President's election," 12/18/1975; *Ta Nea*'s headline: "So that he won't lose the Coca-Cola franchise" "Pappas to Ford: 'Help (me) so I can help (you),'" 12/18/1975

53 "Greek Businessman Joins Ford Camp as Fundraiser," *NYT*, 12/19/1975

54 Kiesling (*Urban*), 9; Lawrence Stern, "CIA Agent's Murder Spurs Accusations," *WP*, 12/25/1975; John Cooley and Peter Melias "Anti-CIA Press Cited in Slaying," *Christian Science Monitor*, 12/25/1975; Athan G. Theoharis, Richard H. Immerman: *The Central Intelligence Agency: Security Under Scrutiny* (Greenwood, 2006), 207

28: FIGHTING FOR VINDICATION

1 Russell Howe and Sarah Hays Trott, "The Foreign Agent," *Washingtonian*, 12/1974; EPD, LTEs, *Washingtonian*, 2/1975

2 EPD, *Washingtonian*, LTE, 2/1975

3 Howe and Trott, *Power Peddlers: How Lobbyists Mold American Foreign Policy*, 1977

4 "Comments of Elias P. Demetracopoulos on Galley Proof of Doubleday & Co. Book Titled, *The Power Peddlers* by Russell Warren Howe and Sarah Hays Trott" (undated); Dobrovir legal memorandum re: Howe book (undated)

5 Russell Warren Howe, "Asset Unwitting: Covering the World for the CIA: Correspondent Tells of Employment by Secretly Funded Agency News Service," *MORE*, 5/1978, 20–7

6 McGovern letter to Churchill, 6/25/1974; Churchill to McGovern, 2/28/1977

7 McGovern letter to Senator John Sparkman, chairman, Senate Foreign Relations Committee, 3/1/1977; Walter Taylor, "McGovern's Objection Blocks 557 Promotions," *Washington Star*, 3/1/1977; Lawrence Pezzullo, Deputy Assistant Secretary for Congressional Affairs (transmitting Churchill answers) to McGovern, 2/28/1977; Pezzullo to John Holum, 3/4/1977; Dobrovir to EPD, 3/10/1977; Holum to Pezzullo, 3/29/1977; McGovern to Douglas Bennett, Assistant Secretary for Congressional Relations, 6/7/1977; Bennet to McGovern, 8/4/1977; Bennet to McGovern, 8/18/1977

8 McGovern, letter to Inouye, 10/29/1976, EPDP

9 Holum, emails and telephone interviews, 10/4–7/2011

10 "Pinochet 'Personally Ordered' Washington Car Bombing," GWU National Security Archive, archive2.gwu.edu/NSAEBB/NSAEBB532-The-Letelier-Moffitt-Assassination-Papers/; "Nixon on Chile Intervention: White House Tape Acknowledges Instructions to Block Salvador Allende," National Security Archive Electronic Briefing Book no. 110, 2/3/2004; Kornbluth, *The Pinochet File*.

11 Senator James Abourezk made explicit the kidnapping link in the *Congressional Record*, S17381, 9/30/1976, inserting an EPD interview with *Ta Nea*, 1/7/1976

12 Inouye to McGovern, 3/4/1977

13 Anderson, "McGovern urges CIA Probe," *Daily Item* (Sunberry, PA), 3/15/1977

14 Ross Evans, "Did US Help Greek Exile's Harassment?" *Washington Star*, 3/15/1977

15 Douglas J. Bennet Jr., letter to Sen. George S. McGovern, 8/4/1977.

16 William A. Dobrovir, Dobrovir, Oakes & Gebhardt. Profiled by Steve Nelson, "Private 'Public Interest' Firms Establish Bases," *Legal Times*, 4/19/1982; Gia Cincone, interview, 4/20/2011

17 For more than a decade, beginning on 8/9/1976, EDP and his attorneys sought to get from President Nixon's papers, the White House, the NSC, and Kissinger copies of any records concerning EPD. The White House said the law exempted or prohibited its responding positively. The NSC said there was nothing under his name or pertaining to him, but that there might be some in the Nixon files, which were enjoined from release. When Dobrovir asked about the contents of the five NSC computer indices mentioning his name, one of which referred to "Demetracopoulos Death in Athens Prison," it responded that the NSC was exempt from FOIA/PA. When EPD discovered references to NSC requests from NSC's A. Russell Ash and a "copy to NSC" in FBI documents, NSC said it could find no records relating to him. When they turned to Kissinger, 6/10/1980, for information concerning disclosures in CIA and FBI files that EPD documents went to NSC, while Kissinger was NSC Advisor and Chairman, Kissinger attorneys first refused to answer in writing. Dobrovir also asked about documents in President Ford's October 1974 briefing that referenced the EPD "trace paper," "the blind derogatory memo," and "the long Kissinger memo," "left with General Skowcroft," Ford's NSC advisor. Eventually, on 11/30/1987, Kissinger attorney James E. Wesner wrote

that [unspecified] "efforts were made" to search Kissinger's papers but found nothing. He suggested that EPD return to the other agencies that sent or received the missing documents, which is where EPD's frustrating search began. Kissinger's amended restrictive deed-of-gift limits access to his records held at the Library of Congress. Requests to Yale University, where he has donated some papers, also yielded no success. Years of Dobrovir–federal agency correspondence in EPDP. Anderson, "Nixon-Era Officials Retain Papers," *Topeka Capital Journal*, 11/10/1988

18   In a confidential State Dept. memorandum, 10/25/1966, John K. Adams, Press Officer, USIS, told Donald K. Taylor, PAO, USIS, about a 10/20/1966 conversation in which Harry Boubourellis, political writer at *To Vima*, who had previously been EPD's assistant at *Kathimerini*, said EPD's "mysterious" source of income was not "hidden connections" but the fruits of being a "favorite nephew." This tip escaped all those who sought to portray EPD as a foreign agent.

19   Another project involved working with Michigan congressman Don Riegle to identify the fate of at least nine American citizens still missing in the wake of the 1974 Turkish invasion of Cyprus. Anderson and Whitten, "Missing Americans," *WP*, 3/16/1976

20   7/12/1977 hearing

21   "Statement of the Honorable William E. Schaufele, Jr. of Ohio, Nominated to be Ambassador to Greece," 7/12/1977, *Alderson Reporting Service*; Evans & Novak, "Greek Concern Over Six Missing Words," *WP*, 2/6/1978

22   He would reprise his scooper role again in 1987, with the exposé of the criminal background of George Koskotas, which contributed to the biggest political and financial scandal to hit Greece in decades. From his sources in federal law enforcement, he learned in January 1987 that the banking and publishing magnate had been indicted by a New York grand jury on sixty-four counts of US tax fraud in 1980, but never arrested. He tipped off Jack Anderson about the issue, two months before Koskotas bought *Kathimerini*, Elias's first paper, which was still being run by Eleni Vlachou. The IRS refused to confirm or deny the allegation and it wasn't until Koskotas was about to visit the Reagan White House in October 1987 that he was arrested. The story shifted to Greece, where it dominated headlines, prompted government investigations about the sources of his wealth and illegal business practices, and contributed to the downfall of the Andreas Papandreou government. Jack Anderson, "The Greeks in Trouble," *San Francisco Chronicle*, 10/29/1987; Jack Anderson, "Scandal Wracks Greek Government," *Oakland Tribune*, 1/11/1989; Joe Spear, "People's will defeats a demagogue," *Newspaper Enterprise Association*, 7/31/1989; William Montalbano, "Embattled Papandreou at Center of Storm in Greece," *Los Angeles Times*, 1/15/1989; "Papandreou, Accused of Taking Bribes, Goes on Trial in Athens," *NYT*, 3/12/1991; "Greek Ex-Premier Not Guilty in Bank Scandal," *NYT*, 1/17/1992

23   "More Tyranny for Greece", *NYT*, 12/30/1970

24   Litsa Tsitera, friend since listening to EPD's MIT speech in 1969

25   Binder, "Ubiquitous Hand Guides Relations of U.S. and Greece," *NYT*, 12/6/1977

26   Joseph C. Goulden, "Fit to Print: A. M. Rosenthal and His Times," used the Elias episode as one of three egregious "instances that illustrate vividly the nigh-impossibility of persuading the *New York Times* that it should confess error on a story and set the record straight." Daniel Chomsky, "The mechanisms of management control at the *New York Times*," Media, Culture & Society, vol. 21, issue 5, 9/1/ 1999, 587–90 https://doi.org/10.1177/016344399021005001

27   *NYT*, 1/4/1978

28   After the *Times* refused to print a correction, EPD considered bringing a libel suit against the paper or Binder but declined, as he similarly decided with Howe, because to do so would have placed him in the "distasteful position of forcing another journalist to reveal confidential sources." Dobrovir to EPD, 11/29/1978

29   CIA, 1/5/1978

30   Evans & Novak, "The CIA: Harassing the Spy Who Never Was," *WP*, 12/23/1977

31   Evans & Novak, *WP*, 12/31/1977

32   Boland, House Hearings of Permanent Select Committee on Intelligence on "The CIA and the Media," 12/7/1977, 1

33   Bernstein, "CIA and the Media," *Rolling Stone*, 10/20/1977

34   Statement of Morton H. Halperin, Director, Center for National Security Studies, 1/4/1978, at "The CIA and the Media" Hearings before the Subcommittee on Oversight of the Permanent Se-

lect Committee on Intelligence, House of Representatives, 188–215
35 UPI, "An Editor Bids CIA Give Data on Press," NYT, 1/5/1978; Compare with Richard Dudman, "CIA Manipulated US Public Opinion, Halperin Charges," St. Louis Post-Dispatch, 1/4/1978; John Jacobs, "Halperin Alleges 4 Instances of CIA Exploitation of Media," WP, January 5, 1978; Jim Adams, AP, "CIA Manipulated Press Willfully, Panel Told," Shreveport Times, 1/5/1978, which dealt with EPD and NYT; telephone interview and JHB email exchange with John Crewdson, 12/22–23/2011
36 Jack Anderson, "CIA Retreating Into Its Shell," WP, 8/30/1978
37 Fowler to Casey, 6/17/1983
38 McMahon, Acting Director of Central Intelligence, to Fowler, 8/16/1983
39 Fowler to EPD, 8/20/1983
40 Allegations Against Greek Refuted by CIA, NYT, 9/29/1983
41 Ibid.
42 Alexander Cockburn, "Elias and 'Ilias'," Village Voice, 10/4/1983
43 Caryle Murphy, 'Vindication' Rewards a Six-Year Struggle," WP, 10/20/1983
44 "It cost me approximately a hundred thousand dollars and six years of my life," Elias recalled, "Six years that I could've devoted to other more important things. But I'm a Greek, and we Greeks are tough when you touch our honor." Ibid.
45 "A Greek Journalist Is Finally Cleared of CIA-Leaked Smear," Newsday, 5/7/1984
46 Robert Bannerman, A/SY/OPS/DO, Memorandum for the Files, 1/20/1983
47 Murphy, WP, op. cit.
48 Elias P. Demetracopoulos v. Federal Bureau of Investigation, Civil Action no. 78 –2209, United States District Court, District of Columbia, January 30, 1981; 510 F. Supp. 529 (1981) 1978; Dobrovir memorandum on Greene Memorandum and Order, EPDP; Statement of EPD on Freedom of Information Act before the Subcommittee on Government Information and Individual Rights, Committee on Government Operations, U.S. House of Representatives, 9/22/1981; Conyers, letter to Webster, 2/25/1982; FBI response 3/11/1982; Webster to Mintz, 3/18/1982. The Bureau denied his request.
49 Letter, Rosenthal to Attorney Gen. William French Smith, 4/19/1982; FBI memorandum letter from Chairman Rosenthal, Commerce, Consumer and Monetary Affairs Subcommittee of the Committee on Government Operations Requesting Information Concerning the FBI's Investigation of Elias Demetracopoulos, 4/28/1982; letter, FBI Director Webster to Rosenthal, 6/8/1982; Jack Anderson, "Rep. Rosenthal Pursues Ghost of Watergate," WP, 12/18/1982
50 Webster to Edwards, 4/11/1984
51 Edwards to Webster, 10/17/1983
52 Webster to Edwards, 12/7/1983
53 Edwards to Webster, 2/24/1984
54 Webster to Edwards, 4/11/1984
55 Edwards to EPD, 4/30/1984
56 Robert Parry, "FBI Concedes 10 Year Probe Found Nothing on Greek Journalist," AP, 6/28/1984; Jack Anderson, "A Greek Journalist Is Finally Cleared of CIA-Leaked Smear," Newsday (Garden City, NY), 5/7/1984
57 EPD to Edwards, 5/31/1984; EPD, "CIA Covert Action and Greece: A Case Study of the Usefulness of the Freedom of Information Act," presentation to Yale Center for International and Area Studies, Yale University, 4/9/1988
58 Robert Tait, "Personal Politics," The Scotsman (Edinburgh), 1/23/2001, 4
59 Republican Cong. Paul Findley "Personal and Confidential" to President Ford, 8,10/1976, EPDP; UPI, "White House File on Connally Includes 1972 Campaign 'Tricks'"; Washington Star, 9/4/1977; Evans & Novak, "Discreet Probe of Connally," WP, 9/3/1977; Jack Anderson, "1972 Skeleton in Connally's Closet," WP, 9/22/1979; Anderson, "Smugglers . . . ," WP, 12/24/1980; Reston, 551–3
60 Hitchens, "Kissinger in Greek Hit Plan?" Counterpunch, 2/16–28/1997, 5

29: LATER YEARS

1 "Washington's Ten Perfect Gentlemen," Washington Dossier, 11/1976, 32
2 Anderson, "Solving a Watergate Mystery," WP, 6/13/1982

3   "Kissinger Says Hersh Charge 'a Slimy Lie'," *Baltimore Sun*, 6/3/1983

4   Hitchens, "Watergate—The Greek Connection," *The Nation*, 5/31/1986

5   Xan Smiley of the *London Telegraph* told Christopher Hitchens about the Helms assessment. Helms knew that Smiley's father, "supposedly" part of the model for the Le Carré character, had been a famous British intelligence agent. Xan Smiley then prepared a Watergate anniversary article, believing that the Republicans broke in to "find something they wanted to keep quiet rather than made public." Christopher Hitchens to EPD, 7/1/92

6   Kempster, 1990, Hackett, 1992; "Why did they do it? . . . I don't know . . ." Ben Bradlee on *The Charlie Rose Show*, WNET[13], 10/21/1993; John Dean concluded it was a "badly botched" "fishing expedition" searching for "no specific information." He also pointed out that Magruder said to Liddy, "while you're in there photograph whatever you can find," and Hunt told the first-wave burglars to "look for financial documents—anything with 'numbers on them,'" especially if it involved "foreign contributions," Dean (*End of the Story*), 521

7   Liddy, 237; Gordon Liddy wrote that Jeb Magruder ordered him to photograph O'Brien's "shit file" on Nixon. "The purpose of the second Watergate break-in," Liddy claimed, "was to find out what O'Brien had of a derogatory nature about us, not for us to get something on him or the Democrats."; Kutler (*Wars*), 204–5; "Liddy, et al wanted more than Hughes material in that break-in. They wanted to get information concerning Tom Pappas and his carrying of Greek CIA money to the 1968 Nixon campaign." Kutler, letter to Jeb Stuart Magruder, 11/24/1987

8   Gary Skolnik, Director of Global Research Strategy and Analytics to EPD, 8/30/1995. Citibank letter to EPD. "Since the early 1980's, our international research efforts have benefitted considerably from your vast experience and personal networks in the fields of Washington policy developments, emerging market politics, and international finance."

9   In response to his complaint to the 2007 FRUS, the State Dept. issued an ERRATA indicating "the reference to Androutsopoulos is incorrect." However, because "it was not clear whether Tasca and Kissinger misspoke or whether the note taker recorded the wrong name," it would not make any further correction. A spokesman told JHB in 2014 "it is up to an outside historian to correct the record."

10 Weiner (*Legacy*), 632. When on a book tour, Weiner was asked by a caller in Silver Spring, MD, why he failed to credit Demetracopoulos as his source for what the reader considered the book's best chapter. Weiner replied: "Mr. Demetracopoulos is an honorable man, but I prefer to tell this tale through American eyes." *WP Book World*, July 24, 2007

11 Edwards, speech in *Congressional Record*, June 17, 1993, p. H 3777. Edwards explained: "This transaction was not only a violation of federal law which prohibits foreign governments from contributing to presidential campaigns, but also was a significant violation of the CIA's founding charter which prohibits any intervention in US domestic affairs. If this disclosure had been known to the American people in 1968 candidate Nixon may well not have won the very close race with Hubert Humphrey, and consequently Watergate would never have happened at all . . . [I'm delighted] to bring to the attention of my colleagues the story of Elias P. Demetracopoulos, a tenacious seeker of the truth, who persevered in his quest for justice in spite of the powers that were brought to bear in the effort to harass him into silence and to discredit him. His devotion to democracy and to the truth is truly inspirational."

12 EPD, "It Didn't Start with Clinton," *WP*, 6/15/1997 and "Beware a Revived Ministry of Lies," *Roll Call Daily*, 2/26/2002; Navy Institute Proceedings, 1/2000 and 5/2001

13 Dr. James Herzog, email to JHB, July 13, 2015; Herzog, "World Beyond Metaphor," in Bergmann, Kestenberg and Jucovy (eds.), *Generations of the Holocaust*, New York: Basic Books, 1982

14 William H. Webster to EPD, 4/6/1993; *Henry S. Reuss*, letter to EPD, 9/8/1996

15 Caryle Murphy,"'Vindication' Rewards a Six-Year Struggle," *WP*, October 20, 1983

16 Kutler, interview, November 2011; Aristotle, *Nichomachean Ethics*, "Three Types of Friendship" in Book VIII.

17 Interviews, Betinakis and Tsalapatis, 6/2/2012

18 Invitation from Ambassador Alexandros Mallias, 12/17/2007; "Veteran Greek Journalist Elias Demetrakopoulos Honoured," http://greeknewsonline.com, 1/14/2008

19 "US 'Sorry' for Junta Support," *Independent* (Burns), 1/15/1998; *AP*, "Clinton leaves Greece after apology for past policies," 11/21/1999; Andrew Cain, "Clinton Says US did not support Greek de-

mocracy: regrets support for junta in 1967," *Washington Times*, 11/21/1999; Terrence Hunt, "Clinton concedes regret for U.S. support of Greek junta, *Topeka Capital-Journal*, 11/21/1999; James Gerstanzang and Richard Boudreaux, "Clinton Says US Regrets Aid to Junta in Cold War," *Los Angeles Times*, 11/21/1999; "A look back at Clinton's 1999 visit to Athens," *Kathimerini*, 7/11/2016

20 "Elias Demetracopoulos Receives Award in D.C.," *National Herald*, 1/12/2008

21 Ibid.

22 James H. Barron, "Time for Compromise, Not Payback, in Greece," *Global Post*, 6/14/2012

23 The project began as a documentary, "Elias Demetracopoulos—THE MAN WHO SUED THE CIA, Maria Gentekou, Kalliopi Legaki, producers, Portlanos Films prospectus, 7/6/2010; Abed Alloush, "Greek Journalist's Story Inspires Documentary," March 17, 2014; YouTube: "It's Time for Heroes, 8 min Trailer" by Maria Gentekou, http://youtu.be/KJE3iRgldhw, March 19, 2013; Basil Tsiokos, "It's All Greek to Me: Championing Regional Filmmaking at the 15th Anniversary Thessaloniki Doc Fest," indiewire.com, 3/25/2013

24 Among the congratulatory notes received were one from historian Robert Dallek, who described him as "a force for honest government and investigative journalism. We are all better for his many years of effective work" (email to JHB, 11/14/2013), and one from John Holum, who recalled "it was a pleasure to work with you not only because of the warmth of your friendship and the righteousness of your cause, but also because, as a skilled journalist you always backed up your assertions with facts." Email to JHB, 11/15/2013

25 Martin Baron, email to JHB, 9/1/2014

26 Barbara LaRosa, interview, 6/26/2015

27 The account of EPD's last days in Athens are distilled from personal accounts of Kostas Loukopoulos, Stefanos Manouelidis, Persa Metaxas, and Christina Moustaklis, 5/2015–4/2016.

28 Kaklamanis served from 1993 to 2004.

29 "New Greek law permits cremation," NYT, 3/2/2006; Helena Smith, "Greece defies church with step towards first crematorium," *The Guardian*, 3/12/2019

SELECTED BIBLIOGRAPHY

BOOKS, THESES, AND REPORTS

Abbot, G. F. *Greece and the Allies 1914–1922*. London: Methuen & Co., 1922; Hotfreebooks.com.

Agee, Philip, and Louis Wolf. *Dirty Work: The CIA in Western Europe*. New York: Dorset Press, 1987.

Agnew, Spiro Theodore. *Go Quietly . . . or Else*. New York: Morrow, 1980.

Alastos, Doros. *Venizelos: Patriot, Statesman, Revolutionary*. London: P. Lund Humphries & Company, 1942.

Albright, Joseph. *What Makes Spiro Run: the Life and Times of Spiro Agnew*. New York: Dell, 1973.

Alexander, George Martin. *The Prelude to the Truman Doctrine: British Policy in Greece, 1944–1947*. Oxford: Clarendon Press, 1982.

Ambrose, Stephen E. *Nixon: Education of a Politician, 1913–1962*, New York: Touchstone, 1987.

Amnesty International (with Jonathan Caplan). *Torture in Greece: The First Torturers' Trial 1975*. London: Amnesty International Publications, 1977.

Anderson, Jack, and James Boyd. *Confessions of a Muckraker: The Inside Story of Life in Washington During the Truman, Eisenhower, Kennedy and Johnson Years*. New York: Ballantine Books, 1980.

Angelos, James. *The Full Catastrophe: Travels among the New Greek Ruins*. New York: Crown, 2016.

Apostolidis, Pavlos. *Intelligence Services in the National Security System: The Case of EYP*. OP07.03, Athens: ELIAMEP, 2007.

Apple, R. W., and Richard M. Nixon. *The White House Transcripts: Submission of Recorded Presidential Conversations to the Committee on the Judiciary of the House of Representatives*. Toronto: Bantam Books, 1974.

Aristotle. *Nichomachean Ethics* (trans. David Ross). London: Oxford University Press, 1961.

"Athenian" [Rodis Rouphos]. *Inside the Colonels' Greece*. New York: Norton, 1972.

Bailyn, Bernard. *The Ideological Origins of the American Revolution*. Cambridge, MA: Harvard University Press, 1967.

Baker, Bobby, and Larry L. King. *Wheeling and Dealing*. New York: Norton, 1978.

Barkman, Carl D. *Ambassador in Athens*. London: Merlin Press, 1989.

Barrett, David M. *The CIA & Congress: The Untold Story from Truman to Kennedy*. Lawrence, KS.: University Press of Kansas, 2017.

Bartlett, Donald L., and James B. Steele. *Empire: The Life, Legend, and Madness of Howard Hughes*. New York: W. W. Norton, 1980.

Beale, Betty. *Power at Play: A Memoir of Parties, Politicians and the Presidents in My Bedroom*. Regnery, 1993.

Beaton, Roderick. *George Seferis: Waiting for the Angel: A Biography*. New Haven: Yale University Press, 2003.

Becket, James, and Claiborne Pell. *Barbarism in Greece: A Young Lawyer's Inquiry into the Use of Torture in Contemporary Greece with Case Histories and Documents*. New York: Tower Publishing, 1970.

Beiser, Frederick C. *The German Historicist Tradition*. Oxford: Oxford University Press, 2011.

Bellett, Gerald. *Age of Secrets: The Conspiracy That Toppled Richard Nixon and the Hidden Death of Howard Hughes*. Maitland: Voyageur North America, 1995.

Bellou, Fotini, Theodore A. Couloumbis, and Theodore C. Kariotis (eds.). *Greece in the Twentieth Century*. New York: Frank Cass Publishers, 2005.

Bernstein, Carl, and Bob Woodward. *All the President's Men*. New York: Simon & Schuster, 1974.

Blum, John Morton. *Years of Discord: American Politics and Society, 1961–1974*. New York: W. W. Norton, 1992.

Blum, William. *Killing Hope: U.S. Military and CIA Interventions Since World War II*. Monroe, ME: Common Courage, 2004.

Bobotinos, Iannis. *Istoria Ethnikis Antistaseos – OAG* [History of National Resistance O.A.G. 1941–1945] Athens, 1954.

Bone, Drummond (ed.). *The Cambridge Companion to Byron*. Cambridge, UK: Cambridge University Press, 2004.

Bradford, James (ed.). *Quarterdeck Bridge and Pentagon: Two Centuries of American Naval Leadership*. Annapolis, Maryland: Naval Institute Press, 1996.

Brewer, David. *Greece, The Hidden Centuries: Turkish Rule from the Fall of Constantinople to Greek Independence*. London: I. B. Tauris, 2013.

Briggs, Ellis Ormsbee. *Proud Servant: The Memoirs of a Career Ambassador*. Kent, OH: Kent State University Press, 1998.

Brock, Peter, and David Binder. *Media Cleansing: Dirty Reporting Journalism and Tragedy in Yugoslavia*. Los Angeles: GM Books, 2006.

Brownworth, Lars. *Lost to the West: The Forgotten Byzantine Empire That Rescued Western Civilization*. New York: Crown Publishers, 2010.

Brugioni, Dino A. *Eyeball to Eyeball: The Inside Story of the Cuban Missile Crisis*. New York: Random House, 1990.

Bucar, Annabelle. *The Truth about American Diplomats*. Moscow: Literaturnaya Gazeta, 1949.

Burr, William (ed.). *The George Polk Case: CIA Has Lost Records on CBS Reporter Murdered in Greece in 1948, and Destroyed FOIA File on Case*, National Security Archive Electronic Briefing Book No. 226, August 10, 2007.

Campbell, John Kennedy, and Philip Sherrard. *Modern Greece*. New York: Praeger, 1969.

Caro, Robert A. *The Passage of Power: The Years of Lyndon Johnson*. New York: Alfred A. Knopf, 2012.

Chester, Lewis, Godfrey Hodgson, and Bruce Page. *An American Melodrama: The Presidential Campaign of 1968*. New York: Viking, 1969.

Churchill, Winston. *The Second World War*. London: Cassell, 1964.

Clark, Bruce. *Twice a Stranger. The Mass Expulsions that Forged Modern Greece and Turkey*. Cambridge, MA: Harvard University Press, 2006.

Clogg, Richard. *Parties and Elections in Greece: The Search for Legitimacy*. Durham, NC: Duke University Press, 1987. [PARTIES]

Clogg, Richard, and George Yannopoulos (eds.). *Greece Under Military Rule*. New York: Basic Books, 1972.

Clogg, Richard. *Greece, 1981–1989: The Populist Decade*. Houndmills: St. Martin's Press, 1993.

Clogg, Richard. *A Concise History of Greece*. Cambridge, UK: Cambridge University Press, 2016. [CONCISE]

Close, David H. *The Greek Civil War*. London: Routledge, 1993. [CIVIL WAR]

Close, David H. *Greece since 1945: Politics, Economy and Society*, London: Routledge, 2002.

Close, David H. *The Origins of the Greek Civil War*. London: Routledge, Taylor & Francis Group, 2015. [ORIGINS]

Cohen, Richard M., and Jules Witcover. *A Heartbeat Away*. New York: Viking, 1974.

Conason, Joe, and Gene Lyons, *Hunting the President*. New York: St. Martin's Press, 2000.

Condit, D. M. *Case Study in Guerrilla War: Greece During WWII*. Special Warfare Research Division, Special Operations Research Office, The American University, 1961.

Constandinos, Andreas. *America, Britain and the Cyprus Crisis of 1974: Calculated Conspiracy or Foreign Policy Failure?* Milton Keynes, UK: Author House, 2009.

Conispoliatis, Helen. *Facing the Colonels: British and American Diplomacy towards the Colonels' Junta in Greece, 1967–1970*. PhD Thesis, Leicester, 2003.

Cottrell, Richard. *Blood on Their Hands: The Killing of Ann Chapman*. London: Grafton, 1987.

Couloumbis, Theodore A., *The Greek Junta Phenomenon: A Professor's Notes*, New York: Pella Publishing Company, Inc., 2004.

Couloumbis, Theodore A. *Greek Political Reaction to American and NATO Influences*. New Haven: Yale University, 1977.

Couloumbis, Theodore A., John Anthony Petropoulos, and Harry J. Psomiades. *Foreign Interference in Greek Politics: An Historical Perspective.* New York: Pella Publications, 1976.

Couloumbis, Theodore A., and John O. Iatrides. *Greek-American Relations: A Critical Review.* New York: Pella Publications, 1980.

Crespino, Joseph. *Strom Thurmond's America: A History.* New York: Farrar, Straus and Giroux, 2012.

Crouse, Timothy. *The Boys on the Bus.* New York: Random House, 1973.

Cunningham, David. *There's Something Happening Here: The New Left, the Klan, and FBI Counterintelligence.* Berkeley: University of California Press, 2004.

Dallek, Matthew. *The Right Moment: Ronald Reagan's First Victory and the Decisive Turning Point in American Politics.* Oxford: Oxford University Press, 2004.

Dallek, Robert. *Flawed Giant: Lyndon Johnson and His Times 1961-1973.* Oxford: Oxford University Press, 1999.

Dallek, Robert. *Harry S Truman.* New York: Times Books, 2008.

Dallek, Robert. *Nixon and Kissinger: Partners in Power.* London: Penguin Books, 2008.

Dallek, Robert. *An Unfinished Life: John F. Kennedy, 1917-1963.* New York: Back Bay Books/Little, Brown and Company, 2013.

Dallek, Robert. *Camelot's Court: Inside the Kennedy White House.* New York: HarperCollins, 2013.

Dean, John W. *Blind Ambition, Updated Edition: The End of the Story.* Palm Springs, CA: Polimedia Publishers, 2009.

Deane, Philip [Gerasimos Gigantes]. *I Should Have Died.* New York: Atheneum, 1977.

Delaporta, Eleftheria. *The Role of Britain in Greek Politics and Military Operations: 1947-1952.* PhD Thesis, Department of History, Faculty of Arts, University of Glasgow, February 2003.

Demetracopoulos, Elias P. *The Royal Hellenic Navy in the Defense of Greece* (in Greek and English). Athens, December 1954.

Demetracopoulos, Elias P. *The Threat of Dictatorship* (in Greek). Athens: G. Fexis, 1967.

Dent, Harry. *Coverup.* San Bernadino, CA: Here's Life Publishers, 1986.

Dietrich, Noah, and Bob Thomas. *Howard: The Amazing Mr. Hughes.* Greenwich, CT: Fawcett, 1972.

Dimitrakis, Panagiotis. *Greece and the English: British Diplomacy and the Kings of Greece.* London: I. B. Tauris, 2009.

Dinges, John, and Saul Landau. *Assassination on Embassy Row.* New York: Pantheon, 1980.

Djilas, Milovan, and Joseph Stalin. *Conversations with Stalin.* New York: Harcourt, Brace and World, Inc., 1962.

Dobrovir, William A. *The Offenses of Richard M. Nixon: A Guide to His Impeachable Crimes.* New York: Quadrangle/The New York Times Book Co., 1974.

Dobrovir, William A. *Corporate Corruptors* (unpublished manuscript). Washington, D.C., 1982.

Donner, Frank J. *The Age of Surveillance: The Aims and Methods of America's Political Intelligence System.* New York: Vintage Books, 1981.

Dorrill, Stephen M. *MI6: Inside the Covert Words of Her Majesty's Secret Intelligence Service.* New York: Simon & Schuster, 2000.

Dorsen, Norman, and Stephen Gillers. *None of Your Business: Government Secrecy in America.* New York: Penguin Books, 1975.

Doulis, Thomas. *The Iron Storm: The Impact on Greek Culture of the Military Junta, 1967-1974.* Bloomington, IN: Xlibris, 2013.

Douzenis, Athanassios. "Starvation and Neglect of the Mentally Ill in Greece during WWII," M.Med. Sci, MRCPsych, PhD, Assistant Professor in Forensic Psychiatry, Athens University Medical School, 2nd Department of Psychiatry, Attikon Hospital, 1 Rimini St, Athens, Greece (undated).

Draenos, Stan. *Andreas Papandreou: The Making of a Greek Democrat and Political Maverick.* London: I. B. Tauris, 2012.

Drew, Elizabeth. *Washington Journal: The Events of 1973-1974.* New York: Macmillan, 1984.

Drosnin, Michael, and Howard Hughes. *Citizen Hughes.* New York: Broadway Books, 2004.

Duke, Simon. *United States Military Forces and Installations in Europe, Stockholm International Peace Research Institute.* Oxford: Oxford University Press, 1989.

Eisner, Robert. *Travelers to an Antique Land: The History and Literature of Travel to Greece.* Ann Arbor: University of Michigan Press, 1994.

Emery, Fred. *Watergate: The Corruption of American Politics and the Fall of Richard Nixon.* New York: Touchstone, 1995.

Evans, Peter. *Nemesis, the True Story: Aristotle Onassis, Jackie O, and the Love Triangle That Brought Down the Kennedys.* New York: Regan Books, 2005.

Evans, Rowland, and Robert D. Novak. *Nixon in the White House: The Frustration of Power.* New York: Random House, 1971.

Fallaci, Oriana. *A Man.* London: Arrow, 1993.

Farber, David R. *The Age of Great Dreams: America in the 1960s.* New York: Hill and Wang, 2000.

Feldstein, Mark. *Poisoning the Press: Richard Nixon, Jack Anderson, and the Rise of Washington's Scandal Culture.* New York: Farrar, Straus and Giroux, 2010.

Fermor, Patrick Leigh. *Roumeli: Travels in Northern Greece.* New York: New York Review of Books, 2004.

Finer, Leslie, and Spiros Vassiliou. *Passport to Greece.* London: Longmans, 1964.

Finlay, George, and Henry Fanshawe Tozer. *A History of Greece from Its Conquest by the Romans to the Present Time: B.C. 146 to A.D. 1864.* New York: AMS Press, 1970.

Fleischer, Hagen, Steven B. Bowman, and John O. Iatrides. *Greece in the 1940s: A Bibliographic Companion.* Hanover, NH: University Press of New England, 1981.

Fleming, Amalia. *A Piece of Truth.* Boston: Houghton Mifflin, 1973.

Fleming, Deena Frank. *The Cold War and Its Origins, 1917–1960.* New York: Doubleday, 1961.

Frank, Jeffrey. *Ike and Dick: Portrait of a Strange Political Marriage.* New York: Simon & Schuster Paperbacks, 2013.

Frazier, Robert. *Anglo-American Relations with Greece: The Coming of the Cold War, 1942–47.* New York: St. Martin's Press, 1991.

Fulbright, J. William. *The Arrogance of Power.* Harmondsworth: Penguin, 1970.

Fulsom, Don. *Nixon's Darkest Secrets.* New York: Thomas Dunne Books, 2012.

Gaddis, John Lewis. *We Now Know: Rethinking Cold War History.* New York: Oxford University Press, 1997.

Gage, Nicholas. *Hellas.* New York: Villard Books, 1987.

Garment, Leonard. *Crazy Rhythm: Richard Nixon and All That Jazz.* New York: Times Books, 1997.

Garment, Leonard. *In Search of Deep Throat: The Greatest Political Mystery of Our Time.* New York: Basic Books, 2000.

Genevoix, Maurice, and Dorothy Trollope. *The Greece of Karamanlis.* London: Doric Publications, 1973.

Gerolymatos, André. *The British and the Greek Resistance, 1936–1944: Spies, Saboteurs, and Partisans.* Lantham, MD: Lexington Books, 2018.

Gerolymatos, André. *Guerrilla Warfare and Espionage in Greece, 1940–1944.* New York: Pella Publishing, 1992. [GUERRILLA]

Gerolymatos, André. *Red Acropolis, Black Terror: The Greek Civil War and the Origins of Soviet-American Rivalry, 1943–1949.* New York: Basic Books, 2004. [RED]

Giannopoulos, Georgios N., and Richard Clogg. *Greece under Military Rule.* London: Secker and Warburg, 1972.

Gibbons, Herbert Adams. *Venizelos.* Ann Arbor: University of Michigan, 2009.

Gitlin, Todd. *The Sixties: Years of Hope, Days of Rage.* New York: Bantam, 1993.

Gkotzaridis, Evi. *A Pacifist's Life and Death: Grigorios Lambrakis and Greece in the Long Shadow of Civil War.* Newcastle upon Tyne: Cambridge Scholars Publishing, 2016.

Goebbels, Joseph, and Louis Paul Lochner. *The Goebbels Diaries: 1942–1943.* Garden City: Doubleday, 1948.

Goldstein, Tom. *The News at Any Cost: How Journalists Compromise Their Ethics to Shape the News.* New York: Simon & Schuster, 1985.

Goldwater, Barry M. *The Conscience of a Conservative.* Shepherdsville, KY: Victor Publishing Company, Inc., 1960.

Goldwater, Barry M. *With No Apologies: The Personal and Political Memoirs of United States Senator Barry M. Goldwater.* New York: William Morrow, 1979.

Gomery, Douglas. *Media in America: The Wilson Quarterly Reader.* Baltimore: The Johns Hopkins University Press, 1998.

Goodman, Melvin A. *Failure of Intelligence: The Decline and Fall of the CIA.* Lanham, MD: Rowman & Littlefield, 2008.

Gould, Lewis L. 1968: *The Election that Changed America*. Chicago: Ivan R. Dee, 1993.

Goulden, Joseph C. *Fit to Print: a.m. Rosenthal and His Times*. Secaucus, NJ: Lyle Stuart, 1988.

Grady, Henry Francis, and John T. MacNay. *The Memoirs of Ambassador Henry F. Grady from the Great War to the Cold War*. Columbia, MO: University of Missouri Press, 2009.

Green, Mark J. *The Other Government: The Unseen Power of Washington Lawyers*. New York: Grossman Publishing, 1975.

Grigoriadis, Solon. *Istoria tis Diktatorias* (History of the Dictatorship) (3 volumes). Athens, 1975.

Grose, Peter. *Gentleman Spy: The Life of Allen Dulles*. Boston: Houghton Mifflin Company, 1994.

Halberstam, David. *The Best and the Brightest*. New York: Random House, 1972.

Halberstam, David. *The Powers That Be*. New York: Alfred A. Knopf, 1979.

Haldeman, H. R., and Stephen E. Ambrose. *The Haldeman Diaries: Inside the Nixon White House*. New York: Berkley Books, 1995.

Hamilton, James. *The Power to Probe: A Study of Congressional Investigations*. New York: Random House, 1976.

Hansen, Stephen A. *Kalorama Triangle: The History of a Capital Neighborhood*. Charleston, SC: History Press, 2011.

Hansen, Stephen A. *A History of Dupont Circle: Center of High Society in the Capital*. Charleston, SC: History Press, 2014.

Haritos-Fatouros, Mika. *The Psychological Origins of Institutionalized Torture*. London: Routledge, 2003.

Hatzivassiliou, Evanthis. *Greece and the Cold War: Front-line State, 1952–1967*. London: Routledge, 2011.

Heer, Hannes and Klaus Naumann (eds). *War of Extermination: The German Military in World War II, 1941–1944*. New York: Berghahn Books, 2004.

Helms, Richard. *A Look Over My Shoulder: A Life in the Central Intelligence Agency*. New York: Random House, 2003.

Hersh, Seymour M. *The Price of Power: Kissinger in the Nixon White House*. New York: Summit Books, 1983. [PRICE]

Hersh, Seymour M. *The Dark Side of Camelot*. Thorndike, ME: Thorndike Press, 1998. [CAMELOT]

Heurtley, W. A. *A Short History of Greece: From Early Times to 1964*. Cambridge, MA: Cambridge University Press, 1965.

Hewitt, Evan C. *Rolling Around the World*. Dartford, UK: Xlibris Publishing Co., 2014.

Higham, Charles. *Howard Hughes: Secret Life*. New York: Putnam, 1993.

Hionidou, Violetta. *Famine and Death in Occupied Greece, 1941–1944*. Cambridge, UK: Cambridge University Press, 2006.

Hitchens, Christopher. *Cyprus*. London: Quartet Books, 1984.

Hitchens, Christopher. *Hostage to History: Cyprus from the Ottomans to Kissinger*. London: Verso, 1999.

Hitchens, Christopher. *The Trial of Henry Kissinger*. London: Verso, 2001.

Hoffman, Paul. *Spiro!* New York: Tower Publications, 1971.

Holden, David. *Greece without Columns: The Making of the Modern Greeks*. London: Faber and Faber, 1972.

Hondros, John Louis. *Occupation and Resistance: the Greek Agony, 1941–44*. New York: Pella, 1983.

Hougan, Jim. *Spooks: The Haunting of America: The Private Use of Secret Agents*. New York: Bantam Books, 1979.

Hougan, Jim. *Secret Agenda: Watergate, Deep Throat, and the CIA*. New York: Random House, 1984.

Hourmouzios, Stelios. *No Ordinary Crown: A Biography of King Paul of the Hellenes*. London: Weidenfeld and Nicolson, 1972.

Housepian, Marjorie. *Smyrna 1922: The Destruction of a City*. New York: Newmark Press, 1998.

Howe, Russell Warren. *Truth at Any Price: A Reporter's Six Decades on Five Continents*. West Conshohocken, PA: Infinity Publishing, 2006.

Howe, Russell Warren, and Sarah Hays Trott. *The Power Peddlers: How Lobbyists Mold America's Foreign Policy*. Garden City, NY: Doubleday, 1977.

Humphrey, Hubert H. *The Education of a Public Man: My Life in Politics*. Minneapolis: University of Minnesota Press, 1991.

Hunt, E. Howard. *Undercover; Memoirs of an American Secret Agent*. London: W.H. Allen, 1975.

Iatrides, John O. *Revolt in Athens: The Greek Communist "Second Round," 1944–1945*. Princeton, NJ: Princeton University Press, 1972.

Iatrides, John O. (ed.), *Ambassador MacVeagh Reports: Greece, 1933–1947*, Princeton, NJ: Princeton University Press, 1980.

Iatrides, John O. (ed.). *Greece in the 1940s: A Nation in Crisis*. Hanover, NH: University Press of New England, 1981.

Iatrides, John O. *Greece at the Crossroads: The Civil War and Its Legacy*. University Park, PA: Pennsylvania State University Press, 1995.

Ilias-Tembos, Evangelos. *The Military Campaigns of the Axis Against Greece Observed*. Doctor of Philosophy, University of York, 1996.

Ioannides, Chris P. *Realpolitik in the Eastern Mediterranean: From Kissinger and the Cyprus Crisis to Carter and the Lifting of the Turkish Arms Embargo*. New York: Athens Printing Company, 2001.

Isaacson, Walter. *Kissinger: A Biography*. New York: Simon & Schuster Paperbacks, 2005.

Jamieson, Kathleen Hall. *Dirty Politics: Deception, Distraction, and Democracy*. New York: Oxford University Press, 1992.

Jamieson, Kathleen Hall. *Packaging the Presidency: A History and Criticism of Presidential Campaign Advertising*. New York: Oxford University Press, 1996.

Janeway, Eliot. *Prescriptions for Prosperity*. New York: Times Books, 1983.

Jeffrey, Keith. *MI6: The History of the Secret Intelligence Service, 1909–1949*. London: Bloomsbury, 2010.

Jenkins, Roy. *Churchill: A Biography*. New York: Farrar, Straus and Giroux, 2001.

Joes, Anthony James. *Modern Guerrilla Insurgency*. Westport, CT: Praeger Publishers, 1992.

Johnson, David K. *The Lavender Scare: The Cold War Persecution of Gays and Lesbians in the Federal Government*. Chicago: University of Chicago Press, 2004.

Johnson, Loch K. *America's Secret Power: The CIA in a Democratic Society*. New York: Oxford University Press, 1991.

Jones, Ken, and Hubert Kelley. *Admiral Arleigh (31-Knot) Burke: The Story of a Fighting Sailor*. Annapolis, MD: Naval Institute Press, 2001.

Judt, Tony. *Postwar: A History of Europe Since 1945*. London: William Heinemann, 2005.

Kagan, Donald. *Pericles of Athens and the Birth of Democracy*. New York: Free Press, 1991.

Kakaounakis, Nikos. *2650 Meronychta Synomosias* (2650 Days and Nights of Conspiracies). Athens: Papazisis, 1976, Vol. 2.

Kalb, Bernard, and Marvin L. Kalb. *Kissinger*. Boston: Little, Brown and Company, 1979.

Kalyvas, Stathis N. *Modern Greece: What Everyone Needs to Know*. New York: Oxford University Press, 2015.

Kamiya, Gary. *Shadow Knights: The Secret War Against Hitler*. New York: Simon & Shuster, 2010.

Kapsis, Iannis (aka John Capsis). *Peninta Xronia sto Kourmpeti* (50 Years on the Beat). Athens: Livanis Publishing Co., 2003.

Karakatsanis, Neovi M., and Jonathan Swarts. *American Foreign Policy towards the Colonels' Greece: Uncertain Allies and the 1967 Coup d'État*. New York: Palgrave, 2018.

Katris, John A. *Eyewitness in Greece: The Colonels Come to Power*. St. Louis, New Critic's Press, 1971.

Keeley, Edmund. *The Salonika Bay Murder*. Princeton, NJ: Princeton University Press, 1989. [SALONICA BAY]

Keeley, Edmund. *Inventing Paradise: The Greek Journey, 1937–47*. Evanston, IL: Northwestern University Press, 2002.

Keeley, Robert V. *The Colonels' Coup and the American Embassy*. University Park, PA: Penn State Press, 2010.

Keegan, John. *The Second World War*. New York: Viking, 1989.

Kennedy, Jacqueline, *Historic Conversations on Life with John F. Kennedy*. New York: Grand Central Publishing, 2011.

Keogh, James. *President Nixon and the Press*. New York: Funk & Wagnalls, 1972.

Kiesling, John Brady. *Diplomacy Lessons: Realism for an Unloved Superpower*. Washington, D.C.: Potomac Books, 2007.

Kiesling, John Brady. *Greek Urban Warriors: Resistance and Terrorism 1967–2014*. Athens: Lycabettus Press, 2014.

Kimball, Penn. *The File.* New York, NY: Harcourt Brace, 1983.

Kinzer, Stephen. *The Brothers: John Foster Dulles, Allen Dulles, and Their Secret World War.* New York: Times Books, 2013.

Kirtz, Neil J. (ed.). *Transitional Justice: How Emerging Democracies Reckon with Former Regimes: Vol. II: Country Studies.* Washington: United States Institute of Peace Press, 1995.

Kissinger, Henry. *Years of Upheaval.* Boston: Little, Brown and Company, 1982.

Kissinger, Henry. *Years of Renewal.* New York: Simon & Schuster, 1999.

Kiste, John Van Der. *King of the Hellenes: The Greek Kings 1863–1974.* Gloucestershire: Sutton Publishing Limited, 1999.

Klarevas, Louis. "Were the Eagle and Phoenix Birds of a Feather? The United States and the Greek Coup of 1967," Discussion Paper No. 15, Hellenic Observatory-European Institute, London School of Economics, February 2004.

Klein, Herbert G. *Making It Perfectly Clear.* Garden City, NY: Doubleday, 1980.

Knudson, Jerry W. *In the News: American Journalists View Their Craft.* Wilmington, DE: SR Books, 2000.

Kofas, Jon V. *Under the Eagle's Claw: Exceptionalism in Postwar U.S.-Greek Relations.* Westport, CT.: Praeger, 2003.

Koliopoulos, John S. *Brigands with a Cause: Brigandage and Irredentism in Modern Greece, 1821–1912.* Oxford: Clarendon Press, 2011.

Koliopoulos, John S., and Thanos Veremis. *Greece: The Modern Sequel.* New York: New York University Press, 2002.

Kornbluth, Peter. *The Pinochet File: A Declassified Dossier of Atrocity and Accountability.* New York: The New Press, 2013.

Kornetis, Kostis. *Children of the Dictatorship: Student Resistance, Cultural Politics and the Long 1960s in Greece.* New York: Berghahn Books, 2016.

Kousoulas, Dimitrios Georgios. *Revolution and Defeat: The Story of the Greek Communist Party.* London: Oxford University Press, 1965.

Kousoulas, D. George. *Modern Greece: Profile of a Nation.* New York: Scribners, 1974.

Kubly, Herbert. *Gods and Heroes.* New York: Doubleday, 1969.

Kutler, Stanley I. *The Wars of Watergate: The Last Crisis of Richard Nixon.* New York: Knopf, 1990.

Kutler, Stanley I. *Abuse of Power: The New Nixon Tapes.* London: Touchstone, 1999.

Lasky, Victor. *It Didn't Start with Watergate.* New York: Dell, 1978.

Lawlor, Sheila. *Churchill and the Politics of War.* Cambridge: Cambridge University Press, 1994.

Leeper, Reginald. *When Greek Meets Greek.* London: Chatto and Windus, 1950.

Legg, Keith R. *Politics in Modern Greece.* Stanford, CA: Stanford University Press, 1969.

Lenzer, Terry. *The Investigator.* New York: Blue Rider Press, 2013.

Leon, George B. *Greece and the Great Powers 1914–17.* Thessaloniki, Institute of Balkan Studies, 1974.

Leontis, Artemis. *Greece: A Traveler's Literary Companion.* San Francisco: Whereabouts Press, 1997.

Lewis, Michael. *Boomerang: Travels in the New Third World.* New York: W. W. Norton & Company, 2012.

Liddy, G. Gordon. *Will: The Autobiography of G. Gordon Liddy.* New York: St. Martin's Paperbacks, 1980.

Louizos, Evangelos. *My Father Had This Luger: A True Story of Hitler's Greece.* Kansas City, MO: Truman Publishing, 2012.

Lucas, Jim G. *Agnew: Profile in Conflict.* New York: Award Books, 1970.

Lukas, J. Anthony. *Nightmare: The Underside of the Nixon Years.* New York: Viking, 1976.

MacNeill, William Hardy. *The Metamorphosis of Greece since World War II.* 1978.

MacPherson, Myra. *"All Governments Lie": The Life and Times of Rebel Journalist I. F. Stone.* New York: Scribners, 2008.

Madinger, John. *Money Laundering: A Guide for Criminal Investigators, Third Edition.* Boca Raton, FL: CRC Press, 2016.

Magruder, Jeb Stuart. *An American Life: One Man's Road to Watergate.* New York: Pocket Books, 1975.

Maheu, Robert, and Richard Hack. *Next to Hughes.* New York, NY: Harper Paperbacks, 1993.

Mallinson, William. *Cyprus: A Modern History*. London: I. B. Tauris, 2009.

Mankiewicz, Frank. *Perfectly Clear: Nixon from Whittier to Watergate*. New York: Quadrangle/The New York Times Book Co., 1973.

Manolopoulos, Jason. *Greece's 'Odious Debt': The Looting of the Hellenic Republic by the Euro, the Political Elite and the Investment Community*. London: Anthem Press, 2011.

Marchak, Patricia. *No Easy Fix: Global Responses to Internal Wars and Crimes Against Humanity*. Montreal: McGill-Queens's University Press, 2008.

Marchetti, Victor, and John D. Marks. *The CIA and the Cult of Intelligence*. New York: Dell Publishing, 1989.

Margolis, Susan. *Fame*. San Francisco: San Francisco Book Company, 1977.

Martin, Ralph G. *Henry & Clare: An Intimate Portrait of the Luces*. New York: Putnam, 1991.

Marton, Kati. *The Polk Conspiracy: Murder and Cover-Up in the Case of CBS News Correspondent George Polk*. New York: Times Books, 1992.

Marwick, Christine M. *Litigation under the Amended Federal Freedom of Information Act*. Washington, D.C.: Center for National Security Studies, 1978.

Mateos, Natalia Ribas. *The Mediterranean in the Age of Globalization: Migration, Welfare & Borders*. Piscataway, NJ: Transaction Publishers, 2005.

Mayes, Stanley. *Makarios: A Biography*. New York: St. Martin's Press, 1981.

Mazower, Mark. *Inside Hitler's Greece: The Experience of Occupation, 1941–1944*. New Haven: Yale, 1993. [INSIDE]

Mazower, Mark. *After the War Was Over: Reconstructing the Family, Nation, and State in Greece, 1943–1960*. Princeton, NJ: Princeton University Press, 2000. [AFTER]

Mazower, Mark. *Salonica: City of Ghosts: Christians, Muslims and Jews, 1430–1950*. New York: Vintage Books, 2006.

Mazower, Mark (ed.). *Networks of Power in Modern Greece: Essays in Honor of John Campbell*. New York: Columbia University Press, 2008.

McCullough, David G. *Truman*. New York: Simon & Schuster, 1992.

McDonald, Robert. *Pillar and Tinderbox: The Greek Press and the Dictatorship*. New York: Boyars, 1983.

McDougall, J. B. "Tuberculosis in Greece: An Experiment in the Relief and Rehabilitation of a Country," World Health Organization, 1948 [Bull World Health Organ. 1948; 1(1): 103–196]. https://www.ncbi.nlm.nih.gov/pmc/articles/PMC2556139/.

McGinniss, Joe. *The Selling of the President*. New York: Trident, 1969.

McLendon, Winzola, and Scottie Smith. *Don't Quote Me: Washington Newswomen & the Power Society*. New York: Dutton, 1970.

McNeill, William H. *The Greek Dilemma*. London: Gollancz, 1947.

McNeill, William H. *The Metamorphosis of Greece Since World War II*. Chicago: University of Chicago Press, 1978. [METAMORPHOSIS]

Mercouri, Melina. *I Was Born Greek*. New York: Dell Publishing, 1973.

Meyer, Cord. *Facing Reality*. New York: Harper & Row, 1980.

Miller, Hope Ridings. *Embassy Row: The Life and Times of Diplomatic Washington*. New York: Holt, Rinehart and Winston, 1969.

Miller, James Edward. *The United States & The Making of Modern Greece: History and Power, 1950–1974*. Chapel Hill, NC: University of North Carolina Press, 2009. [JE MILLER]

Mintz, Morton, Jerry S. Cohen, and Ralph Nader. *America Inc.* New York: Dial Press, 1971.

Mitrakos, Alexander S. *France in Greece During World War I: A Study in the Politics of Power*. Boulder: East European Monographs distributed by Columbia University Press, 1982.

Monos, Dimitrios I. *Upward Mobility, Assimilation, and the Achievements of the Greeks in the United States with Special Emphasis on Boston and Philadelphia*: Ann Arbor, MI: University Microfilms International, 1980.

Moran, Christopher. *Company Confessions: Secrets, Memoirs, and the CIA*. New York: Thomas Dunne Books, 2015.

Moskos, Charles C. *Greek Americans: Struggle and Success*. Englewood Cliffs, NJ: Prentice-Hall, 1980.

Munn, Donald C. *Military Dictatorship and Greece (1967–1964): The Genesis of Greek Anti-American-*

ism. Monterey, CA: Naval Postgraduate School, 1980.

Murtagh, Peter. *The Rape of Greece: The King, the Colonels and the Resistance.* London: Simon & Schuster, 1994.

Myers, E.C.W. *Greek Entanglement.* Gloucester: Sutton, 1985.

Mylonas, George. *Escape from Amorgos.* New York: Scribner's, 1974.

Nafpliotis, Alexandros. *Britain and the Greek Colonels: Accommodating the Junta in the Cold War.* London: I. B. Tauris, 2013.

Nalmpantis, Kyriakos. "Time on the Mountain: The Office of Strategic Services in Axis-Occupied Greece, 1943–1944." Kent State University PhD dissertation, 2010, https://etd.ohiolink.edu/.

Napolitan, Joseph. *The Election Game and How to Win It.* New York: Doubleday, 1972.

Nash, Philip. *The Other Missiles of October: Eisenhower, Kennedy and the Jupiters, 1957–1963.* Chapel Hill, NC: University of North Carolina Press, 1997.

Neer, Robert M. "Napalm, An American Biography." Doctor of Philosophy, Graduate School of Arts and Sciences, Columbia University, 2011. Users/jamesbarron/Downloads/Neer_columbia_0054D_10287%20(12).pdf

"Nixon on Chile Intervention: White House Tape Acknowledges Instructions to Block Salvador Allende." National Security Archive Electronic Briefing Book no. 110, February 2, 2004.

Nixon, Richard M. *Six Crises.* Garden City, NY: Doubleday, 1962.

Nixon, Richard M. *Memoirs of Richard Nixon.* New York: Simon & Schuster, 1990.

Nohlen, Dieter, and Phillip Stover. *Elections in Europe: A Data Handbook.* Oxford: Oxford University Press, 2010.

Nomikos, John M. "Greek Intelligence Service (NIS-EYP): Past, Present and Future," National Security and the Future 1–2 (9) 2008. https://fas.org/irp/world/greece/nomikos2.pdf

Novak, Robert D. *The Prince of Darkness: 50 Years Reporting in Washington.* New York: Crown Forum, 2007.

O'Ballance, Edgar, and C. M. Woodhouse. *The Greek Civil War, 1944–1949.* London: Faber and Faber, 1966.

O'Brien, Lawrence F. *No Final Victories: A Life in Politics, from John F. Kennedy to Watergate.* New York: Ballantine Books, 1976.

O'Connor, Bernard. *Sabotage in Greece.* Lulu.com, 2018.

O'Connor, Brendan (ed.). *Anti-Americanism: History, Causes, Themes, Vol. 3, Comparative Perspectives.* Oxford, Westport, CT: Greenwood World Publishing, 2007.

O'Donnell, Guillermo, Phillipe C. Schmitter, and Laurence Whitehead. *Transitions from Authoritarian Rule: Southern Europe.* Baltimore: Johns Hopkins Press, 1986.

Olmstead, Kathryn S. *Challenging the Secret Government: The Post-Watergate Investigations of the CIA and FBI.* Chapel Hill, NC: University of North Carolina Press, 1966.

Olmstead, Kathryn S. *Conspiracy Theories and American Democracy, World War I to 9/11.* Oxford: Oxford University Press, 2009.

O'Malley, Brendan, and Ian Craig. *The Cyprus Conspiracy: America, Espionage and the Turkish Invasion.* London: I. B. Tauris, 2009.

Onassis, Jacqueline Kennedy, Arthur Meier Schlesinger, Caroline Kennedy, and Michael R. Beschloss. *Historic Conversations on Life with John F. Kennedy.* New York: Hyperion, 2011.

Panagiotakos, Konstantinos. *Stin Proti Grammi Aminis* (At the First Line of Defense). Athens: 1982.

Panourgia, Neni. *Dangerous Citizens: The Greek Left and the Terror of the State.* New York: Fordham University Press, 2009.

Papahelas, Alexis, O. *Biasmos tis Ellenikis Dimokratias: O Amerikanikos paragon 1947–1967* (The Rape of Greek Democracy: The American Factor, 1947–1967). Athens: Estia, 2009.

Papandreou, Andreas. *Democracy at Gunpoint: The Greek Front.* New York: Doubleday & Company, 1970.

Papandreou, Margaret Chant. *Nightmare in Athens.* Englewood Cliffs, NJ: Prentice-Hall, 1970.

Pelt, Mogens. *Tying Greece to the West: US–West German–Greek Relations: 1949–74.* Copenhagen: Museum Tusculanum Press, 2006.

Perlstein, Rick. *Nixonland: The Rise of a President and the Fracturing of America.* New York: Scribner's, 2009.

Pike, Otis M., and Aaron Latham. *The CIA Report the President Doesn't Want You to Read.* New York:

Village Voice, 1976.

Plato. *The Dialogues of Plato, Vol. II* (trans. Benjamin Jowett). New York: Random House, 1937.

Potter, Elmer B. *Admiral Arleigh Burke.* New York: Random House, 1990.

Powers, Thomas. *The Man Who Kept the Secrets: Richard Helms and the CIA.* New York: Alfred A. Knopf, 1987.

Prados, John, and Arturo Jimenez-Bacardi (eds.). "White House Efforts to Blunt 1975 Church Committee Investigation into CIA Abuses Foreshadowed Executive-Congressional Battles after 9/11," National Security Archive, The George Washington University, National Security Archive Electronic Briefing Book No. 522, Posted July 20, 2015.

Price, Raymond. *With Nixon.* New York: Viking, 1977.

Psilos, Dr. Diomedes D., and Dr. Richard M. Westebbe. Public International Development Financing: A Research Project of the Columbia University School of Law, Report Number 10, Greek Center of Economic Research, Athens, NY, September 1964.

Pyrros, James G. "Memories of the Anti-Junta Years," Special Collections (The Pyrros Papers), University of Michigan, 1991.

Pyrros, James G. *The Cyprus File, Washington, D.C.: A Diary of the Cyprus Crisis in the Summer of 1974.* New York: Pella Publishing, 2010.

Quinn, William W. *Buffalo Bill Remembers: Truth and Courage.* Fowlerville, MI: Wilderness Adventure Books, 1991.

Ranelagh, John. *The Agency: The Rise and Decline of the CIA.* New York: Simon & Schuster, 1986.

Rarick, Ethan. *California Rising: The Life and times of Pat Brown.* Berkeley: University of California Press, 2006.

Reisman, W. Michael, and James E. Baker. *Regulating Covert Action: Practices, Contexts, and Policies of Covert Coercion Abroad in International and American Law.* New Haven: Yale University Press, 2011.

Renouard, Joe. *Human Rights in American Foreign Policy: From the 1960s to the Soviet Collapse.* Philadelphia: University of Pennsylvania Press, 2016.

Reston, James Jr. *The Lone Star: The Life of John Connally.* New York: Harper & Row, 1989.

Richardson, John H. *My Father the Spy: An Investigative Memoir.* New York: Harper Perennial, 2006.

Richter, Heinz. *British Intervention in Greece: From Varkiza to Civil War, February 1945 to August 1946.* London: Merlin Press, 1986.

Riefenstahl, Leni. *Leni Riefenstahl: A Memoir.* New York: St. Martin's Press, 1987.

Rigopoulos, Rigas. *Secret War: Greece-Middle East, 1940-1945.* Paducah, KY: Turner, 2003.

Rivers, William L. *The Other Government: Power & the Washington Media.* New York: Universe Books, 1982.

Roehrig, Terence. *The Prosecution of Former Military Leaders in Newly Democratic Nations: The Cases of Argentina, Greece and South Korea.* Jefferson, NC: McFarland & Co., 2002.

Roessel, David. *In Byron's Shadow: Modern Greece in the English and American Imagination.* Oxford: Oxford University Press, 2002.

Rosen, James. *The Strong Man: John Mitchell and the Secrets of Watergate.* New York: Doubleday, 2008.

Rosenfeld, Seth. *Subversives: The FBI's War on Student Radicals, and Reagan's Rise to Power.* New York: Farrar, Straus and Giroux, 2012.

Rossides, Gene. *Kissinger & Cyprus.* Washington, D.C.: American Hellenic Institute Foundation, 2014.

Roubatis, Yiannis P. *Tangled Webs: The U.S. in Greece, 1947-1967.* New York: Pella, 1987.

Rousseas, Stephen. *The Death of a Democracy: Greece and the American Conscience.* New York: Grove Press, 1967.

Rummel, Rudolf J. *Death by Government.* New Brunswick, NJ: Transaction Publishers, 1994.

Rumsfeld, Donald. "Confidential Memo – 1968 Meeting to Discuss Vice Presidential Nomination, August 8, 1968."

Russell, Richard L. *Sharpening Strategic Intelligence: Why the CIA Gets It Wrong, and What Needs to Be Done to Get It Right.* New York: Cambridge University Press, 2007.

Safire, William. *Before the Fall.* Garden City, NY: Doubleday, 1975.

Sakkas, John. *Britain and the Greek Civil War, 1944-1949: British Imperialism, Public Opinion and the Coming of the Cold War.* Berlin: Franz Philipp Rutzen-Verlag, 2013.

Salinger, Pierre. *PS: A Memoir.* New York: MacMillan, 2001.

Santas, Apostolos (Lakis). *One Night in Acropolis.* Athens: Vivliorama Editions, 2010.

Sarafis, Marion. *Greece: From Resistance to Civil War.* Nottingham: Spokesman, 1980.

Sarrinikolaou, George. *Facing Athens: Encounters with the Modern City.* New York: North Point Press, 2004.

Schlesinger, Arthur Meier. *A Thousand Days: John F. Kennedy in the White House.* New York: Fawcett Publications, 1967.

Schmitz, David F. *The United States and Right-Wing Dictatorships, 1965–1989.* Cambridge, UK: Cambridge University Press, 2006.

Schudson, Michael. *Watergate in American Memory: How We Remember, Forget, and Reconstruct the Past.* New York: Basic Books, 1992.

Shaarda, Daniel A. "Admiral Arleigh Burke: A study in strategic leadership, A thesis presented to the Faculty of the U.S. Army Command and General Staff College in partial fulfillment of the requirements for the degree Master of Military Art and Science Military History," Fort Leavenworth, KS, 2004.

Shaw, George Bernard. *Heartbreak House.* Project Gutenberg Ebook, 2009.

Shermer, Elizabeth Tandy. *Barry Goldwater and the Remaking of the American Political Landscape.* Tucson: University of Arizona Press, 2013.

Sherrill, Robert, and Harry W. Ernst. *The Drugstore Liberal: Hubert H. Humphrey in Politics.* New York: Grossman, 1968.

Shesol, Jeff. *Mutual Contempt: Lyndon Johnson, Robert Kennedy, and the Feud that Defined a Decade.* New York: W. W. Norton & Co., 1997.

Shuster, Alvin. *Washington, D.C.: The New York Times Guide to the Nation's Capital.* Cambridge, MD: Luce, 1967.

Sikkink, Kathryn. *The Justice Cascade: How Human Rights Prosecutions are Changing World Politics.* New York: W. W. Norton, 2011.

Simpson, Christopher. *Blowback: U.S. Recruitment of Nazis and Its Effects on the Cold War.* New York, NY: Weidenfeld & Nicolson, 1988.

Site of Historical Memory 1941–1944: 4 Korai Street Ethniki Insurance Mansion. Athens: Ethniki Insurance Company (undated).

Skamnakis, Antonis. *Politics, Media and Journalism in Greece.* Dublin: City University, School of Communications, 2006.

Smith, Adam (George Goodman). *The Money Game.* New York: Vintage, 1967.

Smith, Malcolm E., Jr. *Kennedy's 13 Greatest Mistakes in the White House.* New York: National Forum, 1968.

Smith, Michael Llewellyn. *Athens: A Cultural and Literary History.* Northampton, MA: Interlink Publishing, 2004.

Smith, Richard. *OSS: The Secret History of America's First Central Intelligence Agency.* Guilford, CT: The Lyons Press, 2005.

Smith, Walter Bedell. *My Three Years in Moscow.* New York: J. B. Lippincott Co., 1950. [MOSCOW]

Solberg, Carl. *Hubert Humphrey: A Biography.* New York: Norton, 1984.

Spear, Joseph C. *Presidents and the Press: The Nixon Legacy.* Cambridge, MA: MIT Press, 1984.

Sperber, Ann M. *Murrow, His Life and Times.* New York: Bantam, 1986.

Stans, Maurice H. *One of the Presidents' Men: Twenty Years with Eisenhower and Nixon.* Washington, D.C.: Brasseys, 1995.

Stauber, Ronni (ed.). *Collaboration with the Nazis: Public Discourse after the Holocaust.* Abingdon (UK): Routledge, 2010.

Stavrinides, Zenon. *The Cyprus Conflict: National Identity and Statehood.* [Place of publication not identified.] Zenon Stavrinides, 1975.

Stearns, Monteagle. *Entangled Allies: U.S. Policy toward Greece, Turkey, and Cyprus.* New York: Council on Foreign Relations Press, 1992.

Stearns, Monteagle. *Talking to Strangers: Improving American Diplomacy at Home and Abroad.* Princeton, NJ: Princeton University Press, 1999.

Steel, Ronald. *Walter Lippmann and the American Century.* New York: Vintage Books, 1980.

Stenner, Karen. *The Authoritarian Dynamic.* Cambridge: Cambridge University Press, 2005.

Stephanidis, Ioannis D. *Stirring the Greek Nation: Political Culture, Irredentism and Anti-Americanism in Post-war Greece, 1945–1967.* Aldershot, UK: Ashgate, 2007.

Stern, Laurence. *The Wrong Horse: The Politics of Intervention and the Failure of American Diplomacy.* New York: Times Books, 1977.

Stockton, Bayard. *Phoenix with a Bayonet; a Journalist's Interim Report on the Greek Revolution.* Ann Arbor, MI: Georgetown Publications, 1971.

Stone, I. F. *The Trial of Socrates.* Boston: Little Brown, 1988.

Stone, Roger. *Nixon's Secrets.* New York: Skyhorse Publishing, 2014.

Sulzberger, C. L. *A Long Row of Candles: Memoirs & Diaries, 1934–1954.* New York: Macmillan Company, 1969.

Sulzberger, C. L. *Postscript with a Chinese Accent: Memoirs and Diaries, 1972–73.* New York: Macmillan, 1974. [POSTSCRIPT]

Sulzberger, C. L. *An Age of Mediocrity: Memories and Diaries 1963–1972.* New York: Macmillan, 1978. [MEDIOCRITY]

Summers, Anthony, and Robbyn Swan. *The Arrogance of Power: The Secret World of Richard Nixon.* New York: Viking, 2000.

Talese, Gay. *The Kingdom and the Power.* New York: Marion Boyarsnal, 1969.

Tayfur, M. Fatih. *Semiperipheral Development and Foreign Policy: The Cases of Greece and Spain.* Aldershot, UK: Ashgate, 2003.

Theodorakis, Mikis, *Journals of Resistance.* [Translated from the French by Graham Webb.] London: Hart-Davis MacGibbon, 1973.

Theodorakopulos, Takis. *The Greek Upheaval: Kings, Demagogues, and Bayonets.* New Rochelle, NY: Caratzas, 1978.

Theodos, Peter A. "Tuberculosis in Greece: Present Conditions and Future Considerations," *Diseases of the Chest,* Vol. 12, Issue 6, November–December 1946, 571–92.

Theoharis, Athan G. and Richard H. Immerman, *The Central Intelligence Agency: Security Under Scrutiny.* Greenwood, 2006.

Thomopoulos, Elaine. *The History of Greece.* Santa Barbara, CA: Greenwood/ABC-CLIO, LLC, 2012.

Tifft, Susan E., and Alex S. Jones. *The Trust: The Private and Powerful Family Behind The New York Times.* Boston: Little, Brown and Company, 2000.

Tomai, Photini. *Documentary History of Greece, 1943–1951: Truman Doctrine and Marshall Plan.* Zalokosta: Hellenic Ministry of Foreign Affairs, 2011.

Tsatos, Jeanne. *The Sword's Fierce Edge: A Journal of the Occupation of Greece.* Nashville, TN: Vanderbilt University Press, 1969.

Tsoucalas, Constantine. *The Greek Tragedy.* Baltimore: Penguin Books, 1969.

Ureneck, Lou. *Smyrna.* New York: Ecco Press, 2016.

Uslu, Nasuh. *The Turkish-American Relationship Between 1947 and 2003: The History of a Distinctive Alliance.* New York: Nova Science Publishers, 2003.

Vanezis, P. N. *Makarios: Faith and Power.* London: Abelard-Schuman, 1972.

Van Steen, Gonda. *Stage of Emergency: Theater and Public Performance Under the Greek Military Dictatorship of 1967–1974.* Oxford: Oxford University Press, 2015.

Vassilikos, Vassilis, and Marilyn Calmann. *Z.* New York: Ballentine, 1968.

Vatikiotis, Panayiotis Jerasimof. *Popular Autocracy in Greece: 1936–41: A Political Biography of General Ioannis Metaxas.* London: F. Cass, 1998.

Veremis, Thanos. *The Military in Greek Politics: From Independence to Democracy.* London: C. Hurst, 1997.

Veremis, Thanos M., and Mark Dragoumis. *Historical Dictionary of Greece.* Metuchen, NJ: Scarecrow, 1995.

Vidalis, Orestis E. *Confronting the Greek Dictatorship in the U.S.: Years of Exile: A Personal Diary (1968–1975).* New York: Pella, 2009.

Vlachos, Helen. *House Arrest.* Boston: Gambit, 1970.

Vlanton, Elias, and Zak Mettger. *Who Killed George Polk?: The Press Covers Up a Death in the Family.* Philadelphia: Temple University Press, 1996.

Vlavianos, Haris. *Greece, 1941–49: From Resistance to Civil War: The Strategy of the Greek Communist Party.* New York: St. Martin's Press, 1992.

Voglis, Polymeris. *Becoming a Subject: Political Prisoners in the Greek Civil War, 1945–1950.* New York:

Berghahn Books, 2002.

Walldorf, Charles William. *Just Politics: Human Rights and the Foreign Policy of Great Powers*. Ithaca: Cornell University Press, 2008.

Weiner, Tim. *Blank Check: The Pentagon's Black Budget*. New York: Warner Books, 1991. [BLACK]

Weiner, Tim. *Legacy of Ashes: The History of the Central Intelligence Agency*. New York: Doubleday, 2007. [LEGACY]

Weiner, Tim. *The Enemies*. New York: Random House, 2013.

Weiner, Tim. *One Man Against the World: The Tragedy of Richard Nixon*. New York: Henry Holt and Company, 2015.

White, Theodore H. *The Making of the President 1960*. London: Cape, 1962.

White, Theodore H. *The Making of the President 1964*. New York: Atheneum, 1965.

White, Theodore H. *The Making of the President 1968*. New York: Atheneum, 1969.

White, Theodore H. *The Making of the President 1972*. New York: Atheneum, 1973.

Wilford, Hugh. *The Mighty Wurlitzer: How the CIA Played America*. Cambridge: 2008.

Williams, Paul Kelsey. *Dupont Circle*. Charleston, SC: Arcadia, 2000.

Wills, Gary. *Nixon Agonistes: The Crisis of the Self-Made Man*. New York: Open Road Integrated Media, 2017.

Wise, David. *The Politics of Lying: Government Deception, Secrecy, and Power*. New York: Random House, 1973.

Wise, David, and Thomas B. Ross. *The Invisible Government*. New York: Random House, 1974.

Witcover, Jules. *The Resurrection of Richard Nixon*. New York: Putnam, 1970.

Witcover, Jules. *White Knight: The Rise of Spiro Agnew*. New York: Random House, 1972.

Witcover, Jules. *The Year the Dream Died: 1968 in America*. New York: Warner Books, 1998.

Witcover, Jules. *Very Strange Bedfellows: The Short and Unhappy Marriage of Richard Nixon and Spiro Agnew*. New York: Public Affairs, 2008.

Wittner, Lawrence S. *American Intervention in Greece: 1943–1949*. New York: Columbia University Press, 1982.

Wittner, Lawrence S. *Cold War America: From Hiroshima to Watergate*. New York: Holt, Rinehart and Winston, 1990.

Wittner, Lawrence S. *The Struggle Against the Bomb. Resisting the Bomb: A History of the World Nuclear Disarmament Movement, 1954–1970*. Stanford, CA: Stanford University Press, 2003.

Woodhouse, C. M. *Karamanlis: The Restorer of Greek Democracy*. Oxford: Clarendon Press, 1982. [KARAMANLIS]

Woodhouse, C. M. *The Rise and Fall of the Greek Colonels*. London: Granada, 1985. [RISE]

Woodhouse, C. M. *Modern Greece: A Short History*. London: Faber, 1991. [MODERN]

Woodhouse, Christopher Montague, and Richard Clogg. *The Struggle for Greece: 1941–1949*. Chicago: I. R. Dee, 2003.

Woodward, Bob, and Carl Bernstein. *The Final Days: Bob Woodward, Carl Bernstein*. New York: Simon and Schuster, 1976.

Xydis, Stephen G. *Cyprus: Reluctant Republic*. The Hague: Mouton, 1973.

Yearbook of the European Convention on Human Rights, the European Commission and European Court of Human Rights (Annuaire De La Convention Européenne Des Droits De L'homme, Commission Et Cour Européennes Des Droits De L'homme). The Hague: Martinus Nijhoff, 1971.

Yearbook of the European Convention on Human Rights; The European Commission and European Court of Human Rights: 1969: The Greek Case, The Hague: Martinus Nijhoff, 1972.

Young, Nancy Beck. *Wright Patman: Populism, Liberalism, & the American Dream*. Dallas: Southern Methodist University Press, 2000.

Zaharopoulos, Thimios, and Manny Paraschos. *Mass Media in Greece: Power, Politics, and Privatization*. Westport, CT: Praeger, 1993.

Zotos, Stephanos. *Greece: The Struggle for Freedom*. New York: Crowell, 1967.

ARTICLES

"3 Senators Assail State Department," *New York Times*, December 20, 1970.

"2 Foes of Greek Regime Get U.S. Legislators Greeting." *New York Times*, January 12, 1972.

"The 1972 Campaign," *New York Times*, July 23, 1972.

"The 1972 Campaign," *New York Times*, July 26, 1972.

Abadi, Jacob. "Constraints and Adjustments in Greece's Policy," *Mediterranean Quarterly*, Fall 2000 (www.scribd.com/doc/23018215/Greece-Israel).

Adams, Jim. "CIA manipulated press willfully, panel told," *Shreveport Times*, January 5, 1978.

"Admiral Burke's Views Disturb Pentagon Again," *Washington Star*, February 16, 1961.

"The Administration. Housecleaning," *TIME*, April 7, 1952.

Agnew, Spiro. "Remarks by Governor Spiro Agnew," National Press Club Transcript, Friday, September 27, 1968.

"Agnew, the Junta and the CIA Link with the Nixon camp," *The Times* (London), September 29, 1968.

"Agnew Denies Funding from Greek Junta," *New York Times*, August 2, 1975.

"Agnew's Response," *Baltimore Sun*, July 16, 2016.

"'A Good Word' for Agnew," *New York Times*, August 10, 1968.

Anonymous. "Athens: Black November—The Slaughter of the Innocents, by an Eyewitness," November 1973.

Anastaplo, George. "Greece Today and the Limits of American Power," *Southwest Review*, Winter 1969, 1–24.

"A Native Goes Home," Thomas A. Pappas, *New York Times*, December 21, 1966.

Anderson, Jack, "The man in the helicopter," *New York Post*, November 11, 1971.

Anderson, Jack, "Senate Probes Wealthy Boss of Esso in Greece," *Baytown Sun*, November 11, 1971.

Anderson, Jack, "US Ignored Pleas from Karamanlis," *Washington Post*, July 29, 1974.

Anderson, Jack, "Greek Military Hero, Now in US, Seeks Treatment," *El Paso Times*, December 9, 1974.

Anderson, Jack and Les Whitten, "US Officials Harassed Greek Exile," *Washington Post*, February 12, 1975.

Anderson, Jack with Les Whitten, "The Plot to Snatch Demetracopoulos," *Washington Post*, April 26, 1975; "Junta Plotted Washington Kidnapping," *The Daily Journal*, April 26, 1975.

Anderson, Jack and Les Whitten, "Greek Probe of Funds Cancelled," *Washington Post*, July 5, 1975.

Anderson, Jack, "Government Burglaries," *Boston Globe*, February 2, 1977.

Anderson, Jack, "McGovern asks probe of CIA Greek link," *Boston Globe*, March 15, 1977.

Anderson, Jack, "CIA Retreating into Its Shell," *Washington Post*, August 30, 1978.

Anderson, Jack "1972 Skeleton in Connally's Closet," *Washington Post*, September 22, 1979; "Connally Tied to Another Dirty Trick, *Capital Times*, September 21, 1979.

Anderson, Jack, "Reagan Aide was Suspected of Lobbying for Greek Junta," *Washington Post*, October 25, 1980.

Anderson, Jack, "Henry Tried a Sex Smear," *New York Post*, April 21, 1991; "Greek is target of Kissinger," *Clinton* (IA) *Herald*, April 28, 1981.

Anderson, Jack, "Remembering Watergate: How Nixon killed the first probe," *United Features Syndicate*, June 13, 1982; "Solving a Watergate Mystery," *Washington Post*, June, 13, 1982.

Anderson, Jack, "Rep. Rosenthal pursues ghost of Watergate," *Washington Post*, December 18, 1982; "FBI Won't Reveal How It Got Look At Bank Account," *Burlington Free Press*, December 18, 1982.

Anderson, Jack, "'Greek Connection' enabled Nixon to obtain CIA money," *Newark Star Ledger*, September 2, 1983; "CIA Funds to Nixon Campaign Watergate key?" Lafayette (IN) *Journal and Courier*, September 2, 1983; "Did Nixon Use Oil Magnate to Funnel CIA Funds?" *The Tennessean* (Nashville), September 2, 1983; "Trail of Money Ties CIA Funds to Nixon's bid," *Portland Oregonian*, September 2, 1983; "How Greek Connection Figured in Watergate," Camden (NJ) *Courier Post*, September 2, 1983; "Can Watergate Be Traced to Greece?" *Paterson* (NJ) *News*, September 2, 1983; "Greek Connection May Have Been Part of Nixon's Downfall," *Sioux Falls Argus-Leader*, September 2, 1983.

Anderson, Jack "A Greek Journalist Is Finally Cleared of CIA-Leaked Smear," *Newsday*, Garden City, NY, May 7, 1984; "CIA tried to smear Greek writer," *Enterprise Journal*, May 6, 1984.

Anderson, Jack and Joseph Spear, "Meese Wants to Avoid Bank Privacy Act," *Washington Post*, December 20, 1985.

Anderson, Jack and Joseph Spear, "Watergate Fallout Continues," *Washington Post*, June 17, 1986.

Anderson, Jack and Joseph Spear, "CIA Has Routinely Spread Disinformation," Camden (NJ) *Courier-Post*, January 24, 1987.

Anderson, Jack and Dale Van Atta, "Into the Labyrinth," *Washington Post*, January 17, 1988; "Kissinger

May Hold Clues to Mystery of Greek Journalist," *Toledo Blade*, January 17, 1988.

Anderson, Jack, "Watergate's Untold Story," *San Francisco Chronicle*, November 10, 1988; "Nixon-Era Officials Retain Papers," *Topeka Capital Journal*, November 10, 1988; "Watergate Era Papers Still Under Wraps," *Washington Post*, November 10, 1988; Haig, Kissinger Help Block Watergate Truth, *"Jacksonville Times-Union*, November 10, 1988.

Anderson, Jack and Michael Binstein, "Watergate and the 'Greek Connection,'" United Features Syndicate, Inc., June 16, 1993.

Anderson, Jack and Michael Binstein, "Did JFK Victimize an American Hero?" *Merry Go-Round*, January 14, 1996.

Anderson, Jack and Jan Moller, "Foreign Cash and U.S. Elections," United Features Syndicate, Sunday, November 3, 1996.

Anderson, Jack and Jan Moller, "New Book Reveals Nixon's Greek Connection," United Features Syndicate, Inc., November 3, 1997.

Anderson, Jack and Jan Moller, "Did the Mistrust of Kennedy Butcher the Bay of Pigs?" Lompoc (CA) *Record*, November 21, 1997.

"Appointment in Gargalianoi," *TIME*, November 1, 1971.

Associated Press, "Block of Ambassador's Approval Planned to Protest Greek Policies," *Arizona Republic*, December 11, 1969.

Associated Press, "Goodell Ends Stall on Envoy," Wilmington (DE) *Evening Journal*, December 12, 1969.

Associated Press, "Nixon Donor's Ties to Greek Junta Eyed," *Washington Post*, September 21, 1971; "Nixon Backer Faces Probe on Ties with Greek Junta, Louisville (KY) *Times*, December 20, 1971.

Associated Press, "Watergate Probers get McGovern's Greek file," *Syracuse Herald-Journal*, May 17, 1973.

Associated Press, "Papadopoulos Safe in Villa; Believe Aware of Coup Plan," *Hartford Courant*, December 10, 1973.

Associated Press, "Partially Paralyzed Greek War Hero Going Home After Medical Treatment;" "Agony of a Greek War Hero," *Oakland Tribune*, January 27, 1975; Associated Press, January 27, 1975.

Associated Press, "Junta-CIA link; Exile to Testify," April 8, 1975.

Associated Press, "Greece Coup-CIA Probe," Bristol (CT) Press, September 4, 1975.

Associated Press, "A Four Year Old Confidential Memorandum," September 24, 1975.

Associated Press, "Book says Greek CIA contributed to Nixon," *Akron Beacon Journal*, June 2, 1983; "Book Claims Greece donated to Nixon's 1968 race," Chillicothe (OH) *Gazette*, June 2, 1983.

Associated Press, "Papers Back Theory on Watergate Case," *St. Louis Post-Dispatch*, May 25, 1986; "Newly Pevealed Papers Tie Greek-American to Watergate Scandal," *Salt Lake City Deseret News*, May 25, 1986.

Associated Press, "Clinton leaves Greece after apology for past policies," November 21, 1999.

"Athens Challenges Motives of Exile," *New York Times*, December 30, 1970.

Barker, Karlyn and Walter Pincus, "Watergate Revisited; 20 Years After the Break-in, the Story Continues to Unfold," *Washington Post*, June 14, 1992.

Barrett, Matt. History of Greece.com in https://www.ahistoryofgreece.com/index.htm

Barron, James H. "Time for Compromise, Not Payback, in Greece," *Global Post/Public Radio International*, June 14, 2012.

Becket, James "The Greek Case Before the European Rights Commission," 1 Hum. Rts. 91 (1970–1971).

Belser, Lee, "Gore Letter Seen Vital in Senate Probe of CIA," *Baltimore News American*, July 17, 1975.

Bernstein, Carl, "CIA and the Media," *Rolling Stone*, October 20, 1977.

Bernstein, Carl and Bob Woodward, "Woodward and Bernstein: 40 years After Watergate, Nixon Was Far Worse than We Thought," *Washington Post*, June 8, 2012.

Binder, David, "Ubiquitous Hand Guides Relations of U.S. and Greece," *New York Times*, December 6, 1977.

Blackman, Ann, "Victim of Torture Going Home," *Miami Herald*, January 28, 1975.

Braestrup, Peter, "Johnson Assures Greeks on U.S. Aid," *New York Times*, September 4, 1962.

Brelis, Dean, "Greece 1971: Stay Silent, Stay Alive," *Boston Globe Magazine*, August 29, 1971.

"Brother of Nixon and Onassis in Deal," *New York Times*, June 4, 1970.

Burrell, Hedley, "House consultant hits diplomacy in Greece," *Washington Post*, November 14, 1971.

Burrell, Hedley, "Amb. Tasca, State Differ on Foreign Aid to Greek Junta," *Washington Post*, December 12, 1971.

Cain, Andrew, "Clinton Says US Did Not Support Greek Democracy: Regrets Support for Junta in 1967," *Washington Times*, November 21, 1999.

Cambanis, Thanassis. "A Crusade Vindicated," *Odyssey*, January/February 1998, 19–20.

Cambanis, Thanassis. "Nine Greek Americans to Receive Honors of High Distinction from Greece," *National Herald*, January 2, 2007.

Childs, Marquis. "Agnew Plunges into the Greek Tragedy," *Baltimore Sun*, October 11, 1971.

Chomsky, Daniel, "The mechanisms of management control at the New York Times," *Media, Culture & Society*, 1999, Vol. 21: 579–99.

Claffey, Charles E., "Exile Greek Claims Agnew Supports Junta," *Boston Globe*, October 17, 1971.

Claffey, Charles E. "Pappas Poses Nixon Issue," *Boston Globe*, November 13, 1971.

Clement, Alain, *Le Monde*, September 29–30, 1968.

Clogg, Richard, "'Cousins and Allies:' British and American Misunderstandings over Greece During the Second World War." *Journal of Modern Hellenism*, Vol. 14, 1997. [COUSINS]

Cockburn, Alexander, "Elias and 'Ilias'," *Village Voice*, October 4, 1983.

Cody, Edward, "Papandreou Embroiled in Love, Money," *Washington Post*, December 2, 1988.

Contis, Angelike, "Joy of the Scoop: the Demetracopoulos Files," *National Herald*, August 28– September 3, 2010.

Converse, Philip E., Warren E. Miller, Jerrold G. Rusk, and Arthur C. Wolfe, "Continuity and Change in American Politics: Parties and Issues in the 1968 Election," *The American Political Science Review*, Vol. 63, No. 4 (December 1969), 1083–1105.

Cooley, John and Peter Melias, "Anti-CIA Press Cited in Slaying," *Christian Science Monitor*, December 25, 1975.

Cotts, Cynthia, "Now You CIA Me; Now You Don't," *Village Voice*, May 29, 2001.

Cplakidas, "Transcript of signal sent by Cmdr Nikolaos Pappas signal during Velos Mutiny.jpg," *Creative Commons*, April 7, 2013.

Craig, Phyllis, "United States and the Greek Dictatorship," *Journal of Hellenic Diaspora*, Vol. 3 (1976) 5–15.

Curry, Leonard (*UPI*), "Industrialist Tied to Questionable Contributions: Pappas joins Ford fund-raising committee," *Dominion News*, Morgantown, WV, December 19, 1975.

Dallek, Robert, "Three New Revelations About LBJ," *The Atlantic*, April 1998.

Danopoulos, Constantine P., "Military Professionalism and Regime Legitimacy in Greece, 1967–1974," *Political Science Quarterly*, Vol. 98, no. 3 (Autumn, 1983), 485–506.

Daskalothannis, Harilaos H. "The President vs. the Admiral and the Greek in Their Midst," *National Herald*, November 22–23, 1997.

Davis, Saville R., "Nixon Congress Collision: Back-door US Arms Aid to Greece Strikes Congress Sparks," *Christian Science Monitor*, May 6, 1970.

Davis, Saville R., "US Cools toward Greece," *Christian Science Monitor*, June 17, 1970.

Davis, Saville R., "Greek Nuclear Incident Points to Risk in NATO Alliance," *Christian Science Monitor*, December 7, 1970.

"Decoration of Greek Newspaperman," *Kathimerini*, October 5, 1950.

Delis, Panagiotis. "The British Intervention in Greece: The Battle of Athens, December 1944," *Journal of Modern Greek Studies*, Vol. 35, Number 1, May 2017, 211–237.

Demetracopoulos, Elias P. (Interview with Admiral Arleigh Burke). "Surprise Attack? Impossible" *Philadelphia Bulletin*, February 15, 1961; "Sea Borne Missile Strength Holds Russia in Check, Burke Says," *St. Louis Globe-Democrat*, February 16, 1961; "America Power to Destroy Russia; Outspoken Remarks By Navy Chief," *The Times* (London), February 17, 1961.

Demetracopoulos, Elias P. "Coming De Gaulle Visit Worries Officials in Greece," *New York Herald Tribune*, May 14, 1963.

Demetracopoulos, Elias P. (NANA), "Athens Cautioned on Dictatorship," *The Press*, Jamaica, NY. September 15, 1965.

Demetracopoulos, Elias P., "A Greek Exile Looks at the Colonels," *Wall Street Journal*, April 21, 1969.

Demetracopoulos, Elias P. "Admirals Strike a Blow for the Free Press," Navy Institute Proceedings, Vol. 127, no. 5 (May 2001), 66–73.

Demetracopoulos, Elias P. "Budding Presidential Candidate Speaks to Post," ADP, October 13, 1963.

Demetracopoulos, Elias P. "Muzzling Admiral Burke," Navy Institute Proceedings, 126, no. 1 (1/2000), 64–70.

Demetracopoulos, Elias P. "Statement Made by the Greek Political Editor in Exile, Mr. Elias P. Demetracopoulos, on Thursday, October 31, 1968, Washington DC at 6 PM."

Demetracopoulos, Elias P. "Greece: A New Vietnam?" Hudson Institute Discussion Paper (H-1241-DP), August 1, 1969.

Demetracopoulos, Elias P. "It Didn't Start With Clinton," Washington Post, June 15, 1997.

Demetracopoulos, Elias P. "Beware a Revived Ministry of Lies," Roll Call Daily, February 26, 2002.

Democratic National Committee, "O'Brien Asks Explanation of Nixon-Agnew Relationships with Pappas," Press Release, October 31, 1968.

Dixon, Ymelda, "People at Lunch," Washington Star, January 24, 1972.

"Donor's Ties to Greek Juntas Eyed," Washington Post, September 21, 1971.

Draenos, Stan, "United States Foreign Policy and the Liberal Awakening in Greece, 1958–1967," The Historical Review/La Revue Historique, Institute for Neohellenic Research, Vol. V (2008), 121–149.

Draenos, Stan, "Papandreou's Exile Politics: The First Phase (1968–70)," The Historical Review/La Revue Historique (2014), 11, 35–66.

Drew, Elizabeth B. "Democracy on Ice: a Study of American Policy toward Dictatorship in Greece," The Atlantic Monthly, July 1968, 56–67.

Dudman, Richard, "CIA Manipulated US Public Opinion, Halperin Charges," St. Louis Post-Dispatch, January 4, 1978.

Editorial, "Haven for Persecuted," Boston Globe, November 3, 1967.

Editorial, "Greek Tragedy," Fall River Herald News, November 7, 1967.

Editorial, "More Tyranny for Greece," New York Times, December 30, 1970.

Editorial "Arms for the Colonels," New York Times, July 3, 1970.

Editorial, "Money and Power," St. Louis Post-Dispatch, September 25, 1971.

Editorial, "The Colonels Disagree," Baltimore Sun, August 9, 1972.

Elias, Nicholas. "Greece, Three Years After," New York Times, May 3, 1970.

"Elias Demetracopoulos, Greek dissident, 87," Philadelphia Inquirer, February 29, 2016.

"Elias Demetracopoulos Receives Award in D.C.," National Herald, January 12, 2008.

"Elias P. Demetracopoulos: the loss of a prominent Greek journalist and human rights activist," Hellenic News, February 17, 2016.

"Entrepreneurs: The Greek for Go-Between," TIME, February 14, 1969.

Evans, Ross, "Did US Help Greek Exile's Harassment?" Washington Star, March 15, 1977.

Evans, Rowland and Novak, Robert. "State Official Aided Greek Junta in Trying to Bar Political Refugee," Washington Post, November 2, 1967.

Evans, Rowland and Robert Novak, "Pentagon Says Greece Must Work Own Fate," Boston Globe, November 29, 1968; "Memo Reveals US Attitude on Rightist Juntas," Washington Post, November 29, 1968.

Evans, Rowland and Robert Novak, "Greek Junta Cynicism," Washington Post, November 16, 1969.

Evans, Rowland and Robert Novak, "Greece versus the World Bank," Washington Post, May 19, 1970.

Evans, Rowland and Robert Novak "World Bank Assails Greek Junta for Bid to Play Politics with Loan," Financial Times, WP, May 21, 1970.

Evans, Rowland and Robert Novak, "Another Greek Tragedy," Washington Post, December 23, 1970.

Evans, Rowland and Robert Novak, "Sen. Fulbright vs. the Junta," Washington Post, January 31, 1971; "Fulbright Checking Up on Greek Colonels, Toledo Blade, February 1, 1971.

Evans, Rowland and Robert Novak, "The Greek Colonels' Friend," Washington Post, Sept 19, 1971.

Evans, Rowland and Robert Novak, "Greek Gifts for President," Boston Globe, July 20, 1972.

Evans, Rowland and Robert Novak, "Odyssey of the US Navy," Washington Post, August 4, 1972.

Evans, Rowland and Robert Novak, "Greek Aid and Israeli Safety: Scuttling the Nixon Connection," Washington Post, February 17, 1972.

Evans, Rowland and Robert Novak, "A Routine Staff Trim for Agnew—or a Sign of His Political Decline?" Washington Post, January 21, 1973.

Evans, Rowland and Robert Novak, "Distorting Agnew's View on Greece," *Washington Post*, April 22, 1973.

Evans, Rowland and Robert Novak, "Election '72: Another Propaganda Letter," *Washington Post*, May 13, 1973.

Evans, Rowland and Robert Novak, "Policy on Greece Backfires on US," *Boston Globe*, November 30, 1973.

Evans, Rowland and Robert Novak, "The Greek Coup: Where Does It Leave the US?" *Washington Post*, November 30, 1973.

Evans, Rowland and Robert Novak, "US Policy in a Straitjacket on Greece," *Washington Post*, December 24, 1973.

Evans, Rowland and Robert Novak, World Bank Loans and the Greek Junta, *Washington Post*, January 27, 1974.

Evans, Rowland and Robert Novak, "A Greek Military Scandal," *Washington Post*, August 28, 1974.

Evans, Rowland and Robert Novak, "Mr. Ford and the Greek Archbishop," *Washington Post*, November 11, 1974.

Evans, Rowland and Robert Novak, "Why Did Agnew Shift on Greek Junta?" *Boston Globe*, July 16, 1975; "Agnew's Turnaround on Greece," *Washington Post*, July 16, 1975; "A Mystery: Agnew and the Greek Junta," *Ithaca Journal*, July 16, 1975; "Senators Curious About Agnew Support of Greek Junta," *South Bend Tribune*, July 18, 1975.

Evans, Rowland and Robert Novak, "A NATO Defense Triangle of Worsening Relations," *Washington Post*, April 13, 1976.

Evans, Rowland and Robert Novak, "A Covert Operation that Failed," *Washington Post*, July 17, 1976.

Evans, Rowland and Robert Novak, "Discreet Probe of Connally," *Washington Post*, September 3, 1977.

Evans, Rowland and Robert Novak, "The CIA: Harassing the Spy Who Never Was," *Washington Post*, December 23, 1977.

Evans, Rowland and Robert Novak, "Greek Concern Over Six Missing Words," *Washington Post*, February 6, 1978.

Evans, Rowland and Robert Novak, "CIA vs Reporter: Someone's Lying," *New York Post*, September 4, 1978.

Evans, Rowland and Robert Novak, "The Demetracopoulos Affair," *Washington Post*, September 3, 1979.

Farrell, David, "Politics was always on the menu," *Boston Globe*, August 7, 1983.

Farrell, John Aloysius, "Yes, Nixon Scuttled the Vietnamese Peace Talks," *Politico Magazine*, June 9, 2014.

"Fascist Junta in Greece Financing Nixon's Campaign" [Andreas Papandreou interview], Tidsignal in Stockholm, October 1, 1968.

Feldstein, Mark, Memorandum to Jim Barron Re: Nixon & Demetracopoulos, August 29, 2013.

Fitch, Robert, "Jackie and Ari and Tom and George and Spiro and . . . ," *Ramparts*, January 1972, 36–51.

Fort, Bob, "Smear Letter by Georgian Is Investigated," *Atlanta Constitution*, May 15, 1973.

Frangos, Steve, "The Picture Bride Era in Greek American History," *National Herald*, March 12, 2005.

Friendly, Alfred, Jr., "Bostonian Pappas Means Esso in Greece," *New York Times*, May 4, 1969.

Gerstanzang, James and Richard Boudreaux, "Clinton Says US Regrets Aid to Junta in Cold War," *Los Angeles Times*, November 21, 1999.

Gilmore, Daniel F. (UPI), "Bank Apologizes for Watergate Snooping," *News Journal* (Murphreesboro, TN), December 22, 1985; "Bank Gives Reluctant Apology to Depositor Irate Since 1972," *Herald Journal*, (Logan, UT) December 25, 1985.

Gilmore, Daniel F. (UPI), "Watergate: A Greek connection," May 24, 1986.

Gkotzaridis, Evi. "'Who ?' Grigoris Lambrakis and the Nonaligned Peace Movement in Post–Civil War Greece: 1951 to 1964," *Journal of Modern Greek Studies* 30 (2012) 299–338.

Glaser, Vera and Malvina Stephenson, "Millionaire Nixon Pal Pappas Faces Capitol Hill Fire," *Knight Newspapers, Miami Herald*, August 29, 1971.

Gounardes, Andrew S. and Maria Avgitidis Pyrgiotakis, "No Greeks Need Apply," *National Herald*, August 8, 2017.

"Gravel on Greek Incident," *Washington Post*, December 28, 1970.

"Greece: A Dilemma for the West," *Newsweek*, January 19, 1970, 31–37.

"Greece: Answering to History," *TIME*, September 1, 1975.

"Greece Denies US Statements that Bases Help Protect Israel," *Athens News*, August 6, 1972.

"Greece Reports Foiling Plot by King's Supporters," *New York Times*, July 14, 1973.

"Greece: The King's Wife," *TIME*, October 26, 1953.

"Greek and Foreign Spies in Greece," *Stavros Magazine*, October 8, 1950.

"Greek Businessman Joins Ford Camp as Fundraiser," *New York Times*, December 19, 1975.

"Greek Colonels Said to Have Planned Seizure of US Nuclear Missiles," *The Times* (London) November 25, 1970.

"Greek Exile Asks US to Stop Military Assistance to Regime," *New York Times*, July 13, 1971.

"Greek Façade Topples: Greece Steps Backward" Jasper (AL) *Daily Mountain Eagle*, December 10, 1973.

"Greek On Trial with 33, Asserts He Was Tortured," *New York Times*, March 28, 1970.

"Greek Regime Denies Rumor That It Is Financing Nixon," *New York Times*, October 15, 1968.

Grimes, Paul, "Senators Stall on Envoy to Greece," *Philadelphia Bulletin*, December 10, 1969.

Grose, Peter, "Agnew in His Farewell, Hails Greek Regime," *New York Times*, October 24, 1971.

Hackett, Clifford P., "The Nixon Pardon (LTE)," *The Atlantic*, November 1983.

Hackett, Clifford P., "Congress and Greek American Relations: The Embargo Example," *Journal of the Hellenic Diaspora*, Spring-Summer 1988, 15, 1&2, 5–32.

Hackett, Clifford P., "Watergate's 'Greek Connection' Theory: Burglars Sought Evidence That Nixon Backed Junta in Exchange for Cash," *St. Louis Post-Dispatch*, June 17, 1992.

Hartmann, Robert T., "Taped Goldwater Interview Proves Factor in Upsetting Caramanlis," *Washington Post*, November 11, 1963.

Hatfield, Mark O., "Vice Presidents of the United States: Spiro Theodore Agnew (1969–1973)," Senate Historical Office, Washington: US GPO, 1997.

"Hill Probers Eye Session with Nixon," *Washington Post*, July 29, 1975.

"Historian backs writer's Greek connection theory," [Rochester] *Democrat and Chronicle*, August 5, 1990.

Hitchens, Christopher, "Minority Report," *The Nation*, April 16, 1983.

Hitchens, Christopher, "Minority Report" *The Nation*, June 30, 1984.

Hitchens, Christopher, "Minority Report," *The Nation*, February 16, 1985.

Hitchens, Christopher, "Minority Report," *The Nation*, January 11, 1986.

Hitchens, Christopher, "Watergate—The Greek Connection," *The Nation*, May 31, 1986.

Hitchens, Christopher, "Minority Report," *The Nation*, June 5, 1989.

Hitchens, Christopher, "Minority Report," *The Nation*, June 25, 1990.

Hitchens, Christopher, "Kissinger in Greek Hit Plan?" *Counterpunch*, February 16–28, 1997, 5.

Hitchens, Christopher, "Nixon's Tapes & the Greek Connection," Minority Report, *The Nation*, November 24, 1997, 8.

Hoffman, Paul, "Italy Gives Asylum to Rebel Commander of Greek Destroyer and 30 of His Men," *New York Times*, May 27, 1973.

"House Lawmakers Bewildered by Classified Greek Document," *Chicago Tribune*, July 14, 1971.

Hovey, Graham, "Making Foreign Policy," *New York Times*, January 22, 1973.

Howe, Russell Warren, "Asset Unwitting: Covering the World for the CIA: Correspondent Tells of Employment by Secretly Funded Agency News Service," *MORE*, May 1978, 20–27.

Howe, Russell Warren and Sarah Hays Trott, "The Foreign Agent," *Washingtonian*, December 1974.

Hunter, John Patrick, "Book Confirms Major Reason for Watergate," Madison (WI) *Capital Times*, August 2, 1990.

Jacobs, John, "Halperin Alleges 4 Instances of CIA Exploitation of Media," *Washington Post*, January 5, 1978.

Johnson, Haynes, "Last Respects Paid Truman at Simple Cathedral Service," *Washington Post*, January 6, 1973.

Kaff, Al, "People . . . ," *Overseas Press Club Bulletin*, December 1977.

Kakissis, Joanna, "American's Death Still a Greek Mystery, 65 Years Later," Weekend Edition Sunday PBS, October 27, 2013.

Kantor, Seth, "Greek Junta's Role in U.S Politics Questioned," Detroit News, January 27, 1974.

Karagiorgas, George, "After the Slander Against Makarios, CIA Launched an Anti-Greek Campaign in Order to Have the Aid to Turkey Approved," Ta Nea, February 22, 1977.

Kempe, Frederick, "The worst day of JFK's life," Reuters.com/berlin1961/2011/05/27/the-worst-day-of-jfks-life/.

Kempster, Norman, "Admiral: Government Burglarized Files," Los Angeles Times, February 4, 1977.

Kempster, Norman, "Watergate Motive – Break-in Held Effort to Hide Nixon's Money Link to Greece," Los Angeles Times, August 1, 1990.

Kilpatrick, James J., "McGovern Writes a Foolish Letter on Greece," Washington Star, July 30, 1972.

Kilpatrick, James J., "Columnist Eats Crow in Three Great Gulps," Saginaw (MI) News, August 13, 1972.

"Kissinger Says Hersh Charge 'a Slimy Lie'," Baltimore Sun, June 3, 1983.

Kondracke, Morton, "McGovern Against Greek Aid," Chicago Sun-Times, July 23, 1972.

Konstandaras, Nikos, "Book sheds light on claims linking the junta to Nixon and Johnson," Kathimerini, February 26, 2004.

Langer, Emily, "Elias Demetracopoulos: Enigmatic Expatriate Who Opposed Greek Junta from Washington, Dies at 87," Washington Post, February 26, 2016.

Lardner, George Jr., "McGovern Would End Greek Aid," Washington Post, July 23, 1972.

Lardner, George Jr., "Senate Probe Urged of Exile's Charges," Washington Post, February 13, 1975.

Lewis, Flora, "Ambassador Extraordinary: John Peurifoy," New York Times, July 18, 1954.

"Life 'Too Fast' For Greek Hubby," Palm Beach Post, July 19, 1955.

Ling, Robert B., "Agnew's Money," Philadelphia Inquirer, July 30, 1975.

Lydon, Christopher, "Thomas Pappas: Portrait of a Wealthy Immigrant, Political Kingmaker," Boston Globe, October 31, 1968, 21.

Maniatis, Lydia, "The man who knew too much," Odyssey, January/February 2004.

Maragkou, Konstanina, "The foreign factor and the Greek Colonels coming to power on 21 April 1967," Southeast European and Black Sea Studies, Vol. 6, 2006, issue 4, 427–443, published online 23 November 2006.

Markaris, Petros, "Greece: the other side of 1968," in 1968: 1984 Memories and Legacies.

Maury, John M., "The Greek Coup: A Case of CIA Intervention? No, Says Our Man in Athens," Washington Post, May 1, 1977.

McDonald, Robert, "Greece: April 21, 1967," Massachusetts Review, Vol. 9, No. 1, Winter, 1968, 59–78.

McGrory, Mary, "Getting Away with Dirty Stables," Boston Globe, Oct 8, 1972.

McMahon, Robert, "Human Rights Reporting and US Foreign Policy," Council on Foreign Relations, March 25, 2009.

McMasters, Theresa, "Pappas influence cited," Boston Herald Traveler, September 20, 1971

Micchiche, S. J. "Pappas to testify on funding for Watergate defendants," Boston Globe, February 5, 1974.

Millinship, William, "US may probe financier's role in aid to Greece," London Observer, September 25, 1971.

Modiano, Mario S., "Stans, in Athens, Hails the Regime," New York Times, April 24, 1971.

Modiano, Mario S., "Lady Fleming Creates a Dilemma for Greek Government by Deciding to Refuse Deportation," The Times (London), September 30, 1971.

Modiano, Mario S., "Amnesty is given to 300 in Greece," The Times (London), August 21, 1973.

Mouat, Lucia, "House Report Hints GOP–Greek Junta Ties," Christian Science Monitor, September 20, 1971.

Murphy, Caryle, "'Vindication' Rewards a Six-Year Struggle," Washington Post, October 20, 1983.

Nelson, Warren L. (UPI), "Greek Coup Is Connected to Watergate," Denver Rocky Mountain News, December 11, 1973.

Nesmith, Jeff, "Did CIA Ransack Greek Journalist's Office?" Cox News Service, January 7, 2000.

Nicodemus, Charles, "Greek Premier Fibs About His Past Here," Chicago News, February 9, 1974.

Novak, Josephine, "Poker Player Louise Gore Looks Ahead to High Stakes Race to Be Governor,"

Baltimore Evening Sun, March 25, 1974.

Oldfield, Col. Barney, "After Elk Creek: Everything; Encounters with Arthur Sylvester, Assistant Secretary of Defense, Public Affairs" (undated).

Oliphant, Thomas, "Documents Indicate Pappas Was Spared in Watergate Probe," *Boston Sunday Globe*, May 25, 1986.

Oliphant, Thomas, "Watergate's Boston Connection," *Boston Globe*, November 10, 1997.

Opotowsky, Stan, "The Fuse Was on Delay," *New York Post*, February 16, 1961.

Othman, Muhammad, "Khashoggi and Demetracopoulos," dissidentvoice.org, October 17, 2018.

Panos, Lou. "Greek Trip Dims for Agnew," *Baltimore Sun*, September 22, 1971.

Parry, Robert, "FBI Concedes 10 year Probe Found Nothing on Greek Journalist," Associated Press, June 28, 1984.

"Patriarch of Alexandria Honors Distinguished Wartime Hero," *Empros*, October 5, 1980.

Pearson, Drew and Jack Anderson, "Agnew's Junta Ties Disturb NATO." *Washington Post*, November 1, 1968.

Pedaliu, Effie G. H., "A discordant note: Nato and the Greek junta, 1967–1974," *Diplomacy & Statecraft*, Vol. 22, 2011, issue 1.

"Pinochet 'Personally Ordered' Washington Car Bombing," GWU National Security Archive.

"Policy Toward Greece," *New York Times*, April 27, 1969.

Polier, Rex, "Watching the Wandering Greek in Exile," *Philadelphia Bulletin*, March 12, 1970.

Polk, James (Associated Press), "Bankers Pay Patman $1500; Hear Him Assail Their Policies," *Gettysburg Times*, June 21, 1971.

Polk, James, "False Campaign Money" (undated).

Pollis, Adamantia, "Social Change and Nationhood," *Massachusetts Review*, Vol. 9, No. 1, Winter, 1968, 123–132.

Price, G. Jefferson III, "A Newsman Who Knew Too Much," *Baltimore Sun*, April 6, 2003.

"Reed Harris Quits as 'Voice' Official,'" *New York Times*, April 15, 1953.

"Rep. Rosenthal Incited Disorders, Greek Says," *New York Times*, March 5, 1973.

Roberts, Sam, "Elias Demetracopoulos, 87, Dies; Journalist Linked Greek Junta to Nixon," *New York Times*, February 26, 2016.

"Rogers Defends Sixth Fleet Using Home Port in Greece," *Washington Post*, August 25, 1972.

"Rogers Rejects Pressure on Greece as 'Arrogance'," *New York Times*, August 25, 1972.

Rosenbaum, Ron, "Woodward and Bernstein Don't Know Who Ordered Watergate," *Slate*, June 18, 2012.

Rossos, Andrew, "Incompatible Allies: Greek Communism and Macedonian Nationalism in the Civil War in Greece, 1943–1949," *Journal of Modern History*, Vol. 69, No. 1 (3/1997), 42–76.

Rummel, Rudolph and Louis Horowitz. "Turkey's Genocidal Purges."

Sakkas, John, "Greece and the Mass Exodus of the Egyptian Greeks," *Journal of the Hellenic Diaspora*, 1956–66, 101–115.

Schaefer, Jack, "The CIA and Riggs Bank: A Wall Street Journal story that the press gang should chase," *Slate*, January 7, 2005.

Sedgwick, A. C., "Greek Army Opens Grammos Assault: Advance to Albanian Border Is Made on North in Drive in Last Main Rebel Zone." *New York Times*, August 26,1949.

Sedgwick, A. C., "Athens Hails Arrival of Makarios," *New York Times*, April 18, 1957.

Sedgwick, Theodore, "Books Behind the Coup," *Harvard Crimson*, February 28, 1970.

"Self-exiled Greek 'Voice of Democracy' in U.S. Returns," *Athens News*, May 17, 1975.

Semple, Robert B. Jr., "Electoral Pact Pushed by Nixon," *New York Times*, October 30, 1968.

Sheehan, Neil, "A Student Group Concedes It Took Funds from the CIA," *New York Times*, February 14, 1967.

"Shock Expressed in U.N. at defeat of Aid Measure," *New York Times*, October 30, 1971.

Spear, Joseph, "This Watergate theory takes the cake," *Viewpoint, Newspaper Enterprise Association*, August 21, 1991.

Spear, Joseph, "After 20 years, Watergate persists," *Viewpoint, Newspaper Enterprise Association*, June 16, 1993.

Spear, Joseph, "Empty promises, hypocrisy and twaddle," *Star Democrat* (Eastern Maryland), November 27, 1996.

Spear, Joseph, "Bill Clinton's deft courtship of the military," *Star Democrat*, November 23, 1997.

"Spiro Agnew and the Golden Age of Corruption in Maryland Politics: An interview with Ben Bradlee and Richard Cohen of The Washington Post," Center for the Study of Democracy, Vol. 2, No. 1, Fall 2006.

Steele, Jonathan, "How the CIA mudslingers use the media," *The Guardian*, January 5, 1978.

Steinem, Gloria, "Gloria Steinem on Learning to Live with Nixon," *New York*, October 28, 1968.

Stern, Sol, "A Short Account of International Student Politics & the Cold War with Particular Reference to the NSA, CIA, Etc.," *Ramparts*, March 1967, 29–39.

Sulzberger, C. L., "Greece Under the Colonels," Foreign Affairs 48(2), January 1970. https://www.foreignaffairs.com/articles/europe/1970-01-01/greece-under-colonels.

Tait, Robert, "Personal Politics," *The Scotsman* (Edinburgh), January 23, 2001, 6–7.

Tait, Robert, "Kissinger's War of Words," *The Scotsman*, July 2, 2001, 10–11.

"Tasca Given Senate OK as Greek Envoy," *Philadelphia Inquirer*, December 20,1969.

"Thailand. Smilin' Jack," *TIME*, August 22, 1955.

"That's Burke's Story," *Washington Star*, February 16, 1961.

"Theft at Admiral's Office? Senate Panel Is Checking," *Washington Star*, February 6, 1977.

Thimmesch, Nick, "Birth of a Salesman," *New York Times Magazine*, October 26, 1975.

Thrall, Nathan and Jesse James Wilkins, "Kennedy Talked, Khrushchev Triumphed," *New York Times*, May 22, 2008.

Tonge, David, "The émigré eminence," *The Guardian*, April 18, 1975.

Tonge, David, "Check on junta plan for kidnap," *The Guardian*, April 28, 1975.

Tumulty, Karen, "Obama Struggles to Get Beyond a Scandal Trifecta," *Washington Post*, May 15, 2013.

Unger, Craig, "Tom Pappas: The Bostonian Behind the Greek Junta," *Boston After Dark*, October 12, 1971.

UPI, "A Good Word' for Agnew," *New York Times*, August 10, 1968.

UPI, "Student Sets Self Ablaze in Genoa," Newport News (VA) *Daily Press*, September 20, 1970.

UPI, "US A-Bombs Abroad in '61," October 11, 1970.

UPI, "Pappas," *Newswire*, September 19, 1971.

UPI, "Tortured Greek Hero Arrives in US for Medical Treatment," *Las Vegas Sun*, December 22, 1974.

UPI, "White House File on Connally Includes 1972 Campaign 'Tricks'"; *Washington Star*, September 4, 1977.

UPI, "An Editor Bids CIA Give Data on Press," *New York Times*, January 5, 1978.

UPI, "Magazine Uncovers Greek Connection in Watergate," *Syracuse Herald Journal*, May 25, 1986.

UPI, "Now, the 'Why' of Watergate," *Kankakee Jour*nal, May 25, 1986.

UPI, "Tycoon's Athens Ties to Nixon May be Key to Watergate Break-in," *Arizona Republic*, May 28, 1986.

"US Denies Refusing Visa to Greek Exile," *Washington Post*, November 3, 1967.

"US Fears Revelations," *Athens News*, August 15, 1975.

"US Senate Committee to Investigate Alleged CIA Involvement in Demetracopoulos Kidnap plot," *Athens News*, May 2, 1975.

"US Silence Approval of Greece Revolt," *Palo Alto Peninsula Bulletin*, December 8, 1973.

"Veteran Greek Journalist Elias Demetrakopoulos Honoured," http://greeknewsonline.com, January 14, 2008.

Vlanton, Elias, "Murder and Its Meaning," *The Nation*, January 28, 1991, 93–95.

Vulliamy, Ed and Helena Smith, "Athens 1944: Britain's Dirty Secret," *The Guardian*, November 30, 2014.

Warden, Philip, "An Achilles Heel—The Greek Post," *Chicago Tribune*, August 12, 1969.

Washington, Barbara Bright. "Congressman Seeks US Aid for Greek Political Prisoners," *Washington Post*, March 11, 1973.

Washington, Lee Daniels, "2 Greeks Consider the Future," *Washington Post*, July 31, 1974.

"Washington's Ten Perfect Gentlemen," *Washington Dossier*, Vol. 2, no. 6, November 1976, 32.

"Watergate scandal had a Greek side, and historians ask if burglars sought evidence of it," Ekathimerini.com, October 30, 2002.

Wechsler, James A., "July 4 in Athens," *New York Post*, July 3, 1970.
Wermiel, Stephen, "Pappas Says He Never Gave Assent for Hush Money," *Boston Globe*, May 2, 1974.
"What the Germans Did to Greece," *LIFE*, November 27, 1944.
"White House to Investigate Demetracopoulos Case," *Athens News*, December 29, 1970.
Wilson, Theo, "Pappas, the Rich Mystery Man Behind Agnew," *New York Daily News*, August 9, 1968.
Wise, David, "The Secret Committee Called 40," *New York Times*, January 19, 1975.
Xydis, Stephen G., "Coups and Countercoups in Greece, 1967–1973," *Political Science Quarterly*, Vol. 89, no. 3 (Autumn, 1974).
Yeager, Debra Sue, "Victim of Greek Junta Gains Entry to Walter Reed Center," *Washington Post*, December 21, 1974.

ARCHIVES

United Nations
  Speeches, UN Security Council
United Kingdom, National Archives, Kew, London
  Foreign Office (FO)
  Prime Minister Records [PREM]
  Cabinet Papers
Churchill War Rooms, Imperial War Museum
United States National Archives (NARA) College Park, MD
  Declassified Central Intelligence Records (CREST)
  General Records of Department of State, RG59; Central Policy Files; Political and Defense; GREECE
Foreign Relations of the United States Diplomatic Papers (FRUS)
  FRUS, 1945, Vol. 8, The Near East and Africa
  FRUS, 1949, Vol. 5, Eastern Europe, The Soviet Union
  FRUS, 1961–1963, Vol. 16, Eastern Europe; Cyprus: Greece; Turkey
  FRUS, 1964–1968, Vol. 16, Cyprus: Greece; Turkey
  FRUS, 1969–1972, Vol. 41, Western Europe; NATO
  FRUS, 1973–1976, Vol. 30, Cyprus: Greece; Turkey
FOIA searches for federal records concerning Elias P. Demetracopoulos (and alternative spellings), Thomas A. Pappas, and Celia A. Was and responses from (partial list):
Department of State (StateDep), Department of Defense, Department of Justice, White House, National Security Council, Department of Justice, Central Intelligence Agency (CIA), Federal Bureau of Investigation (FBI), Department of Army, Department of Navy.

ORAL HISTORIES

Association for Diplomatic Studies and Training (ADST), Washington, D.C.

Norbert L. Anschutz	Ronald D. Flack	Harry I. Odell
Frank Athanason	Katherine (Kay) Folger	John P. Owens
Richard W. Barham	David Fritzlan	Stuart W. Rockwell
Lucius D. Battle	Lindsey Grant	Walter J. Silva
Tapley Bennett, Jr.	Douglas Hartley	Abraham M. Sirkin
Archer K. Blood	Robert V. Keeley	Wells Stabler
Frederick Z. Brown	Charles Stuart Kennedy	Victor L. Stier
Thomas D. Boyatt	Barrington King	Peter B. Swiers
Herbert Daniel Brewster	Jack B. Kubisch	August Velletri
Elizabeth Ann Brown	William B. Macomber	James C. Warren, Jr.
William R. Crawford, Jr.	Robert J. McCloskey	John A. Williams
Ben Franklin Dixon	Edward W. Mulcahy	Daniel Z. Zachary

PRESIDENTIAL LIBRARIES

Harry S. Truman (HSTL), Independence, MO
Dwight D. Eisenhower (DDEL), Abeline, KS
Thomas Pappas
Maxwell Rabb
John F. Kennedy (JFKL), Boston, MA
  National Security File
  President's Daily Diary
  Arleigh A. Burke Oral History interview January 20, 1967
  Ira Kapenstein Personal Papers
  Lawrence O'Brien Personal Papers
Lyndon B. Johnson (LBJL), Austin, TX
  National Security File
  Confidential File, Co. 94, Greece
  President's Daily Diary
  Lawrence O'Brien Personal Papers
  Drew Pearson Papers
Richard M. Nixon (RMNL), Yorba Linda, CA
  National Security File
  President's Daily Diary
  Watergate Tapes [nixontapes.org]
Gerald R. Ford (GRFL), Grand Rapids, MI
  National Security File
  President's Daily Diary

UNIVERSITY AND STATE COLLECTIONS

Jack Anderson Papers, Special Collections Research Center, The George Washington University
Deena Clark Papers, University of Maryland Special Collections in Mass Media & Culture
Don Edwards Congressional Archives, Special Collections and Archives, San Jose State University (closed archives)
Donald M Fraser Papers, Manuscripts Collection, Minnesota Historical Society (restricted)
Louise Gore, Maryland State Archives Special Collections
Harilaos Lagoudakis Collection in Special Collections at Boston University
John A. McCone Papers, Bancroft Library Collections, University of California, Berkeley
James G. Pyrros, The Pyrros Papers (A Collection on the Anti-Junta Struggle, The Labadie Collection of Social and Political Protest Literature, University of Michigan, Hatcher Graduate Library, Special Collections)
Leslie Hunter Whitten, Jr. Papers, Lehigh University Special Collections, Folder 75.14, Elias Demetracopoulos, Greek journalist

U.S. GOVERNMENT DOCUMENTS

Don Edwards, "Watergate and the Greek Connection," Speech in Congressional Record, June 17, 1993, page H 3777.
Watergate Special Prosecution Force, Department of Justice, Legal Memoranda, December 1973–February 1974.
Recommendation for Assistance to Greece and Turkey, Address of the President of the United States Delivered Before a Joint Session of the Senate and House of Representatives, Recommending Assistance to Greece and Turkey, March 12, 1947 (Truman Doctrine), www.ourdocuments.gov.
U.S. Congress, Senate, Hearings before the Subcommittee of the Committee on Appropriations, Departments of State, Justice, Commerce, and the Judiciary Appropriations for 1951, 81st Congress, 2nd Session, 28 February 1950.
"Military Cold War Education and Speech Review Policies," Report by Special Preparedness Subcommittee of the Committee on Armed Services, United States Senate, 1962.
Economic Concentration: Hearings before the US Senate Committee on the Judiciary, Subcommittee on Antitrust and Monopoly, 90th Congress, second session, on April 2, 3, 5, 8, 10, 11, and 17,

1968. Part 7 [concentration outside the US].

United States Security Agreements and Commitments Abroad, United States Forces in Europe, Hearing before the Subcommittee on United States Security Agreements and Commitments Abroad of the Committee on Foreign Relations, United States Senate, 91st Congress, Second Session, Part 10, May 25 and 26, June 16 and 24, and July 15, 1970.

Greece: February 1971; A Staff Report Prepared for the Use of the Committee on Foreign Relations, United States Senate, March 4, 1971 ["Moose/Lowenstein report"].

Greece, Spain, and the Southern NATO Strategy, Hearings before the Subcommittee on Europe of the Committee on Foreign Affairs House of Representatives, 92nd Congress, First Session, July 2, 14, 19, and 21; August 3; September 9 and 15, 1971 [HCFA].

"Hackett Report," Report of Staff Study by the House Subcommittee on Europe, Athens, August–September 1971 [Hackett].

Political and Strategic Implications of Homeporting in Greece," Joint Hearings Before the Subcommittee on Europe and the Subcommittee on the Near East of the Committee on Foreign Affairs House of Representatives, 92nd Congress, Second Session, March 7 and 8; April 12, 13, and 18, 1972 [Homeporting].

Final Report of the Select Committee on Presidential Campaign Activities, United States Senate pursuant to S. Res 60, February 7, 1973; A Resolution to establish a select committee of the Senate to investigate and study illegal or improper campaign activities in the presidential election of 1972, June 1974.

U.S. Intelligence Agencies and Activities: Committee Proceedings, Proceedings of the Select Committee on Intelligence, US House of Representatives, 94th Congress, First Session, 1975, September 10, 29, October 1, November 4, 6, 13, 14, and 20, 1975.

"The CIA and the Media," Hearings Before the Subcommittee on Oversight of the Permanent Select Committee on Intelligence, House of Representatives, 95th Congress, First and Second Sessions, December 27, 28, and 29, 1977 January 4, 5, and April 20, 1978 [CIA and Media].

Freedom of Information Act Oversight, Hearings Before a Subcommittee of the Committee on Government Operations, House of Representatives, 97th Congress, First Session, July 14, 15, and 16, 1981.

Hearings before the Subcommittee on The United States Security Agreements and Commitments Abroad, Senate Committee on Foreign Relations, June 9 and 11, 1970.

"Controlling the Damage: US Policy Options for Greece," Special Study Mission to Greece, January 18–21, 1974, for Committee on Foreign Affairs, US House of Representatives, February 22, 1974 [Fraser Report].

LEGAL CASES

Ingrid Rodenberg v. Robert R. Rodenberg, Civil Action No. D 3741-67, District of Columbia Court of General Sessions, Domestic Relations Branch.

Elias P. Demetracopoulos v. Department of State, Civil Action No. 79-1741, United States District Court, District of Columbia, July 6, 1976.

Elias P. Demetracopoulos v. Federal Bureau of Investigation, Civil Action No. 78-2209, United States District Court, District of Columbia, January 30, 1981; 510 F. Supp. 529 (1981).

Elias P. Demetracopoulos v. Central Intelligence Agency, Civil Action No. 80-1625, United States District Court, District of Columbia (*Demetracopoulos v. Central Intelligence Agency*, 3 GDS ¶ 82,508 at 83,283 (D.D.C. 1982)).

Elias P. Demetracopoulos v. Central Intelligence Agency, Civil Action No. 81-1127, United States District Court, District of Columbia.

FILMS

"Agent #1" (Polish), Dir. Zbignieu Kuzminski, Agent #1, Polart Video, 2006.

"A Time for Heroes" (Greek), Dir. Aggelos Kovotsos & Kalliopi Legaki, Prod. Maria Gentekou, Portolanos Films, 2014.

"Elias Demetracopoulos: The Man Who Sued the CIA," Aggelos Kovotsos, Portolanos Films, 2010.

"The Eleventh Day: Crete 1941," Dir. Ian Ashenbremer, Archangel Films, 2006.

"Polk File on the Air" (Greek: O fakellos Polk ston aera), Dir. Dionysis Grigoratos, New Star Publishing & Entertainment Group, 1988.

"The Rehearsal" (Greek: I Dokimi), Dir. Jules Dassin, Dassin & Mercouri, 1974.

"Your Neighbor's Son: The Making of a Torturer" (Danish: Din nabos søn), Dir. Jorgen Flindt Pedersen and Erik Stephensen, Prod: Ebbe Preisler Vimeo, 1981.

"Z" (French), Dir. Costa-Gavras, Prod. Ahmed Rachedi, 1969.

BROADCAST TRANSCRIPTS AND SPEECHES

The Advocates, "Should the United States discontinue military aid to Greece?" WGBH/KCET, on PBS-TV, March 23, 1971.

Ben Bradlee on "The Charlie Rose Show," WNET[13], October 21, 1993.

"Dallek, Robert Interview with Dan Noble, USIA on Voice of America," 10–10:30 a.m., April 27, 1998 (first US government broadcast of 1968 Greek campaign money to Nixon campaign).

Dekemvriana 1944] (flv) (Television production). tvxs (Reporters Without Frontiers), Stelios Kouloglou. 2006-05-01. https://www.youtube.com/watch?v=L9km1I5tuaY Retrieved December 12, 2011.

Demetracopoulos, Elias P. "Greece: a New Vietnam?" Hudson Institute Discussion Paper (H-1241-DP), August 1, 1969.

Demetracopoulos, Elias P. "Greece—A New Vietnam?" MIT Lecture, WGBH-FM Radio, April 21, 1971.

Demetracopoulos, Elias P. "How to Control the Damage: Greece and Cyprus," Speech Before the Women's National Democratic Club," January 30, 1975; Speech to Aristotle Greek Society, New York University, November 6, 1975.

Demetracopoulos, Elias P. "The Death of Greek Democracy, April 21, 1967, Thoughts and Lessons 11 Years Later," Hellenic Society and Modern Greek Studies Program, Columbia University, April 21, 1978.

Demetracopoulos, Elias P. "Greece: 12 Years After the Coup," The Atheneum, University Club of Washington, D.C., April 6, 1979.

Demetracopoulos, Elias P. "CIA Covert Action and Greece: A Case Study of the Usefulness of the Freedom of Information Act," Presentation to Yale Center for International and Area Studies, Yale University, April 9, 1988.

"Greece Today: Two Points of View" [Professor Demetri Kousoulas, Howard University, co-author of the new Greek constitution and E. P. Demetracopoulos, a leader of the Greek resistance in the United States], "Passport," WMAR-TV (CBS), September 27, 1970, Radio-TV Monitoring Service, Inc., Washington D.C.

Maury Povich, "Interview with Elias Demetracopoulos," "Panorama," WTTG-TV, Washington D.C., May 29, 1969.

"Jerry Williams Show," Interview with Elias Demetracopoulos, WBZ Radio (Boston), April 21, 1971.

Louis Lyons News & Comment: Interview with Elias Demetracopoulos, April 20, 1971 Show, WGBH-FM (Boston).

"Pro-Democracy Fighter Elias Demetracopoulos Honored in Washington," produced by George Bistis, Voice of America, January 17, 2008.

"Freedom of Information in West Germany and the United States," Politischer Bericht, Bayerischer Rundfunk, November 7, 1978.

NBC News, Agnew's Trip to Greece, October 19, 1971, Vanderbilt Archives Record: 454357.

Transcript of a television interview given by Jack Anderson, syndicated columnist, and Elias P. Demetracopoulos, Greek journalist, to Dennis Wholey, host of the PBS show: "Late Night America," on Channel 32, Washington, D.C. Subject: the manipulation of the media by the CIA, taped October 2, 1984.

Martin Agronsky's "Evening Edition," WETA Washington, D.C., March 12, 1973.

Manthoulis, Robert. "Watergate—La Connexion Greque," Y productions, Paris, 1999.

INDEX

Abourezk, Jim, 360–61
Abshire, David, 285, 286
The Advocates (PBS program), 272
Agnew, Spiro, 172–73, 208–12, 228–31, 233, 242, 287–88, 303–4, 317, 326, 363
Akropolis (Greek newspaper), 104, 349
Albert, Carl, 286, 290, 370
Allen, George, 103, 118–19
Allende, Salvador, 371, 379
Alsop, Joe, 74, 86
American Nazi Party, 248
American Newspaper Association, 305
American School of Classical Studies (Athens), 14, 54
American-Hellenic Chamber of Commerce, 72
Amerika (US State Department magazine), 80
Amerika, Amerika (Kazan play), 333
Amnesty International, 351–52
Ampatielos, Antonios, 148
Ampatielos, Betty Bartlett, 148–49
Anastasopoulos, George, 107
Anderson, George W., 125, 136, 145–46, 357–59
Anderson, Jack, 220, 231, 258, 353–54, 371–72, 382, 385, 391
Andreotti, Giulio, 308
Androulidakis, Efangelos, 60, 64, 69, 356
Androulidakis, George, 60, 64, 69, 267
Androutsopoulos, Adamantios, 325, 328, 339
Angulo, Jeanne Oates, 389, 390–91, 393, 395–96, 397, 400
Anne-Marie, Princess of

Denmark, 166, 191
Anschutz, Norbert, 177, 202
Apostolides, Pavlos, 219
Apostolou, Christos, 43
Arapakis, Petros, 339–40
Arbenz, Jacobo, 91
Ash, A. Russell, 299
Aspida, 168–69, 174
Aspin, Les, 367–68, 379–80
Astrinidis, Floros, 357
Athens Daily Post, 107, 132, 136, 146, 154, 155, 164, 172, 185–86
Athens News, 296, 356, 361
Athens School of Economics and Commercial Services, 58
Averof, Efangelos, 272, 340
Averof Prison (Athens), 32, 40–43, 44, 53, 58, 84, 282, 385

Back, Jean, 187, 189
Baker, Howard, 208
Baltimore Sun, 172
Bandung Conference (1955), 96
Bannerman, Robert B., 382
Barham, Richard, 169
Barkas, Angelos, 26, 31
Barker, Bernard, 299
Barkley, Alben W., 76, 83, 86
Baron, Marty, 399
Barton, Lewis, 205
Batlle Berres, Luis, 160
Bay of Pigs invasion, 133, 136–37, 152, 256, 299
BBC, 27, 247, 269, 356
Ben Gurion, David, 124
Bennett, Robert S., 202
Berger, Sam, 123
Bernstein, Carl, 379
Binder, David, 376–81
Bissel, Richard M., 136
Bitsios, Dimitrios, 359–60

Bobotinos, Ioannis "John," 25, 30, 31, 37, 71
Bohlen, Charles "Chip," 195
Bokolas, Costas, 29, 42–43, 374
Boland, Edward, 378–79
Boos, Jack, 365, 366
Boston Globe, 228–29, 231, 233
Botsis Foundation for the Promotion of Journalism, 396–97
Boyatt, Thomas, 233
Boyle, John W., 87–89
Brademas, John, 353
Bradlee, Ben, 249–50, 394
Brewster, Daniel, 194
Bridges, Styles, 135–36, 159
Briggs, Ellis Ormsebee, 120–23, 125–27, 133–35, 137–39, 147
Brimberg, Robert, 195–97, 204–5, 238–39, 246, 374, 392
British Labour Party, 101, 153
Broder, David, 227
Brown, Charles B., 121–22, 125
Brown, Edmund G. "Pat," 186, 195–96, 221–23, 246
Brown, Elizabeth, 297, 323
Brown, George, 153
Brucker, Wilbur, 262
Brugioni, Dino A., 145
Brunswig Drug Company, 239
Bryte, Walter, 200, 204
Bucar, Annabelle, 80–82
Bullock, Roy, 286
Bundy, McGeorge, 141
Burdick, Quentin, 251, 264, 274, 288
Burke, Arleigh, 93, 121–22, 125, 130–37, 142–43, 152, 166, 286, 315–16, 388, 390
Burns, Arthur, 387
Burns, Nicholas, 397
Buzhardt, Fred, 209, 315–17, 319
Byrd, Robert, 297

Byzantine Empire, 5, 6–7

C. Pappas Co. Inc., 158
Callas, Maria, 270–71
Camelot's Court (Dallek), 235
Carney, William, 93
Carter, Jimmy, 371
Casey, William, 380
Cassavetes, Nicholas, 298
Castro, Fidel, 123, 248
Castro, Raoul, 123–24
Caulfield, Jack, 248
Celler, Emanuel, 194, 195–96, 205
Center for Strategic and International Studies (CSIS) at Georgetown University, 142
Center Union Party, 147, 153–56, 162–65, 169, 174–76, 256, 349
Central Bank of Greece, 179, 217–19, 366
Central Intelligence Agency (CIA), 66, 73, 77–78, 81–87, 94, 97, 109–10, 114–15, 122, 125–27, 142–45, 152, 171–72, 206, 217, 305–6, 365–66, 372–73, 376–82
Central Intelligence and Investigation Service (KYP) (Greece), 73, 83, 92, 113, 178, 189, 216–20
The Challenges We Face (Nixon), 161
Chant, Margaret, 76
Cheney, Richard "Dick," 364
Chennault, Anna, 248, 254
Chicago Tribune, 250
Chotiner, Murray, 281–82, 292–93, 314, 354
Chourmouzios, Aimilios, 64–65, 68–70, 74, 85–86, 97, 102
Christian Science Monitor, 247, 254, 258
Church, Frank, 303, 354, 360–61
Church Committee (Senate Select Committee on Intelligence), 354–55, 361–68, 370–71
Churchill, George, 285, 286, 360, 370
Churchill, Winston, 20–21, 35, 47, 50–51, 54, 55–56, 186

Citibank Global Asset Management, 387, 392
Clark, Blake, 200
Clark, Deena, 200, 247, 375, 388–89, 391, 393, 395
Clements, William, Jr., 350
Clinton, Bill, 293, 394, 395, 397
Clinton, Hillary, 386
Colby, William, 355, 363, 372, 380–81
Colson, Charles, 304, 317
Committee for Democracy in Greece, 294
Committee to Reelect the President (CREEP), 281, 289–90, 320
Common Heritage (magazine), 257
Congressional Record, 136, 213, 242
Connally, John, 298, 314, 385–86
Conscience of a Conservative (Goldwater), 117–18
Constantine II, King of Greece, 166, 168–69, 172, 174–76, 191, 200–201, 240, 308
Conway, LaVerne, 257
Conyers, John, 383
Cooper-Church Amendment, 259
Corporation for Public Broadcasting, 256
Corriere della Sera (Rome newspaper), 317
Costa-Gavras, 150
Couloumbis, Theodore, 277
Council of Europe, 244–45, 250–51, 272, 295
Crane, Kent, 248
Crawford, William, 343
Cuban Missile Crisis, 145
Cuban revolution, 123–24
Curie, Eve, 138
Curlin, William, Jr., 300
Cyprus, 94–98, 101–8, 111–13, 124–25, 147, 327–41, 342–52
Cyprus Radio, 335

Dallek, Robert, 232, 235, 397
Damaskinos, Archbishop, 42–43, 54, 71
Dandonaki, Fleuri, 387
Daniels, Clifton, xiii

Dassin, Jules, 247, 332
Davies, Rodger, 244, 270, 277, 286–87, 292, 346
Davos, Ioannis "John," 340
Day, John, 325, 327
de Gaulle, Charles, 149
Dean, Deborah Gore, 389, 398
Dean, John, 289, 290, 315, 319
Dean, Mary Gore, 292
Deegan, Thomas, 219–20
Defense Intelligence Agency, 142
Degiannis, John, 363–64
Dekemvriana ("December events"), 50–51, 56
Demetracopoulos, Panagiota Bokolas, 4–5, 13–18, 22, 26–29, 39, 40, 43, 45, 48, 55–59, 71, 89, 103
Demetracopoulos, Panagiotis, 3–5, 11–18, 21–23, 26–29, 43, 45, 49, 55–58, 61, 76, 89, 188, 255, 263–69
"Demetracopoulos Affair," 269, 274–75
Democracy in Greece Committee, 233
Democratic Army of Greece, 57, 61, 63
Democratic Defense (DD), 247, 256
Democratic National Committee, 230, 293
Democratic National Convention in Chicago (1968), 220
Democratic National Convention in Miami Beach (1972), 294
Dent, Harry, 143, 209, 226, 317
Desautels, Claude, 223
Detroit News, 329
Deutsche Welle, 269
Dewey, Thomas E., 73
Dimas, Stavros, 343
Dimitriou, Nikos, 335
Dirksen, Everett, 250
Dixon, Ymelda, 204
Dobrovir, William, 373, 376, 378, 404
Donovan, Robert J., 122, 125–26, 140–41
Dovas, Konstantinos, 100, 105–6, 176, 178
Drossopoulos, Antonis, 11, 395, 401

Dukakis, Olympia, 333
Duke, Bill, 256
Dulles, Allen, 89, 91, 94, 110,
114–15, 122, 152, 379
Dulles, John Foster, 120, 160
Dumont, Nat, 195

Eagleton, Thomas, 348, 353
EAM (*Ethniko Apeleftherotikon
Metopo*) (National
Liberation Front), 24–25,
34–35, 48–51, 55–56
Eastland, James, 205–6
EC (*Enosis Kentrou*) party,
137–38
Ecevit, Bülent, 339, 345
Economic Cooperation
Administration (ECA), 70
EDA (United Democratic Left)
party, 108, 112, 137, 148,
155, 176
EDES (*Ethnikos Dimokratikos
Elefterotikon Ellinikos
Syndesmos*) (National
Republican Greek League),
24–25, 35
Edwards, Don, 240, 244, 257,
324, 361, 368, 383–84, 393
EENA (National Union of
Young Greek Officers), 113,
138, 150, 177–78, 181
Efetas, Epameinondas, 64–65
Eginition Home for the Insane
(Athens), 43–45, 58, 71, 84
Ehrlichman, John, 248, 315
Eisenberg, Leon, 313
Eisenhower, Dwight D., 87,
101, 121–22, 130–31,
159–61
Eisenhower, Earl, 372
ELAS (*Ellinikos Laikos
Apeleftherotikos Stratos*)
(Greek People's Liberation
Army), 24–25, 34–35,
48–52, 55–57
Eleftheria (Greek newspaper),
29, 106, 155, 184
Eleftheros Kosmos (Greek
newspaper), 296
Elizabeth, Queen, 153
Ellsberg, Daniel, 231, 315
Enislides, George, 10
EOKA-B (Cypriot paramilitary
organization), 333, 334,
339
ERE (National Radical Union)

party, 98, 108, 134, 137–38,
153, 155–56, 169, 176, 349
ESA (Greek Military Police),
311–12, 321, 340, 351
Esso (Standard Oil of New
Jersey), 161–63
Esso-Pappas, 162, 167, 169–70,
173, 183–84
Estia (Greek newspaper), 108,
296
Ethnos (Greek newspaper),
106–8, 122–23, 131–32,
164–66, 170, 185, 188, 257
European Commission on
Human Rights, 251
European Convention on
Human Rights and
Fundamental Freedoms,
251
European Economic
Community (EEC), 137,
295
Evans, Rowland, 220, 268, 281,
284, 295, 348, 363, 378
Evert, Angelos, 50
EYP (National Intelligence
Service), 219

Fair Play for Cuba Committee,
248
Farmakis, Nikos, 50, 177
Federal Bureau of Information
(FBI), 81, 86–87, 237,
290–92, 300, 305–6,
383–85
Federal Privacy Act, 379
Feldstein, Mark, 231
Fetsis, Konstantinos, 362
Fielding, Fred, 290
Finch, Robert, 208
First Pacifist Rally in Athens
(April 1963), 148–50
Fisher, Roger, 272
Fleming, Amalia, 305, 310–11,
343
Fleming, Ian, 72
Foisie, Philip, 152
Folger, Kay, 286
Ford, Gerald, 300, 344, 348,
359, 367, 368, 385
Ford Foundation, 344
Foreign Agents Registration
Act, 220, 279, 291, 295–96
Foreign Assistance Act, 309
Foreign Policy Research
Institute, 272

Foreign Press Association of
Greece, 126–28, 139–40,
147
Foreign Press Division of the
Greek Ministry of the
Press, 140
*Foreign Relations of the United
States, 1969–1976, Vol.
XXX, Greece, Cyprus,
Turkey, 1973–1976*, 393
Fowler, Wyche, 380
Fraser, Don, 233, 240, 244,
257, 275, 331, 350
Frederika, Queen of Greece,
91, 148–49, 153, 166, 167,
172, 175–76, 178, 191
Freedom of Information and
Privacy Act (FOIA), xii,
198, 268, 368, 373, 378,
383, 385, 404
Freeman, Mona, 171
Friendly, Fred, 152
Fulbright, J. William, 243,
250–51, 258, 262, 264, 274,
333–34, 337–38, 397

Gaddafi, Muammar, 245
Galanis, Dimitrios, 218–19,
224, 366
Garment, Len, 226
Garoufalias, Petros, 167,
168–69, 176
Gaston, Nick, 116
Georgakis, Kostas, 260–61
George Washington
University, 242–43, 273
Gerolymatos, André, 49
Giallelis, Stathis, 333
Giannatos, Dimitrios, 30, 32
Giannatos, Kostas, 16, 22,
24–25, 43–44, 71
Giannatos, Mariana, 30
Giantiskos, Menelaos, 37–38
Gingrich, Newt, 394
Giscard d'Estaing, Valéry,
340–41
Gizikis, Phaedon, 340
Gkikas, Solon, 111–12
Glaser, Vera, 292
Goldberg, Lucianne, 72, 293,
298, 314, 317
Goldberg, Sid, 131–32, 204,
292–93
Golden Dawn party, 398

Goldwater, Barry, 117–18, 132, 147, 153–56, 177, 250, 372
Goodell, Charles, 212, 251, 281
Goodpaster, Andrew, 345
Gore, H. Grady, 116–17
Gore, Louise, 116–18, 129, 131, 153, 172, 197, 208–11, 216, 236, 247, 284, 290, 295, 302, 353–54, 363, 368, 375, 388–89, 393, 395
Gozanni, Guido, 37–38
Grady, Henry F., 70, 71
Grande Bretagne Hotel (Athens), 30–31, 52, 68, 100, 167, 186, 341, 356
Gravel, Mike, 264, 266–67, 274
Gray, L. Patrick, 298–99, 306
Grazzi, Emanuele, 17
Great Fire of Smyrna (1922), 8
Greece (English language journal), 72
Greek Civil War (1944–49), 35–36, 47–54, 57–63, 73
Greek Communist Party (KKE), 15–16, 25, 34–35, 55–57, 61, 63. See also EDA (United Democratic Left) Party
Greek Foreign Trade Administration, 155, 162
Greek Herald, 398
Greek Ministry of Foreign Affairs, 126, 140
Greek Ministry of National Defense, 72, 100, 105–6, 175, 278
Greek National Schism, 7, 9
The Greek Proclamation Committee, 298
Greek Report, 241
Greek-American Cultural Institute, 72
Greenup, Leonard, 122, 382
Gregory V, Patriarch of Constantinople, 42
Grivas, Georgios, 51, 95, 111, 113
Grogan, Stanley, 122, 125–27, 133–34

Hackett, Clifford, 275, 280–81, 286, 331, 388, 398–400
Haldeman, H. R., 293, 304
Halperin, Morton, 379
Handrinos, Angeliki, 51–52
Handrinos, Maritsa, 182

Handrinos, Spyros, 51–54, 181–82, 255, 267
Handrinos, Vassilis, 51–54
Hanna, Richard T., 301
Harriman, W. Averill, 249
Harris, Reed, 151–52
Harrison, George, 207
Hartke, Vance, 150–51, 173, 195, 205–6, 213, 262–64, 404
Hatfield, Mark, 288
Hays Amendment, 291
Healy, Robert, 228–29, 233, 235
Hellenic Chronicle (Boston newspaper), 254, 298
Hellenic Red Cross, 49
Hellman, Lillian, 333
Helms, Richard, 129, 144, 221, 223–26, 232–33, 239, 366, 392
Hemingway, Ernest, 72
Hersh, Seymour, xi, 233, 258, 365, 391–92, 397, 398
Herter, Christian, 122, 161
Hill, William, 142–43, 144
Hise, James C., 279
Hitchens, Christopher, 284, 357, 391, 392, 393, 397
Hitler, Adolf, 15, 16, 19–22, 23, 182
Holum, John, 294–95, 365, 369–71, 372, 382
Hooper, Robert, 318
Hoover, J. Edgar, 72, 81, 206, 236, 279, 283–84
Hostage to History (Hitchens), 393
House Banking and Currency Committee, 273, 299, 395
House Committee on Un-American Activities (HUAC), 81
House Foreign Affairs Committee, 244, 273, 274, 280, 295, 338, 347
House Foreign Affairs Subcommittee on Europe, 277, 291, 331
House Intelligence Committee, 370, 378–79
House Judiciary Committee, 194, 205, 334
House Select Committee on Intelligence (Pike Committee), 361, 365–68

House Subcommittee on Commerce, Consumer, and Monetary Affairs, 383
House Subcommittee on Europe, 275
Howe, Russell Warren, 369–70
Hudson Institute, 243, 273
Hughes, Howard, 161, 222–23, 225–27
Hulse, Stacy, 362
Human Events (conservative weekly), 297
Humphrey, Frances Howard, 195
Humphrey, Hubert, xi, 173, 195, 207, 214–16, 222, 227, 232, 338
Hunt, Al, 273
Hunt, Howard, 293
Hussein, King, 261
Hussein, Saddam, 206

I Led Three Lives (Philbrick), 140
Iakovos, Archbishop, 348
IDEA (The Sacred Band of Greek Officers), 112–13, 115, 138, 150, 178
Immigration and Naturalization Service (INS), 204, 212–13, 246
Independent Carpathian Rifle Brigade, 30
Inouye, Daniel, 370, 371–72, 376, 378, 382
International Federation of Newspaper Publishers, 305
International Monetary Fund (IMF), 193, 261, 271
International Red Cross, 275
Ioannidis, Dimitrios, 303, 318–19, 323–24, 327–41, 364
It's Time for Heroes (film), 398
Ivanof (Jerzy Iwanow-Szajnowicz), 29–33, 41

Jack Ruby, 329
Jackson, Henry, 118
Jackson, Nancy, 171, 235
Jamieson, Kathleen Hall, 220
Janeway, Eliot, 173, 195, 196
Javits, Jacob, 212, 297
Jenkins, Reuben, 75
Jeppesen, Svend Sandager, 192
Jockey Club (Washington,

D.C. restaurant), 197, 224, 251, 271, 281–82, 360, 375, 387–88, 396
Johnson, Lyndon, 130, 136, 146–47, 170, 173, 195–96, 207, 208, 221–26, 230–32
Joint US Military Aid Group, 75, 93
Joyce, Vincent, 164–65

Kahn, Herman, 243, 297
Kaklamanis, Apostolos, 401
Kanellopoulos, Panagiotis, 87–88, 90, 94, 174, 176–77, 179, 181, 207, 247, 276, 340
Kann, William F., 212
Kantor, Seth, 329
Kapenstein, Ira, 223, 224, 228–31, 233–34
Karamanlis, Konstantinos, 71, 97–98, 101, 105–9, 123, 125, 137–38, 146–48, 153, 162–64, 207, 240, 245–47, 302–3, 308, 340–41, 345, 348–49, 356, 360, 362, 364
"Karamanlis solution," 245, 302–3
Karamessines, Thomas Hercules, 73–74, 78, 83–85, 91–92, 171, 206, 239
Karayannopoulou, Mary-Louise, 182
Karditsis, Nikolaos, 59
Kariotis, Theodore "Ted," 388
Kathimerini (Greek newspaper), 16, 20, 60, 64–78, 83–88, 93, 97–98, 101–4, 106–7, 116, 180, 184–85, 346
Kazan, Elia, 333
Kazantzakis, Nikos, 69, 396
Kefauver, Estes, 87, 133
Kelly, Clarence M., 355
Kendall, George, 300
Kennedy, Edward M., 146, 225, 248, 252, 254, 264, 268, 303, 350, 360
Kennedy, Jackie, 137, 138, 170, 225, 271
Kennedy, John F., 118, 129–39, 145, 152, 156, 161, 235, 329
Kennedy, Robert, 133, 135, 146–47, 152, 207, 215, 228
KGB, 81, 378

Khrushchev, Nikita, 121, 130, 137, 248
Kilduff, Malcolm "Mac," 141, 150
Kilpatrick, James J., 296–97
Kimball, Dan, 83
King, Jim, 235
King, Martin Luther, Jr., 206
Kissinger, Henry, 100, 237–38, 242, 253, 273, 274, 276–77, 280, 301, 303–4, 309–10, 324–25, 328–41, 342–50, 353–60, 365–67, 370–73, 386, 391
Kitner, William, 272
KKE. *See* Greek Communist Party (KKE)
Klein, Herb, 226
Komer, Robert, 141, 166
Konstantinos, King of Greece, 7–9, 95
Koppel, Ted, 391
Korean Central Intelligence Agency, 301
Korean War, 72, 73
Koryzis, Alexandros, 21
Kothris, Emmanouil, 270
Kotsos, Emanuel, 87
Kousoulas, Demetrios, 305
Kovach, William, 381
Kovotsos, Angelos, 398, 401
Krag, Jens Otto, 191–92
Kubisch, Jack, 344, 350
Kutler, Stanley, 232–33, 236, 391, 396

Labouisse, Henry, 138–39, 146, 147, 155
Lagoudakis, Charlios "Charlie," 178
Laird, Melvin, 242
Lamprakis, Grigorios, 148–50, 256
Lamprias, Panagiotis, 357
Lapschin, Konstantin, 81
LaRosa, Barbara, 399
Lausanne Peace Treaty, 8, 95
Lawrence, Robert, 104, 109–10
Le Monde, 211–12
Legacy of Ashes (Weiner), 393
LeMay, Curtis, 145
Lemnitzer, Lyman, 136
Leopold, King of Belgium, 92
Letelier, Orlando, 371
Lewinsky, Monica, 293

Lewis, J. K., 41, 49
Liddy, G. Gordon, 289
Life magazine, 80, 88
Lindsay, John, 208
Linen, James A., III, 87–89
Lisi, Virna, 171
Lodge, Henry Cabot, 171
London School of Economics, 249, 294
London *Sunday Times*, 230
LOOK magazine, 243–44
Los Angeles Times, 155
Loukopoulos, Kostas, 400–402
Luce, Clare Booth, 96, 120
Luce, Henry, 88–89, 120, 379
Lydon, Christopher, 229–30
Lykourezos, Alexandros, 363–64

MacArthur, Douglas, 67
Macomber, William, 286
MacVeagh, Lincoln, 14–15, 24
Magruder, Jeb S., 289
Maheu, Robert, 222–23
Mahoney, George, 172
Makarezos, Nikolaos, 187–88, 247, 364
Makarios III of Cyprus, 95–96, 101–3, 111–13, 124, 291, 333–38, 342–43, 345
Makedonia (Greek newspaper), 62, 88, 98–99, 106–8, 131–32, 135, 164, 185, 294
Makedonia/Thessaloniki (Greek newspaper), 72, 294
The Making of the President 1968 (White), 216
Mallias, Alexandros, 397
Manning, Robert J., 146
Manthoulis, Robert, 398
Manuelides, Stefan, 400–402
Marcos, Ferdinand, 234
Marcy, Carl, 285
Mardian, Robert, 282
Margolis, Susan, xii–xiii
Markezinis, Spyros, 318–19, 340
Markopoulos, Giannis, 333
Marlowe, Walter and Lydia, xiii
Marriott Corporation, 260
Marshall, Oliver K., 165, 189
Marshall Plan, 66, 70, 155

Martin Marietta Corporation, 249
Martinovic, Veselin, 111
Matsas, Alexandros, 166
Maury, Jack, 303, 366
Mavros, George, 162–63, 177, 247, 340, 345, 348–49, 356
Mayer, Susan, 272
McCarthy, Eugene, 206–7, 215, 228
McCarthy, Joseph, 72–73, 151, 159, 160, 235
McChristian, Joseph, 112
McCloskey, Robert, 267
McCone, John, 143, 152, 166
McCormack, John, 159, 170, 173, 177, 194, 385
McGee, Gale W., 338
McGinnis, Joe, 215
McGovern, George, 251, 252, 290, 294–97, 314, 338, 354, 361, 368, 369–72, 376, 382, 397
McGrory, Mary, 210
McGurn, Barrett, 118
McMahon, John N., 380
McNamara, Robert, 131, 145–46, 151, 152, 278
Meet the Press, 200, 342
"Megali Idea," 6–7, 94
Meir, Golda, 124
Melina Mercouri: I Was Born Greek (television documentary), 256
Mercouri, Melina, 247, 256, 260–61, 272, 286–87, 310, 332–33, 343
Mercouris, Spyros, 247
Mesta, Perle, 254, 290
Metaxas, Ioannis, 9, 13, 15–18, 19, 34
Metaxas, Persa, 104–5, 155, 179–80, 188, 247, 254–55, 263–67, 336, 350, 356, 389, 393, 400–402
MI6, 24, 31
MI9, 24
Military Sales Act, 258–59
Miller, Arthur, 333
Miller, James, 278, 336
Minis, Tasos, 351
Mitchell, John, 216, 223, 236, 250, 278–79, 281, 283–84, 289–90, 292, 295, 301, 304, 319–20, 354, 358, 368
Mitsotakis, Konstantinos,

308, 310
Modiano, Inci, 179–80
Modiano, Mario, 108, 179–80, 219, 388, 395
Moeller, Hans Severin, 191, 193–94
Moffitt, Ronni, 371
Morse, Wayne, 205, 212
Morton, Rogers, 208
Moss, Frank, 213, 251, 264, 274
Mount Lycabettos (Athens), 3, 45, 59, 402
Mountbatten, Lord, 93
Mouskouri, Nana, 387
Moustaklis, Christina, 311–13, 350–51, 396, 401–2
Moustaklis, Natalie, 401
Moustaklis, Spyros, 306–7, 311–13, 349–52, 356, 385–86, 397
Moynihan, Daniel Patrick, 257
Murrow, Edward R., 151
Muskie, Edmund, 289–90
Mussolini, Benito, 15, 17–18, 21, 30–31, 36, 304
Mutual Security Administration (MSA), 70
Mylonas, George, 310

Naftemboriki (Greek newspaper), 104
Nakis, Sam, 297–98
Napalm B, 63
Napolitan, Joe, 150, 222–23, 227, 233–34
Nasser, Gamal Abdel, 96, 123–24, 138
The Nation, 392
National Bank of Greece, 174, 185, 257
National Organization of Cypriot Fighters (EOKA), 95–96
National Press Club, 210–11
National Security Agency (NSA), 145, 178
National Security Council (NSC), 175, 268, 299, 328–29, 359, 373
Natsinas, Alexandros, 123, 178
Nedzi, Lucien, 240, 273–74
Nehru, Jawaharlal, 96
Nelson, Warren, 367
New England Center for Investigative Reporting, xi

New York City Police Department, 248
New York Daily News, 230
New York Herald Tribune, 118–19, 121–22, 125–28, 130, 135, 139–41, 142–44, 152, 394
New York Herald Tribune News Service, 121, 125–28, 143–44
New York magazine, 216
New York Post, 133
New York Times, xii, 127, 172, 175, 185, 221, 226, 233, 245, 247, 254, 258–59, 267, 269, 294, 346, 376–81
Niarchos, Stavros, 162
Nicholson, Donald L., 82
Nightmare in Athens (Papandrou), 186–87
Nikolopoulos, Petros, 83–84
Nixon, Donald, 226, 260
Nixon, Pat, 209
Nixon, Richard, xi, 87, 94, 117–18, 159–61, 185, 208–11, 214–16, 226–27, 230, 234, 267, 287, 290, 303–4, 315–20, 338
Norstad, Lauris, 109, 176
North American Newspaper Alliance (NANA), 72, 107, 131–32, 196, 204, 292
North-Atlantic Treaty Organization (NATO), 73, 92–93, 97, 105–6, 122–23, 150–51, 261–63, 295, 307–9
Novak, Robert, 185, 194, 195, 220, 258, 268, 272, 284–85, 295, 348, 363, 377–78, 397
Noyes, Newbold, 144
Nuclear Test Ban Treaty, 153–54

OAG (Organosis Anastaseos Genous), 24–26, 29–33, 35–37, 41, 54, 71
Oates, Jeanne. See Angulo, Jeanne Oates
O'Brien, Hugh, 171
O'Brien, Larry, 150, 221–36, 290, 293, 330, 392
O'Donnell, Kenny, 150, 229, 235
Office of International

Education, 81
Office of War Information, 80
Olivier, Laurence, 333
Olson, Theodore, 96
Olympic Airways, 260, 358
Onassis, Aristotle, 101, 162, 225, 238, 252, 260, 271
Operation Barbarossa, 20
Operation Gemstone, 289–90
Operation Prometheus, 262
Operation Torch, 63
Organization for the Protection of the People's Struggle (OPLA), 51–52
Oswald, Lee Harvey, 329
Otto Friedrich Ludwig, Prince, 6
Ottoman Empire, 5–7, 45, 94

Pabst, G. W., 182
Palamas, Christos, 266
Pampoukis, George, 71
Pan Hellenic Liberation Movement (PAK), 240–41, 260–61
Panagiotakos, Constantine, 359–60
Panagoulis, Alekos, 207, 236, 267, 305, 310
Panhellenic Socialist Movement (PASOK), 348
Panorama (television program), 244
Papadopoulos, Charalampos "Babis," 360
Papadopoulos, Georgios, 115, 178, 183, 184, 187–89, 191, 207, 217, 236, 247, 251–54, 259–60, 264, 308–11, 318–19, 322–24, 358, 364
Papagos, Alexander, 9, 63, 69–70, 74, 83, 85
Papandreou, Andreas, 75, 76, 162–65, 168–70, 174–76, 178, 207, 210, 221, 240–41, 247, 256, 260–61, 286–87, 291, 297, 308, 310, 323, 325, 346, 349
Papandreou, George, 46, 48–50, 75, 88, 94, 98, 137–38, 147, 153, 155–56, 162–70, 176–77, 179, 207, 217, 235–36, 240
Papandreou, George Andreas, 400
Papandreou, Margaret, 170,

176, 186–87, 240
Papaspyrou, Dimitrios, 270, 296
Papathanassiadis, Theodosis, 100
Papoulis, Karolos, 396–97
Pappas, Bessie, 167
Pappas, John, 158, 160, 170, 175
Pappas, Nikolaos, 306–8
Pappas, Tom, xi, 154, 157–73, 175, 183–84, 207–10, 216–20, 223, 228–36, 238, 246, 248, 250, 260, 270–73, 281–88, 290, 295, 303–4, 310, 319–20, 327–30, 344, 354, 358–68, 369–74, 382, 385, 391–93
Paris Peace Talks, 227, 234
Parthenon, 12, 22–23, 402
Pathfinder News Magazine, 72
Patman, J. Wright, 273–74, 299–301
Pattakos, Stylianos, 183, 251–52, 256, 260, 303, 364
Paul, King of Greece, 91, 153, 166, 170
Pearson, Drew, 220, 226–27, 231, 330
Peiramatikon Gymnasium (Athens), 10–11, 24, 51, 58
Pell, Claiborne, 250–51, 270, 338
Pell, John, 270–71
Pell, Pyma, 270
Pentagon Papers, 289, 315
"Percentages Agreement" (1944), 47
Percy, Charles, 208–9
"Pericles Plan," 168
Pesmazoglou, John, 179, 218, 340, 349, 356
Peterson, Dave, 367
Petrounakos, Dimitrios, 362
Peurifoy, John Emil, 70, 72–74, 78, 82–87, 91–92
Philbrick, Herbert, 140
Pike, Otis, 365–67
Pinochet, Augusto, 371
Pipilis, Ioannis, 111–12
Pipinelis, Panagiotis, 176, 251, 259
Plastiras, Nikolaos, 54, 69
Plumbers, 289, 314
Political Subjects (Greek weekly magazine), 324

Polk, George, xii, 61–62, 64, 99
Polk, James, 273–74, 330
Polytechnic Institute (Athens), 304–5, 320–25, 332–33
Potter, E. B., 136
Potts, Jim, 287, 297, 358
Prague Spring, 206
The Price of Power (Hersh), 365, 391–92
Proto Nekrotafeio Cemetery (Athens), 103, 265–66, 356
Pyrros, Jim, 240, 257–58, 273–74, 334, 336, 345, 347

Quinn, Sally, 249–50
Quinn, William W. "Buffalo Bill," 93, 96, 142, 166, 212, 249–50, 391

Radford, Arthur, 93
Radio Free Greece, 63, 166
Rallis, George, 362
Rand Corporation, 243
Reagan, Ronald, 208, 221
The Rehearsal (film), 332–33
Reid, Ogden, 119
Republican National Convention in Chicago (1944), 159
Republican National Convention in Chicago (1960), 161
Republican National Convention in Detroit (1980), 385
Republican National Convention in Miami Beach (1968), 209
Republican National Convention in Philadelphia (1948), 159
Republican National Finance Committee, 159
Reuss, Henry, 395
Ribbentrop, Joachim von, 181
Richardson, Eliot, 315
Richardson, John, 100, 202, 239
Riddleberger, Antonia, 114
Riddleberger, James, 109, 114, 139
Ridgway, Matthew, 94
Rigas, John, 67

Rivers, Mendel, 194
Roche, Constance Booras, 298
Rockefeller, Nelson, 100, 208
Rodenberg, Ingrid, 200–204, 213
Rodenberg, Robert, 201–4
Rogers, William P., 238, 251, 260, 265–66, 269, 276–79, 293, 309–10
Roosevelt, Franklin D., 14, 54
Rorick, Rosemary, 150–51
Rosenthal, A. M., 377
Rosenthal, Ben, 273, 275, 280, 284–86, 305, 348, 350, 353, 366, 383, 397
Rossides, Eugene, 347
Rostow, Walt, 175
Roufogalis, Michael, 217–18, 357–58, 366
Rousakis, John, 298, 314
The Royal Hellenic Navy in the Defense of Greece (Demetracopoulos), 93
Rusk, Dean, 136, 150, 152, 175, 196
Russell, Bertrand, 153
Russell, Richard, 142–43

Sacred Squadron, 49
Salazar, António de Oliveira, 186
Salinger, Pierre, 132–34, 141, 144, 150–52, 156, 171, 235, 383
Saltonstall, Leverett, 159
Samaras, Antonis, 400
Sampson, Nikos, 333, 335, 336–37
Sarbanes, Paul, 353
Sartorius & Co., 273, 300, 354
Sartzetakis, Christos, 150
Saunders, Harold, 280
Scarelli, Jacques, 271
Schaufele, William, 375–77
Schell, Maximilian, 333
Schlesinger, James, 365
Schlitter, Daisy, 181–82, 188–89, 218–19, 270
Schlitter, Oscar, 181, 200
Schurr, Peter, 313
Scobie, Ronald, 49, 50
Scott, Hugh, 274
Scowcroft, Brent, 348, 367
Sedgwick, A. C., 127–28
The Selling of the President (McGinnis), 215

Senate Armed Services Committee, 142
Senate Foreign Affairs Committee, 173
Senate Foreign Relations Committee, 250–51, 262, 274, 288, 338, 375
Senate Foreign Relations Subcommittee on Security Arrangements, 258
Senate Judiciary Committee, 205–6, 360
Senate Select Committee on Intelligence (Church Committee), 354–55, 361–68, 370–71
Senate Select Committee on Presidential Elections (Watergate Committee), 314–17
Senate Subcommittee on Near Eastern and South Asian Affairs, 370
Shanahan, Eileen, 226
Shaw, George Bernard, 59
Sheridan, Frank, 153
Sherman, Norman, 232
Shields, Mark, 220
Shore, Dinah, 171
Sisco, Joseph, 244, 258, 269, 276–77, 280, 292, 338–40, 350
Skouras, George, 107, 186
Skouras, Spyros, 161, 270–71
Smith, Walter Bedel, 80–82
Socrates, 13
Sotiria clinic (Athens), 58–59
Southern Strategy, 215, 226
Spaak, Paul Henri, 247
Spantidakis, Grigorios, 175
Spear, Joe, 382
Sputnik, 105, 106
Staktopoulos, Grigoris, 62, 99
Stalin, Josef, 47, 57, 63
Stamatopoulos, Byron, 296
Stans, Maurice, 216, 219, 223, 290, 299, 330
Staude, Elmer, 239
Stavros magazine, 40
Stearns, Monteagle, 114
Stennis, John, 135–36
Stern, Larry, 393, 394
Stevenson, Adlai, 87
Stott, Bill, 161
Suez Canal, 101
Sukarno, 96

Sullivan, Ed, 171
Sulzberger, C. L., 127–28, 175, 185, 379
Sylvester, Arthur, 131, 132, 151
Symington, Stuart, 262

Ta Nea (Greek newspaper), 16, 104
Tagmata Asfaleias (Greek Security Battalions), 35, 48, 115
Talbot, Phillips, 151, 156, 175–76, 188, 193, 205, 233, 238, 249, 365
Tasca, Henry, 219, 249–52, 253, 260, 265–68, 274–80, 286–87, 297, 301, 303–4, 309–10, 318, 320, 323, 331–32, 360, 365–66
Taylor, Maxwell D., 96, 152
Thant, U, 188–89
Theodorakis, Mikis, 256, 310, 333, 343
Thessaloniki (Greek newspaper), 150
Thimmesch, Nick, 365
Third Mountain Brigade, 49
Thisavros (Greek newsmagazine), 72
The Threat of Dictatorship (Demetracopoulos), 177, 179
303 Committee, 175
Thurmond, Strom, 142–43, 194, 209, 297, 315
Time magazine, 80, 87–89, 394
Time-Life, Inc., 87–89, 118
Times of London, 107, 179, 212, 216, 294
Timmons, William, 268
Tito, Josip Broz, 57, 63
To Vima (Greek newspaper), xiii, 104, 106, 295, 322–23
Today Show, 342
Tolstoy, Leo, 18, 59
Tonge, David, 356
Topping, Seymour, 377
Totomis, Paul, 184
Tower, John, 363
Tranos, Konstantinos, 124–25
Treaty of Sèvres, 7
Tripp, Linda, 293
Truman, Harry S., 60–61, 73, 76, 83, 86, 303, 393
Truman, Margaret, xiii
Truman Doctrine, 60, 76, 303

Tsakalotos, Thrasyvoulos, 111
Tsalapatis, Dimitrios, 267, 401
Tsimas, Kostas, 219
Tsolakoglou, Georgios, 21
Tsouderou, Virginia, 179

Ulascewitz, Tony, 248
Ulmer, Al, 73
UN Editors' Roundtable
    (1967), 187–89, 190–94
UNESCO, 247, 302
United Nations, 101–2, 111,
    187–89
United Nations Relief
    and Rehabilitations
    Administration
    (UNRRA), 57
United Nations Security
    Council, 338–39
University of Athens, 10, 23,
    48, 58
US Committee for Democracy
    in Greece (USCDG), 240,
    244–45, 257
US Department of Defense,
    85, 175, 292
US Foreign Service, 80
US Information Agency
    (USIA), 118–19, 122
US Information Service
    (USIS), 71, 82, 96, 122,
    123–24
US Naval Operations, 93,
    121–22, 130, 291
US Operations Missions in
    Greece, 118
US Sixth Fleet, 93, 104, 121,
    125, 130, 133, 136, 145,
    261, 291, 337–38
US State Department Bureau
    of Intelligence and
    Research, 178, 290–91,
    309
US State Department's
    Personnel Security Branch,
    81–82
USAID, 138

Vafeiadis, Markos, 61, 62
Valuchek, Andrew, 223
Van Der Stoel, Max, 272
Varhol, Helen, 317–18
Varkiza Agreement (1945), 56
Vellidis, Ioannis, 98–99,
    107–8, 185, 294, 374

Venizelos, Eleftherios, 7, 9–10,
    13, 48, 83
Venizelos, Nikitas, 308
Vidalis, Orestis, 257–58, 310,
    335
Vietnam War, 171, 206–7, 215,
    230–31
Vigderman, Al, 248, 258
Vlachos, Angelos, 360
Vlachos, George, 20, 65, 74,
    97–98
Vlachou, Eleni, 65, 97–98,
    106–7, 116, 180, 184–85,
    200–201, 207, 240–41,
    247, 310, 345–46
Voice of America, 165, 398
Volcker, Paul, 239
Volpe, John, 208–9, 308
von Cramm, Marion Schlitter,
    196, 218–19, 224
Votsadopoulos, Efangelos, 29
Voutselas, Angelique, 225, 254
Vradyni (Greek newspaper),
    247, 305, 324

Wade, Leigh, 75
Walker, Everett, 143
Wall Street Journal, 254, 273
Wallace, George, 215, 298
Walter Reed Army Medical
    Center, 313, 350
Warren Commission report,
    379
The Wars of Watergate (Kutler),
    392
Was, Celia, 71, 79–90, 92,
    102–3, 117, 144, 248–49,
    259, 317–18, 390–91, 396
Washington Dossier, 389
Washington Magazine, 369
Washington Post, xii, 90, 122,
    152, 155–56, 227, 247,
    254, 334, 343, 354, 378,
    381–82, 383, 394–95
Washington Star, 143, 144, 152,
    204, 210, 394
Webster, William, 383–84,
    395, 397
Weiner, Tim, 393
Welch, Richard, 368, 379
Westebbe, Richard, 155,
    162–63, 223, 398
Wheeler, Earle, 145
White, Robert, 139–40, 144
White, Theodore, 216

White Star (insurance firm),
    64
Whitney, Craig, 381
Whitney, John Hay, 142
Whitten, Les, 231, 258,
    353–59, 362, 371–72
Wiggins, Jim, 122
Wiggins, Russell, 152
Williams, Harrison, 330
Wilson, Harold, 153
Winship, Tom, 229–30
Wisner, Frank, 114–15
Witten, Roger M., 329–30
Women's News Service, 293
Woods, Rose Mary, 319
Woods, Warren, 314
World Bank, 193, 194–95, 239,
    261–62, 271, 343–44
World War I, 7–8
World War II, 16–18, 19–33,
    34–46, 115
World War II Greek War Relief
    campaign, 160
Wren, Christopher S., 243–44
The Wrong Horse (Stern), 393

"X" (Greek right-wing
    organization), 49, 50–51,
    95, 177
Xanthopoulos-Palamas,
    Christos, 323

Yad Vashem, 124
Yerxa, Fendall W., 122,
    126–28, 139–40, 144
Yiounis, Sotiris, 360
Yom Kippur War (1973), 325
Young, Kenneth, 272

Z (film), 150, 256
Zachariadis, Nikos, 61, 62, 63
Zafeiropoulos, Konstantinos,
    98
Zagorianakos, Dimitrios, 322
Zimmerman, John, 76–77, 87
Zolotas, Xenophon, 218, 340,
    356
Zumwalt, Elmo R., 291–92